Mathematical Methods and Operation Research in Logistics, Project Planning, and Scheduling

Mathematical Methods and Operation Research in Logistics, Project Planning, and Scheduling

Editors

Zsolt Tibor Kosztyán
Zoltán Kovács

MDPI • Basel • Beijing • Wuhan • Barcelona • Belgrade • Manchester • Tokyo • Cluj • Tianjin

Editors
Zsolt Tibor Kosztyán
University of Pannonia
Hungary

Zoltán Kovács
University of Pannonia
Hungary

Editorial Office
MDPI
St. Alban-Anlage 66
4052 Basel, Switzerland

This is a reprint of articles from the Special Issue published online in the open access journal *Mathematics* (ISSN 2227-7390) (available at: https://www.mdpi.com/si/mathematics/Operation_Research).

For citation purposes, cite each article independently as indicated on the article page online and as indicated below:

LastName, A.A.; LastName, B.B.; LastName, C.C. Article Title. *Journal Name* **Year**, *Volume Number*, Page Range.

ISBN 978-3-0365-6372-5 (Hbk)
ISBN 978-3-0365-6373-2 (PDF)

© 2023 by the authors. Articles in this book are Open Access and distributed under the Creative Commons Attribution (CC BY) license, which allows users to download, copy and build upon published articles, as long as the author and publisher are properly credited, which ensures maximum dissemination and a wider impact of our publications.
The book as a whole is distributed by MDPI under the terms and conditions of the Creative Commons license CC BY-NC-ND.

Contents

About the Editors .... **vii**

Zsolt Tibor Kosztyán and Zoltán Kovács
Preface to the Special Issue on "Mathematical Methods and Operation Research in Logistics, Project Planning, and Scheduling"
Reprinted from: *Mathematics* **2023**, *11*, 232, doi:10.3390/math11010232 .... **1**

Eduardo Álvarez-Miranda and Jordi Pereira
A Districting Application with a Quality of Service Objective
Reprinted from: *Mathematics* **2022**, *10*, 13, doi:10.3390/math10010013 .... **5**

Daniela Ambrosino and Carmine Cerrone
A Rich Vehicle Routing Problem for a City Logistics Problem
Reprinted from: *Mathematics* **2022**, *10*, 191, doi:10.3390/math10020191 .... **27**

Md Al-Amin Khan, Ali Akbar Shaikh, Leopoldo Eduardo Cárdenas-Barrón, Abu Hashan Md Mashud, Gerardo Treviño-Garza and Armando Céspedes-Mota
An Inventory Model for Non-Instantaneously Deteriorating Items with Nonlinear Stock-Dependent Demand, Hybrid Payment Scheme and Partially Backlogged Shortages
Reprinted from: *Mathematics* **2022**, *10*, 434, doi:10.3390/math10030434 .... **41**

Ferenc Bognár and Csaba Hegedűs
Analysis and Consequences on Some Aggregation Functions of PRISM (Partial Risk Map) Risk Assessment Method
Reprinted from: *Mathematics* **2022**, *10*, 676, doi:10.3390/math10050676 .... **65**

Mohammed Alkahtani
Mathematical Modelling of Inventory and Process Outsourcing for Optimization of Supply Chain Management
Reprinted from: *Mathematics* **2022**, *10*, 1142, doi:10.3390/math10071142 .... **85**

Esteban Ogazón, Neale R. Smith and Angel Ruiz
Reconfiguration of Foodbank Network Logistics to Cope with a Sudden Disaster
Reprinted from: *Mathematics* **2022**, *10*, 1420, doi:10.3390/math10091420 .... **113**

Zsuzsanna Nagy, Ágnes Werner-Stark and Tibor Dulai
An Artificial Bee Colony Algorithm for Static and Dynamic Capacitated Arc Routing Problems
Reprinted from: *Mathematics* **2022**, *10*, 2205, doi:10.3390/math10132205 .... **133**

László Radácsi, Miklós Gubán, László Szabó and József Udvaros
A Path Planning Model for Stock Inventory Using a Drone
Reprinted from: *Mathematics* **2022**, *10*, 2899, doi:10.3390/math10162899 .... **171**

Jia-Xuan Yan; Na Ren; Hong-Bin Bei; Han Bao and Ji-Bo Wang
Scheduling with Resource Allocation, Deteriorating Effect and Group Technology to Minimize Total Completion Time
Reprinted from: *Mathematics* **2022**, *10*, 2983, doi:10.3390/math10162983 .... **191**

Zoltán Kovács, Tibor Csizmadia, István Mihálcz and Zsolt T. Kosztyán
Multipurpose Aggregation in Risk Assessment
Reprinted from: *Mathematics* **2021**, *10*, 3166, doi:10.3390/math10173166 .... **207**

Jie Zhang, Yifan Zhu, Xiaobo Li, Mengjun Ming, Weiping Wang and Tao Wang
Multi-Trip Time-Dependent Vehicle Routing Problem with Split Delivery
Reprinted from: *Mathematics* **2022**, *10*, 3527, doi:10.3390/math10193527 . . . . **227**

Zaher Abusaq, Muhammad Salman Habib, Adeel Shehzad, Mohammad Kanan and Ramiz Assaf
A Flexible Robust Possibilistic Programming Approach toward Wood Pellets Supply Chain Network Design
Reprinted from: *Mathematics* **2022**, *10*, 3657, doi:10.3390/math10193657 . . . . **251**

About the Editors

Zsolt Tibor Kosztyán

Zsolt Tibor Kosztyán, is a full professor and head of the Department of Quantitative Methods, University of Pannonia. His research interest is the development of methodologies to manage complex management problems and systems relating to mathematical models and algorithms of project management, production, maintenance, and network science. This research area is on the frontier between Management Science, Applied Informatics, and Applied Network Science.

Zoltán Kovács

Zoltán Kovács is a full professor at the Department of Supply Chain Management, University of Pannonia, and the former dean of the Faculty of Business and Economics. Zoltán received his MSc in Industrial Engineering from the University of Pannonia, in 1980, and his PhD from the Budapest University of Technology and Economics. He was awarded a six-month Fulbright Scholarship, in 1993–94 in the USA. Zoltán started his career in the meat industry as the head of the quality control lab and later worked for a coal mining company as an IT associate. Within SCM, he has a special interest in production and service management, logistics, and maintenance. He extensively uses statistical methods and the Monte Carlo simulation. Zoltán is the author of the books 'Operations Management' and 'Logistics' and co-authored—among others—'Reliability and Maintenance'.

Editorial

Preface to the Special Issue on "Mathematical Methods and Operation Research in Logistics, Project Planning, and Scheduling"

Zsolt Tibor Kosztyán [1,*] and Zoltán Kovács [2,*]

1. Department of Quantitative Methods, Institute of Management, Faculty of Business Administration and Economics, University of Pannonia, 8200 Veszprem, Hungary
2. Department of Supply Chain Management, Institute of Management, Faculty of Business Administration and Economics, University of Pannonia, 8200 Veszprem, Hungary
* Correspondence: kosztyan.zsolt@gtk.uni-pannon.hu (Z.T.K.); kovacs.zoltan@gtk.uni-pannon.hu (Z.K.)

In the last decade, the Industrial Revolution 4.0 brought flexible supply chains and flexible design projects to the fore. Nevertheless, the recent pandemic, the accompanying economic problems, and the resulting supply problems have further increased the role of logistics and supply chains. Therefore, planning and scheduling procedures that can respond flexibly to changed circumstances have become more valuable both in logistics and projects. The aim of this Special Issue was to gather novel, original publications that offer new methods and approaches in the field of planning and scheduling in logistics and project planning that are able to respond to the challenges of the changing environment. The response of the scientific community has been significant, with many papers being submitted for consideration, and, finally, twelve papers were accepted after going through a careful peer-review process based on quality and novelty criteria.

The paper by Abusaq et al. [1] suggests a decision support system for optimizing biomass-based wood pellet production supply chain network design (WPP-SCND). The WPP-SCND decision system minimizes the total supply chain (SC) cost of the system while also reducing carbon emissions associated with wood pellet SC activities. A fuzzy flexible robust possibilistic programming (fuzzy-FRPP) technique is developed for solving the suggested uncertain WPP-SCND model.

The paper authored by Zhanh et al. [2] proposes a mathematical formulation of the multi-trip time-dependent vehicle routing problem with split delivery (MTTDVRP-SD). It analyzes the pattern of the solution, including the delivery routing and delivery quantity. The paper develops an algorithm based on the simulation anneal (SA) framework. The proposed algorithm is compared with random–simulation anneal–CPLEX (R-SA-CPLEX), auction–genetic algorithm–CPLEX (A-GA-CPLEX), and auction–simulation anneal–CPLEX (A-SA) on 30 instances at three scales, and its effectiveness and efficiency are statistically verified.

In the paper by Kovács et al. [3], the authors identify different aggregation scenarios in risk assessment. They summarize the requirements of aggregation functions and characterize different aggregations according to these requirements. They critique the multiplication-based risk priority number (RPN) used in existing applications and propose using other functions in different aggregation scenarios. The behavior of certain aggregation functions in warning systems is also examined. The authors find that, depending on the aggregation location within the organization and the purpose of the aggregation, considerably more functions can be used to develop complex risk indicators.

The paper by Yan et al. [4] studies a single-machine problem with resource allocation and deteriorating effect. Under group technology and limited resource availability, the goal was to determine the schedules of groups and jobs within each group such that the total completion time was minimized.

Citation: Kosztyán, Z.T.; Kovács, Z. Preface to the Special Issue on "Mathematical Methods and Operation Research in Logistics, Project Planning, and Scheduling". *Mathematics* **2023**, *11*, 232. https://doi.org/10.3390/math11010232

Received: 22 December 2022
Accepted: 26 December 2022
Published: 3 January 2023

Copyright: © 2023 by the authors. Licensee MDPI, Basel, Switzerland. This article is an open access article distributed under the terms and conditions of the Creative Commons Attribution (CC BY) license (https://creativecommons.org/licenses/by/4.0/).

In the paper by Radácsi et al. [5], a model and solution are shown for controlling the inventory of a logistics warehouse in which neither satellite positioning nor IoT solutions can be used. The proposed model involves three steps. In the first step, a traversal path definition provides an optimal solution, which is pre-processing. This is in line with the structure and capabilities of the warehouse. In the second step, the pre-processed path determines the real-time movement of the drone during processing, including camera movements and image capture. The third step is post-processing, i.e., the processing of images for QR code identification, the interpretation of the QR code, and the examination of matches and discrepancies for inventory control.

The paper by Nagy et al. [6] solves the Dynamic Capacitated Arc Routing Problem (DCARP) combinatorial optimization problem by the Artificial Bee Colony (ABC) algorithm. The problem requires identifying such route plans on a given graph to several vehicles that generate the least total cost, and it considers dynamic changes in the problem. The proposed algorithm excels in finding a relatively good quality solution in a short amount of time, which makes it a competitive solution.

The paper by Ogazón et al. [7] focuses on foodbank networks. Foodbank networks provide adequate infrastructure and perform logistics activities to supply food to people in need on a day-to-day basis. The paper proposes a mathematical formulation for the design of logistics processes, including collection, transshipment, and aid distribution, over a network of foodbanks inspired by the real case of Bancos de Alimentos de México (BAMX).

The paper authored by Alkahtani [8] formulates mathematical models and provides an optimization algorithm for process outsourcing, considering imperfect production with variable quantities for effective supply chain management. The numerical experiment was performed based on the data taken from the industry for the application of the proposed outsourcing-based SCM model.

The paper by Bognár and Hegedűs [9] proposes a new risk assessment method. The proposed PRISM (partial risk map) methodology is a risk assessment method developed as the combination of the failure mode and effect analysis and risk matrix from the risk assessment methods. Based on the new concept of partial risks, three different aggregation functions are presented for assessing incident risks.

The paper by Khan et al. [10] presents an inventory model that involves non-instantaneous deterioration, nonlinear stock-dependent demand, and partially backlogged shortages by considering the length of the waiting time under a hybrid prepayment and cash-on-delivery scheme. The corresponding inventory problem is formulated as a nonlinear constraint optimization problem.

In the paper by Ambrosino and Cerrone [11], a variation of the Rich Vehicle Routing Problem (RVRP) is solved in city logistic problems. The authors deal with a multi-period vehicle routing problem with a heterogeneous fleet of vehicles, with customers' requirements and company restrictions to satisfy, in which the fleet composition has to be defined daily. A mixed integer programming model was proposed, and an experimental campaign was presented to validate it.

The paper by Álvarez-Miranda and Pereira [12] proposes a hybrid method for designing delivery zones with an objective based on improving the quality of express delivery services. The proposed method combines a preprocess based on the grouping of demand in areas according to the structure of the territory, a heuristic that generates multiple candidates for the distribution zones, and a mathematical model that combines the different distribution zones generated to obtain a final territorial design.

As Guest Editors of this Special Issue, we are grateful to all authors who contributed their articles. We would also like to express our gratitude to all reviewers for their valuable comments on the improvement of the submitted papers. The goal of this Special Issue was to attract quality and novel papers in the field of "Mathematical Methods and Operation Research in Logistics, Project Planning, and Scheduling". It is hoped that these selected research papers will be found to be impactful by the international scientific community and that these papers will motivate further operations research for solving complex problems in various disciplines and application fields.

Conflicts of Interest: The authors declare no conflict of interest.

References

1. Abusaq, Z.; Habib, M.S.; Shehzad, A.; Kanan, M.; Assaf, R. A Flexible Robust Possibilistic Programming Approach Toward Wood Pellets Supply Chain Network Design. *Mathematics* **2022**, *10*, 3657. [CrossRef]
2. Zhang, J.; Zhu, Y.; Li, X.; Ming, M.; Wang, W.; Wang, T. Multi-Trip Time-Dependent Vehicle Routing Problem with Split Delivery. *Mathematics* **2022**, *10*, 3527. [CrossRef]
3. Kovács, Z.; Csizmadia, T.; Mihálcz, I.; Kosztyán, Z.T. Multipurpose Aggregation in Risk Assessment. *Mathematics* **2022**, *10*, 3166. [CrossRef]
4. Yan, J.X.; Ren, N.; Bei, H.B.; Bao, H.; Wang, J.B. Scheduling with Resource Allocation, Deteriorating Effect and Group Technology to Minimize Total Completion Time. *Mathematics* **2022**, *10*, 2983. [CrossRef]
5. Radácsi, L.; Gubán, M.; Szabó, L.; Udvaros, J. A Path Planning Model for Stock Inventory Using a Drone. *Mathematics* **2022**, *10*, 2899. [CrossRef]
6. Nagy, Z.; Werner-Stark, Á.; Dulai, T. An Artificial Bee Colony Algorithm for Static and Dynamic Capacitated Arc Routing Problems. *Mathematics* **2022**, *10*, 2205. [CrossRef]
7. Ogazón, E.; Smith, N.R.; Ruiz, A. Reconfiguration of Foodbank Network Logistics to Cope with a Sudden Disaster. *Mathematics* **2022**, *10*, 1420. [CrossRef]
8. Alkahtani, M. Mathematical Modelling of Inventory and Process Outsourcing for Optimization of Supply Chain Management. *Mathematics* **2022**, *10*, 1142. [CrossRef]
9. Bognár, F.; Hegedűs, C. Analysis and Consequences on Some Aggregation Functions of PRISM (Partial Risk Map) Risk Assessment Method. *Mathematics* **2022**, *10*, 676. [CrossRef]
10. Khan, M.A.A.; Shaikh, A.A.; Cárdenas-Barrón, L.E.; Mashud, A.H.M.; Treviño-Garza, G.; Céspedes-Mota, A. An Inventory Model for Non-Instantaneously Deteriorating Items with Nonlinear Stock-Dependent Demand, Hybrid Payment Scheme and Partially Backlogged Shortages. *Mathematics* **2022**, *10*, 434. [CrossRef]
11. Ambrosino, D.; Cerrone, C. A Rich Vehicle Routing Problem for a City Logistics Problem. *Mathematics* **2022**, *10*, 191. [CrossRef]
12. Álvarez-Miranda, E.; Pereira, J. A Districting Application with a Quality of Service Objective. *Mathematics* **2022**, *10*, 13. [CrossRef]

Disclaimer/Publisher's Note: The statements, opinions and data contained in all publications are solely those of the individual author(s) and contributor(s) and not of MDPI and/or the editor(s). MDPI and/or the editor(s) disclaim responsibility for any injury to people or property resulting from any ideas, methods, instructions or products referred to in the content.

Article

A Districting Application with a Quality of Service Objective

Eduardo Álvarez-Miranda [1,*] and Jordi Pereira [2,3]

1 School of Economics and Business, Universidad de Talca, Talca 3460000, Chile
2 Faculty of Engineering and Sciences, Universidad Adolfo Ibáñez, Av. Padre Hurtado 750, Viña del Mar 2520000, Chile; jorge.pereira@uai.cl or jordi.pereira@bsm.upf.edu
3 UPF Barcelona School of Management, Universitat Pompeu Fabra, C. Balmes 132-134, 08008 Barcelona, Spain
* Correspondence: ealvarez@utalca.cl

Abstract: E-commerce sales have led to a considerable increase in the demand for last-mile delivery companies, revealing several problems in their logistics processes. Among these problems, are not meeting delivery deadlines. For example, in Chile, the national consumer service (SERNAC) indicated that in 2018, late deliveries represented 23% of complaints in retail online sales and were the second most common reason for complaints. Some of the causes are incorrectly designed delivery zones because in many cases, these delivery zones do not account for the demographic growth of cities. The result is an imbalanced workload between different zones, which leads to some resources being idle while others fail to meet their workload in satisfactory conditions. The present work proposes a hybrid method for designing delivery zones with an objective based on improving the quality of express delivery services. The proposed method combines a preprocess based on the grouping of demand in areas according to the structure of the territory, a heuristic that generates multiple candidates for the distribution zones, and a mathematical model that combines the different distribution zones generated to obtain a final territorial design. To verify the applicability of the proposed method, a case study is considered based on the real situation of a Chilean courier company with low service fulfillment in its express deliveries. The results obtained from the computational experiments show the applicability of the method, highlighting the validity of the aggregation procedure and improvements in the results obtained using the hybrid method compared to the initial heuristic. The final solution improves the ability to meet the conditions associated with express deliveries, compared with the current situation, by 12 percentage points. The results also allow an indicative sample of the critical service factors of a company to be obtained, identifying the effects of possible changes in demand or service conditions.

Keywords: districting; last-mile delivery; hybrid heuristics

Citation: Álvarez-Miranda, E.; Pereira, J. A Districting Application with a Quality of Service Objective. *Mathematics* **2022**, *10*, 13. https://doi.org/10.3390/math10010013

Academic Editors: Zsolt Tibor Kosztyán, Zoltán Kovács and Frank Werner

Received: 22 September 2021
Accepted: 15 December 2021
Published: 21 December 2021

Publisher's Note: MDPI stays neutral with regard to jurisdictional claims in published maps and institutional affiliations.

Copyright: © 2021 by the authors. Licensee MDPI, Basel, Switzerland. This article is an open access article distributed under the terms and conditions of the Creative Commons Attribution (CC BY) license (https://creativecommons.org/licenses/by/4.0/).

1. Introduction

A supply chain is the set of elements that allows the development and delivery of a product or service to its customers. Among the stages that can be found in a chain, one of the most important is the final stage, which is usually known as the last-mile service.

The last mile is the process by which a product is transported from the closest distribution center to the final customer [1]. This last-mile concept has been gaining increasing importance due to the enormous growth of e-commerce as well as the current COVID-19 pandemic situation, which limits people's mobility. This is demonstrated, for example, by statistical data from Statista, where one can see that in mid-2014, online sales generated 1.3 trillion dollars worldwide, reaching 4.2 trillion dollars in 2020 [2].

Currently, the last-mile logistics process is considered one of the most crucial in the supply chain, not only because of the current importance of e-commerce but also because of how decisive it is and the impact it has in terms of customer satisfaction. It is also one of the points along the chain experiencing the most problems and that generates the most costs in the entire chain [3].

These problems can be structured in several groups. On the one hand, there are environmental problems that have to do with the ecological vision and commitment of each company. On the other hand, there are transportation problems caused, among other causes, by road congestion in densely packed areas, which prevents the efficient distribution of products. There are also problems associated with the relationship between the service and the customer with respect to the delivery of the product, such as not meeting delivery deadlines, failed delivery attempts due to the recipient not being present at the destination address, deliveries rejected by the customer given the poor condition of the packaging, and even deliveries not fulfilled due to lost packages. In summary, this final distribution phase presents several problems that need to be specifically addressed for an efficient operation.

The process of distribution to the final customer is usually carried out in two different ways: either by the workers of the company itself that sells the product or by outsourcing it to a logistics and transport company that performs the service of transfer of documents, parcels, or luggage of various customers from one origin to a destination (courier). This outsourcing is known as third-party logistics (3PL), is frequently used internationally, and is the most widespread in the Chilean market, since 3PLs have more experience, which leads them to having sustainable competitive advantages over time [4].

The courier market in Chile has experienced considerable changes in demand due to e-commerce, resulting in lower customer service metrics since it has been difficult for distribution companies to adapt to the increase in demand. This can be observed in the statistical data of customer satisfaction in the 2019 semiannual report of the ProCalidad de Chile organization and by the data provided by the website of the National Consumer Service (Servicio Nacional del Consumidor—SERNAC). In the ProCalidad data, the Couriers sector is classified into a group of many problems [5].

On the other hand, the National Consumer Service in 2018 received a total of 330,000 complaints, of which 33% were associated with retail. The online retail sales complaints were broken down into 53% due to noncompliance with the contracted conditions, 23% due to delays in the delivery of what was purchased, and 11.7% due to poor quality of service [6]. In addition, in 2020 and only during the first semester (during the period of pandemic caused by COVID-19), 72,000 complaints were received related to the delay of deliveries of products sold through e-commerce [7].

These statistics shows the relevance of proper on-time delivery as an integral part of any Customer Relationship Management (CRM) [8] strategy of a successful courier company. A CRM strategy should lead to improved customer satisfaction metrics, that helps to ensure loyal customers [9,10]. In order to achieve these results, a delivery company requires an effective logistic strategy, in which last-mile logistics play an important role. In fact, last-mile logistic were identified as a critical step with successful logistic strategies in early e-commerce literature, see [11] for an example, being delivery speed and delivery reliability two of the required capabilities of any successful last-mile logistics implementation [4].

This research originates from and studies a case observed in a courier company operating in the city of Antofagasta (Chile). Antofagasta is the mining capital of the country, and due to being isolated, suffers from a situation in which the distribution problems mentioned above are exacerbated. The company currently works with a distribution model that divides the city into 10 delivery zones, each of them assigned to a third-party delivery person who works with a long-term contract, freely organizing their operations within the assigned zone. The company offers various products that basically depend on the agreed delivery time. The most important service with the greatest number of problems is the *Overnight* (ON) service. *Overnight* service requires delivery before 11:00 a.m., with noncompliance of that deadline leading to the highest number of customer complaints and the highest noncompliance with internal service quality metrics. As an indicator, the initial service situation at the time this study was conducted showed that only 83% of deliveries met this condition, with the company's short-term goal being to reach a level of service quality equal to 90%.

To alleviate the problems identified, the company needs to reevaluate its last-mile operations, moving from a cost-saving to a customer-based operational focus. Among the different changes that the company has to implement, this work focuses on the redesign of the delivery zones geared towards the fulfillment of the express delivery service needs.

Note that while the design of delivery areas falls within a broader class of problems known as districting in the scientific literature, see Section 2 for a review, our proposal differs from previous work on the metric used to evaluate the candidate districting plans. While the districting literature usually focuses on finding districts with a "fair" (i.e., even) distribution among them, our goal is to optimize a quality of service associated to the total expected number of late deliveries. This change modifies the structure of the problem, as the proposed method focuses on an overall metric built from the contributions of the selected delivery zones rather than on a similarity operational metric among delivery zones.

To solve this novel problem, a multi-stage hybrid optimization method is proposed that will be able to design new zones considering the critical factors of service. These delivery zones are defined by keeping in mind the quality of overnight service considering the time available for delivery and an estimate of the expected number of on-time deliveries according to the characteristics of the proposed delivery areas. The proposed procedure performs a preprocessing of the zone based on practical recommendations to add the deliveries in basic units assignable to the delivery zones, which allows maintaining some of the current practices' territorial boundaries between distributors. Subsequently, a procedure is used that combines a random territory generator and a local improvement procedure, which generates alternative territorial configurations. Finally, these alternative configurations are combined through an integer linear program to obtain a final proposal. This procedure is tested in instances derived from the daily operations of the company, as well as in a case study situation, showing significant improvements with respect to current operations. Specifically, it is possible to achieve a level of quality of service greater than 95%, which illustrates the improvement obtained by the proposed process. Our experiments show the advantages of the different elements of our solution methodology. First, the aggregation approach balances computational requirements with solution quality, as more fine-grained aggregation schemes increase computational times without leading to better solutions in terms of quality. Second, the proposed constructive procedure followed by a local search method is able to provide high-quality delivery areas. Moreover, the generated areas are sufficiently diverse to provide a pool of partial solutions, which the combination procedure is able to use to obtain new and better districting plans.

The rest of the work is structured as follows. Section 2 performs a study of the available literature associated with the design of territories. Section 3 describes the problem addressed and the data processing performed. Section 4 describes the proposed resolution procedure, while Section 5 details the results of the experiments performed. Finally, Section 6 describes the conclusions reached and the possible extensions to be made in the work.

2. Literature Review

The problem of territory design or district design is a problem that consists of grouping small geographic areas, called basic units, into larger geographic groups called districts or territories in such a way that these territories are acceptable according to the planning criteria considered [12]. In the 1960s, Hess et al. [13] proposed the first works on the design of territories in an electoral context. In his research, the authors use a mathematical model and a heuristic to create electoral districts. The intention was to find territories with a similar number of voters (i.e., following the premise of "one man, one vote") while avoiding the manipulation of electoral constituencies to favor certain candidates or parties (a defect known as "gerrymandering" in the literature). Subsequently [14] extended the same approach to a problem of the design of sales territories. In this case, the objective is to achieve equitable territories with respect to the associated workload between different vendors.

These investigations served as a starting point for the area, which was later expanded to a wide range of applications and resolution methods, both exact and heuristic or metaheuristic. Within the different applications, we can find both in the areas already mentioned, that is, the design of political territories [15–17] and that of sales territories [18–20], as in other areas, such as the design of service areas, in settings as diverse as home health care [21,22], police patrolling [23,24], the design of school districts [25], the design of energy distribution networks [26], or waste collection [27,28]. Finally, and of special interest for this work are the applications related to the design of distribution territories [29,30], which is the area in which this work is focused. The design of distribution territories consists of designing zones for the pick up and/or delivery of products to customers residing in the zone. Each of these areas is assigned one or more carriers, which will establish one or more service routes each day, starting from a warehouse where the products are stored.

Regardless of how the territories obtained are applied, there are a series of requirements and attributes that all the problems of territory design share and that serve as a point of comparison between the different studies [31]. Within the requirements, there is a unique assignment that implies that each basic unit, that is, each geometric object associated with customers or users, must be assigned to a single territory. Another criterion is the balance between different territories according to some measure. For example, in the distribution of goods, the measure is usually the workload, whose balance seeks to avoid comparative differences between workers. This workload can be represented, for example, by the number of customers in each zone [30].

The compactness of the generated territories is another of the typical requirements for this type of problem. The geometric interpretation of compactness corresponds to a preference for territories with rounded or rectangular shapes that do not have distortions or holes. This helps, for example, that the districts include customers that are close to each other, favoring efficient operations (for example, delivery routes). Finally, another typical requirement is that of contiguity, which is defined as the ability to travel between basic units of the same territory without having to leave it. Although these last two criteria have specific definitions, there is no single representation of the concepts of compactness and contiguity since they depend largely on the problem and its attributes.

Among the attributes of the problem, we highlight those linked to the type and characteristics of the basic units (the representation of the units or customers to be grouped) and of the districts (the groups to be created). For example, the type of basic unit indicates how customers are represented in space and may correspond to coordinates [29], lines, or geometric figures that define urban blocks [32], while the characteristics of the districts, such as the number of territories to be created, are usually fixed according to the characteristics of the system being designed (for example, it can be equal to the number of carriers that the distribution service provider has) or the variables that are to be optimized [29,33,34].

Considering that the territory design problem corresponds to an optimization problem in which one tries to optimize some objective function that indicates the quality of the solution offered by an optimization method, it is necessary to review the resolution methods that have been used in the literature for the problem of territory design and specifically for the design of territories in the area of logistics and distribution.

Among the methods that can be found are the exact methods based on mathematical programming techniques, which seek to obtain a global optimum as a solution to the problem. Optimality has only been achieved in cases with few customers due to the computational complexity of the territory design problem, which is a computationally NP-hard problem [35]. Among the different exact methods are [21,26,36].

Another type of available procedure is one that combines heuristics or metaheuristics with mathematical programming techniques, usually called matheuristics [37]. In [29] a large-scale design of territories is performed using data from up to 45,000 delivery points, in which the objective is to divide a set of customers into the minimum possible number of territories that satisfy the geometric condition of having a rectangular shape, as well as considerations of vehicle capacity and the time limit of the distribution service. To do this, ref. [29] apply a column generation procedure based on an extension of the capacitated clustering problem with which they search for candidate territories that meet the conditions and considerations described above, combining it with a metaheuristic based on the tabu search to select the best candidates.

Another type of research that also combines a heuristic method with another based on an exact method is that by [38]. In this work, territories are designed by partitioning concentric rings around the distribution center with the objective of minimizing transportation costs. These costs include vehicle operating expenses, such as the cost per mileage and delivery time, as well as an extra cost in case of exceeding the service time limit. It is important to mention that to reduce the computational effort, the Beardwood approximation [39] is used to calculate the service time and the distance traveled in each territory. The method used to solve this problem is an extension of a gradient method combined with a genetic algorithm. The procedure differs from a previous version by the same researchers [34] in that the formulation of the variables is continuous, which avoids cumbersome data preparation and the creation of disjoint concentric cell partitions.

In [33] a hybrid approach is also carried out in the design of territories for a meat distribution company. In this case, two K-means algorithms are used to partition the area and create candidate territories, which are then combined with a mathematical model based on formulations of a set covering model, which seeks to minimize the number of territories needed to perform the distribution service. It is important to mention that in this research, the level of service is represented, approximating the time it takes for the distribution service with the formula proposed in [40] since it allows an approximation with differently shaped territories without assuming a distribution of the customers in the zone.

A different resolution method consists of using tools derived from computational geometry. Generally, these methods are based on Voronoi diagrams to define territories. A Voronoi diagram consists of partitioning a plane from the intersection of the bisectors of a set of points. Through the intersection of these bisectors, polygons are formed that represent the area that contains the positions closest to the points of the set. In [41] the use of a weighted multiplicative version of these diagrams to define territories was studied. The weighted multiplicative version allows greater flexibility to create territories with a balanced number of customers. In this research, the balance criterion approximates the time it takes for vehicles to deliver to customers in each territory using the Beardwood formula, adding the round-trip distance to the warehouse and considering the service time for each customer.

Finally, there are heuristic methods that are ad hoc procedures for solving the problem. Within these are the metaheuristics that can be classified into three groups according to the basic ideas they represent: constructive procedures, neighbor exploration procedures, and population procedures. The constructive procedures yield a final solution through small steps in which simple decisions are made (for example, the inclusion of a basic unit in a district) and, generally, they take the one that seems the best choice in each step. On the other hand, metaheuristics based on neighbor exploration begin from an initial solution of the problem that is progressively improved through small modifications.

Finally, population-based metaheuristics procedures imitate the process of biological evolution, which consists of constructing new solutions from the combination of others. Among the numerous metaheuristics available for this type of problem, the most common are the Greedy Randomized Adaptive Search procedure, GRASP, metaheuristic [30,42–44], genetic algorithms [45], simulated annealing [23] and the tabu search [46].

Finally, it should be noted that although the bulk of the literature considers problems with a single objective, there are several studies that try to optimize two or more functions together in the field of service territories [47], political territories [48], or sales territories [32].

3. Problem Description

This section describes the problem addressed in this work, indicating the requirements and attributes of the problem, the starting data, and the objective sought in it.

As a starting point, there is a historical log of addresses with deliveries made in a delivery zone—in our case a city. The basic demarcations of the city are known (geographic limits, streets, and main avenues). These demarcations constitute the set of geographical characteristics that the company and the distributors use to designate the boundaries of the distribution territories. For each customer, their spatial coordinates are available (that is, their latitude and longitude) as well as the days in which a delivery was made to the customer (so the frequency of deliveries for each customer can be obtained, that is, the percentage of days in which the customer has had one or more scheduled deliveries). We also know the spatial location of the warehouse from which the deliveries begin, the traffic speed on expressways (such as "beltways" and highways) and within the city (through the streets), as well as the number, k, of territories to be designed.

In the first phase of preprocessing, basic demarcations are used to group customers into basic units. To do this, the city is divided using these demarcations, which are the same ones that the distributors use to delimit their areas in a logical way (that is, through avenues, main streets, and other physical divisions of the territory). The use of these demarcations has two benefits: first, it allows creating logical territorial groupings with the daily operations observed in practice; and second, it ensures that the territories (distribution zones) are better adopted by the workers and the managers of the company. This is an important step to ensure the applicability of the solutions provided by our solution method. Due to the particularities of the operations considered in our case study, see Section 5.2, the aggregation into basic units helps stakeholders to voice their opinion on how clients should be grouped into small areas that are to be serviced together.

Figure 1 shows an example of the divisions created in one zone of the city.

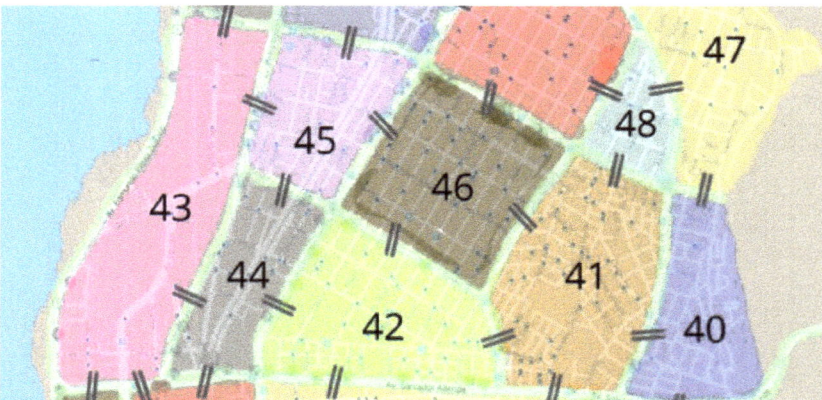

Figure 1. Divisions created in a zone of the city studied in the case study. The different groupings are shown in different colors, while the roads used to delimit the territories are highlighted in green. Additionally, the adjacency among basic units are shown through the inclusion of two lines between adjacent territories.

Two basic units are said to be adjacent if they share a boundary. Figure 1 indicates these adjacency relationships through two lines. Computationally, the adjacency relations are coded through a graph $G(V, E)$, where the vertices, V, are equivalent to the basic units and the edges, E, correspond to the adjacency relations between the basic units associated with both ends of the edges.

Each basic unit also has two associated labels that correspond to its equivalent workload and its center of mass. The equivalent workload of a basic unit is equivalent to the sum of the delivery frequencies of its addresses, the blue dots that can be seen in Figure 1, that is, the expected number of daily deliveries associated with customers located in that basic unit. The center of mass of each basic unit corresponds to the average of the coordinates of the customers weighted by their delivery frequency.

The basic units should be grouped into k territories under conditions of contiguity and quality of service. The quality of service plays the role of balance in other problems of territory design, although it does not necessarily imply that a regular distribution of deliveries is generated. Note that compactness, as described in Section 2 is not considered explicitly, but the blocks used to design the basic units inherently include an aspect of compactness, and the quality of service function that will be shown below penalizes the creation of unbalanced territories or odd structures in terms of their shape or size.

The condition of contiguity is established as a hard condition, that is, as a constraint that all solutions must meet to be considered valid and that forces the vertices of the basic units making up a territory to be connected in graph $G(V, E)$. This condition can be verified by checking whether the subgraph induced by the subset of vertices associated with the basic units making up the territory constitutes a connected graph. This operation is easy to evaluate through an algorithm such as that of Hopcroft and Tarjan [49].

The quality of service will be the objective criterion used to evaluate the different territorial proposals and corresponds to an approximation of the expected number of late deliveries based on the proposed territorial design. Note that these characteristics makes our work depart from other works, as we focus on a service objective and estimate number of deliveries and not the cost of performing the delivery. The approach adopted in this work is constructed through an estimation of the time required by three components: (1) the time required to reach the territory from the logistics center (the warehouse) and (2) the service time required to deliver to each of the customers in the territory, and (3) the travel time in the territory between the various customers. The time to return to the warehouse is not taken into account since after making express deliveries, other deliveries will continue to be distributed throughout the day. The estimation of the service time allows the calculation of the number of maximum deliveries that can be made within the delivery window set by the service, and the difference between the expected number of deliveries and the maximum number of possible deliveries—in case such a difference is positive, it will be our estimate of the quality of service.

Each of the three time estimates is determined as follows.

The time it takes for the carrier to go from the distribution center to a territory, which we call T_0, is calculated as the minimum distance between the distribution center and the territory multiplied by the average speed of travel on expressways. The calculation of this distance is performed by looking up the minimum distance between each basic unit that makes up the territory and the distribution center and selecting the minimum between them.

To determine the expected route time within the territory, the tour length to visit the customers is estimated. Generally, this step would correspond to the resolution of a traveling salesman problem (TSP) in case of knowing the specific customers that must be served. Given that the exact customers of each workday are unknown and the TSP is a complex problem in itself [50], it is decided to estimate the tour length using a "distribution-free" approximation as proposed in [40] and then multiply the length of the route by the average speed of travel observed within the urban center, which we denote as s_w.

The estimation of the length of the tour, d, associated with the problem corresponds to (1)

$$d = 2.791\sqrt{n\hat{\sigma}'_x\hat{\sigma}'_y} + 0.2669\sqrt{\frac{\hat{\sigma}_x\hat{\sigma}_y}{\bar{d}_x\bar{d}_y}}nA_s, \qquad (1)$$

where:

- $\bar{d}_x$ ($\bar{d}_y$) is the average of the distances between the delivery points and the central horizontal axis (central vertical axis);

- $\hat{\sigma}_x$ ($\hat{\sigma}_y$) is the standard deviation of Tpoints;
- $\hat{\sigma}'_x$ ($\hat{\sigma}'_y$) is the standard deviation of the absolute distance of the delivery points with the central horizontal axis (central vertical axis);
- A_s is the area of the territory on which the approximation will be made;
- n is the number of delivery points within the territory.

As in [40], the central horizontal axis and the central vertical axis are defined as the midpoint of the space in which the distributions are made.

Finally, the service time per delivery, which we call T_s, corresponds to an estimate of the time it takes for the recipient of the package to open the door, receive the package and sign the document that proves receipt of the delivery. This time must be multiplied by the number of deliveries to be made.

By combining the three factors, Equation (2), an estimate of the total time required to serve a territory, T, is obtained:

$$T = T_0 + T_s n + ds_w. \tag{2}$$

Given that it is intended to determine the maximum number of customers to serve in the time available for deliveries and that all the parameters of (2) are known except the number of customers n, the procedure to determine the quality of the service will obtain the value maximum of n such that (2) is less than the available time window for deliveries, and then this number will be compared with the number of deliveries within the territory. If the maximum number is less than the number of deliveries that must be made, then the difference between both will correspond to the number of late deliveries of the territory; otherwise, it is estimated that all deliveries can be made on time so the quality of service would be 100%, i.e., no late deliveries. Note that the description and the implementation aim to minimize the expected number of late deliveries, a measure of "disservice", rather than to maximize the number of deliveries on-time. For all intents and purposes, both objectives are identical and, while the code internally minimizes disservice, solutions are reported in terms of quality of service.

In summary, the problem can be formulated as the assignment of the basic units to k groups in such a way that:

1. Each basic unit belongs to a single grouping (i.e., to a single territory);
2. The basic units of each grouping generate a related subgraph;
3. The sum of the average number of late deliveries in the set of territories is minimized.

As mentioned above, the model does not verify the compactness of the solution, but the function that determines the length of the delivery route, Equation (1), favors the construction of compact districts when evaluating the deviations of the coordinates of the deliveries. Another important aspect of the model described is that when estimating the load of each basic unit as the value observed for the deliveries made during a period of time in that geographical area, the model does not work directly with customer history. This avoids the biases that could be created by assigning the past locations of customers as the only existing basic units. Furthermore, it is no longer assumed that historical delivery locations will be the same as future deliveries, nor will the distribution of deliveries in the future be similar to the historical distribution.

4. Proposed Solution Methodology

This section details the hybrid procedure proposed to solve the problem. This procedure is divided into two parts. The first part, which is described in Sections 4.1 and 4.2, corresponds to a multi-start procedure that generates alternative solutions to the problem through a constructive procedure followed by a local improvement procedure. Although the multi-boot procedure has certain requests with a GRASP metaheuristic, it differs from it in the use of a completely random constructive strategy against GRASP in that the constructive phase limits the selection made at each step to a subset of candidates. This part does not use the quality of service function shown in Section 3 but rather optimizes an alternative function with less computational calculations, which significantly reduces the total time required by the algorithm.

In the second part, the level of service of each territory generated in the first part is evaluated, and a mathematical model is solved that attempts to combine the territories constructed by the multi-boot procedure looking for new and better combinations of territories that configure the final territory design. The evaluation of the quality of the proposed method, as well as the contribution of the second phase to the quality of the final procedure, is shown in Section 5.

4.1. Constructive Heuristic

The constructive phase is responsible for forming feasible territories, which will act as initial solutions for local improvement. The constructive method is detailed in Algorithm 1.

Algorithm 1 Description of the constructive algorithm

Input: Number of territories k; Graph $G(V,E)$; Coordinates of each basic unit.
Output: Solution of the problem with k territories.
1: Select k different basic units at random and assign to each territory.
2: **repeat**
3:     **for** each territory κ and basic unit v **do**
4:         **if** v is not part of a territory but is adjacent to the territory κ **then**
5:             Add the pair (v, κ) to the list of iteration candidates.
6:     Select a candidate pair according to (3) and assign the basic unit v to the κ territory.
7: **until** Base units remain unassigned

The first step of the constructive phase is to generate an amount of "seeds" for the territories equal to the number of clusters to be constructed. Each of these seeds corresponds to a different basic unit and will serve as a point from which the different territories will "grow".

The next step is to find the basic units that can be assigned to the clusters under construction. Initially, the basic assignable units are those that are adjacent to the seeds of the clusters and that do not yet form a territory. Subsequently, they will correspond to any basic unit that is not part of a territory and that is adjacent to another basic unit that is part of a territory. Note that by restricting the search for candidates to basic units adjacent to basic units that are part of a territory, the connectivity condition of the resulting groupings is ensured.

After determining the candidates, we proceeded to calculate the distance between each of the candidates and the "seed" of its adjacent territory, considering as the distance between two basic units the Euclidean distance between the centers of mass of both basic units and a candidate-seed pair whose probability is proportional to the inverse of the distance between the "seed" and the district is chosen (that is, the shorter the distance of the basic unit with the seed, the greater the probability of being chosen). Let $d_{v\kappa}$ be the distance between a candidate basic unit v and a territory κ and let V'_κ be the set of all candidates to be assigned to district κ. Then, (3) indicates the probability that the basic unit v is selected during this phase and is assigned to territory κ,

$$p_{v\kappa} = \frac{d_{v\kappa}}{\sum_{\kappa'=1}^{k} \sum_{v' \in V'_k} d_{v'\kappa'}}. \qquad (3)$$

Equation (3) gives each pair of candidate basic unit and territory a probability proportional to its distance between the basic unit and the "seed" of the district, d_{vk} the numerator of the equation. The denominator ensures that the sum of probabilities of all candidates equals 1, by dividing each numerator by the total sum among all numerators of the pairs of candidate basic units and territories.

This approach, in which a probability is assigned to any candidate instead of limiting the decision to the best candidate or a subset of candidates, allows increasing the diversity of solutions facing the subsequent steps of local improvement and solution combinations.

This process of candidate identification and the assignment of a candidate to a grouping is repeated until all basic units are part of a territory. These solutions do not take into account the objective of the problem directly but do try to obtain compact territories by assigning basic units, seeking to minimize distances with respect to a central unit.

4.2. Local Search Procedure

With the initial solution constructed, a local search is performed to "improve" this solution with respect to a metric that describes the balance of deliveries between different districts. The development of the local search phase is summarized in Algorithm 2.

Algorithm 2 Description of the local search phase

Input: Initial solution; Number of territories k; Graph $G(V,E)$; Workload of each basic unit.
Output: Solution of the problem with k territories.

1: **repeat**
2:     Initialize *better change* to *null change*
3:     **for** each basic unit v **do**
4:         **for** each territory κ **do**
5:             **if** the assignment of v to κ is feasible **then**
6:                 Evaluate balance load, bl, according to Equation (4)
7:                 **if** the solution is improved **and** *better change* is improved **then**
8:                       Save v and κ as *better change*
9:     **if** *better change* is not *null change* **then**
10:         Implement change
11: **until** *better change* is *null change*

The neighborhood used in the improvement process is defined by changing the assignment of a basic unit. Such change corresponds to extracting a basic unit (other than the seed of a territory) from some grouping and adding it to another grouping, maintaining the condition of contiguity (connectivity of territories). After moving, it is verified if the movement is feasible, that is, the two territories affected by the change continue to define related subgraphs in $G(V,E)$, and it is evaluated whether there were improvements with respect to an auxiliary function that allows us to analyze the balance in the workload of the resulting territories. For this (4) is evaluated where v is the basic unit that leaves district κ and becomes part of district κ', $c(v)$ is the workload of the basic unit and $C(\kappa)$ and $C(\kappa')$ are the current workloads of districts κ and κ' respectively. In the case that bl, Equation (4), is positive, the move is considered an improvement since it reduces the load of the most loaded district associated with the change.

$$bl = \max\{C(\kappa); C(\kappa')\} - \max\{C(\kappa) - c(v); C(\kappa') + c(v)\}. \quad (4)$$

Equation (4) evaluates the effect on the workload balance between the districts involved in the change. By comparing the workloads among the most loaded districts, Equation (4) helps to identify candidate districting plans in which the workload differences among districts are small.

Note that the verification performed in (4) does not correspond directly with the objective function of the problem, but the calculation time of (4) is less, and preliminary computational experiments showed that territories with similar workloads had better quality of service values. The logic behind this result is that distributing deliveries equitably between delivery zones helps to obtain territories with similar workloads and avoids concentrating many deliveries in some districts, while others do not have enough; see Section 5.2 for an analysis of the associated importance to balance the number of deliveries for each district. In addition, seeing the equal distribution of work between the different distribution zones is easily interpreted within the operations of the company.

The local search is organized as a "best-improvement" procedure; that is, all possible feasible insertions are considered, of which the one that generates the greatest impact on the balance is kept. When all the changes have been reviewed, the change that leads to the greatest improvement in the auxiliary function is applied, and then all possible changes are checked again. The algorithm ends when there is no feasible change that improves the value of the auxiliary function. The implementation chooses to organize the search as "first improvement" since the second option showed biases in the order in which the basic units were considered within the procedure. In the case of using a "best-improvement" type move, it is observed that the algorithm tends to vary the districts and basic units involved in the changes made more frequently than in the "first-improvement" type search.

4.3. Combination of Solutions through Integer Programming

As the aforementioned heuristic generates many feasible solutions and the territories that comprise it have not been directly evaluated with the quality of service metric that is sought to be optimized, it is important to carry out a process that evaluates the territories according to the final metric and selects the best combination of territories according to this criterion. For this reason, the third step of the proposed method proposes a mathematical model that selects the best subset of territories among those found by the feasible solutions of the heuristic to reduce the average number of expected late deliveries. This third step also contributes to a better use of the solutions found during the first phase and can be seen as a phase of search intensification similar to a common "path relinking" in many implementations of the GRASP metaheuristic [51].

Let I be the set of feasible territories obtained as a result of the first phase. Each territory $i \in I$ has an associate number of late deliveries τ_i obtained as indicated in Section 3 and a vector a_i of length $|J|$ which has value 1, $a_{ij} = 1$, if the territory i includes the basic unit j ($j \in J$) and value 0, $a_{ij} = 0$, if not. For each territory $i \in I$ a binary variable x_i is defined that will take value 1 if the territory is selected and 0 if not.

With these data and variables, Formulations (5)–(8) constitute a valid formulation for the problem of selecting territories among those available.

$$z^* = \min \sum_{i \in I} \tau_i x_i \tag{5}$$

$$\text{s.t} \quad \sum_{i \in I} x_i = k \tag{6}$$

$$\sum_{i \in I} a_{ij} x_i = 1, \ \forall j \in J \tag{7}$$

$$x_i \in \{0,1\}, \ \forall i \in I \tag{8}$$

Equation (5) represents the objective function, which seeks to find a design of territories that has the least number of late deliveries. This objective is achieved by adding the number of late deliveries, τ_i, of the districts selected by the solution to the formulation, those districts whose variable τ_i take value 1. Constraint (6) indicates that the set of territories chosen must be composed of a number of k territories by enforcing that the number of districts whose variable take cvalue equal to 1 is exactly equal to a predetermined constant k which is a parameter of the problem. Constraint set (7) indicates that all urban blocks have to be assigned to a territory, by ensuring that exactly one district is selected, its variable takes value equal to 1, if it includes the urban block, that is, if $a_{ij} = 1$. Finally, the decision variable is defined as a binary variable, as observed in condition (8). The resolution of the mathematical model is performed through a standard integer linear programming solver; see details in the next section. The model corresponds to a set partitioning problem with the additional condition that exactly k districts must be chosen among the $|I|$ available.

Given that each of the territories of the set of territories meets the conditions of connectivity, that the model ensures unique assignment of each basic unit to a territory and that the number of districts to be constructed is chosen, the resulting solution of optimizing (5)–(8) is a valid solution for the design of territories analyzed. In addition, this model always has a feasible solution since each solution obtained during the local search procedure is a feasible solution to the problem. Note that this step can be generalized to any other districting problem in which the combination of different districting solutions can be seen as a partition problem and the objective function can be obtained through the summation of the aggregation of each district.

Finally, it is important to comment that sometimes the proposal presented can generate solutions that do not meet some additional conditions of service that are useful in practice. In practice, these conditions are presented in such a way that two basic units cannot be assigned to the same territory. In this case, the model can be adapted to the requirement by eliminating those territories that do not meet the indicated condition without needing to change the model. Although this characteristic is not discussed in the computational results shown in Section 5, it does contribute to the practical applicability of the resolution procedure described.

5. Computational Experiments

This section presents the results of the computational experiments and the analysis of the results obtained by the procedures shown under different conditions and parameters.

The procedures described in the document were programmed in C language using IBM ILOG CPLEX version 12.10 to solve the integer linear program described in Section 4.3. The experiments were performed on a computer running an Intel i5 8600K processor at 3.6 GHz, 16 GB of RAM under the Windows 10 professional operating system.

The instances used in the experiments come from the delivery database of a courier company that operates in the city of Antofagasta (Chile). This database includes 21,025 deliveries made over 19 business days. Of the described deliveries, 4768 correspond to express parcel service, while the rest correspond to regular service. The delivery schedule begins at 9 a.m., and the limit imposed for express deliveries set by service conditions is 11 a.m., so 2 h are available for express deliveries. The number of territories (delivery zones) to be created is set at 10 since this is the value currently used and corresponds to hiring 10 independent distributors who work exclusively for the company. Finally, the time associated with each delivery is equal to 2 min, and the speeds within the city are at 14 km/h, while the speed on the main roads is 31 km/h. These values come from a study conducted by the traffic control operational unit in Chile. Note that while the instances and constants specifically refer to a particular situation, there is no reason to think that there is a bias introduced within the results due to this decision.

The set of instances was obtained by sampling for three demand scenarios: low demand (half of that observed in the data collection period), medium demand (that observed in that period), and high demand (double that observed) which are equivalent to 2384, 4768, and 9536 deliveries over 19 days. For the medium demand, those registered in the database are used as deliveries, while for the low demand, half of them are randomly chosen. For the scenario with high demand, an identical number of new deliveries chosen at random from the locations of the regular service deliveries are added to the deliveries considered in the medium-demand case. Although they are services performed at different times, they have similar demand behaviors, so this option is chosen to generate instances with higher demand.

During the preprocessing, three levels of granularity are considered in the definition of basic units, that is, different amounts of urban blocks (basic units) into which the city is divided during the preprocessing. These levels correspond to 43, 85, and 128 urban blocks.

For each of these combinations of demand levels and number of basic units, the territorial distribution is designed with different numbers of territories (for the low demand level, 5 and 7 districts are designed, for the medium level 5, 7, 10, and 12 districts and for high demand 5, 7, 10, 12, 15, 20, 22l and 25 districts).

Finally, a limit is imposed on the number of solutions proposed by the constructive heuristic equal to 50, 100, 200, 500, 1000, 5000, and 10,000 solutions, and the resolution time of the mathematical model is limited to 600 s. Given the reduced computation times of the proposed heuristic, which uses a simplified evaluation function to speed up the calculations, the total calculation times never reached 1200 s, a time that is considered reasonable in the practical environment analyzed since the design of territories is carried out every several years. The computation times of the heuristic solutions and of the integer programming procedure are also considered separately since it is possible to reuse the solutions constructed by the heuristic to obtain alternative solutions with the mathematical model if required.

5.1. Results from the Experiments

The results of Tables 1–3 show the detailed results for each instance, identified by the number of basic units (column 'BUs'), the number of districts to build (column '#'), and the number of solutions generated by the first phase of the procedure (columns '50' to '10,000'). The number reported is the estimated number of late deliveries, so the level of service would correspond to 1 minus the fraction between the number of late deliveries and the total number of deliveries to be made as indicated in the description of each table.

Table 1. Average of late deliveries on the worst day by the number of solutions generated during the first phase of the algorithm, Columns '50', '100', '200', '500', '1000', '5000', and '10,000' and instance parameters (number of basic units in column 'BU', and number of generated districts in column '#') for instances with low demand.

BUs	#	50	100	200	500	1000	5000	10,000
43	5	94.26	94.54	94.6	94.74	95.01	95.39	95.68
	7	99.77	99.95	100	100	100	100	100
85	5	94.1	94.23	94.33	94.63	94.8	95.16	95.27
	7	99.88	100	100	100	100	100	100
127	5	94.39	94.46	94.68	94.83	95.06	95.33	95.38
	7	99.97	99.98	99.98	99.98	100	100	100

Table 2. Average of late deliveries on the worst day by number of solutions generated during the first phase of the algorithm, Columns '50', '100', '200', '500', '1000', '5000', and '10,000' and instance parameters (number of basic units, column 'BU', and number of districts generated, column '#') for instances with medium demand.

BUs	#	50	100	200	500	1000	5000	10,000
43	5	77.77	78	78.12	78.35	78.5	78.59	78.6
	7	84.9	85.21	85.4	85.49	85.58	85.78	85.83
	10	94.52	94.87	95.15	95.48	95.57	95.85	95.87
	12	98.13	98.61	98.98	99.19	99.3	99.45	99.48
85	5	77.74	77.74	77.98	78.05	78.11	78.35	78.42
	7	84.93	84.96	85.02	85.36	85.53	85.67	85.72
	10	93.98	94.27	94.9	95.32	95.5	95.75	95.81
	12	97.73	98.14	98.73	99.26	99.41	99.65	99.68
127	5	77.58	77.77	77.82	77.87	78.05	78.09	78.17
	7	84.52	84.71	84.8	84.92	85.12	85.43	85.53
	10	93.54	93.95	94.11	94.52	94.97	95.6	95.71
	12	95.51	96.74	97.57	98.7	99.27	99.73	99.79

Table 3. Average of late deliveries on the worst day by number of solutions generated during the first phase of the algorithm, Columns '50', '100', '200', '500', '1000', '5000', and '10,000' and instance parameters (number of basic units, column 'BU', and number of districts generated, column '#') for instances with high demand.

BUs	#	50	100	200	500	1000	5000	10,000
43	5	70.36	70.4	70.54	70.69	70.73	70.8	70.8
	7	74.25	74.27	74.48	74.61	74.63	74.66	74.67
	10	79.78	79.89	80.04	80.08	80.1	80.19	80.23
	12	83.14	83.37	83.49	83.56	83.59	83.7	83.75
	15	87.86	88.12	88.35	88.55	88.62	88.8	88.82
	17	90.34	90.7	90.89	91.15	91.31	91.5	91.56
	20	92.22	92.25	92.26	92.26	92.26	92.26	92.26
	22	92.26	92.26	92.26	92.26	92.26	92.26	92.26
	25	92.26	92.26	92.26	92.26	92.26	92.26	92.26
85	5	70.35	70.35	70.37	70.41	70.52	70.62	70.68
	7	77.8	77.83	77.98	78.15	74.38	74.48	74.51
	10	79.4	79.68	79.79	79.91	79.99	80.12	80.19
	12	82.95	83.18	83.37	83.52	83.61	83.72	83.76
	15	87.59	88.17	88.41	88.65	88.74	88.91	88.97
	17	90.96	91.26	91.43	91.81	91.95	92.12	92.18
	20	93.12	94.06	94.65	94.98	95.2	95.38	95.43
	22	94.74	95.35	95.64	95.93	96.09	96.22	96.23
	25	95.81	96.33	96.38	96.38	96.38	96.75	96.75
127	5	70.22	70.3	70.31	70.6	70.6	70.6	70.6
	7	74.02	74.09	74.11	74.14	74.28	74.44	74.47
	10	79.24	79.46	79.55	79.89	80.06	80.29	80.38
	12	82.79	82.9	83.19	83.5	83.68	83.92	83.96
	15	87.31	87.78	88.29	88.67	88.94	89.2	89.25
	17	88.58	90.02	91.13	91.8	92.22	92.58	92.66
	20	92.66	93.66	94.93	95.94	96.28	96.84	96.93
	22	94.55	96.21	96.82	97.4	97.7	97.97	98.05
	25	96.6	97.56	98.14	98.25	98.28	98.28	98.28

In the three scenarios, it can be observed that when the number of territories (or delivery zones) increases, the number of late deliveries decreases considerably, which shows that increasing the number of districts positively influences the level of service. This conclusion is logical and shows that there is a possibility of improving the quality of service through an increase in current subcontracted services, although there comes a time when increasing the number of districts does not generate great benefits. Specifically, for the current demand scenario, with a medium level of demand and 10 districts, an increase of 20% in the number of districts (going from 10 to 12 districts) would lead to substantial improvements and an expected fulfillment of almost 100% of the on time deliveries. If the results associated with changes in demand are compared, it can be seen that the current delivery service would not be able to cope with a significant increase in demand (a high number of deliveries scenario), requiring a significant growth in the number of districts to be able to adapt to this change.

With respect to the procedure of aggregating urban blocks, it can be seen that in the scenarios with low and medium demand, there are no appreciable differences in the results, which indicates that the grouping factor applied does not influence the results obtained. On the other hand, in the high demand scenario, it can be observed that increasing the granularity (a greater number of basic units) has a positive effect on the results obtained using this method. From this result, it can be inferred that the correct level of granularity depends on the number of deliveries to be analyzed and that if the level of aggregation is correct, the effect on the results is minimal. It should be emphasized that greater granularity implies a greater computational effort with respect to the resolution method, so it is important to define a degree of grouping consistent with the practical needs of the problem (for example, maintaining assigned distribution zones that make sense for the distributor) and the possible improvements derived from subdividing the territory into zones that are increasingly difficult to operate from a day-to-day operations point of view.

Regarding the number of independent executions of the first phase of the procedure, it is observed that when increasing their number, there is a small decrease in the number of late deliveries in the three respective scenarios. However, these increases are sometimes lower and imply an increase in computational effort, so it is necessary to know to what extent these changes are significant and thus reduce the run time of the procedure.

To measure how significant the use of different initial solutions is, a parametric ANOVA with blocking factors test is performed. In this case, the comparison element is the number of independent runs of the first phase of the procedure, that is, 50, 100, 200, 500, 1000, 5000, and 10,000 independent runs. A block design is chosen so that the test considers that part of the variations are caused by the different instances used (number of districts, granularity). The test performed takes as a null hypothesis that the treatments are equal, which leads to a negative outcome since the treatments show significance with a p-value of 2.2×10^{-16}. Additionally, a nonparametric test, the Page test [52], is performed to avoid possible problems of the nonnormality of the residuals. This test also rejects the null hypothesis with a p-value of 2.2×10^{-16}, which leads us to conclude that the number of independent runs of the metaheuristic impacts the results obtained by the algorithm.

To identify which treatments are significantly different, a nonparametric hypothesis test called the "Distribution free Two-Sided all-treatments multiple comparisons based on Friedman rank sums" (Wilcoxon, Nemenyi, McDonald, and Thompson) is applied, which performs multiple comparisons between pairs of treatments. The results of the test are shown in Table 4.

Table 4. Results of the Wilcoxon, Nemenyi, McDonald, and Thompson test to identify possible improvements associated with the generation of a greater number of solutions during the first phase of the analyzed procedure.

	50	100	200	500	1000	5000
100	2.4×10^{-8}	-	-	-	-	-
200	$<2 \times 10^{-16}$	8.6×10^{-8}	-	-	-	-
500	$<2 \times 10^{-16}$	$<2 \times 10^{-16}$	1.1×10^{-9}	-	-	-
1000	$<2 \times 10^{-16}$	$<2 \times 10^{-16}$	$<2 \times 10^{-16}$	2×10^{-6}	-	-
5000	$<2 \times 10^{-16}$	$<2 \times 10^{-16}$	$<2 \times 10^{-16}$	$<2 \times 10^{-16}$	4×10^{-10}	-
10,000	$<2 \times 10^{-16}$	$<2 \times 10^{-16}$	$<2 \times 10^{-16}$	$<2 \times 10^{-16}$	5.7×10^{-14}	0.019

The results of the nonparametric pairwise comparison test show that each increase in the multi-boot level implies a significant difference between the medians with a significance level of 95%. However, the comparison between 5000 and 10,000 has low significance and may not justify the additional computational cost.

In the previous tables of the 3 scenarios, when going from 5000 to 10,000 executions of the heuristic, it can be observed that the average change is smaller compared to the other increases in the number of executions of the heuristic.

Finally, Table 5 evaluates the effect of adding the second phase of the method, that is, the resolution of the mathematical model on the performance of the proposed procedure. For this, the percentage decrease in the number of late deliveries recorded by using the mathematical model is evaluated. This value results from dividing the difference between the expected number of late deliveries of the best solution of the first phase and the second phase by the expected number of late deliveries of the first phase. In this case, a different behavior can be observed according to the levels of grouping (number of basic units), number of solutions generated, and number of territories to be constructed. Specifically, it is observed that as the number of territories and alternative solutions increases, the differences are very significant, especially when a greater number of districts are constructed.

Table 5. Percentage of improvement obtained by the use of the second phase of the proposed procedure (number of districts generated, column '#').

#	Solutions	43 Units	85 Units	127 Units
10	50	12.3	3.8	0
	100	16.2	6	0.1
	200	19.8	12.9	1.1
	500	15.6	16.6	5.4
	1000	17.3	16.5	9.1
	5000	20.5	16.4	14.7
	10,000	18.7	17.1	16.3
12	50	61.9	17.9	2
	100	65	30.8	14.9
	200	73.4	48.5	33.6
	500	73.7	65.2	54.6
	1000	73.6	69.1	57.3
	5000	73.1	75	79.4
	10,000	71.5	75.3	82.8

5.2. Results from the Case Study

Considering the analysis performed in Section 5.1 with respect to the solutions obtained, it is decided to offer a solution to the new territorial design using the original conditions considered by the company (10 districts, medium demand) using a configuration of the procedure that uses 5000 iterations of the constructive heuristic followed by the combination of territories following the mathematical model.

In addition, given that the differences between the medium and high granularity levels were not significant for the scenarios with current demand, a medium granularity was chosen to offer solutions. This combination of characteristics of the procedure allows generating the number of initial solutions indicated and offering an optimal solution for the resulting mathematical model in a total of less than two minutes of run time.

The final solution proposal is shown in Figure 2. It should be noted that some territories have a reduced number of basic units; for example, there is a territory with a single basic unit that corresponds to a zone with a strong presence of industries and offices, while other zones include a large number of basic units (zones with less population and/or economic activity). This disparity is logical and is due to the structure of the city considered in the case study.

The final solution is capable of obtaining an average quality of service of 95.7%, which represents an improvement of 12 points compared to the current service level, which is 83% and allows a certain buffer with respect to the company's goal to reach a service level of 90%.

For a more detailed analysis of the behavior for each of the 19 days available in the study, see Table 6, shows a disparity of service levels throughout the different days, showing that on the day of greatest demand (Day 8) the service index worsens significantly.

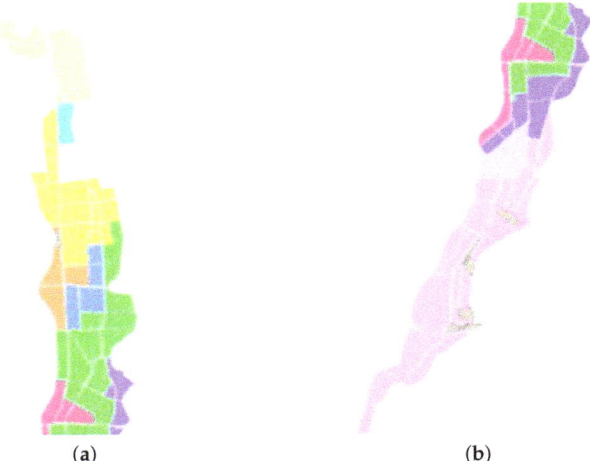

(a)   (b)

Figure 2. Divisions created in a zone of the city studied in the case study (figure (**a**) shows the north and central area, while figure (**b**) shows the central and south area). The territories are shown in different colors with the basic units delimited by white lines.

Table 6. Level of service reached by the proposed solution for each of the 19 days where which information is available.

Day	Level	Day	Level
1	100%	11	100%
2	100%	12	98.3%
3	96.7%	13	91.8%
4	100%	14	91.8%
5	100%	15	100%
6	100%	16	100%
7	100%	17	95.5%
8	78.6%	18	82.5%
9	88.9%	19	94.5%
10	100%		

Analyzing the individual results of each day, it is observed that one of the causes of greater service delays corresponds to a strong variability in the demand depending on the day. In addition, there is no pattern based on the day of the week or the month that justifies this variability. While an increase in the number of delivery zones would improve the level of service on those critical days, the change would lead to an oversized delivery service in most days since optimal levels, 100% of deliveries, are reached in most days of service.

Another important analysis to perform is the effect of service time on the quality of the solution. The service time is defined as the time it takes the carrier to stop the vehicle at the delivery destination, deliver the package, and resume the route. The company assumes that this time is two minutes per delivery, but the variability is high, and given the reduced time available to make all the express deliveries, even small variations can significantly vary the results. To respond to this problem, it was checked what the result would be if the service time were increased to 2 min and 15 s and to 2 min and 30 s.

The results of this change indicate that the quality of service decreases to 93.6% when the increase is only 15 s and to 90.3% when service time is increased by 30 s. These results translate into large variations on the worst day, in which the quality of service drops to 70.4% and 64.1%, respectively. Therefore, one of the improvements available to be made in the daily operation of the system corresponds to maintaining and/or improving that delivery time, which is of vital importance for managing a large number of shipments in smaller time windows.

6. Conclusions and Future Work

In the present work, a procedure and a case study are proposed for the design of delivery zones subject to quality of service conditions in express deliveries. The procedure considers a preprocess of grouping customers into basic units that, on the one hand, helps to generate solutions with the characteristics expected by both the management of the company and by the carriers and, on the other hand, reduces the computational needs of the design method.

The method for designing territories consists of an initial phase in which a set of alternatives are generated that are subsequently combined through a mathematical model to obtain a final territorial design. The mathematical model is general and can be used in other districting problems that feature similar characteristics in terms of the objective function and districts interactions. Moreover, and to minimize computation times, an alternative objective function is used in the initial search phase and to evaluate a more detailed estimate of the level of service offered by each territory considered only in the last phase of the algorithm. This procedure yields quality solutions in shorter times.

Our results show that while a very coarse granularity when grouping clients may hinder the quality of the solution, increasing granularity impacts algorithmic performance but may not directly translate into better solutions. Consequently, there is a "sweet spot" in which a proper degree of aggregation has a positive impact on the algorithmic performance and the properties expected from the proposed districting plans. While this result makes intuitive sense, previous literature on districting problems has not given much attention to it, focusing its attention on other issues, such as defining compactness metrics to try to reach similar results to those than can be obtained through aggregation.

If the results of the case study are examined, it is clear that the proposed territorial design leads to evident and achievable improvements in the company's service indices. The redesigned delivery zones allow reaching a level of service equivalent to 95.7% without internal operational changes. Moreover, the districting plan make sense from a practical point of view as the borders between districts are defined by major roads and streets as in manually generated districts. It is also observed that given the sensitivity of the average service time, it is essential that there is a correct functioning in this process. This point is critical in overall system performance, and incorrect functioning of the system could lead to significant deterioration of the system.

Note that the conclusions reached within the case study may vary in different countries or even in different areas within a country. While the proposed methodology is agnostic to the area under study, data availability, or cultural particularities, the application of this research results to other countries or situations may or may not be possible. For instance, our methodology considers that the old territorial design can be ignored, while there are cases in which changes between the previous and the new territorial design should be minimal or units that need to be assigned to specific territories for some particular reasons. We also consider that all *overnight* deliveries are identical and no preference must be given to some of them. Other operational features, such as the existence of multiple product offerings with different express delivery deadlines would also impact the methodology and require changes to our approach, even if the overall methodological scheme would still be valid.

Among the possibilities for improvement and study, we highlight the inclusion of standard service or pickup operations, such as returns, within the express service in the same territorial design process. This work did not take this combined approach because the view of the company in the case study is that the standard service does not entail major problems and can be performed without taking its limiting factors into account, but this condition may not be true for other scenarios or settings. In this case, it would be necessary to approach the problem from a multicriteria perspective, evaluating the trade-off between the different needs and objectives of each type of service offered by the company.

Similarly, this study does not consider other side constraints that may impact the operational viability of the territories, such as the physical capacity of the vehicle or the size of the items delivered. While these conditions need to be considered in some applications and require additional study within the districting literature, they were not considered necessary in this study because most overnight deliveries are small parcels and letters that represent a small fraction of the total capacity of the vehicles used for delivery.

Finally, it would also be interesting to study the case where the number of districts is not specified as an input. Such a situation is less frequent in delivery companies as changes in their operations should take previous decisions (i.e., the number of territories) into account, but it is a problem of practical relevance that deserves proper attention. However, in some circumstances it may be interesting to reduce operational costs and given the structure of the delivery service, where territories are handed out to independent contractors to actually perform delivery operations, "district minimization" translates into "cost minimization". While the proposed solution method does not provide a direct solution approach for such a problem, it does provide a tool to evaluate the effect on the quality of service metric when a different number of districts, parameter k, are used, and thus it can be seen as a possible decision-aiding tool to manually evaluate the pros and cons of alternative plans.

Author Contributions: Conceptualization, E.Á.-M. and J.P.; methodology, E.Á.-M. and J.P.; software, J.P.; validation, E.Á.-M. and J.P.; formal analysis, E.Á.-M. and J.P.; investigation, E.Á.-M. and J.P.; resources, E.Á.-M. and J.P.; data curation, J.P.; writing—original draft preparation, J.P.; writing—review and editing, E.Á.-M.; visualization, J.P.; supervision, E.Á.-M. and J.P.; funding acquisition, E.Á.-M. and J.P. All authors have read and agreed to the published version of the manuscript.

Funding: E. Álvarez-Miranda acknowledges the support of the National Agency of Research and Development (ANID), Chile, through the grant FONDECYT N.1180670 and through the Complex Engineering Systems Institute ANID PIA/BASAL AFB180003. J. Pereira acknowledges the support of ANID through the grant FONDECYT N.1180670.

Institutional Review Board Statement: Not applicable.

Informed Consent Statement: Not applicable.

Data Availability Statement: Due to non disclosure agreements, the data used in this work cannot be provided. More detailed aggregated results are available upon request to the authors.

Acknowledgments: Both authors acknowledge to Benjamín Conejeros for his involvement in early stages of this research.

Conflicts of Interest: The authors declare no conflict of interest.

References

1. Gevaers, R.; Van de Voorde, E.; Vanelslander, T. Characteristics and Typology of Last-mile Logistics from an Innovation Perspective in an Urban Context. In *City Distribution and Urban Freight Transport*; Macharis, C., Melo, S., Eds.; Edward Elgar Publishing: Cheltenham, UK, 2011; pp. 56–71.
2. Retail e-Commerce Sales Worldwide from 2014 to 2024. Available online: https://www.statista.com/statistics/379046/worldwide-retail-e-commerce-sales/ (accessed on 18 August 2021).
3. Chopra, S. Designing the Distribution Network in a Supply Chain. *Transp. Res. Part E* **2003**, *39*, 123–140. [CrossRef]
4. Cho, J.; Ozment, J.; Sink, H. Logistics Capability, Logistics Outsourcing and Firm Performance in an E-commerce Market. *Int. J. Phys. Distrib. Logist Manag.* **2008**, *38*, 336–359.
5. Índice Nacional de Satisfacción de Clientes: Informe de Resultados Generales. Available online: Https://procalidad.cl/indice-procalidad/ (accessed on 18 August 2021).
6. Servicio Nacional del Consumidor: Un 88% de los Reclamos Recibidos por el SERNAC Fueron en Contra de Grandes Empresas. Available online: Https://www.sernac.cl/portal/604/w3-article-55432.html (accessed on 18 August 2021).
7. Servicio Nacional del Consumidor: SERNAC Analiza Reclamos por Compras Online y Exige Compensaciones. Available online: Https://www.sernac.cl/portal/604/w3-article-58698.html (accessed on 18 August 2021).
8. Kumar, V.; Reinartz, W. *Customer Relationship Management*, 3rd ed.; Springer: Berlin/Heidelberg, Germany, 2018.

9. Gajewska, T.; Zimon, D.; Kaczor, G.; Madzík, P. The impact of the level of customer satisfaction on the quality of e-commerce services. *Int. J. Product. Perform. Manag.* **2019**, *69*, 666–684. [CrossRef]
10. Madzík, P.; Hrnčiar, M. Accuracy in measuring customer satisfaction. *Int. J. Serv. Ind. Manag.* **2021**, *38*, 161–187. [CrossRef]
11. Kotzab, H.; Madlberger, M. European retailing in e-transition? An empirical evaluation of Web-based retailing—Indications from Austria. *Int. J. Phys. Distrib. Logist Manag.* **2001**, *31*, 440–462. [CrossRef]
12. Kalcsics, J. Districting Problems. In *Location Science*; Laporte, G., Nickel, S., Saldanha da Gama, F., Eds.; Springer: New York, NY, USA, 2015; pp. 585–622.
13. Hess, S.; Weaver, J.; Siegfeldt, H.; Whelan, J.; Zitlau, P. Nonpartisan political redistricting by computer. *Oper. Res.* **1965**, *13*, 998–1008. [CrossRef]
14. Hess, S.; Samuels, S. Experiences with a sales districting model: Criteria and implementation. *Manag. Sci.* **1971**, *18*, 41–54. [CrossRef]
15. Ricca, F.; Scozzari, A.; Simeone, B. Political Districting: From classical models to recent approaches. *Ann. Oper. Res.* **2013**, *204*, 271–299. [CrossRef]
16. Bucarey, V.; Ordóñez, F.; Bassaletti, E. Shape and balance in police districting. In *Applications of Location Analysis*; Eiselt, H., Marianov, V., Eds.; Springer: New York, NY, USA, 2015; pp. 329–347.
17. Dugošija, D.; Savić, A.; Maksimović, Z. A new integer linear programming formulation for the problem of political districting. *Ann. Oper. Res.* **2020**, *288* 247–263. [CrossRef]
18. Fleischmann, B.; Paraschis, J.N. Solving a Large-Scale districting problem: A case report. *Comput. Oper. Res.* **1988**, *15*, 521–533. [CrossRef]
19. Zoltners, A.; Sinha, P. Sales territory design: Thirty years of modeling and implementation. *Mark Sci.* **2005**, *24*, 313–331. [CrossRef]
20. Salazar-Aguilar, M.A.; Ríos-Mercado, R.Z.; Cabrera-Ríos, M. New Models for Commercial Territory Design. *Netw. Spat. Econ.* **2011**, *11*, 487–507. [CrossRef]
21. Benzarti, E.; Sahin, E.; Dallery, Y. Operations management applied to home care services: Analysis of the districting problem. *Decis. Support. Syst.* **2013**, *55*, 587–598. [CrossRef]
22. Lin, M.; Chin, K.; Fu, C.; Tsui, K. An effective greedy method for the Meals-On-Wheels service districting problema. *Comput. Ind. Eng.* **2017**, *106*, 1–19. [CrossRef]
23. D'Amico, S.; Wang, S.; Batta, R.; Rump, C. A simulated annealing approach to police district design. *Comput. Oper. Res.* **2002**, *29*, 667–684. [CrossRef]
24. Chen, H.; Cheng, T.; Ye, X. Designing efficient and balanced police patrol districts on an urban street network. *Int. J. Geogr. Inf. Sci.* **2019**, *33*, 269–290. [CrossRef]
25. Caro, F.; Shirabe, T.; Guignard, M.; Weintraub, A. School redistricting: Embedding GIS tools with integer programming. *J. Oper. Res. Soc.* **2004**, *55*, 836–849. [CrossRef]
26. Ríos-Mercado, R.; Bard, J. An exact algorithm for designing optimal districts in the collection of waste electric and electronic equipment through an improved reformulation. *Eur. J. Oper. Res.* **2019**, *276*, 259–271. [CrossRef]
27. Lin, H.; Kao, J. Subregion districting analysis for municipal solid waste collection privatization. *J. Air Waste Manag. Assoc.* **2008**, *58*, 104–111. [CrossRef]
28. Cortinhal, M.; Mourão, M.; Nunes, A. Local search heuristics for sectoring routing in a household waste collection context. *Eur. J. Oper. Res.* **2016**, *255*, 68–79. [CrossRef]
29. Jarrah, A.; Bard, J. Large-scale pickup and delivery work area design. *Comput. Oper. Res.* **2012**, *39*, 3102–3118. [CrossRef]
30. González-Ramírez, R.; Smith, N.; Askin, R.; Camacho-Vallejo, J.; González-Velarde, J. A GRASP-Tabu Heuristic Approach to Territory Design for Pickup and Delivery Operations for Large-Scale Instances. *Math. Probl. Eng.* **2017**, *2017*, 4708135. [CrossRef]
31. Kalcsics, J.; Nickel, S.; Schröder, M. Towards a unified territorial design approach—Applications, algorithms and GIS integration. *TOP* **2005**, *13*, 1–56. [CrossRef]
32. Salazar-Aguilar, M.; Ríos-Mercado, R.; González-Velarde, J. GRASP strategies for a bi-objective commercial territory design problem. *J. Heuristics* **2013**, *19*, 179–200. [CrossRef]
33. Moreno, S.; Pereira, J.; Yushimito, W. A hybrid K-means and integer programming method for commercial territory design: A case study in meat distribution. *Ann. Oper. Res.* **2020**, *286*, 87–117. [CrossRef]
34. Novaes, A.; Graciolli, O. Designing multi-vehicle delivery tours in a grid-cell format. *Eur. J. Oper. Res.* **1999**, *119*, 613–634. [CrossRef]
35. Altman, M. Is automation the answer: The computational complexity of automated redistricting. *Rutgers K Comput. Technol. Law* **1997**, *23*, 81–141.
36. Sandoval, M.; Díaz, J.; Ríos-Mercado, R. An Improved Exact Algorithm for a Territory Design Problem with p-Center-Based Dispersion Minimization. *Expert Sys. Appl.* **2020**, *146*, 113150. [CrossRef]
37. Maniezzo, V.; Boschetti, M.; Stützle, T. *Matheuristics. Algorithms and Implementations*, 1st ed.; Springer: New York, NY, USA, 2021.
38. Novaes, A.; Souza De Cursi, J.; Graciolli, O. A continuous approach to the design of physical distribution systems. *Comput. Oper. Res.* **2000**, *27*, 877–893. [CrossRef]
39. Beardwood, J.; Halton, J.; Hammersley, J. The shortest path through many points. *Math. Proc. Camb. Philos. Soc.* **1959**, *55*, 299–327. [CrossRef]

40. Çavdar, B.; Sokol, J. A distribution-free tsp tour length estimation model for random graphs. *Eur. J. Oper. Res.* **2015**, *243*, 588–598. [CrossRef]
41. Galvao, L.; Novaes, A.; Cursi, E.; Souza, J. A multiplicatively-weighted Voronoi diagram approach to logistics districting. *Comput. Oper. Res.* **2006**, *33*, 93–114. [CrossRef]
42. Ríos-Mercado, R.; Fernández, E. A reactive GRASP for a commercial territory design problem with multiple balancing requirements. *Comput. Oper. Res.* **2009**, *36*, 755–776. [CrossRef]
43. Fernández, E.; Kalcsics, J.; Nickel, S. A novel maximum dispersion territory design model arising in the implementation of the WEEE-directive. *J. Oper. Res. Soc.* **2010**, *61*, 503–514. [CrossRef]
44. Gonzalez-Ramírez, R.; Smith, N.; Askin, R.; Kalashnikov, V. A heuristic approach for a logistics districting problem. *Int. J. Innov. Comput. Inf. Control* **2010**, *6*, 3551–3562.
45. Lei, H.; Wang, R.; Laporte, G. Solving a multi-objective dynamic stochastic districting and routing problem with a co-evolutionary algorithm. *Comput. Oper. Res.* **2016**, *67*, 12–24. [CrossRef]
46. Bozkaya, B.; Erkut, E.; Laporte, G. A tabu search heuristic and adaptive memory procedure for political districting. *Eur. J. Oper. Res.* **2003**, *144*, 12–26. [CrossRef]
47. Tavares-Pereira, F.; Figueira, J.; Mousseau, V.; Roy, B. Multiple criteria districting problems: The public transportation network pricing system of the Paris region. *Ann. Oper. Res.* **2007**, *154*, 69–92. [CrossRef]
48. Ricca, F.; Scozzari, A.; Simeone, B. Weighted Voronoi region algorithms for political districting. *Math. Comput. Model.* **2007**, *48*, 1468–1477. [CrossRef]
49. Hopcroft, J.; Tarjan, R. Algorithm 447: Efficient algorithms for graph manipulation *Commun. ACM* **1973**, *16*, 372–378. [CrossRef]
50. Garey, M.; Johnson, D. *Computers and Intractability: A Guide to the Theory of NP-Completeness (Series of Books in the Mathematical Sciences)*, 1st ed.; W. H. Freeman: New York, NY, USA, 1979.
51. Resende M.; Ribeiro C.; Path-relinking. In *Optimization by GRASP*; Springer: New York, NY, USA, 2016; pp. 167–188.
52. Hollander, M.; Wolfe, D.; Chicken, E. *Nonparametric Statistical Methods*, 3rd ed.; Wiley: Hoboken, NJ, USA, 2014.

Article

A Rich Vehicle Routing Problem for a City Logistics Problem

Daniela Ambrosino * and Carmine Cerrone

Department of Economics and Business Studies, University of Genova, 16126 Genova, Italy; carmine.cerrone@unige.it
* Correspondence: ambrosin@economia.unige.it

Abstract: In this work, a Rich Vehicle Routing Problem (RVRP) is faced for solving city logistic problems. In particular, we deal with the problem of a logistic company that has to define the best distribution strategy for obtaining an efficient usage of vehicles and for reducing transportation costs while serving customers with different priority demands during a given planning horizon. Thus, we deal with a multi-period vehicle routing problem with a heterogeneous fleet of vehicles, with customers' requirements and company restrictions to satisfy, in which the fleet composition has to be daily defined. In fact, the company has a fleet of owned vehicles and the possibility to select, day by day, a certain number of vehicles from the fleet of a third-party company. Routing costs must be minimized together with the number of vehicles used. A mixed integer programming model is proposed, and an experimental campaign is presented for validating it. Tests have been used for evaluating the quality of the solutions in terms of both model behavior and service level to grant to the customers. Moreover, the benefits that can be obtained by postponing deliveries are evaluated. Results are discussed, and some conclusions are highlighted, including the possibility of formulating this problem in such a way as to use the general solver proposed in the recent literature. This seems to be the most interesting challenge to permit companies to improve the distribution activities.

Keywords: rich vehicle routing problem (RVRP); heterogeneous fleet; fleet dimensioning; VRP with time windows (VRPTW); multi-period VRP; combinatorial optimization

1. Introduction

Distribution activities in urban areas represent a considerable part of the total cost of transport and are intended to grow for the emerging increment in the number of requests for pick up and deliveries [1]. For these reasons, companies are required to find logistics solutions in such a way as to reduce costs caused by inefficiency and ineffectiveness [2]. Moreover, efficient solutions are required by the law restrictions (for example, to limit noise and air pollution) imposed to preserve social interests.

Nowadays, companies pay more attention to their city logistics activities and try to include in their decisional process external costs related to transports, together with total logistic costs [3]. The optimization of the number of vehicles used together with the better usage of the vehicles' capacity permit to reduce the negative impacts of transportation activities.

When dealing with the optimization of transportation activities, one of the most studied combinatorial optimization problems is the vehicle routing problem (VRP).

The basic form of VRP can be used when a fleet of homogeneous vehicles is available in a depot to serve a set of customers. Each customer is characterized by a given location and a given demand and must be visited once. Each vehicle starts its route at the depot, visits a subset of customers in such a way that the total delivered demand is less or equal to its capacity, and finally returns to the depot. Moreover, the objective is to minimize the total routing costs, often expressed in terms of total travelled distance. VRP has been quickly recognized as a useful model for facing logistics problems and for supporting supply chain managers; thus, a set of additional attributes and constraints have been added

to its first definition, and researchers have defined a new class of these problems: the rich VRP (RVRP) [4].

Many logistics problems requiring operative and tactical decisions are faced by an RVRP. The distribution network can be more complex than the simple one considered in VRP: more than one depot and more layers can characterize the supply chain, different kinds of depots can be operative in the supply chain and can play different roles (i.e., maintaining inventories and being a cross-docking point). The planning of distribution activities refers to more than one period when the problem cannot be decomposed into single period problems since some decisions refer to and impact more than one period. Examples of these problems can be found in the enormous literature related to VRP and its extensions, including the multi-depot VRP [5], the periodic-VRP [6–8], and the inventory-routing problems [9].

VRP has also been combined with location decisions in the network design problems; thus, location-routing problems are defined and studied [10].

The dynamic version of the problem represents a useful instrument to guide companies that have to serve both customers with a known demand at the beginning of the planning horizon and new customers with requests arriving over it.

Moreover, when dealing with real-life logistics activities, constraints related to many operational aspects are relevant and must be included in the VRP model.

Customers are often characterized by priorities, by multi-product demands, they can either require to be served in defined time windows or have other requirements.

On the other hand, distribution companies may have either a heterogeneous fleet of vehicles or an undefined fleet (when they refer to third parties for having trucks); they must respect law restrictions for drivers and, finally, may have policies to follow that can impose distribution conditions in respect to serving customers (i.e., related to the customer service level to grant, to the lead time to grant, and to the discounts that can be applied in case of delays).

All these aspects generate new constraints that characterize the faced problem as an RVRP. Comprehensive classifications of RVRP problems can be found in [4,11,12].

As far as the objective functions are considered, new and interesting objectives characterizing the management of distribution activities include the minimization of the number of vehicles used and of extra hours worked by drivers as well as of the postponed service (in case of soft time windows), and the balance of the routes in terms of duration or/and number of clients visited; readers can refer to [13] for an overview of the different objectives used in VRP. Finally, environmental performance evaluations, together with business evaluations, are included in VRP; the authors refer to green VRP (GVRP) [14]. Recent papers related to distribution activities in urban areas include environmental aspects in their model [15,16].

In this paper, we are involved with an RVRP with additional constraints due to:

- Multi-periods planning, as in [17], together with a distribution policy of the company that permits the postponement of services;
- Customer requirements: time windows for serving customers, and products with different priorities, as in [18];
- Fleet of vehicles: a heterogenous fleet in terms of capacity and costs, as in [19], since the company has its own and third-party vehicles.

To the authors' knowledge, the problem investigated here has never been proposed in the literature, and the above three cited papers have only some common elements with the RVRP analyzed. In particular, ref. [17] deals with a multi-period distribution of pharmaceutical products that is characterized by a heterogeneous fleet, restrictions on routes (a maximum duration and a maximum number of clients are fixed), and flexible customer time windows. The authors analyze a multi-depot network, where it is also possible to use auxiliary depots for improving routing costs and permitting to anticipate deliveries; moreover, incompatibilities between customers and vehicles are considered. This is different from our problem because we permit the postponement of a part of customers' demand following different demand priorities. Priorities are also included in [18]; in case of not enough vehicles (the fleet is fixed), it is possible to postpone customer services until the next day (depending on the priorities given) or to allow extra time to drivers, differently from our case in which there is the possibility of postponing the delivery of some products until one or two days.

Finally, in [19], the authors consider a fleet composed of company vehicles and vehicles of third-party, thus a heterogeneous fleet for the costs and the possibility of outsourcing the last mile transport of some specific deliveries. Furthermore, this problem is different from ours because the company we are involved with can increase the available vehicles due to third-party ones but without distinguishing between long-haul transport and last mile, and without using third-party depots. Heuristics approaches for heterogeneous fleet VRP (HFVRP) have been reviewed in [20]. In [21], the authors propose a Branch-Cut-and-Price algorithm (BCP) for solving HFVRP; they also show how to transform the MD-VRP and the site-dependent VRP in an HFVRP.

Many RVRP, based on a multi-period analysis, are present in the literature in addition to the previous ones. In [20], a survey of heuristics approaches for periodic VRP is presented. To cite some other recent papers, ref. [22] is related to food distribution in Portugal and presents a RVRP with multiple time windows, multi-products, and site-dependent incompatible constraints; ref. [23] considers a multi-depot network, but customers can be visited only once in the planning horizon with a heterogeneous fleet and respecting some site-dependent incompatible constraints; in [24], multiple periods and multi-depot RVP is analyzed, and the authors also include in the analysis inventory management.

In the recent literature, many papers offer exact algorithms to solve some of the variants of VRP cited above, such as VRPTW, HFVRP, and MD-VRP. The new challenge was to find a general solver for tackling a wide class of VRPs. Heuristics and meta-heuristics for many variants of VRP were reviewed by [20]; the authors defined Muli-attribute-VRP (MAVRP). A Unified Hybrid Genetic Search metaheuristic as a general-purpose algorithm for solving MAVRP was proposed by [25]. Recently, ref. [26] proposed a BCP algorithm that is able to solve most of the studied VRP variants. The authors also offer a generic way to model different attributes of VRP that permits them to be solved by BCP.

The problem under investigation will be deeply analyzed and defined in the next section, while in Section 3, the proposed method for solving it is presented. A computational campaign for validating the proposed model and for evaluating the impact of the company policy on distribution activities and costs is reported in Section 4. A discussion together with some conclusions are reported in Section 5.

2. Problem under Investigation

In this work, the problem under investigation can be defined as a multi-period VRP with time windows for serving customers, with a heterogeneous fleet of vehicles, in which the fleet composition must be defined by searching for the best mix of subcontracting transportation to add to an owned fleet. The number and type of vehicles to be used each day of a given planning horizon have to be defined, together with the routes for the selected vehicles.

The company, which has a fleet of owned vehicles and has the possibility of using extra vehicles of a third party company, adopts a distribution strategy for obtaining an efficient usage of the vehicles and for reducing routing costs, which must be minimized together with the number of vehicles used.

In more detail, given a depot with a heterogeneous fleet of vehicles, a set of extra vehicles that can be required daily to a third part company, and a set of customers characterized by demand over a planning horizon for products with three different priorities, determine the best way to serve the customers in such a way to satisfy their demands by respecting required time windows, minimize the total kilometers traveled and the number of additional vehicles required to serve customers, while respecting law restrictions for drivers (i.e., the maximum route duration and the maximum drive time per route).

The daily customer demand is characterized by three different priorities, in the sense that a part of the demand must be delivered on the exact day the request refers, another part can be delayed to the day after, and another part (with the low priority) can be postponed by two days. This means that a part of the customer demand can be split into two or three days. An example is reported in Figure 1. Let us consider a planning horizon of 5 working days (Day 1, Day 2, ... Day 5) and suppose to have to supply to a given client the following quantities 10, 11, and 5 (in pallets) in three days of the week: Day 1, Day 3, and Day 4, split into $p0$, $p1$, and $p2$ according to the required delivery priorities (i.e., 10 is given by $p0 = 5$, $p1 = 4$, and $p2 = 1$ as reported in the bottom of Figure 1). This means that if it is necessary to reduce the transportation costs, the company can deliver either part of $p1$ or the whole $p1$ in Day 2, and $p2$ either in Day 2 or Day 3. Suppose there are vehicles with nine-pallet capacity, as shown in Figure 1, it is possible to note that when the split strategy is permitted, the demand of Day 1 is not completely served in the required day, and $p2$ for example, is supplied in Day 3, together with a part of the demand of Day 3. The demand of Day 3 for products $p1$ and $p2$ is satisfied in Day 4 together with the demand of Day 4. In this way, we are able to use only one vehicle each day, while without the split strategy in Day 1 and Day 3, two vehicles are required.

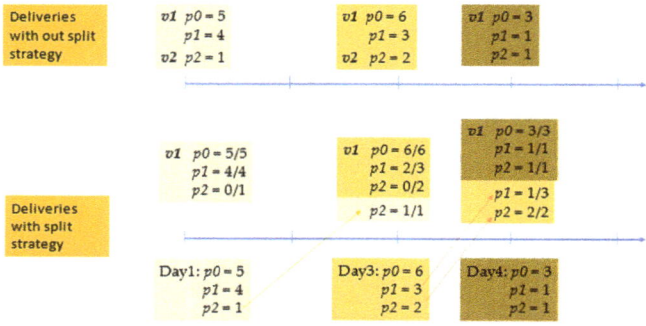

Figure 1. Example of deliveries without and with the postponing strategy.

This distribution policy is based on the different priorities associated with the customers' demand and has a positive impact on both the costs of the company for the third part vehicles and the external costs paid by the society due to better usage of the vehicle capacity.

The above described distribution policy can be adopted for reducing the impact of negative externalities of transport activities. Cooperation among different actors of the supply chain (in this case, between the distribution company and the customers) is an important way that must be investigated for improving efficiency. In the next section, we introduce the optimization model for solving this distribution problem.

3. Method: An Optimization Model

In this section, the mathematical programming model proposed to solve the problem described above is introduced. We begin with useful notations, which are outlined below.
Sets:
N is set of nodes
C is set of customers
A is set of arcs
P is set of types of products characterized by different priorities (i.e., $p0, p1, p2$)
V is set of vehicles
V' is set of vehicles of the third party
D is set of working days

Parameters:
c_{ij} $\forall (i,j) \in A$ is transport cost associated to arc (i,j)
s_{ij} $\forall (i,j) \in A$ is transport time associated to arc (i,j)
d_{jpd} $\forall j \in C, \forall p \in P, \forall d \in D$ is demand of customer j for product p in day d
a_j $\forall j \in C$ is least time for visiting customer j
b_j $\forall j \in C$ is last time for visiting customer j
t_j $\forall j \in C$ is time required to serve customer j
e_k $\forall k \in V'$ is cost associated to vehicle k of the third party
q_k $\forall k \in V \cup V'$ is capacity of vehicle k
md_k $\forall k \in V \cup V'$ is maximum driver time for vehicle k
ms_k $\forall k \in V \cup V'$ is maximum service time for vehicle k (i.e., max route duration)

Decision variables:
$x_{ijkd} \in \{0,1\}$, $\forall (i,j) \in A, k \in V \cup V', d \in D$
$x_{ijkd} = 1$ if vehicle k travel on arc (i,j) in day d
$y_{kd} \in \{0,1\}$, $\forall k \in V, d \in D$ $y_{kd} = 1$ if vehicle k is used during day d
$z_{kd} \in \{0,1\}$, $\forall k \in V', d \in D$ $z_{kd} = 1$ if vehicle k of third party is used during day d
$t_{ikd} \geq 0$ $\forall i \in N, k \in V, d \in D$ is arrival time of vehicle k at customer i in day d
$q0_{ipkd} \geq 0$ $\forall i \in C, p \in P, k \in V \cup V', d \in D$ is quantity of product p shipped on time to customer i by vehicle k in day d
$q1_{ipkd} \geq 0$ $\forall i \in C, p \in P\setminus\{p0\}, k \in V \cup V', d \in D$ is quantity of product p (either a product $p1$ or $p2$) shipped with 1 day-delay to customer i by vehicle k in day d
$q2_{ipkd} \geq 0$ $\forall i \in C, p \in P\setminus\{p0, p1\}, k \in V \cup V', d \in D$ is quantity of product $p2$, shipped with 2 days-delay to customer i by vehicle k in day d

The resulting model is the following:

$$\text{Min} \sum_{(i,j)\in A} \sum_{k \in V \cup V'} \sum_{d \in D} c_{ij} x_{ijkd} + \sum_{k \in V'} \sum_{d \in D} e_k z_{kd} \quad (1)$$

$$\sum_{(i,j)\in A} \sum_{k \in V \cup V'} x_{ijkd} \leq 1 \quad \forall j \in C, \forall d \in D \quad (2)$$

$$\sum_{(n_0,j)\in A} \sum_{k \in V \cup V'} x_{ijkd} \leq \sum_{k \in V} y_{kd} + \sum_{k \in V'} z_{kd} \quad d \in D \quad (3)$$

$$\sum_{(n_0,j)\in A} x_{ijkd} \leq 1 k \in V \cup V', \forall d \in D \quad (4)$$

$$\sum_{(i,j)\in A} x_{ijkd} \leq M y_{kd} k \in V, \forall d \in D \quad (5)$$

$$\sum_{(i,j)\in A} x_{ijkd} \leq M z_{kd} k \in V', \forall d \in D \quad (6)$$

$$\sum_{(i,j)\in A} s_{ij} x_{ijkd} \leq t_d k \in V \cup V', \forall d \in D \quad (7)$$

$$\sum_{(i,j)\in A} (s_{ij} + t_j) x_{ijkd} \leq t_d k \in V \cup V', \forall d \in D \quad (8)$$

$$\sum_{k \in V \cup V'} q0_{j0kd} = d_{j0d} \forall j \in C, \forall d \in D \quad (9)$$

$$\sum_{k \in V \cup V'} q0_{j0kd} + q1_{j1k(d-1)} = d_{j1d} \forall j \in C, \forall d \in D \quad (10)$$

$$\sum_{k \in V \cup V'} q0_{j0kd} + q1_{j1k(d-1)} + q1_{j2k(d-2)} = d_{j2d} \quad \forall j \in C, \forall d \in D \quad (11)$$

$$\sum_{j \in C} q0_{j0kd} + q0_{j1kd} + q0_{j2kd} + q1_{j1k(d-1)} + q1_{j2k(d-1)} + q2_{j2k(d-2)} \leq q_k k \in V \cup V', \forall d \in D \quad (12)$$

$$\sum_{(i,j)\in A} x_{ijkd} d_{jpd} \geq q0_{jpkd} \forall j \in C, \forall p \in P, k \in V \cup V', \forall d \in D \quad (13)$$

$$\sum_{(i,j)\in A} x_{ijkd} d_{jpd} \geq q1_{jpkd} \forall j \in C, \forall p \in P, k \in V \cup V', \forall d \in D \quad (14)$$

$$\sum_{(i,j)\in A} x_{ijkd} d_{jpd} \geq q2_{jpkd} \forall j \in C, \forall p \in P, k \in V \cup V', \forall d \in D \quad (15)$$

$$\sum_{k \in V \cup V'} t_{jkd} \leq b_j \forall j \in C, \forall d \in D \quad (16)$$

$$\sum_{k \in V \cup V'} t_{jkd} \geq a_j \forall j \in C, \forall d \in D \quad (17)$$

$$t_{jkd} - t_{ikd} \geq s_{ij} + t_i + M(x_{ijkd} - 1) \forall (i,j) \in A, k \in V \cup V', \forall d \in D \quad (18)$$

Equation (1) aims at minimizing the routing costs and the number of vehicles of third party used during the time horizon. Equation (2) impose that each day of the planning horizon, each customer can be visited no more than 1 time by a vehicle (either an owned or a third-party vehicle). Equations (3)–(6) refer to the usage of vehicles: the maximum number of vehicles used each day must be no greater than the number of owned vehicles and the number of vehicles available due to the third party (Equation (3)) and each vehicle can be used at most for one route per day (Equation (4)). Equations (5) and (6) are used to define variables y and z related to the usage of owned and third-party vehicles respectively.

Equations (7) and (8) are related to the maximum duration of each route associated with a vehicle; in particular, Equations (7) refer to the drive time, while Equation (8) to the service time that includes the time spent at the customer's location for delivering goods in addition to time spent driving.

Equations (9)–(11) are related to the customer demand, for the products having 3 different priorities. The capacity of each vehicle is verified due to Equation (12). Moreover, Equations (13)–(15) link variables x and those representing the quantities supplied to customers: only if vehicle k visits customer j in day d, it can supply a given amount of product p to the customer, no greater than the demand of the customer for that product.

Equations (16)–(18) are related to the time windows. For each customer, Equations (16) and (17) verify that the vehicle arrives within his time window. Equation (18) permit to compute, in the correct way, the time of arrival at each couple of customers visited in sequence by the same vehicle k (i.e., when arc (i,j) is used by vehicle k).

The validation of the proposed model is presented in the next section.

4. Results

Some experimental tests have been realized with the aim of validating the proposed model and evaluating the effect of the strategy of postponing some deliveries in such a way to reach more sustainable solutions, in terms of number of vehicles used and better usage of vehicle capacity. All tests have been implemented in Java, using CPLEX version 12.8 as a solver. The computational tests were performed on a MacBook Pro, with a 2.9 GHz Intel i9 processor, and 32 GB of RAM. Different kinds of instances have been generated. In particular, we have tested instances characterized by a different space distribution of clients (i.e., a circular region and a rectangular one) and a different position of the depot in the considered region; the depot can be either centred in the area or positioned near a border of the area as depicted in Figure 2.

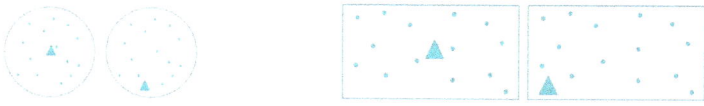

Figure 2. Circular and rectangular region with different depot locations.

We consider a time horizon of a week (5 working days) and instances with 10 and 20 clients with a random generated demand for three types of products:

- $p0$ product to serve in time;
- $p1$ product to serve no more than 1 day late;
- $p2$ product to serve no more than 2 days late.

The demand distribution among these three products is 50% $p0$, 30% $p1$ and 20% $p2$. Moreover, different demand distributions within the time horizon are generated: each client has a demand distributed among 2 days or 5 days of the week. Finally, different time window durations are considered: from 0 h to 1 h, from 1 h to 2 h, and from 2 h to 3 h.

In the following, we will use Instance Id for identifying the instance characteristics in the following order: shape, depot position, number of clients, time windows duration, i.e., C_C_10_1 refers to a circular area with a depot in the centre, 10 customers with time windows of 1 hour, while R_L_20_3 refers to a rectangular area with a depot near a border, 20 customers to serve with time windows from 2 to 3 h.

The experimental campaign has the following main aims:

1. To evaluate the impact of some of the characteristics of the generated instances on both the model behavior (in terms of computational time and optimality gap) and the quality of the solutions in terms of service level to grant to the customers (i.e., delayed deliveries);
2. To evaluate the benefits that can be obtained when postponing deliveries.

4.1. First Analysis: Model Behavior and Customer Service Level

In this section, we report some results obtained solving randomly generated instances by the models (1)–(18) within a time limit of 30 min.

Each set of instances (**Id_Ist**) are shown in Table 1: the objective function values (**Obj**), the computational time in seconds (**CPU time**), and the optimality gap (**Gap**). The last three columns are related to the quality of the solutions, and the delays in the delivery are reported. In particular, the ratio between the quantities delivered with one (two) day(s) delay and the total customer demand (**l1/tot [l2/tot]**) are computed together with the total amount of goods delayed (l1 + l2) with respect to the total demand (**(l1 + l2)/tot**). Instances characterized by 10 customers have 3640 variables and 3965 constraints, while those with 20 customers have 11,240 variables and 11,805 constraints.

Data reported in Table 1 are the average values of two instances. From Table 1, we can note that it is possible to solve up to optimality instances with 10 customers and instances with 20 customers and a time window duration of less than 1 h. When larger time windows are considered, often the time limit of half an hour is reached, and only the best solutions found by CPLEX are returned. Solutions with an average gap of 0.05 and 0.11 are obtained for instances with time windows less than 2 and 3 h, respectively. About 50% of instances characterized by 20 customers and time windows from 1 to 2 h have been solved up to optimality.

Table 1. Results obtained by using mode (1)–(18).

Id_Ist	Obj	CPU	Gap	l1/tot	l2/tot	l1 + l2/tot
CC_10_1	6809.77	0	0.00	5.11	0.0	5.1
RC_10_1	5552.58	1	0.00	5.84	0.0	5.8
CL_10_1	8859.78	0	0.00	5.11	0.0	5.1
RL_10_1	6786.45	1.5	0.00	5.11	0.0	5.1
CC_10_2	6532.14	0.5	0.00	4.38	0.0	4.4
RC_10_2	5347.37	3	0.00	5.84	0.0	5.8
CL_10_2	8567.69	25	0.00	4.38	0.0	4.4
RL_10_2	6274.39	32	0.00	5.84	0.0	5.8
CC_10_3	6425.10	4.5	0.00	5.84	0.0	5.8
RC_10_3	5275.17	28	0.00	5.11	0.0	5.1
CL_10_3	8038.77	975	0.02	6.57	0.0	6.6
RL_10_3	6310.80	915.5	0.07	5.11	0.0	5.1
CC_20_1	11,116.72	8	0.00	4.99	0.6	5.6
RC_20_1	10,405.45	25.5	0.00	6.16	0.0	6.2
CL_20_1	14,342.25	48	0.00	4.69	0.0	4.7
RL_20_1	11,527.94	210	0.00	5.28	0.0	5.3
CC_20_2	8816,25	1018.5	0.01	4.11	0.0	4.1
RC_20_2	8527.19	1141	0.01	4.40	0.6	5.0
CL_20_2	12,797.78	1800	0.06	4.99	0.3	5.3
RL_20_2	10,527.72	1800	0.11	4.40	0.3	4.7

Table 1. *Cont.*

Id_Ist	Obj	CPU	Gap	l1/tot	l2/tot	l1 + l2/tot
CC_20_3	9093.23	1800	0.03	4.69	0.6	5.3
RC_20_3	7600.76	1800	0.05	4.40	1.5	5.9
CL_20_3	11,785.21	1800	0.19	4.40	0.3	4.7
RL_20_3	9097.86	1800	0.18	4.88	0.0	4.9

The following figures are useful to understand what the main factors are impacting the difficulty when solving the model. In particular, the graph in Figure 3 reports an increasing trend of the computational time spent by the model when increasing the number of customers, when changing the position of the depot: instances characterized by a depot located in the center of the region seems to be easier to be solved, and also, the shape of the area in which customers are located (from circle to rectangular) seems to have an effect on the solution time and gap.

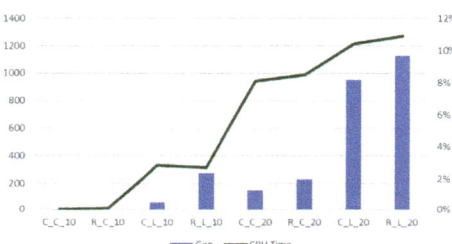

Figure 3. Optimality gap (%) and computational time (secs).

But what are the main factors impacting the CPU time and optimality gap? In the following graphs, we are able to stress the main influencer factor on the CPU, on the Gap, and on the quality of the solution in terms of delays.

In graphs reported in Figure 4, we can compare the average Gap in percentage (Figure 4a) and average CPU time in seconds (Figure 4b) of instances characterized by different areas' shape, different depots position and a different number of customers (number C). In Figure 4a, we can observe by the orange line, that when customers are distributed in a rectangular area, the Gap is a little higher; the lateral position of the depot has a greater impact on the Gap as the larger number of customers. In Figure 4b the orange line represents in all cases the longest solution time, but the impact on the CPU time is low for the area shape, larger for the depot position, and influenced by the number of customers.

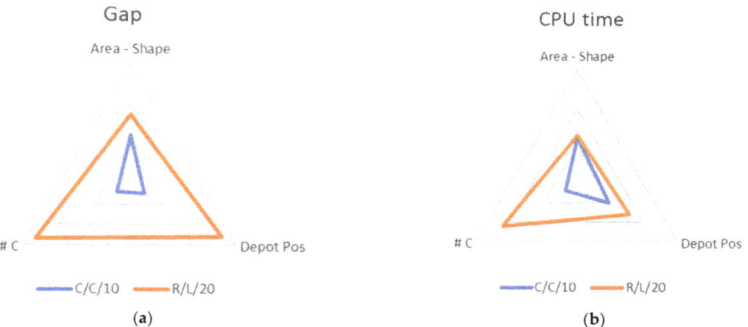

Figure 4. Factors influencing the model behavior: (**a**) impact on the optimality gap; (**b**) impact on computational time.

From Figure 5, we can note that the considered factors (number C, depot position, and shape) seem not to have a strong impact on the postponed deliveries (percentage of postponed customers' demand). All the differences are in the range −6.0 + 4.3%

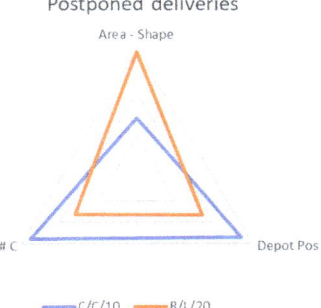

Figure 5. Postponed deliveries.

Finally, we show in the graph of Figure 6 the impact of time window durations on the complexity of the model. We can easily note that larger time windows have an impact on both CPU time and the optimality gap. In particular, instances with a 1-h time window are solved up to optimality in an average CPU time of 36.75 s, while 727.50 and 1140.38 s are required to solve instances with 2- and 3-h time windows. The average gaps have the same trend and pass from 0 to 0.02 and 0.07.

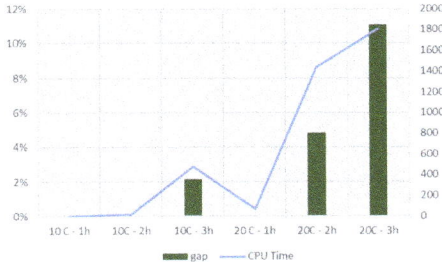

Figure 6. Impact of time window durations on optimality gap (%) and computational time (secs).

We are also interested in evaluating the impact of time windows duration on the quality of the solutions. In the graph shown in Figure 7, we can observe the relation between the time window duration and the total quantities of delayed deliveries. The time window durations seem to have a soft effect on the delayed deliveries.

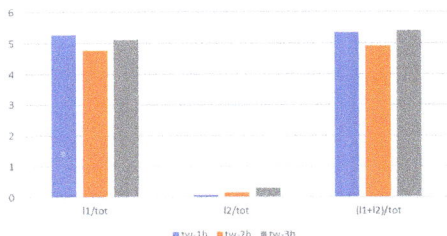

Figure 7. Time window durations and % of postponed deliveries.

Impact of Time Windows Duration on the Routing Costs

When analyzing the different solutions obtained varying the time window (TW) durations, we noted some differences in the planned routes and their related costs. As an example of these differences, in Figure 8 we report the solution for a specific day of the week in which we have to serve a subset of 20 customers, assuming to have 1 h (Figure 8a) and 3 h (Figure 8b) time windows. The number of routes is unchanged, but the paths (i.e., the sequences of visited customers) are different.

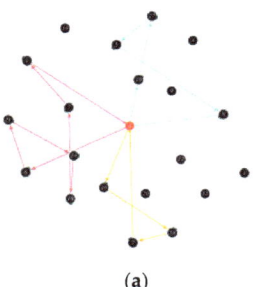
(a)

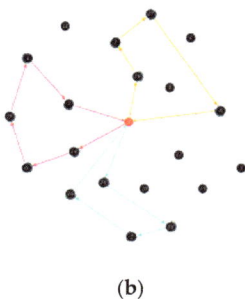
(b)

Figure 8. Planned routes: (**a**) distribution plan for serving customers respecting 1-h TW; (**b**) distribution plan for serving customers respecting 3-h TW.

As far as transportation costs are considered, the savings due to larger time windows durations can be computed looking at Table 1 (obj column). On average, passing from time windows less than 1 h to time windows from 1 to 2 h, we obtain a saving of 4.6%, while from less than 1 h to time windows from 2 to 3 h the saving is 7%.

4.2. Second Analysis: Effects of Postponing Deliveries

The policy of distribution companies for reducing routing costs may include split deliveries. In this paper, the split delivery can be used to postpone part of the customer's demand by either one or two days. The split considered here is possible only for a part of the customer demand in accordance with the priorities (as already explained in the previous sections). In this section, we show the benefits that can be obtained by using this distribution strategy. We compare the results reported in Table 1, related to the following situation $p0 = 50\%$, $p1 = 30\%$, and $p2 = 20\%$ with those obtained considering two opposite and extreme cases:

- *free*: there is not a limitation on the products that can be postponed (i.e., $p0 = p1 = 0\%$ and $p2 = 100\%$);
- *fixed*: it is not possible to postpone deliveries (i.e., $p0 = 100\%$, $p1 = p2 = 0$).

From Figure 9, we can note that the transportation costs are lower for case *free*. In this case, there is a higher level of postponed deliveries, which is double with respect to the case 50-30-20; the delayed deliveries pass from 4.52% to more than 9%. Concerning the costs, we can say that the distribution strategy investigated here permits the cost reduction of about 2.4%, while the saving passes to 5.4% in the ideal case, which is when the company is free to decide when to deliver goods (in any case within 2 days).

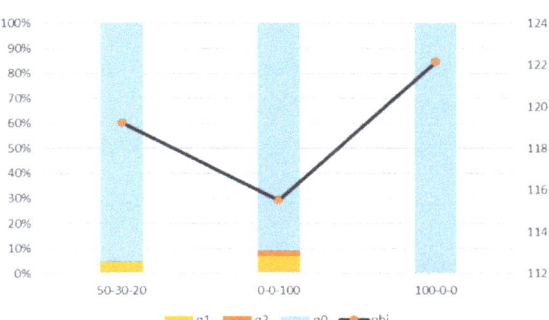

Figure 9. Impact of different distribution policies on the routing costs.

5. Discussion and Conclusions

In this work, we have analyzed a distribution strategy for reducing routing costs and the number of vehicles used for serving customers (that is, for reducing the impact of negative externalities of transport activities). In particular, the scope of the present work has been to investigate the advantages that should be obtained with more flexibility in serving customers. This flexibility can be obtained by solving a period VRP for a planning horizon during which split delivery is permitted for a part of the customer's demand. In fact, each customer's demand is partitioned into three sets in accordance with different priorities. The split delivery in this case consists in postponing part of the demand and depends on the priority.

Note that, the distribution strategy based on split deliveries, while permitting to optimize transportation costs, can represent a reduction of the customer's service level. Thus, part of the savings in the transportation costs could be shared with customers; in this way, the cooperation among companies and their customers will produce a gain for both.

We can conclude in stressing that cooperation among different actors of the supply chain is an important avenue that must be investigated for improving efficiency.

For evaluating this strategy, we have proposed a mixed integer programming model, that can be included in the class of RVRP. Despite the objective function that minimizes the sum of two objectives, in the present paper we have not investigated the proposed RVRP as a bi-objective optimization problem. In future work, it should be interesting to furnish the distribution company with a set of Pareto efficient solutions by facing the problem, for example, with the epsilon constraints method.

We have solved some small instances with 10 and 20 customers. Larger instances have been solved up to optimality, only when time windows duration is less than 1 h. For larger time windows, it was not possible to obtain optimal solutions within half an hour. Larger instances will require a different approach for being solved in reasonable CPU times.

The future challenge is to furnish a tool able to support the distribution company we are involved with during its decisional process for serving customers. Thus, in future works, we will deeply analyze the solution methods for solving this RVRP. The performances of the proposed model can be improved by adding sub-tour cuts for couples of nodes and for cycles of three nodes. We tested them solving the larger instances and have noted a CPU time reduction that ranges from 20 to 70%. Moreover, in the recent literature generic solver for RVRP has been proposed. The idea is to investigate how to transform our RVRP in such a way to use the generic solver. Some kinds of transformations are described in [21], but unfortunately, we deal with a period VRP with split delivery among the periods of the planning horizon, and this case is quite different from those proposed in some recent papers.

Author Contributions: The author contributions are considered equal in all parts of the article. All authors have read and agreed to the published version of the manuscript.

Funding: This research received no external funding.

Institutional Review Board Statement: Not applicable.

Informed Consent Statement: Not applicable.

Data Availability Statement: The data presented in this study are available on request from the corresponding author.

Conflicts of Interest: The authors declare no conflict of interest.

References

1. Bosona, T. Urban Freight Last Mile Logistics—Challenges and Opportunities to Improve Sustainability: A Literature Review. *Sustainability* **2020**, *12*, 8369. [CrossRef]
2. Sicilia, J.A.; Quemada, C.; Royo, B.; Escuín, D. An optimization algorithm for solving the rich vehicle routing problem based on Variable Neighborhood Search and Tabu Search metaheuristics. *J. Comput. Appl. Math.* **2016**, *291*, 468–477. [CrossRef]
3. Ambrosino, D.; Ferrari, C.; Sciomachen, A.; Tei, A. Intermodal nodes and external costs: Re-thinking the current network organization. *Res. Transp. Bus. Manag.* **2016**, *19*, 106–117. [CrossRef]
4. Lahyani, R.; Khemakhem, M.; Semet, F. Rich vehicle routing problems: From a taxonomy to a definition. *Eur. J. Oper. Res.* **2015**, *241*, 1–14. [CrossRef]
5. Montoya-Torres, J.; Franco, J.; Isaza, S.; Jiménez, H.; Herazo-Padilla, N. A literature review on the vehicle routing problem with multiple depots. *Comput. Ind. Eng.* **2015**, *79*, 115–129. [CrossRef]
6. Vidal, T.; Crainic, T.G.; Gendreau, M.; Lahrichi, N.; Rei, W. A Hybrid Genetic Algorithm for Multidepot and Periodic Vehicle Routing Problems. *Oper. Res.* **2012**, *60*, 611–624. [CrossRef]
7. Rahimi-Vahed, A.; Crainic, T.G.; Gendreau, M.; Rei, W. Fleet-sizing for multi-depot and periodic vehicle routing problems using a modular heuristic algorithm. *Comput. Oper. Res.* **2015**, *53*, 9–23. [CrossRef]
8. Francis, P.; Smilowitz, K.; Tzur, M. The period vehicle routing problem and its extensions. In *The Vehicle Routing Problem: Latest Advances and New Challenges*; Golden, B., Raghavan, S., Wasil, E., Eds.; Springer: New York, NY, USA, 2008; pp. 73–102.
9. Andersson, H.; Hoff, A.; Christiansen, M.; Hasle, G.; Løkketangen, A. Industrial aspects and literature survey: Combined inventory management and routing. *Comput. Oper. Res.* **2010**, *37*, 1515–1536. [CrossRef]
10. Prodhon, C.; Prins, C. A survey of recent research on location-routing problems. *Eur. J. Oper. Res.* **2014**, *238*, 1–17. [CrossRef]
11. Cáceres-Cruz, J.; Arias, P.; Guimarans, D.; Riera, D.; Juan, A.A. Rich vehicle routing problem: Survey. *ACM Comput. Surv.* **2015**, *47*, 1–28. [CrossRef]
12. Toth, P.; Vigo, D. *Vehicle Routing: Problems, Methods, and Applications*, 2nd ed.; Society for Industrial and Applied Mathematics—SIAM: Philadelphia, PA, USA, 2014. [CrossRef]
13. Vidal, T.; Laporte, G.; Matl, P. A concise guide to existing and emerging vehicle routing problem variants. *Eur. J. Oper. Res.* **2020**, *286*, 401–416. [CrossRef]
14. Lin, C.; Choy, K.L.; Ho, G.T.S.; Chung, S.H.; Lam, H.Y. Survey of Green Vehicle Routing Problem: Past and future trends. *Expert Syst. Appl.* **2014**, *41*, 1118–1138. [CrossRef]
15. Cerulli, R.; Dameri, R.; Sciomachen, A. Operations management in distribution networks within a smart city framework. *IMA J. Manag. Math.* **2018**, *29*, 189–205. [CrossRef] [PubMed]
16. Cerrone, C.; Cerulli, R.; Golden, B. Carousel greedy: A generalized greedy algorithm with applications in optimization. *Comput. Oper. Res.* **2017**, *85*, 97–112. [CrossRef]
17. Kramer, R.; Cordeau, J.-F.; Iori, M. Rich vehicle routing with auxiliary depots and anticipated deliveries: An application to pharmaceutical distribution. *Transp. Res. Part E Logist. Transp. Rev.* **2019**, *129*, 162–174. [CrossRef]
18. De Armas, J.; Melian-Batista, B. Variable Neighborhood Search for a Dynamic Rich Vehicle Routing Problem with time windows. *Comput. Ind. Eng.* **2015**, *85*, 120–131. [CrossRef]
19. Alcaraz, J.J.; Caballero-Arnaldos, L.; Vales-Alonso, J. Rich vehicle routing problem with last-mile outsourcing decisions. *Transp. Res. Part E Logist. Transp. Rev.* **2019**, *129*, 263–286. [CrossRef]
20. Vidal, T.; Crainic, T.G.; Gendreau, M.; Prins, C. Heuristics for multi-attribute vehicle routing problems: A survey and synthesis. *Eur. J. Oper. Res.* **2013**, *231*, 1–21. [CrossRef]
21. Pessoa, A.; Sadykov, R.; Uchoa, E. Enhanced Branch-Cut-and-Price algorithm for heterogeneous fleet vehicle routing problems. *Eur. J. Oper. Res.* **2018**, *270*, 530–543. [CrossRef]
22. Amorim, P.; Parragh, S.; Sperandio, F.; Almada-Lobo, B. A rich vehicle routing problem dealing with perishable food: A case study. *TOP* **2014**, *22*, 489–508. [CrossRef]
23. Mancini, S. A real-life Multi Depot Multi Period Vehicle Routing Problem with a Heterogeneous Fleet: Formulation and Adaptive Large Neighborhood Search based Matheuristic. *Transp. Res. Part C Emerg. Technol.* **2016**, *70*, 100–112. [CrossRef]
24. Bertazzi, L.; Coelho, L.C.; De Maio, A.; Laganà, D. A matheuristic algorithm for the multi-depot inventory routing problem. *Transp. Res. Part E Logist. Transp. Rev.* **2019**, *122*, 524–544. [CrossRef]

25. Vidal, T.; Crainic, T.G.; Gendreau, M.; Prins, C. A unified solution framework for multi-attribute vehicle routing problems. *Eur. J. Oper. Res.* **2014**, *234*, 658–673. [CrossRef]
26. Pessoa, A.; Sadykov, R.; Uchoa, E.; Vanderbeck, F. A generic exact solver for vehicle routing and related problems. *Math. Program.* **2020**, *183*, 483–523. [CrossRef]

Article

An Inventory Model for Non-Instantaneously Deteriorating Items with Nonlinear Stock-Dependent Demand, Hybrid Payment Scheme and Partially Backlogged Shortages

Md Al-Amin Khan [1], Ali Akbar Shaikh [2], Leopoldo Eduardo Cárdenas-Barrón [3,*], Abu Hashan Md Mashud [4], Gerardo Treviño-Garza [3] and Armando Céspedes-Mota [3]

[1] Department of Mathematics, Jahangirnagar University, Dhaka 1342, Bangladesh; alaminkhan@juniv.edu
[2] Department of Mathematics, The University of Burdwan, Burdwan 713104, India; aakbarshaikh@gmail.com
[3] School of Engineering and Sciences, Tecnologico de Monterrey, Ave. Eugenio Garza Sada 2501, Monterrey 64849, Mexico; trevino@tec.mx (G.T.-G.); acespede@tec.mx (A.C.-M.)
[4] Department of Mathematics, Hajee Mohammad Danesh Science and Technology University, Dinajpur 5200, Bangladesh; mashud@hstu.ac.bd
* Correspondence: lecarden@tec.mx; Tel.: +52-81-83284235; Fax: +52-81-83284153

Abstract: This research work presents an inventory model that involves non-instantaneous deterioration, nonlinear stock-dependent demand, and partially backlogged shortages by considering the length of the waiting time under a hybrid prepayment and cash-on-delivery scheme. The corresponding inventory problem is formulated as a nonlinear constraint optimization problem. The theoretical results for the unique optimal solution are presented, and eight special cases are also identified. Moreover, a salient theoretical result is provided: a certain condition where the optimal inventory policy may or may not involve deterioration. Finally, two numerical examples are provided using a sensitivity analysis to show the validity range of the inventory parameters.

Keywords: inventory; non-instantaneous deterioration; partial backlogging; stock-dependent demand

Citation: Khan, M.A.-A.; Shaikh, A.A.; Cárdenas-Barrón, L.E.; Mashud, A.H.M.; Treviño-Garza, G.; Céspedes-Mota, A. An Inventory Model for Non-Instantaneously Deteriorating Items with Nonlinear Stock-Dependent Demand, Hybrid Payment Scheme and Partially Backlogged Shortages. *Mathematics* 2022, 10, 434. https://doi.org/10.3390/math10030434

Academic Editors: Zsolt Tibor Kosztyán, Zoltán Kovács and Frank Werner

Received: 13 October 2021
Accepted: 13 January 2022
Published: 29 January 2022

Publisher's Note: MDPI stays neutral with regard to jurisdictional claims in published maps and institutional affiliations.

Copyright: © 2022 by the authors. Licensee MDPI, Basel, Switzerland. This article is an open access article distributed under the terms and conditions of the Creative Commons Attribution (CC BY) license (https://creativecommons.org/licenses/by/4.0/).

1. Introduction

Harris [1] was the first researcher to design an economic order quantity (EOQ) inventory model by presenting the concept of inventory to encounter future demand by storing products in warehouses for an appropriate period of time. Notwithstanding, his inventory model incorporated many practical scenarios in simple forms, for instance, demand is constant and known, the quality level of the products during the storing period is uniform, products are delivered instantaneously after the order has been made, the payment is entirely dependent on the products delivery time, and products are always available to meet market demand. Nowadays, inventory management has become more much complicated because of the emergence of competitive market globalization, and hence, a substantial number of researchers in the inventory field have been developing several efficacious inventory models by taking more realistic assumptions that perfectly model the reality of businesses into consideration. A recent report by [2] indicates that about half of the total number of stored items in any US grocery industry are perishable while the remaining half consists of non-perishable foods and non-food items. Subsequently, the gross revenue of any grocery practitioner depends considerably upon how to manage these perishable items by increasing operational efficiency through the entire business with the help of proper purchasing coordination and by fulfilling the market demand on time. However, a plethora of perishable items (for instance, vegetables, fruits, milk, meat, among others) deteriorate during the storage time period due to their physical ingredients or due to other reasons. Additionally, for many other types of products (for instance, perfumes, radioactive materials, alcohol, among others), practitioners can observe the decay these items over their storage time durations. Due to the deterioration of these products, practitioners' profits may be badly affected, and hence, the impact of deterioration must be considered in the inventory management of these items. Due to the original quality of the items (for instance, vegetables, fruits, milk, meat, among others), deterioration may not start at the moment when the products are received by the practitioner and might begin sometime after from the items have been received by the practitioner. This kind of phenomenon is termed as non-instantaneous deterioration. In general, customers always prefer to buy what they want from a place where a substantial number of items in perfect condition are stored. This study demonstrates the client inclinations to stock a huge amount product storage as a nonlinear stock-dependent function. In order to improve the operational efficiency of the inventory management for non-instantaneous deteriorating items, this research work outlines an inventory model with nonlinear stock-dependent demand and partial backlogged shortage with a hybrid advance and cash payment agreement. Under this agreement, for a product that is in high demand or a product that is in limited supply in markets, the retailer pays a fraction or the total of the purchase cost prior to receiving the delivery for the purpose of an on-time delivery.

The remaining portion of this research work is systematized as follows: Section 2 presents a literature review. Section 3 states the notation, description, and formulation of the inventory model as a nonlinear constraint optimization problem. Section 4 develops the solution procedure. Section 5 identifies some particular cases. Section 6 studies the impacts of the parameters of the advance payment scheme on the total cost. Section 7 solves some numerical examples to show the validity range of the inventory parameters. Finally, Section 8 provides conclusions and some opportunities for future research.

2. Literature Review

This section articulates the research gap and previous research contributions by describing existing studies related to this research work and then compares the studies in a tabular form.

Considering a constant deterioration rate, Ghare and Schrader [3] formulated an EOQ inventory model. After that, a plethora of inventory models were developed by several researchers by observing the characteristics of different deteriorating items to help practitioners reduce the losses incurred from the impact of deterioration efficaciously by maintaining the order size in a competent manner. Taleizadeh et al. [4] studied a vendor-managed inventory model for deteriorating items by adopting the Stackelberg approach. Some other correlated studies were conducted by Shaikh et al. [5], Tavakoli and Taleizadeh [6], Pando et al. [7], Khan et al. [8], Shaikh et al. [9], Khan et al. [10], Khan et al. [11], and Das et al. [12]. As a matter of fact, due to the original quality of the items (for instance, vegetables, fruits, milk, meat, among others), deterioration may not start from the moment when the products are received by the practitioner, and it might begin after some time the items have been received by the practitioner. This kind of phenomenon is termed as non-instantaneous deterioration. Musa and Sani [13] explored the impact of delayed deterioration on the inventory management policies of practitioners when they allowed a delay in the payment environment. Later, Sarkar and Sarkar [14] further investigated the consequences of delayed deterioration on the retailer's best stock policy when the demand is related to a linear form of the current stock amount. In this direction, it is worth referring to the following recent works: Tyagi et al. [15], Mashud et al. [16], Rastogi et al. [17], Khan et al. [18], Sundararajan et al. [19], and Sundararajan et al. [20].

According to Levin et al. [21], a large number of customers are attracted by the display of huge amounts of stock with lots of variety in super-shops, resulting in the market demand increasing. This is termed as stock-dependent demand. Valliathal and Uthayakumar [22] established an economic production quantity (EPQ) inventory model for time-reliant deteriorating goods with current stock-dependent market demand and partial backordering, and then they solved the problem by proposing a computational methodology. Later, Min et al. [23] extended Valliathal and Uthayakumar [22]'s production–inventory model by including the consequences incurred by delaying payments and solved the problem mathematically by developing theoretical results. Pando et al. [24] analyzed another inventory management policy by considering the nonlinear stock-dependent market demand instead of the linear demand pattern when the carrying cost is proportional to power form of the current stock amount. Sarkar and Sarkar [14] further investigated the effect of delayed deterioration when the demand is related to a linear form of the current stock amount. Again, Pando et al. [25] extended the previous study by Pando et al. [24] by improving the carrying cost proportionally to the power form of both the current stock amount and the storage duration. Following that, Yang [26] described two inventory models on the basis of the terminal condition under power form of the current stock amount related to demand when the carrying cost is proportional to the nonlinear form of the current stock amount. Sarkar et al. [27] investigated a seasonal product related inventory model with preservation facilities and linearly stock-dependent item demand along with time-dependent partial backordering. Later, Pando et al. [7] considered the nonlinear stock amount-related consumption rate for decaying products with zero terminating scenario and obtained an optimal solution. Again, Pando et al. [28] and Pando et al. [29] further examined the power form of the stock amount-related consumption rate under the objective of optimizing the profit and cost ratio. Recently, Cárdenas-Barrón et al. [30] improved the inventory model developed by Yang [26] by allowing a delay in payments into two inventory models according to the terminal conditions. All of the aforementioned studies related to nonlinear stock-dependent client demand are formulated for non-deteriorating items, except for in a single study Pando et al. [7]. However, Pando et al. [7] considered the moment at which deterioration began as the moment at which the items began to be stored in the warehouse. Consequently, it is critical to make inventory management more robust and flexible to delay deteriorating items under nonlinear stock-dependent client demand by developing efficient and effective inventory models.

Most recently, during the global coronavirus pandemic, the stay-at-home orders have markedly stimulated online grocery shopping, i.e., e-shopping transactions that depend on advanced payment and cash-on-delivery. When online shopping, suppliers typically require a certain segment of the purchasing price in advance of delivery, after the order has been placed, and asks for the rest of the purchasing price when the order is delivered, i.e., cash-on-delivery. By receiving the advanced payment segment for the ordered goods, suppliers cannot only obtain assurance about the orders but can also earn interest from this segment. Relaxing the cash-on-delivery policy from typical inventory models, Zhang [31] introduced an advance payment strategy in the inventory management system for the first time. Connected to this, the researchers developed some noteworthy works, such as an EOQ inventory model, by allowing multiple prepayment payment opportunities (Taleizadeh et al. [32]); multiple prepayment payments opportunities for deteriorating items (Taleizadeh [33]); the inclusion of prepayment opportunities in the supply chain environment (Zhang et al. [34]), multiple prepayment models under capacity constraints (Khan et al. [18], Khan et al. [35] and Shaikh et al. [36]); price discount opportunities on the basis of full or partial prepayment (Tavakoli and Taleizadeh [6], and Khan et al. [11]); and multiple prepayment opportunities for a perishable item with a certain lifetime (Khan et al. [37]).

Practitioners are frequently confronted with two distinct situations during shortages, namely (i) backorders and (ii) sales opportunity when shortages appear due to uncertainty in the marketplaces. In fact, when shortages occur, the customers may wait for new products to arrive or may move to other available sources that are able to meet their requirements. When all of the customers wait for the new product they want to arrive, the situation is termed as complete backordering (Shaikh et al. [5], and San-José et al. [38], and San-José et al. [39]); moreover, when some customers wait for new products to arrive, the situation is defined as partial backordering. Many researchers have been studying partial backordering situations by assuming that a fixed portion of the customers wait for a backordered item, i.e., a constant backlogging rate (Yang [26]; Taleizadeh [33]; Singh et al. [40], Khan et al. [11], Khan et al. [35], and Cárdenas-Barrón et al. [30]). In fact, whether customers wait for backorders or not depends on the duration of the waiting time. Hence, relaxing the concept of constant backlogging by waiting time, which is sensitive to the backlogging rate, some researchers have described several inventory policies (Sarkar and Sarkar [14]; Tyagi et al. [15]; Sarkar et al. [27]; Khan et al. [8], Khan et al. [37]; Shaikh et al. [36], and Panda et al. [28]). In addition, a comparison of the aforementioned studies and the proposed inventory model is presented in Table 1.

Table 1. A comparison of the inventory models.

Authors	EOQ/EPQ Inventory Model	Stock-Dependent Demand		Deterioration		Payment Scheme		Partial Backordering Rate	
		Linear	Nonlinear	Instantaneous	Non-Instantaneous	Advance	Cash on Delivery	Constant	Waiting Time Dependent
Shaikh et al. [5]	EOQ	√			√		√		
Pando et al. [7]	EOQ		√	√			√		
Khan et al. [11]	EOQ	√			√	√		√	
Sarkar and Sarkar [14]	EOQ	√			√		√		√
Tyagi et al. [15]	EOQ	√			√		√		√
Mashud et al. [16]	EOQ	√			√		√	√	
Valliathal and Uthayakumar [22]	EPQ	√		√			√		√
Min et al. [23]	EPQ	√		√			√		
Pando et al. [24]	EOQ		√				√		
Pando et al. [25]	EOQ		√				√		
Yang [26]	EOQ		√				√	√	
Sarkar et al. [27]	EOQ	√		√			√		√
Pando et al. [28]	EOQ		√				√		
Pando et al. [29]	EOQ		√				√		
Cárdenas-Barrón et al. [30]	EOQ		√				√	√	
Alshanbari et al. [41]	EOQ		√			√	√		√
Rahman et al. [42]	EOQ	√		√		√		√	
This paper	EOQ		√		√	√	√		√

Table 1 indicates that few works have explored the impacts of the nonlinear form of stock amount-related market demand on inventory policies and only a single work (Pando et al. [7]) in the literature has been conducted on decaying items under the nonlinear form of the stock amount-related consumption rate. In Pando et al. [7], deterioration commences as soon as the products are stored in the warehouse of the practitioner. However, they ignored the fact that a plethora of items (for instance, vegetables, fruits, milk, meat, fish, among others) has certain time intervals within the deterioration time span that do not commence immediately due to the original quality of the products. Moreover, Pando et al. [7] considered that products are delivered instantaneously after the practitioner has made the order and that the payment is entirely accomplished when the product is delivered. However, for a product that is in high or limited on the market, practitioners want to pay a fraction or total of the purchase cost prior to receiving the delivery for the purposes of having an on-time delivery. On the other hand, suppliers require a certain segment of the purchasing price after the product has been ordered and in advance of the rest of the segment that is paid when the order is delivered, i.e., cash-on-delivery, in order to obtain assurance about their orders. In addition, Pando et al. [7] did not take another practical scenario in marketplaces into consideration: backordering.

The salient findings of this research work can be abridged as follows: (i) the effects of the power form of the stock amount-related market demand on inventory policies for delayed or deteriorated items are investigated; (ii) a hybrid prepayment and cash-on-delivery payment scheme for the retailer is adopted; (iii) partial backordering on the basis of the length of the customer waiting time is incorporated; and (iv) a certain condition is provided to decide whether the optimal inventory policy involves deterioration. The combination of these four claims made by the present research work is unique in the inventory management literature.

3. Notation, Description and Formulation of the Inventory Model

This research work defines an inventory model for non-instantaneous deteriorating items with stock-dependent demand and partial-backlogged shortages with a hybrid payment system.

3.1. Notation

The following notation is used throughout the development of the inventory model:

Parameter	Units	Description
C_0	USD/order	replenishment cost
c_p	USD/unit	purchasing cost
c_h	USD/unit/unit of time	holding cost per unit per unit of time
c_b	USD/unit/unit of time	shortage cost per unit per unit of time
c_d	USD/unit/unit of time	deterioration cost per unit per unit of time
c_l	USD/unit/unit of time	opportunity cost per unit per unit of time
η	$\eta > 0$	scaling constant for demand rate
θ	$0 < \theta < 1$	deterioration rate
γ	$0 \leq \gamma < 1$	inventory level elasticity of demand rate
δ	$\delta \geq 0$	backloging parameter
t_s	unit of time	time at which the inventory starts to deteriorate with a rate of θ
$\aleph$	integer value	number of installments to prepay
σ	unit of time	time interval to accomplish the prepayment
ω	%	portion of the purchase price to prepay
i_c	%/unit of time	interest charged for the loan
$I(t)$	units	inventory level at any time t where $0 \leq t \leq t_1 + t_2$
X	USD/cycle	the total cost per cycle
$TC(t_1, t_2)$	USD/unit of time	the total cost per unit of time
Dependent Decision variables		
S	units	maximum stock per cycle
R	units	maximum shortages level
Decision variables		
t_1	unit of time	time at which the inventory level becomes zero
t_2	unit of time	time duration at which the inventory level is negative

3.2. Description of the Inventory Model

Initially, a retailer places an order to a supplier following a hybrid advanced and cash payment scheme. According to this scheme, the order is made by giving the ω portion of the total purchase price with the help of $\aleph$ equal installments during σ time units, and when the order is received by the person paying, then the remaining $(1 - \omega)$ amount is paid instantaneously. The replenishment rate is deemed as infinite. This paper considers that the demand is a power function of the stock level at time t, then it is:

$$D(t) = \begin{cases} \eta[I(t)]^\gamma, & \text{when } I(t) > 0 \\ \eta, & \text{when } I(t) \leq 0 \end{cases} \quad \text{where } \eta > 0 \text{ and } 0 \leq \gamma < 1.$$ Notice that when $I(t) > 0$, the demand is dependent on stock, and when $I(t) \leq 0$, demand is constant. This type or demand has been used previously by Pando et al. [7]; Pando et al. [25]; Yang [26]; and Cárdenas-Barron et al. [30]. In this inventory model, an infinite planning horizon is considered. It is well-known that product deterioration is a critical phenomenon in inventory management. Moreover, every deteriorating product has a fresh lifetime; after that time, it begins to deteriorate increasingly over time or constantly. Bearing its importance to inventory management, it is incorporated into the proposed inventory model, and the deterioration rate is considered as constant (Taleizadeh et al. [4]; Shaikh et al. [5]; Tavakoli and Taleizadeh [6]; Pando et al. [7]; and Sarkar and Sarkar [14]). In contrast, when there is no stock available in the retailer's warehouse, i.e., there is no deterioration during the shortage time. The $I_1(t)$ denotes the inventory level at any time $t \in [0, t_s]$ when deterioration has no effect on the product on the stock amount. $I_2(t)$ represents for the inventory level at any time $t \in [t_s, t_1]$ when there is product deterioration, while $I_3(t)$ represents the inventory level at any time $t \in [t_1, t_1 + t_2]$ when shortages have appeared. Due to the vagueness of the demand some time, it is difficult for the retailer to foresee how much stock needs to be preserved for the customers. Therefore, natural shortages are inevitable for variable demands. Moreover, it is important to satisfy the shortages more meticulously through proper management. In this inventory model, the backlogging rate depends on the customer waiting time, which is anticipated as $\frac{1}{1+\delta y}$, where y is the customer waiting time (Khan et al. [8], Sarkar et al. [27] and Khan et al. [37]).

Initially, the company places an order for a unique product with $S + R$ units by providing the $\omega c_p(S + R)$ amount, creating loans from a third party (i.e., a bank) through $\aleph$ equal installments during σ time units, and when the order is received, then the remaining $(1 - \omega)$ portion is paid at $t = 0$. The inventory level follows the pattern depicted in Figure 1.

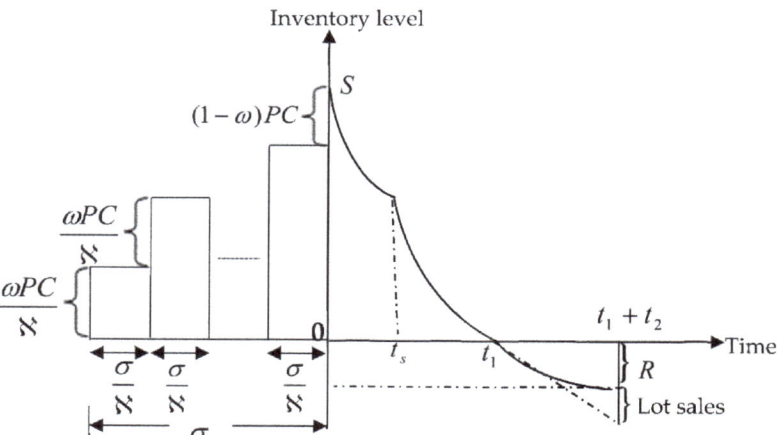

Figure 1. Inventory system for non-instantaneous deterioration with partial backlogging.

3.3. Formulation of the Inventory Model

In the beginning, the inventory is declined due to customer consumption alone. However, after t_s units of time, the stock is not only depleted to satisfy customer demand but also due to deterioration and consequently, the inventory amount reaches zero at time $t = t_1$. Shortly after, shortages appear, and these are partially backlogged shortages with a rate that depends upon the customer waiting time. Therefore, the inventory amount at any moment preserves the following differential equations:

$$\frac{dI_1(t)}{dt} = -\eta[I_1(t)]^\gamma \quad 0 \leq t \leq t_s \tag{1}$$

with the condition $I_1(0) = S$, and $I_1(t)$ is continuous at $t = t_s$.

$$\frac{dI_2(t)}{dt} + \theta\, I_2(t) = -\eta[I_2(t)]^\gamma \quad t_s < t \leq t_1 \tag{2}$$

with the subsidiary condition $I_2(t_1) = 0$, and $I_2(t)$ is continuous at $t = t_1$.

$$\frac{dI_3(t)}{dt} = -\frac{\eta}{1 + \delta(t_1 + t_2 - t)} \quad t_1 < t \leq t_1 + t_2 \tag{3}$$

with the auxiliary condition $I_3(t_1 + t_2) = -R$.

Utilizing the condition $I_1(0) = S$ from Equation (1), one has

$$I_1(t) = \left[S^{1-\gamma} - \eta t(1-\gamma)\right]^{\frac{1}{1-\gamma}} \quad 0 \leq t \leq t_s \tag{4}$$

Again, employing $I_2(t_1) = 0$, from Equation (2), one finds

$$I_2(t) = \eta^{\frac{1}{1-\gamma}} \theta^{-\frac{1}{1-\gamma}} \left\{e^{\theta(1-\gamma)(t_1-t)} - 1\right\}^{\frac{1}{1-\gamma}} \quad t_s \leq t \leq t_1 \tag{5}$$

Using $I_3(t_1 + t_2) = -R$, from Equation (3), one has

$$I_3(t) = \frac{\eta}{\delta}\ln|1 + \delta(t_1 + t_2 - t)| - R \quad t_1 < t \leq t_1 + t_2 \tag{6}$$

Considering the continuity of the current inventory at $t = t_s$ and $t = t_1$, one has

$$S = [\eta t_s(1-\gamma) + \Delta_1]^{\frac{1}{1-\gamma}} \tag{7}$$

$$R = \frac{\eta}{\delta}\ln|1 + \delta t_2| \tag{8}$$

where $\Delta_1 = \frac{\eta}{\theta}\left\{e^{\theta(1-\gamma)(t_1-t_s)} - 1\right\}$.

The following costs are involved in the inventory model.

(a) The ordering cost per cycle is:

$$OC = C_0 \tag{9}$$

(b) The purchasing cost per cycle is:

$$PC = c_p(S + R) \tag{10}$$

(c) The loan cost per cycle from Figure 1 is: $LC = i_c\left[\left(\frac{\omega PC}{\aleph}\right)\left(\frac{\sigma}{\aleph}\right)(1 + 2 + \ldots + \aleph)\right]$

$$LC = \frac{i_c \omega \sigma(\aleph + 1)c_p(S + R)}{2\aleph} \tag{11}$$

(d) The inventory holding cost per cycle is: $HC = c_h\left[\int_0^{t_s} I_1(t)dt + \int_{t_s}^{t_1} I_2(t)dt\right]$

$$HC = \frac{c_h}{\eta + \alpha}\left[(t_s\alpha + \Delta_1)^{\frac{\eta+\alpha}{\alpha}} - \Delta_1^{\frac{\eta+\alpha}{\alpha}} + \{\alpha(t_1 - t_s)\}^{\frac{\eta+\alpha}{\alpha}}\right] \tag{12}$$

where $\alpha = \eta(1 - \gamma)$.

(e) The deterioration cost per cycle is: $DC = c_d \left[I_2(t_s) - \eta \int_{t_s}^{t_1} [I_2(t)]^\gamma dt \right]$

$$DC = c_d \left[\Delta_1^{\frac{1}{1-\gamma}} + (\gamma - 1)\alpha^{\frac{\gamma}{1-\gamma}}(t_1 - t_s)^{\frac{1}{1-\gamma}} \right] \quad (13)$$

(f) The shortage cost per cycle is: $SC = -c_b \int_{t_1}^{t_1+t_2} I_3(t) dt$

$$SC = \frac{c_b \eta}{\delta} \left[t_2 - \frac{\ln|1 + \delta t_2|}{\delta} \right] \quad (14)$$

(g) The opportunity cost per cycle is: $OC = c_l \eta \int_{t_1}^{t_1+t_2} \left[1 - \frac{1}{1+\delta(t_1+t_2-t)} \right] dt$

$$OC = c_l \eta \left[t_2 - \frac{\ln|1 + \delta t_2|}{\delta} \right] \quad (15)$$

Detailed calculations of HC and DC are given in Appendix A.

Therefore, the total inventory cost is determined as the sum of the ordering cost, purchasing cost, loan cost, holding cost, deterioration cost, shortage cost, and opportunity cost, that is, $X = C_0 + PC + LC + HC + DC + SC + OC$.

Hence, the total inventory cost per unit of time is

$$TC(t_1, t_2) = \frac{1}{t_1 + t_2} \begin{bmatrix} C_0 + c_p \left\{ 1 + \frac{i_c \omega \sigma(\aleph+1)}{2\aleph} \right\} \left(\{ \eta t_s (1-\gamma) + \Delta_1 \}^{\frac{1}{1-\gamma}} + \frac{\eta}{\delta} \ln|1 + \delta t_2| \right) \\ + \frac{c_h}{\eta + \alpha} \left[(t_s \alpha + \Delta_1)^{\frac{\eta+\alpha}{\alpha}} - \Delta_1^{\frac{\eta+\alpha}{\alpha}} + \{\alpha(t_1 - t_s)\}^{\frac{\eta+\alpha}{\alpha}} \right] \\ + c_d \left[\Delta_1^{\frac{1}{1-\gamma}} + (\gamma - 1)\alpha^{\frac{\gamma}{1-\gamma}}(t_1 - t_s)^{\frac{1}{1-\gamma}} \right] + (c_l + \frac{c_b}{\delta}) \eta \left[t_2 - \frac{\ln|1+\delta t_2|}{\delta} \right] \end{bmatrix} \quad (16)$$

where $\Delta_1 = \frac{\eta}{\theta} \left\{ e^{\theta(1-\gamma)(t_1-t_s)} - 1 \right\}$ and $\alpha = \eta(1-\gamma)$.

Considering the total inventory cost, the nonlinear optimization problem is written as follows:

$$\text{Problem: Minimize } TC(t_1, t_2) = \frac{X}{t_1 + t_2}$$
$$\text{Subject to } 0 < t_s \leq t_1 \leq t_1 + t_2 \quad (17)$$

4. Solution Procedure

The optimization problem given in (17) can be solved by the following solution procedure.

Computing the first and second order partial derivatives of $TC(t_1, t_2)$ with respect to t_1 and t_2, one obtains

$$\frac{\partial TC(t_1, t_2)}{\partial t_1} = -\frac{X}{(t_1 + t_2)^2} + \frac{1}{t_1 + t_2} \frac{\partial X}{\partial t_1} \quad (18)$$

$$\frac{\partial^2 TC(t_1, t_2)}{\partial t_1^2} = \frac{2X}{(t_1 + t_2)^3} - \frac{2}{(t_1 + t_2)^2} \frac{\partial X}{\partial t_1} + \frac{1}{t_1 + t_2} \frac{\partial^2 X}{\partial t_1^2} \quad (19)$$

$$\frac{\partial TC(t_1, t_2)}{\partial t_2} = -\frac{X}{(t_1 + t_2)^2} + \frac{1}{t_1 + t_2} \frac{\partial X}{\partial t_2} \quad (20)$$

$$\frac{\partial^2 TC(t_1, t_2)}{\partial t_2^2} = \frac{2X}{(t_1 + t_2)^3} - \frac{2}{(t_1 + t_2)^2} \frac{\partial X}{\partial t_2} + \frac{1}{t_1 + t_2} \frac{\partial^2 X}{\partial t_2^2} \quad (21)$$

Now, the necessary conditions for optimizing $TC(t_1, t_2)$ are:

$$\frac{\partial TC(t_1, t_2)}{\partial t_1} = 0 \quad (22)$$

$$\frac{\partial TC(t_1, t_2)}{\partial t_2} = 0 \quad (23)$$

Using Equations (22) and (23), the reduced forms of Equations (18)–(21) can be obtained as follows:

$$X = (t_1 + t_2)\frac{\partial X}{\partial t_1} \tag{24}$$

$$\frac{\partial^2 TC(t_1, t_2)}{\partial t_1^2} = \frac{1}{t_1 + t_2}\frac{\partial^2 X}{\partial t_1^2} \tag{25}$$

$$X = (t_1 + t_2)\frac{\partial X}{\partial t_2} \tag{26}$$

$$\frac{\partial^2 TC(t_1, t_2)}{\partial t_2^2} = \frac{1}{t_1 + t_2}\frac{\partial^2 X}{\partial t_2^2} \tag{27}$$

Combining Equations (24) and (26), one writes

$$\frac{\partial X}{\partial t_1} = \frac{\partial X}{\partial t_2} \tag{28}$$

where $\frac{\partial X}{\partial t_1}$ and $\frac{\partial X}{\partial t_2}$ are computed as

$$\begin{aligned}\frac{\partial X}{\partial t_1} &= \frac{c_p}{1-\gamma}\left\{1 + \frac{i_c\omega\sigma(\aleph+1)}{2\aleph}\right\}\left\{\eta t_s(1-\gamma) + \Delta_1\right\}^{\frac{\gamma}{1-\gamma}}\frac{\partial \Delta_1}{\partial t_1} + c_d\left[\frac{1}{1-\gamma}\Delta_1^{\frac{\gamma}{1-\gamma}}\frac{\partial \Delta_1}{\partial t_1} - \alpha^{\frac{\gamma}{1-\gamma}}(t_1-t_s)^{\frac{\gamma}{1-\gamma}}\right] \\ &+ \frac{c_h}{\alpha}\left[(t_s\alpha + \Delta_1)^{\frac{\eta}{\alpha}}\frac{\partial \Delta_1}{\partial t_1} - \Delta_1^{\frac{\eta}{\alpha}}\frac{\partial \Delta_1}{\partial t_1} + \alpha^{\frac{\eta+\alpha}{\alpha}}(t_1-t_s)^{\frac{\eta}{\alpha}}\right],\end{aligned} \tag{29}$$

$$\frac{\partial X}{\partial t_2} = \frac{c_p\eta}{1+\delta t_2}\left\{1 + \frac{i_c\omega\sigma(\aleph+1)}{2\aleph}\right\} + \left(c_l + \frac{c_b}{\delta}\right)\eta\left(1 - \frac{1}{1+\delta t_2}\right) \tag{30}$$

Based on the performed analysis, the following lemma is proposed:

Lemma 1. *If* $c_p\left\{1 + \frac{i_c\omega\sigma(\aleph+1)}{2\aleph}\right\} \geq \left(c_l + \frac{c_b}{\delta}\right)$, *then the optimization problem given in (17) does not have an optimal solution.*

Proof. See Appendix B. □

It follows from Equation (28) that

$$\begin{aligned}\frac{c_p\eta}{1+\delta t_2}\left\{1 + \frac{i_c\omega\sigma(\aleph+1)}{2\aleph}\right\} - \left(c_l + \frac{c_b}{\delta}\right)\eta\frac{1}{1+\delta t_2} &= \frac{c_p}{1-\gamma}\left\{1 + \frac{i_c\omega\sigma(\aleph+1)}{2\aleph}\right\}\left\{\eta t_s(1-\gamma) + \Delta_1\right\}^{\frac{\gamma}{1-\gamma}}\frac{\partial \Delta_1}{\partial t_1} \\ &- \left(c_l + \frac{c_b}{\delta}\right)\eta + c_d\left[\frac{1}{1-\gamma}\Delta_1^{\frac{\gamma}{1-\gamma}}\frac{\partial \Delta_1}{\partial t_1} - \alpha^{\frac{\gamma}{1-\gamma}}(t_1-t_s)^{\frac{\gamma}{1-\gamma}}\right] \\ &+ \frac{c_h}{\alpha}\left[(t_s\alpha + \Delta_1)^{\frac{\eta}{\alpha}}\frac{\partial \Delta_1}{\partial t_1} - \Delta_1^{\frac{\eta}{\alpha}}\frac{\partial \Delta_1}{\partial t_1} + \alpha^{\frac{\eta+\alpha}{\alpha}}(t_1-t_s)^{\frac{\eta}{\alpha}}\right].\end{aligned} \tag{31}$$

After performing some simplifications, from Equation (31), one has

$$t_2 = \frac{\eta}{\delta}\left[\frac{c_p\left\{1 + \frac{i_c\omega\sigma(\aleph+1)}{2\aleph}\right\} - \left(c_l + \frac{c_b}{\delta}\right)}{\Phi(t_1)} - \frac{1}{\eta}\right] \tag{32}$$

where

$$\begin{aligned}\Phi(t_1) &= \frac{c_p}{1-\gamma}\left\{1 + \frac{i_c\omega\sigma(\aleph+1)}{2\aleph}\right\}\left\{\eta t_s(1-\gamma) + \Delta_1\right\}^{\frac{\gamma}{1-\gamma}}\frac{\partial \Delta_1}{\partial t_1} \\ &- \left(c_l + \frac{c_b}{\delta}\right)\eta + c_d\left[\frac{1}{1-\gamma}\Delta_1^{\frac{\gamma}{1-\gamma}}\frac{\partial \Delta_1}{\partial t_1} - \alpha^{\frac{\gamma}{1-\gamma}}(t_1-t_s)^{\frac{\gamma}{1-\gamma}}\right] \\ &+ \frac{c_h}{\alpha}\left[(t_s\alpha + \Delta_1)^{\frac{\eta}{\alpha}}\frac{\partial \Delta_1}{\partial t_1} - \Delta_1^{\frac{\eta}{\alpha}}\frac{\partial \Delta_1}{\partial t_1} + \alpha^{\frac{\eta+\alpha}{\alpha}}(t_1-t_s)^{\frac{\eta}{\alpha}}\right].\end{aligned} \tag{33}$$

Equation (32) reveals that t_2 is a function of t_1. Now, the existence of the unique time at which the inventory level becomes zero, i.e., t_1, is explored.

Performing differentiation with respect to t_1 on both sides of Equation (31), one obtains

$$-\frac{\left[c_p\left\{1+\frac{i_c\omega\sigma(\aleph+1)}{2\aleph}\right\}-\left(c_l+\frac{c_b}{\delta}\right)\right]\eta\delta}{(1+\delta t_2)^2}\frac{dt_2}{dt_1} = c_d\left[\begin{array}{c}\frac{1}{1-\gamma}\left\{\frac{\gamma}{1-\gamma}\Delta_1^{\frac{2\gamma-1}{1-\gamma}}\left(\frac{\partial\Delta_1}{\partial t_1}\right)^2+\Delta_1^{\frac{\gamma}{1-\gamma}}\frac{\partial^2\Delta_1}{\partial t_1^2}\right\}\\+\alpha^{\frac{\gamma}{1-\gamma}}\frac{\gamma}{\gamma-1}(t_1-t_s)^{\frac{2\gamma-1}{1-\gamma}}\end{array}\right]$$
$$+\frac{c_h}{\alpha}\left[\begin{array}{c}\frac{\eta}{\alpha}(t_s\alpha+\Delta_1)^{\frac{\eta-\alpha}{\alpha}}\left(\frac{\partial\Delta_1}{\partial t_1}\right)^2+(t_s\alpha+\Delta_1)^{\frac{\eta}{\alpha}}\frac{\partial^2\Delta_1}{\partial t_1^2}\\-\frac{\eta}{\alpha}\Delta_1^{\frac{\eta-\alpha}{\alpha}}\left(\frac{\partial\Delta_1}{\partial t_1}\right)^2-\Delta_1^{\frac{\eta}{\alpha}}\frac{\partial^2\Delta_1}{\partial t_1^2}+\alpha^{\frac{\eta+\alpha}{\alpha}}\frac{\eta}{\alpha}(t_1-t_s)^{\frac{\eta-\alpha}{\alpha}}\end{array}\right] \quad (34)$$
$$+\frac{c_p}{1-\gamma}\left\{1+\frac{i_c\omega\sigma(\aleph+1)}{2\aleph}\right\}\left[\begin{array}{c}\frac{\gamma}{1-\gamma}\{\eta t_s(1-\gamma)+\Delta_1\}^{\frac{2\gamma-1}{1-\gamma}}\left(\frac{\partial\Delta_1}{\partial t_1}\right)^2\\+\{\eta t_s(1-\gamma)+\Delta_1\}^{\frac{\gamma}{1-\gamma}}\frac{\partial^2\Delta_1}{\partial t_1^2}\end{array}\right],$$

where $\frac{\partial\Delta_1}{\partial t_1}=\eta(1-\gamma)e^{\theta(1-\gamma)(t_1-t_s)}$ and $\frac{\partial^2\Delta_1}{\partial t_1^2}=\eta\theta(1-\gamma)^2e^{\theta(1-\gamma)(t_1-t_s)}$.

Since $\frac{\partial^2\Delta_1}{\partial t_1^2} > 0$, $\frac{\eta}{\alpha}\left(\frac{\partial\Delta_1}{\partial t_1}\right)^2\left\{(t_s\alpha+\Delta_1)^{\frac{\eta-\alpha}{\alpha}}-\Delta_1^{\frac{\eta-\alpha}{\alpha}}\right\} > 0$, and $\frac{\partial^2\Delta_1}{\partial t_1^2}\left\{(t_s\alpha+\Delta_1)^{\frac{\eta}{\alpha}}-\Delta_1^{\frac{\eta}{\alpha}}\right\} > 0$, the expression on the right-hand side of Equation (34) is always positive. Consequently,

$$\frac{\left[c_p\left\{1+\frac{i_c\omega\sigma(\aleph+1)}{2\aleph}\right\}-\left(c_l+\frac{c_b}{\delta}\right)\right]\eta\delta}{(1+\delta t_2)^2}\frac{dt_2}{dt_1} < 0 \quad (35)$$

Employing Equation (31) and accomplishing some simplifications, Equation (22) reduces to

$$\frac{1}{(t_1+t_2)^2}\left[\begin{array}{c}(t_1+t_2)\left[\frac{c_p\eta}{1+\delta t_2}\left\{1+\frac{i_c\omega\sigma(\aleph+1)}{2\aleph}\right\}+\left(c_l+\frac{c_b}{\delta}\right)\eta\left(1-\frac{1}{1+\delta t_2}\right)\right]\\-C_0-\left(c_l+\frac{c_b}{\delta}\right)\eta\left[t_2-\frac{\ln|1+\delta t_2|}{\delta}\right]-\frac{c_h}{\eta+\alpha}\left[(t_s\alpha+\Delta_1)^{\frac{\eta+\alpha}{\alpha}}-\Delta_1^{\frac{\eta+\alpha}{\alpha}}+\{\alpha(t_1-t_s)\}^{\frac{\eta+\alpha}{\alpha}}\right]\\-c_d\left[\Delta_1^{\frac{1}{1-\gamma}}-(1-\gamma)\alpha^{\frac{\gamma}{1-\gamma}}(t_1-t_s)^{\frac{1}{1-\gamma}}\right]-c_p\left\{1+\frac{i_c\omega\sigma(\aleph+1)}{2\aleph}\right\}\left(\begin{array}{c}\{\eta t_s(1-\gamma)+\Delta_1\}^{\frac{1}{1-\gamma}}\\+\frac{\eta}{\delta}\ln|1+\delta t_2|\end{array}\right)\end{array}\right]=0 \quad (36)$$

For convenience, let us define the auxiliary function $\Psi(t_1)$ from Equation (36) as follows:

$$\Psi(t_1) = (t_1+t_2)\left[\frac{c_p\eta}{1+\delta t_2}\left\{1+\frac{i_c\omega\sigma(\aleph+1)}{2\aleph}\right\}+\left(c_l+\frac{c_b}{\delta}\right)\eta\left(1-\frac{1}{1+\delta t_2}\right)\right]$$
$$-C_0-\left(c_l+\frac{c_b}{\delta}\right)\eta\left[t_2-\frac{\ln|1+\delta t_2|}{\delta}\right]-\frac{c_h}{\eta+\alpha}\left[(t_s\alpha+\Delta_1)^{\frac{\eta+\alpha}{\alpha}}-\Delta_1^{\frac{\eta+\alpha}{\alpha}}+\{\alpha(t_1-t_s)\}^{\frac{\eta+\alpha}{\alpha}}\right] \quad (37)$$
$$-c_d\left[\Delta_1^{\frac{1}{1-\gamma}}-(1-\gamma)\alpha^{\frac{\gamma}{1-\gamma}}(t_1-t_s)^{\frac{1}{1-\gamma}}\right]-c_p\left\{1+\frac{i_c\omega\sigma(\aleph+1)}{2\aleph}\right\}\left(\{\eta t_s(1-\gamma)+\Delta_1\}^{\frac{1}{1-\gamma}}+\frac{\eta}{\delta}\ln|1+\delta t_2|\right),$$

where $t_1 \in [t_s, \infty)$.

Differentiating $\Psi(t_1)$ with respect to t_1, one obtains

$$\frac{d\Psi(t_1)}{dt_1} = \left[\frac{c_p\eta}{1+\delta t_2}\left\{1+\frac{i_c\omega\sigma(\aleph+1)}{2\aleph}\right\}+\left(c_l+\frac{c_b}{\delta}\right)\eta\left(1-\frac{1}{1+\delta t_2}\right)\right]-c_d\left[\frac{1}{1-\gamma}\Delta_1^{\frac{\gamma}{1-\gamma}}\frac{\partial\Delta_1}{\partial t_1}-\alpha^{\frac{\gamma}{1-\gamma}}(t_1-t_s)^{\frac{\gamma}{1-\gamma}}\right]$$
$$-(t_1+t_2)\frac{\eta\delta}{(1+\delta t_2)^2}\frac{dt_2}{dt_1}\left[c_p\left\{1+\frac{i_c\omega\sigma(\aleph+1)}{2\aleph}\right\}-\left(c_l+\frac{c_b}{\delta}\right)\right] \quad (38)$$
$$-\frac{c_p}{1-\gamma}\left\{1+\frac{i_c\omega\sigma(\aleph+1)}{2\aleph}\right\}\{\eta t_s(1-\gamma)+\Delta_1\}^{\frac{\gamma}{1-\gamma}}\frac{\partial\Delta_1}{\partial t_1}-\frac{c_h}{\alpha}\left[(t_s\alpha+\Delta_1)^{\frac{\eta}{\alpha}}\frac{\partial\Delta_1}{\partial t_1}-\Delta_1^{\frac{\eta}{\alpha}}\frac{\partial\Delta_1}{\partial t_1}+\alpha^{\frac{\eta+\alpha}{\alpha}}(t_1-t_s)^{\frac{\eta}{\alpha}}\right].$$

Using the expression in Equation (31), the first order derivative of $\Psi(t_1)$ is expressed as

$$\frac{d\Psi(t_1)}{dt_1} = -(t_1+t_2)\frac{\eta\delta}{(1+\delta t_2)^2}\frac{dt_2}{dt_1}\left[c_p\left\{1+\frac{i_c\omega\sigma(\aleph+1)}{2\aleph}\right\}-\left(c_l+\frac{c_b}{\delta}\right)\right] > 0 \quad (39)$$

Equation (39) reveals that the auxiliary function $\Psi(t_1)$ strictly increases in $t_1 \in [t_s, \infty)$. In addition, at $t_1 = t_s$, from Equation (32), one has

$$t_2 = \frac{1}{\delta}(\xi_1 - 1) \tag{40}$$

where $\xi_1 = \dfrac{c_p\left\{1 + \frac{i_c\omega\sigma(\aleph+1)}{2\aleph}\right\} - \left(c_l + \frac{c_b}{\delta}\right)}{c_p\left\{1 + \frac{i_c\omega\sigma(\aleph+1)}{2\aleph}\right\}(\alpha t_s)^{\frac{\gamma}{1-\gamma}} - \left(c_l + \frac{c_b}{\delta}\right) + \frac{c_h}{\eta}(\alpha t_s)^{\frac{1}{1-\gamma}}}$ (41)

Now, the expression of the auxiliary function $\Psi(t_1)$ at $t_1 = t_s$ is:

$$\Psi(t_s) = \left\{t_s + \frac{(\xi_1-1)}{\delta}\right\}\left[\frac{c_p\eta}{\xi_1}\left\{1 + \frac{i_c\omega\sigma(\aleph+1)}{2\aleph}\right\} + \left(c_l + \frac{c_b}{\delta}\right)\eta\left(1 - \frac{1}{\xi_1}\right)\right] - C_0 - \frac{c_h}{\eta+\alpha}(t_s\alpha)^{\frac{\eta+\alpha}{\alpha}}$$
$$- \left(c_l + \frac{c_b}{\delta}\right)\frac{\eta}{\delta}(\xi_1 - 1 - \ln|\xi_1|) - c_p\left\{1 + \frac{i_c\omega\sigma(\aleph+1)}{2\aleph}\right\}\left\{(\alpha t_s)^{\frac{1}{1-\gamma}} + \frac{\eta}{\delta}\ln|\xi_1|\right\}(= \Omega, \text{ say}) \tag{42}$$

It is easy to show that when t_1 becomes larger, $\Psi(t_1)$ tends to be ∞.

Now, two cases for the optimal t_1 are recognized on the basis of the sign of Ω, i.e., $\Psi(t_s)$, as follows:

Case 1: When $\Omega < 0$, employing the intermediate value theorem, one can straightforwardly observe that Equation (22) represents a unique situation, say $\tilde{t}_1 \in (t_s, \infty)$, which is the unique optimal t_1 minimizing the total inventory cost per unit of time. Moreover, the corresponding optimal shortages duration, say $\tilde{t}_2$, is calculated from Equation (32). Now, the convexity of $TC(t_1, t_2)$ at the point $(\tilde{t}_1, \tilde{t}_2)$ is explored as follows:

Computing the second order partial derivatives of $TC(t_1, t_2)$ at the point $(t_1, t_2) = (\tilde{t}_1, \tilde{t}_2)$, one has

$$\left.\frac{\partial^2 TC(t_1,t_2)}{\partial t_1^2}\right|_{(t_1,t_2)=(\tilde{t}_1,\tilde{t}_2)} = \frac{1}{\tilde{t}_1+\tilde{t}_2}\begin{bmatrix} \frac{c_p}{1-\gamma}\left\{1+\frac{i_c\omega\sigma(\aleph+1)}{2\aleph}\right\}\begin{bmatrix} \frac{\gamma}{1-\gamma}\{\eta t_s(1-\gamma)+\Delta_1\}^{\frac{2\gamma-1}{1-\gamma}}\left(\frac{\partial\Delta_1}{\partial t_1}\right)^2 \\ +\{\eta t_s(1-\gamma)+\Delta_1\}^{\frac{\gamma}{1-\gamma}}\frac{\partial^2\Delta_1}{\partial t_1^2} \end{bmatrix} \\ +\frac{c_h}{\alpha}\begin{bmatrix} \frac{\eta}{\alpha}(t_s\alpha+\Delta_1)^{\frac{\eta-\alpha}{\alpha}}\left(\frac{\partial\Delta_1}{\partial t_1}\right)^2+(t_s\alpha+\Delta_1)^{\frac{\eta}{\alpha}}\frac{\partial^2\Delta_1}{\partial t_1^2} \\ -\frac{\eta}{\alpha}\Delta_1^{\frac{\eta-\alpha}{\alpha}}\left(\frac{\partial\Delta_1}{\partial t_1}\right)^2-\Delta_1^{\frac{\eta}{\alpha}}\frac{\partial^2\Delta_1}{\partial t_1^2}+\alpha^{\frac{\eta+\alpha}{\alpha}}\frac{\eta}{\alpha}(t_1-t_s)^{\frac{\eta-\alpha}{\alpha}} \end{bmatrix} \\ +c_d\begin{bmatrix} \frac{1}{1-\gamma}\left\{\frac{\gamma}{1-\gamma}\Delta_1^{\frac{2\gamma-1}{1-\gamma}}\left(\frac{\partial\Delta_1}{\partial t_1}\right)^2+\Delta_1^{\frac{\gamma}{1-\gamma}}\frac{\partial^2\Delta_1}{\partial t_1^2}\right\} \\ +\alpha^{\frac{\gamma}{1-\gamma}}\frac{\gamma}{\gamma-1}(t_1-t_s)^{\frac{2\gamma-1}{1-\gamma}} \end{bmatrix} \end{bmatrix}_{(t_1,t_2)=(\tilde{t}_1,\tilde{t}_2)} + \tag{43}$$

Since $\frac{\partial^2\Delta_1}{\partial t_1^2} > 0$, $\frac{\eta}{\alpha}\left(\frac{\partial\Delta_1}{\partial t_1}\right)^2\left\{(t_s\alpha+\Delta_1)^{\frac{\eta-\alpha}{\alpha}} - \Delta_1^{\frac{\eta-\alpha}{\alpha}}\right\} > 0$, and $\frac{\partial^2\Delta_1}{\partial t_1^2}\left\{(t_s\alpha+\Delta_1)^{\frac{\eta}{\alpha}} - \Delta_1^{\frac{\eta}{\alpha}}\right\} > 0$, the expression on the right-hand side of Equation (43) is always positive. Consequently,

$$\left.\frac{\partial^2 TC(t_1,t_2)}{\partial t_1^2}\right|_{(t_1,t_2)=(\tilde{t}_1,\tilde{t}_2)} > 0 \tag{44}$$

$$\left.\frac{\partial^2 TC(t_1,t_2)}{\partial t_2^2}\right|_{(t_1,t_2)=(\tilde{t}_1,\tilde{t}_2)} = \frac{\eta\delta}{(\tilde{t}_1+\tilde{t}_2)(1+\delta\tilde{t}_2)^2}\left\{\left(c_l+\frac{c_b}{\delta}\right)-c_p\left\{1+\frac{i_c\omega\sigma(\aleph+1)}{2\aleph}\right\}\right\} \tag{45}$$

$$\left.\frac{\partial^2 TC(t_1,t_2)}{\partial t_1\partial t_2}\right|_{(t_1,t_2)=(\tilde{t}_1,\tilde{t}_2)} = \left.\frac{\partial^2 TC(t_1,t_2)}{\partial t_2\partial t_1}\right|_{(t_1,t_2)=(\tilde{t}_1,\tilde{t}_2)} = 0 \tag{46}$$

Since $\left.\frac{\partial^2 TC(t_1,t_2)}{\partial t_1^2}\right|_{(t_1,t_2)=(\tilde{t}_1,\tilde{t}_2)} > 0$ and, from Equations (44)–(46), one can straightforwardly observe that $\left.\frac{\partial^2 TC(t_1,t_2)}{\partial t_1^2}\right|_{(t_1,t_2)=(\tilde{t}_1,\tilde{t}_2)} \left.\frac{\partial^2 TC(t_1,t_2)}{\partial t_2^2}\right|_{(t_1,t_2)=(\tilde{t}_1,\tilde{t}_2)} - \left[\left.\frac{\partial^2 TC(t_1,t_2)}{\partial t_1 \partial t_2}\right|_{(t_1,t_2)=(\tilde{t}_1,\tilde{t}_2)}\right]^2$ is only positive when $c_p\left\{1 + \frac{i_c \omega \sigma (\aleph+1)}{2\aleph}\right\} < \left(c_l + \frac{c_b}{\delta}\right)$.

Taking the above results into consideration, the following theorem can be proposed to achieve the optimal replenishment policy.

Theorem 1. *If $\Omega < 0$ and $c_p\left\{1 + \frac{i_c \omega \sigma (\aleph+1)}{2\aleph}\right\} < \left(c_l + \frac{c_b}{\delta}\right)$, then a unique $t_1^* = \tilde{t}_1$ and $t_2^* = \tilde{t}_2$ exist, where $\tilde{t}_1$ and $\tilde{t}_2$ satisfy Equations (22) and (32), respectively, and $TC(t_1, t_2)$ achieves the global minimum value at $(t_1^*, t_2^*) = (\tilde{t}_1, \tilde{t}_2)$.*

Case 2: When $\Omega \geq 0$, then the total inventory cost per unit of time is an increasing function for $t_1 \in [t_s, \infty)$, as $\Psi(t_1) > 0$ for all $t_1 \in (t_s, \infty)$. Consequently, the value of t_1 satisfying Equation (22) does not exist in this case, and hence, the unique optimal t_1 for minimizing the total cost is achieved at t_s. In this case, there only one decision variable exists, i.e., t_2, and the corresponding nonlinear optimization problem becomes

$$\text{Problem : Minimize } \Pi(t_2) = TC(t_s, t_2) = \frac{\widetilde{X}}{t_s + t_2} \quad (47)$$
$$\text{Subject to } 0 < t_s = t_1 \leq t_s + t_2$$

where

$$\widetilde{X} = C_0 + c_p\left\{1 + \frac{i_c \omega \sigma (\aleph+1)}{2\aleph}\right\}\left\{(\alpha t_s)^{\frac{1}{1-\gamma}} + \frac{\eta}{\delta}\ln|1 + \delta t_2|\right\}$$
$$+ \frac{c_h}{\eta+\alpha}(t_s \alpha)^{\frac{\eta+\alpha}{\alpha}} + \left(c_l + \frac{c_b}{\delta}\right)\eta\left\{t_2 - \frac{\ln|1+\delta t_2|}{\delta}\right\}.$$

The first order derivative of $\Pi(t_2)$ is

$$\Pi'(t_2) = \frac{1}{(t_s+t_2)^2}\left[-\widetilde{X} + (t_s+t_2)\frac{d\widetilde{X}}{dt_2}\right] \quad (48)$$

For notational convenience, let us define the auxiliary function $Z(t_2)$ from Equation (48) as follows:

$$Z(t_2) = -\widetilde{X} + (t_s+t_2)\left[\frac{c_p \eta}{1+\delta t_2}\left\{1 + \frac{i_c \omega \sigma (\aleph+1)}{2\aleph}\right\} + \left(c_l + \frac{c_b}{\delta}\right)\eta\left(1 - \frac{1}{1+\delta t_2}\right)\right] \quad (49)$$

where $t_2 \geq 0$.

In addition, at $t_2 = 0$, the value of $Z(t_2)$ is

$$Z(0) = -\begin{array}{l} C_0 - c_p\left\{1 + \frac{i_c \omega \sigma (\aleph+1)}{2\aleph}\right\}(\alpha t_s)^{\frac{1}{1-\gamma}} - \frac{c_h}{\eta+\alpha}(t_s\alpha)^{\frac{\eta+\alpha}{\alpha}} \\ + t_s c_p \eta\left\{1 + \frac{i_c \omega \sigma (\aleph+1)}{2\aleph}\right\} \end{array} \quad (50)$$

Approaching t_2 tends to ∞, and one can straightforwardly observe that

$$\lim_{t_2 \to \infty} Z(t_2) = \infty \quad (51)$$

Differentiating $Z(t_2)$ with respect to t_2, one has

$$\frac{dZ(t_2)}{dt_2} = (t_s+t_2)\frac{\eta \delta}{(1+\delta t_2)^2}\left[\left(c_l + \frac{c_b}{\delta}\right) - c_p\left\{1 + \frac{i_c \omega \sigma (\aleph+1)}{2\aleph}\right\}\right] \quad (52)$$

To investigate the characteristics of Equation (48), let

$$\chi_1 = C_0 + c_p\left\{1 + \frac{i_c\omega\sigma(\aleph+1)}{2\aleph}\right\}(\alpha t_s)^{\frac{1}{1-\gamma}} + \frac{c_h}{\eta+\alpha}(t_s\alpha)^{\frac{\eta+\alpha}{\alpha}}$$

and $\chi_2 = t_s c_p \eta \left\{1 + \frac{i_c\omega\sigma(\aleph+1)}{2\aleph}\right\}$.

Theorem 2.
(a) If $\chi_1 = \chi_2$ and $c_p\left\{1 + \frac{i_c\omega\sigma(\aleph+1)}{2\aleph}\right\} < \left(c_l + \frac{c_b}{\delta}\right)$, then Equation (48) has a unique root at $t_2 = 0$.
(b) If $\chi_1 > \chi_2$ and $c_p\left\{1 + \frac{i_c\omega\sigma(\aleph+1)}{2\aleph}\right\} < \left(c_l + \frac{c_b}{\delta}\right)$, then Equation (48) has a unique root of t_2 in $(0,\infty)$.
(c) If $\chi_1 < \chi_2$, then Equation (48) has no real root of t_2.

Proof.
(a) When $\chi_1 = \chi_2$, then $t_2 = 0$ is a root of Equation (48). Moreover, if $\left(c_l + \frac{c_b}{\delta}\right) - c_p\left\{1 + \frac{i_c\omega\sigma(\aleph+1)}{2\aleph}\right\} > 0$, then Equation (52) reveals that $Z(t_2)$ is strictly an increasing function of t_2, and hence, $t_2 = 0$ is the unique root of Equation (48). On the other hand, if $\left(c_l + \frac{c_b}{\delta}\right) - c_p\left\{1 + \frac{i_c\omega\sigma(\aleph+1)}{2\aleph}\right\} \leq 0$, then Equation (52) shows that $Z(t_2)$ is either a strictly decreasing or constant function of t_2 in $(0,\infty)$, which contradicts the result of Equation (51).
(b) If $\chi_1 > \chi_2$, then $Z(0) < 0$. When $\left(c_l + \frac{c_b}{\delta}\right) - c_p\left\{1 + \frac{i_c\omega\sigma(\aleph+1)}{2\aleph}\right\} \leq 0$, then Equation (52) exposes the fact that $Z(t_2)$ is either a strictly decreasing or constant function of t_2 in $(0,\infty)$, and consequently, Equation (48) has no real root of t_2. Again, if $\left(c_l + \frac{c_b}{\delta}\right) - c_p\left\{1 + \frac{i_c\omega\sigma(\aleph+1)}{2\aleph}\right\} > 0$, then $Z(t_2)$ is strictly an increasing function of t_2 in $(0,\infty)$. Since $\lim_{t_2\to\infty} Z(t_2) = \infty$, Equation (48) has a unique real root of t_2 in $(0,\infty)$.
(c) Finally, when $\chi_1 < \chi_2$, one can observe from Equation (50) that $Z(0)$ is positive. As a result, Equation (48) has no real root of t_2 in $[0,\infty)$ when $\left(c_l + \frac{c_b}{\delta}\right) - c_p\left\{1 + \frac{i_c\omega\sigma(\aleph+1)}{2\aleph}\right\} \geq 0$ because $Z(t_2)$ becomes either a strictly increasing or constant function of t_2 in $(0,\infty)$ in this case. On the other hand, if $\left(c_l + \frac{c_b}{\delta}\right) - c_p\left\{1 + \frac{i_c\omega\sigma(\aleph+1)}{2\aleph}\right\} < 0$, then the function $Z(t_2)$ is a strictly a decreasing function of t_2 in $(0,\infty)$, which opposes the result $\lim_{t_2\to\infty} Z(t_2) = \infty$. □

Theorem 3. If $c_p\left\{1 + \frac{i_c\omega\sigma(\aleph+1)}{2\aleph}\right\} < \left(c_l + \frac{c_b}{\delta}\right)$, then $\Pi(t_2)$ is strictly pseudo-concave in t_2, and hence, a sole optimal t_2^* exists for which $\Pi(t_2)$ is minimized.

Proof. For notational suitability, let us define

$$\begin{aligned}Z_1(t_2) &= C_0 + c_p\left\{1 + \frac{i_c\omega\sigma(\aleph+1)}{2\aleph}\right\}\left\{(\alpha t_s)^{\frac{1}{1-\gamma}} + \frac{\eta}{\delta}\ln|1+\delta t_2|\right\} \\ &\quad + \frac{c_h}{\eta+\alpha}(t_s\alpha)^{\frac{\eta+\alpha}{\alpha}} + \left(c_l + \frac{c_b}{\delta}\right)\eta\left\{t_2 - \frac{\ln|1+\delta t_2|}{\delta}\right\},\end{aligned} \quad (53)$$

$$Z_2(t_2) = t_s + t_2 > 0 \quad (54)$$

As a result, $\Pi(t_2)$ is repressed as follows: $\Pi(t_2) = \frac{Z_1(t_2)}{Z_2(t_2)}$. Moreover, $Z_1(t_2)$ is strictly positive as the sum of all of the inventory-associated costs. Taking the differentiation of $Z_1(t_2)$ two times with respect to t_2, one finds

$$\frac{dZ_1(t_2)}{dt_2} = \frac{c_p\eta}{1+\delta t_2}\left\{1 + \frac{i_c\omega\sigma(\aleph+1)}{2\aleph}\right\} + \left(c_l + \frac{c_b}{\delta}\right)\eta\left(1 - \frac{1}{1+\delta t_2}\right) \quad (55)$$

$$\frac{d^2 Z_1(t_2)}{dt_2^2} = \frac{\eta\delta}{(1+\delta t_2)^2}\left[\left(c_l + \frac{c_b}{\delta}\right) - c_p\left\{1 + \frac{i_c\omega\sigma(\aleph+1)}{2\aleph}\right\}\right] \quad (56)$$

The second order derivative $\frac{d^2 Z_1(t_2)}{dt_2^2}$ is positive only when $c_p\left\{1 + \frac{i_c\omega\sigma(\aleph+1)}{2\aleph}\right\} < \left(c_l + \frac{c_b}{\delta}\right)$. Therefore, $Z_1(t_2)$ is a differentiable and strictly convex in t_2 if $c_p\left\{1 + \frac{i_c\omega\sigma(\aleph+1)}{2\aleph}\right\} < \left(c_l + \frac{c_b}{\delta}\right)$. Moreover, $Z_2(t_2) = t_s + t_2$ is a positive and affine function of t_2. This implies that $\Pi(t_2)$ is a strictly pseudo-convex function in t_2, and therefore, there a unique optimal solution of t_2^* exists. This completes the proof of the theorem. □

Setting $\frac{d\Pi_1(t_2)}{dt_2}$, the necessary condition to achieve t_2^* is:

$$(t_s + t_2)\left\{\frac{c_p\eta}{1+\delta t_2}\left\{1 + \frac{i_c\omega\sigma(\aleph+1)}{2\aleph}\right\} + \left(c_l + \frac{c_b}{\delta}\right)\eta\left(1 - \frac{1}{1+\delta t_2}\right)\right\} - \widetilde{X} = 0 \quad (57)$$

Taking the above results into consideration, the following theorem can be proposed to achieve the optimal replenishment policy for $\Omega \geq 0$.

Theorem 4. *If $\Omega \geq 0$, $\chi_1 \geq \chi_2$ and $c_p\left\{1 + \frac{i_c\omega\sigma(\aleph+1)}{2\aleph}\right\} < \left(c_l + \frac{c_b}{\delta}\right)$, then $\Pi(t_2)$ is strictly pseudo-concave in t_2, and hence, $TC(t_1, t_2)$ achieves the global minimum value at $t_1^* = t_s$ and t_2^*, which satisfies Equation (57).*

Proof. The proof is immediate from Theorems 2 and 3. □

5. Special Cases

The proposed inventory model involves the following inventory models as particular cases:

(i) If the value of δ is chosen as 0, then the backlogging rate of the current inventory model becomes 1, that is, shortages are completely backlogged.
(ii) If $\delta \to \infty$, one has $t_2 \approx 0$ from Equation (32), and hence, the current inventory model reduces to the inventory model without shortages.
(iii) When $t_s = 0$ and $\delta = 0$, then the current inventory model becomes the inventory model with instantaneous deterioration and is fully backlogged.
(iv) If $t_s = 0$ and $\delta \to \infty$, then one has $t_2 \approx 0$ from Equation (32), and therefore, the current inventory model transforms into the inventory model with instantaneous deterioration without shortages.
(v) If $\omega = 1$, then the current inventory model involves a fully advance payment scheme. On the other hand, when $\omega = 0$ and $\gamma = 0$, then the present inventory model does not involve any advance payment policy under constant demand and hence involves a payment policy that is similar to the one seen in the classical EOQ inventory model.
(vi) If $\aleph = 1$, then the present model includes a single installment opportunity for prepayment, whereas when $\aleph = 1$ and $\omega = 1$, then the present inventory model becomes a fully advance payment scheme with single installment instead of multiple installment opportunities.

6. Sensitivity Analysis

The impacts of the parameters of the advance payment scheme on the total cost per unit of time are examined in this section.

(a) Calculating the derivative of $TC(t_1, t_2)$ with respect to $\aleph$, one has

$$\frac{dTC(t_1,t_2)}{d\aleph} = -\frac{1}{t_1+t_2}\left[\left(\frac{i_c\omega\sigma c_p}{2\aleph^2}\right)\left(\{\eta t_s(1-\gamma)+\Delta_1\}^{\frac{1}{1-\gamma}}+\frac{\eta}{\delta}\ln|1+\delta t_2|\right)\right] < 0 \quad (58)$$

Equation (58) implies that increasing the number of installments to accomplish the prepayment decreases the total cost per unit of time.

(b) Taking the derivative of $TC(t_1,t_2)$ with respect to σ, one obtains

$$\frac{dTC(t_1,t_2)}{d\sigma} = \frac{1}{t_1+t_2}\left[c_p\left\{\frac{i_c\omega(\aleph+1)}{2\aleph}\right\}\left(\{\eta t_s(1-\gamma)+\Delta_1\}^{\frac{1}{1-\gamma}}+\frac{\eta}{\delta}\ln|1+\delta t_2|\right)\right] > 0 \quad (59)$$

It reveals that increasing the time duration for accomplishing prepayment opportunities increases the total cost per unit of time.

(c) By performing the first-order differentiation of $TC(t_1,t_2)$ with respect to ω, one obtains

$$\frac{dTC(t_1,t_2)}{d\omega} = \frac{1}{t_1+t_2}\left[c_p\left\{\frac{i_c\sigma(\aleph+1)}{2\aleph}\right\}\left(\{\eta t_s(1-\gamma)+\Delta_1\}^{\frac{1}{1-\gamma}}+\frac{\eta}{\delta}\ln|1+\delta t_2|\right)\right] > 0 \quad (60)$$

It follows that the total cost per unit of time increases when the portion of the total purchase price for accomplishing the prepayment scheme increases.

(d) By taking the derivative of $TC(t_1,t_2)$ with respect to i_c, one obtains

$$\frac{dTC(t_1,t_2)}{di_c} = \frac{1}{t_1+t_2}\left[c_p\left\{\frac{\omega\sigma(\aleph+1)}{2\aleph}\right\}\left(\{\eta t_s(1-\gamma)+\Delta_1\}^{\frac{1}{1-\gamma}}+\frac{\eta}{\delta}\ln|1+\delta t_2|\right)\right] > 0 \quad (61)$$

Therefore, Equation (61) exposes that the total cost per unit of time increases when the interest charging rate for the borrowed amounts increases.

7. Numerical Examples

To demonstrate the applicability of the inventory model, several numerical examples are solved in this section.

Example 1. *The values of the input parameters for the example are from Pando et al. [25] and Khan et al. [37] with some additional data that were adopted in the present work the present work. Let $C_0 = 10$, $c_p = 50$, $c_h = 0.5$, $c_b = 20$, $c_d = 50$, $c_l = 10$, $\eta = 1$, $\theta = 0.05$, $\gamma = 0.1$, $\delta = 0.1$, $t_s = 0.5$, $\aleph = 3$, $\sigma = 5$, $\omega = 0.4$ and $i_c = 0.05$. The values of all of the parameters are in their appropriate units, and LINGO18.0 software was used to solve the example. Now,*

$$\Omega = \left\{t_s + \frac{(\xi_1-1)}{\delta}\right\}\left[\frac{c_p\eta}{\xi_1}\left\{1+\frac{i_c\omega\sigma(\aleph+1)}{2\aleph}\right\}+\left(c_l+\frac{c_b}{\delta}\right)\eta\left(1-\frac{1}{\xi_1}\right)\right]$$
$$-C_0 - \frac{c_h}{\eta+\alpha}(t_s\alpha)^{\frac{\eta+\alpha}{\alpha}} - \left(c_l+\frac{c_b}{\delta}\right)\frac{\eta}{\delta}(\xi_1-1-\ln|\xi_1|)$$
$$-c_p\left\{1+\frac{i_c\omega\sigma(\aleph+1)}{2\aleph}\right\}\left(\{\eta t_s(1-\gamma)\}^{\frac{1}{1-\gamma}}+\frac{\eta}{\delta}\ln|\xi_1|\right) = -10.95273$$

Since $c_p\left\{1+\frac{i_c\omega\sigma(\aleph+1)}{2\aleph}\right\} = 53.333$ and $\left(c_l+\frac{c_b}{\delta}\right) = 210$, one can observe that $c_p\left\{1+\frac{i_c\omega\sigma(\aleph+1)}{2\aleph}\right\} < \left(c_l+\frac{c_b}{\delta}\right)$. Therefore, based on Theorem 1, the optimal time durations for positive and negative stock amounts are determined from Equations (22) and (32) and are given by $t_1^* = 1.1771$ and $t_2^* = 0.2718$. Moreover, the global minimum the total cost per unit of time is $TC^* = 57.4792$ (see Figure 2).

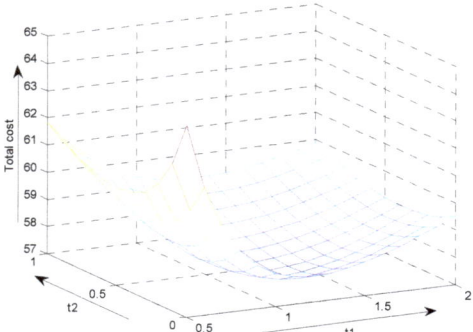

Figure 2. Graphical presentation of the convexity of TC against t_1 and t_2 when $\Omega < 0$.

Example 2. *Let $C_0 = 10$, $c_p = 100$, $c_h = 15$, $c_b = 40$, $c_d = 100$, $c_l = 20$, $\eta = 1.2$, $\theta = 0.05$, $\gamma = 0.05$, $\delta = 0.4$, $t_s = 0.6$, $\aleph = 3$, $\sigma = 5$, $\omega = 0.4$, and $i_c = 0.05$. The values of all of the parameters are in their appropriate units, and LINGO18.0 software was used to solve the example. In this case, the value of Ω is:*

$$\Omega = \left\{ t_s + \tfrac{(\xi_1 - 1)}{\delta} \right\} \left[\tfrac{c_p \eta}{\xi_1} \left\{ 1 + \tfrac{i_c \omega \sigma (\aleph + 1)}{2\aleph} \right\} + \left(c_l + \tfrac{c_b}{\delta} \right) \eta \left(1 - \tfrac{1}{\xi_1} \right) \right]$$
$$- C_0 - \tfrac{c_h}{\eta + \alpha} (t_s \alpha)^{\tfrac{\eta + \alpha}{\alpha}} - \left(c_l + \tfrac{c_b}{\delta} \right) \tfrac{\eta}{\delta} (\xi_1 - 1 - \ln|\xi_1|)$$
$$- c_p \left\{ 1 + \tfrac{i_c \omega \sigma (\aleph + 1)}{2\aleph} \right\} \left(\{\eta t_s (1 - \gamma)\}^{\tfrac{1}{1-\gamma}} + \tfrac{\eta}{\delta} \ln|\xi_1| \right) = 0.6191346 > 0$$

Since $\chi_1 = 84.4558$, $\chi_2 = 64$, $c_p \left\{ 1 + \tfrac{i_c \omega \sigma (\aleph + 1)}{2\aleph} \right\} = 106.6667$, and $\left(c_l + \tfrac{c_b}{\delta} \right) = 120$, one can observe that $\chi_1 > \chi_2$ and $c_p \left\{ 1 + \tfrac{i_c \omega \sigma (\aleph + 1)}{2\aleph} \right\} < \left(c_l + \tfrac{c_b}{\delta} \right)$. Consequently, according to Theorem 4, the optimal time duration for positive stock amounts is $t_1^* = t_s = 0.6$, and the optimal time duration for the negative stock amounts is obtained from Equation (52) and is provided by $t_2^* = 1.5487$. In addition, the global minimum of the total cost per unit of time is $TC^* = 134.1203$ (see Figure 3). Figure 3 reveals that the cost function $TC(t_1, t_2)$ is strictly increasing for $t_1 \in [t_s, \infty)$, and hence, $t_1^* = t_s$.

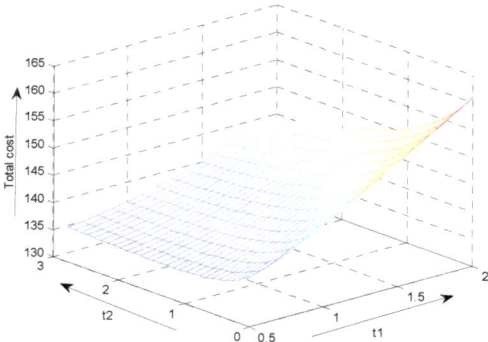

Figure 3. Graphical presentation of the convexity of TC against t_1 and t_2 when $\Omega \geq 0$.

Example 3. *The solutions of the special cases mentioned in Section 5 are investigated with the same data from Example 1 and the corresponding conditions for the cases. The computational results are summarized in Table 2.*

Table 2. Optimal solutions for the special cases.

Special Case	t_1^*	t_2^*	TC^*
(i) when $\delta = 0$	1.1856	0.2119	57.5717
(ii) when $\delta \to \infty$	1.22	0	57.9451
(iii) when $t_s = 0$ and $\delta = 0$	1.0833	0.2889	59.112
(iv) when $t_s = 0$ and $\delta \to \infty$	1.1481	0	59.8604
(v) when $\omega = 1$	1.1292	0.2553	62.1095
(vi) when $\omega = 0$ and $\gamma = 0$	1.7639	0.4864	57.4215
(vii) when $\aleph = 1$	1.1606	0.2666	59.025
(viii) when $\aleph = 1$ and $\omega = 1$	1.0928	0.2396	65.9521

Example 4. *By adopting Example 1 in this example, the consequence of estimating the parameters of the optimal results of t_1, t_2 and total cost TC is explored. The percentage of variations in the optimal results are taken as measures of the analysis, increasing and decreasing the parameters by -20% to $+20\%$. These results are obtained by altering a single parameter value at a time and by keeping the rest of the parameters values unchanged. The outcomes of the analysis are presented in Table 3. The * denotes the optimal solution.*

Table 3. Consequence of changing the parameters of the proposed inventory model.

Parameter	% Changes of Parameters	% Changes in TC^*	% Changes in			
			S^*	R^*	t_1^*	t_2^*
δ	−20	0.04	0.19	−5.04	0.17	−5.35
	−10	0.02	0.10	−2.59	0.09	−2.75
	10	−0.02	−0.10	2.73	−0.09	2.91
	20	−0.04	−0.21	5.61	−0.19	5.99
γ	−20	1.53	9.99	21.62	6.76	21.98
	−10	0.79	4.85	11.16	3.25	11.33
	10	−0.85	−4.60	−11.88	−3.02	−12.02
	20	−1.75	−8.97	−24.52	−5.85	−24.77
C_0	−20	−2.61	−12.90	−36.56	−11.48	−36.88
	−10	−1.25	−6.26	−17.52	−5.54	−17.71
	10	1.16	5.95	16.31	5.21	16.57
	20	2.24	11.63	31.64	10.16	32.20
θ	−20	−0.27	4.79	−3.83	4.40	−3.88
	−10	−0.13	2.28	−1.85	2.10	−1.88
	10	0.12	−2.09	1.75	−1.93	1.77
	20	0.24	−4.02	3.41	−3.71	3.45
c_b	−20	−0.22	−1.13	30.68	−0.99	31.22
	−10	−0.10	−0.50	13.28	−0.44	13.48
	10	0.08	0.40	−10.48	0.35	−10.61
	20	0.14	0.73	−18.96	0.64	−19.17
c_h	−20	−0.07	0.59	−1.02	0.52	−1.03
	−10	−0.04	0.30	−0.51	0.26	−0.51
	10	0.04	−0.29	0.50	−0.26	0.51
	20	0.07	−0.59	1.01	−0.52	1.02

Table 3. Cont.

Parameter	% Changes of Parameters	% Changes in TC^*	% Changes in			
			S^*	R^*	t_1^*	t_2^*
c_p	−20	−17.31	11.85	9.91	10.35	10.06
	−10	−8.63	5.54	5.42	4.86	5.50
	10	8.59	−4.90	−6.42	−4.33	−6.50
	20	17.14	−9.27	−13.92	−8.22	−14.08
c_l	−20	−0.01	−0.04	1.19	−0.04	1.20
	−10	−0.004	−0.02	0.59	−0.02	0.60
	10	0.004	0.02	−0.58	0.02	−0.59
	20	0.01	0.04	−1.16	0.04	−1.17
η	−20	−13.10	−70.15	78.60	−57.52	127.00
	−10	–	–	–	–	–
	10	12.29	−20.49	42.26	−25.65	29.84
	20	23.14	−37.42	64.34	−44.91	37.63
t_s	−20	0.41	−2.24	5.76	5.84	−2.24
	−10	0.20	−1.15	2.79	2.83	−1.14
	10	−0.19	1.22	−2.63	−2.66	1.19
	20	−0.36	2.49	−5.09	−5.16	2.44

From Table 3, the following interpretations are given:

(i) The total cost (TC) is decreased; consequently, with the increase in the inventory level elasticity parameter (γ), the total stock (S), maximum shortage (R), and the time where the stock becomes zero (t_1) sharply fall. This same tendency is also identified in the shortage period (t_2).

(ii) When the value of the backlogging parameter (δ) increases, the total cost of the system (TC) declines as well as the stock amount (S). In contrast, the value of the shortage amount (R) intensifies; contrasting observations are noticed at point (t_1), where shortages are started. This reveals that an increase in the backlogging parameter triggers the customer demand; as a result, the stock is consumed quickly; consequently, it decreases the time (t_1) at which the shortages commence. The duration of the shortage period (t_2) increase significantly simultaneously as the backlogging parameter (δ) increases.

(iii) It is observed that an intensification of the ordering cost triggers the value of the stock (S), shortage (R), and the time (t_1), resulting in stock becoming zero. This means that the retailer has much more time to sell their own products without any interruptions (i.e., shortages). It also affects the total cost (TC) positively. This is a positive sign for the retailer, as the ordering cost neutralizes the holding cost of the system. However, an increase in the holding cost (c_h) results in a significant increase in total cost (TC), as the practitioner has to hold the products for a long time before they can be sold.

(iv) It can be concluded that an upsurge in the purchase cost badly affects the total cost (TC) because the retailer has to buy goods at a high cost. Thence, the retailer reduces the capacity to purchase products, affecting the stock (S) and shortage amount (R).

(v) As the value of the lost sale cost per unit (c_l) increases, the total cost (TC) decreases, and it has a significant effect on the shortage amount (R), where it diminishes as the lost sale cost increases. The length where the (t_1) shortage commences is less sensitive with regard to the lost sale cost per unit (c_l), while it is moderately sensitive with respect to the rest of the parameters. It should also be noted that the investment in shortage cost (c_b) intensifies the total cost (TC) as well as increases the amount of shortages (R).

(vi) The total cost (TC) upsurges as the rate of deterioration increases (θ); consequently it reduces the stock (S) in the retailer's warehouse. This is exhibited by the fact that an intensification in the deterioration rate diminishes the on-hand inventory of the retailer, as deterioration is considered as the obsolesce or decay of products. A massive effect is noted with the increase in the scaling factor of the demand rate (η). When it increases, the total cost (TC) and the stock (S) significantly increases resulting in some of losses in business for the retailer.

(vii) When the deterioration free time (t_s) increases, the total cost (TC) decreases. Nonetheless, the practitioner's stock rises at the same time because during this period, there is no deterioration, so the stock only depletes due to customer demand. Moreover, a higher fresh item period reduces the number of shortages (R) and, consequently, the duration of the shortages (t_2) as well. In contrast, a proliferation in the fresh item period prolongs the shortage-free duration (t_1), which provides more flexibility to the retailer to sell his products according to market demand. As a result, the retailer can maintain the products' original quality for a longer period of time by providing a better holding environment.

8. Conclusions

This research studies an inventory model that considers the effect of delayed deterioration under nonlinear stock-dependent market demand and partial backlogged shortages with respect to the length of the customer waiting time. In the inventory procedure, demand is modeled as a power function of the inventory level when the inventory level is positive while it is constant during shortage periods. The inventory model was formulated as a nonlinear optimization problem, which was solved mathematically. The convexity was proven mathematically as well as numerically. A certain condition was found for the existence of the optimal solution to the problem. Moreover, a salient theoretical result was obtained that guarantees whether the optimal inventory policy involves deterioration or not. The executed analysis points out that a proliferation in the fresh-item period prolongs the shortage-free duration, which provides more flexibility to the inventory manager to sell his/her products according to market demand. This result has a direct influence on the inventory policy to reduce the cost of inventory management. The total cost increases as the deterioration rate increases because it consequently reduces the stock in the retailer's warehouse. This exhibits the fact that an intensification in the deterioration rate diminishes the on-hand inventory of the retailer, as deterioration is considered the obsolescence or decay of products.

In this research work, an optimal policy for an economic order quantity inventory model was derived under the following limitations:

(i) The proposed inventory model was derived based on deteriorating products, nonlinear stock-dependent demand, and partially backlogged shortages. However, preservation technology was not applied to reduce the rate of deterioration.

(ii) Advanced payment with an installment facility was considered for the development of this inventory model. Other facilities such as delay in payment, all unit discount facility, among others are not considered here.

In the future, on the one hand, the inventory model can be expanded for various kinds of variable demands that are dependent on the displayed stock-level, time, quantity discount, etc. On the other hand, the inventory model can also be generalized by including single-level trade credit or two-level credit policies. Finally, one can also explore this inventory model in fuzzy and interval environments. Due to the high nonlinearity of the objective function, soft computing techniques, metaheuristic algorithms, and uncertainty techniques can be applied in order to solve the proposed inventory model.

Author Contributions: Conceptualization, M.A.-A.K., A.A.S., L.E.C.-B., G.T.-G. and A.C.-M.; data curation, M.A.-A.K., A.A.S. and L.E.C.-B.; formal analysis, M.A.-A.K., A.A.S., L.E.C.-B., A.H.M.M., G.T.-G. and A.C.-M.; investigation, M.A.-A.K., A.A.S., L.E.C.-B., A.H.M.M., G.T.-G. and A.C.-M.; methodology, M.A.-A.K., A.A.S., L.E.C.-B., A.H.M.M., G.T.-G. and A.C.-M.; supervision, L.E.C.-B.; validation, M.A.-A.K., L.E.C.-B. and A.H.M.M.; writing—original draft, M.A.-A.K., A.A.S. and A.H.M.M.; writing—review and editing, L.E.C.-B., G.T.-G. and A.C.-M. All authors have read and agreed to the published version of the manuscript.

Funding: This research received no external funding.

Institutional Review Board Statement: Not applicable.

Informed Consent Statement: Not applicable.

Data Availability Statement: All data are contained in the paper.

Conflicts of Interest: The authors declare no conflict of interest.

Appendix A

Holding cost (HC): $HC = c_h \left[\int_0^{t_s} I_1(t)dt + \int_{t_s}^{t_1} I_2(t)dt \right]$

$$\text{Now,} \int_0^{t_s} I_1(t)dt = \int_0^{t_s} [\eta t_s(1-\gamma) + \Delta_1 - \eta t(1-\gamma)]^{\frac{1}{1-\gamma}} dt$$

$$= \int_0^{t_s} [\alpha(t_s - t) + \Delta_1]^{\frac{1}{1-\gamma}} dt, \text{ where } \alpha = \eta(1-\gamma)$$

$$= \frac{1}{\eta + \alpha}\left[(t_s\alpha + \Delta_1)^{\frac{\eta+\alpha}{\alpha}} - \Delta_1^{\frac{\eta+\alpha}{\alpha}}\right]$$

$$\text{Again,} \int_{t_s}^{t_1} I_2(t)dt = \int_{t_s}^{t_1} \eta^{\frac{1}{1-\gamma}} \theta^{-\frac{1}{1-\gamma}} \left\{ e^{\theta(1-\gamma)(t_1-t)} - 1 \right\}^{\frac{1}{1-\gamma}} dt$$

$$= \eta^{\frac{1}{1-\gamma}} \theta^{-\frac{1}{1-\gamma}} \int_{t_s}^{t_1} \left\{ 1 + \frac{\theta\alpha(t_1-t)}{\eta} - 1 \right\}^{\frac{\eta}{\alpha}} dt$$

$$= \alpha^{\frac{\eta}{\alpha}} \int_{t_s}^{t_1} (t_1 - t)^{\frac{\eta}{\alpha}} dt = \frac{1}{\eta+\alpha}\{\alpha(t_1 - t_s)\}^{\frac{\eta+\alpha}{\alpha}}$$

Therefore, $HC = \frac{c_h}{\eta+\alpha}\left[(t_1\alpha + \Delta_1)^{\frac{\eta+\alpha}{\alpha}} - \Delta_1^{\frac{\eta+\alpha}{\alpha}} + \{\alpha(t_1-t_s)\}^{\frac{\eta+\alpha}{\alpha}}\right].$

Deterioration cost (DC): $DC = c_d\left[I_2(t_s) - \eta \int_{t_s}^{t_1} [I_2(t)]^\gamma dt\right]$

$$DC = c_d\left[\Delta_1^{\frac{1}{1-\gamma}} - \eta^{\frac{1}{1-\gamma}} \theta^{-\frac{\gamma}{1-\gamma}} \int_{t_s}^{t_1} \left[\left\{e^{\theta(1-\gamma)(t_1-t)} - 1\right\}^{\frac{\gamma}{1-\gamma}}\right] dt\right]$$

$$= c_d\left[\Delta_1^{\frac{1}{1-\gamma}} - \eta^{\frac{1}{1-\gamma}} \theta^{-\frac{\gamma}{1-\gamma}} \int_{t_s}^{t_1} \left[\left\{e^{\frac{\theta\alpha(t_1-t)}{\eta}} - 1\right\}^{\frac{\gamma}{1-\gamma}}\right] dt\right]$$

$$DC \approx c_d\left[\Delta_1^{\frac{1}{1-\gamma}} - \eta^{\frac{1}{1-\gamma}} \theta^{-\frac{\gamma}{1-\gamma}} \int_{t_s}^{t_1} \left[\left\{1 + \frac{\theta\alpha(t_1-t)}{\eta} - 1\right\}^{\frac{\gamma}{1-\gamma}}\right] dt\right]$$

$$DC = c_d\left[\Delta_1^{\frac{1}{1-\gamma}} - \alpha^{\frac{\gamma}{1-\gamma}} \int_{t_s}^{t_1} (t_1-t)^{\frac{\gamma}{1-\gamma}} dt\right] = c_d\left[\Delta_1^{\frac{1}{1-\gamma}} - (1-\gamma)\alpha^{\frac{\gamma}{1-\gamma}}(t_1-t_s)^{\frac{1}{1-\gamma}}\right]$$

Appendix B

From Equation (29), one has

$$\frac{\partial X}{\partial t_1} = \frac{c_p}{1-\gamma}\left\{1 + \frac{i_c\omega\sigma(\aleph+1)}{2\aleph}\right\}\{\eta t_s(1-\gamma) + \Delta_1\}^{\frac{\gamma}{1-\gamma}}\frac{\partial \Delta_1}{\partial t_1} + c_d\left[\frac{1}{1-\gamma}\Delta_1^{\frac{\gamma}{1-\gamma}}\frac{\partial \Delta_1}{\partial t_1} - \alpha^{\frac{\gamma}{1-\gamma}}(t_1-t_s)^{\frac{\gamma}{1-\gamma}}\right] \\ + \frac{c_h}{\alpha}\left[(t_s\alpha + \Delta_1)^{\frac{\eta}{\alpha}}\frac{\partial \Delta_1}{\partial t_1} - \Delta_1^{\frac{\eta}{\alpha}}\frac{\partial \Delta_1}{\partial t_1} + \alpha^{\frac{\eta+\alpha}{\alpha}}(t_1-t_s)^{\frac{\eta}{\alpha}}\right] \quad (A1)$$

The expression on the right-hand side of (A1) only involves the decision variable t_1 where $t_1 \in [t_s, \infty)$. Now at $t_1 = t_s$,

$$\left.\frac{\partial X}{\partial t_1}\right|_{t_1=t_s} = c_p\eta\left\{1 + \frac{i_c\omega\sigma(\aleph+1)}{2\aleph}\right\}(\alpha t_s)^{\frac{\gamma}{1-\gamma}} + c_h(t_s\alpha)^{\frac{\eta}{\alpha}} > 0 \quad (A2)$$

Moreover,

$$\frac{d}{dt_1}\left(\frac{\partial X}{\partial t_1}\right) = \frac{c_p}{1-\gamma}\left\{1 + \frac{i_c \omega \sigma (\aleph+1)}{2\aleph}\right\}\left[\frac{\gamma}{1-\gamma}\{\eta t_s(1-\gamma) + \Delta_1\}^{\frac{2\gamma-1}{1-\gamma}}\left(\frac{\partial \Delta_1}{\partial t_1}\right)^2 + \{\eta t_s(1-\gamma) + \Delta_1\}^{\frac{\gamma}{1-\gamma}}\frac{\partial^2 \Delta_1}{\partial t_1^2}\right]$$

$$+ c_d\left[\frac{1}{1-\gamma}\left\{\frac{\gamma}{1-\gamma}\Delta_1^{\frac{2\gamma-1}{1-\gamma}}\left(\frac{\partial \Delta_1}{\partial t_1}\right)^2 + \Delta_1^{\frac{\gamma}{1-\gamma}}\frac{\partial^2 \Delta_1}{\partial t_1^2}\right\} + \alpha^{\frac{\gamma}{1-\gamma}}\frac{\gamma}{\gamma-1}(t_1-t_s)^{\frac{2\gamma-1}{1-\gamma}}\right]$$

$$+ \frac{c_h}{\alpha}\left[\frac{\eta}{\alpha}(t_s\alpha + \Delta_1)^{\frac{\eta-\alpha}{\alpha}}\left(\frac{\partial \Delta_1}{\partial t_1}\right)^2 + (t_s\alpha + \Delta_1)^{\frac{\eta}{\alpha}}\frac{\partial^2 \Delta_1}{\partial t_1^2} - \frac{\eta}{\alpha}\Delta_1^{\frac{\eta-\alpha}{\alpha}}\left(\frac{\partial \Delta_1}{\partial t_1}\right)^2 - \Delta_1^{\frac{\eta}{\alpha}}\frac{\partial^2 \Delta_1}{\partial t_1^2}\right.$$

$$\left. + \alpha^{\frac{\eta+\alpha}{\alpha}}\frac{\eta}{\alpha}(t_1-t_s)^{\frac{\eta-\alpha}{\alpha}}\right], \quad (A3)$$

where $\frac{\partial \Delta_1}{\partial t_1} = \eta(1-\gamma)e^{\theta(1-\gamma)(t_1-t_s)}$ and $\frac{\partial^2 \Delta_1}{\partial t_1^2} = \eta\theta(1-\gamma)^2 e^{\theta(1-\gamma)(t_1-t_s)}$.

Since $\frac{\partial^2 \Delta_1}{\partial t_1^2} > 0$, $\frac{\eta}{\alpha}\left(\frac{\partial \Delta_1}{\partial t_1}\right)^2 \left\{(t_s\alpha + \Delta_1)^{\frac{\eta-\alpha}{\alpha}} - \Delta_1^{\frac{\eta-\alpha}{\alpha}}\right\} > 0$, and $\frac{\partial^2 \Delta_1}{\partial t_1^2}\left\{(t_s\alpha + \Delta_1)^{\frac{\eta}{\alpha}} - \Delta_1^{\frac{\eta}{\alpha}}\right\} > 0$, the expression on the right-hand side of Equation (A3) is always positive. Therefore, $\frac{\partial X}{\partial t_1} > 0$ for all $t_1 \in [t_s, \infty)$. Combining Equations (28) and (30) and then by performing some simplifications one can write

$$\frac{1}{1+\delta t_2} < \frac{\left(c_l + \frac{c_b}{\delta}\right)}{\left[\left(c_l + \frac{c_b}{\delta}\right) - c_p\left\{1 + \frac{i_c \omega \sigma(\aleph+1)}{2\aleph}\right\}\right]} \quad (A4)$$

Since the left-hand side of the inequality (B4) is always positive, the inequality (A4) will be true only if $\left(c_l + \frac{c_b}{\delta}\right) - c_p\left\{1 + \frac{i_c \omega \sigma(\aleph+1)}{2\aleph}\right\} > 0$. Otherwise, if $\left(c_l + \frac{c_b}{\delta}\right) - c_p\left\{1 + \frac{i_c \omega \sigma(\aleph+1)}{2\aleph}\right\} \leq 0$, then one can find $t_2 < 0$, which contradicts the assumption $t_2 \geq 0$. Consequently, if $\left(c_l + \frac{c_b}{\delta}\right) \leq c_p\left\{1 + \frac{i_c \omega \sigma(\aleph+1)}{2\aleph}\right\}$, then there is no optimal solution for $TC(t_1, t_2)$.

References

1. Harris, F.W. How many parts to make at once. *Factory. Mag. Manag.* **1913**, *10*, 135–136.
2. First Research. *Industry Profile: Grocery Stores and Supermarkets*; Technical Report; D&B Hoovers: Austin, TX, USA, 2013.
3. Ghare, P.M.; Schrader, G.F. A model for exponentially decaying inventory. *J. Ind. Eng.* **1963**, *14*, 238–243.
4. Taleizadeh, A.A.; Noori-Daryan, M.; Cárdenas-Barrón, L.E. Joint optimization of price, replenishment frequency, replenishment cycle and production rate in vendor managed inventory system with deteriorating items. *Int. J. Prod. Econ.* **2015**, *159*, 285–295. [CrossRef]
5. Shaikh, A.A.; Mashud, A.H.M.; Uddin, M.S.; Khan, M.A.A. Non-instantaneous deterioration inventory model with price and stock dependent demand for fully backlogged shortages under inflation. *Int. J. Bus. Forecast. Mark. Intell.* **2017**, *3*, 152–164. [CrossRef]
6. Tavakoli, S.; Taleizadeh, A.A. An EOQ model for decaying item with full advanced payment and conditional discount. *Ann. Oper. Res.* **2017**, *259*, 415–436. [CrossRef]
7. Pando, V.; San-José, L.A.; García-Laguna, J.; Sicilia, J. Optimal lot-size policy for deteriorating items with stock-dependent demand considering profit maximization. *Comput. Ind. Eng.* **2018**, *117*, 81–93. [CrossRef]
8. Khan, M.A.A.; Shaikh, A.A.; Panda, G.C.; Konstantaras, I.; Taleizadeh, A.A. Inventory system with expiration date: Pricing and replenishment decisions. *Comput. Ind. Eng.* **2019**, *132*, 232–247. [CrossRef]
9. Shaikh, A.A.; Khan, M.A.A.; Panda, G.C.; Konstantaras, I. Price discount facility in an EOQ model for deteriorating items with stock-dependent demand and partial backlogging. *Int. Trans. Oper. Res.* **2019**, *26*, 1365–1395. [CrossRef]
10. Khan, M.A.A.; Ahmed, S.; Babu, M.S.; Sultana, N. Optimal lot-size decision for deteriorating items with price-sensitive demand, linearly time-dependent holding cost under all-units discount environment. *Int. J. Syst. Sci. Oper. Logist.* **2020**, 1–14. [CrossRef]
11. Khan, M.A.A.; Shaikh, A.A.; Panda, G.C.; Konstantaras, I.; Cárdenas-Barrón, L.E. The effect of advance payment with discount facility on supply decisions of deteriorating products whose demand is both price and stock dependent. *Int. Trans. Oper. Res.* **2020**, *27*, 1343–1367. [CrossRef]
12. Das, S.; Khan, M.A.A.; Mahmoud, E.E.; Abdel-Aty, A.H.; Abualnaja, K.M.; Shaikh, A.A. A production inventory model with partial trade credit policy and reliability. *Alex. Eng. J.* **2021**, *60*, 1325–1338. [CrossRef]
13. Musa, A.; Sani, B. Inventory ordering policies of delayed deteriorating items under permissible delay in payments. *Int. J. Prod. Econ.* **2012**, *136*, 75–83. [CrossRef]
14. Sarkar, B.; Sarkar, S. An improved inventory model with partial backlogging, time varying deterioration and stock-dependent demand. *Econ. Model.* **2013**, *30*, 924–932. [CrossRef]

15. Tyagi, A.P.; Pandey, R.K.; Singh, S. An optimal replenishment policy for non-instantaneous deteriorating items with stock-dependent demand and variable holding cost. *Int. J. Oper. Res.* **2014**, *21*, 466–488. [CrossRef]
16. Mashud, A.; Khan, M.; Uddin, M.; Islam, M. A non-instantaneous inventory model having different deterioration rates with stock and price dependent demand under partially backlogged shortages. *Uncertain Supply Chain. Manag.* **2018**, *6*, 49–64. [CrossRef]
17. Rastogi, M.; Singh, S.R.; Kushwah, P. An inventory model for non-instantaneous deteriorating products having price sensitive demand and partial backlogging of occurring shortages. *Int. J. Oper. Quant. Manag.* **2018**, *24*, 59–73.
18. Khan, M.A.A.; Shaikh, A.A.; Panda, G.C.; Bhunia, A.K.; Konstantaras, I. Non-instantaneous deterioration effect in ordering decisions for a two-warehouse inventory system under advance payment and backlogging. *Ann. Oper. Res.* **2020**, *289*, 243–275. [CrossRef]
19. Sundararajan, R.; Palanivel, M.; Uthayakumar, R. An inventory system of non-instantaneous deteriorating items with backlogging and time discounting. *Int. J. Syst. Sci. Oper. Logist.* **2020**, *7*, 233–247. [CrossRef]
20. Sundararajan, R.; Palanivel, M.; Uthayakumar, R. An EOQ model of non-instantaneous deteriorating items with price, time-dependent demand and backlogging. *J. Control Decis.* **2021**, *8*, 135–154. [CrossRef]
21. Levin, R.I. *Production Operations Management: Contemporary Policy for Managing Operating Systems*; McGraw-Hill Companies: New York, NY, USA, 1972.
22. Valliathal, M.; Uthayakumar, R. Designing a new computational approach of partial backlogging on the economic production quantity model for deteriorating items with non-linear holding cost under inflationary conditions. *Optim. Lett.* **2011**, *5*, 515–530. [CrossRef]
23. Min, J.; Zhou, Y.W.; Liu, G.Q.; Wang, S.D. An EPQ model for deteriorating items with inventory-level-dependent demand and permissible delay in payments. *Int. J. Syst. Sci.* **2012**, *43*, 1039–1053. [CrossRef]
24. Pando, V.; García-Laguna, J.; San-José, L.A.; Sicilia, J. Maximizing profits in an inventory model with both demand rate and holding cost per unit time dependent on the stock level. *Comput. Ind. Eng.* **2012**, *62*, 599–608. [CrossRef]
25. Pando, V.; San-José, L.A.; García-Laguna, J.; Sicilia, J. An economic lot-size model with non-linear holding cost hinging on time and quantity. *Int. J. Prod. Econ.* **2013**, *145*, 294–303. [CrossRef]
26. Yang, C.T. An inventory model with both stock-dependent demand rate and stock-dependent holding cost rate. *Int. J. Prod. Econ.* **2014**, *155*, 214–221. [CrossRef]
27. Sarkar, B.; Mandal, B.; Sarkar, S. Preservation of deteriorating seasonal products with stock-dependent consumption rate and shortages. *J. Ind. Manag. Optim.* **2017**, *13*, 187–206. [CrossRef]
28. Pando, V.; San-José, L.A.; Sicilia, J. Profitability ratio maximization in an inventory model with stock-dependent demand rate and non-linear holding cost. *Appl. Math. Model.* **2019**, *66*, 643–661. [CrossRef]
29. Pando, V.; San-José, L.A.; Sicilia, J. A new approach to maximize the profit/cost ratio in a stock-dependent demand inventory model. *Comput. Oper. Res.* **2020**, *120*, 104940. [CrossRef]
30. Cárdenas-Barrón, L.E.; Shaikh, A.A.; Tiwari, S.; Treviño-Garza, G. An EOQ inventory model with nonlinear stock dependent holding cost, nonlinear stock dependent demand and trade credit. *Comput. Ind. Eng.* **2020**, *139*, 105557. [CrossRef]
31. Zhang, A.X. Optimal advance payment scheme involving fixed per-payment costs. *Omega* **1996**, *24*, 577–582. [CrossRef]
32. Taleizadeh, A.A.; Pentico, D.W.; Jabalameli, M.S.; Aryanezhad, M. An economic order quantity model with multiple partial prepayments and partial backordering. *Math. Comput. Model.* **2013**, *57*, 311–323. [CrossRef]
33. Taleizadeh, A.A. An EOQ model with partial backordering and advance payment for an evaporating item. *Int. J. Prod. Econ.* **2014**, *155*, 185–193. [CrossRef]
34. Zhang, Q.; Zhang, D.; Tsao, Y.C.; Luo, J. Optimal ordering policy in a two-stage supply chain with advance payment for stable supply capacity. *Int. J. Prod. Econ.* **2016**, *177*, 34–43. [CrossRef]
35. Khan, M.A.A.; Shaikh, A.A.; Panda, G.C.; Konstantaras, I. Two-warehouse inventory model for deteriorating items with partial backlogging and advance payment scheme. *RAIRO Oper. Res.* **2019**, *53*, 1691–1708. [CrossRef]
36. Shaikh, A.A.; Das, S.C.; Bhunia, A.K.; Panda, G.C.; Khan, M.A.A. A two-warehouse EOQ model with interval-valued inventory cost and advance payment for deteriorating item under particle swarm optimization. *Soft Comput.* **2019**, *23*, 13531–13546. [CrossRef]
37. Khan, M.A.A.; Shaikh, A.A.; Konstantaras, I.; Bhunia, A.K.; Cárdenas-Barrón, L.E. Inventory models for perishable items with advanced payment, linearly time-dependent holding cost and demand dependent on advertisement and selling price. *Int. J. Prod. Econ.* **2020**, *23*, 107804. [CrossRef]
38. San-José, L.A.; Sicilia, J.; Alcaide-López-de-Pablo, D. An inventory system with demand dependent on both time and price assuming backlogged shortages. *Eur. J. Oper. Res.* **2018**, *270*, 889–897. [CrossRef]
39. San-José, L.A.; Sicilia, J.; González-De-la-Rosa, M.; Febles-Acosta, J. Best pricing and optimal policy for an inventory system under time-and-price-dependent demand and backordering. *Ann. Oper. Res.* **2020**, *286*, 351–369. [CrossRef]
40. Singh, S.; Sharma, S.; Singh, S.R. Inventory model for deteriorating items with incremental holding cost under partial backlogging. *Int. J. Math. Oper.* **2019**, *15*, 110–126. [CrossRef]

41. Alshanbari, H.M.; El-Bagoury, A.A.A.H.; Khan, M.; Mondal, S.; Shaikh, A.A.; Rashid, A. Economic Order Quantity Model with Weibull Distributed Deterioration under a Mixed Cash and Prepayment Scheme. *Comput. Intell. Neurosci.* **2021**, *2021*, 9588685. [CrossRef]
42. Rahman, M.S.; Khan, M.A.A.; Halim, M.A.; Nofal, T.A.; Shaikh, A.A.; Mahmoud, E.E. Hybrid price and stock dependent inventory model for perishable goods with advance payment related discount facilities under preservation technology. *Alex. Eng. J.* **2021**, *60*, 3455–3465. [CrossRef]

Article

Analysis and Consequences on Some Aggregation Functions of PRISM (Partial Risk Map) Risk Assessment Method

Ferenc Bognár [1,*] and Csaba Hegedűs [2]

1 Department of Management and Business Economics, Budapest University of Technology and Economics, H-1117 Budapest, Hungary
2 Department of Supply Chain Management, University of Pannonia, H-8200 Veszprém, Hungary; hegedus.csaba@gtk.uni-pannon.hu
* Correspondence: bognar.ferenc@gtk.bme.hu; Tel.: +36-1-463-4014

Abstract: The PRISM (partial risk map) methodology is a novel risk assessment method developed as the combination of the failure mode and effect analysis and risk matrix risk assessment methods. Based on the concept of partial risks, three different aggregation functions are presented for assessing incident risks. Since the different aggregation functions give different properties to the obtained PRISM numbers and threshold surfaces (convex, concave, linear), the description of these properties is carried out. Similarity analyses based on the sum of ranking differences (SRD) method and rank correlation are performed and robustness tests are applied related to the changes of the assessment scale lengths. The PRISM method provides a solution for the systematically criticized problem of the FMEA, i.e., it is not able to deal with hidden risks behind the aggregated RPN number, while the method results in an expressive tool for risk management. Applying new aggregation functions, proactive assessment can be executed, and predictions can be given related to the incidents based on the nature of their hidden risk. The method can be suggested for safety science environments where human safety, environmental protection, sustainable production, etc., are highly required.

Keywords: partial risk map; PRISM; PRISM number; failure mode and effect analysis; FMEA; RPN; risk matrix; risk assessment; safety science; systems safety

MSC: 90B50; 90B25

Citation: Bognár, F.; Hegedűs, C. Analysis and Consequences on Some Aggregation Functions of PRISM (Partial Risk Map) Risk Assessment Method. *Mathematics* **2022**, *10*, 676. https://doi.org/10.3390/math10050676

Academic Editor: Christoph Frei

Received: 22 January 2022
Accepted: 19 February 2022
Published: 22 February 2022

Publisher's Note: MDPI stays neutral with regard to jurisdictional claims in published maps and institutional affiliations.

Copyright: © 2022 by the authors. Licensee MDPI, Basel, Switzerland. This article is an open access article distributed under the terms and conditions of the Creative Commons Attribution (CC BY) license (https://creativecommons.org/licenses/by/4.0/).

1. Introduction

Nowadays, the development of risk assessment methodologies is clearly visible in the industry and service sector as well. One typical development direction is to combine different mathematical methodologies with a platform risk assessment methodology such as FMEA—failure mode and effect analysis [1,2], RM—risk matrix [3], HAZOP—hazard and operability analysis [4], FTA—fault tree analysis [5], etc. The typical aim of these studies is to develop the platform methodology, increasing its strengths and/or decreasing its weaknesses by adding new, typically mathematical features. Another major development direction is to combine a risk assessment methodology with another one [6–8]. Typically, the aim is to combine the strength of the risk assessment methodologies in this case. Throughout the decades of development, the reliability, effectiveness, usefulness, applicability, etc., of the platform risk assessment methodologies were significantly increased by dominantly mathematic-based methodological developments [9–12].

In our understanding, the risk is not just the probability of an incident but a composite of all the characteristics that are relevant to the incident and its possible outcome. In this paper, just the probability of the occurrence, the severity of the consequences, and the degree of undetectability are considered, but other aspects or features of the incident can be regarded as a component of the risk (e.g., criticality, range/expansion of the effects, controllability, etc.). The number of such characteristics that are considered can vary method by method; in most of the cases, these characteristics are described with values and condensed into a single value for each incident.

Based on the combination of the FMEA and RM methodologies, a novel risk assessment methodology called partial risk map (PRISM) was described. Although, the application of the methodology was presented in a case study related to the assessment of compliance risks in the banking sector [13], the PRISM risk assessment method is more generic and can be applied in different operational fields as well, where the risk assessment is based on similar rating factors to the FMEA, and the identification of hidden risks is essential. Thus, the method can be offered for safety science environments, where human health, environmental protection, and sustainable production are in the focus, and also applied to those fields, where the incident consequences can be generally high. Since the methodology is quite novel, it still has potential to improve in different descriptive, comparative, and developmental directions. Although, the methodology builds on the strengths of both the FMEA and RM methods, the mathematical process of the incident ranking is still not defined [13]. The purpose of this work is the mathematical development and description of the ranking algorithm of the PRISM method. The aim is to create, describe, and compare some aggregation functions for the incident characteristics to determine and to detail the application of the PRISM number. Since PRISM methodology applies the same risk assessment dimensions as FMEA, the paper also focuses on putting the results related to the PRISM number into the context of the RPN (risk priority number) of FMEA. Thus, the aim of the paper is to create the formal description of the theory of partial risks and to compare the newly developed formulas to each other and to the formula of RPN. The main results and innovations of the paper are the following:

- Three functions are developed for assessing partial risks (one algorithm is sensitive for incidents, having a high risk level at one rating factor, one algorithm is sensitive for middle risk levels at all the rating factors, one is a balanced algorithm). Applying the new functions, proactive assessment can be executed, and predictions can be given related to the incidents based on the nature of their hidden risk.
- The developed functions have an exact description based on the distribution of their possible values and these are compared to the distribution of RPN number.
- The rankings of the functions are compared to each other by applying different analyses, and detailed discussion of the theoretical differences is given based on the comparison.
- The rankings are robust related to the change of evaluation factor scales. This test is important, since, in the practical field, the evaluation scale lengths can be different.

Therefore, the work aims to identify the evaluation specialties of the different methods, and based on the comparisons, possible application suggestions are given for the practitioners and other research gaps are presented for future research and development.

Since the PRISM methodology builds off of some key specialties of FMEA and RM as well, in Section 1.1, a brief introduction of these two methodologies is given, and in Section 1.2, the description of the PRISM method is presented. All the methods featured in these subsections evaluate the risk of the incidents based on several risk factors and use some aggregation of these factors to provide an order of priority among the incidents. The applied method influences the priorities and directs the focus of risk mitigation in a different way.

1.1. Brief Description of the RM and FMEA

In this subsection, the focus is on the brief introduction of two methodologies, which have significant impacts on the aim of this study. Thus, RM and FMEA are introduced here since the PRISM method builds on some key features of these methodologies [14]. The introduction aims to describe the basic structures of the methods and to refer to some important notes of existing developments. There is no focus on the complete introduction of these methods, their practical applications, and all the consequences in the field of risk assessment techniques.

The methodology of the risk matrix is a widely applicable method of risk assessment. The structure of risk matrices is built up by factors developed to assess the risk of particular objects [15]. Risk matrices are usually based on two independent rating factors, which are the probability of occurrence and the severity of consequences [16]. In most cases, RM estimates the risk on ordinal or higher measurement scales having usually four to five different values. The higher the factor-related risk of the object, the higher the value of the factor.

The risk assessment is generally based on the score of the probability of occurrence and the severity of consequences factors [17]. In the case of having high values related to both rating factors, the associated risk is usually interpreted as high, while in the case of having low values related to the factors, the indicated risk level is low. However, other categories can be created as well. The visualization of the methodology is usually represented with a matrix as shown in Figure 1.

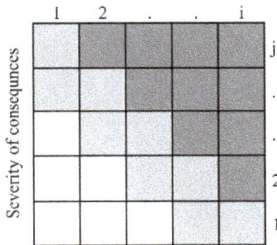

Figure 1. Visualization example of the risk matrix.

Selection of the set of the riskiest incidents that must be averted, mitigated, eliminated, etc., can be executed using a given or calculated threshold level. Once an aggregated value reaches the threshold level, it signals to the control system. In Figure 1, two threshold levels are visualized on the frontiers of the white, light gray, and dark gray cells as examples. The darker the region, the higher the priority.

Similar to the risk matrices, the failure mode and effect analysis methodology also estimates risks of certain incidents by different rating factors. In the case of FMEA, the estimation is based on the aggregation of three rating factor values (probability of occurrence, severity of consequences, and degree of undetectability). The most typical aggregation of these values is multiplication, as many scientific papers refer to it [1,2,18–20].

As for the result of the multiplication, the RPN can be calculated. Based on the RPN value, it can be decided whether any risk reduction action is necessary to be launched or not in case of certain incidents. Over the past decades, the RPN is widely criticized by scientists, highlighting a couple of weaknesses of the RPN.

One of the most criticized properties of the RPN is that some hidden or latent risks can be unestimated or misestimated because different combinations of the three factors can result in the same RPN [13,21–25]. Thus, these hidden risks can later lead to unexpected errors.

Despite structured criticisms [22,23,26–29], the method is used quite frequently in the latest publications as well without modifications applied to it. As for example, an application is given for the classical failure mode and effects analysis in the context of smart grid cyber–physical systems [30].

1.2. Brief Description of the Partial Risk Map (PRISM) Methodology

The PRISM methodology is a novel risk assessment methodology [13], and it builds on the synergies of some key properties of both the FMEA and RM methods. Similar to the FMEA method, PRISM applies three risk assessment factors (probability of occurrence, severity of consequences, degree of undetectability). Since the PRISM methodology defines and visualizes the phenomena of partial risk, the method describes well all the potentially existing hidden risks that are not taken into consideration by the RPN. Many criticisms said that the relative importance of the three rating factors is not highlighted in the case of FMEA [31–36], the PRISM method also solves this problem as well as the latent or hidden risk problem of FMEA. The method is offered to apply in situations when safety and reliability has a high priority.

According to [37], based on parametrization, the methodology gives the possibility of focusing either on the FMEA or PRISM-related assessment results. In the context of the method, the partial risk is a combination of any two of the applied assessment factors, and the risk level of an incident can be estimated partially regarding this factor combination.

According to [38], the PRISM methodology can be applied as a sophisticated approach option of risk analysis in the field of project management, since the partial risks of a certain project can be estimated and visualized by it.

The structure of the PRISM method is a set of three sub-matrices, as visible in Figure 2. Some theoretical priority levels are also visualized as previously modeled in Figure 1.

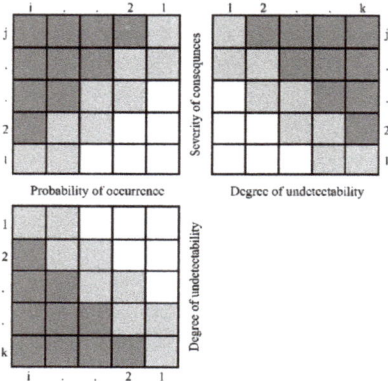

Figure 2. Visualization example of the partial risk map.

Based on the scores of the rating factors, a certain incident can be visualized in the Partial Risk Map [13]. If a partial risk is in any of the gray cells in at least one of the three matrices, it will signal the need for control. The location of a partial risk in the map indicates the direction of the action, mitigation, etc., that should be performed.

Although the basic idea of the PRISM methodology has already been described, the deeper analysis of the method cannot be executed without the formal description of the methodology and the definition of aggregation functions for the calculation of the PRISM number. Based on the formal description, the comparison of the RPNs and PRISM numbers determined by different aggregation functions can be executed, the differences can be described, and suggestions can be made for the practical application of the methodology.

2. Materials and Methods

In this section, the focus is on the formal description of different aggregation functions for the PRISM methodology.

The first step is to define incidents and their characteristics. Denote as $m : (o, s, d)$ a failure mode or incident that has three characteristics: o probability of occurrence (occurrence), s severity of consequences (severity), and d degree of undetectability (detection). The characteristics have the following values, $o \in [1, 2, \cdots, i]$, $s \in [1, 2, \cdots, j]$ and $d \in [1, 2, \cdots, k]$. For every failure mode or incident, some aggregate risk value can be calculated from the o, s, and d values by applying the $\otimes$ aggregation function. As mentioned in Section 1, this aggregate value is used to prioritize the incidents, and the higher the aggregated value, the higher the risk of the incident compared to the cases that are assessed with the same aggregation method.

The risk assessment is three dimensional in the case of FMEA, so the RPN value is a point in the three-dimensional space represented by Equation (1).

$$A = (a_{o,s,d}) \in \mathbb{N}_+^{i \times j \times k}. \tag{1}$$

Denote $r(m) = r(o,s,d) = (o \otimes s \otimes d)$ a three-dimensional risk evaluation function of m incident in the case of FMEA. For the calculation of the RPN, the typical aggregation method in the industry is the multiplication of o, s, and d values, as shown by Equation (2).

$$\mathbb{N}_+^3 \to \mathbb{R}: \ RPN(m) = o \cdot s \cdot d. \tag{2}$$

The PRISM methodology observes partial risks that describe three paired characteristics of m incident [13]. Formally, the Partial Risk Map can be described, with a set of three matrices represented by Equations (3)–(5).

$$A_{o,s} = (a_{o,s}) \in \mathbb{N}_+^{i \times j}. \tag{3}$$

$$A_{d,s} = (a_{s,d}) \in \mathbb{N}_+^{j \times k}. \tag{4}$$

$$A_{o,d} = (a_{o,d}) \in \mathbb{N}_+^{i \times k}. \tag{5}$$

Since the PRISM methodology calculates the aggregate values of the paired characteristics of m incident, denote $p(m) = p(o,s,d) = (o \otimes s, o \otimes d, d \otimes s)$ as the PRISM pattern of an incident. The representation of a theoretical PRISM pattern is visible in Figure 3.

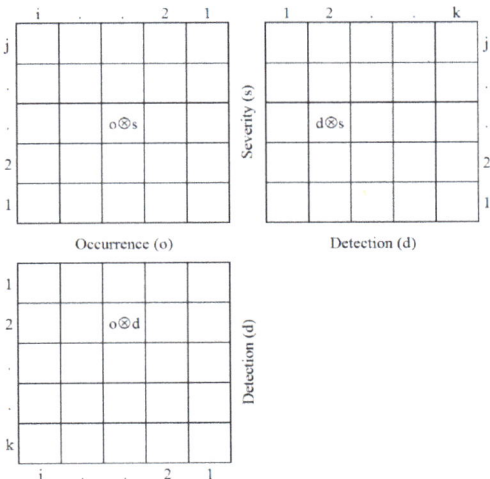

Figure 3. The visualization of the PRISM pattern in the partial risk map.

Let M denote the maximal number of m incidents with different risk characteristic combinations, this can be formulated as follows.

$$M = |Re(o)| \cdot |Re(s)| \cdot |Re(d)| \tag{6}$$

In most of the practical cases, $o \in [1, 2, \cdots, 10]$, $s \in [1, 2, \cdots, 10]$, and $d \in [1, 2, \cdots, 10]$; thus, the value of M is 1000.

The PRISM number of incident m can be given by selecting the maximal value of the three aggregates of $p(m)$. Let $PRISM(m)$ denote the PRISM number of a certain incident. The calculation of the PRISM number is as follows:

$$PRISM(m) = \max\{o \otimes s,\ o \otimes d,\ d \otimes s\}. \tag{7}$$

In this study, three different formulas are proposed for the PRISM number calculation, as shown by Equations (8)–(10). Note that, the PRISM method is for considering partial risks, no formula is previously given for any calculations.

$$\mathbb{N}_+^3 \to \mathbb{R}\colon A(m) = \max\{o+s,\ o+d,\ d+s\} \tag{8}$$

$$\mathbb{N}_+^3 \to \mathbb{R}\colon M(m) = \max\{o \cdot s,\ o \cdot d,\ d \cdot s\} \tag{9}$$

$$\mathbb{N}_+^3 \to \mathbb{R}\colon S(m) = \max\left\{o^2+s^2,\ o^2+d^2,\ d^2+s^2\right\} \tag{10}$$

Let N denote the size of the image set of an aggregation function, i.e., the number of different output values that can be given by an aggregation function. Applying different aggregation functions can result in different N values. In the cases of the applied $A(m)$, $M(m)$, and $S(m)$ aggregation functions, the followings can be given, when $o \in [1, 2, \cdots, 10]$, $s \in [1, 2, \cdots, 10]$, and $d \in [1, 2, \cdots, 10]$:

$$N_{A(m)} := |\mathrm{Im}(A(m))| = 19 \tag{11}$$

$$N_{M(m)} := |\mathrm{Im}(M(m))| = 42 \tag{12}$$

$$N_{S(m)} := |\mathrm{Im}(S(m))| = 52 \tag{13}$$

In the case of $RPN(m)$, the following formula can be given, when $o \in [1, 2, \cdots, 10]$, $s \in [1, 2, \cdots, 10]$, and $d \in [1, 2, \cdots, 10]$:

$$N_{RPN(m)} := |\mathrm{Im}(RPN(m))| = 120 \tag{14}$$

The generated values of the PRISM numbers are visualized in Figure 4 including the PRISM pattern representation of four different (m_1, m_2, m_3, m_4) incidents. Based on the PRISM numbers, the ranks of the incidents are also given in Figure 4 as well as the ranks by the RPNs. The higher the value of the PRISM number, the lower the rank. Changing the aggregation function could also change the order of incident priorities as well.

Putting more focus on the application of thresholds, there is an option for further profiling the incident set—instead of only ranking the incidents. As previously described, a threshold is a maximal value of the aggregated result of different m incident patterns that cannot be reached or exceeded by the aggregated result of an incident pattern; otherwise, it signals to the control system. Naturally, the aggregation function of the PRISM number affects also the threshold surface, and the number of steps can be applied from the least strict threshold level to the strictest one (in the case of $A(m)$ from 20 to 2, in the case of $M(m)$ from 100 to 1, and in the case of $S(m)$ from 200 to 2.) The maximum number of different effective threshold levels naturally equals the number of N.

Based on the number N of the aggregation function, the sensitivity for a given threshold can be characterized. Since the $A(m)$ function has the lowest N value, it has sectioning with the largest steps available. In the case of the $S(m)$ function, the N value is the highest, so thresholds can be set by the smallest units. The aggregation function also determines the threshold surface; thus, it affects the set of incidents that need to be treated.

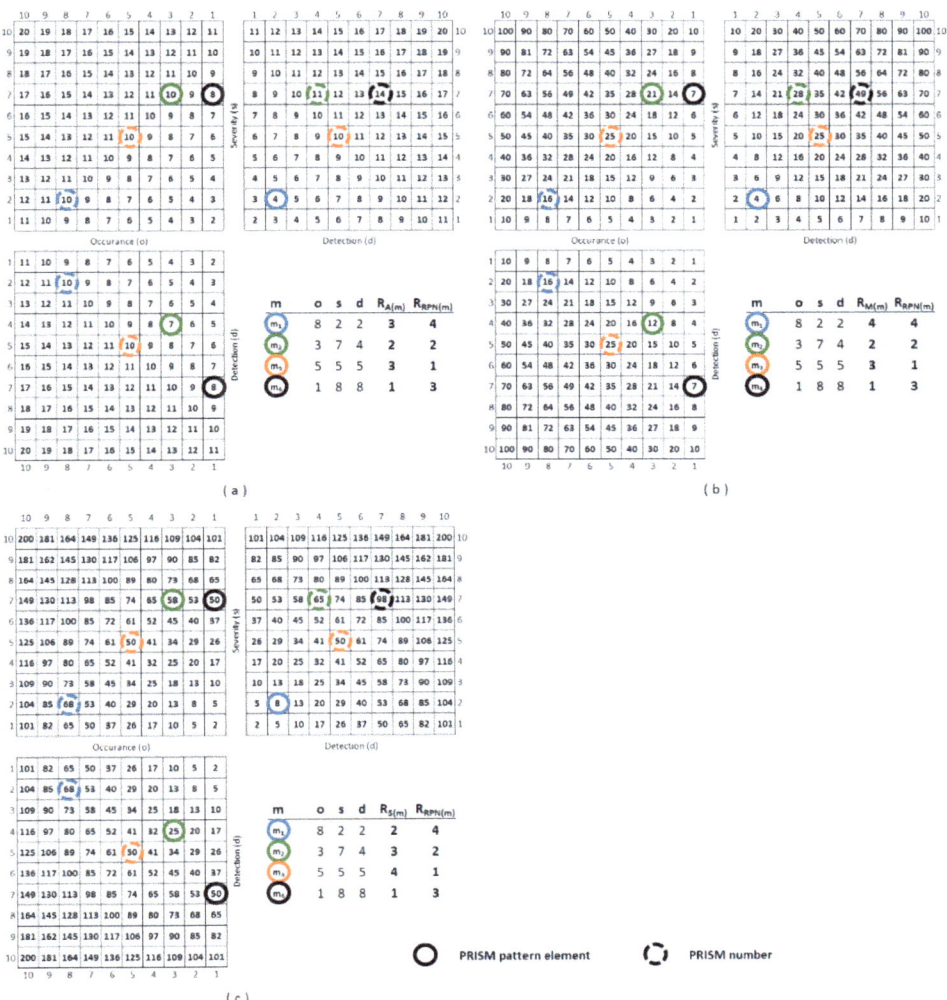

Figure 4. The visualization of the PRISM patterns and PRISM numbers in the case of $A(m)$, $M(m)$, and $S(m)$ functions. Picture part (**a**) shows all the results of $p(m)$ and $PRISM(m)$ in the case of $A(m)$, part (**b**) represents the results for $M(m)$, while part (**c**) shows the results for $S(m)$.

Figure 5 shows an example for the different threshold surfaces in the case of each of the applied aggregation functions. $A(m)$ function results in a linear threshold surface, $M(m)$ results in a convex, and $S(m)$ results in a concave one. In Appendix A, Figure A1 shows the colored partial risk maps, representing all the possible threshold surfaces related to the three aggregation functions.

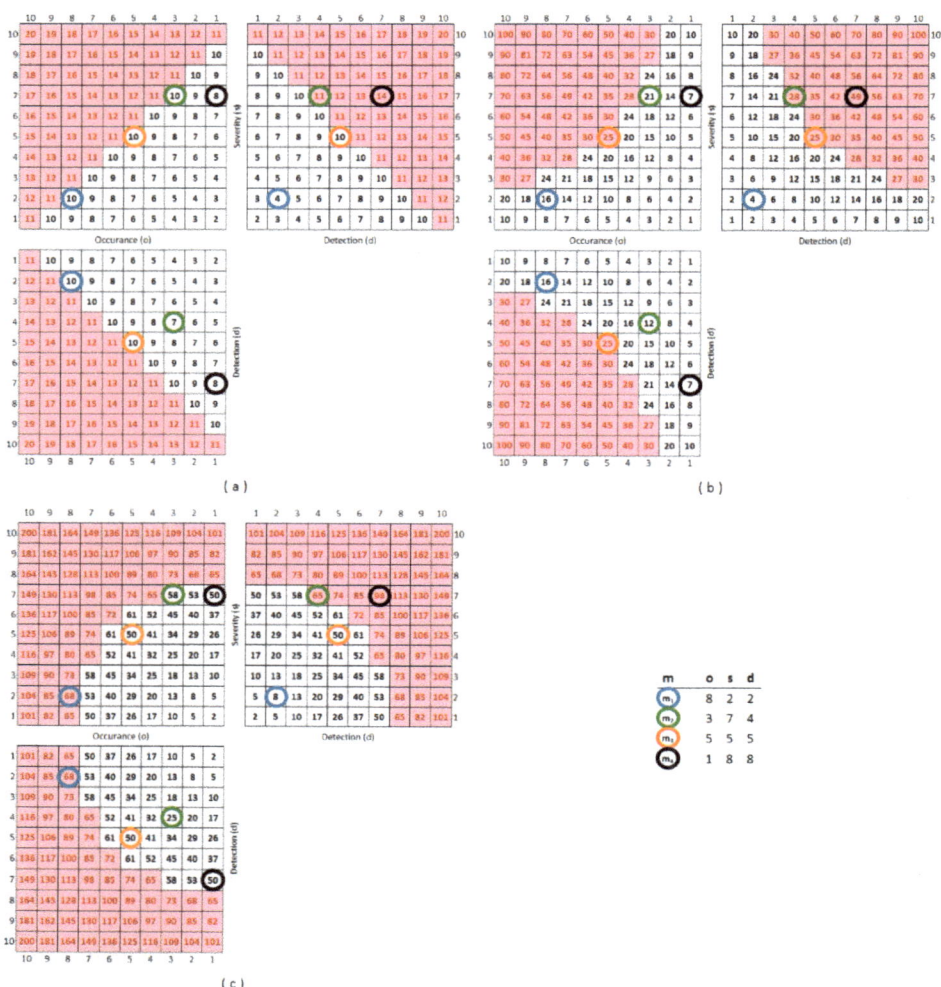

Figure 5. The example thresholds are set at the 25th percentiles of all the incidents. (**a**) The threshold surface in the case of $A(m)$, (**b**) the threshold surface in the case of $M(m)$, and (**c**) the threshold surface in the case of $S(m)$.

In Figure 6, the set of m_1, m_2, m_3, and m_4 incidents are profiled by applying increasingly stricter threshold levels until all the PRISM pattern elements exceed this threshold.

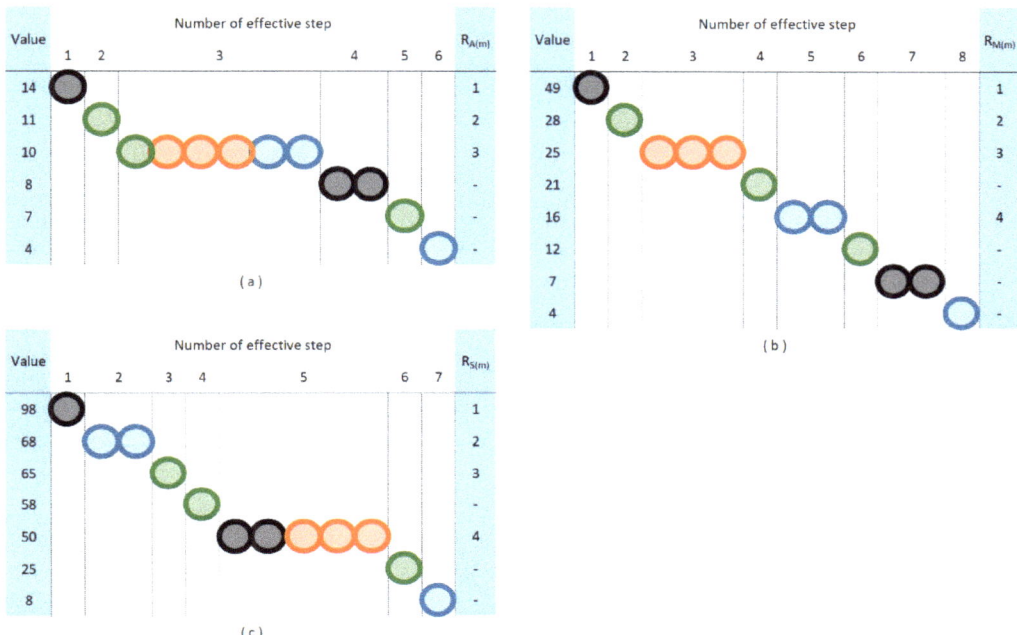

Figure 6. (**a**) The profile of the incident set in the case of $A(m)$, (**b**) the case of $M(m)$, and (**c**) the case of $S(m)$.

Of course, the ranking by the PRISM number will not change, but further information on the nature of the risk set can be described as well, which gives a more detailed picture to the decision-makers.

3. Results

In this section, descriptive statistics of the set of PRISM numbers produced by the presented aggregation functions and the set of traditional RPN numbers are described and compared. Some key relations between the aggregation functions of the PRISM method are also presented in this section. Robustness tests of the rankings based on PRISM numbers determined by different aggregation functions are described as well.

3.1. Descriptive Statistics

The descriptive statistics of the three different sets of the PRISM numbers and the set of traditional RPN numbers are shown in Table 1.

Changing to the PRISM aggregation functions from $RPN(m)$, the number of distinct values (N) drops off from 120 to 19, 42, and 52 for the $A(m)$, $M(m)$, and $S(m)$ versions, respectively, that also decrease the variability of the values. The coefficient of variation (the standard deviation over the mean) is between the quarter and the half of the same value of the traditional RPN. However, the PRISM spreads the values more evenly around the mean, and the absolute values of skewness are also lower than that for the traditional RPN (see Figure 7).

Figure 7 shows that, while the traditional RPN has exponential-like distribution with most of the values close to the lower end of the scale, the PRISM produces more cases on the upper half of its scale.

Table 1. Descriptive statistics related to the different PRISM numbers and the traditional RPN number.

		$A(m)$	$M(m)$	$S(m)$	$RPN(m)$
Number of incidents (M)		1000	1000	1000	1000
Mean		13.48	46.32	102.64	166.38
Std. error of mean		0.117	0.791	1.483	5.424
Mode		14	90	181	60
Std. deviation		3.704	25.012	46.901	171.509
Variance		13.721	625.594	2199.668	29,415.400
Coefficient of variation		0.275	0.540	0.457	1.031
Skewness		−0.383	0.274	0.044	1.672
Kurtosis		−0.398	−0.838	−0.727	2.828
Number of different ranks (N)		19	42	52	120
Range		18	99	198	999
Minimum		2	1	2	1
Maximum		20	100	200	1000
Percentiles	25	11.00	25.00	65.00	42.00
	50	14.00	45.00	101.00	105.00
	75	16.00	64.00	136.00	240.00

3.2. Comparison of the Methods

The incidents are ranked by the RPN and the PRISM numbers from the highest to the lowest, ties are resolved by giving the same rank to incidents with the same value—the arithmetic mean of the ranks, i.e., fractional ranking is applied.

All the three PRISM rankings have high (Spearman's rho) rank correlation to the ranking of traditional RPN, $\rho(R_{RPN(m)}, R_{A(m)}) = 0.820$, $\rho(R_{RPN(m)}, R_{M(m)}) = 0.842$, and $\rho(R_{RPN(m)}, R_{S(m)}) = 0.778$. To evaluate the similarity of the rankings made by the studied methods, the sum of ranking differences (SRD) method [39] is applied. The sum of ranking differences (SRD) [40] method assesses ranking methods according to the sum of the absolute differences in ranks of the objects (i.e., the Manhattan distance) compared to an ideal ranking (a golden standard). If the ideal rank is not known or cannot be explicitly determined, the average rank of the objects can be used since the errors of the different methods cancel each other and the maximum likelihood principle ensures that the most probable ranking is provided by the average [40]. This method is non-parametric and robust, and it is used in several fields of science, see, e.g., [41,42]. In contrast to other statistical methods, such as Spearman's rho, Kendall's tau, and Mann–Whitney U test, the SRD not only provides pairwise comparison but also puts all the assessed rankings (aggregation methods) into an order according to their similarity (or dissimilarity) to the golden standard [40]. In this way, SRD also can distinguish groupings and outliers among the ranking methods. Considering all the possible permutations in a ranking, the probability distribution of the SRD values can be determined. This probability distribution is then used to assess the significance of a ranking, i.e., how low is the probability of receiving this ranking as a random permutation.

For the SRD, no universally applicable ranking can be created as a reference in this case because the three characteristics of m are not commensurable with each other, and their relative importance is appraised subjectively. Thus, the average ranking was calculated for each of the 1000 combinations of o, s, and d values. Alongside the traditional RPN and the previously introduced three PRISM aggregations, the total sum ($o + s + d$), and total squared sum ($o^2 + s^2 + d^2$) of the three characteristics were used as a rank determining method. This was necessary to avoid the bias toward the three new PRISM-based approaches (similar to each other) against the singleton of the traditional RPN. This setting has equal number of approaches for the pairwise holistic comparison and also for each aggregation. The normalized SRD distances from this reference are shown in Table 2. For the normalization, the theoretical maximum of SRD was calculated and it received the value 1 on the scale. Considering all the possible permutations of the M = 1000 cases, the normalized SRD values can be described with a normal distribution with 0.6667 mean and 0.0133 standard deviation.

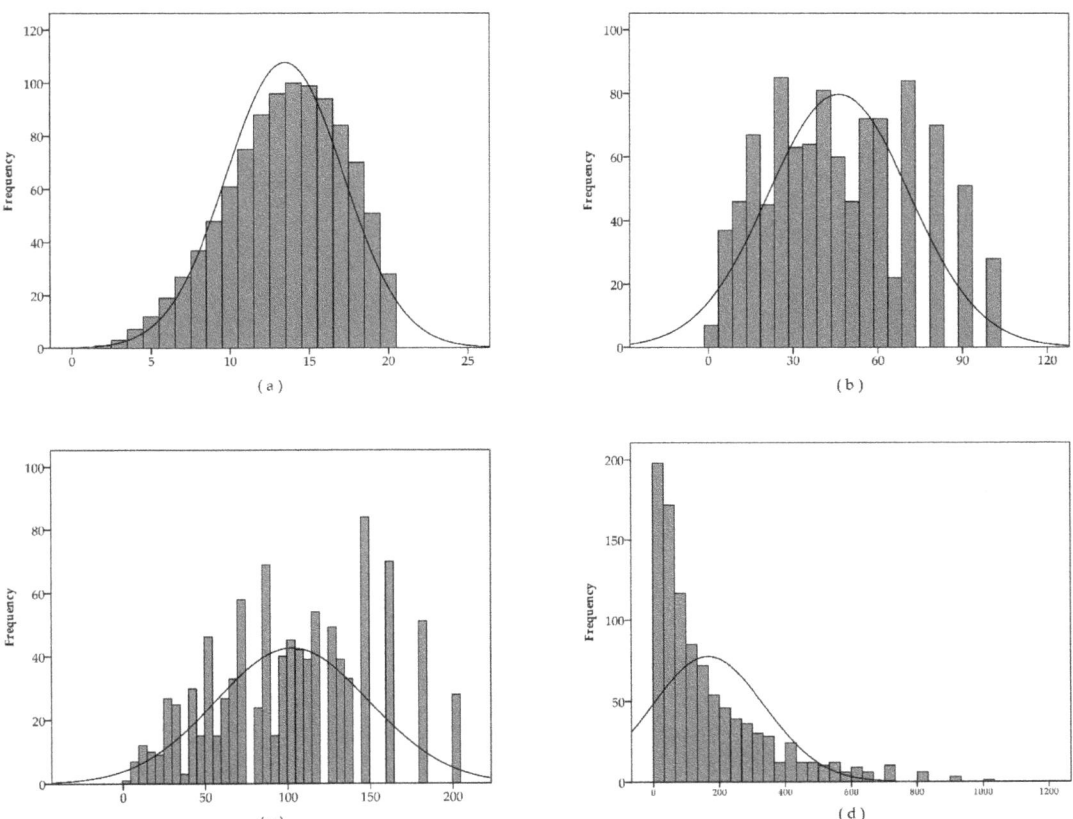

Figure 7. The histograms of all the possible results of the assessment algorithms, when o, s, and d $\in [1,2,\ldots,10]$. Picture part (**a**) shows the histogram of $A(m)$, part (**b**) shows the histogram of $M(m)$, part (**c**) shows the histogram of $S(m)$ while part (**d**) shows the histogram of $RPN(m)$.

Table 2. Sum of ranking differences compared to the average rankings.

Method	Formula	SRD
$RPN(m)$	$o \cdot s \cdot d$	0.2074
$A(m)$	$\max\{o+s,\ o+d,\ d+s\}$	0.0653
$M(m)$	$\max\{o \cdot s,\ o \cdot d,\ d \cdot s\}$	0.0897
$S(m)$	$\max\{o^2+s^2, o^2+d^2, d^2+s^2\}$	0.0967

The average ranking of the three PRISM aggregations is used as a reference when only these functions are compared to each other. The SRD of the three methods to this reference is shown in the diagonal of Table 3. The upper triangle of the table gives the pairwise distance of the methods. From the results, it can be inferred that the additive PRISM gives the closest ranking to the average, and it is at an equal distance from the other two methods. The Spearman rho coefficients are in the lower triangle and indicate high rank correlations between the rankings.

Table 3. Sum of ranking differences (SRD) between each PRISM aggregation pair in the upper triangle, SRD compared to the average of PRISM rankings in the diagonal, Spearman's rho values in the lower triangle.

	$A(m)$ Ranking	$M(m)$ Ranking	$S(m)$ Ranking
$A(m)$ ranking	$SRD_A = 0.0170$	$SRD_{AM} = 0.0594$	$SRD_{AS} = 0.0596$
$M(m)$ ranking	$\rho_{MA} = 0.990$	$SRD_M = 0.0606$	$SRD_{MS} = 0.1182$
$S(m)$ ranking	$\rho_{SA} = 0.988$	$\rho_{SM} = 0.957$	$SRD_S = 0.0624$

The method-by-method change in ranking or classification can also be visualized with alluvial diagrams (Figure 8).

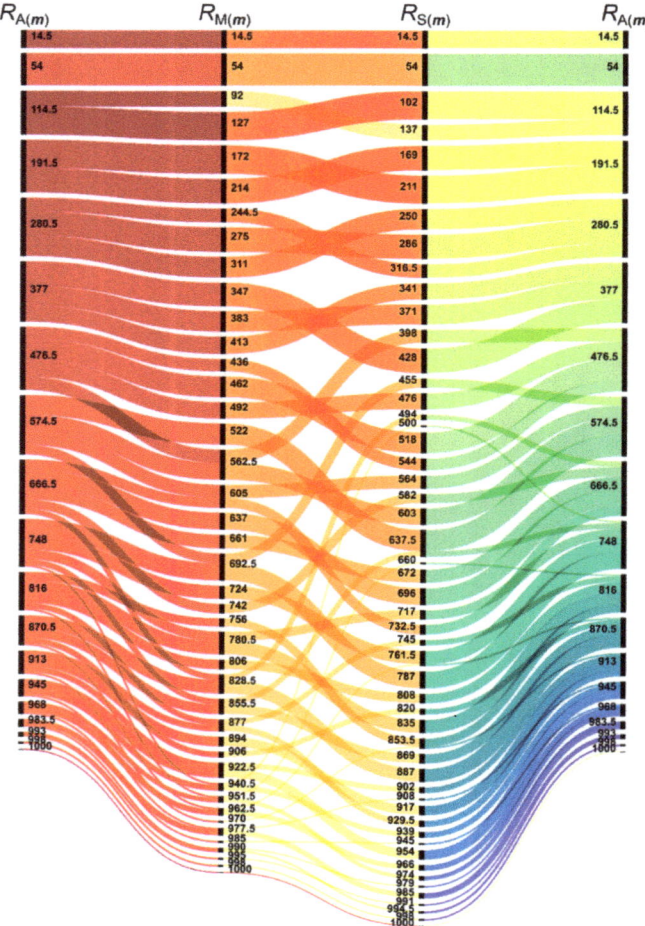

Figure 8. The alluvial diagram of the rankings of the three PRISM methods. One node represents the incidents with the same fractional rank (the value on the node).

The three algorithms rank the most important 79 (28 + 51) cases from the 1000 in the same way (see Figure 8). After that, there are some rearrangements in the rankings. The addition and the multiplication have almost the same order in the first half of the possible 1000 cases, multiplication just breaks the ties of the addition; however, the multiplication ranks further back some cases in the second half of the cases. The sum of squares produces a very different order and breaks the ties of the addition in the opposite order than the multiplication does immediately after the first 79 cases.

Let denote $R_A(m)$, $R_M(m)$, and $R_S(m)$ denote the ranks of m incident according to the value produced by $A(m)$, $M(m)$, and $S(m)$ aggregation or evaluation functions, respectively. The rank here means an order of importance and $R_A(m) \succ R_A(l) \sim R_A(k)$ means that incident m is more important than incident l, and incident k has the same importance as l.

In Figure 8, several groups can be identified in which the methods give different priority orders, for instance, see Equations (15)–(17).

$$R_M(10, 6, 1\ldots 6) \prec R_M(9, 7, 1\ldots 7) \prec R_M(8, 8, 1\ldots 8) \tag{15}$$

$$R_S(10, 6, 1\ldots 6) \succ R_S(9, 7, 1\ldots 7) \succ R_S(8, 8, 1\ldots 8) \tag{16}$$

$$R_A(10, 6, 1\ldots 6) \sim R_A(9, 7, 1\ldots 7) \sim R_A(8, 8, 1\ldots 8) \tag{17}$$

Evidently, any permutation of the scores of m produces the same output value, and thus, the same rank for the given evaluation function. The points in Equation (17) are on three perpendicular frontiers of $A(m)$ that are between the concave and convex frontiers of $S(m)$ and $M(m)$ as the SRD values also indicated in Table 2.

3.3. Effect of the Scale

The ranking can vary not only when the evaluation method is altered but also with the change of resolution of characteristics of the incidents while the same evaluation method is maintained. If the resolution of the scale that is used for the specification of the o, s, and d values decreases from range 10 ($R_{A(m)}10$, $R_{M(m)}10$, and $R_{S(m)}10$) to 6 ($R_{A(m)}6$, $R_{M(m)}6$, and $R_{S(m)}6$), 5 ($R_{A(m)}5$, $R_{M(m)}5$, and $R_{S(m)}5$), or 4 ($R_{A(m)}4$, $R_{M(m)}4$, and $R_{S(m)}4$), the rank of the incidents can change even within the same evaluation method. However, according to the Spearman's rank correlations (see Table 4), the rankings can maintain most of their priority order even with a rougher scale, the correlation coefficient between the original and any investigated lower-resolution scale with the same aggregation is not lower than 0.938. The correlation is even higher if one switches between methods but keeps the same scale of the risk factor scores (o, s, and d); see the shaded cells in Table 4. Comparing the SRD values in the Tables 2 and 4, it can be seen that even using PRISM with fewer steps results in a lower distance from the golden standard than the cumulative Manhattan distance of the RPN (0.2073).

Table 4. Spearman rho rank correlations between the ranks determined by additive ($R_{A(m)}$), multiplicative ($R_{M(m)}$), or sum of squares ($R_{S(m)}$) aggregations based on o, s, and d scores with 10, 6, 5, and 4 categories on their scale. $R_{M(m)}6$ means the ranks come from a multiplicative aggregation of score values on a six-category-long scale. The last row contains the SRD values of the rankings.

	$R_{A(m)}6$	$R_{A(m)}5$	$R_{A(m)}4$	$R_{M(m)}10$	$R_{M(m)}6$	$R_{M(m)}5$	$R_{M(m)}4$	$R_{S(m)}10$	$R_{S(m)}6$	$R_{S(m)}5$	$R_{S(m)}4$
$R_{A(m)}10$	0.982	0.981	0.958	0.990	0.980	0.970	0.951	0.988	0.969	0.969	0.943
$R_{A(m)}6$		0.955	0.965	0.966	0.990	0.932	0.947	0.977	0.993	0.958	0.959
$R_{A(m)}5$			0.950	0.974	0.949	0.990	0.939	0.966	0.946	0.987	0.939
$R_{A(m)}4$				0.945	0.954	0.929	0.987	0.951	0.959	0.951	0.989
$R_{M(m)}10$					0.982	0.981	0.957	0.957	0.939	0.942	0.913
$R_{M(m)}6$						0.944	0.956	0.956	0.968	0.932	0.930
$R_{M(m)}5$							0.938	0.936	0.909	0.954	0.900
$R_{M(m)}4$								0.923	0.924	0.917	0.953
$R_{S(m)}10$									0.980	0.976	0.954
$R_{S(m)}6$										0.965	0.968
$R_{S(m)}5$											0.960
SRD	0.106	0.107	0.143	0.090	0.109	0.124	0.153	0.097	0.129	0.128	0.162

Figure 9 shows the rankings in the case of range 10 ($R_{A(m)}10$, $R_{M(m)}10$ and $R_{S(m)}10$), 6 ($R_{A(m)}6$, $R_{M(m)}6$ and $R_{S(m)}6$), 5 ($R_{A(m)}5$, $R_{M(m)}5$ and $R_{S(m)}5$), and 4 ($R_{A(m)}4$, $R_{M(m)}4$ and $R_{S(m)}4$) of the methods, and whether or how they change on transferring from one to the another. The most robust ranking is made by $A(m)$; here, just a few swaps happen between neighboring categories. In the case of the other aggregation methods ($M(m)$ and $S(m)$), the lower resolution makes the incident skip categories in both directions, which alters the priority order considerably. The higher the number of crossings on the alluvial diagrams (Figure 9), the lower is the correlation between the rankings (Table 4).

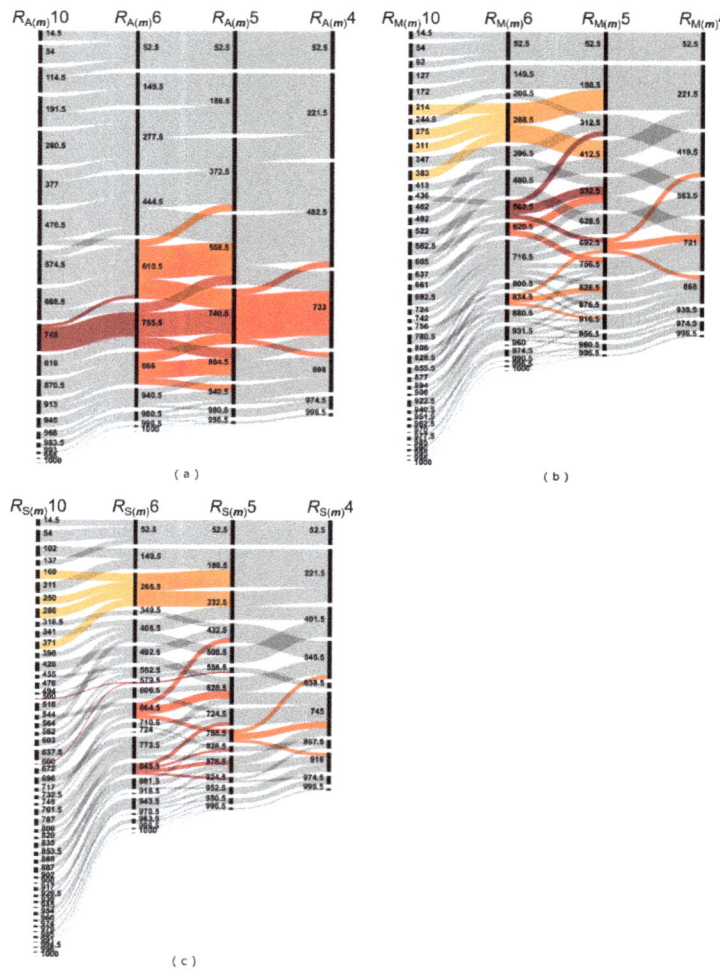

Figure 9. The alluvial diagram of the rankings of the three PRISM methods—addition (**a**), multiplication (**b**), and the sum of squares (**c**)—when the range of the scores (*o*, *s*, *d*) decreases from 10 to 6, 5, and 4. Some cases are colored to make them more distinguishable.

4. Discussion

The PRISM method is effective in identifying risks, where there is a high partial risk; however, the entire risk level does not make any signal for the control system. In the cases of high partial risks, the possibility of sudden failures can be higher, which can lead to unexpected costs, loss of availability, unplanned breakdowns, unnecessary environmental impacts, etc. Similar to the FMEA methodology, the PRISM method also gives high priority to those incidents, where all the factor values (o, s, d) are relatively high, but PRISM puts also more focus on those cases where only two of the factor values are relatively high while the third one is relatively low [13]. In these cases, a relatively small increase in the value of the third factor can result in a significant increase in the entire risk level.

Applying different aggregation functions for the calculation of the PRISM number generates different partial risk maps, with different properties. Instead of conventional FMEA, which applies multiplication [43] for aggregating the three factors, PRISM creates the opportunity of application in scenarios related to the risk assessment process.

In the case of the $S(m)$ function (sum of squares), an additional focus exists besides the attention to partial risks. Since the $S(m)$ function provides a concave threshold surface, the additional focus is on the higher priority of those incidents, which have a very high value at one factor. An example for this case is m_1 in Figure 5. Applying the $S(m)$ function, the relative priority of m_1 significantly increases; however, when applying other functions for creating the PRISM number, this incident stays in the background.

This function can be proposed for practical cases, where signaling of very high values of any factor is important. Since a new trend is unfolding in the automotive industry, special attention is given to the severity factor in the new AIAG-VDA FMEA handbook [44]. The $S(m)$ PRISM function can be useful in a risk assessment environment where the focus is on high-priority incidents that have high severity values. The $S(m)$ function is also offered for testing, modification, and development in safety-related cases as well, such as in the energy industry [45], healthcare industry [46], or in the field of compliance management [47].

In the case of the $M(m)$ function (multiplication), the focus is on the "mid-values" since this function provides a convex surface (see Figure A1). The outputs of the $M(m)$ function have the highest correlation to the RPN(m) outputs. Thus, the application of $M(m)$ can be offered in cases where the application experience of RPN is high, but the possible effects of the partial risks should be useful to be considered. For assessing compliance risks, multiplication is applied for constructing the risk matrix [17], but the results cannot be as detailed as applying the $M(m)$ function of the PRISM method.

As is clearly visible in the results, the $A(m)$ function stays between the previously discussed two functions. Based on the normalized SRD values (see Table 3), the $A(m)$ function is almost definitely in the center between the $M(m)$ and $S(m)$ functions. This can be visually proved by Figure 8 since there are significantly more changes in the rankings between the $M(m)$ and $S(m)$ functions than between the $A(m)$ and $M(m)$ or the $A(m)$ and $S(m)$ ones. Although an addition function is already applied for creating a risk matrix of o and s [7], the analysis could be more detailed by applying the $A(m)$ function of PRISM.

The priority order provided by the PRISM method is robust to the resolution of the scales of the risk factors o, s, and d. If the number of distinct categories decreases from the conventional 10 to a reasonable low value, the PRISM keeps a high rate of the original order. This also means that it is applicable for fuzzy approaches, since in fuzzification, reducing the number of categories of the crisp set to the fuzzy set with help of the membership function is the same as coherently using broader risk factor categories (in Table 4 and Figure 9).

Applying any of the PRISM functions, the nature of the incident risk can be described more precisely than in the case of [30], where only the RPN function is applied. According to [13,37], the combined application of the traditional RPN and PRISM number can result in a balanced risk assessment since the effects of partial risks and risk priority number can be adjusted using any of the PRISM functions.

When more incidents have the same PRISM number, the one that has its value in more submatrices should be prioritized. As a management tool, the PRISM methodology gives a better option than traditional RM [17] or FMEA [30] in visualizing the risk assessment results, and the estimated outcomes after risk reduction actions were executed were more favorable.

Although applying PRISM functions can improve the usability of the partial risk map methodology [13], other potentials of the method can be developed in future works. Based on many lessons learned related to other previously created platform risk assessment methods (FMEA, RM, FTA, HAZOP, etc.), possible development directions of the PRISM method can be forecasted. Since the most methodological similarity can be identified between PRISM and FMEA, based on some systematic and rigorous literature reviews of FMEA developments [28,48,49], some developmental fields can be highlighted for the PRISM method as well.

Although many criticisms expressed that different combinations of o, s, and d can result in the same RPN while the hidden risk content behind the RPN is different [21–25,47,50,51], the PRISM method solves this problem, since it describes hidden risks with different aggregation functions and visualizes hidden risks via the PRISM pattern. On the other hand, realizing more potentials for the methodology, one development direction can be of the future of applying MCDM methods such as AHP [1,52] or ANP [32] or multilevel methods such as TREF [53] for solving the possible subjective ranking issues of the evaluators. Another major direction in the future can be to describe the nature and applicability of different partial risk maps using different aggregation functions in different submatrices of the map.

5. Conclusions

Risk assessment and mitigation is an evergreen topic among practitioners and scholars. One of the most widespread tools to evaluate and prioritize risky incidents is FMEA, which condenses several risk factors into one variable, the RPN. However, this simple condensing operation neglects a lot of information about the investigated incidents. Several methods try to enhance this risk evaluation and prioritization process by balancing between the information loss and handling a multicriteria decision-making problem.

The PRISM method and some of its possible aggregation functions are studied in this paper to describe how it relates to the traditional FMEA and which properties of the PRISM method and its functions make it suitable for risk evaluation and prioritization in different cases. The PRISM method can focus the user's attention to such incidents where just some of the risk factors are high and the RPN of the traditional FMEA falls below the stimulus threshold of the process but a small change in the lower value factor(s) would launch up the aggregated value. Choosing the appropriate aggregation method can fine-tune this feature of the PRISM, increasing ($S(m)$) or decreasing ($M(m)$) its sensitivity toward these kinds of incidents.

Though the PRISM can reveal some hidden potential risks, it cannot tell how one can eliminate or mitigate these risks, the PRISM is just a risk assessment method and not a risk management tool. Thus, it cannot decide for the user where (on what level) the threshold should be drawn, but the priority order given by the PRISM and resource constraints can specify a set of incidents to be treated.

As a limitation of the PRISM, it can be stated that its capability depends on the exactitude of its inputs: although the uncertainty or fuzziness in the determination risk factor values does not radically change the priority order of the incidents, a biased evaluation of o, s, or d can turn the focus of risk management to a wrong direction. The effects of biased risk factor evaluation or using weights for these factors in the aggregation is a possible topic of future research.

Author Contributions: Conceptualization, methodology, formal analysis, visualization, writing—original draft preparation, and writing—review and editing, F.B. and C.H. All authors have read and agreed to the published version of the manuscript.

Funding: The work was supported by the TKP2020-NKA-10 project financed under the 2020-4.1.1-TKP2020 Thematic Excellence Program by the National Research, Development, and Innovation Fund of Hungary.

Data Availability Statement: Not applicable.

Conflicts of Interest: The authors declare no conflict of interest.

Appendix A

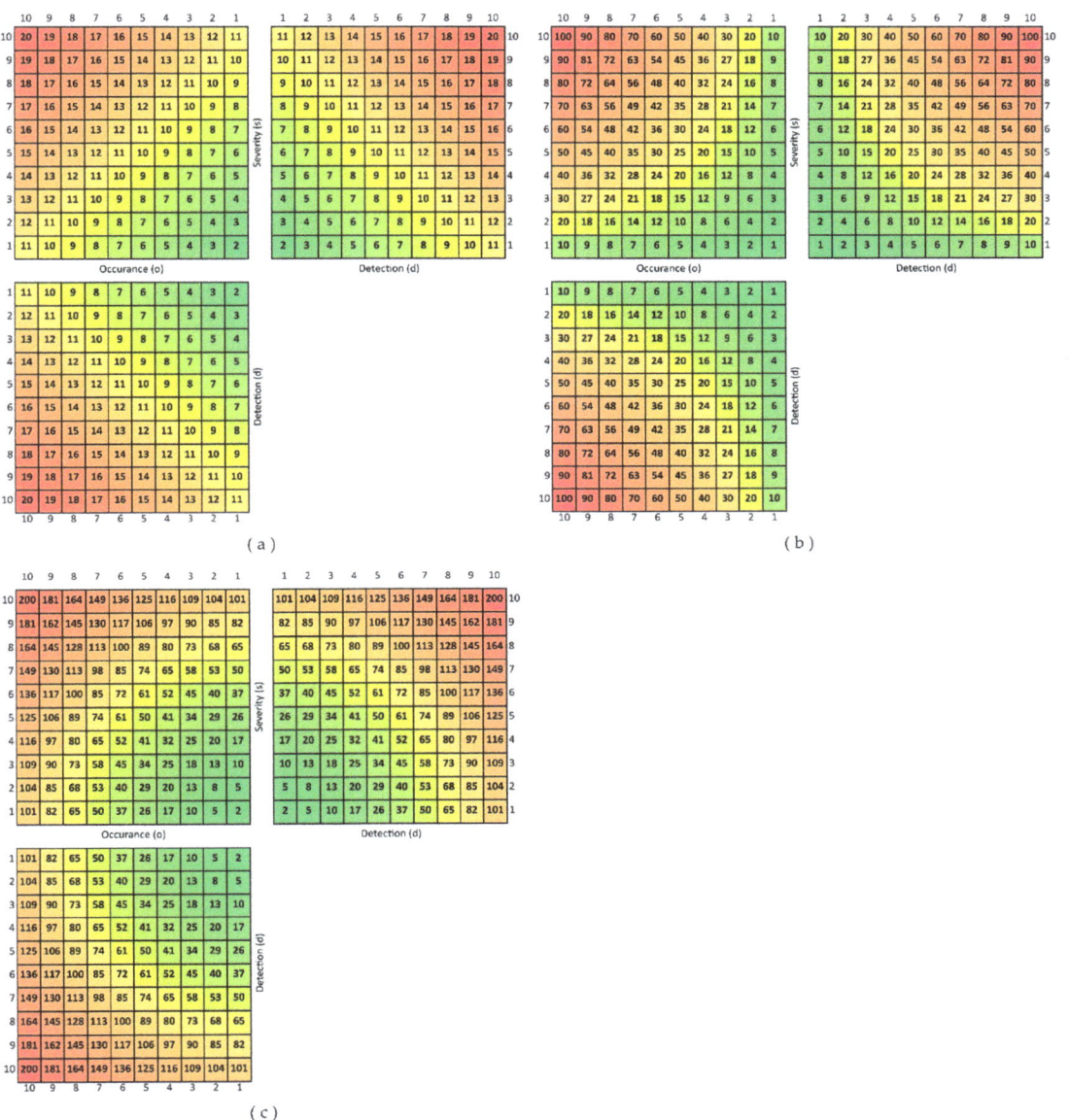

Figure A1. Colored visualization of the possible thresholds of the partial risk maps. (**a**) The threshold surfaces in the case of $A(m)$, (**b**) threshold surfaces in the case of $M(m)$, and (**c**) threshold surfaces in the case of $S(m)$.

References

1. Braglia, M. MAFMA: Multi-attribute failure mode analysis. *Int. J. Qual. Reliab. Manag.* **2000**, *17*, 1017–1033. [CrossRef]
2. Shan, H.; Tong, Q.; Shi, J.; Zhang, Q. Risk Assessment of Express Delivery Service Failures in China: An Improved Failure Mode and Effects Analysis Approach. *J. Theor. Appl. Electron. Commer. Res.* **2021**, *16*, 2490–2514. [CrossRef]
3. Somi, S.; Seresht, N.G.; Fayek, A.R. Developing a risk breakdown matrix for onshore wind farm projects using fuzzy case-based reasoning. *J. Clean. Prod.* **2021**, *311*, 127572. [CrossRef]
4. Marhavilas, P.K.; Filippidis, M.; Koulinas, G.K.; Koulouriotis, D.E. Safety-assessment by hybridizing the MCDM/AHP & HAZOP-DMRA techniques through safety's level colored maps: Implementation in a petrochemical industry. *Alex. Eng. J.* **2022**, *61*, 6959–6977. [CrossRef]
5. Zhang, J.; Kang, J.; Sun, L.; Bai, X. Risk assessment of floating offshore wind turbines based on fuzzy fault tree analysis. *Ocean Eng.* **2021**, *239*, 109859. [CrossRef]
6. Shafiee, M.; Enjema, E.; Kolios, A. An Integrated FTA-FMEA Model for Risk Analysis of Engineering Systems: A Case Study of Subsea Blowout Preventers. *Appl. Sci.* **2019**, *9*, 1192. [CrossRef]
7. Schafer, H.L.; Beier, N.A.; Macciotta, R. A Failure Modes and Effects Analysis Framework for Assessing Geotechnical Risks of Tailings Dam Closure. *Minerals* **2021**, *11*, 1234. [CrossRef]
8. Bradley, J.R.; Guerrero, H.H. An Alternative FMEA Method for Simple and Accurate Ranking of Failure Modes. *Decis. Sci.* **2011**, *42*, 743–771. [CrossRef]
9. Kang, J.; Sun, L.; Sun, H.; Wu, C. Risk assessment of floating offshore wind turbine based on correlation-FMEA. *Ocean Eng.* **2017**, *129*, 382–388. [CrossRef]
10. Ivančan, J.; Lisjak, D. New FMEA Risks Ranking Approach Utilizing Four Fuzzy Logic Systems. *Machines* **2021**, *9*, 292. [CrossRef]
11. Fabis-Domagala, J.; Domagala, M.; Momeni, H. A Concept of Risk Prioritization in FMEA Analysis for Fluid Power Systems. *Energies* **2021**, *14*, 6482. [CrossRef]
12. Carnero, M.C. Waste Segregation FMEA Model Integrating Intuitionistic Fuzzy Set and the PAPRIKA Method. *Mathematics* **2020**, *8*, 1375. [CrossRef]
13. Bognár, F.; Benedek, P. A Novel Risk Assessment Methodology—A Case Study of the PRISM Methodology in a Compliance Management Sensitive Sector. *Acta Polytech. Hung.* **2021**, *18*, 89–108. [CrossRef]
14. Bognár, F.; Benedek, P. Case Study on a Potential Application of Failure Mode and Effects Analysis in Assessing Compliance Risks. *Risks* **2021**, *9*, 164. [CrossRef]
15. Qazi, A.; Shamayleh, A.; El-Sayegh, S.; Formaneck, S. Prioritizing risks in sustainable construction projects using a risk matrix-based Monte Carlo Simulation approach. *Sustain. Cities Soc.* **2021**, *65*, 102576. [CrossRef]
16. Wang, R.; Wang, J. Risk Analysis of Out-drum Mixing Cement Solidification by HAZOP and Risk Matrix. *Ann. Nucl. Energy* **2020**, *147*, 107679. [CrossRef]
17. Losiewicz-Dniestrzanska, E. Monitoring of compliance risk in the bank. *Procedia Econ. Financ.* **2015**, *26*, 800–805. [CrossRef]
18. Jeon, H.; Park, K.; Kim, J. Comparison and Verification of Reliability Assessment Techniques for Fuel Cell-Based Hybrid Power System for Ships. *J. Mar. Sci. Eng.* **2020**, *8*, 74. [CrossRef]
19. Zheng, H.; Tang, Y. Deng Entropy Weighted Risk Priority Number Model for Failure Mode and Effects Analysis. *Entropy* **2020**, *22*, 280. [CrossRef]
20. Lv, Y.; Liu, Y.; Jing, W.; Woźniak, M.; Damaševičius, R.; Scherer, R.; Wei, W. Quality Control of the Continuous Hot Pressing Process of Medium Density Fiberboard Using Fuzzy Failure Mode and Effects Analysis. *Appl. Sci.* **2020**, *10*, 4627. [CrossRef]
21. Lo, H.W.; Liou, J.J.H.; Huang, C.N.; Chuang, Y.C. A novel failure mode and effect analysis model for machine tool risk analysis. *Reliab. Eng. Syst. Saf.* **2019**, *183*, 173–183. [CrossRef]
22. Liou, J.J.H.; Liu, P.C.Y.; Lo, H.W. A Failure Mode Assessment Model Based on Neutrosophic Logic for Switched-Mode Power Supply Risk Analysis. *Mathematics* **2020**, *8*, 2145. [CrossRef]
23. Chang, T.W.; Lo, H.W.; Chen, K.Y.; Liou, J.J.H. A Novel FMEA Model Based on Rough BWM and Rough TOPSIS-AL for Risk Assessment. *Mathematics* **2019**, *7*, 874. [CrossRef]
24. Lo, H.W.; Liou, J.J.H. A novel multiple-criteria decision-making-based FMEA model for risk assessment. *Appl. Soft Comput.* **2018**, *73*, 684–696. [CrossRef]
25. Ghoushchi, S.J.; Yousefi, S.; Khazaeili, M. An extended FMEA approach based on the Z-MOORA and fuzzy BWM for prioritization of failures. *Appl. Soft Comput.* **2019**, *81*, 105505. [CrossRef]
26. Chanamool, N.; Naenna, T. Fuzzy FMEA application to improve decision-making process in an emergency department. *Appl. Soft Comput.* **2016**, *43*, 441–453. [CrossRef]
27. Liu, H.C.; Liu, L.; Liu, N.; Mao, X.L. Risk evaluation in failure mode and effects analysis with extended VIKOR method under fuzzy environment. *Expert Syst. Appl.* **2012**, *39*, 12926–12934. [CrossRef]
28. Liu, H.C.; Liu, L.; Liu, N. Risk evaluation approaches in failure mode and effects analysis: A literature review. *Expert Syst. Appl.* **2013**, *40*, 828–838. [CrossRef]
29. Kutlu, A.C.; Ekmekçioğlu, M. Fuzzy failure modes and effects analysis by using fuzzy TOPSIS-based fuzzy AHP. *Expert Syst. Appl.* **2012**, *39*, 61–67. [CrossRef]
30. Zúñiga, A.A.; Baleia, A.; Fernandes, J.; Branco, P.J.D.C. Classical Failure Modes and Effects Analysis in the Context of Smart Grid Cyber-Physical Systems. *Energies* **2020**, *13*, 1215. [CrossRef]

31. Sharma, R.K.; Kumar, D.; Kumar, P. Modeling and analysing system failure behaviour using RCA, FMEA and NHPPP models. *Int. J. Qual. Reliab. Manag.* **2007**, *24*, 525–546. [CrossRef]
32. Zammori, F.; Gabbrielli, R. ANP/RPN: A multi criteria evaluation of the risk priority number. *Qual. Reliab. Eng. Int.* **2011**, *28*, 85–104. [CrossRef]
33. Gargama, H.; Chaturvedi, S.K. Criticality assessment models for failure mode effects and criticality analysis using fuzzy logic. *IEEE Trans. Reliab.* **2011**, *60*, 102–110. [CrossRef]
34. Braglia, M.; Frosolini, M.; Montanari, R. Fuzzy criticality assessment model for failure modes and effects analysis. *Int. J. Qual. Reliab. Manag.* **2003**, *20*, 503–524. [CrossRef]
35. Seyed-Hosseini, S.M.; Safaei, N.; Asgharpour, M.J. Reprioritization of failures in a system failure mode and effects analysis by decision making trial and evaluation laboratory technique. *Reliab. Eng. Syst. Saf.* **2006**, *91*, 872–881. [CrossRef]
36. Abdelgawad, M.; Fayek, A.R. Risk management in the construction industry using combined fuzzy FMEA and fuzzy AHP. *J. Constr. Eng. Manag.* **2010**, *136*, 1028–1036. [CrossRef]
37. Forgács, A.; Lukács, J.; Horváth, R. The Investigation of the Applicability of Fuzzy Rule-based Systems to Predict Economic Decision-Making. *Acta Polytech. Hung.* **2021**, *18*, 97–115. [CrossRef]
38. Rosenberger, P.; Tick, J. Multivariate Optimization of PMBOK, Version 6 Project Process Relevance. *Acta Polytech. Hung.* **2021**, *18*, 9–28. [CrossRef]
39. Kollár-Hunek, K.; Héberger, K. Method and model comparison by sum of ranking differences in cases of repeated observations (ties). *Chemom. Intell. Lab. Syst.* **2013**, *127*, 139–146. [CrossRef]
40. Héberger, K.; Kollár-Hunek, K. Sum of ranking differences for method discrimination and its validation: Comparison of ranks with random numbers. *J. Chemom.* **2011**, *25*, 151–158. [CrossRef]
41. Ipkovich, Á.; Héberger, K.; Abonyi, J. Comprehensible Visualization of Multidimensional Data: Sum of Ranking Differences-Based Parallel Coordinates. *Mathematics* **2021**, *9*, 3203. [CrossRef]
42. Mizik, T.; Gál, P.; Török, Á. Does Agricultural Trade Competitiveness Matter? The Case of the CIS Countries. *AGRIS On-Line Pap. Econ. Inform.* **2020**, *12*, 61–72. [CrossRef]
43. Wang, Q.; Jia, G.; Jia, Y.; Song, W. A new approach for risk assessment of failure modes considering risk interaction and propagation effects. *Reliab. Eng. Syst. Saf.* **2021**, *216*, 108044. [CrossRef]
44. AIAG; VDA. *FMEA Handbook*, 1st ed.; Automotive Industry Action Group: Southfield, MI, USA, 2019.
45. Koval, K.; Torabi, M. Failure mode and reliability study for Electrical Facility of the High Temperature Engineering Test Reactor. *Reliab. Eng. Syst. Saf.* **2021**, *210*, 107529. [CrossRef]
46. Abrahamsen, A.B.; Abrahamsen, E.B.; Høyland, S. On the need for revising healthcare failure mode and effect analysis for assessing potential for patient harm in healthcare processes. *Reliab. Eng. Syst. Saf.* **2016**, *155*, 160–168. [CrossRef]
47. Benedek, P. Compliance management—A new response to legal and business challenges. *Acta Polytech. Hung.* **2012**, *9*, 135–148.
48. Liu, H.C.; Chen, X.Q.; Duan, C.Q.; Wang, Y.M. Failure mode and effect analysis using multi-criteria decision making methods: A systematic literature review. *Comput. Ind. Eng.* **2019**, *135*, 881–897. [CrossRef]
49. Huang, J.; You, J.X.; Liu, H.C.; Song, M.S. Failure mode and effect analysis improvement: A systematic literature review and future research agenda. *Reliab. Eng. Syst. Saf.* **2020**, *199*, 106885. [CrossRef]
50. Tay, K.M.; Lim, C.P. Enhancing the failure mode and effect analysis methodology with fuzzy inference techniques. *J. Intell. Fuzzy Syst.* **2010**, *21*, 135–146. [CrossRef]
51. Zhang, Z.F.; Chu, X.N. Risk prioritization in failure mode and effects analysis under uncertainty. *Expert Syst. Appl.* **2011**, *38*, 206–214. [CrossRef]
52. Ilangkumaran, M.; Shanmugam, P.; Sakthivel, G.; Visagavel, K. Failure mode and effect analysis using fuzzy analytic hierarchy process. *Int. J. Product. Qual. Manag.* **2014**, *14*, 296–313. [CrossRef]
53. Kosztyán, Z.T.; Csizmadia, T.; Kovács, Z.; Mihálcz, I. Total Risk Evaluation Framework. *Int. J. Qual. Reliab. Manag.* **2020**, *37*, 575–608. [CrossRef]

Article

Mathematical Modelling of Inventory and Process Outsourcing for Optimization of Supply Chain Management

Mohammed Alkahtani

Industrial Engineering Department, College of Engineering, King Saud University, Riyadh 11421, Saudi Arabia; moalkahtani@ksu.edu.sa

Abstract: Outsourcing is one of the major challenges for production firms in the current supply chain management (SCM) due to limited skilled workers and technology resources. There are too many parameters involved in the strategic decisions of the outsourcing level, quantity, quality, and cost. The outsourcing process removes the burden of capital investment; however, still it creates crucial concerns related to inventory control and production management by adding extra inventories. The semi-finished products are outsourced for a few processes due to limited resources and then returned to the manufacturer for the finishing operations. The article is based on the mathematical modeling and optimization of the process outsourcing considering imperfect production with variable quantity for the effective supply chain management. The numerical experiment was performed based on the data taken from the industry for the application of the proposed outsourcing-based SCM model. The results are significant in finding optimal production and outsourcing quantity with a minimum total cost of SCM. The sensitivity analysis was performed to see how important the effect of input parameters is on the total cost. The research is an important contribution in developing a mathematical model of process outsourcing in SCM. The research study is beneficial for managers to find the economic feasibility of process outsourcing for managing inventory and supply chain between manufacturer and outsourcing vendor.

Keywords: process outsourcing; inventory management; imperfect production; mathematical modeling; supply chain management

1. Introduction

In the present socio-economic scenario, outsourcing is a dominant production mode that is rampant around the globe. To compete in this technologically advanced age, the market is saturated in terms of product variety and product life cycle [1]. Further, to take advantage of the competitor, an organization must focus on specialized processes and outsource other activities [2]. Nowadays, it is difficult to meet all customers' needs; therefore, the basic objective of outsourcing should be flexibility enhancement and letting the organization focus on their specialized activities [3]. Initially, firms would usually outsource the non-specialized activities, but how each activity can be outsourced irrespective of the specialized or non-specialized activity has changed with the times [4].

Outsourcing has become the prime attention of organizations due to several advantages, e.g., low initial investment, reduction of cost, and enhanced customer services [2]. In the basic production order quantity model, it is assumed that a complete lot of products that are produced are non-defective; however, in real-life productions, there are some defective items. These defective products are discarded, while others are reprocessed to ensure good-quality products. An example of outsourcing is an anime figure designing company in Japan that outsources its production activities to its CM. They outsource the coloring process, which is a difficult task and usually takes more time to complete the duplicated figure. The CM to which this company outsources its activities reduces the estimated amount by about 25%.

Outsourcing in a supply chain (SC) is an epithet of economic globalization, which, on the other hand, decentralizes the SC and encounters the OPM with uncertainty. A few years back, a survey conducted by Deloitte depicted that almost 71% of a pool of 600 executives from worldwide companies observe SC risk as a significant factor affecting the company's strategic decisions [5]. Particularly, the original product manufacturer (OPM) designs a new product due to technological advantage in developed countries. Later on, it outsources its manufacturing to a contract manufacturer from a developing country. The advantages are obvious, such as freeing up the capital, labor cost reduction, and worker productivity [6].

Several researchers have attempted to deal with yield uncertainty in which they have typically used multiplicative fashion to model it. However, these researchers have assumed a case in which the items produced are exactly equal to the ordered quantity, which is physically not always possible. A production environment that follows make-to-order scenario may face a lack of the Requisite products. Still, there is certain research work in which the researchers have picked production and order quantity of their own choice [7,8]. In these cases, the optimization of both the production as well as of order quantity is equally important. Several researchers have done work on product outsourcing, but very little work is available on process outsourcing and its mathematical model's development. The purpose of this project takes into consideration the process of outsourcing in an imperfect environment for optimization to minimize the cost. Organizations with restricted resources require outsourcing to satisfy customer demands. Additionally, in the proposed research, the mathematical models for the supply chain are developed and tested using the data, which provides a platform to the decision makers to minimize total cost by optimizing the lot size and outsourcing quantity.

Due to certain restrictions, i.e., production programing in some SMEs, which produces some kind of special products as per make-to-order policy or manufacture commodities, reprocessing of imperfect products is not possible. Therefore, such organizations outsource the reprocessing of these imperfect products to some other firms, i.e., repair stores. Moreover, reprocessing these imperfect products, some specific operations i.e., welding, milling/lath machines, or any other kind of equipment that may not be available at the facility and purchasing of that equipment, may not reasonable. On the other hand, imperfect products have a significant value to a company, and therefore, the rework of imperfect items is outsourced. It is assumed that in the after-repair process, the products are as good as perfect ones, especially in the case of remanufacturing. It is considered that the HC of repaired products is higher than the initial HC [9–11]. Additionally, it is assumed that in a repair shop, the repair process is always under control, and all the imperfect products can be repaired. Furthermore, the repaired items are added to inventory in the same production cycle.

2. Literature

Outsourcing is considered as a prime factor to gain the best possible performance by an organization [12]. For flexible, low-cost production in a supply chain, outsourcing from suppliers is critical. In this regard, better supplier selection as an outsourcer is important. Kumar et al. developed a logical method in which, for multi-objective modeling, they used three different types of fuzzy logic and some hard constraints. In addition to this, they also opted for goal programming for the problem solution [13]. To simultaneously find the order quantity and formulation impression, more sophisticated fuzzy multi-objective methods have been considered by [14]. In another study, [15] developed a model in which the consumer needs to determine the goods that need to be ordered, the amounts, the suppliers, and the times. To find the best suppliers and how to assign orders among them, Karpak et al. [16] used goal programming, evaluating trade-offs between multiple objectives, such as cost, quality, and delivery, simultaneously.

Next, outsourcing strategies are also one of the important aspects of production business schemes of specific operations. While outsourcing some of their operations, the organizations can have a special focus on their core operations. In conventional outsourcing, only the non-specialized activities are outsourced except the activities that may have a competitive advantage [17–19]. In a production environment, different researchers have modeled several optimal batch problems considering different production conditions to minimize the total system cost. For instance, E.W. Taft [20] is among the pioneers who developed Economic Production quantity (EPQ) inventory model. Subsequently, this basic model was modified and expanded by other researchers. Previous research studies have shown that small perturbations in parameters of EOQ and EPQ models do not impose any significant impact on the solution of a problem. Owing to this, the Economic Production quantity (EPQ) model emerged as an optimal substitute, which shows promising results for a production environment when applied with some assumptions.

In an actual production environment, the system runs with some imperfections. The imperfections in a production system produce low-quality items for several reasons, namely defects in raw materials, changes in machine capabilities, backorders, rework, and differences in the experience of the operators. Some research studies are available in the literature in which the proposed models have considered these imperfections. For example, Jamal et al. [21] studied the EPQ model to obtain the optimum Batch size. The proposed model is considered a re-work process after several production cycles. Expanding the contributions of Jamal et al. [21], Sarkar et al. [22] formulated the same problem with additional terms of backorders. The model proposed by Cardenas-Barron [23] encompasses numerous parameters. The model undertakes the reworked production quantities and other production system defects. Wee et al. [24] adopted the same methodology and developed a model that considered the development of refurnished products with non-conformities. It was concluded that in repeated manufacturing cycles, there is an effective way to reprocess faulty products. The data obtained confirmed the critical aspects could be more related to the manufacturing cost and the service expenditures of the process. An identical model was presented by [25], which focused on the inflation effect. It was shown that the prolonged use of the manufacturing units could potentially damage the smooth operating of the system, i.e., could produce defects in the system. The focus of the research was on how to overcome the defects produced during the smooth operation and to reprocess the defective products. The overtime of the workers could be the potential reason for the introduction of defects into the system, or it could be due to unrealized reasons. Lastly, the study of Talizadeh et al. [26] is emphatic towards dealing with imperfection in an outsourcing supply chain environment.

Another factor in outsourcing is optimally tweaking the resources. In this area, Alvarez and Stenbacka [27] and Benaroch et al. [28] researched flexible sourcing models for finding the optimal expected time to change resources. The outsourcing cost per transaction in their considered dynamic models is variable. Inderfurth and Kelle [29] and Spinler and Huchzermeier [30] took the outsourcing strategy when both cost and demand are not certain. Liu and Nagurney [31] put forward a model with a global outsourcing and quick-response mechanism. Vibrational inequality theory was used for investigation by considering uncertainty in cost and demand. Some cases were analyzed to take both demand and production costs into account. Nosoohi and Nookabadi [32] developed a model of outsourcing for the industrialist to study optimal ordering policy under the uncertainty of customer demand and final processing costs. They used different options contracts for neutralizing the effect of uncertainty in cost parameters. Chen et al. [33] studied the outsourcing and coordination mechanism for two Stackelberg game models by considering numerous uncertainty parameters, such as disruption risk, demand, and capacity. They concluded that the manufacturer will not be interested in outsourcing if the disruption-risk/production capacity is low/high. Zhao et al. [34]

studied a situation where an industrialist outsources a portion of his production to a supplier. They considered the ordering behavior of companies that outsource their products over long distances. Min [35] considered the usual outsourcing techniques of logistics operations in factories of the United States and recognized the significant elements of outsourcing in logistics operations.

Research has also been carried out on outsourcing risk from various perspectives. Lacity et al. [36] stated that risk is the degree to which a transaction exposes a party to a chance of damage or loss. Qin et al. [37] studied the risks linked with ITO in Chinese institutions and concluded that mismatch in culture and goals, limited choice of vendors, and IT literacy are the significant risks. Oh et al. [38] utilized the stock market's reaction to study the perceived transactional risks linked with ITO engagement. They determined the market's reaction based on the cultural similarity with the vendor and the asset specification of the IT resources. Earl [39] pinpointed the role of inexperienced staff, lack of innovation, organizational learning, and hidden costs as risks in outsourcing. Gewald and Dibbern [40] determined the levels of perceived risk as well as benefits for finding the extent to which banks would select to outsource their processes.

Research on service outsourcing has been carried out widely by different researchers. Choi et al. [41] performed research and suggested service outsourcing as a critical topic in service supply chain management. Tsai et al. [42] examined the potential risks structural relationships that can lead to failure in an outsourcing relationship. Typically, business is linked with forward and reverse flows of products. Yet, customers are vastly involved in the service process. The valuation of the service level is critical to the market demand [43]. Nowadays, outsourcing is a major development in the service industry for increasing the level of service. Chen et al. [44] considered an outsourced supply chain that consists of one original equipment manufacturer, one contract manufacturer, and a retailer. They studied the results of encroachment on the profit. Akan et al. [45] investigated two outsourcing settings, namely order fulfillment and call center, and examined how asymmetric demand information will affect the two parties. Xin et al. [46] compared the proactive inventory of relief items both in the presence and absence of outsourcing. They concluded that social efficiency improvement depends on the monitoring costs and the perishable rates under the outsourcing strategy. Wu et al. [47] investigated the incentives for information shared with two retailers in Cournot competition and with multiple suppliers in Bertrand competition. Li et al. [48] also studied the service channel choice. Huang et al. [49] investigated the quality risk from the viewpoint of a 4PL and considered asymmetric information in between 3PL and 4PL. Zhang et al. [50] discussed the retailer's information-sharing strategies when the service is delegated to the retailer or undertaken by the manufacturer. Yue and Ryan [51] carried out a comparison between single sourcing and multi-sourcing. They found that buyers always desire single sourcing to multi-sourcing. Ching et al. [52] used time-based competition for analyzing the model of outsourcing to multiple make-to-order suppliers. Ding et al. [53] used the customized integration service chain model for evaluating the business performance and found that it extends the service supply chain with multiple service providers in the oilfield service industry. Summing up the literature on outsourcing, an ample amount of work has been done by various researchers in service as well as manufacturing streams considering imperfection, outsourcing strategies, supplier selection, risk assessments of outsourcing products, etc., as illustrated in Table 1. However, mathematical modelling of outsourcing the processes with attributes of imperfection and recycling has not been pondered by any researcher, and this work provides insight into this gap.

Table 1. Authors Contribution.

Author	Corporate SC	Outsourcing		Recycling	Imperfection	Outsource		Modeling
		Process	Product			Single	Multiple	
Ching et al. [51]			x				x	x
Ding et al. [52]		x					x	
Yue and Ryan [50]	x		x	x		x	x	x
Choi et al. [40]	x		x				x	
Stenbacka [26]	x		x		x		x	x
Nosoohi and Nookabadi [31]	x		x					x
Chen et al. [32]	x		x	x	x	x		
Talizadeh et al. [26]	x		x		x	x	x	x
Proposed Study	x	x		x	x	x		x

3. Mathematical Modelling

A supply chain management model was developed, considering manufacturer and multi-vendor, to deal with the inventory and production control by modelling process outsourcing operation. The assumptions, notations, and model formulation are part of mathematical modelling. The centralized inventory diagram of the proposed mathematical model is given in Figure 1.

3.1. Assumptions

Before proceeding with the modeling, the following assumptions are considered:

- Due to a lack of in-house resources, the manufacturer outsources certain operations;
- The demand of customers is only fulfilled in phase 3;
- The demand and production rates are known and constant;
- A single type of item is considered in the model;
- Raw material holding cost per unit item is smaller than the unit holding cost of work in process;
- Phase A has a higher production rate than phase 2, which is higher than phase 3; therefore, there are no shortages. ($P_1 > \sum P_{vi} > P_3 > D$);
- The inspection is performed during the production and rework phase;
- The scrape is zero in the production phase as well as in the rework phase;
- The rate of reworking is the same as the production rate;
- Inventory holding cost is based on the average inventory;
- The screening cost is considered negligible in this model.

As shown in Figure 1, there are three production phases to the inventory diagram. Manufacturer activities are included in phase 3, whereas outsourcing processes are represented in phase 2. T_1, T_2, and T_3 are the three portions of the total time T, which are further subdivided into t_1, t_2, t_3, t_4, t_5, t_6, t_7, t_8, and t_9. The customer demand rate is denoted by "D". In the first and third phases I_{max1} and I_{max3} represent maximum inventories, I_{max11} and I_{max31} represent the inventories produced after the rework of defective parts, and I_{max12} and I_{max32} indicates production Quantities without defective items. In the second phase, I_{max2i} indicates the maximum inventory level of the ith outsourcer, I_{max2i1} indicates inventory produced after the rework of defective parts for ith outsourcer, and I_{max2i2} indicates ith outsourcer production quantity without defective items. The manufacturer produced amount Q_1 in the first phase, which is distributed into n number of vendors in optimal Quantities Q_{21}, Q_{22}, ..., Q_{2n}. In the second step, vendors perform operations and send it back to the manufacturer. Finally, the products enter the manufacturer's third phase, where they are turned into final products and distributed to customers.

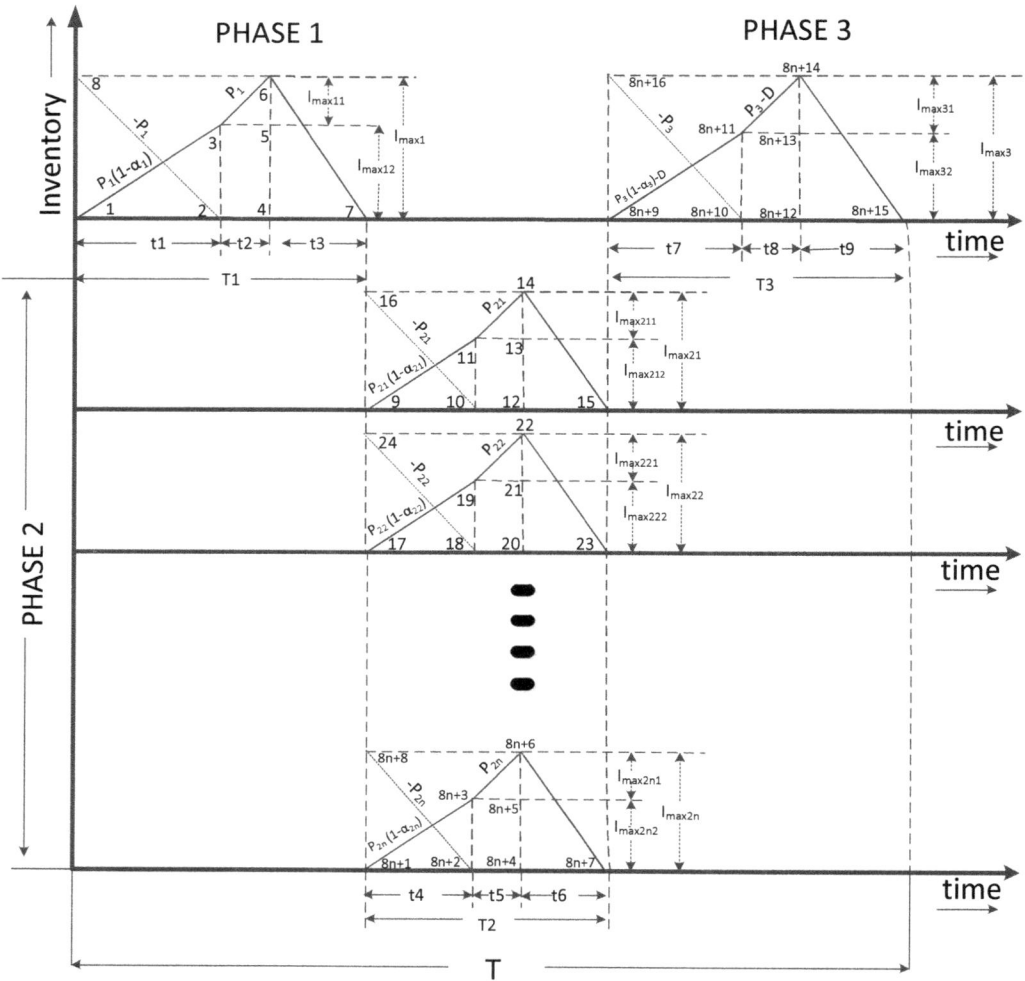

Figure 1. Inventory diagram of the supply chain management considering process outsourcing.

3.2. Notation

The decision variables are "$Q, Q_1, Q_2, Q_3, \ldots, Q_n$". Q is the production quantity for manufacture. Q_1 is the production quantity for the first vendor, Q_2 is the production quantity for the second vendor, and Q_3 is the production quantity for the third vendor, while Q_n is the production quantity for nth vendor. To express the mathematical model discussed in this study, certain notations were adopted in this research. The table below contains and explains these notations.

3.3. Modelling

The SCM model is divided into three phases (first, second, and third phases). Raw material inventory decreases when production starts during time t_1, t_4, and t_7 in phases 1, 2, and 3, respectively, and similarly, the quantity of products continues increasing and approaching its maximum level. The first and the last phase is of the manufacturer and the second phase include all vendors. The demand of the customer is fulfilled only in the third phase. The objective function of our model is to minimize the total cost of supply chain TC, which is equal to the total cost of the manufacturer and total cost of vendors.

$$TC = TC_m + \sum TC_{vi} \tag{1}$$

In addition,

$$\sum TC_{vi} = TC_{v1} + TC_{v2} + TC_{v2} + \ldots TC_{vn} \tag{2}$$

The cost of manufacturer is given as

$$TC_m = S_m + PC_m + H_m + CE_m + IC_m \tag{3}$$

Similarly, the cost of the ith vendor will be

$$TC_{vi} = S_{vi} + M_{2i} + H_{vi} + CE_{vi} + IC_{vi} \tag{4}$$

where $i = 1, 2, 3, \ldots, n$.

3.3.1. Cost of Manufacturer and Outsourcer

The manufacturing process is divided into two phases: phase 1 and phase 3. Both phases have their own set of costs. The setup cost, production cost, holding cost, carbon emission cost, inspection cost, and rework cost are all included in the manufacturing cost.

Setup Cost

This is a fixed cost that is unaffected by quantity or time. This cost includes costs such as tool setup, changeovers, and so on. It is the cost of setting up the production system for the first time. Manufacturers' setup costs are determined by

$$S_m = \frac{s_m \times D}{Q} \tag{5}$$

Similarly, vendors' setup costs can be shown as

$$S_{vi} = \frac{s_{vi} \times D}{Q} \tag{6}$$

Manufacturing and Rework Cost

This cost is primarily dependent on the demand for manufactured goods. Processing, machine, labor, and material costs are all included in this cost. For the same phase, the manufacturing cost per unit item and the reworks cost per unit item are assumed to be equal. As a result, the manufacturing and rework costs for phases A and C are provided.

Phase A Manufacturing Cost

$$M_1 = m_1 \times D \times (1 + \alpha_1) \tag{7}$$

Phase C Manufacturing Cost

$$M_3 = m_3 \times D \times (1 + \alpha_3) \tag{8}$$

Manufacturing and rework cost for outsourcer is given in Equation (9)

$$M_{2i} = m_{2i} \times D(1 + \alpha_{2i}) \tag{9}$$

Holding Cost

Holding cost is the cost incurred through carrying an inventory of raw material and semi-finished and finished goods. This cost also includes the transportation cost of semi-finished goods between manufacturer and supplier. Mathematically, this can be depicted from Equation (10).

$$H_m = \frac{Q}{2}(h_m X + h_{r1} + h_{r3}) \tag{10}$$

where

$$X = \left\{D\frac{(1-\alpha_1)}{P_1}\right\}(1+2\alpha_1) + \frac{\alpha_1^2 D}{P_1} + \left(1 - \frac{D}{P_1} - \frac{\alpha_1 D}{P_1}\right) + \frac{D}{P_3}\left(1 - \frac{D}{P_3} - \alpha_3\right)(1+2\alpha_3) + \frac{\alpha_3^2 D}{P_3}\left(1 - \frac{D}{P_3}\right) + \left(1 - \frac{D}{P_3} - \frac{\alpha_3 D}{P_3}\right)^2 \tag{11}$$

The derivation of holding cost is given in Appendix B for all three phases. Similarly, the holding cost of outsourcers is given in Equation (12):

$$H_{vi} = \frac{Q}{2}(h_{vi} Y_i + h_{r2i}) \tag{12}$$

where $i = (1, 2, 3)$, and

$$Y_i = \frac{Q_{2i}}{2}\left\{\frac{D(1+\alpha_{2i})}{P_{2i}}(1+2\alpha_{2i}) + \frac{\alpha_{2i}^2 D}{P_{2i}} + \left(1 - \frac{D}{P_{2i}} - \frac{\alpha_{2i} D}{P_{2i}}\right)\right\} \tag{13}$$

Carbon Emission Cost

During the production process, carbon emission occurs. Minimized carbon emission is of great concern for not only government and industries, but the customer also demands green products. This production model includes carbon emission costs for managerial concerns. For the manufacturer, the cost of carbon emission per unit production can be represented by Equation (14):

$$CE_m = e_m \times f_m \times D \tag{14}$$

For outsourcers, it is shown by Equation (15):

$$CE_{vi} = e_{vi} \times f_{vi} \times D \tag{15}$$

Inspection Cost

To ensure customers receive 100% good products, inspection is done at all the phases of manufacturing. Defective parts are sent back for rework, and good items are sent for packing. The cost of inspection for the manufacturer is given in Equation (16):

$$IC_m = (I_1 + I_3) \times D \tag{16}$$

For vendors, the inspection cost will transform, as represented in Equation (17):

$$IC_{vi} = I_{2i} \times D \tag{17}$$

Total Manufacturing Cost

Overall manufacturing cost is the addition of setup cost, production cost, holding cost, carbon emission cost, and inspection cost of the manufacturer. According to Equations (5), (7), (8), (10), (12) and (14), the total cost of the manufacturer in Equation (3) can be represented as Equation (18):

$$TC_m = \left[\frac{Q}{2}(h_m X + h_{r1} + h_{r3}) + \frac{s_m D}{Q} + M_1 D(1+\alpha_1) + M_3 D(1+\alpha_3) + e_m f_m D + (I_1 + I_3)D\right] \tag{18}$$

Total Cost of Outsourcers

Similarly, the general equation for the total cost of all the vendors can be shown as Equation (19) by inserting the Equations (6), (9), (11), (13), and (15) in Equation (4):

$$TC_v = M_R \left[\sum_{i=1}^{n} \left[\frac{Q}{2}(h_{vi}Y_{vi} + h_{r2i}) + \frac{s_{vi}D}{Q} + m_{2i}D(1 + \alpha_{2i}) + e_{vi}f_{vi}D + I_{2i}D \right] \right] \qquad (19)$$

Total Cost of the Supply Chain

Combining Equations (18)–(19) into Equation (1) to obtain the overall cost of the supply chain, Equation (20) is as follows:

$$TC = \left[\frac{Q}{2}(h_m X + h_{r1} + h_{r3}) + \frac{s_m D}{Q} + M_1 D(1 + \alpha_1) + M_3 D(1 + \alpha_3) + e_m f_m D + (I_1 + I_3)D \right] \\ + M_R \left[\sum_{i=1}^{n} \left[\frac{Q}{2}(h_{vi}Y_{vi} + h_{r2i}) + \frac{s_{vi}D}{Q} + m_{2i}D(1 + \alpha_{2i}) + e_{vi}f_{vi}D + I_{2i}D \right] \right] \qquad (20)$$

The first-order derivative can be written as

$$TC' = \left[\frac{1}{2}(h_m X + h_{r1} + h_{r3}) - \frac{s_m D}{Q^2} \right] + M_R \left[\sum_{i=1}^{n} \left[\frac{1}{2}(h_{vi}Y_{vi} + h_{r2i}) - \frac{s_{vi}D}{Q^2} \right] \right] \qquad (21)$$

3.3.2. Constraints

The actual manufacturing system has some constraints. The following constraints are defined to make the mathematical model behave like a real-life scenario. Both equality and non-equality constraints are included.

Production constraint
Total production quantity at all three phases is the same:

$$Q_1 = Q_2 = Q_3 \qquad (22)$$

where,

$$Q_2 = Q_{21} + Q_{22} + Q_{23} + \ldots + Q_{2n} = \sum_{i=1}^{n} Q_{2i} \qquad (23)$$

Demand constraint

$$Q = Q_1 = Q_2 = Q_3 \cong D \qquad (24)$$

Space constraint

$$c * Q \leq C_m \qquad (25)$$

$$c * Q_{2i} \leq C_{vi} \qquad (26)$$

To avoid shortage

$$P_1 \geq \sum_{i=1}^{n} P_{2i} \geq P_3 \geq D \qquad (27)$$

Non-negativity constraint

$$Q_1, Q_2, Q_3 \geq 0 \qquad (28)$$

3.3.3. Algorithm

The problem at hand is a complex quadratic problem. Because no existing basic optimization method can solve the problem, this study presents a solution algorithm to solve the model.

Step 1
Define the function

$TC\ (Q, Q_{2i})$, shown in Equation (19) noted $Q = \sum Q_{2i}$

Define the derivative of the function $TC'(Q, Q_{2i})$, shown in Equation (20)

Step no 2
Initially, guess
$$Q_0 = 1$$
where
$$Q_0 = Q_{21} + Q_{22} + Q_{23} \ldots + Q_{2n}$$
Find
$$TC(Q_0)$$
Then,
$$TC'(Q_0), \text{ noted } Q_0 = Q_{21} + Q_{22} + Q_{23} \ldots + Q_{2n}$$

Step no 3
Find
$$Q_1 = Q_0 - TC(Q_0)/TC'(Q_0)$$
Then,
$$Q_2 = Q_1 - TC(Q_1)/TC'(Q_1) \text{ and so on} \ldots Q_{r+1} = Q_r - TC(Q_r)/TC'(Q_r)$$

Step no 4
Stop iteration when
$$Q_{r+1} = Q_r$$

Step no 5
When $Q_{r+1} = Q_r$, it means Q_r is optimal, represented as Q^*
As we know,
$$Q = Q_{21} + Q_{22} + Q_{23} \ldots + Q_{2n}$$
To find
$$Q^*_{21}, Q^*_{22}, Q^*_{23} \ldots, Q^*_{2n}$$
Repeat the same steps for each Q_{2i}.
Finally,
$$Q^* = Q^*_{21} + Q^*_{22} + Q^*_{23} \ldots + Q^*_{2n}$$
for n number of outsourcers.

4. Numerical Example

To check the model validity, a numerical example was performed for which the data were acquired from the previous literature review based on the automobile spare-part industry. Parameters such as production rate, demand, setup cost, holding cost, and manufacturing cost were taken from the paper of Sarkar et al. (2014) [1]. The data of carbon emission in tons per unit item production were taken from work done by E. Bazan and M.Y. Jaber (2016) [2]. The inspection data were collected from the research study of Sarkar (2016) [3]. Parameters such as defective rates and marginal cost were taken directly from the industry because they depend on industrial conditions and state regulations. All the data for the manufacturing phase are collected in Table 2, given below.

Table 2. Manufacturing data for phase 1 and phase 3 (spare-part-manufacturing industry).

Manufacturer	Demand	Production Rate	Manufacturing Cost	Holding Cost	Setup Cost	Inspection Cost	Carbon Emission Cost	CO_2 Emission/Item	Defectives
Phase 1	300	600	12	50	50	10	23	0.8	0.05
Phase 3	300	400	8	50	50	9	23	0.8	0.02

For the second phase of vendors, the data are given in Table 3, considering only three vendors.

Table 3. Outsourcing data (spare-part-manufacturing industry).

Phase 2 Outsourcers	Production Rate	Manufacturing Cost	Holding Cost	Setup Cost	Rework Cost	Inspection Cost	Carbon Emission Cost	Defectives	CO_2 Emission/Item
1	450	6	56	45	6	9.5	23	0.04	0.18
2	550	7	50	50	7	10	23	0.04	0.2
3	580	8	47	55	8	10.5	23	0.04	0.22

5. Results and Discussion

The mathematical model is a single-objective constraint nonlinear model. Sequential quadratic programming (SQP) methodology is used to solve objective functions. The formulation was coded in MATLAB16, and optimum values of total cost and production quantities were calculated in the optimization toolbox. There are four decision variables in this model. One $Q*$ is for the manufacturer and $Q_{bi}*$ for ith outsourcer, where $i = (1, 2,$ and $3)$. When the product comes out from phase A, it is sent to the outsourcer for further processes that are unavailable in the manufacturing firm. Total * is distributed to vendors such that it gives minimum TC. This mathematical model helps managers to make the best decision in the production of optimal quantity for the manufacturer and the shipment of optimum quality of products to outsourcers that will give the optimum value of TC for the overall supply chain. The output values generated from MATLAB for both experiments are given in Table 4.

Table 4. Mathematical model outputs for different sources of data.

Data Collection Resource	Total Cost (TC)	Manufacturer Optimal Quantity (Q)	1st Outsourcer Optimal Quantity (Q_{21})	2nd Outsourcer Optimal Quantity (Q_{22})	3rd Outsourcer Optimal Quantity (Q_{23})
Research paper	USD 48,332.87	41.27 parts	12.9 parts	13.8 parts	14.6 parts

6. Sensitivity Analysis

Sensitivity analysis is used to learn about a variable that has a significant impact on total production costs and decision variables. Each input parameter is adjusted within the range of (+50 percent to −50 percent) with a 25% increment to examine the sensitivity of variables. The data compiled in Table 5 show the sensitivity analysis of the manufacturer. The sensitivity analyses of all the variables are presented in Appendix A Tables A1–A7.

Table 5 shows the output values of four decision variables as well as the % change in TC values

Table 5. Sensitivity analysis of input parameters.

Parameters	% Age Change	Decision Variables				% Change in the Total Cost
		Q	Q_{21}	Q_{22}	Q_{23}	
s_m	−50	40.35	12.5741	13.49	14.2817	−0.38
	−25	40.81	12.71	13.65	14.45	−0.19
	25	41.72	12.99	13.95	14.78	0.19
	50	42.17	13.12	14.10	14.94	0.37
h_m	−50	45.40	14.09	15.19	16.12	−1.55
	−25	43.19	13.43	14.45	15.31	−0.76
	25	39.59	12.34	13.24	14.01	0.72
	50	38.10	11.89	12.74	13.47	1.42
M_1	−50	41.27	12.85	13.80	14.62	−3.91
	−25	41.27	12.85	13.80	14.62	−1.96
	25	41.27	12.85	13.80	14.62	1.96
	50	41.27	12.85	13.80	14.62	3.91
M_3	−50	41.27	12.85	13.80	14.62	−2.53
	−25	41.27	12.85	13.80	14.62	−1.27
	25	41.27	12.85	13.80	14.62	1.27
	50	41.27	12.85	13.80	14.62	2.53
I_1	−50	41.27	12.85	13.80	14.62	−3.10
	−25	41.27	12.85	13.80	14.62	−1.55
	25	41.27	12.85	13.80	14.62	1.55
	50	41.27	12.85	13.80	14.62	3.10
I_3	−50	41.27	12.85	13.80	14.62	−2.79
	−25	41.27	12.85	13.80	14.62	−1.40
	25	41.27	12.85	13.80	14.62	1.40
	50	41.27	12.85	13.80	14.62	2.79
e_m	−50	41.27	12.85	13.80	14.62	−5.71
	−25	41.27	12.85	13.80	14.62	−2.86
	25	41.27	12.85	13.80	14.62	2.86
	50	41.27	12.85	13.80	14.62	5.71
P_1	−50	39.44	12.30	13.19	13.95	0.79
	−25	40.63	12.66	13.59	14.38	0.27
	25	41.67	12.97	13.94	14.76	−0.16
	50	41.94	13.05	14.03	14.86	−0.27
P_3	−50	41.65	12.97	13.93	14.75	−0.15
	−25	41.39	12.89	13.84	14.66	−0.05
	25	41.20	12.83	13.78	14.59	0.03
	50	41.15	12.81	13.76	14.57	0.05
D	−50	30.82	9.58	10.31	10.93	−47.11
	−25	36.70	11.42	12.28	13.01	−23.41
	25	44.99	14.02	15.05	15.92	23.24
	50	48.12	15.01	16.09	17.02	46.36
M_R	−50	34.27	10.73	11.45	12.09	−29.31
	−25	38.34	11.97	12.82	13.56	−14.59
	25	43.50	13.52	14.55	15.42	14.53
	50	45.25	14.05	15.14	16.06	29.02

Table 5. Cont.

Parameters	% Age Change	Decision Variables				% Change in the Total Cost
		Q	Q_{21}	Q_{22}	Q_{23}	
H_{r1}	−50	42.29	13.16	14.15	14.99	−0.41
	−25	41.77	13.00	13.97	14.80	−0.20
	25	40.78	12.71	13.64	14.44	0.20
	50	40.32	12.56	13.48	14.27	0.40
H_{r3}	−50	42.74	13.29	14.30	15.15	−0.59
	−25	41.99	13.07	14.04	14.88	−0.29
	25	40.59	12.65	13.57	14.37	0.29
	50	39.94	12.45	13.36	14.13	0.57

The data presented in Table 5 and Appendix A Tables A1–A7 conclude the following points:

- Increase in the demand rate "D" increases the total cost TC. The total cost is more influenced by the demand rate. Changing the demand value by 50% can result in a change of 47% in the total cost.
- When the marginal cost M_R increases, it increases the TC. It is the second important metric that has a greater impact on TC. Changing the M_R by 50% will change the TC by 29%.
- High carbon emission will increase the total cost. It is the third biggest variable, with a TC variation of 5.7 percent.
- Increase in the manufacturing cost increases the TC. It can impact TC by 3.9% when varying by 50%.
- Inspection cost (I_1, I_{2i}, I_3) can cause change if there is a 3.5 % change in the TC. Holding cost of inventory (h_m, h_{vi}), raw material holding cost (h_{r1}, $h_{2v,i}$), and setup cost (s_m, s_{vi}) also have a direct impact on the total cost. Increasing these costs can increase the total cost (TC).
- Certain variables have zero impact on decision variables but can cause a significant effect on the total cost. These parameters are M_R, I_a, I_c, I_{bi}, e_m, e_{bi}, M_a, M_c, and M_{bi}.
- Production rate (P_1, P_{2i}, and P_3) has an inverse impact on the total cost. When the production rate increases, then the total cost decreases.

The parameters that managers are worried about are those that have a significant impact on TC. The initial investment is planned to keep these variables under control. One of them is the expense of setup and carbon emissions. Reusable energy sources are used to reduce carbon emissions costs. To reduce rework costs, inline inspection should be strictly followed. To minimize rework costs, inline inspection should be followed strictly, and similarly, to minimize inspection costs, a traditional, human-based inspection can be regulated by automation and technology.

Table 6 shows what effect the decision variables have on the objective function TC when we change their values from the optimum value suggested by our model. It can be seen that iteration number 6 is the only optimal value of Q for the minimum TC.

The below Figure 2 shows the relation of production lot size and total cost of the supply chain.

Figure 3 depicts the graphical representation of sensitivity analysis. The graphical representation indicates that the marginal and demand lines have a higher impact on the total cost %. A minor change in one of these variables will have a significant influence on the total cost. The other variables have a slight impact on the total cost as well. Only when the marginal and demand rates are changed significantly does the total cost abruptly alter. The lines of all the other variables can be recognized through different colors and markers. The marginal rate and demand have a significant impact on output, as this graph indicates. Similarly, the third line is the carbon emission cost line, which has the third greatest impact on total cost and can affect the overall cost with a tiny modification. The manufacturing cost is the fourth item in this category, and similarly, holding cost is the next factor that has higher impact on the total cost.

When the production rate increases, the total cost decreases. The sensitivity analysis for production rate is shown in Appendix C Figure A1. A separate graph of the sensitivity analysis of major parameters, such as holding cost, setup cost, and carbon emission cost, is also given in Appendix C Figures A2–A4.

Table 6. Effect of decision variables on TC.

Iteration	Q	Q_{21}	Q_{22}	Q_{23}	TC
1	30	9.413829	10.02195	10.56422	48,755.3
2	32	10.02961	10.69199	11.2784	48,600.8
3	34	10.64312	11.36237	11.99451	48,487.96
4	36	11.25424	12.0331	12.71265	48,409.84
5	38	11.86283	12.70421	13.43296	48,360.94
6 *	**41.27**	**12.9**	**13.8**	**14.6**	**48,332.87**
7	42	13.07191	14.04756	14.88053	48,334.14
8	44	13.67213	14.71983	15.60804	48,349.78
9	46	14.26932	15.39249	16.33818	48,381.41
10	48	14.86333	16.06557	17.0711	48,427.02
11	50	15.45406	16.73904	17.8069	48,484.95

* Optimal run to achieving the lowest TC.

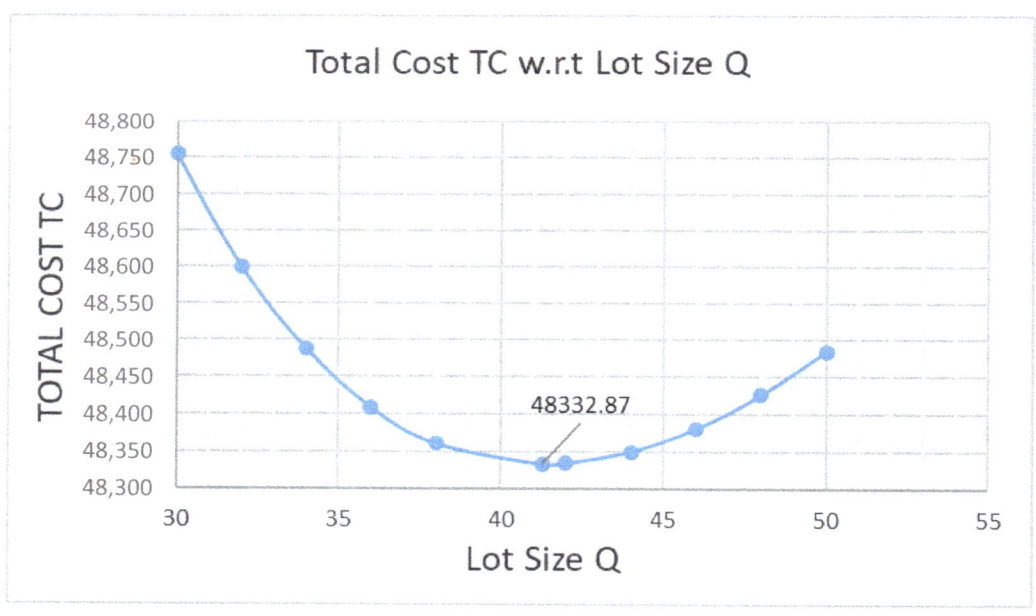

Figure 2. Total cost TC with respect to production lot size Q.

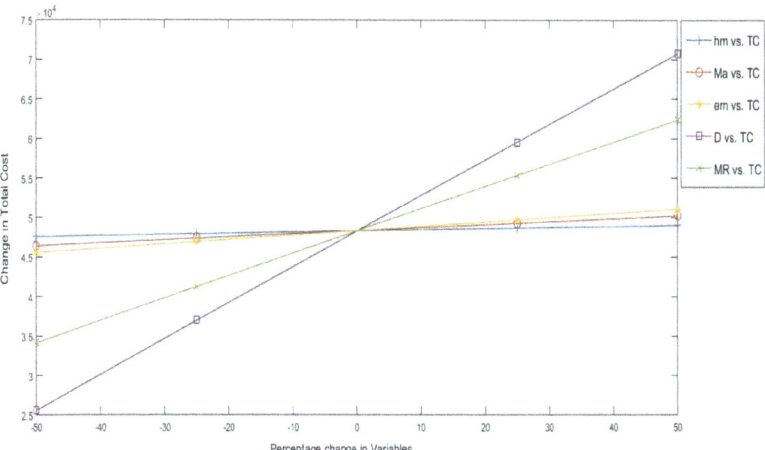

Figure 3. Graphical representation of sensitivity analysis.

7. Conclusions

Process outsourcing has been mathematically modelled for successful management of supply and inventory between manufacturer and multi-vendor. The total cost of supply chain is minimized with the optimization of the production quantity and outsourcing quantity. The parts are outsourced to the vendor and returned back to the manufacturer for remaining operations. The process has been modelled and optimized for effective SCM. The process outsourcing model is one of the significant contributions of the proposed research, which is important for the understanding of the managers and decision makers about the optimal production quantity and managing optimal outsourcing quantity among various vendors. An extra inventory is created at the lower end of the manufacturer, which is managed and controlled well using mathematical modelling for the smooth flow of products in SCM.

The imperfection is modelled in the proposed manufacturer and vendor-based SCM. Inspection is performed on all production and outsourcing quantities, where the defective items are reworked. The sensitivity analysis shows a dramatic relationship; i.e., the change in market demand shows a high-rise curve, the marginal rate of the vendor is also very significant for the management of the outsourcing operation in SCM, and carbon emission cost has an intermediate impact on the total cost, while other all factors have a very low impact on the total cost of SCM. The managers need to see the significant cost parameters for the management of outsourcing in SCM.

Outsourcing is a very important operation of the manufacturing firm. There are too many new research ideas and contributions available in the current field for the development of the outsourcing process in the SCM. The model can be extended by considering variable demand pattern, i.e., price or advertisement cost depending on demand, time-based demand, quality as a function of demand, etc. The deterministic model can be converted into a probabilistic one if the product's demand follows a certain distribution function. Stochastic modelling can be utilized to reflect the real scenario of the market demand pattern as a new paradigm with process outsourcing operations in the proposed SCM. Process outsourcing was modelled in the research study; however, research can be performed to model product outsourcing. Overall, the research work is an important direction in the management of outsourcing and inventory between manufacturers and vendors for effective SCM.

Funding: This work was supported by Researchers Supporting Project Number (RSP-2021/274), King Saud University, Riyadh, Saudi Arabia.

Institutional Review Board Statement: Not applicable.

Informed Consent Statement: Not applicable.

Data Availability Statement: Data available on request due to restrictions.

Acknowledgments: This work was supported by Researchers Supporting Project Number (RSP-2021/274), King Saud University, Riyadh, Saudi Arabia.

Conflicts of Interest: The authors declare no conflict of interest.

Abbreviations

Notation	Description
M	Index for manufacturer
vi	Index for ith vendor
TC	The total cost of the supply chain
TC_m	The total cost of the manufacturer
TC_{vi}	The total cost of ith vendor
H_m	Holding cost of manufacturer
H_{vi}	Holding cost of vendor i
h_m	Holding cost per unit item of manufacturer
h_{vi}	Holding cost per unit item of an ith vendor
h_{r1}	Unit holding cost of raw material for manufacturer of first phase
h_{r3}	Unit holding cost of raw material for manufacturer of third phase
h_{r2i}	Unit holding cost of raw material for vendors of second phase
S_m	Setup cost of manufacturer
S_{vi}	Setup cost of vendor i
s_m	Setup cost per unit item of manufacturer
s_{vi}	Setup cost per unit item of an ith vendor
PCm	Overall production cost of manufacturer
M_1	Production cost of the manufacturer for first phase
M_3	Production cost of a manufacturer for third phase
M_{2i}	Production cost of the ith vendor for second phase
m_1	Production cost per unit item of phase 1 for manufacturer
m_3	Production cost per unit item of phase 3 for manufacturer
m_{2i}	Production cost per unit item of an ith vendor
D	Constant rate of demand
P_1	Production rate of phase 1
P_3	Production rate of phase 3
P_{2i}	Production rate of phase 2 for ith vendor
CE_m	Carbon emission cost for the manufacturer
CE_{vi}	Carbon emission cost for ith vendor
f_m	Carbon emission cost per ton CO_2 emission for manufacturer
e_m	Carbon emission per unit item production for the manufacturer
f_{vi}	Carbon emission cost per ton CO_2 emission for outsourcer i
e_{vi}	Carbon emission per unit item production for outsourcer i
α_1	Rate of rework of first phase for the manufacturer
α_3	Rate of rework of third phase for manufacturer
α_{2i}	rate of rework of second phase for the ith outsourcer
M_R	Marginal cost of outsourcers
IC_m	Inspection cost for the manufacturer
IC_{vi}	Inspection cost for ith vendor
I_1	Inspection cost per unit item at first phase
I_3	Inspection cost per unit item at third phase
I_{2i}	Inspection cost per unit item at second phase for ith outsourcer
c	Capacity of each item (%)
C	T capacity of manufacturer inventory (%)
C_{vi}	Total capacity of ith vendor inventory (%)

Appendix A.

Table A1. Sensitivity analysis for setup cost of manufacturer and outsourcers.

Parameters	% Age Change	Decision Variables				% Change in the Total Cost
		Q	Q_{21}	Q_{22}	Q_{23}	
S_m	−50	40.35	12.58	13.49	14.28	−0.38
	−25	40.81	12.71	13.65	14.45	−0.19
	25	41.72	12.99	13.95	14.78	0.19
	50	42.17	13.12	14.10	14.94	0.37
S_{v1}	−50	37.85	9.17	13.93	14.75	−1.46
	−25	39.70	11.17	13.86	14.67	−0.67
	25	42.65	14.33	13.76	14.57	0.59
	50	43.91	15.66	13.72	14.53	1.13
S_{v2}	−50	37.60	12.98	9.86	14.77	−1.51
	−25	39.59	12.90	12.00	14.68	−0.69
	25	42.76	12.81	15.38	14.57	0.61
	50	44.11	12.78	16.80	14.53	1.17
S_{v3}	−50	37.39	12.99	13.95	10.45	−1.57
	−25	39.49	12.91	13.86	12.72	−0.72
	25	42.85	12.81	13.75	16.28	0.64
	50	44.27	12.77	13.71	17.79	1.21

Table A2. Sensitivity analysis for holding cost of manufacturer and outsourcers.

Parameters	% Age Change	Decision Variables				% Change in the Total Cost
		Q	Q_{21}	Q_{22}	Q_{23}	
h_m	−50	45.40	14.09	15.19	16.12	−1.55
	−25	43.19	13.43	14.45	15.31	−0.76
	25	39.59	12.34	13.24	14.01	0.72
	50	38.10	11.89	12.74	13.47	1.42
h_{v1}	−50	42.42	14.07	13.77	14.58	−0.45
	−25	41.80	13.42	13.79	14.60	−0.22
	25	40.80	12.35	13.82	14.63	0.21
	50	40.38	11.90	13.83	14.65	0.41
h_{v2}	−50	42.40	12.82	15.00	14.58	−0.43
	−25	41.80	12.84	14.37	14.60	−0.21
	25	40.80	12.87	13.30	14.63	0.20
	50	40.37	12.88	12.85	14.65	0.40
h_{v3}	−50	42.41	12.82	13.77	15.82	−0.42
	−25	41.81	12.84	13.79	15.18	−0.21
	25	40.79	12.87	13.82	14.11	0.20
	50	40.36	12.88	13.83	13.64	0.39

Table A3. Sensitivity analysis for manufacturing cost of manufacturer and outsourcers.

Parameters	% Age Change	Decision Variables				% Change in the Total Cost
		Q	Q_{21}	Q_{22}	Q_{23}	
M_1	−50	41.27	12.85	13.80	14.62	−3.91
	−25	41.27	12.85	13.80	14.62	−1.96
	25	41.27	12.85	13.80	14.62	1.96
	50	41.27	12.85	13.80	14.62	3.91
M_3	−50	41.27	12.85	13.80	14.62	−2.53
	−25	41.27	12.85	13.80	14.62	−1.27
	25	41.27	12.85	13.80	14.62	1.27
	50	41.27	12.85	13.80	14.62	2.53

Table A3. Cont.

Parameters	% Age Change	Decision Variables				% Change in the Total Cost
		Q	Q_{21}	Q_{22}	Q_{23}	
M_{21}	−50	41.27	12.85	13.80	14.62	−2.23
	−25	41.27	12.85	13.80	14.62	−1.11
	25	41.27	12.85	13.80	14.62	1.11
	50	41.27	12.85	13.80	14.62	2.23
M_{22}	−50	41.27	12.85	13.80	14.62	−2.60
	−25	41.27	12.85	13.80	14.62	−1.30
	25	41.27	12.85	13.80	14.62	1.30
	50	41.27	12.85	13.80	14.62	2.60
M_{23}	−50	41.27	12.85	13.80	14.62	−2.97
	−25	41.27	12.85	13.80	14.62	−1.48
	25	41.27	12.85	13.80	14.62	1.48
	50	41.27	12.85	13.80	14.62	2.97

Table A4. Sensitivity analysis for inspection cost of manufacturer and outsourcers.

Parameters	% Age Change	Decision Variables				% Change in the Total Cost
		Q	Q_{21}	Q_{22}	Q_{23}	
I_1	−50	41.27	12.85	13.80	14.62	−3.10
	−25	41.27	12.85	13.80	14.62	−1.55
	25	41.27	12.85	13.80	14.62	1.55
	50	41.27	12.85	13.80	14.62	3.10
I_3	−50	41.27	12.85	13.80	14.62	−2.79
	−25	41.27	12.85	13.80	14.62	−1.40
	25	41.27	12.85	13.80	14.62	1.40
	50	41.27	12.85	13.80	14.62	2.79
I_{21}	−50	41.27	12.85	13.80	14.62	−3.39
	−25	41.27	12.85	13.80	14.62	−1.70
	25	41.27	12.85	13.80	14.62	1.70
	50	41.27	12.85	13.80	14.62	3.39
I_{22}	−50	41.27	12.85	13.80	14.62	−3.57
	−25	41.27	12.85	13.80	14.62	−1.78
	25	41.27	12.85	13.80	14.62	1.78
	50	41.27	12.85	13.80	14.62	3.57
I_{23}	−50	41.27	12.85	13.80	14.62	−3.75
	−25	41.27	12.85	13.80	14.62	−1.87
	25	41.27	12.85	13.80	14.62	1.87
	50	41.27	12.85	13.80	14.62	3.75

Table A5. Sensitivity analysis for carbon emission per unit item of manufacturer and outsourcers.

Parameters	% Age Change	Decision Variables				% Change in the Total Cost
		Q	Q_{21}	Q_{22}	Q_{23}	
e_m	−50	41.27	12.85	13.80	14.62	−5.71
	−25	41.27	12.85	13.80	14.62	−2.86
	25	41.27	12.85	13.80	14.62	2.86
	50	41.27	12.85	13.80	14.62	5.71
e_{v1}	−50	41.27	12.85	13.80	14.62	−1.48
	−25	41.27	12.85	13.80	14.62	−0.74
	25	41.27	12.85	13.80	14.62	0.74
	50	41.27	12.85	13.80	14.62	1.48

Table A5. *Cont.*

Parameters	% Age Change	Decision Variables				% Change in the Total Cost
		Q	Q_{21}	Q_{22}	Q_{23}	
e_{v2}	−50	41.27	12.85	13.80	14.62	−1.64
	−25	41.27	12.85	13.80	14.62	−0.82
	25	41.27	12.85	13.80	14.62	0.82
	50	41.27	12.85	13.80	14.62	1.64
e_{v3}	−50	41.27	12.85	13.80	14.62	−1.81
	−25	41.27	12.85	13.80	14.62	−0.90
	25	41.27	12.85	13.80	14.62	0.90
	50	41.27	12.85	13.80	14.62	1.81

Table A6. Sensitivity analysis for demand, marginal, and production rate of manufacturer and outsourcers.

Parameters	% Age Change	Decision Variables				% Change in the Total Cost
		Q	Q_{21}	Q_{22}	Q_{23}	
P_1	−50	39.44	12.30	13.19	13.95	0.79
	−25	40.63	12.66	13.59	14.38	0.27
	25	41.67	12.97	13.94	14.76	−0.16
	50	41.94	13.05	14.03	14.86	−0.27
P_3	−50	41.65	12.97	13.93	14.75	−0.15
	−25	41.39	12.89	13.84	14.66	−0.05
	25	41.20	12.83	13.78	14.59	0.03
	50	41.15	12.81	13.76	14.57	0.05
P_{21}	−50	41.15	12.82	13.76	14.57	0.05
	−25	41.17	12.82	13.77	14.58	0.04
	25	41.42	12.90	13.85	14.67	−0.06
	50	41.60	12.95	13.91	14.74	−0.13
P_{22}	−50	40.92	12.75	13.69	14.49	0.14
	−25	41.05	12.79	13.73	14.54	0.09
	25	41.53	12.93	13.89	14.71	−0.11
	50	41.79	13.01	13.98	14.80	−0.21
P_{23}	−50	40.83	12.72	13.65	14.46	0.18
	−25	41.00	12.77	13.71	14.52	0.11
	25	41.56	12.94	13.90	14.72	−0.12
	50	41.85	13.03	14.00	14.82	−0.23
D	−50	30.82	9.58	10.31	10.93	−47.11
	−25	36.70	11.42	12.28	13.01	−23.41
	25	44.99	14.02	15.05	15.92	23.24
	50	48.12	15.01	16.09	17.02	46.36
M_R	−50	34.27	10.73	11.45	12.09	−29.31
	−25	38.34	11.97	12.82	13.56	−14.59
	25	43.50	13.52	14.55	15.42	14.53
	50	45.25	14.05	15.14	16.06	29.02

Table A7. Sensitivity analysis for holding cost of raw material of manufacturer and outsourcers.

Parameters	% Age Change	Decision Variables				% Change in the Total Cost
		Q	Q_{21}	Q_{22}	Q_{23}	
h_{r1}	−50	42.29	13.16	14.15	14.99	−0.41
	−25	41.77	13.00	13.97	14.80	−0.20
	25	40.78	12.71	13.64	14.44	0.20
	50	40.32	12.56	13.48	14.27	0.40

Table A7. Cont.

Parameters	% Age Change	Decision Variables				% Change in the Total Cost
		Q	Q_{21}	Q_{22}	Q_{23}	
h_{r3}	−50	42.74	13.29	14.30	15.15	−0.59
	−25	41.99	13.07	14.04	14.88	−0.29
	25	40.59	12.65	13.57	14.37	0.29
	50	39.94	12.45	13.36	14.13	0.57
h_{r21}	−50	41.66	12.97	13.93	14.76	−0.16
	−25	41.46	12.91	13.87	14.69	−0.08
	25	41.08	12.79	13.74	14.55	0.08
	50	40.89	12.74	13.68	14.48	0.16
h_{r22}	−50	41.74	12.99	13.96	14.79	−0.19
	−25	41.50	12.92	13.88	14.70	−0.10
	25	41.04	12.78	13.72	14.53	0.10
	50	40.81	12.71	13.65	14.45	0.19
h_{r23}	−50	41.77	13.00	13.97	14.80	−0.20
	−25	41.52	12.93	13.89	14.71	−0.10
	25	41.03	12.78	13.72	14.53	0.10
	50	40.79	12.71	13.64	14.44	0.20

Appendix B.

Appendix B.1. Mathematical Modelling

There are three phases to the inventory diagram. The manufacturer phases are shown in phases 1 and 3, whereas the outsourcer phase is shown in phase 2. T_1, T_2, and T_3 are the three portions of total time T ($T = T_1 + T_2 + T_3$). These three phases of the manufacturer are further broken into t_1, t_2, t_3, t_4, t_5, t_6, t_7, t_8, and t_9 such that $T_1 = t_1 + t_2 + t_3$, $T_2 = t_4 + t_5 + t_6$, and $T_3 = t_7 + t_8 + t_9$. Thus, the total cycle time can be written as $T = t_1 + t_2 + t_3 + t_4 + t_5 + t_6 + t_7 + t_8 + t_9$. From Figure 1, it can be shown as $t_1 = \frac{Q}{P_1}$ $t_2 = \frac{\alpha_1 Q}{P_1}$ $t_3 = \frac{Q}{D}\left[1 - \frac{D}{P_1} - \frac{\alpha_1 D}{P_1}\right]$ $t_4 = \frac{Q}{P_{2i}}$ $t_5 = \frac{\alpha_{2i} Q_{2i}}{P_{2i}}$ $t_6 = \frac{Q_{2i}}{D}\left[1 - \frac{D}{P_{2i}} - \frac{\alpha_{2i} D}{P_{2i}}\right]$ $t_7 = \frac{Q}{P_3}$ $t_8 = \frac{\alpha_3 Q_3}{P_3}$ and $t_9 = \frac{Q}{D}\left[1 - \frac{D}{P_3} - \frac{\alpha_3 D}{P_3}\right]$. The customer demand rate is denoted by the symbol D. The mathematical modelling of each phase is explored in depth below.

Appendix B.2. Phase 1

From Figure A1, the total inventory of phase 1 is equal to the area under the curve, which is

$$\text{Total inventory of first phase} = Inv_1 = \Delta_{123} + \square_{2345} + \Delta_{356} + \Delta_{467} \quad (A1)$$

where area of triangle is represented by symbol (Δ), and area of rectangle is represented by symbol ($\square$), where the subscript represents specific area locations from Figure A1.
Now,

$$\Delta_{123} = \frac{1}{2} I_{max11} \times t_1 \quad (A2)$$

$$I_{max12} = Q(1 - \alpha_1) \quad (A3)$$

$$I_{max11} = Q\alpha_1 \quad (A4)$$

$$\text{slope} = \tan\theta = \frac{\text{perpendicular}}{\text{base}}, \text{ which implies } P_1(1 - \alpha_1) = \frac{I_{max12}}{t_1} \quad (A5)$$

$$\Delta_{123} = Q^2\left(\frac{1 - \alpha_1}{2P_1}\right) \quad (A6)$$

$$\square_{2345} = t_2 \times I_{max12} \quad (A7)$$

$$\square_{2345} = \frac{\alpha_1 Q}{P_1} \times Q(1-\alpha)$$

$$\square_{2345} = \frac{Q^2 \alpha_1 (1-\alpha_1)}{P_1} \tag{A8}$$

$$\Delta_{356} = \frac{1}{2} t_2 \times I_{\max 11} \tag{A9}$$

$$\Delta_{356} = \frac{Q^2 \alpha_1^2}{2 P_1} \tag{A10}$$

$$\Delta_{467} = \frac{1}{2} t_3 \times I_{\max 1} \rightarrow [I_{\max 1} = I_{\max 11} + I_{\max 12}] \tag{A11}$$

$$\Delta_{467} = \frac{Q^2}{2}\left[1 - \frac{D}{P_1} - \frac{\alpha_1 D}{P_1}\right]^2 \tag{A12}$$

Area from 2–4 to 2–7 of the figure, total inventory of first phase will be

$$Inv_1 = \Delta_{123} + \Delta_{2345} + \Delta_{356} + \Delta_{467} \tag{A13}$$

$$= Q^2 \left(\frac{1-\alpha_1}{2P_1}\right) + \frac{Q^2 \alpha_1 (1-\alpha_1)}{P_1} + \frac{Q^2 \alpha_1^2}{2P_1} + \frac{Q^2}{2}\left[1 - \frac{D}{P_1} - \frac{\alpha_1 D}{P_1}\right]^2 \tag{A14}$$

$$Inv_1 = Q^2 \left\{\frac{1-\alpha_1}{2P_1} + \frac{\alpha_1(1-\alpha_1)}{P_1} + \frac{\alpha_1^2}{2P_1} + \frac{1}{2}\left[1 - \frac{D}{P_1} - \frac{\alpha_1 D}{P_1}\right]^2\right\} \tag{A15}$$

Now, divide the upper equation by the total cycle time of phase A $\left[T_1 = \frac{Q}{D}\right]$

$$I_{avg1} = Q^2 \left\{\frac{\frac{1-\alpha_1}{2P_1} + \frac{\alpha_1(1-\alpha_1)}{P_1} + \frac{\alpha_1^2}{2P_1} + \frac{1}{2}\left[1 - \frac{D}{P_1} - \frac{\alpha_1 D}{P_1}\right]^2}{T}\right\} \tag{A16}$$

$$I_{avg1} = Q \left\{\frac{D(1-\alpha)(1+2\alpha)}{2P_1} + \frac{\alpha_1^2 D}{2P_1} + \frac{1}{2}\left[1 - \frac{D}{P_1} - \frac{\alpha_1 D}{P_1}\right]^2\right\} \tag{A17}$$

Raw material inventory for phase 1:

$$\Delta_{128} = \frac{1}{2} t_1 \times Q_1 \tag{A18}$$

$$Inv_{R1} = \frac{Q^2}{2P_1} \tag{A19}$$

$$I_{avgR1} = \frac{Inv_{R1}}{T} = \frac{QD}{2P_1} \tag{A20}$$

Appendix B.3. Phase B

From Figure A1, the first outsourcer total average inventory is given as

$$I_{avg21} = \frac{\Delta_{8910} + \square_{9101112} + \Delta_{101213} + \Delta_{111314}}{T_2} \tag{A21}$$

From Figure A1, the second outsourcer total average inventory is given as

$$I_{avg22} = \frac{\Delta_{151617} + \square_{16171819} + \Delta_{171920} + \Delta_{182021}}{T_2} \tag{A22}$$

From Figure A1, the third outsourcer total average inventory is given as

$$I_{avg23} = \frac{\Delta_{222324} + \square_{23242526} + \Delta_{242627} + \Delta_{252728}}{T_2} \tag{A23}$$

Total average inventory of phase 2 $= I_{avg21} + I_{avg22} + I_{avg23} \ldots I_{avg2n}$ (A24)

$$\Delta_{8910} = Q^2 \left(\frac{1 - \alpha_{2i}}{2P_{2i}} \right) \tag{A25}$$

$$\square_{9101112} = \frac{Q^2 \alpha_{2i}(1 - \alpha_{2i})}{P_{2i}} \tag{A26}$$

$$\Delta_{101213} = \frac{Q^2 \alpha_{2i}^2}{2P_{2i}} \tag{A27}$$

$$\Delta_{111314} = \frac{Q^2}{2} \left[1 - \frac{D}{P_{2i}} - \frac{\alpha_{2i}D}{P_{2i}} \right]^2 \tag{A28}$$

$$I_{avg21} = \frac{\Delta_{8910} + \square_{9101112} + \Delta_{101213} + \Delta_{111314}}{T_2} \tag{A29}$$

$$I_{avg21} = Q \left\{ \left(\frac{D(1 - \alpha_{21})(1 + 2\alpha_{21})}{2P_{21}} \right) + \frac{D\alpha_{21}^2}{2P_{21}} + \frac{1}{2}\left(1 - \frac{D}{P_{21}} - \frac{\alpha_{21}D}{P_{21}}\right) \right\} \tag{A30}$$

Similarly, for outsourcer 2, the average inventory is

$$I_{avg22} = Q \left\{ \left(\frac{D(1 - \alpha_{22})(1 + 2\alpha_{22})}{2P_{22}} \right) + \frac{D\alpha_{22}^2}{2P_{22}} + \frac{1}{2}\left(1 - \frac{D}{P_{22}} - \frac{\alpha_{22}D}{P_{22}}\right) \right\} \tag{A31}$$

Further, for phase 2 and vendor 3, inventory is written as

$$I_{avg23} = Q \left\{ \left(\frac{D(1 - \alpha_{23})(1 + 2\alpha_{23})}{2P_{23}} \right) + \frac{D\alpha_{23}^2}{2P_{23}} + \frac{1}{2}\left(1 - \frac{D}{P_{23}} - \frac{\alpha_{23}D}{P_{23}}\right) \right\} \tag{A32}$$

The general form of average inventory for the ith, outsourcer is given as

$$I_{avg2i} = Q \left\{ \left(\frac{D(1 - \alpha_{2i})(1 + 2\alpha_{2i})}{2P_{2i}} \right) + \frac{D\alpha_{2i}^2}{2P_{2i}} + \frac{1}{2}\left(1 - \frac{D}{P_{2i}} - \frac{\alpha_{2i}D}{P_{2i}}\right) \right\} \tag{A33}$$

$$\text{Let} \quad Y_i = \left(\frac{D(1 - \alpha_{2i})(1 + 2\alpha_{2i})}{P_{21}} \right) + \frac{D\alpha_{2i}^2}{P_{2i}} + \left(1 - \frac{D}{P_{2i}} - \frac{\alpha_{2i}D}{P_{2i}}\right) \tag{A34}$$

$$I_{avg2i} = \frac{Q}{2}(Y_i) \tag{A35}$$

Raw material inventory for phase 2, vendors is

$$\Delta_{91016} = \frac{1}{2} t_4 \times Q_{21} \tag{A36}$$

$$Inv_{R2i} = \frac{Q_{2i}^2}{2P_{2i}} \tag{A37}$$

$$I_{avgR2i} = \frac{Inv_{R2i}}{T} = \frac{Q_{2i}D}{2P_{2i}} \tag{A38}$$

Appendix B.4. Phase C

The inventory of phase C can be found in Figure A1 as

$$\Delta_{293031} = \frac{Q^2}{2P_3}\left[1 - \alpha_3 - \frac{D}{P_3}\right] \quad (A39)$$

$$\Delta_{313334} = \frac{Q^2 \alpha_3^2}{2P_3}\left[1 - \frac{D}{P_3}\right] \quad (A40)$$

$$\square_{30313233} = \frac{\alpha_3 Q^2}{P_3}\left[1 - \alpha_3 - \frac{D}{P_3}\right] \quad (A41)$$

$$\Delta_{323334} = \frac{Q^2}{2D}\left[1 - \frac{D}{P_3} - \frac{\alpha_3 D}{P_3}\right]^2 \quad (A42)$$

Equations (A37)–(A40) imply total average inventory of phase C is

$$I_{avgc} = \Delta_{293031} + \Delta_{313334} + \square_{30313233} + \Delta_{323334} \quad (A43)$$

$$I_{avg3} = QD\left\{\frac{1}{2P_3}\left[1 - \alpha_3 - \frac{D}{P_3}\right][1 + 2\alpha_3] + \frac{\alpha_3^2}{2P_3}\left[1 - \frac{D}{P_3}\right] + \frac{1}{2D}\left[1 - \frac{D}{P_3} - \frac{\alpha_3 D}{P_3}\right]^2\right\} \quad (A44)$$

Raw material inventory of manufacturer for phase 3 is given as

$$\Delta_{(8n+9,8n+10,8n+15)} = \frac{1}{2}t_7 \times Q_3$$

$$Inv_{R3} = \frac{Q_3^2}{2P_3} \quad (A45)$$

$$I_{avgR3} = \frac{Inv_{R3}}{T} = \frac{Q_3 D}{2P_3} \quad (A46)$$

Now, total average inventory of manufacturer will be

$$I_{avgm} = I_{avg1} + I_{avg3}$$

$$I_{avgm} = Q\left\{\frac{D(1-\alpha_1)(1+2\alpha_1)}{2P_1} + \frac{\alpha_1^2 D}{2P_1} + \frac{1}{2}\left[1 - \frac{D}{P_1} - \frac{\alpha_1 D}{P_1}\right]\right\} + QD\left\{\frac{1}{2P_3}\left[1 - \alpha_3 - \frac{D}{P_3}\right][1 + 2\alpha_3] + \frac{\alpha_3^2}{2P_3}\left[1 - \frac{D}{P_3}\right] + \frac{1}{2D}\left[1 - \frac{D}{P_3} - \frac{\alpha_3 D}{P_3}\right]^2\right\} \quad (A47)$$

$$I_{avgm} = \frac{Q}{2}\left[\left\{\frac{D(1-\alpha_1)(1+2\alpha_1)}{P_1} + \frac{\alpha_1^2 D}{P_1} + \left[1 - \frac{D}{P_1} - \frac{\alpha_1 D}{P_1}\right]\right\} + QD\left\{\frac{1}{P_3}\left[1 - \alpha_3 - \frac{D}{P_3}\right][1 + 2\alpha_3] + \frac{\alpha_3^2}{P_3}\left[1 - \frac{D}{P_C}\right] + \frac{1}{D}\left[1 - \frac{D}{P_3} - \frac{\alpha_3 D}{P_3}\right]^2\right\}\right] \quad (A48)$$

Let

$$X = \left[\left\{\frac{D(1-\alpha_1)(1+2\alpha_1)}{P_1} + \frac{\alpha_1^2 D}{P_1} + \left[1 - \frac{D}{P_1} - \frac{\alpha_1 D}{P_1}\right]\right\} + QD\left\{\frac{1}{P_3}\left[1 - \alpha_3 - \frac{D}{P_3}\right][1 + 2\alpha_3] + \frac{\alpha_3^2}{P_3}\left[1 - \frac{D}{P_C}\right] + \frac{1}{D}\left[1 - \frac{D}{P_3} - \frac{\alpha_3 D}{P_3}\right]^2\right\}\right] \quad (A49)$$

$$I_{avgm} = \frac{Q}{2}X \quad (A50)$$

Thus, Equation (A35) is the total average inventory for ith outsourcer, and Equation (A43) is the total average inventory for the manufacturer.

The Equations (A5), (A15), (A29), (A35), (A42) and (A43) gives the total cost of the supply chain in Equation (A44) below.

$$TC = \left[\frac{Q}{2}\left(h_m X + \frac{h_{r1}D}{P_1} + \frac{h_{r3}D}{P_3}\right) + \frac{s_m D}{Q} + m_1 D(1+\alpha_1) + m_3 D(1+\alpha_3) + e_m f_m D + (I_1 + I_3)D\right]$$
$$+ M_R \left[\sum_{i=1}^{n}\left[\frac{Q_{2i}}{2}(h_{2i}Y_i + h_{r2i}) + \frac{s_{vi}D}{Q_{2i}} + m_{2i}D(1+\alpha_{2i}) + e_{vi}f_{vi}D + I_{2i}D\right]\right] \quad (A51)$$

Appendix C.

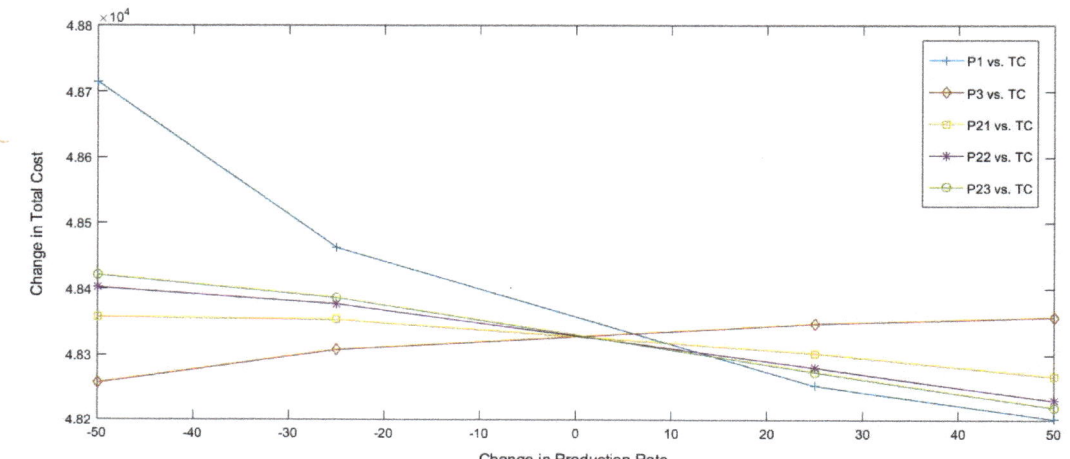

Figure A1. Sensitivity analysis graph for production rate and total cost.

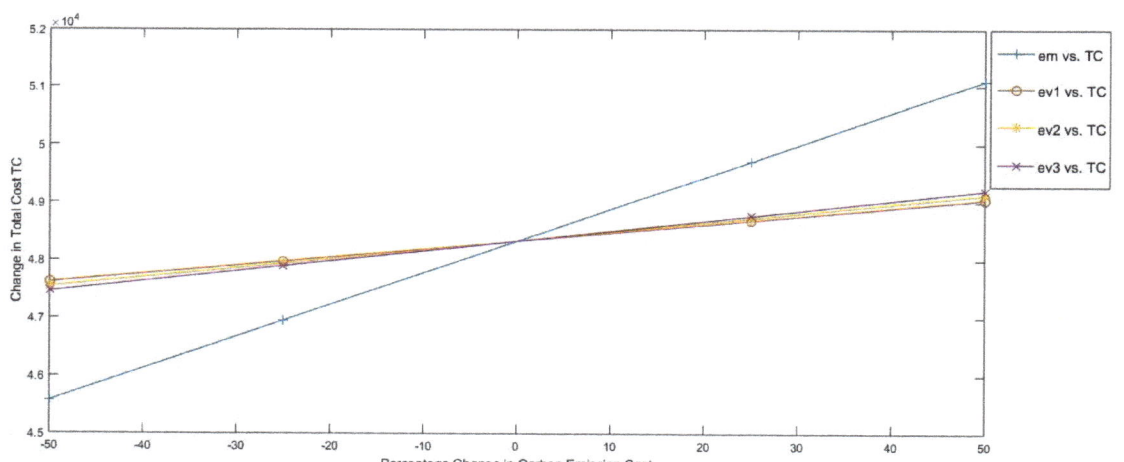

Figure A2. Sensitivity analysis graph for carbon emission and total cost.

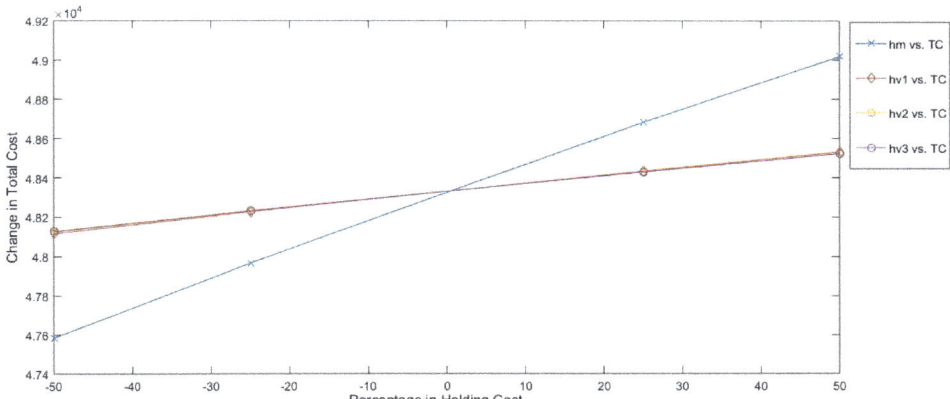

Figure A3. Sensitivity analysis graph for holding cost and total cost.

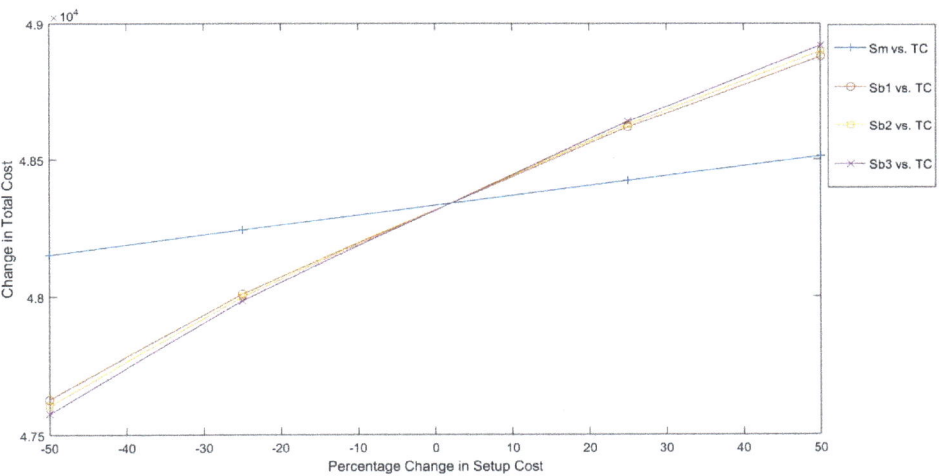

Figure A4. Sensitivity analysis graph for setup cost and total cost.

References

1. Kroes, J.R.; Ghosh, S. Outsourcing congruence with competitive priorities: Impact on supply chain and firm performance. *J. Oper. Manag.* **2009**, *28*, 124–143. [CrossRef]
2. Bernard, K. The effect of outsourcing on supply chain performance at Cadbury Kenya Limited. *Int. J. Logist. Procure. Manag.* **2019**, *1*, 123–138.
3. Hila, C.M.; Dumitrașcu, O. Outsourcing within a Supply Chain Management Framework. In Proceedings of the 8th International Management Conference, Bucharest, Romania, 6–7 November 2014.
4. Kroes, J.R. Outsourcing of supply chain processes: Evaluating the impact of congruence between outsourcing drivers and competitive priorities on performance. *Ga. Inst. Technol.* **2007**.
5. Dolgui, A.; Ivanov, D.; Sokolov, B. Ripple effect in the supply chain: An analysis and recent literature. *Int. J. Prod. Res.* **2018**, *56*, 414–430. [CrossRef]
6. Sun, J.; Tang, J.; Fu, W.; Chen, Z.; Niu, Y. Construction of a multi-echelon supply chain complex network evolution model and robustness analysis of cascading failure. *Comput. Ind. Eng.* **2020**, *144*, 106457. [CrossRef]
7. Gurnani, H.; Yigal, G. Coordination in decentralized assembly systems with uncertain component yields. *Eur. J. Oper. Res.* **2007**, *176*, 1559–1576. [CrossRef]
8. Li, X.; Li, Y.; Cai, X. Double marginalization and coordination in the supply chain with uncertain supply. *Eur. J. Oper. Res.* **2013**, *226*, 228–236. [CrossRef]

9. Jaber, M.Y.; Zanoni, S.; Zavanella, L.E. Economic order quantity models for imperfect items with buy and repair options. *Int. J. Prod. Econ.* **2014**, *155*, 126–131. [CrossRef]
10. Shaban, A.; Costantino, F.; Di Gravio, G.; Tronci, M. A new efficient collaboration model for multi-echelon supply chains. *Expert Syst. Appl.* **2019**, *128*, 54–66. [CrossRef]
11. Tang, S.; Wang, W.; Zhou, G. Remanufacturing in a competitive market: A closed-loop supply chain in a Stackelberg game framework. *Expert Syst. Appl.* **2020**, *161*, 113655. [CrossRef]
12. Hilletofth, P.; Hilmola, O.P. Role of logistics outsourcing on supply chain strategy and management: Survey findings from Northern Europe. *Strateg. Outsourcing Int. J.* **2010**, *3*, 46–61. [CrossRef]
13. Kumar, M.; Vrat, P.; Shankar, R. A fuzzy goal programming approach for vendor selection problem in a supply chain. *Comput. Ind. Eng.* **2004**, *46*, 69–85. [CrossRef]
14. Amid, A.; Ghodsypour, S.; O'Brien, C. A weighted additive fuzzy multiobjective model for the supplier selection problem under price breaks in a supply chain. *Int. J. Prod. Econ.* **2009**, *121*, 323–332. [CrossRef]
15. Rezaei, J.; Davoodi, M. A deterministic, multi-item inventory model with supplier selection and imperfect quality. *Appl. Math. Model.* **2008**, *32*, 2106–2116. [CrossRef]
16. Karpak, B.; Kumcu, E.; Kasuganti, R.R. Purchasing materials in the supply chain: Managing a multi-objective task. *Eur. J. Purch. Supply Manag.* **2001**, *7*, 209–216. [CrossRef]
17. Scott, C.; Lundgren, H.; Thompson, P. Guide to Outsourcing in Supply Chain Management. *Guide Supply Chain Manag.* **2018**, *2*, 189–202.
18. Shy, O.; Stenbacka, R. Strategic outsourcing. *J. Econ. Behav. Organ.* **2003**, *50*, 203–224. [CrossRef]
19. Behara, R.S.; Gundersen, D.E.; Capozzoli, E.A. Trends in information systems outsourcing. *Int. J. Purch. Mater. Manag.* **1995**, *31*, 45–51. [CrossRef]
20. Chiu, S.W.; Liu, C.J.; Li, Y.Y.; Chou, C.L. Manufacturing lot size and product distribution problem with rework, outsourcing and discontinuous inventory distribution policy. *Int. J. Eng. Model.* **2017**, *30*, 49–61.
21. Jamal, A.M.M.; Sarker, B.R.; Mondal, S. Optimal manufacturing batch size with rework process at a single-stage production system. *Comput. Ind. Eng.* **2004**, *47*, 77–89. [CrossRef]
22. Sarkar, B.; Cárdenas-Barrón, L.E.; Sarkar, M.; Singgih, M.L. An economic production quantity model with random defective rate, rework process and backorders for a single stage production system. *J. Manuf. Syst.* **2014**, *33*, 423–435. [CrossRef]
23. Cárdenas-Barrón, L.E. Economic production quantity with rework process at a single-stage manufacturing system with planned backorders. *Comput. Ind. Eng.* **2009**, *57*, 1105–1113. [CrossRef]
24. Widyadana, G.A.; Wee, H.M. An economic production quantity model for deteriorating items with multiple production setups and rework. *Int. J. Prod. Econ.* **2012**, *138*, 62–67. [CrossRef]
25. Sarkar, B.; Sana, S.S.; Chaudhuri, K. An imperfect production process for time varying demand with inflation and time value of money—An EMQ model. *Expert Syst. Appl.* **2011**, *38*, 13543–13548. [CrossRef]
26. Taleizadeh, A.A.; Sari-Khanbaglo, M.P.; Cárdenas-Barrón, L.E. Outsourcing rework of imperfect items in the economic production quantity (EPQ) inventory model with backordered demand. *IEEE Trans. Syst. Man Cybern. Syst.* **2017**, *49*, 2688–2699. [CrossRef]
27. Alvarez, L.H.; Stenbacka, R. Partial outsourcing: A real options perspective. *Int. J. Ind. Organ.* **2007**, *25*, 91–102. [CrossRef]
28. Benaroch, M.; Webster, S.; Kazaz, B. Impact of sourcing flexibility on the outsourcing of services under demand uncertainty. *Eur. J. Oper. Res.* **2012**, *219*, 272–283. [CrossRef]
29. Inderfurth, K.; Kelle, P. Capacity reservation under spot market price uncertainty. *Int. J. Prod. Econ.* **2011**, *133*, 272–279. [CrossRef]
30. Spinler, S.; Huchzermeier, A. The valuation of options on capacity with cost and demand uncertainty. *Eur. J. Oper. Res.* **2006**, *171*, 915–934. [CrossRef]
31. Liu, Z.; Nagurney, A. Supply chain networks with global outsourcing and quick response production under demand and cost uncertainty. *Ann. Oper. Res* **2013**, *208*, 251–289. [CrossRef]
32. Nosoohi, I.; Nookabadi, A.S. Outsource planning through option contracts with demand and cost uncertainty. *Eur. J. Oper. Res.* **2016**, *250*, 131–142. [CrossRef]
33. Chen, K.; Xiao, T. Outsourcing strategy and production disruption of supply chain with demand and capacity allocation uncertainties. *Int. J. Prod. Econ.* **2015**, *170*, 243–257. [CrossRef]
34. Zhao, L.; Langendoen, F.R.; Fransoo, J.C. Supply management of high-value components with a credit constraint. *Flex. Serv. Manuf. J.* **2012**, *24*, 100–118. [CrossRef]
35. Min, H. Examining logistics outsourcing practices in the United States: From the perspectives of third-party logistics service users. *Logist. Res.* **2013**, *6*, 133–144. [CrossRef]
36. Lacity, M.C.; Khan, S.A.; Yan, A. Review of the empirical business services sourcing literature: An update and future directions. *J. Inf. Technol.* **2016**, *31*, 269–328. [CrossRef]
37. Qin, L.; Wu, H.; Zhang, N.; Li, X. Risk identification and conduction model for financial institution IT outsourcing in China. *Inf. Technol. Manag.* **2012**, *13*, 429–444. [CrossRef]
38. Oh, W.; Gallivan, M.J.; Kim, J.W. The market's perception of the transactional risks of information technology outsourcing announcements. *J. Manag. Inf. Syst.* **2006**, *22*, 271–303. [CrossRef]
39. Earl, M.J. The risks of outsourcing IT. *Sloan Manag. Rev.* **1996**, *37*, 26–32.

40. Gewald, H.; Dibbern, J. Risks and benefits of business process outsourcing: A study of transaction services in the German banking industry. *Inf. Manag.* **2009**, *46*, 249–257. [CrossRef]
41. Choi, T.; Wallace, S.W.; Wang, Y. Risk management and coordination in service supply chains: Information, logistics, and outsourcing. *J. Oper. Res. Soc.* **2016**, *67*, 159–164. [CrossRef]
42. Tsai, M.; Lai, K.; Lloyd, A.E.; Lin, H. The dark side of logistics outsourcing—unraveling the potential risks leading to failed relationships. *Transp. Res. Part E Logist. Transp. Rev.* **2012**, *48*, 178–189. [CrossRef]
43. Wang, Y.; Wallace, S.W.; Shen, B.; Choi, T. Service supply chain management: A review of operational models. *Eur. J. Oper. Res.* **2015**, *247*, 685–698. [CrossRef]
44. Chen, J.; Liang, L.; Yao, D.Q. Factory encroachment and channel selection in an outsourced supply chain. *Int. J. Prod. Econ.* **2018**, *215*, 73–83. [CrossRef]
45. Akan, M.; Ata, B.; Lariviere, M.A. Asymmetric Information and Economies of Scale in Service Contracting. *Manuf. Serv. Oper. Manag.* **2011**, *13*, 58–72. [CrossRef]
46. Xin, Y.; Huang, R.; Song, M.; Mishra, N. Pre-positioning inventory and service outsourcing of relief material supply chain. *Int. J. Prod. Res.* **2018**, *56*, 6859–6871.
47. Wu, J.; Wang, H.; Shang, J. Multi-sourcing and information sharing under competition and supply uncertainty. *Eur. J. Oper. Res.* **2019**, *278*, 658–671. [CrossRef]
48. Li, X.; Li, Y.; Cai, X.; Shan, J. Service channel choice for supply chain: Who is better off by undertaking the service? *Prod. Oper. Manag.* **2016**, *25*, 516–534. [CrossRef]
49. Huang, M.; Tu, J.; Chao, X.; Jin, D. Quality risk in logistics outsourcing: A fourth party logistics perspective. *Eur. J. Oper. Res.* **2019**, *276*, 855–879. [CrossRef]
50. Zhang, S.; Zhang, J.; Zhu, G. Retail service investing: An anti-encroachment strategy in a retailer-led supply chain. *Omega* **2019**, *84*, 212–231. [CrossRef]
51. Yue, J.; Ryan, J.K. Price and service competition in an outsourced supply chain. *Prod. Oper. Manag.* **2012**, *21*, 331–344.
52. Ching, W.K.; Choi, S.M.; Huang, X. Inducing high service capacities in outsourcing via penalty and competition. *Int. J. Prod. Res.* **2011**, *49*, 5169–5182. [CrossRef]
53. Ding, H.; Chen, X.; Lin, K.; Wei, Y. Collaborative mechanism of project profit allotment in petroleum engineering service chain with customized integration. *Int. J. Prod. Econ.* **2019**, *214*, 163–174. [CrossRef]

Article

Reconfiguration of Foodbank Network Logistics to Cope with a Sudden Disaster

Esteban Ogazón [1], Neale R. Smith [1] and Angel Ruiz [2,*]

[1] Escuela de Ingeniería y Ciencias, Tecnologico de Monterrey, Monterrey 64849, Mexico; estebanogazon@gmail.com (E.O.); nsmith@tec.mx (N.R.S.)
[2] Interuniversity Research Centre on Enterprise Networks, Logistics and Transportation (CIRRELT), Faculty of Business Administration, Université Laval, Québec, QC G1V 0A6, Canada
* Correspondence: angel.ruiz@fsa.ulaval.ca

Abstract: Foodbank networks provide adequate infrastructure and perform logistics activities to supply food to people in need on a day-to-day basis. However, in the case of a sudden event, such as a natural disaster, they must reconfigure themselves to quickly and fairly satisfy the needs of the affected people, despite the rapid changes in supply and demand, as much as possible. In contrast to most of the studies in the humanitarian logistics literature, which have focused on aid distribution—the downstream part of the supply chain—this paper extends the field of view upstream, explicitly considering supply (or, in the case of foodbanks, donors). To this end, we compare several network design strategies in order to assess the potential benefits of centralized decisions in a context where, in practice, there exists no formal protocol to support bank coordination. We propose a mathematical formulation for the design of such logistics processes, including collection, transshipment, and aid distribution, over a network of foodbanks inspired by the real case of Bancos de Alimentos de México (BAMX). The case considers several categories of food and encompasses restrictions on their mixture to ensure the nutritional quality of the delivered food, distinct from other models in the literature. Finally, we assess the differences in the strategies through the use of effectiveness and efficiency performance metrics.

Keywords: humanitarian logistics; relief distribution; network design problem; food banks

MSC: 90B90

1. Introduction

Humanitarian organizations devote their best efforts to helping vulnerable people improve their situation, fighting against poverty, inequality, and discrimination [1]. Access to water, food, medical supplies, and other products are among the immediate needs of vulnerable communities, constituting the primary goal of foodbanks. Food banking systems obtain surplus food and distribute it to the people in need, involving all society sectors such as civil, governments, and businesses in the process. Foodbanks acquire donated food that in most of the cases would otherwise be spoiled, usually from farms, manufacturers, distributors, retail stores, consumers, and other sources, to make it available to people in need [2].

Foodbank networks offer adequate logistics to provide food sources to people in need on a day-to-day basis through a network of community agencies such as school feeding programs, homeless shelters, soup kitchens, after-school programs, and other non-profit programs that support people in need. Furthermore, one of the most important goals of a foodbank is to provide an acceptable nutritional status to the population in need [3]. Indeed, having "something to eat" is not sustainable or sufficient to prevent malnutrition [4]. The ability to offer people a balanced proportion of macronutrients and micronutrients has been shown to have a major impact on the vulnerability of individuals and entire populations facing diseases and health risks [5]. Foodbanks must, therefore, manage the diversity of surplus food provided by donors to achieve "balanced" deliveries to the population, in order to align with the Sustainable Development Goals for 2030 identified by the United Nations [6].

Conceived to mitigate the continuous needs of a given population, these networks must be reconfigured upon the arrival of sudden events, such as natural or man-made disasters, that provoke sudden variations, both in the demand (for example, the number and the needs of the affected population) and the supply (for example, the number of donors and the quantities they supply). This inbound part of the supply chain, which has received limited attention in the humanitarian logistics literature, is the key to improving effectiveness in the case of foodbanks, therefore increasing their ability to better satisfy the needs of the affected population, as well as to do so in a timely manner.

In this context where food banks must quickly reorganize their logistics—which are designed for day-to-day operations—to cope with the humanitarian consequences of a natural disaster, the contributions of this paper are twofold. First, it proposes a mathematical formulation that spans the entire supply chain (from donors to communities) to solve the logistic planning problem. Then, it empirically compares multiple network reconfiguration strategies to shed some light on how the food banks should reorganize their responsibilities with respect to the day-to-day model, and to identify specific decisions that should be prioritized to achieve the highest performance in terms of satisfaction of the affected people's demand and balance of delivered food. To ground the analysis on a real-world logistic network configuration and its requirements, we consider the case of Bancos de Alimentos de México (BAMX), a foodbank network in Mexico.

The remainder of this paper is structured as follows: Section 2 discusses relevant studies in the recent literature devoted to humanitarian aid distribution with emphasis on papers related to food bank operations. Section 3 presents BAMX, describes its day-to-day operations, and details how these operations would be challenged in the case of a sudden humanitarian crisis. Section 4 proposes a mathematical model for BAMX's logistics. Section 5 describes the experimental design used to compare the different network configurations. Section 6 presents the results, where the impacts of the distinct reconfiguration decisions are assessed. Section 7 discusses the managerial insights obtained from the results. Finally, Section 8 presents the conclusions, as well as some future research.

2. Literature Review

The food distribution modeling literature is extensive [7,8], although most of it is dominated by studies focused on for-profit organizations; comparatively, little work has considered non-profit food distribution networks [9]. Contrarily to the profit case, where networks are optimized with respect to cost or food travel time, non-profit operations seek objectives such as equity [10]. This section contains two parts. The first part reviews the notion of fairness in distribution, whereas the second part focuses on food banks operations and the alternative distribution structures proposed in the literature.

Equity or fairness is one of the major decision-making issues in humanitarian operations. The theoretical notion of fairness in humanitarian aid distribution has recently been discussed, and there is still no universal agreement on a definition or metric. Sengul Orgut et al. [11] have stated that equity has two dimensions in the food distribution network context: quantity received per person and quality (or type) of the food received.

Quantity seems to be the prime aspect when addressing relief distribution and its success. Review papers have claimed that most studies tackle the problems of equity in distribution using fairness constraints [12–15]. Anaya-Arenas et al. [16] have discussed the importance of fairness in relief distribution and how it can be defined. Sengul Orgut et al. [17] have presented two robust optimization models focused on the equitable and effective distribution of donated food over a foodbank's service area, considering only the bank-to-community section of the network. The first model allowed the demand point capacities to vary over given ranges, to control the tradeoff between the total amount of food distributed and the robustness of the solution concerning the capacity variations. The second model controlled the overall equity in the system while seeking to maximize the total amount of food shipped. Their results showed that by sacrificing equity at certain locations that may generate a bottleneck in the network, they can considerably increase the total distribution, while most demand points continue to receive food equitably.

Papers dealing with the quality of the distributed food must incorporate multiple types of products and their characteristics [18–20]. Ross, Campbell, and Webb [21] have conducted a survey of 137 foodbanks and concluded that the quality of the distributed food (such as the nutritious value) needs to be improved, which justifies food banks efforts to limit the donation of unhealthy food while minimizing the negative effects on the quantity of the total donated foods [22,23]. For instance, Gómez-Pantoja et al. [20] have proposed a model for the foodbank resource allocation problem which considers inventory management, product–beneficiary compatibilities, and balanced nutrition in terms of calorie consumption. In summary, food banks are more and more concerned by the attributes of the food they deliver, stressing the need for models able to separate products into categories according to their respective contributions to the individual needs.

If we focus now on the transportation facet of aid distribution, many optimization models have been suggested to improve transportation planning in humanitarian logistics, especially during the last 20 years. Leiras [24], Anaya-Arenas et al. [13], and Yáñez-Sandivari et al. [25] have reviewed 228, 500, and 178 articles related to relief distribution networks, respectively. These studies pointed out that most of the proposed models remain theoretical, with less than 15% of them being tested on real data [24]. These reviews show that most studies have focused on two areas: network design (see, for example, [26–28]) and delivery routing problems (see, for example, [29,30]). They also indicated that limited research had been devoted to the upstream part of the humanitarian supply chains, an area that is central to our work. The material convergence problem becomes even more challenging in the case of a decentralized organization such as BAMX, where each bank in the network operates with a high level of autonomy and, in practice, decides the resources it is willing to engage to support other banks in the network. Whereas the literature from the cooperation perspective of vertical logistics is quite extensive [31–34], academic research on horizontal cooperation in logistics remains limited, especially in terms of humanitarian logistics [25].

As is the case in humanitarian logistics, most of the research concerning food banks has focused on their operations, proposing various models that reflect alternative distribution structures. A recent review on decision support models for managing food aid supply chains (Mahmoudi et al. [35]) has concluded that most studies only consider the resource allocation or transportation between two tiers of the food aid supply chain (for example, between donors and food banks), whereas very few of them have explored this problem as a whole, as it is the case of our paper. In addition, none of the works studied contemplates transshipment between the banks. In the next paragraphs, we have grouped relevant papers into four categories according to the structure of the distribution network they propose.

Resource allocation problems (RAP). The aim is to plan the allocation of supplies among communities or charities over a period or a set of periods. In most of the cases, the problem seeks to maximize the utility of the delivered food. Sengul Orgut et al. [11] considered the allocation of available donations to charities over one month as a single period problem. Sengul et al. [17] extended the previous problem to incorporate variability on the charity capacities. These works do not handle donations that are assumed to be available at banks and consider food as a single commodity. Gómez-Pantoja et al. [20] also dealt with a resource allocation problem, but they modeled food demand in a more detailed manner. Indeed, they considered product-beneficiary compatibilities, balanced nutrition, and priority of beneficiaries to decide who will be served, what kind of products, and how many of them will be supplied. Alkaabneh et al. [19] addressed a similar food allocation model where supply is uncertain, so the models' objective is to maximize the expected utility of charities. However, all of the resource allocation problems adopt a rather strategic perspective and they do not consider the transportation of the food.

Location-routing problems (LRP). They seek to simultaneously determine (1) the location of intermediate food distribution points (FDP) where charities or people in need travel to grab the food, and (2) the routes that, starting at the bank's warehouse, visit food collection points (donors) and FDP's. Naji-Azimi et al. [36] and Boostani et al. [37] proposed Location-Routing problems seeking to locate satellite distribution centers in the context of humanitarian logistics. Concerning food banks, Davis et al. [38] studied a version of the Location-Routing problem where the objective is to minimize the number of FDPs and transportation costs. Similar situations were presented in Solak et al. [39] and in Reihaneh et al. [40], but they proposed different solution approaches. All of the mentioned location-routing works consider food as a single commodity.

Sequential Resource Allocation (SAR) problems. This family of problems also aims to build routes mixing collection and distribution of food in such a way that it is required to set the quantity of food to collect (usually at the first or the firsts stops) and the quantity to deliver at the charities or communities. Gunes et al. [41] studied a deterministic version of this problem and proposed various approaches to model it. Lien et al. [9] and Balcik et al. [42] addressed versions of a SAR where the demand at each delivery point is not known in advance, the challenge of the problem is therefore to decide the amount of food to be left at each delivery stop in order to minimize the wasted (unused) food at the time that equity is maximized. A similar context is presented in Eisenhandler and Tzur [43] and Eisenhandler and Tzur [44], where the food bank decides which charities to visit, in what order, and how much to pick up or distribute to each donor or charity. The SAR has been extended to multiple periods in the so-called food rescue problem (FRP). The FRP is a multi-period problem where food suppliers and charities are chosen in order to form routes that meet the required service levels in such a way that the total transportation cost is minimized and operational constraints are satisfied [45,46]. The routes depart from a depot, collect food from suppliers, and deliver it to charities before returning to the depot.

Location-routing and SAR problems are based on mixed-routes that visit donors and distribution points or charities. Therefore, they are appropriate for modelling situations where donors and charities are geographically close. To cope with situations where the geographical scope of the problem covers a whole region or even a country, food banks often adopt structures inspired by two-stage distribution networks, the first stage encompassing collection and transportation of food to banks, and the second stage the distribution of food to charities or communities.

Two-stage Supply Chain problems. Horne and Downs [26] proposed a 2-echelon relief distribution network where aid travels from a warehouse to points of distribution (POD) or break-of-bulk points (BOB) to which people in need (or agencies) travel to grab the aid. Martins et al. [47] is probably the closest work to ours. They considered a multi-period, multi-echelon food bank supply chain network for the collection of food donations and their distribution to charitable agencies. Contrarily to our problem, Martins et al. [47] did not consider transportation of food to communities. Indeed, charities travel and collect food at their designated food bank on specific days. Moreover, in Martins et al. [47], the donors to banks assignments are given and cannot be modified. Furthermore, although they considered several families of products to distribute, they are handled independently because transportation and storage capacities at banks are dedicated to each family of products. From a transportation standpoint, that means that a donor offering products of two families should be visited for collection two times or by different means.

Table 1 reports the main attributes of the reviewed works, including the type of distribution network they propose, the manner in which they model food (single or multiple commodity), the constraints they consider concerning the execution time, and lastly, the nature of the objective to optimize (F = equity, E = efficiency, T = transportation cost, A = access cost for charities to deliver, U = utility of the food delivered, W = waste, S = a multicriteria function encompassing the three aspects of sustainability).

Table 1. Main attributes of reviewed papers presenting food aid distribution models.

References	Donors to Banks (SC)	Donors to Comm. (SC)	Bank to Bank (SC)	RAP	LRP	SAR	Single/Multi Product	Constraints on Delivery Time	Objective
Davis et al. [38]					✓		S	Driving time	T
Solak et al. [39]					✓		S		T + A
Reihaneh and Ghoniem [40]					✓		S	Truck capacity	T + A
Lien et al. [9]						✓	S	Route length	F + W
Balcik et al. [42]						✓	S	Route length	F + W
Gunes et al. [41]						✓	S	Route length	T
Eisenhandler and Tzur [43]						✓	S	Route length	F + E
Eisenhandler and Tzur [44]						✓	S	Route length	F + E
Nair et al. [45]						✓	M	Route length	T
Rey et al. [46]						✓	M	Route length	F + E
Alkaabneh et al. [19]				✓			M		U
Gómez-Pantoja et al. [20]				✓			M		U
Sengul Orgut et al. [17]				✓			S		F + W
Sengul Orgut et al. [11]				✓			S		F + W + R
Horner et al. [26]	✓	✓					S		T
Martins et al. [47]	✓		✓				M		S
This work	✓	✓	✓				M	Makespan	F

Table 1 shows that, to the best of our knowledge, no previous work simultaneously encompasses decisions on both stages of the food banks supply chain, including food transshipments between banks. Furthermore, Horne and Downs [26] consider a single donor (the warehouse) and a single commodity, for which there is no limitation on the supply. Therefore, food transshipment between PODs or BOBs is not necessary. As Martins et al. [47], our paper considers multiple nutritional products but, as will be shown later, we intend to achieve this by imposing a restriction limiting the proportion of each type of product in the delivered food. This restriction is used by BAMX to deliver a balanced proportion of macronutrients and micronutrients to prevent malnutrition. Finally, it is worth mentioning that our problem is different from all of the papers reviewed in at least 1 of the following aspects: (1) we consider an urgent situation where operations must be achieved within a target deadline or makespan, and (2) we do not only seek a solution to a problem, but to assess the impact that the decisions taken at each stage of the supply chain (for example, assignment of donors to banks, food transshipment between banks, and assignment of communities to banks) have on the total performance of the network.

3. Problem Description

Bancos de Alimentos de México (BAMX) is a Mexican non-profit civil organization, member, and co-founder of the Global FoodBanking Network (GFN). BAMX is the only foodbank network in México and the second largest in the world, federating more than 50 foodbanks distributed across the country. BAMX is focused on rescuing food that would otherwise be spoiled at manufacturing plants, farms, supermarkets, restaurants, and hotels, with the aim of fighting hunger. Over 25,000 people staff the network, 90% of whom are volunteers. BAMX supported more than 1.137 million Mexicans in 2018 [48].

On a day-to-day basis, BAMX works in a decentralized manner. Donors, the start of the BAMX supply chain, are assigned to specific banks, and each bank covers the needs of a geographical region. Donor-to-bank assignments are made according to their distance, the demand for the donor's products within the area covered by the bank, and the bank's logistic capabilities. The bank processes the donor's products by validating them and returning reports and acknowledgments of the goods they have received to the donor. Each bank, which is responsible for a demand region, organizes and coordinates deliveries to individuals in need in relevant communities. Additionally, it produces forecasts of its region's needs and receives a budget from the headquarters to ensure its operations. As manpower is mostly provided by volunteers, the budget is basically devoted to logistics expenses (for example, warehouses, truck hire, fuel). However, as the volume and the nature of the products supplied by each donor vary greatly, it is almost impossible to achieve a donor-to-bank assignment that perfectly matches the supply and demand. Moreover, as BAMX seeks to deliver a balanced proportion of macronutrients and micronutrients to prevent malnutrition, lateral transshipments between banks may need to be organized to achieve the right quantity and mixture of products required by each community. The receiving bank bears the cost of such transshipments within their operating budget.

However, on the arrival of a sudden man-made or natural disaster such as floods provoked by a hurricane strike or an earthquake, food banks must adapt their day-to-day operations to cope with the event's consequences, which can last from several days up to a few weeks. During that period, the needs in the affected region rapidly increase so that the capacity of the local bank in charge of the area exceeds. On the other end of the supply chain, solidarity and generosity typically cause the number and volume of donations to grow very quickly, which leads to several managerial challenges, as (1) the donors may be outside of the affected region and scattered across the whole country; (2) new donors that have never collaborated with BAMX need to be assigned to a specific bank; (3) the growing number of donations may exceed the bank's capacities, in terms of transportation, storage, or handling resources; and (4) products donated by new donors to a bank, or the extra quantities from regular donors, may or may not fit the nutritional restrictions targeted by BAMX. To put it mildly, the rather decentralized logistic plans designed to cope with the day-to-day operations by BAMX are not adequate for the extraordinary requirements of sudden humanitarian situations.

In such situations, BAMX's central logistics management (CLM) office must make quick decisions to adapt the network to the surging supply and demand. However, according to the managers of the organization, specialized protocols for these kinds of situations do not exist. Indeed, although each bank is willing to cooperate, the arrival of a disaster triggers a rather unstructured process, where some more proactive banks contact other banks or make available part of their resources, while other rather reactive banks wait to see how their help is specifically requested. The timeframe (see Figure 1) for BAMX to draw up a collection plan, collect donations at donor locations and move them to the selected banks, process items at banks, and deliver food to communities is indeed very short, with the goal being to provide first relief to the people in need as soon as possible after the event. In this context, the lack of formal collaborative processes and the urgency of the matter may result in a poorly organized cooperative logistic plan, where most of the decisions are made after the collection of donations has started (or, in some cases, even finished), thus reducing the effectiveness and the aid that the network can bring to people.

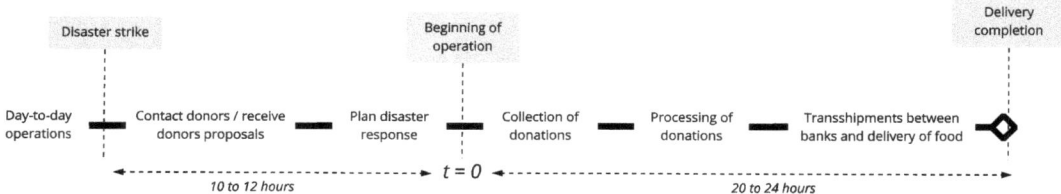

Figure 1. BAMX's response to a sudden natural disaster.

4. A Mixed-Integer Linear Programming Formulation

The BAMX supply chain can be modeled as a two-echelon distribution network, composed of three sets of nodes—donors, foodbanks, and the communities to which aid must be delivered, denoted as D, B, and C, respectively—and three sets of oriented arcs, representing the transitable roads connecting donors to foodbanks (set A), banks to banks (set N), and banks and communities to communities (set M). As is the case in most works devoted to two-echelon relief distribution networks [17,49], the goal is to decide the assignments of donors to banks and banks to communities, as well as the quantities of products transported from donors to banks, between banks, and from banks to communities, in order to satisfy the demand of the communities as much as possible, while respecting the desired proportion of nutrients in the products delivered to communities and some additional operational restrictions. However, our aim is not only to find the optimal solution, but to also consider the extent to which different organizational strategies (such as levels of decision centralization) impact the network performance. Therefore, it is necessary to elaborate a formulation that captures the assumptions and practices observed at BAMX, and which can model more flexible configurations, as is detailed in the Numerical Experiments section.

A donor can supply only one bank and each bank can receive goods from several donors in the regular (day-to day) plan. Donations must be processed by the original recipient bank, which is responsible for delivering reports to the donor institutions, and transshipments between banks are allowed. Two operational phases are considered: (1) donation collection and processing, and (2) donation re-allocation, and donation delivery. We assume that each bank must complete phase (1) before to begin phase (2). Moreover, if one bank receives food from other banks during phase (2), deliveries cannot start until all the receptions have been completed. Food needs to be processed only when it is directly received from a donor. As per the assignments of communities to banks, BAMX follows a single sourcing strategy, meaning that each community receives food from a single bank. This method has been also reported in the literature. Sengul Orgut et al. [11,49] and Martins et al. [47], among others, describe food bank networks having the same structure as BAMX, and the single sourcing strategy is used by their partner organizations. In our case, BAMX justified the use of this strategy because it allows better contact with the communities, and better knowledge and control on the communities' needs. Even more importantly, it helps in developing a trustful relationship with the communities. BAMX considers that a single source is easier to manage and overall, the advantage of single source outweighs the fact that it is not optimal from a transportation perspective.

Indeed, several communities can be visited into a single route starting from a given bank. Each bank's official team plans the delivery to a list of communities, which will be visited in succession by a convoy of vehicles. However, schedules for vehicles and the assignment of vehicles to routes are beyond the scope of the proposed work.

BAMX needs to plan food collection and transportation to banks, processing at banks, and deliveries to communities, in such a way that the latest delivery is performed within a maximum time $Tmax$. The model considers various types of transport vehicles, defined in a set O, including owned vehicles and those of third-party companies (3PL), mostly Less-Than-TruckLoad partners. Each type of available vehicle has a given capacity. Notice also that the distance to be traveled by a vehicle depends on the vehicle's type. 3PL companies only consider the distance from the pickup location (the donor) to the destination (the bank) whereas owned vehicles must travel from the bank to the donor and back. Costs are computed according to the travelled distances, but since 3PL's rates per kilometer are much higher than the owned vehicles' cost per kilometer, in most of the cases using 3PL is more expensive. The acquisition of additional vehicles is not considered in the short span of the problem's planning horizon. Therefore, only variable transportation costs are considered. Multiple trips are not allowed. Indeed, as our goal is not to find the optimal distribution plan, but to discuss the impact of reconfiguration tactics on the network performance, this is an assumption that we deem acceptable. Furthermore, this assumption is also in alignment with the BAMX's objective of a fast response. Nonetheless, this assumption may be relaxed when the actual distribution plans are executed.

As per the quality of the distributed food, the model considers a set F of the various types or families of food and restricts their mixture to provide a balanced diet. This is achieved by ensuring that the quantity of each type of food f (for example, sugary drinks) delivered to each community does not exceed the proportion given by parameter $Fprop_f$, which is set by BAMX. The units of food that do not meet these proportions may not be delivered. Notice that these restrictions ensure a minimum level of quality, whereas the demand at each community is expressed as kilograms of food, independently of its type.

Banks must complete the collection of donations, donation processing, and reception of all of the food coming from other banks before shipping food to the communities. Finally, each bank has a limited budget. When food is transported between banks, the one receiving the food assumes the expenses. Table 2 lists the sets and indices used in the model formulation.

Table 2. Sets and indices used in the model formulation.

Indices or Sets	
$d \in D$	Index and set of donors
$b \in B$	Index and set of food bank
$c \in C$	Index and set of communities to deserve
$f \in F$	Index and set of food types
$o \in O$	Index and set of vehicle types
A	Set of arcs connecting nodes $(d,b) : (d \in D, b \in B)$
N	Set of arcs connecting nodes $(i,j) : (i \in B, j \in B, i \neq j)$
M	Set of arcs connecting nodes $(i,c) : (i \in B \cup C, c \in C)$

Several sets of variables are used to formulate the model. Sets of continuous variables x_{ofdb}, y_{ofij}, and z_{obic} decide the quantities of each food type $f \in F$ shipped using vehicles of type $o \in O$ from donors to banks, between banks, and from banks and communities to communities, respectively. Binary variables sz_{bc} represent the assignment of banks to communities. Auxiliary variables αx_{db}, αy_{ij}, and αz_{bc}, which, similarly to the assignment ones, are set to one only if food is transported between the referred nodes. Integer variables (vx_{odb}, vy_{oij}, and vz_{obc}) determine the number of trucks of each type allocated by each bank to perform food transportation from donors, to or from other donors, and to communities, respectively. Auxiliary continuous variables wx_b, wy_b, and wz_c represent the latest arrival time of food shipped from donors to banks, from a bank to another bank, and from banks to communities, respectively. Finally, the continuous variable u_c computes the percentage of unmet demand at each community. Sets of variables are defined in Table 3.

Table 3. Sets of variables used in the model formulation.

If there is a figure in wide page, please release command

Variables	
x_{ofij}	Kilograms of food type $f \in F$ shipped on vehicles of type $o \in O$ from donor i to bank $j \mid (i,j) \in A$
y_{ofij}	Kilograms of food type $f \in F$ shipped on vehicles of type $o \in O$ from bank i to bank $j \mid (i,j) \in N$
z_{ofbij}	Kilograms of food type $f \in F$ shipped on vehicles of type $o \in O$ from node i to community $j \mid (i,j) \in M$, originally shipped from bank $b \in B$
θ_{fbc}	Kilograms of food type $f \in F$ delivered at community $c \in C$
sz_{bc}	Takes value of 1 if bank $b \in B$ is assigned to community $c \in C$; zero otherwise
αx_{db}	Takes value 1 if food is shipped from donor d to bank $b \mid (d,b) \in A$; zero otherwise
αy_{ij}	Takes value 1 if food is shipped from bank i to bank $j \mid (i,j) \in N$; zero otherwise
αz_{bij}	Takes value 1 if food is shipped from bank $b \in B$ and uses the arc connecting node i to community $j \mid (i,j) \in M$; zero otherwise
vx_{oij}	Number of vehicles of type $o \in O$ assigned to donor i from bank $j \mid (i,j) \in A$
vy_{oij}	Number of vehicles of type $o \in O$ assigned to bank i from bank $j \mid (i,j) \in N$
vz_{ob}	Number of vehicles of type $o \in O$ assigned to bank $b \in B$ for delivery to communities
wx_b	Latest arrival time of food shipped from donors to bank $b \in B$ (minutes)
wy_b	Latest arrival time of food shipped from banks to bank $b \in B$ (minutes)
wz_c	Latest arrival time of food shipped from a bank or community to community $c \in C$ (minutes)
u_c	Unmet demand at community $c \in C$ (expressed as a percentage)
$\overline{u}$	Mean unmet demand over all the communities
u_{max}	The largest unmet demand over all the communities

Finally, the parameters and constants reported in Table 4 are used in the formulation.

Table 4. Parameters used in the model formulation.

Parameters	
Don_{fd}	Kilograms of food type $f \in F$ offered by donor $d \in D$
$Bcap_b$	Capacity in kilograms of food that bank $b \in B$ can process
$Fprop_f$	Maximum proportion of food type $f \in F$ a bank can deliver
$Vcap_o$	Capacity of vehicles type $o \in O$ in kilograms
Vav_{ob}	Number of vehicles of type $o \in O$ available at bank $b \in B$
Vsp	Mean transportation speed
Dem_c	Demand in kilograms of food at community $c \in C$
Tid_{oij}	Distance (km) between donor i and bank $j \mid (i,j) \in A$, using vehicle of type $o \in O$
Tib_{ij}	Distance (km) between bank i and bank $j \mid (i,j) \in N$
Tic_{ij}	Distance (km) between node i and community $j \mid (i,j) \in M$
Tp_b	Processing time of a metric ton (1000 kg) of food at bank $b \in B$
$Tmax$	Latest arrival time allowed in the network for food delivery to a community
Bud_b	Available budget for bank $b \in B$
Tc_{ofb}	Transportation cost of food type $f \in F$ per kilometer, using vehicle of type $o \in O$ for bank $b \in B$

The model's objective is to minimize the average fraction of unmet demand computed as $\bar{u} = \sum_{c \in C} u_c / |C|$. However, to avoid the case where the average shortage is minimized by sending more supplies to small or low-demand communities, we also minimize the largest unmet demand, $u_{max} = \max_c(u_c)$. The formulation is expressed as follows:

$$\text{minimize } U = \bar{u} + u_{max} \tag{1}$$

subject to:

$$\sum_{\substack{o \in O \\ (i,j) \in A}} \sum_{j \in B} x_{ofij} \leq Don_{fi} \quad \forall f \in F, i \in D \tag{2}$$

$$\sum_{o \in O} \sum_{f \in F} \sum_{\substack{i \in D \\ (i,j) \in A}} x_{ofij} \leq Bcap_j \quad \forall j \in B \tag{3}$$

$$\sum_{\substack{i \in D \\ (i,j) \in A}} vx_{oij} \leq Vav_{oj} \quad \forall o \in O, j \in B \tag{4}$$

$$\sum_{\substack{j \in B \\ (i,j) \in N}} vy_{oij} + vz_{oj} \leq Vav_{oi} \quad \forall o \in O, i \in B \tag{5}$$

$$\sum_{f \in F} x_{ofij} \leq Vcap_o vx_{oij} \quad \forall o \in O, (i,j) \in A \tag{6}$$

$$\sum_{f \in F} y_{ofij} \leq Vcap_o vy_{oij} \quad \forall o \in O, (i,j) \in N \tag{7}$$

$$\sum_{j \in C} z_{oiij} \leq Vcap_o vz_{oi} \quad \forall o \in O, (i,j) \in M \tag{8}$$

$$\theta_{fbc} \leq Fprop_f \left(\sum_{o \in O} \sum_{\substack{i \in C \cup B \\ (i,c) \in M}} \sum_{w \in F} z_{owbic} - \sum_{o \in O} \sum_{\substack{j \in C \\ (c,j) \in M}} \sum_{w \in F} z_{owbcj} \right) \quad \forall f \in F, b \in B, c \in C \tag{9}$$

$$\theta_{fbc} \leq \sum_{o \in O} \sum_{\substack{i \in C \cup B \\ (i,c) \in M}} z_{ofbic} - \sum_{o \in O} \sum_{\substack{j \in C \\ (c,j) \in M}} z_{ofbcj} \quad \forall f \in F, b \in B, c \in C \tag{10}$$

$$\sum_{o \in O} \sum_{\substack{c \in C \\ (b,c) \in M}} z_{ofbbc} \leq \sum_{o \in O} \sum_{\substack{i \in D \\ (i,b) \in A}} x_{ofib} + \sum_{o \in O} \sum_{i \in B} y_{ofib} - \sum_{o \in O} \sum_{j \in B} y_{ofbj} \quad \forall f \in F, b \in B \tag{11}$$

$$\sum_{o \in O} \sum_{\substack{j \in B \\ (b,j) \in N}} y_{ofbj} \leq \sum_{o \in O} \sum_{\substack{i \in D \\ (i,b) \in A}} x_{ofib} \qquad \forall b \in B, f \in F \qquad (12)$$

$$\sum_{o \in O} \sum_{\substack{j \in C \\ (i,j) \in M}} z_{ofbij} \leq \sum_{o \in O} \sum_{\substack{j \in C \cup B \\ (j,i) \in M}} z_{ofbji} \qquad \forall f \in F, b \in B, i \in C \qquad (13)$$

$$\sum_{\substack{i \in B \cup C \\ (i,j) \in M}} \alpha z_{bij} \leq 1 \qquad \forall j \in C, b \in B \qquad (14)$$

$$\sum_{\substack{j \in C \\ (i,j) \in M}} \alpha z_{bij} \leq 1 \qquad \forall i \in C, b \in B \qquad (15)$$

$$\sum_{j \in B} \alpha x_{ij} \leq 1 \qquad \forall i \in D \qquad (16)$$

$$\sum_{o \in O} \sum_{f \in F} x_{ofij} \leq Bcap_j \alpha x_{ij} \qquad \forall i \in D, j \in B \qquad (17)$$

$$\sum_{i \in B} sz_{ij} \leq 1 \qquad \forall j \in C \qquad (18)$$

$$\sum_{o \in O} \sum_{\substack{i \in C \cup B \\ (i,c) \in M}} z_{ofbic} - \sum_{o \in O} \sum_{\substack{j \in C \\ (c,j) \in M}} z_{ofbcj} \qquad \forall b \in B, c \in C, f \in F \qquad (19)$$
$$\leq \sum_{f \in F} \sum_{d \in D} Don_{fd} sz_{bc}$$

$$\sum_{o \in O} \sum_{f \in F} x_{ofij} \leq Bcap_b \alpha x_{ij} \qquad \forall (i,j) \in A \qquad (20)$$

$$\sum_{o \in O} \sum_{f \in F} y_{ofij} \leq Bcap_i \alpha y_{ij} \qquad \forall (i,j) \in N \qquad (21)$$

$$\sum_{o \in O} \sum_{f \in F} z_{ofbij} \leq \sum_{f \in F} \sum_{d \in D} Don_{fd} \alpha z_{bij} \qquad \forall b \in B, (i,j) \in M \qquad (22)$$

$$\frac{Tid_{oij}}{Vsp} \alpha x_{ij} + \sum_{w \in O} \sum_{f \in F} \sum_{\substack{i \in D \\ (i,j) \in A}} \frac{Tp_b}{1000} x_{wfij} \leq wx_j \qquad \forall o \in O, (i,j) \in A \qquad (23)$$

$$\frac{Tib_{ij}}{Vsp} \alpha y_{ij} + wx_i \leq wy_j \qquad \forall j \in B, (i,j) \in N \qquad (24)$$

$$\frac{Tic_{ij}}{Vsp} \alpha z_{iij} + wy_i \leq wz_j \qquad \forall j \in C, (i,j) \in M \qquad (25)$$

$$\frac{Tic_{ij}}{Vsp} \alpha z_{bij} + wz_i \leq wz_j \qquad \begin{array}{l} \forall b \in B, \\ (i,j) \in M | (i \notin B) \end{array} \qquad (26)$$

$$wz_c \leq Tmax \qquad \forall c \in C \qquad (27)$$

$$\sum_{o \in O} \sum_{\substack{i \in D \\ (i,j) \in A}} \sum_{f \in F} Tc_{ofb} Tid_{oib} x_{ofib}$$
$$+ \sum_{o \in O} \sum_{\substack{j \in B \\ (b,j) \in N}} \sum_{f \in F} Tc_{ofb} Tib_{bj} y_{ofbj} \qquad \forall b \in B \qquad (28)$$
$$+ \sum_{o \in O} \sum_{(i,j) \in M} \sum_{f \in F} Tc_{ofb} Tic_{ij} z_{ofbij}$$
$$\leq Bud_b$$

$$\frac{1}{Dem_c} \left(Dem_c - \sum_{f \in F} \sum_{b \in B} \theta_{fbc} \right) \leq u_c \qquad \forall c \in C \qquad (29)$$

$$u_c \leq u_{max} \qquad \forall c \in C \qquad (30)$$

$$xz_{bc}, sz_{bc}, \alpha x_{db}, \alpha y_{ij}, \alpha z_{bic} \in \{0,1\} \qquad \begin{array}{l} \forall (b,c) \in A, (b,c) \in M, \\ (i,j) \in N, (i,c) \in M \end{array} \qquad (31)$$

$$x_{ofdb}, y_{ofij}, z_{ofbic}, wx_b, wy_b, wz_c, r_{fb}, u_c \geq 0 \qquad \forall o \in O, f \in F, d \in D, b \in B, c \in C, (i,j) \in N, (i,c) \in M \qquad (32)$$

$$vx_{odb}, vy_{oij}, vz_{ob} \in \mathbb{Z}^+ \qquad \forall o \in O, d \in D, b \in B, (i,j) \in N \qquad (33)$$

Constraints (2) ensure that the flow of each type of food from each donor $d \in D$ to banks $b \in B$ is not greater than the donor's offer Don_{fd}. Constraints (3) enforce that the food flow received at each bank $b \in B$ is not greater than its capacity $Bcap_b$ for processing donations. As the food only needs to be processed once by the network, food shipped between banks does not impact the recipient bank´s capacity $Bcap_b$.

Constraints (4) require that the number of vehicles of every type $o \in O$ assigned by a bank $b \in B$. to collect food from all of its donors $d \in D$ is not greater than Vav_{ob}, the number of vehicles available for each vehicle's type. As mentioned before, multiple trips are not allowed; however, once all of the food collected from donors is received—in the first transportation phase of the supply chain—and processed by the banks, the vehicles can be used to transport the donations to other banks or communities (in the second transportation phase). Constraint (5) limits the usage of vehicles in the second transportation phase. Since banks can simultaneously send food to other banks and communities, both usages are considered together for the transportation capacity of the second transportation phase. Constraints (6)–(8) limit the flow of food across the different stages of the network, considering the number of vehicles assigned and their capacity $Vcap_o$.

The quality of the food delivered to communities is handled by Constraints (9) and (10). Constraints (9) ensure that the food sent by each bank to the communities it serves respects the proportions set by the parameter $Fprop_f$ by computing the total amount of food delivered at the community and setting an upper bound for the proportion allowed of each food type. However, as it is possible that the available quantity of a given type is lower than its bound, all of the available food would most probably not be delivered. For this reason, Constraints (10) compute the actual quantity of each food type that can be delivered at each community, setting another upper bound on θ_{fbc}.

Constraints (11) establish the flow balance between banks and communities, whereas Constraints (12) establish the balance of the flows between banks, and Constraints (13) concern the flow balance between communities. Constraints (14) and (15) limit a single arc in set M to be used to reach and leave each community $c \in C$, respectively. Constraints (16) limit each donor $d \in D$ to supply at most one bank $b \in B$, and Constraints (17) identify which of these assignments are made, using the bank capacity $Bcap_b$ as a flow upper bound. Constraints (18) require that each community $c \in C$ be assigned to, at most, one bank $b \in B$ through the binary variable sz_{bc}. Constraints (19) ensure that a bank $b \in B$ can deliver food to a community c only if c is assigned to bank b by the variable sz_{bc}. The first and second terms in equation (19) compute the community's food inflow and outflow, respectively. The right-hand side of the equation bounds their difference by the community-to-bank assignment variable multiplied by a "Big quantity", which is set to the sum of the donations available. Therefore, if the community is not assigned to the bank ($sz_{bc} = 0$), the food coming to the community cannot be greater than the food leaving the community. Otherwise, the difference between the inflow and the outflow provides the quantity delivered at the community. Notice that it might be helpful for a bank to use a route that visits a community which is not assigned to it in order to reach other communities, particularly these within the disaster zone. Therefore, Constraints (19) do not forbid the flow through the communities when $sz_{bc} = 0$. In such cases, Constraints (19) ensure that the community's outflow is not lower than the inflow, meaning that no food can be delivered. Therefore, Constraints (19) and (13) work together to ensure flow continuity, thus allowing banks to use communities that are not assigned to them as passthrough nodes.

Constraints (20)–(22) help to track which arcs are being used to transport food by setting the associated auxiliary variables αx_{db}, αy_{ij}, and αz_{bic} to 1, respectively. Constraints (19)–(22) use the total donation supply or bank's capacity as flow upper limits. Together, Constraints (23)–(27) ensure that all the activities of collection, processing, and delivering to communities are completed within a maximum timespan $Tmax$. Constraints (23) track the latest arrival times wx_b of each food type $f \in F$ transported from donors $d \in D$ to each bank $b \in B$, which includes the travel time Tid_{odb}/Vsp and processing time at banks, Tp_b. The latest times wx_b can be interpreted as the time at which shipments to a bank are consolidated for shipment to another node. Constraints (24) track the latest arrival times wy_b of food type $f \in F$ transported from banks $i \in B$ to banks $b \in B$ with the addition of the previous arrival times wx_i. This represents the time at which the delivery to the communities $c \in C$ can start for every bank $b \in B$. Similarly, Constraints (25) track the time wz_c in which food $f \in F$ arrives from a bank $b \in B$ to a community $c \in C$, and Constraints (26) track the time wz_c for the cases in which the transportation is between communities. Constraints (27) limit the arrival time wz_c to every community $c \in C$ to $Tmax$, ensuring that food arrives to the communities on time, thus limiting the length of the distribution routes.

Constraints (28) limit the expenditures of each bank $b \in B$ to their budget Bud_b. Constraints (29) track the fraction of unmet demand u_c at each community $c \in C$, and Constraints (30) calculate the largest proportion of unmet demand among banks in the network. Notice that u_c measures only the total quantity of food delivered at the community since the quality is ensured by Constraints (9) and (10). Finally, Constraints (31) and (32), and (33) define the domains of variables.

5. Numerical Experiments

The objective of this section is to empirically assess the extent to which network design decisions at different stages of the supply chain may contribute to achieving better performance under a disaster scenario, assuming that the current structure of the supply chain will need to be modified in response to a disaster. By doing so, we intend to identify the decisions having the highest impact on the network effectiveness, such that managers can focus their efforts on them. First, the instances designed to reproduce the distribution process of an organization such as BAMX are described. Then, different network reconfigurations focusing on specific types of decisions are proposed and their impact on both system effectiveness and efficiency are assessed by solving a testbed of random instances.

5.1. Instances

To generate a comprehensive testbed, we followed a two-step process. First, instances representing the regular (such as day-to-day) operations of an organization such as BAMX were generated. Then, for each instance, the effect of a random disaster was applied, such that regular supply and demand, as well as the state of the transit arcs, is affected. The instances were designed to emulate common scenarios discussed and validated with the logistics managers of BAMX. However, they do not correspond to a particular event faced by BAMX in the past.

Let us start by describing the regular instances. A regular instance consists of a set with $|B| = 15$ banks, $|D| = 45$ donors, and $|C| = 15$ communities uniformly located in a 1000 km × 1000 km territory. To each community, we associate a random demand that represents the needs of the surrounding population. To this end, two kinds of demand distributions are used: a uniform distribution where each community's demand is drawn from a $U(\underline{d}, \overline{d})$ distribution, and a distribution where the demand assigned to communities is inversely proportional to the square of their distance to the territory's center. We refer to the latter as a "dense" distribution as it concentrates demand near the center of the territory (see Figure 2).

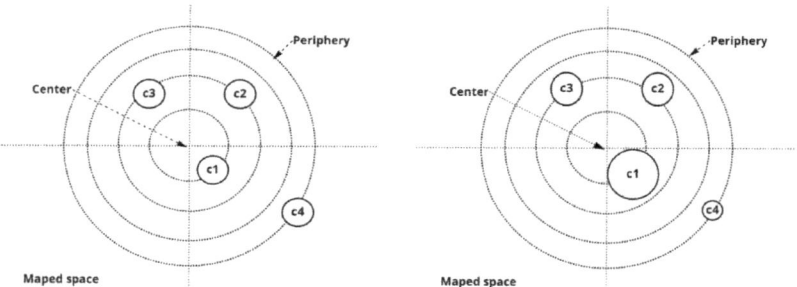

Figure 2. Representation of a "uniform" distribution (**left**) and a "dense" distribution (**right**). The size of the circles C representing the communities is proportional to the size of the community's demand.

The total demand of the network is computed as the sum over all of the communities and, to emulate the historical performance of the bank network, the total network supply is set to satisfy only 90% of the total demand. For this supply, 3 types ($|F| = 3$) of food are considered. A total of 2 possible profiles of supply mixes are considered: a "good" mix, where the proportions of the three food types supplied by the donor match those targeted by the parameter $Fprop_f$ (70%, 20%, and 10%), and a "bad" mix (50%, 30%, and 20%), which has a higher proportion of products of types 2 and 3 than desired. The total quantity offered by each donor is drawn from a probabilistic distribution. Again, two profiles of distribution (uniform and dense) are considered. In the latter, supplies available for each donor are inversely proportional to the square of their distance to the territory's center. We assume the bank's capacity, budget, and quantity of owned vehicles to be tied together as a single factor of network resources, in order to represent the size of each bank. The distribution of these network resources can be uniform or dense. In addition to the owned vehicles, rented vehicles with the same speed but different travel costs are available.

Then, to simulate the effect of a disaster, a point is selected as the disaster's epicenter. Two cases are considered: a "centered" case, where the disaster is on the center of the territory, and a peripheral case, where it strikes on the edge of the mapped territory. In both cases, the affected area is generated by drawing a circular area around the disaster's epicenter, which contains at least 10% of the communities. Within the affected zone, we define a critical zone around the same epicenter but with half the radius of the affected area. To model the fact that traveling an arc in the disaster zone is more difficult, we decided to increase the arc's length and keep the vehicle speed constant. Hence, the length of arcs connected to any node located within the affected zone is increased by 20%. However, if the arc connects to at least one node in the critical zone, the length of the arc is increased by 50%, instead of 20%.

Once the disaster zone is created, the disaster demand—which refers to the increase in demand of the affected communities—is generated. To this end, the demand of the communities inside the affected and critical zones is multiplied by a disaster factor, the value of which is set to 2. The total donations to the network are increased accordingly and, to simulate the existence of an emergency budget, the monetary resources of the banks are increased by 20%.

As described above, several instance features, such as the demand distribution, might use two alternative distributions or parameters. Adopting the design of experiment terminology, we refer to these features as factors, and to the available choices as levels. Since each of the five factors has two possible levels (which are arbitrarily denoted as low and high), up to 32 combinations of levels of the five factors are possible. Each combination is referred to as a scenario. The five factors, their corresponding model parameters, and their levels are reported in Table 5. Finally, a Monte Carlo approach was used to sample the chosen random distributions in each scenario, in order to generate the desired number of regular and disaster replicates.

Table 5. Factors and levels considered to generate the scenarios.

Factor	Related Parameters	Levels (Low/High)
DDO	Don_{fd}	Uniform/dense
QDM	Don_{fd}	Good (70%, 20%, 10%)/bad (50%, 30%, 20%)
DDE	Dem_c	Uniform/dense
DNR	$Bcap_b$, Bud_b, and Vav_{ob}	0 = uniform/1 = dense
DL	Dem_c, Tid_{odb}, Tib_{ij}, and Tic_{ic}	0 = centered/1 = peripheral

DDO: distribution of donations; QDM: quality of donation mixture; DDE: distribution of the demand; DNR: distribution of network resources (capacity, budget, and vehicles); DL: disaster location.

All of the computations were performed on a 64-bit Windows computer with a Ryzen 5600 @ 4.6 GHz CPU and 16 GB RAM. The Gurobi v9.0 software was used to solve the formulation. Computational times depended strongly on the network configuration, ranging from an average time of 0.4 s. up to 82 s. All of the instances were solved to optimality. These computational times were deemed as short and, therefore, acceptable by the BAMX manager, in the context of planning the response to a natural disaster.

5.2. Experiments

As our objective was to shed some light on how the foodbanks in the network should re-organize their operations, with respect to the day-to-day model, we first solved each regular or day-to-day instance. These solutions provide the donor-to-bank assignments, the community-to-bank assignments, and the food quantities that flow through the network, constituting our baseline. We then solved the corresponding disaster versions of the instances. Three types of network reconfigurations were proposed. Each configuration allowed for the reviewing of specific decisions with respect to the day-to-day solution. To this end, the problem formulation was solved, but only variables related to the decisions allowed by the reconfiguration were free; the remainder were set to the values produced in the day-to-day solution. The motivation for this strategy is that, in a decentralized network such as that of BAMX, each change or modification implies a series of calls and negotiations between bank managers. Considering the limited time available to redesign and implement the changes in the network, it is of utmost importance to identify the modifications or aspects to negotiate that maximize the outcome and the potential added value that longer discussions may achieve.

From a practical standpoint, considering network changes based on the supply chain levels is a straightforward way to segment network reconfigurations. Therefore, three possible reconfigurations (low, mid, and high level) are proposed with respect to the day-to-day solution (referred to as configuration 1). A low-level reconfiguration (configuration 4) corresponds to the case where only distribution decisions (banks to communities) are modified. Furthermore, the single-source assumption is relaxed, such that several banks are allowed to send food to the same community. The implementation of such modifications in practice is rather easy, as they involve coordination between two or among a low number of banks. In a mid-level reconfiguration (configuration 3), shipments of products between banks can be modified, but distribution decisions remain the same as in the day-to-day case. In a high-level reconfiguration (configuration 2), assignments of donors to banks can be modified. It is worth noting that banks are generally reluctant to allow others to interact with "their" suppliers. A bank would only be open to such a possibility if doing so would result in an important improvement in network performance. Finally, we also propose a full reconfiguration alternative (configuration 5), where all of the previous modifications are allowed. Figure 3 illustrates the reconfiguration alternatives.

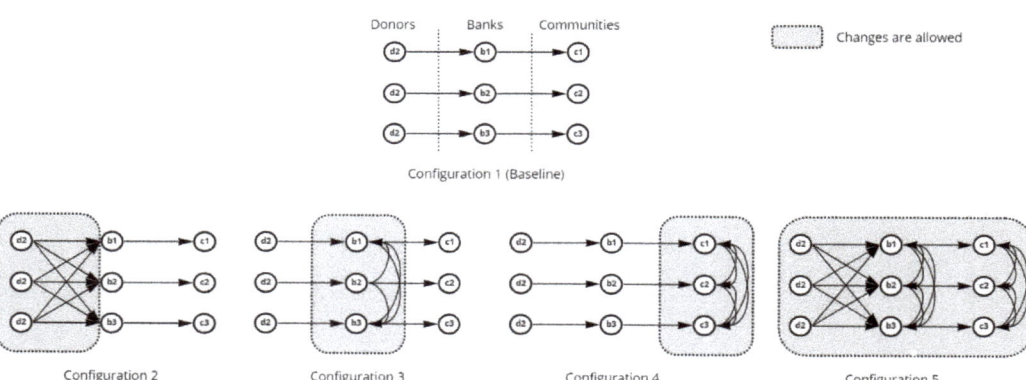

Figure 3. Considered reconfiguration alternatives. The gray boxes identify the part of the network in which changes are allowed, with respect to the day-to-day solution.

6. Numerical Results

We first analyzed how the network performance metrics were impacted by the factors characterizing the different scenarios. To this end, Table 6 reports the average unmet demand $\overline{\overline{U}}$ and the maximum unmet demand $\overline{maxU}$, as well as the half of their confidence intervals at 95% (HW), when each factor was set to its low and high levels. We also report $\Delta \overline{\overline{U}}$ and $\Delta \overline{maxU}$, which are the changes in $\overline{\overline{U}}$ and $\overline{maxU}$, respectively, when a given factor changes from its low to high level while keeping all other factors constant. Note that only the results for which $\Delta \overline{\overline{U}}$ and $\Delta \overline{maxU}$ show a statistically significant difference are reported.

Table 6. Sensitivity analysis of the scenario factors.

Factor	Level	$\overline{\overline{U}}$	HW ($\overline{\overline{U}}$)	$\Delta\overline{\overline{U}}$	$\overline{\max U}$	HW ($\overline{\max U}$)	$\Delta\overline{\max U}$
DDO	low	41.60%	±1.65%	−5.57%	60.42%	±2.22%	−4.19%
	high	36.49%	±1.43%		56.23%	±2.23%	
QDM	low	37.23%	±1.56%	3.62%	56.99%	±2.23%	
	high	40.85%	±1.52%		59.66%	±2.22%	
DDE	low	42.10%	±1.66%	−6.11%	55.31%	±2.35%	6.04%
	high	35.99%	±1.40%		61.35%	±2.09%	
DNR	low	37.79%	±1.47%	2.51%	54.07%	±1.79%	8.52%
	high	40.30%	±1.64%		62.59%	±2.55%	
DL	low	40.70%	±1.43%	−3.32%	63.07%	±2.04%	−9.48%
	high	37.38%	±1.66%		53.59%	±2.33%	

DDO: distribution of donations; QDM: quality of donation mixture; DDE: distribution of the demand; DNR: distribution of network resources (capacity, budget, and vehicles); DL: disaster location.

Table 6 shows that all of the factors similarly impacted the network performance, with two exceptions. Firstly, QDM did not seem to affect the metric $\overline{\max U}$. Secondly, DNR and DL had a much greater impact than other factors on the metric $\overline{\max U}$. This larger effect can be explained, at least partially, by the fact that disasters increase the demand and transportation costs in the affected zone. Therefore, banks with relatively low resources exhaust their budget rapidly when they are within the disaster zone; hence, a network where resources are unevenly distributed is more susceptible to bottlenecks caused by banks with limited capacity, and banks with low availability of resources have a greater impact on the performance of the network than the location of the disaster.

Regarding the remaining factors, a poor food mix quality provided by the donors reduced the aid distributed by the network. If one type of product is less available, it limits the quantity of the other types that can be delivered, even if the banks have plenty of them. Although the model tries to correct unbalance on the mix of the donations by reassigning donors to banks or by transferring food between banks, these activities incur logistic costs that in some cases exceed the available budget or the amount of food that a bank can process. On average, instances having a "bad" composition of food mix increased $\overline{\overline{U}}$ by 3.62% but had no significant increase in $\overline{\max U}$. Furthermore, the factors DDE and DDO showed similar impacts on $\overline{\overline{U}}$ and $\overline{\max U}$, which means that the performance of the network is sensitive to the location of the demand and the location of the supply. These effects were diminished when the demand was equally distributed among the communities. Finally, it is worth mentioning that analysis of variance of the full factorial experimental design indicated that the disaster scenarios only explained 12.3% of the variation of $\overline{\overline{U}}$ and 18.7% of the variation of $\overline{\max U}$, while the configurations explained 80% and 64%, respectively.

Next, we analyzed how the different reconfigurations affected the effectiveness and the efficiency of the network. Table 7 reports, for each configuration, the average computational time $\overline{T}$ in seconds to solve each instance to optimality, effectiveness metrics $\overline{\overline{U}}$ and $\overline{\max U}$ and the metrics related to efficiency $\overline{Don}$, the ratio between quantities actually delivered to communities and the available donations, and $\overline{Bud}$, the average usage of each bank's budget. These are relevant metrics for the banks, as spending their entire budget on a single response operation will leave them vulnerable to future disasters. Higher values of $\overline{Bud}$ indicate that more resources of the network are spent, but not necessarily that the cost is translated to higher performance. Therefore, we also report an efficiency metric, $\overline{E} = (1 - U)/\overline{Bud}$, based on the percentage of met demand and the percentage of budget spent among banks. Additionally, we measured the usage of the flexibility granted by each network reconfiguration, in order to quantify its potential. In the case of the first stage (donation collection), we report $\overline{DB}$, which is computed as the percentage of donors whose assignment has changed with respect to the day-to-day operations. Regarding the second level (transshipment), $\overline{BB}$ reports the percentage of donations received by each bank that is transferred to another bank. Finally, $\overline{BC}$ provides the ratio between the number of goods delivered from each bank to communities that it does not serve in the regular operations and its total output flow.

Table 7. Aggregated results produced by each configuration to the 320 instances.

Conf.	$\overline{T}$	$\overline{\overline{U}}$		$\overline{\max U}$		$\overline{Don}$	$\overline{Bud}$	$\overline{E}$	$\overline{DB}$	$\overline{BB}$	$\overline{BB}$
		%	hw	%	hw						
0	–	19.4%	±1.4%	31.9%	±4.7%	87.2%	38.0%	2.1%	-	-	-
1	0.4	55.8%	±1.1%	75.2%	±1.1%	49.7%	83.3%	0.5%	-	-	-
2	25.7	27.9%	±1.1%	70.4%	±1.1%	80.9%	98.2%	0.7%	91.5%	-	-
3	0.15	48.13%	±1.1%	54.9%	±0.6%	54.8%	99.9%	0.5%	-	16.7%	-
4	58.04	44.54%	±1.2%	65.0%	±2.1%	58.2%	96.8%	0.6%	-	-	27.4%
5	82.0	19.99%	±1.5%	25.9%	±2.5%	87.3%	99.1%	0.8%	86.8%	18.7%	20.1%

Before starting the performance analysis, let us briefly discuss the reported computational times. As it was mentioned earlier, times depend strongly on the configuration applied, varying from a fraction of a second for configurations 1 and 3 up to 82 s. in the case of configuration 5.

Table 7 shows that, compared to the day-to-day performance (configuration 0), the levels of unmet demand were significantly higher in disaster scenarios when the baseline configuration used (configuration 1). Indeed, the results obtained for the day-to-day scenarios are uniquely presented as an upper bound for reference on how much the performance of the network could be diminished in a disaster setting—even if the ratio of total available donations to total demand remained basically the same—and to identify differences in the use of the network. Table 7 also shows that the best performance, in terms of $\overline{\overline{U}}$ and $\overline{\max U}$, was achieved by the most flexible configuration (configuration 5), although the results in $\overline{\overline{U}}$ produced by configuration 2 were close. The better performance of configurations 2 and 5 can be explained, as shown by metric $\overline{DB}$, by their ability to perform the re-assignment of donors to banks.

Figure 4 shows, for both levels of the factor DNR, the results for $\overline{\max U}$. It can be seen that when the resources were densely distributed (for example, DNR = 1), the results produced by configuration 2 were greatly deteriorated. The poorest performances were produced by configurations 1 (the baseline) and 4, which demonstrated that reassigning communities to banks alone is ineffective in the rebalancing of supply and demand in the case of a disaster.

As per the efficiency-oriented metrics, configurations 2 and 5 had the highest percentage of donations delivered ($\overline{Don}$), consistent with the results obtained for $\overline{\overline{U}}$ and $\overline{\max U}$, whereas configuration 1 and 3 achieved the poorest values. Concerning the budget utilization $\overline{Bud}$, configurations 1 and 4 had the lowest values, whereas configurations 2, 3, and 5 were close to 100% budget utilization. The efficiency indicator $\overline{E}$ showed, again, that configurations 2 and 5 offered the best results under disaster scenarios, displaying the highest amount of demand satisfied per percentage of budget spent for both levels of the network resource distribution factor. On the other hand, configuration 3 was among the least efficient. To summarize, a network reconfiguration in the highest level of the distribution chain is beneficial for performance and more cost-effective than reconfigurations in the lower levels.

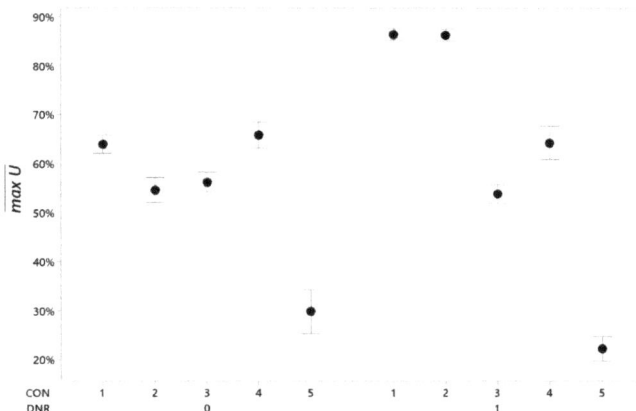

Figure 4. Confidence intervals for maximum unmet demand ($\alpha = 0.05$).

7. Discussion

Altogether, the numerical results of the experiments demonstrated that the transition from day-to-day operations to a crisis is critical from a logistics planning standpoint. Moreover, a significant deterioration of the network performance can be expected if the network does not adapt its configuration, even if the total amount of donated food increases in the same proportion as the demand.

To cope with urgent situations, such as those in the aftermath of a natural disaster, the decentralized management approach, as practiced by BAMX, needs to be replaced by cooperative strategies focused on the reallocation of resources to achieve a higher and fairer fulfillment of the needs of the affected people. The results confirmed that situations where resources, such as capacity and budget, are unevenly distributed throughout the network, although efficient in day-to-day operations, tend to cause bottlenecks in the lowest-capacity nodes, which may cause high levels of unmet demand in the disaster zones, depending on the distribution strategy used. This may suggest that an alternative strategy, in which specific resources for emergencies are managed in a centralized rather than decentralized manner, should lead to better results.

Our experiments also indicated that a partial reconfiguration, limited to the reassignment of food donors to banks, can yield very good results in a budget-balanced network and, as such reallocations are the most efficient, the negotiations between managers to cope with urgent situations should focus on them. Furthermore, the food mixture constraints can be better handled if they are considered within the upper-level decisions of the distribution chain; that is, during the planning of food collection from donors. Once a donation of the wrong mix reaches a bank, it becomes very costly, in terms of time and money, to execute redistribution among banks, creating a bottleneck in the network.

We also observed that trying to adapt the distribution part of the supply chain to mitigate an imbalance in food mixture and availability leads to transport routes that are too expensive or require too much time, delaying delivery beyond the acceptable target. Whereas donors can be reassigned easily to a new bank, banks often need to create less efficient routes to distribute to other regions. However, this conclusion strongly depends on the topological characteristics of the considered instance.

To summarize, the proposed mathematical model and its various configurations can be used to help guide foodbank managers in the challenging process of adapting their day-to-day operations to cope with the extreme requirements in the aftermath of a natural disaster. Considering the short time available to make decisions and the fact that, in practice, there is no formal protocol to support bank coordination, knowing that a rather small set of decisions have the most impact on network performance may help managers to focus first on these decisions and establish prioritized lines of action, in order to better respond to disaster situations.

8. Conclusions

We considered the problem of re-organizing foodbank logistics to cope with the extraordinary needs resulting from the occurrence of a natural disaster. Inspired by the real case of Bancos de Alimentos de México (BAMX), a food bank network in Mexico, this paper contributes a mathematical formulation that extends existing ones to encompass the whole supply chain, from donors to communities. Furthermore, it considers several types of products and incorporates restrictions on their proportions to guarantee the quality of the food delivered to communities from a nutritional perspective. Finally, it empirically analyzed the performance of five different options for network reconfiguration in terms of effectiveness and efficiency. From a practical standpoint, the empirical results offer insights that can be useful guiding foodbank managers in the challenging process of adapting their day-to-day operations to cope with the extreme requirements in the aftermath of a natural disaster. In particular, the experiments showed that the demand satisfaction levels at the communities served by the foodbanks may decrease drastically when the distribution of the demand changes, even if there is a rise in food supply and budget to cope with it. Additionally, the results showed that an uneven distribution of network resources can have a negative impact on the performance of a foodbank network when the day-to-day configuration is used or when only the upper section of the supply chain is modified. Finally, the results demonstrate that different network configurations from the centralized decision-maker perspective can lead to interesting results. As expected, giving responsibility to the whole range of decisions to the CLM offers the most effective performance. Despite this, the results showed that a network configuration focused only on the reassignment of food donors to the banks gives similar results in most scenarios. This is because the model can better deal with the food mixture constraints if they are addressed in the upper level of the distribution chain, which may give different results in networks that lack constraints of this type. Once a donation of the wrong mix reaches a bank, it tends to become too costly, in terms of time and money, to redistribute to other banks, thus creating a bottleneck in the network. With the prior knowledge of this, the process of negotiation between banks and the CLM can be accelerated, thereby improving the crucial response time when a disaster strikes, which may also help in the implementation of long-term interbank cooperation policies for the organization.

This work raises the need for additional research in certain directions. First, it is necessary to address the fairness of the measures taken by the CLM from the perspective of the individual banks, as well as the impact on performance when there is resistance to cooperation. Second, the variable nature of the donation volumes could be considered in a stochastic approach to the presented model. This implies a shift of focus from response execution to response planning. Finally, this work focuses on the first response offered by food banks to relief the affected people in the aftermath of a natural disaster. However, it does not consider the continuity of the operations between this first response and the moment the communities get back to normal and the food banks return to their day-to-day activities. Additional research is required to develop models supporting decision makers in this dynamic transition where the population's needs, and the consequences of the disaster dynamically evolve.

Author Contributions: Conceptualization, E.O., N.R.S. and A.R.; methodology, E.O., N.R.S. and A.R.; software, E.O.; validation, N.R.S. and A.R.; writing—original draft, E.O.; writing—review and editing, N.R.S. and A.R. All authors have read and agreed to the published version of the manuscript.

Funding: This research was partially supported by Conacyt and the School of Engineering and Sciences of the Tecnológico de Monterrey.

Institutional Review Board Statement: Not applicable.

Informed Consent Statement: Not applicable.

Data Availability Statement: The data presented in this study are available from the corresponding author upon request.

Acknowledgments: The authors thank Adrian Alvarez Alvarado, logistics manager of BAMX, for providing ample information and for his constructive comments and valuable insights.

Conflicts of Interest: The authors declare no conflict of interest.

References

1. Moshtari, M.; Altay, N.; Heikkilä, J.; Gonçalves, P. Procurement in humanitarian organizations: Body of knowledge and practitioner's challenges. *Int. J. Prod. Econ.* **2021**, *233*, 108017. [CrossRef]
2. The Global Food Banking Network, Why We Exist—The Global FoodBanking Network, (n.d.). Available online: https://www.foodbanking.org/why-we-exist/ (accessed on 14 March 2021).
3. Martin, K.S.; Wolff, M.; Callahan, K.; Schwartz, M.B. Supporting Wellness at Pantries: Development of a Nutrition Stoplight System for Food Banks and Food Pantries. *J. Acad. Nutr. Diet.* **2019**, *119*, 553–559. [CrossRef] [PubMed]
4. Scrinis, G. Reframing malnutrition in all its forms: A critique of the tripartite classification of malnutrition. *Glob. Food Sec.* **2020**, *26*, 100396. [CrossRef]
5. Adepoju, A.A.; Allen, S. Malnutrition in developing countries: Nutrition disorders, a leading cause of ill health in the world today. *Paediatr. Child Health* **2019**, *29*, 394–400. [CrossRef]
6. THE 17 GOALS | Sustainable Development, (n.d.). Available online: https://sdgs.un.org/goals (accessed on 20 June 2021).
7. Zhu, Z.; Chu, F.; Dolgui, A.; Chu, C.; Zhou, W.; Piramuthu, S. Recent advances and opportunities in sustainable food supply chain: A model-oriented review. *Int. J. Prod. Res.* **2018**, *56*, 5700–5722. [CrossRef]
8. Grunow, M.; van der Vorst, J. Food production and supply chain management. *OR Spectr.* **2010**, *32*, 861–862. [CrossRef]
9. Lien, R.W.; Iravani, S.M.R.; Smilowitz, K.R. Sequential Resource Allocation for Nonprofit Operations. *Oper. Res.* **2014**, *62*, 301–317. [CrossRef]
10. Huang, M.; Smilowitz, K.; Balcik, B. Models for relief routing: Equity, efficiency and efficacy. *Transp. Res. Part E Logist. Transp. Rev.* **2012**, *48*, 2–18. [CrossRef]
11. Orgut, I.S.; Brock, L.G., III; Davis, L.B.; Ivy, J.S.; Jiang, S.; Morgan, S.D.; Uzsoy, R.; Hale, C.; Middleton, E. *Achieving Equity, Effectiveness, and Efficiency in Food Bank Operations: Strategies for Feeding America with Implications for Global Hunger Relief*; Zobel, C.W., Altay, N., Haselkorn, M.P., Eds.; Springer International Publishing: Cham, Switzerland, 2016; pp. 229–256. [CrossRef]
12. Holguín-Veras, J.; Pérez, N.; Jaller, M.; van Wassenhove, L.N.; Aros-Vera, F. On the appropriate objective function for post-disaster humanitarian logistics models. *J. Oper. Manag.* **2013**, *31*, 262–280. [CrossRef]
13. Anaya-Arenas, A.M.; Renaud, J.; Ruiz, A. Relief distribution networks: A systematic review. *Ann. Oper. Res.* **2014**, *223*, 53–79. [CrossRef]
14. Balcik, B.; Smilowitz, K. *Contributions to Humanitarian and Non-Profit Operations: Equity Impacts on Modeling and Solution Approaches*; Springer: Cham, Switzerland, 2020; pp. 371–390. [CrossRef]
15. Anaya-Arenas, A.M.; Ruiz, A.; Renaud, J. *Models for a Fair Humanitarian Relief Distribution*; CIRRELT: Montreal, QC, Canada, 2016.
16. Anaya-Arenas, A.M.; Ruiz, A.; Renaud, J. Importance of fairness in humanitarian relief distribution. *Prod. Plan. Control* **2018**, *29*, 1145–1157. [CrossRef]
17. Orgut, I.S.; Ivy, J.S.; Uzsoy, R.; Hale, C. Robust optimization approaches for the equitable and effective distribution of donated food. *Eur. J. Oper. Res.* **2018**, *269*, 516–531. [CrossRef]
18. Martins, I.; Guedes, T.; Rama, P.; Ramos, J.; Tchemisova, T. Modelling the problem of food distribution by the Portuguese food banks. *Int. J. Math. Model. Numer. Optim.* **2011**, *2*, 313. [CrossRef]
19. Alkaabneh, F.; Diabat, A.; Gao, H.O. A unified framework for efficient, effective, and fair resource allocation by food banks using an Approximate Dynamic Programming approach. *Omega* **2021**, *100*, 102300. [CrossRef]
20. Gómez-Pantoja, J.Á.; Salazar-Aguilar, M.A.; González-Velarde, J.L. The food bank resource allocation problem. *TOP* **2021**, *29*, 266–286. [CrossRef]
21. Ross, M.; Campbell, E.C.; Webb, K.L. Recent Trends in the Nutritional Quality of Food Banks' Food and Beverage Inventory: Case Studies of Six California Food Banks. *J. Hunger Environ. Nutr.* **2013**, *8*, 294–309. [CrossRef]
22. Campbell, E.C.; Ross, M.; Webb, K.L. Improving the Nutritional Quality of Emergency Food: A Study of Food Bank Organizational Culture, Capacity, and Practices. *J. Hunger Environ. Nutr.* **2013**, *8*, 261–280. [CrossRef]
23. Chapnick, M.; Barnidge, E.; Sawicki, M.; Elliott, M. Healthy Options in Food Pantries—A Qualitative Analysis of Factors Affecting the Provision of Healthy Food Items in St. Louis, Missouri. *J. Hunger Environ. Nutr.* **2019**, *14*, 262–280. [CrossRef]
24. Leiras, A.; de Brito, I.; Peres, E.Q.; Bertazzo, T.R.; Yoshizaki, H.T.Y. Literature review of humanitarian logistics research: Trends and challenges. *J. Humanit. Logist. Supply Chain Manag.* **2014**, *4*, 95–130. [CrossRef]
25. Yáñez-Sandivari, L.; Cortés, C.E.; Rey, P.A. Humanitarian logistics and emergencies management: New perspectives to a sociotechnical problem and its optimization approach management. *Int. J. Disaster Risk Reduct.* **2021**, *52*, 101952. [CrossRef]

26. Horner, M.W.; Downs, J.A. Optimizing hurricane disaster relief goods distribution: Model development and application with respect to planning strategies. *Disasters* **2010**, *34*, 821–844. [CrossRef] [PubMed]
27. Hong, X.; Lejeune, M.A.; Noyan, N. Stochastic network design for disaster preparedness. *IIE Trans.* **2015**, *47*, 329–357. [CrossRef]
28. Viswanath, K.; Peeta, S. The multicommodity maximal covering network design problem. In Proceedings of the IEEE 5th International Conference on Intelligent Transportation Systems, Singapore, 6 September 2002; IEEE: Piscataway, NJ, USA, 2002; pp. 505–510. [CrossRef]
29. Huang, X.; Song, L. An emergency logistics distribution routing model for unexpected events. *Ann. Oper. Res.* **2018**, *269*, 223–239. [CrossRef]
30. de la Torre, L.E.; Dolinskaya, I.S.; Smilowitz, K.R. Disaster relief routing: Integrating research and practice. *Socio-Econ. Plan. Sci.* **2012**, *46*, 88–97. [CrossRef]
31. Li, H.; Li, D.; Jiang, D. Optimising the configuration of food supply chains. *Int. J. Prod. Res.* **2020**, *59*, 3722–3746. [CrossRef]
32. Sucky, E. Coordinated order and production policies in supply chains. *OR Spektrum* **2004**, *26*, 493–520. [CrossRef]
33. Safaei, A.S.; Farsad, S.; Paydar, M.M. Robust bi-level optimization of relief logistics operations. *Appl. Math. Model.* **2018**, *56*, 359–380. [CrossRef]
34. Mohammadi, M.; Esmaelian, M.; Atighehchian, A. Design of mathematical models for the integration of purchase and production lot-sizing and scheduling problems under demand uncertainty. *Appl. Math. Model.* **2020**, *84*, 1–18. [CrossRef]
35. Mahmoudi, M.; Shirzad, K.; Verter, V. Decision support models for managing food aid supply chains: A systematic literature review. *Socio-Econ. Plan. Sci.* **2022**, 101255. [CrossRef]
36. Naji-Azimi, Z.; Renaud, J.; Ruiz, A.; Salari, M. A covering tour approach to the location of satellite distribution centers to supply humanitarian aid. *Eur. J. Oper. Res.* **2012**, *222*, 596–605. [CrossRef]
37. Boostani, A.; Jolai, F.; Bozorgi-Amiri, A. Designing a sustainable humanitarian relief logistics model in pre- and postdisaster management. *Int. J. Sustain. Transp.* **2021**, *15*, 604–620. [CrossRef]
38. Davis, L.B.; Sengul, I.; Ivy, J.S.; Brock, L.G.; Miles, L. Scheduling food bank collections and deliveries to ensure food safety and improve access. *Socio-Econ. Plan. Sci.* **2014**, *48*, 175–188. [CrossRef]
39. Solak, S.; Scherrer, C.; Ghoniem, A. The stop-and-drop problem in nonprofit food distribution networks. *Ann. Oper. Res.* **2014**, *221*, 407–426. [CrossRef]
40. Reihaneh, M.; Ghoniem, A. A multi-start optimization-based heuristic for a food bank distribution problem. *J. Oper. Res. Soc.* **2018**, *69*, 691–706. [CrossRef]
41. Gunes, C.; van Hoeve, W.-J.; Tayur, S. Vehicle Routing for Food Rescue Programs: A Comparison of Different Approaches. In Proceedings of the Integration of AI and OR Techniques in Constraint Programming for Combinatorial Optimization Problems: 7th International Conference, CPAIOR 2010, Bologna, Italy, 14–18 June 2010; pp. 176–180. [CrossRef]
42. Balcik, B.; Iravani, S.; Smilowitz, K. Multi-vehicle sequential resource allocation for a nonprofit distribution system. *IIE Trans.* **2014**, *46*, 1279–1297. [CrossRef]
43. Eisenhandler, O.; Tzur, M. The Humanitarian Pickup and Distribution Problem. *Oper. Res.* **2019**, *67*, 10–32. [CrossRef]
44. Eisenhandler, O.; Tzur, M. A Segment-Based Formulation and a Matheuristic for the Humanitarian Pickup and Distribution Problem. *Transp. Sci.* **2019**, *53*, 1389–1408. [CrossRef]
45. Nair, D.J.; Grzybowska, H.; Fu, Y.; Dixit, V.V. Scheduling and routing models for food rescue and delivery operations. *Socio -Econ. Plan. Sci.* **2018**, *63*, 18–32. [CrossRef]
46. Rey, D.; Almi'ani, K.; Nair, D.J. Exact and heuristic algorithms for finding envy-free allocations in food rescue pickup and delivery logistics. *Transp. Res. Part E Logist. Transp. Rev.* **2018**, *112*, 19–46. [CrossRef]
47. Martins, C.L.; Melo, M.T.; Pato, M.V. Redesigning a food bank supply chain network in a triple bottom line context. *Int. J. Prod. Econ.* **2019**, *214*, 234–247. [CrossRef]
48. DATOS QUE ALIMENTAN—BAMX, (n.d.). Available online: https://www.bamx.org.mx/datos-que-alimentan/ (accessed on 28 April 2020).
49. Orgut, I.S.; Ivy, J.; Uzsoy, R. Modeling for the equitable and effective distribution of food donations under stochastic receiving capacities. *IISE Trans.* **2017**, *49*, 567–578. [CrossRef]

Article

An Artificial Bee Colony Algorithm for Static and Dynamic Capacitated Arc Routing Problems

Zsuzsanna Nagy [1,*], Ágnes Werner-Stark [1] and Tibor Dulai [1]

Department of Electrical Engineering and Information Systems, Faculty of Information Technology, University of Pannonia, Egyetem St. 10, 8200 Veszprém, Hungary; werner.agnes@virt.uni-pannon.hu (Á.W.); dulai.tibor@virt.uni-pannon.hu (T.D.)
* Correspondence: nagy.zsuzsanna@virt.uni-pannon.hu

Abstract: The Capacitated Arc Routing Problem (CARP) is a combinatorial optimization problem, which requires the identification of such route plans on a given graph to a number of vehicles that generates the least total cost. The Dynamic CARP (DCARP) is a variation of the CARP that considers dynamic changes in the problem. The Artificial Bee Colony (ABC) algorithm is an evolutionary optimization algorithm that was proven to be able to provide better performance than many other evolutionary algorithms, but it was not used for the CARP before. For this reason, in this study, an ABC algorithm for the CARP (CARP-ABC) was developed along with a new move operator for the CARP, the sub-route plan operator. The CARP-ABC algorithm was tested both as a CARP and a DCARP solver, then its performance was compared with other existing algorithms. The results showed that it excels in finding a relatively good quality solution in a short amount of time, which makes it a competitive solution. The efficiency of the sub-route plan operator was also tested and the results showed that it is more likely to find better solutions than other operators.

Keywords: capacitated arc routing problem; dynamic capacitated arc routing problem; artificial bee colony algorithm; evolutionary optimization; move operator

MSC: 68W50; 90B06; 90B20; 90C27; 90C35; 90C59; 90C90

Citation: Nagy, Z.; Werner-Stark, Á.; Dulai, T. An Artificial Bee Colony Algorithm for Static and Dynamic Capacitated Arc Routing Problems. *Mathematics* **2022**, *10*, 2205. https://doi.org/10.3390/math10132205

Academic Editors: Zsolt Tibor Kosztyán and Zoltán Kovács

Received: 27 May 2022
Accepted: 22 June 2022
Published: 24 June 2022

Publisher's Note: MDPI stays neutral with regard to jurisdictional claims in published maps and institutional affiliations.

Copyright: © 2022 by the authors. Licensee MDPI, Basel, Switzerland. This article is an open access article distributed under the terms and conditions of the Creative Commons Attribution (CC BY) license (https://creativecommons.org/licenses/by/4.0/).

1. Introduction

The Capacitated Arc Routing Problem (CARP) is an NP-hard combinatorial optimization problem that was first introduced by Golden and Wong in [1]. The CARP requires determining the least cost route plans on a graph of a road network for vehicles subject to some constraints. It has many applications in real life, for instance, in winter gritting [2,3] or in urban solid waste collection [4,5]. Since the CARP is an NP-hard problem, instead of exact methods, mainly heuristics and meta-heuristics (e.g., [6–10]) are considered in the literature to find solutions. The existing methods are either too slow or do not give enough good quality solutions, so there is still room for improvements.

The standard CARP assumes a static problem, which is not the closest to real life, where changes may happen during the execution of the solution. These changes modify the instance, and thus, may have an effect on the feasibility and optimality of the current solution [11]. For this reason, the Dynamic CARP (DCARP), which is a variation of the CARP that takes into account dynamic changes, is a better approach. To make the model of the problem under consideration closer to the real-life problem, the changes should be made based on the collected information about the vehicles and the roads. For instance, information can be provided by the drivers of the vehicles about the executed tasks, by the GPS of the vehicles about their current position, and (indirectly) by traffic patrol drones [12] about the current state of the roads.

The Artificial Bee Colony (ABC) algorithm is a swarm intelligence-based algorithm for optimization problems [13]. It was successfully applied on multiple combinatorial optimization problems that are similar to the CARP [14–19] and was shown that the ABC algorithm provides better performance than most of the evolutionary computation-based optimization algorithms [16]. However, the ABC algorithm was never applied before, neither on the CARP nor on the DCARP.

In our previous work [20], we collected all the possible events and analyzed their effects on the model. Based on the results, a data-driven DCARP framework with three event handling algorithms and a rerouting algorithm (RR1) was developed. The framework uses 'the "virtual task" strategy [21] to be able to use static CARP solvers for DCARP instances.

The contributions of this work are as follows:

1. The definition of the first ABC algorithm for the CARP (CARP-ABC).
2. The definition of a new small step-size move operator for the CARP, the sub-route plan operator, which is utilized in the CARP-ABC algorithm.
3. The definition of a new method for creating initial population, the RSG. The purpose of the RSG is to create random but feasible solutions for the CARP quickly.
4. Numerical experiments to test the CARP-ABC algorithm on a variety of CARP and DCARP instances. The same experiments were performed with other algorithms for CARP, then the results were compared. The results showed that for both CARP and DCARP instances, the CARP-ABC algorithm excels in finding a relatively good quality solution in a short amount of time.
5. Numerical experiments to test the efficiency of the sub-route plan operator within the CARP-ABC algorithm, on a variety of CARP instances. The results showed that the sub-route plan operator is more likely to find a better solution than the other operators, especially when a greater modification is needed on the current solution (since it is a randomly generated solution and/or it is a solution of a larger CARP instance).

The rest of the paper is structured as follows. In Section 2, the related works are presented. In Section 3, the basic concepts related to the proposed CARP-ABC algorithm is introduced. In Section 4 and Section 5, the algorithm and the sub-route plan move operator are formulated in detail, respectively. In Section 6, the experiments and their results are discussed. The paper is concluded in Section 7.

2. Related Works

In this section, the related works are introduced. In Section 2.1, the algorithms that were developed for CARP are presented. In Section 2.2, the approaches for DCARP are summarized. In Section 2.3, the ABC algorithms that were developed for problems that are similar to the CARP are presented.

2.1. Algorithms for the CARP

As it was mentioned in Section 1, there are mainly approximate approaches (i.e., heuristics and metaheuristics) for the CARP. For this reason, only the methods that belong to that category are mentioned in this subsection.

2.1.1. Heuristics

Golden et al. developed the first heuristic algorithms for the CARP, namely, the path-scanning and the augment-merge [22]. Other notable heuristics for the CARP are the parallel-insert method [23], Ulusoy's tour splitting method [24], the augment-insert method [25], the path-scanning with ellipse rule [26] and the path-scanning with efficiency rule [27].

2.1.2. Metaheuristics

The metaheuristic algorithms for the CARP can be divided into two main categories (with some exceptions): trajectory-based and population-based.

From the trajectory-based algorithms, the notable ones are the guided local search algorithm [28], the tabu search algorithms [29,30], the variable neighborhood search algorithm [31], and the greedy randomized adaptive search procedure with evolutionary path relinking [32]. It must be mentioned that in [29], two versions of the tabu search algorithm (TSA) were proposed (TSA1 and TSA2), from which the latter performed better. In [33], a global repair operator was developed and embedded into the TSA, creating the repair-based tabu search (RTS), which outperforms the TSA.

From the population-based algorithms, the notable ones are the genetic algorithm [34], the memetic algorithms [6,35], and the ant colony optimization algorithms [8,36,37]. From these, the Memetic Algorithm with Extended Neighborhood Search (MAENS) [6] is the most popular one, even though it only gives relatively good quality solutions and also has slow runtime. There are multiple solutions that try to improve some parts of the MAENS (e.g., [9,10]), but these improvements do not really increase the overall performance of it. The Ant Colony Optimization Algorithm with Path Relinking (ACOPR) [8] gives only relatively good quality solutions, but currently it has the fastest runtime on most of the CARP instances from the benchmark test sets.

The Hybrid Metaheuristic Approach (HMA) [7] is a population-based algorithm that utilizes a randomized tabu thresholding procedure as a part of its local refinement procedure. The HMA gives the best quality solutions among all existing algorithms and has faster runtime than MAENS, but it is still relatively slow on some real-life based CARP instances. The ACOPR gives only relatively good quality solutions, but currently, it has the fastest runtime on most of the CARP instances from the benchmark test sets.

2.2. Approaches for the DCARP

Despite the importance of the DCARP, the number of studies about CARP (or ARP) that consider dynamic changes in the problem during the execution of the solution are relatively small [20,21,38–45]. Moreover, there are only three studies that consider more than two type of changes [20,21,42] and only two of them (including our previous work) considers all the critical changes that can happen [20,21]. (For a more detailed comparison see [11,20].) Critical changes or events may change the problem to such an extent that the current solution is not feasible anymore, so handling them is essential. Both [20,21] propose a framework for the DCARP that, instead of using complex specialized algorithms, allows the use of any static CARP solvers for solving a DCARP instance.

To the best of our knowledge, the data-driven solution for the DCARP introduced in [20] is the only data-driven approach for DCARP or even CARP.

2.3. The ABC Algorithm and Its Applications

The original ABC algorithm was proposed by Karaboga in [13]. In [46], Karaboga and Görkemli proposed a new definition for the search behavior of the onlooker bees, which improved the convergence performance of the algorithm. For this reason, the new version of the ABC algorithm was named quick ABC (qABC).

The ABC algorithm was introduced as an algorithm for multivariable and multi-modal continuous function optimization, but later it was successfully applied on other types of optimization problems as well. Karaboga and Görkemli introduced an ABC and a qABC algorithm for combinatorial problems (CABC and qCABC, respectively) and applied them to the Traveling Salesman Problem (TSP) [14,15]. Both algorithms use the Greedy Sub Tour Mutation (GSTM) operator [47], which was developed to increase the performance of a genetic algorithm (GA) that solves the TSP. It was proven that the GSTM is significantly faster and and more accurate than other existing mutation operators [47]. Furthermore, it was shown that the ABC and the qABC algorithm provide better performance than many evolutionary computation-based optimization algorithms [16]. Since the TSP is similar to the CARP, in the hope that an ABC algorithm with a mutation operator such as GSTM will perform well, we developed the CARP-ABC algorithm (Section 4) with the sub-route plan operator (Section 5).

There are also ABC algorithms for the Vehicle Routing Problem (VRP) [48] and its variations [17,18]. However, there is only one ABC algorithm for the CARP and even that is for just a variation of CARP, the undirected CARP with profits [19]. Therefore, to the best of our knowledge, currently there are no ABC algorithms, neither for the CARP nor for the DCARP.

3. Problem Formulations

This section introduces basic concepts related to the proposed CARP-ABC algorithm to help to understand how it works. The concepts are introduced only briefly, for a more detailed description the corresponding works are referred to.

In this section, first, the static CARP, then the (data-driven) DCARP is formulated. It is followed by the introduction of the basic ABC algorithm and the existing move operators for CARP (which are used in the proposed CARP-ABC solution). The notations used for the CARP and the DCARP are collected in Table A1 in Appendix A.

3.1. The CARP

In the existing works, as the input graph, some assume an undirected graph [7], others assume a directed graph [8,49], and other ones a mixed graph [6,34]. In this work, a directed graph is assumed, in which undirected edges are regarded as two oppositely directed edges.

The (directed) graph of the CARP can be described the following way: $G = (V, A)$, with a set of vertices V and a set of arcs (directed edges) A. A set of tasks $T \subseteq A$ is also given, which defines the arcs that have tasks assigned to them. If the graph of a CARP instance contains (undirected) edges, then an edge is added to A as a pair of arcs, one for each direction. For instance, if (v_i, v_j) is an edge and $v_i, v_j \in V$, then the arcs (v_i, v_j) and (v_j, v_i) are added to A. Similarly, if (v_i, v_j) is an edge with tasks assigned to it and $v_i, v_j \in V$, then the arcs (v_i, v_j) and (v_j, v_i) are added to T. The graph also has a special vertex v_0 ($v_0 \in V$), the depot, and a dummy task $t_0 = (v_0, v_0)$, the significance of which is explained later.

The tasks are performed by a fleet of w homogeneous vehicles of capacity q. Every vehicle starts and ends its route at the depot (v_0). Each task must be performed in a single operation, and each vehicle can satisfy at most as many demands as its maximum capacity.

The graph can be mapped to a road network where the arcs are road segments. Some of the road segments have tasks. To fulfill the tasks, different amounts but the same type of demand must be served. Each arc is characterized by the following functions:

- *head*: the head vertex of the arc;
- *tail*: the tail vertex of the arc;
- *dc*: the dead-heading or traversing cost, the cost of crossing the arc.

In addition, each task is characterized by the following functions:

- *id*: the unique identifier of the task, which is a positive integer;
- *dem*: (positive) demand, which indicates the load necessary to serve the task;
- *sc*: service cost, which is the cost of executing the task and crossing the arc (i.e., *dc* is included in *sc*).

Although an edge is regarded as two oppositely directed arcs, if a task is assigned to it, then the task should be executed only once, in either direction. Let $t \in T$ be a task of one of the arcs of an edge, then let $inv(t)$ denote the inversion of t, the other task of the edge. If $head(t)$ and $tail(t)$ are the head and the tail vertexes of t, then $head(inv(t)) = tail(t)$ and $tail(inv(t)) = head(t)$ are the head and the tail vertexes of $inv(t)$. The dc, dem and sc values are the same for t and $inv(t)$.

Let the total number of tasks that have to be executed by at least one of the vehicles be denoted by n. The value of n depends on the composition of T: if T only contains arc tasks from edges, then $n = |T|/2$, if T only contains arc tasks from arcs then $n = |T|$.

The minimal total dead-heading cost between two vertices is provided by the mdc : $V \times V \to N$ function, which uses Dijkstra's algorithm as the search algorithm. For instance, $mdc(v_i, v_j)$ denotes the minimal total dead-heading cost traversing from vertex v_i to vertex v_j, where $v_i, v_j \in V$.

A CARP instance (I) is defined as follows:

$$I = (V, v_0, A, T, n, w, q, head, tail, dc, id, dem, sc, inv, mdc) \qquad (1)$$

3.1.1. Solution Representation

A solution for a CARP instance is expressed as a set of route plans. The route plans are sequences of the $t \in T$ tasks that need to be executed in the given order. The consecutive tasks are connected by the shortest paths, which is provided by the mdc function. Therefore, a solution S for a CARP instance can be expressed the following way:

$$S = \{r_1, r_2, \ldots, r_{|S|}\} \tag{2}$$

where $|S|$ is the number of route plans and r_k ($k \in \{1, 2, \ldots, |S|\}$) is the k-th route plan within the solution S. The k-th route plan can be expressed the following way:

$$r_k = \langle t_0, t_{k,1}, t_{k,2}, \ldots, t_{k,l_k}, t_0 \rangle \tag{3}$$

where l_k is the number of (not dummy) tasks and $t_{k,i}$ is the i-th task within the k-th route plan. It must be noted that here, k is an index, which is only used to identify a specific route plan in the solution. The order of the route plans within the solution has no effect on the quality of the solution.

Since every route starts and ends in the depot, the dummy task t_0 – which represents the vehicle being in the depot – is added also as the first and the last element of the route plan sequences. Its id, dc, dem and sc are set to 0, and both the head and the tail vertexes are the depot vertex.

For the solution representation of the CARP, a natural encoding approach can be used, just like in most vehicle routing problems. This means that all route plans can be encoded as an ordered list of ids of the tasks, so a solution can be represented as the concatenation of these lists. However, every route plan starts and ends with the dummy task t_0, so if the encoded route plans are concatenated, then there are consecutive dummy tasks in the resulting list. For the sake of simplicity, only one of each consecutive dummy task is kept in the encoded solution. Figure 1 shows an example of a solution representation.

0	1	4	10	0	8	2	7	3	0	6	9	5	0

Figure 1. An example of a solution representation for a CARP instance with 10 required tasks, where 0 is the id of the dummy task. In this example, there are 3 routes. The first route services the tasks with ids 1, 4 and 10. The second services the tasks with ids 8, 2, 7 and 3. The third services the tasks with ids 6, 9 and 5.

3.1.2. Objective and Constraints

The objective of the CARP is to minimize the total cost of the solution S subject to some constraints, which are defined in this section. The total cost of a solution S (i.e., $TC(S)$) is calculated with the following formula (Equations (4)–(6)):

$$TC(S) = \sum_{k=1}^{|S|} DC(r_k) + SC(r_k) \tag{4}$$

$$DC(r_k) = mdc(t_0, head(t_{k,1})) + \sum_{i=1}^{l_k - 1} mdc(tail(t_{k,i}), head(t_{k,i+1})) + mdc(tail(t_{k,l_k}), t_0) \tag{5}$$

$$SC(r_k) = \sum_{i=1}^{l_k} sc(t_{k,i}) \tag{6}$$

where $DC(r_k)$ and $SC(r_k)$ are the total dead-heading and service cost of the route plan r_k.

The solution S has to satisfy the following constraints. First, each route plan starts and ends at the depot. Second, each task is executed exactly once. Therefore, the total number of tasks executed on each route plan (excluding the dummy task t_0) is equal to n:

$$\sum_{k=1}^{|S|} l_k = n \qquad (7)$$

Moreover, a task cannot be executed more than once, neither in the same route nor in another route:

$$t_{a,i} \neq t_{b,j}, \forall (a,i) \neq (b,j) \qquad (8)$$

where r_a and r_b are route plans within S, $t_{a,i}$ is the i-th task in the route plan r_a, and $t_{b,j}$ is the j-th task in the route plan r_b. If a task t has an inverse (i.e., $\exists inv(t)$), then either t or $inv(t)$ is executed. Both cannot be executed in the same solution. Third, the total demand served each route plan does not exceed the capacity (q) of the vehicle:

$$\sum_{i=1}^{l_k} dem(t_{k,i}) \leq q, \qquad \forall k \in \{1, 2, \ldots, |S|\} \qquad (9)$$

3.2. The Data-driven DCARP

There are various approaches for DCARP, but in this work, the data-driven version of DCARP is considered, which was recently formulated in [20].

In this problem, instead of one static CARP instance, there is a series of DCARP instances (i.e., a DCARP scenario [21]) that needs to be solved. A DCARP scenario is denoted by $\mathcal{I} = \langle I_0, I_1, \ldots, I_i, \ldots, I_{m-1} \rangle$, where m is the number of DCARP instances within the scenario (i.e., the number of dynamic events that occurred and changed the previous DCARP instance is $m-1$). Each I_i ($I_i \in \mathcal{I}$) DCARP instance contains all the information about the current problem. The previous DCARP instance I_{i-1}, the execution of the accepted solution for I_{i-1} and the occurred event(s) define the next DCARP instance I_i, where $0 < i < m$. The initial instance (I_0) can be viewed as a static (data-driven) CARP instance, since initially every vehicle is in the depot (in good state) and no task has been executed yet.

For a data-driven DCARP instance, information needs to be stored about all the vehicles and route plans. For each vehicle, the current location and state have to be known. Furthermore, identifiers are needed to be used for the vehicles and the route plans, since a vehicle may follow multiple route plans (one after another) and it is important to know for each route plan whether a vehicle already executed it, its execution is still in progress, or a vehicle still needed to be assigned to it to start its execution.

Instead of the number of vehicles (w), a set of identifiers of all the vehicles is needed to be defined, which is denoted by H. The set of the identifiers of the (currently) free vehicles is denoted by H_f ($H_f \subseteq H$), which is initially equal to H. The identifier of a vehicle is added to H_f, if the vehicle finishes the execution of a route plan, and the identifier is removed, when a new route plan is assigned to the vehicle. If the execution of all the tasks is finished and all the vehicles are returned to the depot (i.e., there are no broken down vehicles outside on the roads), then $H_f = H$, otherwise $H_f \subset H$.

The set of identifiers of all the route plans is denoted by R, and the set of identifiers of the route plans that currently cannot be modified and not executed by any vehicle is denoted by R_e ($R_e \subseteq R$). When a new route plan is created, its identifier is added to R, and when the execution of it is finished or suspended (due to vehicle breakdown), its identifier is added to R_e. If the execution of all the route plans is finished and there are no more tasks to execute, then $R_e = R$, otherwise $R_e \subset R$. The identifier is removed from R_e only if the vehicle which is assigned to it was broken, but got fixed and can continue the execution of the plan. The function that defines which vehicle is assigned to a specific route plan is denoted by $rv : R \rightarrow H$.

To store the current location of the vehicles in the instance, the virtual task strategy introduced in [21] is used, which replaces the executed tasks in each route plan with "virtual tasks". A "virtual task" is an arc whose *head* is the depot vertex v_0 and *tail* is the current location of the vehicle, vertex v ($v \in V$). For the sake of simplicity, it is assumed that when an unexpected event occurs, every vehicle is located exactly at a vertex. Since this task is "virtual", it cannot be traversed, for this reason, it has an infinite traversing cost (i.e., $dc(v) = \infty$). Furthermore, since it is a "task", there is a demand and a service cost assigned to it, which are calculated according to the provided data: the service cost is the total cost produced by the vehicle so far (i.e., it is the sum of traversing and serving cost of the arcs that were crossed or served by the vehicle), and the demand is the total demand served by the vehicle so far. A route plan can have at most one virtual task. Therefore, if a route plan already has a virtual task, then it is updated taking into account the arcs traversed and the tasks executed since then by the corresponding vehicle. The set of all virtual tasks is denoted by T_v ($T_v \subseteq T$), and the function that defines which virtual task belongs to a specific route plan is denoted by $rt : R \to T_v$.

The set of arc tasks that need to be executed is denoted by T. If according to the gathered information a task t ($t \in T$) was executed by the vehicle h ($h \in H$), then in the new DCARP instance t needs to be removed from T. Furthermore, the virtual task of the route plan of the vehicle (e.g., $t_{k,v}$, where $rv(k) = h$ and $t_{k,v} \in T_v$) needs to be updated. The new virtual task is generated in such a way that t is included in it (along with the other tasks the vehicle executed and arcs the vehicle traversed). If t has an inverse (i.e., $\exists inv(t)$), then it is removed from T as well. Accordingly, the total number of tasks that have to be executed (n) is decreased by one or two.

The initial DCARP instance (I_0) is similar to a static CARP instance. The sets of the route plan identifiers (R) and the function rv are created and filled only after the solution is found for I_0. The set H_f is initially equal to H, then based on rv, all the vehicle identifiers that are assigned to a route plan are removed from H_f. At this stage, the sets R_e and T_v are empty sets, therefore the function rt is an empty function as well. According to these, the initial DCARP instance (I_0) is defined as follows:

$$I_0 = (V, v_0, A, T, n, w, q, H, head, tail, dc, inv, dem, sc, mdc) \quad (10)$$

The subsequent DCARP instances (I_i, where $0 < i < m$) are defined as follows:

$$I_i = (V, v_0, A, T, T_v, n, q, H, H_f, R, R_e, rt, rv, head, tail, dc, inv, dem, sc, mdc) \quad (11)$$

3.2.1. Structure of a Scenario

A new DCARP instance is constructed and added to the DCARP scenario, when an unexpected event happens that changes the current problem to such an extent that it has effect on the currently executed solution. In [21] all the possible events (based on realistic assumptions) were collected and analyzed based on their effect.

It is assumed that the roadmap, the number of vehicles, and the maximum capacity of the vehicles cannot change (at least during the execution of the solution). Therefore, V, v_0, A, $head$, $tail$, inv, q and H are the same in all the DCARP instances of a DCARP scenario.

It is assumed that roads can become closed/opened (it changes dc, thus mdc, too), the traffic can decrease/increase (it changes dc and in some cases sc, thus mdc, too), tasks can get cancelled/added (it changes T, n, dem, and sc) and vehicles can breakdown/restart (it changes R_e), which are unexpected events. The expected events are the events that normally occur during the execution of the solution: a task is executed (it changes T), a vehicle moves (it changes T_v, thus rt, too), or a vehicle returns to the depot (it changes H_f and in some cases rv). The affected components are updated only when a new instance is constructed. If rerouting is performed, then R and rv may change, but the changes are visible only in the next DCARP instance. Therefore, T, T_v, n, H_f, R, R_e, rt, rv, dem, sc, dc, and mdc may be different among the DCARP instances of a DCARP scenario.

Since due to the unexpected events some components of the DCARP instance change, the optimal solution may change, too. It is one's choice to construct a new DCARP instance and reroute when there might be a better solution available, but the current solution is still feasible. However, constructing a new DCARP instance and rerouting is necessary when the current solution is not feasible anymore.

3.2.2. Solution Representation

For each DCARP instance, the solution representation is mainly the same as for static CARP instances. The only difference is that if the route plan has a virtual task assigned to it, then the virtual task is the second task within the route plan (since the first task is always the dummy task t_0). For instance, if the route plan $r_k = \langle t_0, t_{k,1}, t_{k,2}, \ldots, t_{k,l_k}, t_0 \rangle$ has an identifier k ($k \in R$) and there is a virtual task $t_{v,k}$ assigned to it (i.e., $rt(k) = t_{v,k}$), then $t_{k,1} = t_{v,k}$.

3.2.3. Objective and Constraints

For each DCARP instance, the objective and the constraints are mainly the same, as well as for static CARP instances. The only difference is at the second constraint, which requires that the total number of tasks in the solution S (excluding the dummy task t_0) is equal to the sum of the number of tasks that still need to be executed (n) and the total number of virtual tasks ($|T_v|$):

$$\sum_{k=1}^{|S|} l_k = n + |T_v| \qquad (12)$$

The attributes of a virtual task guarantee that a solver will always place the virtual task right after the dummy task within a route plan of a (nearly optimal) solution, so there is no need to add a constraint regarding it.

3.2.4. Finding a Solution

The data-driven DCARP framework allows rerouting when a critical event (i.e., an unexpected event that may change the feasibility of the current solution) occurs. These events are the task appearance, the demand increased and the vehicle breakdown.

The data-driven DCARP framework allows the use of static CARP solvers by converting the current data-driven DCARP instance into a static CARP instance. After a (sufficiently good) solution is found by the CARP solver, the solution is converted into a data-driven DCARP solution.

Converting a data-driven DCARP instance into a static CARP instance works as follows: the sets of vehicle and route plan identifiers (i.e., H, H_f, R, and R_e) are omitted, along with the related functions (rt and rv). Furthermore, all virtual tasks related to finished and suspended route plans are removed from T. For instance, if $rt(k) = t_{v,k}$ ($t_{v,k} \in T$) is the virtual task of the route plan with identifier k ($k \in R$) and $k \in R_e$, then $t_{v,k}$ is removed from T (i.e., $T \setminus \{t_{v,k}\}$).

Converting a static CARP solution into a data-driven DCARP solution works as follows: the virtual tasks that are related to finished and suspended route plans are added to the solution in separate route plans to keep track the total cost of the DCARP scenario. Furthermore, if there are any new route plans within the solution, the framework gives them identifiers and also attempts to assign each of them to a free vehicle. For the other route plans, it can be easily determined which route plan identifier belongs to which route plan, based on the virtual task within them.

3.3. The Basic ABC Algorithm

This section introduces the basic ABC algorithm for combinatorial problems, based on [16]. Just like in the original ABC algorithm [13], the artificial bees are classified into the three groups:

- employed bees, who are exploiting the food sources;
- onlooker bees, who are making the decision about which food source to select;
- scout bees, who are randomly choosing a new food source.

In the ABC algorithm, a food source is corresponded to a solution and the nectar amount of a food source is corresponded to the fitness of a solution.

The ABC algorithm is an iterative process with four phases in total. It begins with the initial phase, then it iterates three bee phases (always in the same order) until a predefined termination criterion is met. In the initial phase, the population is initialized with randomly generated food sources. In the first phase, the employed bee phase, the employed bees are sent to the food sources, where they determine the nectar amounts of the food sources. In the second phase, the onlooker bee phase, the probability value of the sources are calculated based on their nectar amount, then the onlooker bees are sent to the preferred food source to find neighboring food sources and determine their nectar amount. In the third phase, the scout bee phase, the exploitation process of the sources exhausted by the bees are stopped and the scout bees are sent out to randomly discover new food sources within the search area. In each phase, the best food source found so far is memorized. The phases are described in more detail in the subsections below.

3.3.1. Initialization Phase

In the initialization phase, the parameters and the population are initialized. The parameters of the ABC algorithm can be defined as follows:

- sn: the number of food sources, which is also the number of the employed bees and onlooker bees (i.e., for every food source, there is only one employed bee);
- $limit$: the number of trials after which a food source is assumed to be abandoned;
- a termination criterion.

The population is initialized by randomly generating sn number of food sources and assigning one employed bees to each of them. The employed bees evaluate the fitness of these solutions.

3.3.2. Employed Bee Phase

At this phase, each employed bee x_i generates a new food source x_{new} in the neighborhood of its current position. Once x_{new} is obtained, it will be evaluated and compared to x_i. If the nectar amount of x_{new} is equal to or higher than that of x_i, x_{new} replaces x_i and becomes a new member of the population, otherwise x_i is retained. In other words, a greedy selection mechanism is employed between the old and the new candidate solutions.

3.3.3. Onlooker Bee Phase

An onlooker bee evaluates the nectar information taken from all the employed bees and selects a food source x_i depending on its probability value p_i calculated by the following expression:

$$p_i = \frac{fit_i}{\sum_{j=1}^{sn} fit_j} \quad (13)$$

where fit_i is the nectar amount (i.e., the fitness value) of the i-th food source x_i. The higher the value of fit_i is, the higher the probability of that the i-th food source is selected.

Once the onlooker has selected her food source x_i, she produces a modification on x_i by using a local search operator. The local search operator randomly selects a position in the neighborhood of x_i. As in the case of the employed bees, if the modified food source has a better or equal nectar amount than x_i, the modified food source replaces x_i and becomes a new member in the population.

3.3.4. Scout Bee Phase

If a food source x_i cannot be further improved through a predetermined number of trials $limit$, the food source is assumed to be abandoned, and the corresponding employed bee becomes a scout. The scout produces a food source randomly.

In the basic ABC algorithm, in each cycle, at most one scout bee goes outside to search for a new food source.

3.4. Move Operators for the CARP

In population-based evolutionary algorithms, to enrich the diversity of the population, move operators with different levels of step-size are utilized to generate new, neighboring solutions. These move operators can be divided into two main categories: small step-size operators and large step-size operators. Small step-size operators can modify the position and/or the direction of the tasks within one or two route plans. In contrast, large step-size operators are able to modify more than two route plans. The most commonly used small step-size operators in the literature, which are used in this work as well, are inversion, (single) insertion, swap, and two-opt operators [6–8]. In this work, a novel small step-size operator is used as well, the sub-route plan operator, which is introduced in this work, in Section 5. The only large step-size operator used in this work is merge-split, which was introduced in [6]. It is called a large-step-size operator, since it is able to modify more than two route plans.

The inversion and the sub-route operators can only change the direction and the order of the tasks within one route plan, so they do not change the feasibility of the solution. In contrast, the insertion, the swap, and the two-opt operators may change the amount of demand that needs to be served in some of the route plans, so the feasibility of the solution may change, too. For this reason, based on the settings, the output solution of these operators could be different. If infeasible solutions are not accepted and the calculated output solution is infeasible, then the operator returns the original, input solution instead (assuming that the input solution is a feasible solution).

3.4.1. Inversion Operator

The inversion operator randomly selects a task $t \in T$ within the input solution. If this task has an inverse (i.e., $\exists inv(t) \in T$), then the operator replaces t with $inv(t)$ within the solution, else it returns the input solution.

3.4.2. Insertion Operator

The insertion operator randomly selects a task $t_1 \in T$, then replaces (inserts) it before or after another randomly selected task $t_2 \in T$ within the input solution. The selected tasks can be in different route plans or in the same route plan, but they cannot be the same tasks (i.e., $t_1 \neq t_2$).

It creates two potential output solutions, based on where t_1 is inserted (before or after t_2). If t_1 has an inverse, then the operator creates other potential output solutions, which contains the inverse task of the task (i.e., $inv(t_1)$) instead of t_1. It selects the solution as the output solution which has the smallest total cost among the potential output solutions.

3.4.3. Swap Operator

The swap operator randomly selects two tasks (t_1 and t_2, where $t_1, t_2 \in T$), then replaces them with each other (i.e., swaps them). Similarly to the insertion operator, the selected tasks can be from the same route plan or different route plans, but they cannot be the same tasks.

It creates potential output solutions, which contain one or two inverse task(s) of the selected tasks instead of the task(s). All the four possible combinations are considered. It selects the solution as the output solution which has the smallest total cost among the potential output solutions.

3.4.4. Two-Opt Operator

The two-opt operator randomly selects two route plans (e.g., r_1 and r_2) of the solution. Based on the selected two route plans, two cases exist for this move operator. If the selected two route plans are the same (i.e., $r_1 = r_2$), then a sub-route plan (i.e., a part of the route plan) is selected randomly and its direction is reversed. If the selected two route plans are different (i.e., $r_1 \neq r_2$), then these two route plans are randomly cut into four sub-route plans, and then two new potential output solutions are generated by reconnecting the four sub-route plans and the best one from them is selected. For example, r_1 and r_2 are cut into sub-route plans r_{11} r_{12} and r_{21} r_{22}, respectively. Two new solutions are generated by connecting them in the following ways: (1) r_{11} with r_{22} and r_{21} with r_{12} and (2) r_{11} with reversed r_{21} and reversed r_{12} with r_{22}.

3.4.5. Merge-split Operator

As it was mentioned before, the merge-split operator can make large changes in the solution (e.g., it can modify the order of all the tasks within one or more route plans), so it is considered a large step-size operator. This operator randomly selects x number of different route plans in the input solution, where x is a random number ($1 \leq x \leq |S|$). It obtains an unordered list of tasks by merging the tasks of the selected route plans into one list, and then sorts this unordered list with a path scanning heuristic (e.g., [22], which is used in this work as well). The obtained ordered list is then optimally split into new route plans using Ulusoy's splitting procedure [24].

The ordered list is constructed by the path scanning heuristic the following way. First, an empty path is initialized, then, the affected tasks are added one by one into the current path, until no tasks are left in the unordered list. In each iteration, only those tasks are taken into account that can be added to the current path without breaking the capacity constraint. If there are no any tasks like that, then the depot is added to the current path and a new path is initialized (that becomes the current path). When a task or the depot is added to the current path, the task/depot is connected to the end of the current path with the shortest path between them. If there are multiple tasks that can be added, the one that is closest to the end of the current path is added. If there are multiple tasks that are closest to the end of the current path, then one of the following rules are applied to determine which task should be added next:

1. maximize the distance between $head(t)$ and v_0;
2. minimize the distance between $head(t)$ and v_0;
3. maximize the term $\frac{dem(t)}{sc(t)}$;
4. minimize the term $\frac{dem(t)}{sc(t)}$;
5. use rule 1, if the vehicle is less than half-full, otherwise use rule 2.

In the rules above, t ($t \in T$) is a task and v_0 ($v_0 \in V$) is the depot. In one run, only one of the rules can be used. Therefore, the path scanning heuristic is ran five times, which results in five ordered lists.

The Ulusoy's splitting procedure creates five new candidate output solutions from the five ordered lists by splitting the lists into route plans. How the procedure works is best summarized in [50]. The procedure starts with constructing the Directed Acyclic Graph (DAG) from the ordered list. A DAG is a graph with arcs that represent feasible sub-tours of one giant tour. Next, the shortest path through the graph is calculated, which gives the optimal partition of the giant tour into feasible route plans. As the final step, a new candidate solution is created from the untouched route plans of the input solution and the route plans returned by the procedure. From the five candidate solutions the best one is chosen and returned by the operator.

4. The Proposed ABC Algorithm for CARP (CARP-ABC Algorithm)

In this chapter, the ABC algorithm developed for CARP (CARP-ABC algorithm) is presented. The notations used for the CARP-ABC algorithm are collected in Table A2 in Appendix A.

The algorithmic description of the main CARP-ABC algorithm can be seen in Algorithm 1. The main algorithm can be divided into four main phases: initialization, employed bee, onlooker bee, and scout bee phases. The algorithm begins with the initialization phase, then enters a cycle, where it repeats the mentioned phases in the respective order until the termination criterion is satisfied (line 4). In the initialization phase (line 2), the colony (C), the age of the solutions within the colony ($\mathcal{A}$), the global best solution (S^*), and its age (α^*) are initialized. In the employed bee phase (line 6), local search is performed around the members of the colony. In the onlooker bee phase (line 7), a more in-depth local search is performed around one solution from the colony. In the scout bee phase (line 8), global search is performed.

Algorithm 1: Main CARP-ABC algorithm.

input: $I; n_{cs}, n_{mi}, n_{gsl}, n_{lsl}, n_{sal} \in \mathbb{N}$

1 **begin**
2     $C, \mathcal{A}, S^*, \alpha^* \leftarrow initializationP(I, n_{cs})$;
3     $t \leftarrow 0$;
4   **while** $t < n_{mi} \wedge \alpha^* < n_{gsl}$ **do**
5       $\check{C} \leftarrow C$;
6       $C, P \leftarrow employedBP(I, C, n_{lsl})$;
7       $C \leftarrow onlookerBP(I, C, P, n_{cs}, n_{lsl})$;
8       $C, \mathcal{A}, S^*, \alpha^* \leftarrow scoutBP(I, \check{C}, C, \mathcal{A}, S^*, \alpha^*, n_{sal})$;
9       $t \leftarrow t + 1$;
10   **return** S^*;

The parameters of the algorithm are the followings:

- I: a CARP instance;
- n_{cs}: the size of the colony, the number of solutions in the population;
- n_{mi}: the maximum number of iterations of the algorithm;
- n_{gsl}: the global search limit, the maximally allowed number of consecutive iterations in which the currently known global best solution is not improved;
- n_{lsl}: the local search limit, the maximally allowed number of consecutive iterations in which the currently known local best solution is not improved in the employed bee phase and the onlooker bee phase of the algorithm;
- n_{sal}: the solution age limit, the maximally allowed number of consecutive iterations of the algorithm in which a solution is kept in the population;
- a termination criterion, which in default is that either the n_{mi} or the n_{gsl} is reached.

4.1. Initialization Phase

The algorithmic description of the initialization phase of the CARP-ABC algorithm can be seen in Algorithm 2. The algorithm in this phase first initializes the sets for the solutions S_i for $i = 1, 2, \ldots, n_{cs}$ and their age (lines 2–3). To guarantee an initial population with certain quality and diversity, the solutions are generated randomly by using the Random Solution Generation (RSG) algorithm for CARP (line 6), which is introduced in this work (in Section 4.1.1). Other population based evolutionary algorithms usually use the Randomized Path-Scanning Heuristic (RPSH) [22] to generate initial solutions. However, our experiments showed that, in the case of the CARP-ABC algorithm, it does not improve the convergence speed of the algorithm, so only the RSG is used.

After the initialization of the colony, the algorithm selects the solution $S_i \in C$ with the best (highest) fitness value by using the *selectBestSolution* function (line 11). The fitness of a solution S_i is defined by its total cost $TC(S_i)$ (it needs to be as small as possible). Therefore, the fitness value of a solution S_i is computed by the following fit function:

$$fit(S_i) = \frac{LB}{TC(S_i)} \qquad (14)$$

where LB is the lower bound of the solution (i.e., the total service cost of all the tasks, involving only one of each tasks which has an inverse). Its value ranges between 0 and 1. Solutions with greater fitness values are preferred, since greater fitness value means that the total cost of the solution is closer to the lower bound.

Algorithm 2: initializationP (Initialization Phase of the CARP-ABC algorithm).

input: $I; n_{cs} \in \mathbb{N}$

1 **begin**
2     $C \leftarrow \emptyset$;
3     $\mathcal{A} \leftarrow \emptyset$;
4     $i \leftarrow 1$;
5   **while** $i \leq n_{cs}$ **do**
6        $S_i \leftarrow RSG(I)$;
7        $\alpha_i \leftarrow 0$;
8        $C \leftarrow C \cup S_i$;
9        $\mathcal{A} \leftarrow \mathcal{A} \cup \alpha_i$;
10       $i \leftarrow i + 1$;
11     $S^* \leftarrow selectBestSolution(C)$;
12     $\alpha^* \leftarrow 0$;
13   **return** $C, \mathcal{A}, S^*, \alpha^*$;

4.1.1. Random Solution Generation Algorithm

As the first step, the algorithm generates n_{cs} random permutations, which contain positive integers from 1 to n (i.e., the id of every arc task and one of the two *id*s of every edge task) in random order. As the next step, the algorithm reads the *id*s in the permutation one-by-one from left to right, while summing up the demand of the corresponding tasks. If the task assigned to the currently read *id* would break the capacity constraint of the current route plan, the algorithm inserts a "0" (the *id* of the dummy task t_0) before the *id* of the task in the sequence (i.e., the task is added to a new route plan). After it is finished with separating the *id*s of the tasks into route plans, the algorithm checks each task in the solution and, if it has an inverse task, then randomly (e.g., with 0.5 probability) replaces the id of the task with the *id* of its inverse. As the final step, the algorithm inserts a "0" as the first and last task of the solution to make it a valid solution.

4.2. Employed Bee Phase

The algorithmic description of the employed bee phase of the CARP-ABC algorithm can be seen in Algorithm 3. The algorithm in this phase, for each employed bee, generates new candidate solutions in the neighborhood of S_i with each small step-size operator, then evaluates and selects the best solution (lines 2–11). In this phase, only the inversion operator (line 6) and the sub-route plan operator (line 7) are used, because only these operators guarantee that the new candidate solution will be feasible. It is repeated until the known best local solution S_i^* cannot be improved within the defined number of iterations (i.e., its age reached n_{lsl}). If the fitness value of the new candidate solution S_i^* is greater than or equal to the fitness value of the current solution S_i, the new solution replaces the current one in the population (lines 14–15).

As the next step, the algorithm calculates the winning probability values p_i for the solutions S_i (lines 16–19). The probability values p_i are calculated with the same function as in the basic ABC algorithm (Equation (13)).

Algorithm 3: employedBP (Employed Bee Phase of the CARP-ABC algorithm).

input: I; $C = \{S_1, S_2, \ldots, S_i, \ldots, S_{n_{cs}}\}$; $n_{lsl} \in \mathbb{N}$

1 **begin**
2   **forall** $S_i \in C$ **do**
3         $S_i^* \leftarrow S_i$;
4         $\alpha_i^* \leftarrow 0$;
5   **while** $\alpha_i^* < n_{lsl}$ **do**
6             $S_{i,1} \leftarrow inverse(I, S_i)$;
7             $S_{i,2} \leftarrow subRoutePlan(I, S_i)$;
8             $S_i' \leftarrow selectBestSolution(\{S_i^*, S_{i,1}, S_{i,2}\})$;
9   **if** $fit(S_i^*) < fit(S_i')$ **then**
10                 $S_i^* \leftarrow S_i'$;
11                 $\alpha_i^* \leftarrow 0$;
12   **else**
13                 $\alpha_i^* \leftarrow \alpha_i^* + 1$;
14   **if** $fit(S_i) < fit(S_i^*)$ **then**
15             $S_i \leftarrow S_i^*$;
16     $P \leftarrow \varnothing$;
17   **forall** $S_i \in C$ **do**
18         $p_i \leftarrow \dfrac{fit(S_i)}{\sum_{j=1}^{n_{cs}} fit(S_j)}$;
19         $P \leftarrow P \cup p_i$;
20   **return** C, P;

4.3. Onlooker Bee Phase

The algorithmic description of the onlooker bee phase of the CARP-ABC algorithm can be seen in Algorithm 4. The algorithm in this phase, depending on the p_i values, selects a solution S_i with the *selectSolution* function. This function first performs a roulette selection $Int(\sqrt{n_{cs}})$ times to select $Int(\sqrt{n_{cs}})$ number of solutions from the colony. Next, it compares the selected solutions to each other and selects the best one from them (i.e., the one with the greatest fitness value).

As a next step, the algorithm generates n_{cs} number of new candidate solutions $S_{i,j}$ in the neighborhood of S_i (i.e., one solution for each onlooker bee) with the merge-split operator (lines 5–6). It generates new candidate solutions in the neighborhood of these solutions with the small step-size operators, until the known best local solution $S_{i,j}^*$ cannot be improved within the defined number of iterations (i.e., the age of the solution, $\alpha_{i,j}^*$, reaches n_{lsl}) (lines 7–21). In this phase, all the small step-size operators (i.e., inversion, insertion, swap, 2-opt, and sub-route plan) are applied to $S_{i,j}'$, which is the best solution that was found in the previous iteration (lines 11–15). From the resulted solutions, the best one is chosen with the *selectBestSolution* function as the new $S_{i,j}'$ (line 16). If the new $S_{i,j}'$ is better than the currently known best solution in the neighborhood of $S_{i,j}$ (i.e., $S_{i,j}^*$), then it is set as the new best solution $S_{i,j}^*$ (lines 17–19). Otherwise, the age of $S_{i,j}^*$ (i.e., $\alpha_{i,j}^*$) is increased by one (lines 20–21). After the search ends in the neighborhood of $S_{i,j}$, it is checked whether the best solution found (i.e., $S_{i,j}^*$) is better than the best solution found in the whole neighborhood of S_i (i.e., S_i^*). If $S_{i,j}^*$ has a higher fitness value and is also feasible (its total excess demand is zero), then it will be set as the new S_i^* (lines 22–23).

If the best solution found in this phase (i.e., S_i^*) is better than the current solution S_i, then S_i is replaced by S_i^* in the colony (lines 25–26).

Algorithm 4: onlookerBP (Onlooker Bee Phase of the CARP-ABC algorithm).

input: I; $C = \{S_1, S_2, \ldots, S_i, \ldots, S_{n_{cs}}\}$; $P = \{p_1, p_2, \ldots, p_i, \ldots, p_{n_{cs}}\}$; $n_{cs}, n_{lsl} \in \mathbb{N}$

1 **begin**
2 $\quad S_i \leftarrow selectSolution(C, P)$;
3 $\quad S_i^* \leftarrow S_i$;
4 $\quad j \leftarrow 1$;
5 $\quad$ **while** $j \leq n_{cs}$ **do**
6 $\quad\quad S_{i,j} \leftarrow mergeSplit(S_i)$;
7 $\quad\quad S_{i,j}^* \leftarrow S_{i,j}$;
8 $\quad\quad S_{i,j}' \leftarrow S_{i,j}$;
9 $\quad\quad \alpha_{i,j}^* \leftarrow 0$;
10 $\quad\quad$ **while** $\alpha_{i,j}^* < n_{lsl}$ **do**
11 $\quad\quad\quad S_{i,j,1} \leftarrow inverse(I, S_{i,j}')$;
12 $\quad\quad\quad S_{i,j,2} \leftarrow insert(I, S_{i,j}')$;
13 $\quad\quad\quad S_{i,j,3} \leftarrow swap(I, S_{i,j}')$;
14 $\quad\quad\quad S_{i,j,4} \leftarrow twoOpt(I, S_{i,j}')$;
15 $\quad\quad\quad S_{i,j,5} \leftarrow subRoutePlan(I, S_{i,j}')$;
16 $\quad\quad\quad S_{i,j}' \leftarrow selectBestSolution(\{S_{i,j,1}, S_{i,j,2}, S_{i,j,3}, S_{i,j,4}, S_{i,j,5}\})$;
17 $\quad\quad\quad$ **if** $fit(S_{i,j}^*) < fit(S_{i,j}')$ **then**
18 $\quad\quad\quad\quad S_{i,j}^* \leftarrow S_{i,j}'$;
19 $\quad\quad\quad\quad \alpha_{i,j}^* \leftarrow 0$;
20 $\quad\quad\quad$ **else**
21 $\quad\quad\quad\quad \alpha_{i,j}^* \leftarrow \alpha_{i,j}^* + 1$;
22 $\quad\quad$ **if** $fit(S_i^*) < fit(S_{i,j}^*) \wedge totalExcessDem(S_{i,j}^*) = 0$ **then**
23 $\quad\quad\quad S_i^* \leftarrow S_{i,j}^*$;
24 $\quad\quad j \leftarrow j + 1$;
25 $\quad$ **if** $fit(S_i) < fit(S_i^*)$ **then**
26 $\quad\quad S_i \leftarrow S_i^*$;
27 $\quad$ **return** C;

4.4. Scout Bee Phase

The algorithmic description of the scout bee phase of the CARP-ABC algorithm can be seen in Algorithm 5. The algorithm in this phase increases the age of unchanged solutions (lines 3–4) and sets the age to zero for new solutions (lines 8–9) within the colony. Furthermore, if there is an abandoned solution (i.e., a solution which could not be improved through a predetermined number of trials, which is called n_{sal}), the algorithm replaces it with a new solution (lines 5–7), which is generated by using the RSG algorithm (as in the initialization phase).

In this phase, the algorithm also updates the global best solution, S^*. First, the best solution of the new colony is selected with the *selectBestSolution* function as solution S' (line 10). If S' is better than S^*, then S' is set as the new global best solution (lines 11–13). Otherwise, the age of S^* (i.e., α^*) is increased by one (lines 14–15).

Algorithm 5: scoutBP (Scout Bee Phase of the CARP-ABC algorithm).

input: I; $\bar{C} = \{\bar{S}_1, \bar{S}_2, \ldots, \bar{S}_i, \ldots, \bar{S}_{n_{cs}}\}$; $C = \{S_1, S_2, \ldots, S_i, \ldots, S_{n_{cs}}\}$;
$\mathcal{A} = \{\alpha_1, \alpha_2, \ldots, \alpha_i, \ldots, \alpha_{n_{cs}}\}$; S^*; α^*, $n_{sal} \in \mathbb{N}$

1 **begin**
2   **forall** $S_i \in C$ **do**
3   **if** $fit(S_i) = fit(\bar{S}_i)$ **then**
4           $\alpha_i \leftarrow \alpha_i + 1$;
5   **if** $\alpha_i = n_{sal}$ **then**
6              $S_i \leftarrow RSG(I)$;
7              $\alpha_i \leftarrow 0$;
8   **else**
9           $\alpha_i \leftarrow 0$;
10     $S' \leftarrow selectBestSolution(C)$;
11   **if** $fit(S^*) < fit(S')$ **then**
12        $S^* \leftarrow S'$;
13        $\alpha^* \leftarrow 0$;
14   **else**
15        $\alpha^* \leftarrow \alpha^* + 1$;
16   **return** $C, \mathcal{A}, S^*, \alpha^*$;

4.5. Computational Complexity Analysis

In this section, the computational complexity of the proposed CARP-ABC algorithm is discussed. The computational complexity is expressed by using the big-O notation. For the sake of simplicity, approximations are used and the constant values are omitted. The computational complexity of the whole algorithm depends on the given parameter values and the complexity of the input CARP instance, mainly on n (i.e., the number of tasks that have to be executed).

4.5.1. Initialization Phase

The computational complexity of the initialization phase is $O(n_{cs} * n + n_{cs})$, in which $O(n)$ is the complexity of the RSG algorithm and $O(n_{cs})$ is the complexity of selecting the best solution. $O(n)$ is multiplied by n_{cs}, because RSG is executed n_{cs} times to create the initial population.

Within the RSG algorithm, the complexity of generating a random permutation of the task identifiers is $O(n)$, assuming that the Fisher–Yates shuffle algorithm [51] is used for it. After a permutation is generated, the algorithm iterates over each element, which also has $O(n)$ as complexity. Therefore, the complexity of the RSG algorithm is around $O(2*n)$, which is $O(n)$ if the constant multiplier is omitted.

4.5.2. Employed Bee Phase

The computational complexity of the employed bee phase is $O(n_{cs} * n_{lsl} * (n + \log n + n_{max}) + n_{cs})$, in which the complexity of the local search is $O(n_{lsl} * (\log n + n + n_{max}))$. The complexity of the probability calculation is $O(n_{cs})$ (assuming, that the sum of the fitness values is calculated only once). $O(n_{lsl} * (\log n + n + n_{max}))$ is multiplied by n_{cs}, because the local search is executed for all the n_{cs} members of the population.

Within the local search, the complexity of the inversion operator is $O(n)$ and the complexity of the sub-route plan operator is $O(\log n + n + n_{max})$. Within the sub-route plan operator, the complexity of selecting a route plan is $O(\log n)$, since in the worst case $|S| = n$ (i.e., every task is on a separate route). After a route plan is selected, one of the methods of the operator is executed. From the methods, the sub-route plan rotation method has the greatest complexity, which is $O(n + n_{max})$, since in the worst case $l_k = n$ (i.e., there is only one route plan in the solution).

4.5.3. Onlooker Bee Phase

The computational complexity of the onlooker bee phase is $O(n_{cs} + n_{cs} * (\log n + n + n_{lsl} * (n + \log n + n_{max})))$, in which the complexity of selecting a solution from the colony is $O(k * n_{cs})$ or $O(n_{cs})$ is the constant k is omitted. The complexity of the main search is $O(n_{cs} * (\log n + n + n_{lsl} * (n + \log n + n_{max}))$.

Within the main search, the complexity of the merge-split operator is $O(\log n + n)$, because the complexity of selecting the number of route plans is $O(\log n)$ and the complexity of the other components of the operator (i.e., selecting the route plans, collecting the affected tasks, and executing the RPSH) is $O(n)$. The complexity of RPSH is $O(n)$, since in the worst case all the n tasks are affected in the solution. After the merge-split operator returns a solution, search is performed around this solution. The complexity of this search is $O(n_{lsl} * (n + \log n + n_{max}))$, because the complexity of the sub-route plan operator is $O(\log n + n + n_{max})$ and the complexity of the other operators (i.e., inversion, insertion, swap, and two-opt) are $O(n)$.

4.5.4. Scout Bee Phase

The computational complexity of the scout bee phase is $O(n_{cs} * n + n_{cs})$, because in the worst case, all the solutions have to be replaced in the colony for exceeding n_{sal}), so RSG is executed n_{cs} times. Next, the best solution is chosen from the colony, which has O_{cs} complexity.

4.5.5. Whole Algorithm

The computational complexity of the whole CARP-ABC algorithm is composed of the complexity of the initialization phase and the multiplication of the other phases by n_{mi}, since in the worst case the algorithm runs till the maximum number of iterations is reached. If the duplications are removed, then it is the following: $O(n_{cs} * n + n_{cs} + n_{mi} * (n_{cs} * n_{lsl} * (n + \log n + n_{max}) + n_{cs} + n_{cs} * (\log n + n + n_{lsl} * (n + \log n + n_{max}))))$.

If the parameters of the CARP-ABC algorithm and the sub-route plan operator are set to a fixed value, then the computational complexity is the following: $O(n + \log n)$. Therefore, the time complexity of the CARP-ABC algorithm is mostly linear but it contains components with logarithmic time complexity (e.g., when a route plan is selected).

5. Sub-Route Plan Operator

The sub-route plan operator is based on the GSTM operator for TSP [47]. The main differences between the modified version and the original version are due to the differences between the TSP and the CARP. Therefore, the modified version works with arcs instead of nodes. Furthermore, since the solution for a TSP is always one route plan, while the solution for a CARP (usually) consists of more than one route plan, the modified version takes into account only a part of the solution (one route plan) instead of the whole solution.

The sub-route plan operator is a complex move operator which consists of two different greedy search methods (greedy reconnection and sub-route rotation) and a method that provides distortion. In all three methods, inversion of the affected tasks is considered. Inversion of the tasks has real importance when a sequence of tasks is inverted in the sub-route rotation method because when the execution order of the tasks changes, the direction in which the tasks are executed should be changed too, to keep the traveling cost minimal. The used notations within this chapter are collected in Table A3 in Appendix A.

5.1. The Main Algorithm

The algorithmic description of the main algorithm of the sub-route plan operator can be seen in Algorithm 6. As input, a CARP instance I, a solution S of I, and the parameters of the algorithm are expected. The parameters are the following:

- the reconnection probability (p_{rc});
- the correction and perturbation probability (p_{cp});
- the linearity probability (p_l);

- the minimum length of the sub-route plan (l_{min});
- the (maximal) size of the neighborhood of a task arc that is considered (n_{max}).

Algorithm 6: subRoutePlan (main algorithm of the sub-route plan operator).

input: I; S; $p_{rc}, p_{cp}, p_l \in \mathbb{R}$; $l_{min}, n_{max} \in \mathbb{N}^+$
1 **begin**
2     $r_k \leftarrow selectOne(S)$;
3   **if** $l_k \geq l_{min}$ **then**
4        $l_{max} \leftarrow max(\{l_{min}, toInt(\sqrt{l_k})\})$;
5        $r'_k \leftarrow r_k$;
6        $l \leftarrow randInt(l_{min}, l_{max})$;
7        $s \leftarrow randInt(1, l_k - l + 1)$;
8        $e \leftarrow s + l - 1$;
9        $r_k^* \leftarrow \langle t_{k,s}, \ldots, t_{k,e} \rangle$;
10       $r_k^\# \leftarrow removeSubRoutePlan(r_k^*, r_k)$;
11       $p_{rand} \leftarrow randFloat(0, 1)$;
12   **if** $p_{rand} \leq p_{rc}$ **then**
13           $r'_k \leftarrow greedyReconnection(I, r_k, r_k^*, r_k^\#)$;
14   **else**
15           $p_{rand} \leftarrow randFloat(0, 1)$;
16   **if** $p_{rand} \leq p_{cp}$ **then**
17              $r'_k \leftarrow distortion(I, r_k^*, r_k^\#, s, p_l)$;
18   **else**
19              $r'_k \leftarrow subRoutePlanRotation(I, r_k, s, e, n_{max})$;
20     $S \leftarrow (S \setminus r_k) \cup r'_k$;
21 **return** S;

The maximal length of the sub-route plan (l_{max}) is determined after the route plan is selected. In the proposed CARP-ABC algorithm, the parameters of this algorithm are given as constant values, so only I and S are expected.

In the first step of the algorithm, a route plan r_k is selected from the solution S (line 2), then, if the number of (not dummy) tasks within r_k is sufficient (i.e., l_k is greater than or equal to l_{min}, line 3), the algorithm proceeds to the next step. Otherwise, it returns the input solution S unchanged (line 21).

In the following step of the algorithm, the parameters are initialized and the (sub-)route plans are generated. The maximum length of the sub-route plan (l_{max}) is determined based on the number of tasks within r_k (l_k) and the predefined minimum length of the sub-route plan (l_{min}) (line 4), and the new route plan (r'_k) is initialized (line 5). The length of the sub-route plan l is determined randomly based on l_{min} and l_{max} (line 6). The position index of the starting task of the sub-route plan (s) is randomly selected taking into account l (line 7). The position index of the ending task of the sub-route plan (e) is determined by s and l (line 8). The sub-route plan r_k^* is constructed by taking the sub-route plan that is enclosed by the tasks $t_{k,s}$ and $t_{k,e}$ from r_k (line 9). The route plan without r_k^* is denoted by $r_k^\#$ (line 10).

As the next step of the algorithm, a random number is generated (p_{rnd}) between 0 and 1 (line 11), which determines the operation of the operator. If p_{rnd} is less than or equal to the predefined reconnection probability p_{rc} (i.e., $p_{rnd} \leq p_{rc}$, line 12), then the greedy reconnection method is executed (line 13, Section 5.2), otherwise, a new random number is generated (line 15). If the new value of p_{rnd} is less than or equal to the predefined correction and perturbation probability p_{cp} (i.e., $p_{rnd} \leq p_{cp}$, line 16), then distortion is added to r_k (line 17, Section 5.3), otherwise, the sub-route plan rotation method is executed (line 19, Section 5.4). As the final step, the solution S is updated by removing the old route plan r_k and adding the new one, r'_k (line 20), then the updated solution is returned (line 21).

5.2. Greedy Reconnection Method

The greedy reconnection method inserts r_k^* into the position within $r_k^\#$ that generates the least amount of increase in the total cost of the route plan.

5.2.1. Algorithm

The algorithmic description of the greedy reconnection method within the sub-route plan operator can be seen in Algorithm 7. As input, the CARP instance I, the original route plan r_k of the solution S, the selected sub-route plan r_k^*, and the truncated route plan $r_k^\#$ (i.e., r_k without r_k^*) are expected.

Algorithm 7: greedyReconnection (algorithm of the greedy reconnection method within the sub-route plan operator).

input: $I; r_k; r_k^*; r_k^\#$

1 **begin**
2     $r_k' \leftarrow r_k$;
3     $i \leftarrow 1$;
4   **while** $i \leq l_k^\# + 1$ **do**
5        $r_{k,i} \leftarrow insertSubRoutePlan(r_k^*, r_k^\#, i)$;
6   **if** $TC(\{r_{k,i}\}) < TC(\{r_k'\})$ **then**
7           $r_k' \leftarrow r_{k,i}$;
8        $i \leftarrow i + 1$;
9   **return** r_k';

In the first step of the algorithm, the new route plan r_k' is initialized with the current route plan r_k (line 2). The position index i that is used to find the best position for insertion of r_k^* into $r_k^\#$ is initialized as well (line 3). The value "1" refers to the first (not dummy) task within $r_k^\#$ (i.e., $t_{k,1}^\#$). The value "0" would refer to the first dummy task (t_0) and "$l_k^\# + 1$" to the last dummy task within $r_k^\#$ (assuming $l_k^\#$ is the number of not dummy tasks within $r_k^\#$). In the following step, the algorithm checks each position within $r_k^\#$ to find the best one to insert r_k^* into (lines 4–8). In each iteration, before task $t_{k,i}^\#$ within $r_k^\#$, it inserts r_k^* with the *insertSubRoutePlan* function (line 5). The total cost of the resulting route plan ($r_{k,i}$) is then compared with the total cost of r_k' (line 6). If $r_{k,i}$ is better than r_k' (i.e., it has lower total cost), then it becomes the new value of r_k' (line 7).

In the final step of the algorithm, r_k' is returned by the function (line 9).

5.2.2. Example

For a better understanding of the method, see the following example. Let the selected route plan be $r_k = \langle t_0, t_{k,1}, t_{k,2}, \ldots, t_{k,13}, t_0 \rangle$ and the length of the sub-route plan be $l = 3$. Based on these, let the selected starting and ending task be $t_{k,s} = t_{k,5}$ and $t_{k,e} = t_{k,7}$, then the selected sub-route plan is $r_k^* = \langle t_{k,5}, t_{k,6}, t_{k,7} \rangle$ and the route plan r_k without r_k^* is $r_k^\# = \langle t_0, t_{k,1}, t_{k,2}, t_{k,3}, t_{k,4}, t_{k,8}, t_{k,9}, t_{k,10}, t_{k,11}, t_{k,12}, t_{k,13}, t_0 \rangle$. Let us assume that inserting r_k^* between $t_{k,8}$ and $t_{k,9}$ in $r_k^\#$ results in the least amount of increase in the total cost of the solution, then $r_k' = \langle t_0, t_{k,1}, t_{k,2}, t_{k,3}, t_{k,4}, t_{k,8}, t_{k,5}, t_{k,6}, t_{k,7}, t_{k,9}, t_{k,10}, t_{k,11}, t_{k,12}, t_{k,13}, t_0 \rangle$ will be the new k-th route plan in the solution.

The example discussed in the previous paragraph is depicted in Figures 2 and 3. In both figures, the arc tasks served within a route plan are depicted with solid lines, and the other arcs, which are only traversed, are depicted with dashed lines. The original route plan r_k can be seen in Figure 2. In Figure 3, the sub-route plan r_k^* and the truncated route plan $r_k^\#$ are shown, highlighted with red and blue colors, respectively. The selected starting and ending tasks ($t_{k,s}$ and $t_{k,e}$) are depicted with thicker lines.

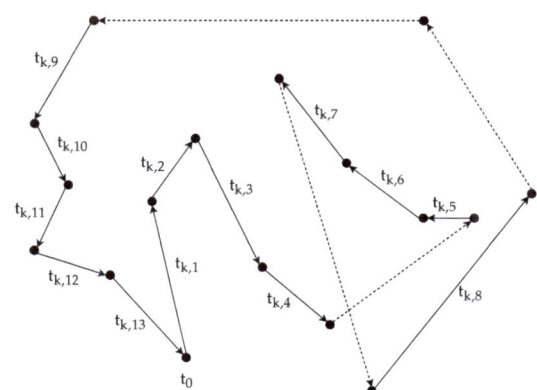

Figure 2. Example route plan r_k.

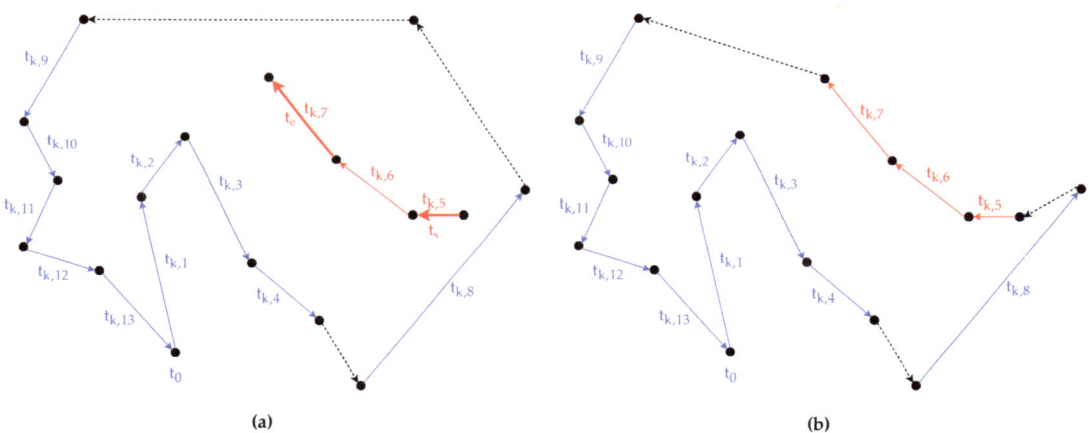

Figure 3. Greedy reconnection method: (**a**) sub-route plan r_k^* subtracted from route plan r_k; (**b**) sub-route plan r_k^* connected to the route plan $r_k^\#$.

5.3. Distortion Method

The distortion method takes the tasks in r_k^* and inserts them one-by-one into $r_k^\#$, starting from the position index s, and by rolling or mixing with the predefined linearity probability (p_l). Rolling means selecting the current last task in r_k^* and mixing means selecting a random task in r_k^*.

5.3.1. Algorithm

The algorithmic description of the distortion method within the sub-route plan operator can be seen in Algorithm 8. As input, the CARP instance I, the selected sub-route plan r_k^*, the truncated route plan $r_k^\#$ (i.e., r_k without r_k^*), the position index s of the starting task of r_k^* within the original route plan r_k, and the linearity probability p_l are expected.

Algorithm 8: Distortion (algorithm of the distortion method within the sub-route plan operator).

input: $l; r_k^*; r_k^\#; s; p_l$
1 **begin**
2     $i \leftarrow s;$
3     $r_k' \leftarrow r_k^\#;$
4   **while** $|r_k^*| \neq 0$ **do**
5        $p_{rnd} \leftarrow randFloat(0,1);$
6        $t \leftarrow t_{k,|r_k^*|}^*;$
7   **if** $p_{rnd} \leq p_l$ **then**
8           $j \leftarrow randInt(1,|r_k^*|);;$
9           $t \leftarrow t_{k,j}^*;$
10        $r_k' \leftarrow insertTask(t, r_k', i);$
11        $r_k^* \leftarrow removeTask(t, r_k^*);$
12        $i \leftarrow i+1;$
13   **return** $r_k';$

In the first step of the algorithm, the position index i is initialized with s (line 2) and the new route plan r_k' is initialized with the truncated route plan $r_k^\#$ (line 3). While there are tasks in r_k^*, the algorithm executes the following steps (lines 4–12). First, a random number is generated (p_{rnd}) between 0 and 1 (line 5) and the last task is selected from r_k^* into t (line 6). If p_{rnd} is less than or equal to p_l, then the value of t is changed into a random task from r_k^* (lines 7–9). The selected task t is then inserted into the position i in r_k' with the *insertTask* function (line 10) and removed from r_k^* with the *removeTask* function (line 11). The task is always inserted right after the previously inserted task. When r_k^* runs out of tasks (i.e., all the tasks within it have been inserted into r_k'), the algorithm returns r_k' (line 13).

5.3.2. Example

For a better understanding of the method, see the following example. Let the selected route plan be $r_k = \langle t_0, t_{k,1}, t_{k,2}, \ldots, t_{k,13}, t_0 \rangle$ and the length of the sub-route plan be $l = 3$. Based on these, let the selected starting and ending task be $t_{k,s} = t_{k,5}$ and $t_{k,e} = t_{k,7}$, then the selected sub-route plan is $r_k^* = \langle t_{k,5}, t_{k,6}, t_{k,7} \rangle$ and the route plan r_k without r_k^* is $r_k^\# = \langle t_0, t_{k,1}, t_{k,2}, t_{k,3}, t_{k,4}, t_{k,8}, t_{k,9}, t_{k,10}, t_{k,11}, t_{k,12}, t_{k,13}, t_0 \rangle$. The length of r_k^* is three, so in this case the algorithm has three iterations. Let the linearity probability be $p_l = 0.2$.

In the first iteration, let the random number be $p_{rnd} = 0.1$. Since it is smaller than p_l, a random task is selected from r_k^*. Let the selected task be $t_{k,6}$. In this case, the new route plan is $r_k' = \langle t_0, t_{k,1}, t_{k,2}, t_{k,3}, t_{k,4}, t_{k,6}, t_{k,8}, \ldots \rangle$ (i.e., $t_{k,6}$ is inserted between $t_{k,4}$ and $t_{k,8}$) and $r_k^* = \langle t_{k,5}, t_{k,7} \rangle$ (i.e., $t_{k,6}$ is removed).

In the second iteration, let the random number be $p_{rnd} = 0.8$. Since it is greater than p_l, the currently last task is selected from r_k^*, which is $t_{k,7}$. In this case, the new route plan is $r_k' = \langle t_0, t_{k,1}, t_{k,2}, t_{k,3}, t_{k,4}, t_{k,6}, t_{k,7}, t_{k,8}, \ldots \rangle$ (i.e., $t_{k,7}$ is inserted between $t_{k,6}$ and $t_{k,8}$) and $r_k^* = \langle t_{k,5} \rangle$.

In the third iteration, since only one task left in r_k^*, regardless of the value of p_{rnd}, $t_{k,5}$ is selected. Therefore, $r_k' = \langle t_0, t_{k,1}, t_{k,2}, t_{k,3}, t_{k,4}, t_{k,6}, t_{k,7}, t_{k,5}, t_{k,8}, \ldots \rangle$ and $r_k^* = \langle t_{k,5} \rangle$. Since r_k^* is now empty, the algorithm returns r_k'.

5.4. Sub-route Plan Rotation Method

The sub-route plan rotation method selects one neighbor task randomly from the neighbors of $t_{k,s}$ and $t_{k,e}$ (t_{k,s^*} and t_{k,e^*}, respectively), then inverts the sequence of tasks enclosed by $t_{k,i}$ and t_{k,i^*} (including t_{k,i^*} in the sequence), where $(i, i^*) \in \{(s, s^*), (e, e^*)\}$. The inversion of the sequence is performed in such a manner, that $t_{k,i}$ and t_{k,i^*} (or $inv(t_{k,i^*})$) become direct neighbors in the new route plan r_k'.

5.4.1. Algorithm

The algorithmic description of the sub-route plan rotation method within the sub-route plan operator can be seen in Algorithm 9. As input, the CARP instance I, the original route plan r_k, the position index s of the starting task and the position index e of the ending task of r_k^* within the original route plan r_k, and the size of the neighborhood n_{max} are expected.

Algorithm 9: subRoutePlanRotation (algorithm of the sub-route plan rotation method within the sub-route plan operator).

---

input: I; r_k; s; e; n_{max}

1 **begin**
2    $s^* \leftarrow selectNeighborTask(r_k, s, n_{max})$;
3    $e^* \leftarrow selectNeighborTask(r_k, e, n_{max})$;
4    $r'_k \leftarrow r_k$;
5   **forall** $(i, i^*) \in \{(s, s^*), (e, e^*)\}$ **do**
6      $r'_{k,i} \leftarrow \langle \rangle$;
7   **if** $i < i^*$ **then**
8        $r'_{k,i} \leftarrow \langle t_0, t_{k,1}, \ldots, t_{k,i} \rangle \cdot \langle t_{k,i^*}, t_{k,i^*-1}, \ldots, t_{k,i+1} \rangle \cdot \langle t_{k,i^*+1}, \ldots, t_{k,l_k}, t_0 \rangle$;
9        $j \leftarrow i^*$;
10   **while** $i < j$ **do**
11   **if** $\exists inv(t_{k,j})$ **then**
12            $r'_{k,i} \leftarrow replaceTask(t_{k,j}, inv(t_{k,j}), r'_{k,i})$;
13          $j \leftarrow j - 1$;
14   **else**
15        $r'_{k,i} \leftarrow \langle t_0, t_{k,1}, \ldots, t_{k,i^*-1} \rangle \cdot \langle t_{k,i-1}, t_{k,i-2}, \ldots, t_{k,i^*} \rangle \cdot \langle t_{k,i}, \ldots, t_{k,l_k}, t_0 \rangle$;
16        $j \leftarrow i - 1$;
17   **while** $i^* \leq j$ **do**
18   **if** $\exists inv(t_{k,j})$ **then**
19            $r'_{k,i} \leftarrow replaceTask(t_{k,j}, inv(t_{k,j}), r'_{k,i})$;
20          $j \leftarrow j - 1$;
21   **if** $TC(\{r'_{k,i}\}) < TC(\{r'_k\})$ **then**
22        $r'_k \leftarrow r'_{k,i}$;
23   **return** r'_k;

In the first step of the algorithm, one position index of the n_{max} closest neighbor tasks is selected randomly for both $t_{k,s}$ and $t_{k,e}$ (s^* and e^*, respectively) with the *selectNeighborTask* function (lines 2–3) and the new route plan r'_k is initialized with the original route plan r_k (line 4). In the next step, for all $(i, i^*) \in \{(s, s^*), (e, e^*)\}$, the following steps are executed (lines 5–22). First, the potential new route plan $r'_{k,i}$ is initialized with an empty sequence (line 6), then, based on the relationship between i and i^*, a sub-route plan is selected and inverted. If $t_{k,i}$ is before t_{k,i^*} (i.e., $i < i^*$) in r_k, then $t_{k,i}$ is directly followed by t_{k,i^*} (or $inv(t_{k,i^*})$) in r'_k (lines 7–8). Otherwise, if t_{k,i^*} is before $t_{k,i}$ in r_k, then t_{k,i^*} (or $inv(t_{k,i^*})$) is directly followed by $t_{k,i}$ in r'_k (lines 14–15). In both cases, each task that has an inverse and is within the inverted sub-sequence, is replaced by its inverse task in the new route plan r'_k with the *replaceTask* function (lines 9–13, lines 16–20). From the sub-route plan rotations, the one that has the lowest total cost is chosen (lines 21–22) and returned by the algorithm (line 23).

5.4.2. Determining the Neighborhood

The neighbors are determined according to the predefined size of the neighborhood (n_{max}). The distance between arc task $t_{k,i}$ and another arc task is calculated based on their order within r_k and whether the other arc task has an inverse task (i.e., it is from an edge task) or not. Let $t_{k,j}$ be an arc task in r_k that is not $t_{k,i}$ (i.e., $t_{k,i} \neq t_{k,j}$). If $t_{k,j}$ is before $t_{k,i}$ in r_k

(i.e., $j < i$) and has inverse task (i.e., $inv(t_{k,j}) \in T$), then the distance between the two arc tasks is the shortest path between the head vertices of $t_{k,j}$ and $t_{k,i}$, so it can be calculated with the expression $mdc(head(t_{k,j}), head(t_{k,i}))$. The shortest path is calculated starting from $head(t_{k,j})$, because during the sub-route plan rotation $t_{k,j}$ gets reversed (i.e., it gets replaced by its inverse in the route plan) and it is known that the head vertex of the task is the same as the tail vertex of the inverse task (i.e., $tail(inv(t_{k,j})) = head(t_{k,j})$). If the task does not have inverse, then the shortest path is calculated starting from $tail(t_{k,j})$. If $t_{k,j}$ is after $t_{k,i}$ in r_k (i.e., $j > i$) and has inverse task, then $mdc(tail(t_{k,i}), tail(t_{k,j}))$ is calculated. If the task does not have inverse, then the shortest path is calculated ending at $head(t_{k,j})$. The reasoning behind what expression to use in each case is summarized in Table 1.

Table 1. Summary table about what expression to use to calculate the distance between an arbitrary arc task $t_{k,j}$ from the route plan r_k and $t_{k,i}$ ($i \in \{s, e\}$).

Is $t_{k,j}$ before or after $t_{k,i}$ in r_k?	Does $t_{k,j}$ Have Inverse Task?	Expression
before	yes	$mdc(head(t_{k,j}), head(t_{k,i}))$
before	no	$mdc(tail(t_{k,j}), head(t_{k,i}))$
after	yes	$mdc(tail(t_{k,i}), tail(t_{k,j}))$
after	no	$mdc(tail(t_{k,i}), head(t_{k,j}))$

5.4.3. Example

For a better understanding of the method, see the following example. Let the selected route plan be $r_k = \langle t_0, t_{k,1}, t_{k,2}, \ldots, t_{k,13}, t_0 \rangle$, the length of the sub-route plan be $l = 3$, and the size of the neighborhood be $n_{max} = 5$. (At this method, l only defines the distance between the two selected arc tasks, it has no effect on the length of the rotated sub-route plans.) Based on these, let the selected two arcs task be $t_{k,s} = t_{k,6}$ and $t_{k,e} = t_{k,8}$. Let us assume that all the arc tasks in r_k are from an edge task, so they all have inverse task.

The route plan, the selected arc tasks, and their neighborhood are illustrated on Figure 4. The arc tasks served within the route plan are depicted with solid lines, and the other arcs, which are only traversed, are depicted with dashed lines. The arc tasks $t_{k,s}$ and $t_{k,e}$ and their neighborhood are highlighted with red and blue color, respectively. Only the arc tasks that are completely covered by the ellipses are part of the neighborhood. It must be noted that the ellipses are only for representational purpose. Since identifying the neighborhood is quite complex due to the distance calculation, this yields to that the shape that covers only the neighbor arc tasks varies. Based on this, for $t_{k,s}$, the set of the neighbor arc tasks is $\{t_{k,2}, t_{k,3}, t_{k,7}, t_{k,8}, t_{k,11}\}$, and for $t_{k,e}$, it is $\{t_{k,4}, t_{k,6}, t_{k,7}, t_{k,9}, t_{k,10}\}$.

For $t_{k,s}$, let us assume that the selected neighbor task is $t_{k,2}$ (i.e., $t_{k,s^*} = t_{k,2}$), then the sub-route plan is $r_k^* = \langle t_{k,2}, t_{k,3}, t_{k,4}, t_{k,5} \rangle$ (Figure 5a). Since t_{k,s^*} precedes $t_{k,s}$ (i.e., $s^* < s$), the sub-route plan is reversed in a manner that in the new route plan $inv(t_{k,s^*})$ is directly followed by $t_{k,s}$. The reversed sub-route plan is $\langle inv(t_{k,5}), inv(t_{k,4}), inv(t_{k,3}), inv(t_{k,2}) \rangle$, therefore the new route plan is $r_k' = \langle t_0, t_{k,1}, inv(t_{k,5}), inv(t_{k,4}), inv(t_{k,3}), inv(t_{k,2}), t_{k,6}, \ldots \rangle$ (Figure 5b).

For $t_{k,e}$, let us assume that the selected neighbor task is $t_{k,10}$ (i.e., $t_{k,e^*} = t_{k,10}$), then the sub-route plan is $r_k^* = \langle t_{k,9}, t_{k,10} \rangle$ (Figure 6a). Since t_{k,e^*} is after $t_{k,e}$ (i.e., $e < e^*$), the sub-route plan is reversed in a manner that in the new route plan $inv(t_{k,e^*})$ directly follows $t_{k,e}$. The reversed sub-route plan is $\langle inv(t_{k,10}), inv(t_{k,9}) \rangle$, therefore the new route plan is $r_k' = \langle t_0, t_{k,1}, \ldots, t_{k,8}, inv(t_{k,10}), inv(t_{k,9}), t_{k,11}, \ldots, t_{k,13}, t_0 \rangle$ (Figure 6b).

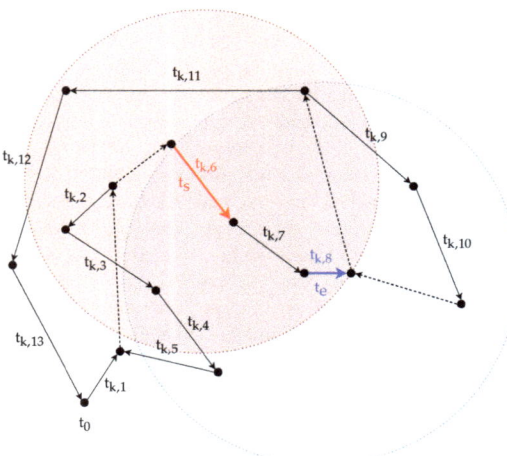

Figure 4. Nearest neighbors of the arc tasks $t_{k,s}$ ($t_{k,6}$) and $t_{k,e}$ ($t_{k,8}$) within the route plan r_k, when $n_{max} = 5$.

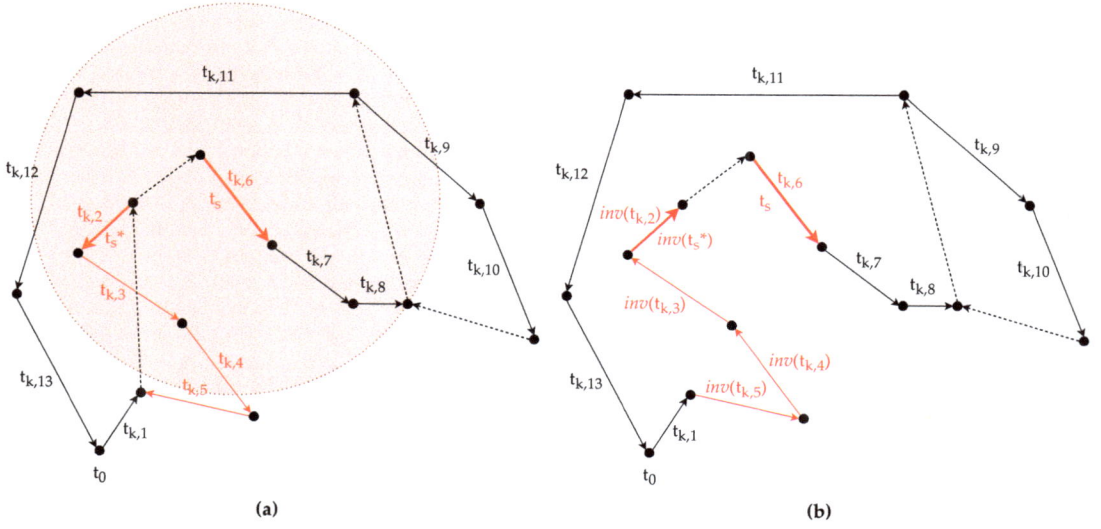

Figure 5. Rotation of the sub-route plan enclosed by t_{k,s^*} and $t_{k,s}$: (**a**) An arc task (here $t_{k,2}$) is randomly selected as t_{k,s^*} from the neighbor list of arc task $t_{k,s}$ ($t_{k,6}$), thus a sub-route plan is obtained; (**b**) The sub-route plan is inverted, so $inv(t_{k,s^*})$ will be directly followed by $t_{k,s}$ in the new route plan r'_k.

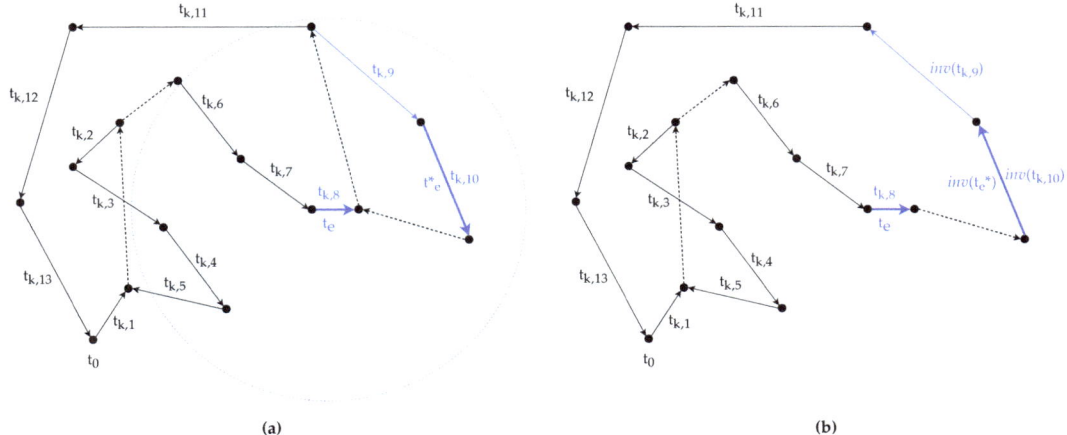

Figure 6. Rotation of the sub-route plan enclosed by $t_{k,e}$ and t_{k,e^*}: (**a**) An arc task ($t_{k,10}$) is randomly selected as t_{k,e^*} from the neighbor list of arc task $t_{k,e}$ ($t_{k,8}$), thus, a sub-route plan is obtained; (**b**) The sub-route plan is inverted, so $t_{k,e}$ will be directly followed by $inv(t_{k,e^*})$ in the new route plan r'_k.

6. Experiments

The proposed CARP-ABC algorithm (ABC algorithm from now on in this section) along with the sub-route plan operator was implemented in Python (3.6) in the Spyder (4.2.1) development environment. To compare the ABC algorithm with other static CARP solvers, the HMA and the ACOPR were also implemented. To test the ABC algorithm and the HMA as complete rerouting algorithms within the DCARP framework and compare them to the minimal rerouting algorithm RR1, the implementations from our previous work [20] were used. Python programming language was chosen for the implementation, because the DCARP framework will be supported in the future with the PM4Py process mining platform, which is written in Python. The experiments were performed on a laptop PC with Windows 10 operation system, equipped with an Intel(R) Core(TM) i5-3320M 2.60 GHz 2-core CPU and 8 GB of RAM.

It must be signified, that the HMA and the ACOPR were implemented based on their algorithmic description (in [7] and in [8], respectively), because the original implemented version of them is not available. Therefore, the implementations used in this work might have errors that decrease the effectiveness of these algorithms.

In this section, first, the setups of the experiments are specified (Section 6.1). Next, the results of the CARP experiments (Section 6.2), the results of the DCARP experiments (Section 6.4), and the results of the operator experiments (Section 6.3) are discussed, in the respective order.

6.1. Experimental Setups

For the CARP experiments, five CARP instances of different sizes were used. The ABC algorithm, the HMA, and the ACOPR were run 30 times with a time limit set to 10 min and applied to the CARP instances, independently, then the recorded outputs were compared and analyzed.

For the DCARP experiments, one CARP instance of medium size was used. Since the initial DCARP instance is fundamentally a static CARP instance and the HMA is the currently known the most accurate metaheuristic for CARP, the HMA was used to obtain the initial solution. The travel and service logs and the events were generated with the algorithms introduced in [20]. For each event type, 15 events were independently generated, then executed on the initial instance, creating new DCARP instances. The RR1 algorithm, the ABC algorithm, and the HMA were run with a time limit set to 1 min and applied to these instances, independently, then the recorded outputs were compared and analyzed.

For the operator experiments, three CARP instances of different sizes were used. The sub-route plan operator and the other small step-size operators for CARP (i.e., inversion, insertion, swap, and two-opt) were used as local search operators within the employed bee phase of the ABC algorithm. The employed bee phase was chosen instead of the onlooker bee phase so the efficiency of the operators can be measured on solutions of different qualities, not only on good quality solutions. The (modified) ABC algorithm was run 30 times with a time limit set to 10 min and applied to the CARP instances, independently, then the recorded outputs were compared and analyzed.

At the CARP and the DCARP experiments, during the execution of each algorithm, the new global best solution and the time it took for the algorithm to find the new global best solution (i.e., the elapsed time since the beginning of the execution of the algorithm) were recorded and analyzed. At the operator experiments, during the execution of the algorithm, the number of search trials in which the move operators found a better local best solution (i.e., S_i^*) was recorded and analyzed.

The used instances and the parameter settings of the used algorithms are specified in the subsections (in Section 6.1.1 and in Section 6.1.2, respectively).

6.1.1. Used Instances

To test the CARP solvers, benchmark test sets are often used in the literature. These test sets can be divided into two main categories: synthetic (e.g., containing randomly generated instances) [52–54] and real-life based (containing examples based on real road networks and tasks) [2,28,29].

Since testing an algorithm on all the instances would be time-consuming, only the following five instances were selected for the CARP experiments:

- "kshs1" from the KSHS set [54];
- "egl-e1-A" and "egl-s1-A" from the EGL set [2];
- "egl-g1-A" and "egl-g2-A" from EGL-Large set [29].

For the DCARP experiments, only the "egl-e1-A" instance was used. For the operator experiments, the "egl-e1-A", "egl-s1-A", and "egl-g1-A" instances were used.

The EGL and the EGL-Large sets originate from the data of a winter gritting application in Lancashire (UK). The EGL set contains 24 instances in which two different graphs are combined with various attribute values. The instances "egl-e1-A" and "egl-s1-A" were selected to represent one of each graph. The EGL-Large set contains 10 instances in which the graph is the same but the number of task edges is 347 in 5 instances and 375 in the other 5 instances. The instances "egl-g1-A" and "egl-g2-A" were selected to represent one from both kinds of instances.

The attributes of all the five selected instances are briefly summarized in Table 2. These CARP instances were selected to represent CARPs of very different sizes, thus requiring very different complexity levels to solve them. It can be seen, that the "kshs1" instance is a small synthetic CARP instance, which means a small search space for the algorithm, so for problem difficulty it can be put into the easy category. The EGL instances are real-life based CARP instances, so they are naturally more complex. Based on their size, the difficulty of the "egl-e1-A" instance is medium, the difficulty of the "egl-s1-A" instance is hard, and the difficulty of the instances "egl-g1-A" and "egl-g2-A" are very hard.

Table 2. Attributes of the used CARP instances.

Name	kshs1 [54]	egl-e1-A [2]	egl-s1-A [2]	egl-g1-A [29]	egl-g2-A [29]
Number of vertices	8	77	140	255	255
Number of task edges	15	51	75	347	375
Number of other edges	0	47	115	28	0
Number of vehicles	4	5	7	20	22
Capacity of the vehicles	150	305	210	28,600	28,000
Lower bound of the total cost	8705	1468	1394	553,696	604,228
Total cost of the best solution [1]	14,661	3548	5018	992,045	1,088,040

[1] Based on the literature.

6.1.2. Parameter Settings

The ABC algorithm was tested with multiple parameter settings. Based on the results, the following settings provided the best quality results without unnecessarily increasing the running time of the algorithm, thus these are used in the experiments:

- n_{cs}: 10;
- n_{mi}: 10,000;
- n_{gsl}: 100;
- n_{lsl}: 20;
- n_{sal}: 20.

According to the investigation in [47], the ideal parameter values for the GSTM operator are the followings: $p_{rc} = 0.5$, $p_{cp} = 0.8$, $p_l = 0.2$, $l_{min} = 2$, $l_{max} = Int(\sqrt{n})$, and $n_{max} = 5$, where n is the number of cities. In the experiments, the same parameter values are used for the sub-route plan move operator. The only difference is that n is the number of tasks within the selected route plan.

For the HMA and the ACOPR, the optimal parameter settings defined by the corresponding works [7,8] were used. For the RR1, no parameters are needed.

6.2. Results of the CARP Experiments

The charts on Figures 7–9 show the convergence speed of 30 independent runs of the algorithms for the selected instances. As it was mentioned before, for these, the new global best solution and the time it took for the algorithm to find the new global best solution were recorded. The y-axis shows the total cost of the solution, and the x-axis shows the elapsed time since the algorithm started running in seconds. The different colors indicate the outputs of the different algorithms. The colored lines indicate the average convergence speed and the colored areas cover all the values that were recorded (i.e., the areas are enclosed by the minimum and maximum values). The closer the line is to the intersection of the axes, the better the convergence speed of the algorithm.

In the case of the "kshs1" instance (Figure 7), it can be seen that the convergence speed of the ACOPR and the ABC algorithm is around twice as fast as the speed of the HMA. However, even though the speed of the ACOPR and the ABC algorithm is nearly the same, the ACOPR algorithm has failed to find the best solution in 30 runs, thus making the ABC algorithm the best solver for CARPs of small size like the "kshs1" instance.

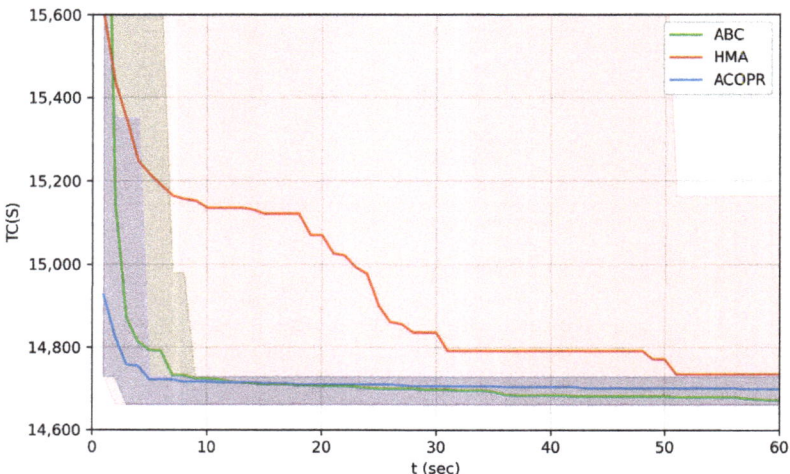

Figure 7. The convergence speed of 30 independent runs of HMA, ACOPR, and ABC algorithms on the "kshs1" instance, plotted on one chart.

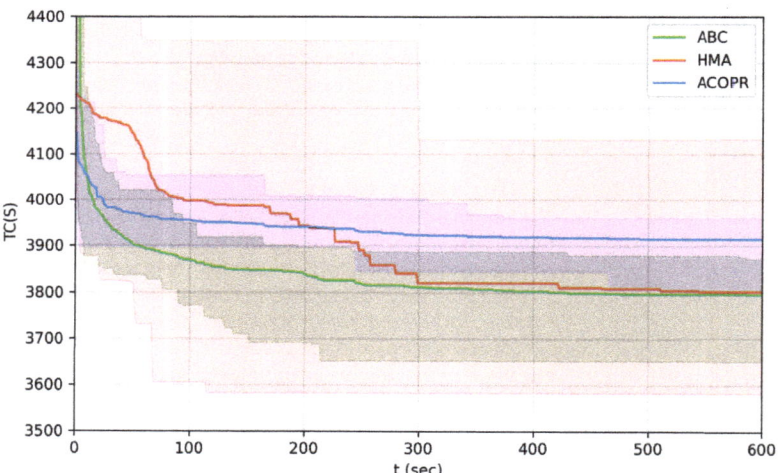

Figure 8. The convergence speed of 30 independent runs of HMA, ACOPR, and ABC algorithm on the "egl-e1-A" instance, plotted on one chart, with time limit ($t \leq 600$ s).

In the case of the "egl-e1-A" instance (Figure 8), the differences between the convergence speed of the algorithms start to show. It can be seen that in all cases, the ABC algorithm provides better solutions and faster, than the ACOPR algorithm. The HMA algorithm has a very slow cycle time, thus it has a very slow convergence speed as well. If time is not taken into account, the HMA can generally provide better solutions than the other algorithms.

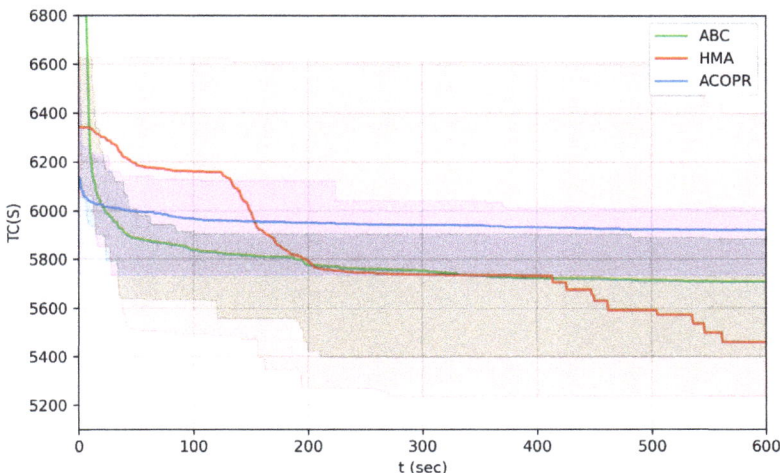

Figure 9. The convergence speed of 30 independent runs of HMA, ACOPR, and ABC algorithm on the "egl-s1-A" instance, plotted on one chart with time limit ($t \leq 600$ s).

In Table 3, the total cost of the globally best solution within different time limits is examined, based on 30 independent runs of the ABC algorithm and the HMA. The calculated statistics are the following: minimum (Min.), maximum (Max.), average (Avg.), and standard deviation (Std.). It can be seen that within 1 min, the ABC algorithm always provided better solutions. Within 5 min, in some cases, the HMA algorithm found better results (it has smaller Min. value), but in average the ABC algorithm still performed better (it has smaller Max. and Avg. values). Nevertheless, within 10 or more minutes, the HMA algorithm provided better solutions. Regardless of the time limit, the ABC algorithm is slightly more stable than the HMA algorithm, in terms of how much the solution varies for different runs (it has smaller Std. values).

Table 3. Statistics of the total cost of the globally best solution of the HMA and the ABC algorithms on the "egl-e1-A" instance, within different time limits.

Algorithm	Statistic Value	Output at Different Time Limits		
		$\leq$1 min	$\leq$5 min	$\leq$10 min
ABC	Min.	3835	3651	3651
	Max.	4021	3887	3872
	Avg.	3894.9	3812.5	3796.23
	Std.	38.02	68.90	65.70
HMA	Min.	3731	3582	3582
	Max.	4357	4133	4133
	Avg.	4091.6	3821.5	3802.4
	Std.	184.92	140.69	148.10

In the case of the "egl-s1-A" instance (Figure 9 and Table 4), the differences between the convergence speed of the HMA and the ABC algorithm is more complex. It can be seen that before 200 s, the ABC algorithm performs better, between 200 and 400 s they perform around the same, then after 400 s the HMA performs better.

Table 4. Statistics of the total cost of the globally best solution of the HMA and the ABC algorithms on the "egl-s1-A" instance, within different time limits.

Algorithm	Statistic Value	Output at Different Time Limits		
		≤1 min	≤5 min	≤10 min
ABC	Min.	5635	5398	5398
	Max.	5977	5903	5883
	Avg.	5876.53	5752.87	5708.5
	Std.	66.73	131.41	130.64
HMA	Min.	5507	5235	5235
	Max.	6628	6611	6401
	Avg.	6176.57	5738.67	5459.87
	Std.	355.71	440.63	209.63

The results were similar for the "egl-g1-A" and "egl-g2-A" instances (Figure 10 and Tables 5 and 6). In most of the runs, the set time limit was not enough for the HMA to improve its initial solution, so only its initial solution was recorded. That is why the graph for the HMA looks like a straight line in Figure 10. As a result of this, in the measured time period, the ABC algorithm performed better than the HMA after around 100 s.

Table 5. Statistics of the total cost of the globally best solution of the HMA and the ABC algorithms on the "egl-g1-A" instance, within different time limits.

Algorithm	Statistic Value	Output at Different Time Limits		
		≤1 min	≤5 min	≤10 min
ABC	Min.	1,272,733	1,224,289	1,222,579
	Max.	2,069,358	1,299,609	1,274,297
	Avg.	1,370,687.2	1,266,411.97	1,244,482.33
	Std.	161,727.50	19,121.17	13,385.36
HMA	Min.	1,245,358	1,245,358	1,245,358
	Max.	1,380,727	1,380,727	1,380,727
	Avg.	1,323,545.83	1,323,544.97	1,323,519.2
	Std.	32,452.85	32,452.53	32,443.37

Table 6. Statistics of the total cost of the globally best solution of the HMA and the ABC algorithms on the "egl-g2-A" instance, within different time limits.

Algorithm	Statistic Value	Output at Different Time Limits		
		≤1 min	≤5 min	≤10 min
ABC	Min.	1,389,720	1,349,032	1,343,764
	Max.	1,897,513	1,416,208	1,385,876
	Avg.	1,527,504.47	1,386,266.17	1,366,140.43
	Std.	163,125.66	7587.12	11,848.98
HMA	Min.	1,356,204	1,356,204	1,356,204
	Max.	1,478,279	1,478,279	1,478,279
	Avg.	1,429,353	1,425,706.43	1,424,908.2
	Std.	30,287.61	33,358.28	34,299.91

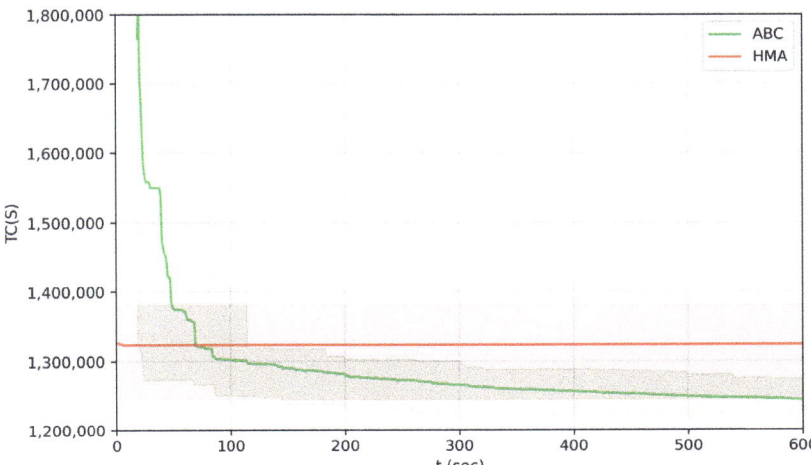

Figure 10. The convergence speed of 30 independent runs of HMA, and ABC algorithm on the "egl-g1-A" instance, plotted on one chart with time limit ($t \leq 600$ s)

Based on the results, it can be concluded that the ABC algorithm can provide a good enough solution within a short amount of time. Since it has a small cycle time, the best global solution can be updated more frequently. The ABC algorithm is better than the ACOPR algorithm in all aspects. The ABC algorithm has faster convergence speed and finds better quality solutions, than the ACOPR algorithm. Furthermore, it is competitive with the HMA, when the running time of the algorithms is set to a short time interval.

6.3. Results of the Operator Experiments

The results of the operator experiments are summarized in Table 7. In each row, the percentage of the number of trials is shown, in which the operator (specified by the column header) found a better solution, compared to the total number of trials in which a better solution was found for the instance (that is specified in the first column). For the sake of simplicity, let us call this measure efficiency. It can be seen that the sub-route plan operator has the highest efficiency in all the three cases, thus, among the examined operators, it has the highest chance to improve the current solution, regardless of the problem size.

A correlation can be observed between the size and complexity of the CARP problem and the efficiency of the operators. As it was mentioned before, the complexity of the "egl-e1-A" instance is medium, the "egl-s1-A" instance is difficult, and the the "egl-g1-A" instance is the most difficult. By increasing the size of the problem, the efficiency of the inversion and the sub-route plan operator increases compared to the other operators, and by decreasing the size of the problem, the efficiency of the insertion, the swap, and the two-opt operators increases compared to the other operators.

Table 7. The efficiency of the move operators compared with each other within the CARP-ABC algorithm, measured on instances of different sizes.

Instance	Efficiency of the Operators				
	Inversion	Insertion	Swap	Two-Opt	Sub-Route Plan
egl-e1-A	15%	26%	17%	16%	27%
egl-s1-A	16%	23%	16%	16%	29%
egl-g1-A	20%	19%	13%	8%	40%

Based on the results, it can be concluded that the sub-route plan operator is more likely to find a better solution than the other operators, especially when a greater modification is needed on the current solution (since it is a randomly generated solution and/or it is a solution of a larger CARP instance).

6.4. Results of the DCARP Experiments

The results for the task appearance events, the demand increase events, and the vehicle breakdown events for the "egl-e1-A" instance can be seen in Table 8, Table 9, and Table 10, respectively. In all the three tables, the first few columns contain the parameter values that can be used to reconstruct the event data components of the problem:

- the travel and service log (with *crc*);
- the task appearance event (with *nt_arc*, *nt_dem*, and *nt_sc*);
- the demand increase event (with *dit_arc*, *dit_dem_inc*, and *dit_sc_inc*);
- the vehicle breakdown event (with *vb_id*).

The best total cost calculated by the RR1 rerouting algorithm, the ABC algorithm, and the HMA are contained by the last three columns. The best total cost of each run is highlighted with bold font.

The results of all the events are summarized in Table 11. It can be seen that in total, the ABC algorithm performed better than the other examined algorithms (RR1 and HMA). The HMA performed better only at the vehicle breakdown events, but the difference is negligible. The RR1 algorithm gave the best results in nearly the same amount of times as the ABC algorithm, in case of task appearance and vehicle breakdown events.

It is not shown in the tables, but the RR1 algorithm has the shortest run time (in the test cases, it was always less than one second). The run time of the other algorithms (ABC and HMA) is approximately the same whether a DCARP or a CARP instance is used as input, since it is the complexity of the problem that mainly defines the convergence speed.

Based on the results, similar conclusions can be made as in the CARP experiments. The ABC algorithm outperforms the HMA for a certain period of time, but then the HMA slowly takes over the lead. If time is the priority, then in the case of task appearance and vehicle breakdown events, the RR1 algorithm should be used. If time and the quality of the solution are equally important, then the ABC algorithm should be used for all events. If the quality of the solution is the priority, then the HMA should be used.

Table 8. The best total costs of 15 independent runs, calculated by the RR1, ABC, and HMA within one minute, after the occurrence of a random task appearance event in the "egl-e1-A" instance.

#	Parameter Values				Outputs of the Algorithm		
	crc	nt_arc	nt_dem	nt_sc	RR1	ABC	HMA
1	315	(25, 75)	58	16	3889	**3702**	3941
2	315	(46, 45)	67	12	**3700**	3705	3799
3	356	(43, 42)	11	11	3720	**3645**	3883
4	379	(42, 57)	20	14	3704	**3647**	4091
5	406	(2, 1)	62	32	**3642**	3658	3671
6	409	(73, 74)	40	25	4077	**3991**	4202
7	419	(9, 8)	37	26	**3693**	3709	3709
8	427	(32, 31)	5	58	4248	**4227**	4235
9	436	(24, 22)	64	4	**3667**	**3667**	**3667**
10	439	(15, 14)	99	7	**3872**	3905	3905
11	457	(6, 5)	46	8	**3714**	**3714**	**3714**
12	490	(41, 40)	207	9	**3764**	**3764**	**3764**
13	517	(22, 75)	66	24	3866	3866	**3841**
14	520	(21, 51)	89	2	**3767**	**3767**	**3767**
15	522	(39, 35)	67	7	**3622**	**3622**	**3622**

Table 9. The best total costs of 15 independent runs, calculated by the RR1, ABC, and HMA within one minute, after the occurrence of a random demand increased event in the "egl-e1-A" instance.

#	Parameter Values				Outputs of the Algorithm		
	crc	dit_arc	dit_dem	dit_sc	RR1	ABC	HMA
1	326	(32, 34)	36	36	4318	**3931**	4171
2	344	(54, 52)	11	11	3749	**3648**	3907
3	345	(50, 52)	15	15	3753	**3636**	3678
4	374	(52, 54)	9	9	3747	**3630**	3814
5	376	(68, 66)	32	32	4036	**3762**	3930
6	384	(44, 45)	18	18	3905	**3668**	3905
7	415	(46, 47)	9	9	3975	**3590**	**3590**
8	431	(44, 59)	11	11	3885	**3632**	3766
9	449	(32, 35)	12	12	4280	**3636**	3683
10	468	(35, 32)	65	65	4334	**4326**	**4326**
11	490	(44, 46)	2	2	3636	**3550**	**3550**
12	490	(32, 33)	28	28	4289	3760	**3674**
13	493	(59, 44)	5	5	3879	3626	**3553**
14	516	(35, 32)	24	24	4293	3756	**3572**
15	545	(35, 41)	13	13	3775	3657	**3559**

Table 10. The best total costs of 15 independent runs, calculated by the RR1, ABC, and HMA within one minute, after the occurrence of a random vehicle breakdown event in the "egl-e1-A" instance.

#	Parameter Values		Outputs of the Algorithm		
	crc	vb_id	RR1	ABC	HMA
1	305	2	**4124**	4217	4737
2	311	1	4060	**4012**	4365
3	342	2	4204	**4126**	4585
4	344	0	**4096**	4112	4303
5	364	0	**4096**	4112	4241
6	399	4	**4004**	4020	4308
7	430	1	**3966**	**3966**	**3966**
8	451	2	4282	**4261**	**4261**
9	463	0	3718	3652	**3639**
10	490	2	4282	**4261**	**4261**
11	495	2	4282	**4261**	**4261**
12	506	0	3621	3621	**3585**
13	507	1	3874	3736	**3572**
14	523	2	**4261**	**4261**	**4261**
15	540	2	**4282**	**4282**	**4282**

Table 11. The total number of the best outputs (and their percentage compared to the total number of outputs) of the algorithms RR1, ABC, and HMA summarized for the "egl-e1-A" instance, for each event type.

Event Type	Outputs of the Algorithm		
	RR1	ABC	HMA
Task appearance	9 (60%)	10 (67%)	6 (40%)
Demand increase	0 (0%)	11 (73%)	7 (47%)
Vehicle breakdown	7 (47%)	8 (53%)	9 (60%)
Total	16 (36%)	29 (64%)	22 (49%)

7. Conclusions and Future Work

In this study, an ABC algorithm for the CARP (CARP-ABC) was developed along with a new move operator, the sub-route plan operator, which is utilized by the proposed CARP-ABC algorithm. The CARP-ABC algorithm was tested both as a CARP and a DCARP solver, then, its performance was compared with other algorithms. The results showed that for both CARP and DCARP instances, the CARP-ABC algorithm excels in finding a relatively good quality solution in a short amount of time. It makes the algorithm highly competitive with the currently most accurate CARP solver, the HMA, when the running time of the algorithms is limited to around one minute.

In the future, the CARP-ABC algorithm will be improved upon, to increase the accuracy of the algorithm without increasing its runtime. The goal is to make the algorithm better than the HMA, even when the running time is unlimited.

Author Contributions: Conceptualization, Z.N.; Formal analysis, Z.N.; Investigation, Z.N.; Methodology, Z.N.; Software, Z.N.; Supervision, Á.W.-S.; Validation, Z.N.; Visualization, Z.N.; Writing—original draft, Z.N.; Writing—review & editing, Z.N., Á.W.-S. and T.D. All authors have read and agreed to the published version of the manuscript.

Funding: This research was funded by Széchenyi 2020 under the EFOP-3.6.1-16-2016-00015.

Institutional Review Board Statement: Not applicable.

Informed Consent Statement: Not applicable.

Data Availability Statement: The used CARP datasets are available at https://www.uv.es/belengue/carp.html (accessed on 21 June 2022). The output data of the experiments discussed in the paper are available at https://drive.google.com/file/d/1LFgct7Z8_W_yx_CppVmN1kAYry3VGM8Q/ (accessed on 21 June 2022).

Acknowledgments: The authors acknowledge support from the Slovenian–Hungarian bilateral project "Optimization and fault forecasting in port logistics processes using artificial intelligence, process mining and operations research", grant 2019-2.1.11-TÉT-2020-00113, and from the National Research, Development and Innovation Office–NKFIH under the grant SNN 129364.

Conflicts of Interest: The authors declare no conflict of interest.

Abbreviations

The following abbreviations are used in this manuscript:

ABC	Artificial Bee Colony
ACOPR	Ant Colony Optimization Algorithm with Path Relinking
CARP	Capacitated Arc Routing Problem
DAG	Directed Acyclic Graph
DCARP	Dynamic Capacitated Arc Routing Problem
GA	Genetic Algorithm
GPS	Global Positioning System
GSTM	Greedy Sub Tour Mutation
HMA	Hybrid Metaheuristic Approach
MAENS	Memetic Algorithm with Extended Neighborhood Search
NP-hard	Non-deterministic Polynomial-time hard
RPSH	Randomized Path-Scanning Heuristic
RSG	Random Solution Generation
TSP	Traveling Salesman Problem
VRP	Vehicle Routing Problem

Appendix A

This appendix shows all the notations that are used in this work, categorized by the context where they appear and along with their meaning.

Table A1. Notations used in the CARP and the DCARP.

Notation	Meaning
G	graph $G = (V, A)$
V	set of vertices
v_0	the depot ($v_0 \in V$)
A	set of arcs
T	set of tasks ($T \subseteq A$)
t_0	the dummy task $t_0 = (v_0, v_0)$
n	the number of tasks that have to be executed
$inv(a)$	the inverse of arc $a \in A$
$head(a)$	the head vertex of arc $a \in A$
$tail(a)$	the tail vertex of arc $a \in A$
$dc(a)$	the dead-heading cost of arc $a \in A$
$id(t)$	the identifier of the task $t \in T$
$dem(t)$	the demand of task $t \in T$
$sc(t)$	the serving cost of task $t \in T$
$mdc(v_i, v_j)$	the minimal total dead-heading cost from vertex v_i to v_j ($v_i, v_j \in V$)
w	the number of vehicles
q	the maximum capacity of a vehicle
r_k	the k-th route plan
l_k	the number of tasks on the k-th route plan
$t(k, i)$	the i-th task in the k-th route plan
$DC(r_k)$	the total dead-heading cost of the route plan r_k
$SC(r_k)$	the total service cost of the route plan r_k
I	a CARP instance
S	a solution for the CARP instance I
$TC(S)$	the total cost of solution S
T_v	set of virtual tasks ($T_v \subseteq T$)
H	set of identifiers of all the vehicles ($|H| = w$)
H_f	set of identifiers of the (currently) free vehicles ($H_f \subseteq H$)
R	set of identifiers of all the route plans
R_e	set of identifiers of the route plans whose execution stopped ($R_e \subseteq R$)
$rt(k)$	the virtual task of the k-th route plan ($k \in R$, $rt(k) \in T_v$)
$rv(k)$	the identifier of the vehicle that is executing the k-th route plan ($k \in R$, $rv(k) \in H$)
m	the number of DCARP instances within a DCARP scenario
$\mathcal{I}$	a DCARP scenario, a set of DCARP instances ($|\mathcal{I}| = m$)
I_i	the i-th DCARP instance within a DCARP scenario ($0 \leq i < m$)
S_i	the accepted solution for the i-th DCARP instance
$TC(S_i)$	the total cost of solution S_i

Table A2. Notations used in the CARP-ABC algorithm.

Notation	Meaning
n_{cs}	the size of the colony
n_{mi}	the maximum number of iterations
n_{gsl}	the global search limit
n_{lsl}	the local search limit
n_{sal}	the solution age limit (within the population)
C	the current colony, a set of solutions ($C = \{S_1, S_2, \ldots\}$, $|C| = n_{cs}$)
$\overline{C}$	the previous colony
$\mathcal{A}$	set of the age of the solutions within C ($\mathcal{A} = \{\alpha_1, \alpha_2, \ldots\}$, $|\mathcal{A}| = n_{cs}$)
P	set of probability values of the solutions within C ($P = \{p_1, p_2, \ldots\}$, $|P| = n_{cs}$)
I	a CARP instance
S^*	the currently known globally best solution
S'	the best solution found within one iteration
S_i^*	the best solution found in the neighborhood of $S_i \in C$
S_i'	the best solution found within one iteration, in the neighborhood of $S_i \in C$
$S_{i,j}^*$	the best solution found in the neighborhood of $S_{i,j}$ ($S_{i,j}$ is a neighbor of $S_i \in C$)
$S_{i,j}'$	the best solution found within one iteration, in the neighborhood of $S_{i,j}$ ($S_{i,j}$ is a neighbor of $S_i \in C$)
α^*	the current age of S^*
α'	the current age of S'
α_i^*	the current age of S_i^*
α_i'	the current age of S_i'

Table A3. Notations used in the description of the sub-route plan operator.

Notation	Meaning
p_{rc}	the reconnection probability
p_{cp}	the correction and perturbation probability
p_l	the linearity probability
p_{rnd}	a random number between 0 and 1
l_{min}	the minimum length of the sub-route plan
l_{max}	the maximal length of the sub-route plan
l	the selected length of the sub-route plan ($l_{min} \leq l \leq l_{max}$)
$t_{k,s}$	the selected starting task of the sub-route plan
$t_{k,e}$	the selected ending task of the sub-route plan
n_{max}	the (maximal) size of the neighborhood of a task arc
t_{k,s^*}	the selected task from the neighborhood of $t_{k,s}$
t_{k,e^*}	the selected task from the neighborhood of $t_{k,e}$
r_k^*	the selected sub-route plan within a route plan r_k
$r_k^\#$	the route plan r_k without the sub-route plan r_k^*
r_k'	the resulting route plan

References

1. Golden, B.L.; Wong, R.T. Capacitated arc routing problems. *Networks* **1981**, *11*, 305–315. [CrossRef]
2. Eglese, R.W. Routeing winter gritting vehicles. *Discret. Appl. Math.* **1994**, *48*, 231–244. [CrossRef]
3. Fink, J.; Loebl, M.; Pelikánová, P. Arc-routing for winter road maintenance. *Discret. Optim.* **2021**, *41*, 100644. [CrossRef]
4. Maniezzo, V. *Algorithms for Large Directed CARP Instances: Urban Solid Waste Collection Operational Support*; Technical Report; University of Bolonha: Bolonha, Italy, 2004.
5. Babaee Tirkolaee, E.; Mahdavi, I.; Seyyed Esfahani, M.M.; Weber, G.W. A hybrid augmented ant colony optimization for the multi-trip capacitated arc routing problem under fuzzy demands for urban solid waste management. *Waste Manag. Res.* **2020**, *38*, 156–172. [CrossRef]
6. Tang, K.; Mei, Y.; Yao, X. Memetic algorithm with extended neighborhood search for capacitated arc routing problems. *IEEE Trans. Evol. Comput.* **2009**, *13*, 1151–1166. [CrossRef]
7. Chen, Y.; Hao, J.K.; Glover, F. A hybrid metaheuristic approach for the capacitated arc routing problem. *Eur. J. Oper. Res.* **2016**, *253*, 25–39. [CrossRef]
8. Ting, C.J.; Tsai, H.S. Ant Colony Optimization with Path Relinking for the Capacitated Arc Routing Problem. *Asian Transp. Stud.* **2018**, *5*, 362–377.
9. Fu, H.; Mei, Y.; Tang, K.; Zhu, Y. Memetic algorithm with heuristic candidate list strategy for capacitated arc routing problem. In Proceedings of the IEEE Congress on Evolutionary Computation, Barcelona, Spain, 18–23 July 2010; IEEE: New York, NY, USA, 2010; pp. 1–8.
10. Chen, X. Maens+: A divide-and-conquer based memetic algorithm for capacitated arc routing problem. In Proceedings of the 2011 Fourth International Symposium on Computational Intelligence and Design, Hangzhou, China, 28–30 October 2011; IEEE: New York, NY, USA, 2011; pp. 83–88.
11. Corberán, Á.; Eglese, R.; Hasle, G.; Plana, I.; Sanchis, J.M. Arc routing problems: A review of the past, present, and future. *Networks* **2021**, *77*, 88–115. [CrossRef]
12. Wu, G.; Zhao, K.; Cheng, J.; Ma, M. A Coordinated Vehicle–Drone Arc Routing Approach Based on Improved Adaptive Large Neighborhood Search. *Sensors* **2022**, *22*, 3702. [CrossRef]
13. Karaboga, D. *An Idea Based on Honey Bee Swarm for Numerical Optimization*; Technical Report; Erciyes University: Kayseri, Turkey, 2005.
14. Karaboga, D.; Görkemli, B. A combinatorial artificial bee colony algorithm for traveling salesman problem. In Proceedings of the 2011 International Symposium on Innovations in Intelligent Systems and Applications, Istanbul, Turkey, 15–18 June 2011; IEEE: New York, NY, USA, 2011; pp. 50–53.
15. Görkemli, B.; Karaboga, D. Quick combinatorial artificial bee colony -qCABC- optimization algorithm for TSP. In Proceedings of the 2nd International Symposium on Computing in Informatics and Mathematics (ISCIM 2013), Tirana, Albania, 26 September 2013; Epoka University: Tirana, Albania, 2013; pp. 97–101.
16. Karaboga, D.; Görkemli, B. Solving traveling salesman problem by using combinatorial artificial bee colony algorithms. *Int. J. Artif. Intell. Tools* **2019**, *28*, 1950004. [CrossRef]
17. Kantawong, K.; Pravesjit, S. An Enhanced ABC algorithm to Solve the Vehicle Routing Problem with Time Windows. *ECTI Trans. Comput. Inf. Technol. (ECTI-CIT)* **2020**, *14*, 46–52. [CrossRef]
18. Mortada, S.; Yusof, Y. A Neighbourhood Search for Artificial Bee Colony in Vehicle Routing Problem with Time Windows. *Int. J. Intell. Eng. Syst.* **2021**, *14*, 255–266. [CrossRef]
19. Cura, T. An artificial bee colony approach for the undirected capacitated arc routing problem with profits. *Int. J. Oper. Res.* **2013**, *17*, 483–508. [CrossRef]

20. Nagy, Z.; Werner-Stark, A.; Dulai, T. A Data-driven Solution for The Dynamic Capacitated Arc Routing Problem. In Proceedings of the IAC in Budapest 2021, Budapest, Hungary, 26–27 November 2021; Kratochvílová, H., Kratochvíl, R., Eds.; Czech Institute of Academic Education z.s.: Prague, Czech Republic, 2021; pp. 64–83.
21. Tong, H.; Minku, L.L.; Menzel, S.; Sendhoff, B.; Yao, X. A Novel Generalised Meta-Heuristic Framework for Dynamic Capacitated Arc Routing Problems. *arXiv* **2022**, arXiv:2104.06585.
22. Golden, B.L.; DeArmon, J.S.; Baker, E.K. Computational experiments with algorithms for a class of routing problems. *Comput. Oper. Res.* **1983**, *10*, 47–59. [CrossRef]
23. Chapleau, L.; Ferland, J.A.; Lapalme, G.; Rousseau, J.M. A parallel insert method for the capacitated arc routing problem. *Oper. Res. Lett.* **1984**, *3*, 95–99. [CrossRef]
24. Ulusoy, G. The fleet size and mix problem for capacitated arc routing. *Eur. J. Oper. Res.* **1985**, *22*, 329–337. [CrossRef]
25. Pearn, W.L. Augment-insert algorithms for the capacitated arc routing problem. *Comput. Oper. Res.* **1991**, *18*, 189–198. [CrossRef]
26. Santos, L.; Coutinho-Rodrigues, J.; Current, J.R. An improved heuristic for the capacitated arc routing problem. *Comput. Oper. Res.* **2009**, *36*, 2632–2637. [CrossRef]
27. Arakaki, R.K.; Usberti, F.L. An efficiency-based path-scanning heuristic for the capacitated arc routing problem. *Comput. Oper. Res.* **2019**, *103*, 288–295. [CrossRef]
28. Beullens, P.; Muyldermans, L.; Cattrysse, D.; Van Oudheusden, D. A guided local search heuristic for the capacitated arc routing problem. *Eur. J. Oper. Res.* **2003**, *147*, 629–643. [CrossRef]
29. Brandão, J.; Eglese, R. A deterministic tabu search algorithm for the capacitated arc routing problem. *Comput. Oper. Res.* **2008**, *35*, 1112–1126. [CrossRef]
30. Hertz, A.; Laporte, G.; Mittaz, M. A tabu search heuristic for the capacitated arc routing problem. *Oper. Res.* **2000**, *48*, 129–135. [CrossRef]
31. Polacek, M.; Doerner, K.F.; Hartl, R.F.; Maniezzo, V. A variable neighborhood search for the capacitated arc routing problem with intermediate facilities. *J. Heuristics* **2008**, *14*, 405–423. [CrossRef]
32. Usberti, F.L.; França, P.M.; França, A.L.M. GRASP with evolutionary path-relinking for the capacitated arc routing problem. *Comput. Oper. Res.* **2013**, *40*, 3206–3217. [CrossRef]
33. Mei, Y.; Tang, K.; Yao, X. A global repair operator for capacitated arc routing problem. *IEEE Trans. Syst. Man Cybern. Part B (Cybern.)* **2009**, *39*, 723–734. [CrossRef]
34. Lacomme, P.; Prins, C.; Ramdane-Chérif, W. A genetic algorithm for the capacitated arc routing problem and its extensions. In *Proceedings of the Applications of Evolutionary Computing (EvoWorkshops 2001: EvoCOP, EvoFlight, EvoIASP, EvoLearn, and EvoSTIM, Como, Italy, 18–20 April 2001 Proceedings)*; Boers, E.J.W., Ed.; Springer: Berlin/Heidelberg, Germany, 2001; pp. 473–483.
35. Lacomme, P.; Prins, C.; Ramdane-Cherif, W. Competitive memetic algorithms for arc routing problems. *Ann. Oper. Res.* **2004**, *131*, 159–185. [CrossRef]
36. Lacomme, P.; Prins, C.; Tanguy, A. First competitive ant colony scheme for the CARP. In *Ant Colony Optimization and Swarm Intelligence (4th International Workshop, ANTS 2004, Brussels, Belgium, 5–8 September 2004)*; Dorigo, M., Birattari, M., Blum, C., Gambardella, L.M., Mondada, F., Stützle, T., Eds.; Springer: Berlin/Heidelberg, Germany, 2004; pp. 426–427.
37. Santos, L.; Coutinho-Rodrigues, J.; Current, J.R. An improved ant colony optimization based algorithm for the capacitated arc routing problem. *Transp. Res. Part B* **2010**, *44*, 246–266. [CrossRef]
38. Tagmouti, M.; Gendreau, M.; Potvin, J.Y. A dynamic capacitated arc routing problem with time-dependent service costs. *Transp. Res. Part C Emerg. Technol.* **2011**, *19*, 20–28. [CrossRef]
39. Archetti, C.; Guastaroba, G.; Speranza, M.G. Reoptimizing the rural postman problem. *Comput. Oper. Res.* **2013**, *40*, 1306–1313. [CrossRef]
40. Mei, Y.; Tang, K.; Yao, X. Evolutionary computation for dynamic capacitated arc routing problem. In *Evolutionary Computation for Dynamic Optimization Problems*; Yang, S., Yao, X., Eds.; Springer: Berlin/Heidelberg, Germany, 2014; pp. 377–401.
41. Yazici, A.; Kirlik, G.; Parlaktuna, O.; Sipahioglu, A. A dynamic path planning approach for multirobot sensor-based coverage considering energy constraints. *IEEE Trans. Cybern.* **2013**, *44*, 305–314. [CrossRef] [PubMed]
42. Liu, M.; Singh, H.K.; Ray, T. A memetic algorithm with a new split scheme for solving dynamic capacitated arc routing problems. In Proceedings of the 2014 IEEE Congress on Evolutionary Computation (CEC), Beijing, China, 6–11 July 2014; IEEE: New York, NY, USA, 2014; pp. 595–602.
43. Monroy-Licht, M.; Amaya, C.A.; Langevin, A.; Rousseau, L.M. The rescheduling arc routing problem. *Int. Trans. Oper. Res.* **2017**, *24*, 1325–1346. [CrossRef]
44. Padungwech, W. Heuristic algorithms for dynamic capacitated arc routing. Ph.D. Thesis, Cardiff University, Cardiff, UK, 2018.
45. Padungwech, W.; Thompson, J.; Lewis, R. Effects of update frequencies in a dynamic capacitated arc routing problem. *Networks* **2020**, *76*, 522–538. [CrossRef]
46. Karaboga, D.; Gorkemli, B. A quick artificial bee colony -qABC- algorithm for optimization problems. In Proceedings of the 2012 International Symposium on Innovations in Intelligent Systems and Applications, Trabzon, Turkey, 2–4 July 2012; IEEE: New York, NY, USA, 2012; pp. 1–5.
47. Albayrak, M.; Allahverdi, N. Development a new mutation operator to solve the traveling salesman problem by aid of genetic algorithms. *Expert Syst. Appl.* **2011**, *38*, 1313–1320. [CrossRef]
48. Bhagade, A.S.; Puranik, P.V. Artificial bee colony (ABC) algorithm for vehicle routing optimization problem. *Int. J. Soft Comput. Eng.* **2012**, *2*, 329–333.

49. Consoli, P.; Yao, X. Diversity-driven selection of multiple crossover operators for the capacitated arc routing problem. In *Evolutionary Computation in Combinatorial Optimisation (14th European Conference, EvoCOP 2014, Granada, Spain, 23–25 April 2014, Revised Selected Papers)*; Blum, C., Ochoa, G., Eds.; Springer: Berlin/Heidelberg, Germany, 2014; pp. 97–108.
50. Willemse, E.J.; Joubert, J.W. Splitting procedures for the mixed capacitated arc routing problem under time restrictions with intermediate facilities. *Oper. Res. Lett.* **2016**, *44*, 569–574. [CrossRef]
51. Durstenfeld, R. Algorithm 235: Random permutation. *Commun. ACM* **1964**, *1477*, 420. [CrossRef]
52. DeArmon, J.S. A Comparison of Heuristics for the Capacitated Chinese Postman Problem. Master's Thesis, University of Maryland, College Park, MD, USA, 1981.
53. Benavent, E.; Campos, V.; Corberán, A.; Mota, E. The capacitated arc routing problem: Lower bounds. *Networks* **1992**, *22*, 669–690. [CrossRef]
54. Kiuchi, M.; Shinano, Y.; Hirabayashi, R.; Saruwatari, Y. An exact algorithm for the capacitated arc routing problem using parallel branch and bound method. In *Spring National Conference of the Operational Research Society of Japan*; INFORMS: Catonsville, MD, USA, 1995; pp. 28–29.

Article
A Path Planning Model for Stock Inventory Using a Drone

László Radácsi, Miklós Gubán, László Szabó * and József Udvaros

Faculty of Finance and Accountancy, Budapest Business School, 1149 Budapest, Hungary
* Correspondence: szabo.laszlo4@uni-bge.hu

Abstract: In this study, a model and solution are shown for controlling the inventory of a logistics warehouse in which neither satellite positioning nor IoT solutions can be used. Following a review of the literature on path planning, a model is put forward using a drone that can be moved in all directions and is suitable for imaging and transmission. The proposed model involves three steps. In the first step, a traversal path definition provides an optimal solution, which is pre-processing. This is in line with the structure and capabilities of the warehouse. In the second step, the pre-processed path determines the real-time movement of the drone during processing, including camera movements and image capture. The third step is post-processing, i.e., the processing of images for QR code identification, the interpretation of the QR code, and the examination of matches and discrepancies for inventory control. A key benefit for the users of this model is that the result can be achieved without any external orientation tools, relying solely on its own movement and the organization of a pre-planned route. The proposed model can be effective not only for inventory control, but also for exploring the structure of a warehouse shelving system and determining empty cells.

Keywords: drone; inventory management; GA model; route planning; warehouse

MSC: 90B05

1. Introduction

In large, lightly structured warehouses in logistics centers, especially those where different products from several companies are stored, it is often difficult to pinpoint the exact location of stored goods. This is primarily the case when storage is not carried out with the help of automatic forklifts, or when errors occur in the registered and actual location of the goods due to mistakes during the picking process. To make matters worse, it is very difficult or in some cases impossible to use GPS-based identifications in these warehouses. If Time of Flight (ToF) cameras are not available, the positioning of the automatic devices is not possible. In this study, a model capable of updating the stock-on-hand registry using a drone is introduced, and the proposed model applies to a specific warehouse.

Storage (loading and unloading) and picking, unit load formation, and labeling take place in the warehouse building. In the warehouse, a double shelving system is used. Between the double shelves, there is a wide corridor in which the drone can travel. A shelf is divided into rows or compartments (cells). Within one compartment there can be one, two, or three locations created. Each unit stored in these locations is identified with a QR code that contains all the important data that are relevant to our solution.

Driving down the aisle, the drone searches for the QR codes placed on the outer cartons, and as soon as the drone camera finds one, a photo is taken and it is sent to a processing device (in our study, it is a large capacity tablet). According to the proposed model, the drone knows its exact location in the warehouse, i.e., the 3D data inside the warehouse are defined. This and the QR code or codes sent (in the case of a multi-cell location) can tell the inventory management model exactly where the product is located, or if the location is empty. Further processing depends solely on the capabilities of the application, which is beyond the scope of this study.

The mid-range drone and its camera can take a good quality picture from the middle of the aisle and identify the stored goods in the picture based on the blue and red colors used on the shelves. This helps the drone to move forward, backward, up, and down in the middle of the aisle, with no right-to-left movement. At the end of the aisle, the dock is manually placed where the battery can be charged and replaced.

After this introduction, an optimal route is described that is optimized primarily for the operating time of the drone, i.e., the drone will continue checking the locations until its battery wears out.

Based on the literature review, we have identified a gap in the research, as we have not encountered an approach such as ours to inventory accounting; therefore, we can say that the drone inventory based on this paper can be considered as a development in the existing discussion in this field.

Our study is founded on the following research question: How can warehouse stocking be automated by drones? Within this question, we pose a sub-question: How can the time of stocking be optimized by drones? In this study, we aimed to develop an algorithm to mathematically answer these questions; thus, we have proposed a model for automated warehouse stocking.

2. Path Planning

Our analysis suggests that there are very different approaches to path planning for the problem we are considering. In general, these studies focus primarily on a specific problem. Furthermore, the solutions that are used also vary (e.g., [1]).

To begin with, we investigated several solution methods. According to the literature, studies have used the Swarm Intelligence approach to solve, for example, the collision avoidance problem of robots in 3D media such as water [2] using a velocity-matching method. The route planning used in this paper is based on the ant algorithm. Our investigations have shown that this solution does not provide sufficient convergence and that the motions in our problem are different from it, but several elements of the basic model can be incorporated into our model. A similar and similarly unsuccessful attempt based on swarm intelligence is presented in [3], where an evolutionary algorithm was also chosen as the suitable approach. Another approach that can be used concerns automatic parking systems. It essentially provides a similar baseline for the path selection in a planar domain to the vertical-plane path-search algorithm. Of course, the authors focus primarily on the narrow setting, i.e., they focus on maneuvering, and their path-finding algorithm focuses on finding a parking space, although this is solved using a less well-known RRT (Rapid-exploring Random Trees) algorithm. The chosen method for the model in [4] provides a useful solution in this direction. In this paper, the route planning of UAVs (Unmanned Aerial Vehicles) under terrain conditions is considered. The path is based on a polynomial model, a solution whereby only discontinuous linear motions need to be simulated. The advantage of their method is that it improves the initial population after construction using an ACO.

Several articles deal with logistics inventory control models and propose a specific solution. In their article, F. Benes et al. describe that, in the case of large outdoor warehouses, general identification methods are lengthy and inadequate. One way to easily and quickly determine the inventory is to deploy a UAV (unmanned aerial vehicle) for product identification. In this case, however, there is a problem in determining the location of the goods. A drone moves at a higher altitude, which can lead to a situation where we cannot accurately determine the location of the goods. This paper deals with the development of the definition of the correct flight level, which is suitable for distinguishing one of the identified elements at a distance of at least 2 m. The evaluation is based on an RSSI (received signal strength indicator) value. The experiment proved that the two objects can be distinguished even at the maximum reading distance of the selected passive UHF RFID tags [5]. This solution does not provide a suitable solution, since in this case the products are placed in one flat, whereas we need to check the inventory of a warehouse with a shelf system (3D).

Indoor drone or unmanned aerial vehicle (UAV) operations in automated or pilot-controlled drone use cases are addressed by Kurt Geebelen et al. Automated indoor flights have stricter requirements for stability and localization accuracy compared to classic outdoor use cases, which rely primarily on (RTK) GNSS for localization. In this paper, the effect of multiple sensors on 3D indoor-position accuracy is investigated using the OASE flexible sensor fusion platform. This evaluation is based on real drone flights in an industrial laboratory, with mm-accurate ground truth measurements provided by motion capture cameras, which enable the sensors to be evaluated based on their deviation from ground reality in 2D and 3D. The sensors considered in the research are: IMU, the sonar, SLAM camera, ArUco markers, and Ultra-Wideband (UWB). The article shows that with this setup, the achievable 2D (3D) indoor localization error varies from 4.4 cm to 21 cm depending on the sensor set selected. They also include cost/accuracy tradeoffs to indicate the relative importance of different sensor combinations depending on the (engineering) budget and use case. These laboratory results were validated in a Proof-of-Concept deployment of an inventory-scanning drone with more than 10 flight hours in a 65,000 m^2 warehouse. By combining the laboratory results and real-world deployment experience, the different subsets of the sensors represent a minimum viable solution for three different indoor use cases, considering accuracy and cost: a large drone with low weight and cost constraints, one or more medium-sized drones, and a swarm of weight- and cost-constrained nano drones [6]. Our solution also eliminates these flight inaccuracies, as the drone takes a picture from the approaching position, which is processed by software (which extracts the QR code from it). Therefore, the inaccuracies recommended in the article are negligible in our case.

As part of their research project, A. Rhiat, L. Chalal and A. Saadane developed a prototype named "Smart Shelf" that simulates a smart warehouse where mobile robots with grips managed by the ROS "Robotic Operating System" can autonomously navigate through inverse kinematics and different obstacles between other robots; on the other hand, RFID and iBeancon technology have a Smart Shelf to manage stocks. All items on the shelf are identified by RFID tags. The connection of the robots must be applicable to the various predefined or non-obstacles to optimize their search and items they encounter and to accessing the local network through a predefined map in the database. In addition, the embedding of Bin Packing Optimization techniques helps to improve the utilization of static volumes. Optimization algorithms can take into account some robotic constraints, including accessibility, improving the quality of placements and minimizing damaged goods. Their project aims to minimize human intervention and gain time [7]. We consider the solution very useful; it can also be used in our case. However, a problem is caused by the fact that we are inspecting the stock during the storage process, while material handling is taking place. Therefore, we have to discard this solution as well, since it is not possible to use the Smart Shelf during the material-handling process.

Haishi Liu et al. show that tobacco companies must regularly take inventory of finished products as well as raw and auxiliary materials, and drones with radio frequency identification (RFID) readers are becoming a major application trend for inventory applications. Under the condition of ensuring the accuracy of the inventory, this paper considers the limitations of the drone's physical performance, the limitations of the RFID reader, etc., and presents the power of the drone with respect to modeling and a task-planning model for the UAV. An inventory library equipped with an RFID reader is recommended. Thus, considering the problem whereby the greedy strategy in the traditional differential evolution (DE) algorithm causes the loss of location information preserved by other individuals, we propose a hybrid DE algorithm based on lion swarm optimization. Finally, the proposed algorithm was verified by environmental modeling based on data from the tobacco industry warehouse [8]. This solution is already similar to our model, but our proposed Generation Algorithm (OGA) simplifies the solution.

Our study also concerns the determination of optimal routes. The location search strategies used during picking can also provide a good basis, as the goal is to work as quickly and accurately as possible. Based on this, two basic strategies are distinguished: in the case of the strategy regarding the increasing horizontal location coordinates, the order of visiting each storage location corresponds to the increase in the horizontal coordinates of the storage sites. The zoning strategy is a variation of the strategy of increasing the horizontal location coordinates, in which the scaffolding field is first divided into (even-numbered) superimposed zones, and storage locations within each zone are accessed in ascending order of the horizontal location coordinates [9]. However, regarding warehouse robotization, in many cases, besides route planning, the other task is to balance the size of the robot fleet and the load stabilizing between the robots, which is not the case of this study [10].

Moving to the next aisle is a manual movement, as the aisles may not be processed in a sequential way, there may be a closed aisle, or the next aisle might be in another part of the building. This adds another aim to our proposed model of enabling the drone to recognize its own position.

These types of solutions are already used in several places, mainly for large multinational companies. There are some excellent solutions such as the Eyesee system developed by the Hardis Group, a comprehensive drone inventory solution that includes a drone capable of flying unmanned and equipped with a system for automatically capturing and identifying barcode data and handling the collected data via Amazon Web Services [11].

A similar problem is analyzed in [12], involving the target tracking of a drone moving in a defined closed area, but this goes beyond the scope of our study, as their goal is to recognize the target and choose its speed; however, it is still of relevance. The article chooses the Fuzzy solution, which is a viable option for this study as well, since in many cases the position of the QR code within the given location is not clear and the camera unfortunately does not see it in all cases. For this reason, fuzzy control after the basic and deterministic movement should be incorporated into the model. This can also be applied to differences due to columns. The authors of [13] solve the positioning of a drone in a GPS-free environment using a ToF camera used in robotics and self-guidance. However, this approach demands considerable investment into hardware as well. The camera is installed on the ceiling, and this monitors the positioning of the drone in the x, y direction and changes in height. Important technical solutions are presented to prevent interference from rotors. With the use of Gaussian function filtering, it was feasible to accurately analyze the situation in 3D. The article also provides an exact algorithm as a solution. Another methodology worth considering for closed-area drone control is presented in [14]. The authors use a voxel model and perform two types of route calculations: one for the shortest route and the other for the cheapest route.

Their problem is mainly the use of obstacle-avoidance image analysis, for which they use the distance transformation method for an abnormal image laid down by A. Rosenfeld and J. L. Pfaltz in *Distance Functions on Digital Pictures*, from the journal *Pattern Recognition* [15]. The obstacles, in the form of shelves, are assumed to be fixed, which is problematic because this is not always the case. Their approach keeps the drone safe from the obstacle within an effective range. Another article suggests a search for known trajectory options [16]. In their proposal, a usable genetic algorithm is used, which would be very useful in choosing the optimal crawl route for our study as well. The initial population is selected by a randomly generated greedy algorithm. An interesting solution is a low-complexity, machine-learning-based algorithm for optimizing the location of DBSs (drone base stations) [17] based on minimizing the collective wireless reception signal strength experienced by active terminals. The proposed algorithm reduces propagation loss in the system and provides a lower bit error rate compared to the Euclidean cost comparison. The main result of this study is the creation of a model that can provide input for a genetic Algorithm and can even be effective as a precise tool. This is pre-operation processing, as all processing can start with the knowledge of the optimum. The second result is a clear position-definition that is in-service and real-time.

3. Materials and Methods

The first step in creating a model is to clarify the notations and their content; therefore, a complete parameter exploration was carried out. The data set was defined with the help of practitioners. The basic data collected were grouped according to their roles in the model. Then, after selecting the parameters needed, it was important to capture their dimensions. In the second step, we created a parametric model of the warehouse and the factory parameters of the drone we wanted to use, improved with the data we had found. We created a manageable simplified model of motion and velocity (the simplification was within reason). The next step was to work out a practical positioning strategy. Then, we created a mathematical model of the operation. After that, the necessary items and environment for the optimization were selected.

During the testing of the GA method, we encountered some inconsistencies, which caused the model to undergo several manual tunings (the main reasons were the discrepancy between the factory and real drone parameters and the not necessarily smooth motion, which could have been due to several reasons, e.g., temperature and stock saturation problems). These inconsistencies, as they required relatively small modifications, were easily eliminated.

3.1. Known Data

In this section, we provide the mathematical model of the problem and the associated known and unknown data. The known data include the most important parameters of the warehouse and the drone: specifically, they were provided by the warehousing company, and the drone parameters are given in the technical specifications. Tables 1 and 2 summarize the data used for the model and provide the notations. We will use each index consistently for the same data, so we will also provide a table of indexes.

Table 1. Summary and notation of known data.

$\mathbf{w} = \mathbf{w}[w_x, w_y]$	The size of the warehouse
h_e	The vertical distance between the storage shelves
h_h	Horizontal distance between storage shelves
m	The number of storage shelves
h_w	The width of the corridor
h_c	The width of the road
n	The number of compartments within the rows
r	The number of rows of shelves
$\mathbf{D} = \mathbf{D}[d_x, d_y, d_z]$	The position of the dock. $d_z = 0$
$\mathbf{P}_l = \mathbf{P}_l[p_{lx}, p_{ly}, 0]$	The position of shelf $\mathbf{P}_1$ is indicated by the red circle in Figure 2. If l is odd, it denotes the left shelf row of the aisle; if l is even, it denotes the right shelf row.
$R_k = R_k(i, j)$	Shows the compartment in the i-th row and j-th column of the k-th shelf ($k = 1; 2$)
$\mathbf{C}_k = \mathbf{C}_k[c_{ix}, c_{iy}, c_{iz}]$	The starting position of the middle guide path between the two shelves, e.g., $c_{kx} = \frac{p_{2l+1,x} + p_{2l+2,x}}{2}$, etc., and ($l = 0, \ldots r - 1$). In Figure 2, it is indicated by a green square. $c_{kz} = \frac{h_e}{2}$, where the z coordinate is equal to half the height of the shelf.
$\overline{\mathbf{C}}_k = \overline{\mathbf{C}}_k[\overline{c}_{ix}, \overline{c}_{iy}, \overline{c}_{iz}]$	The end position of the middle guide path between the two shelves. $\overline{c}_{kx} = \frac{p_{2l+1,x} + p_{2l+2,x}}{2}$, etc., and ($l = 0, \ldots r - 1$). In Figure 2, it is indicated by a green square. $c_{kz} = \frac{h_e}{2}$. Here, the z coordinate is equal to half the height of the shelf.
T_w	At full charge, the operating time of the drone. During this time, a person must get from the charger to the compartments and back
T_{PH}	Time for taking a picture
V_h	Horizontal forward speed
V_a	Speed of ascent
V_d	The rate of descent is $V_a \approx 0.99 \, V_d$; therefore, the two are considered to be equal.
V_r	Rotation speed (degrees)
Δt	Indicates the operating time that must be left on arrival at the charger in case of intermediate charging.
T_{ch}	Charging time

Table 2. Table of indexes.

k, k_1	The number of the shelving system
i, i_1	Indicate the rows of the shelving system
j, j_1	Indicate the columns of the shelving system (as an example, see the $R_k = R_k(i,j)$ in the previous table)
v	Indicates the subindex of the consecutive compartments
u	The running index of the charges

The schematic structure of the shelving system is shown in Figures 1–4.

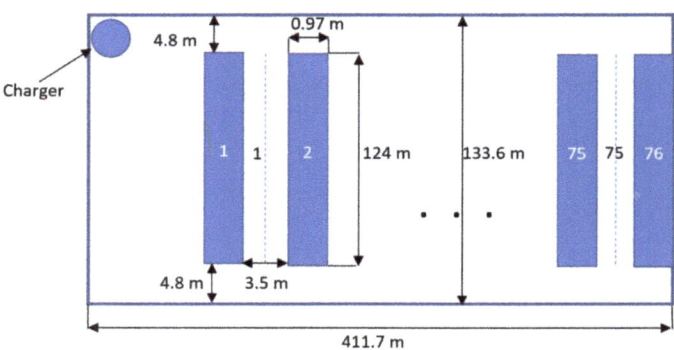

Figure 1. The floor plan of the warehouse with the dimensions. (Source: self-edited figure).

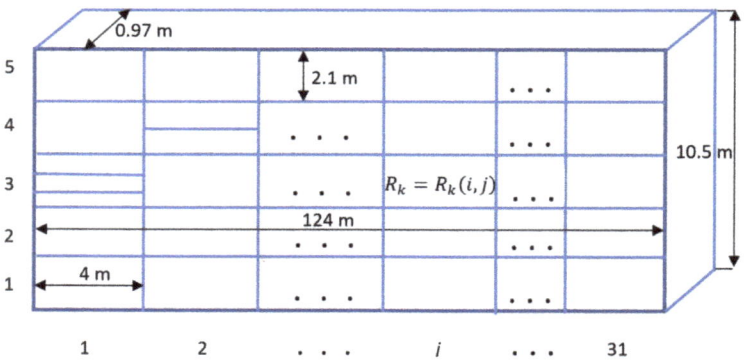

Figure 2. Shelf system details. (Source: self-edited figure).

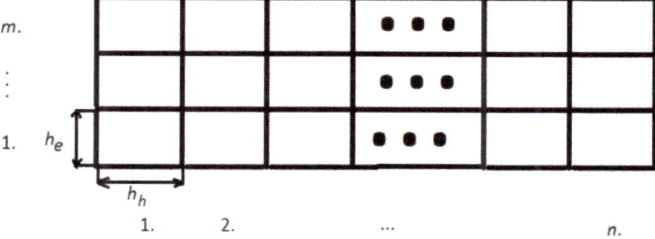

Figure 3. Structure of a shelf. (Source: self-edited figure).

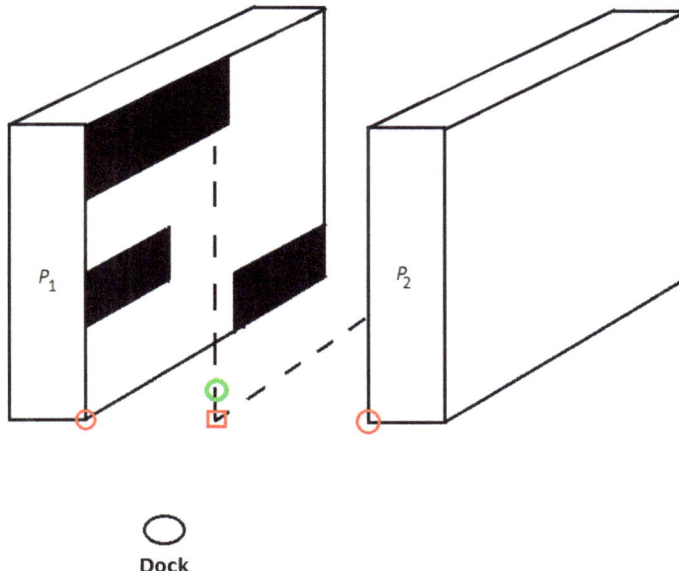

Figure 4. The shelving system to be tested. Black shelves indicate compartments that have already been checked. The green circle is the start position of the examination, the red square is the center of the corridor (reference point). The red circles are reference points. (Source: self-edited figure).

3.2. Variable Data

Search for the
$$S = S((k_1 i_1 j_1), (k_2 i_2 j_2), \ldots, (k_{2mn} i_{2mn} j_{2mn})) \tag{1}$$
series of compartments, where
$$(k_{l_1} i_{l_1} j_{l_1}) \neq (k_{l_2} i_{l_2} j_{l_2}) \text{ ha } l_1 \neq l_2. \tag{2}$$

The drone passes over all the compartments of the two shelving systems during operation. The series of compartments S describes the order of these compartments where the first parameter is the shelf system number (1 or 2) and the other two are the number of shelves (rows) in the shelf system and the number of compartments (columns) within it.

The drone needs to be charged from time to time so it may not be possible to process the two shelf systems with one charge (especially when the batteries are not fully charged from the start). For this reason, the series of compartments S must be divided into parts that can be processed with one charge, i.e., the drone contains compartments processed during operation. (Table 3 shows summary and notation of variable data). Thus, the processing time consists of three parts:

- The drone travels to the first compartment to be processed;
- It processes the compartments;
- It returns to the charger.

Table 3. Summary and notation of variable data.

$\mathbf{x} = \left[x_{k,i,j}\right]$	The number of processing sequence (as the drone moves between each compartment)
$T_f = T_f(S)$	The execution time for the S-compartment series visit
$t_P = t_P(\acute{S})$	The dockless execution time of the $\acute{S}$ series
$t_{T,R_k(i_p,j_p)}$	The time from the dock to the starting point (i_p, j_p)
$t_{R_k(i_q,j_q),T}$	The travel time from (i_q, j_q) to the dock
$t_{R_{k_1}(i_1,j_1),R_{k_2}(i_2,j_2)}$	The travel time from one compartment in one row to another compartment in another row
$T_{R_{k_1}(i_1,j_1),R_{k_2}(i_2,j_2)}(C)$	Time from one row compartment to the other row compartment with a front-of-row change
$T_{R_{k_1}(i_1,j_1),R_{k_2}(i_2,j_2)}(\overline{C})$	Time from one row compartment to another row compartment with end of row change
p	Number of charges—1

The following correlations illustrate the abovementioned 3 points. The drone goes to the charger when it arrives at a compartment in which the available operating time for the previous compartment is still greater than Δt, but in the case of the current compartment it is already less, i.e., the operating time falls below a predefined level.

In addition, it must be fulfilled that the sum of each subchain must be equal to the entire chain, since each compartment must be examined in S order.

Mark the series of compartment tests carried out simultaneously in a corridor

$$\check{S} = \check{S}((k_p i_p j_p), \ldots, (k_q i_q j_q)) \subset S \ (q \geq p) \quad q, p \in \mathbb{N}^+ \tag{3}$$

if the shelving system is to be changed, it will change either in the direction of $\overline{C}$ or in the direction of C.

Let $\check{S}$ denote the corridor change in G, i.e.,

$$G = \begin{cases} (k_p, k_{p+1}, 0), & \text{if it changes in direction } C \\ (k_p, k_{p+1}, -1), & \text{if it changes in direction } \overline{C} \end{cases} \tag{4}$$

Let

$$\acute{S} = \acute{S}\left(\check{S}_1, G_1, \check{S}_2, \ldots, G_{f-1}, \check{S}_f\right) \tag{5}$$

then, the execution time of the $\acute{S}$ series is from the charger to the charger

$$T_f(\acute{S}) = t_{T,R_k(i_p,j_p)} + t_P(\acute{S}) + t_{R_k(i_q,j_q),T} \tag{6}$$

if the following is met

$$0 \leq T_w - T_f(\acute{S}) \leq \Delta t \tag{7}$$

Let

$$S = S((k_1 i_1 j_1), (k_2 i_2 j_2), \ldots, (k_{2mn} i_{2mn} j_{2mn})) = \sum_{u=1}^{r} \acute{S}_u \tag{8}$$

where every $\acute{S}_u$

$$0 \leq T_w - T_f(\acute{S}_u) \leq \Delta t \ (u = 1, \ldots, r-1). \tag{9}$$

The last one no longer needs to meet this condition.

The final report must also include a flight to the charger. For this reason, S must be supplemented with the **D** drone charger in the appropriate places. Its location will be determined by a later algorithm (Target Function Generation Algorithm). The function

$T_f(Ś_u)$ represents the operating time of the drone from a charger to the next charger. The sum of these yields the total operating time.

Then the execution sequence is as follows:

$$S_v = S_v(\mathbf{D}, Ś_1, \mathbf{D}, \ldots, Ś_r, \mathbf{D}). \tag{10}$$

Then the goal is

$$T = \sum_{u=1}^{r} T_f(Ś_u) \rightarrow min! \tag{11}$$

If $T_f(S_v)$ is minimal, then S_v is the optimal route

3.3. The Speed of the Drone

The speed of the drone is determined by knowing the speed of horizontal travel and the speed of vertical travel by projecting it on a diagonal path, as shown in Figure 5. The red arrow indicates velocity as a vector and its magnitude is the magnitude of the current velocity.

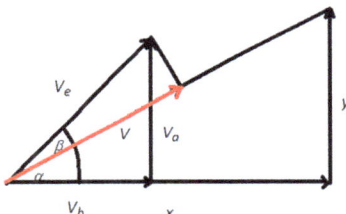

Figure 5. Drone speed (source: self-edited figure).

Ascension:

$$V_e = \sqrt{v_h^2 + v_a^2} \tag{12}$$

$$\alpha = \arctan\frac{y}{x}, \beta = \arctan\frac{v_a}{v_h} \tag{13}$$

Descension:

$$V_e = \sqrt{v_h^2 + v_d^2} \tag{14}$$

$$\beta = \arctan\frac{v_d}{v_h} \tag{15}$$

It follows that the ascension speed of the drone is:

$$V_1(x,y) = V_e \cdot \cos(\beta - \alpha) = V_e \cdot \cos\left(\arctan\frac{v_a}{v_h} - \arctan\frac{y}{x}\right) \tag{16}$$

It follows that the descension speed of the drone is:

$$V_2(x,y) = V_e \cdot \cos\left(\arctan\frac{v_d}{v_h} - \arctan\frac{y}{x}\right) \tag{17}$$

Let i_v, j_v denote the indices of the compartment corresponding to the location of the drone, and i_{v+1}, j_{v+1} denote the indices of the next compartment to be examined by the drone.

If

$$x = abs(j_v - j_{v+1}) \cdot h_h \tag{18}$$

$$y = abs(i_v - i_{v+1}) \cdot h_e. \tag{19}$$

If $x = 0$, then

If $i_v - i_{v+1} > 0$

$$V_3(x,y) = V_d \tag{20}$$

If $i_v - i_{v+1} < 0$

$$V_4(x,y) = V_a \tag{21}$$

then it follows that the speed of the drone is:

$$V = V(x,y) = \begin{cases} j_v - j_{v+1} \geq 0 \text{ és } x \neq 0 \text{ akkor } V_2(x,y) \\ j_v - j_{v+1} < 0 \text{ és } x \neq 0 \text{ akkor } V_1(x,y) \\ j_v - j_{v+1} \geq 0 \text{ és } x = 0 \text{ akkor } V_3(x,y) \\ j_v - j_{v+1} < 0 \text{ és } x = 0 \text{ akkor } V_4(x,y) \end{cases} \tag{22}$$

Thus, substituting $(i_v - i_{v+1}) \cdot h_h$ for x, and substituting $(j_v - j_{v+1}) \cdot h_e$ for y, we obtain the following

$$V_1 = V_1((j_v - j_{v+1}) \cdot h_h, (i_v - i_{v+1}) \cdot h_e) = \\ = V_e \cdot \cos\left(\arctan\left(\frac{v_a}{v_h}\right) - \arctan\left(\frac{abs(i_v - i_{v+1}) \cdot h_e}{abs(j_v - j_{v+1}) \cdot h_h}\right)\right) \tag{23}$$

$$V_2 = V_2((i_v - i_{v+1}) \cdot h_h, (j_v - j_{v+1}) \cdot h_e) = \\ = V_d \cdot \cos\left(\arctan\left(\frac{v_d}{v_h}\right) - \arctan\left(\frac{abs(i_v - i_{v+1}) \cdot h_e}{abs(j_v - j_{v+1}) \cdot h_h}\right)\right) \tag{24}$$

This depends on the horizontal and vertical travel distances.

3.4. The Length and Time of Each Route

The drone begins all processing by centering the two shelving systems, as shown in the green circle's position in Figure 6. This point denotes the center of the bottom row (which can be adjusted if necessary). The drone can take the best shot from the center of the compartments. The steps of processing include:

- The drone travels to the first compartment to be processed;
- It processes compartments;
- It travels back to the charger.

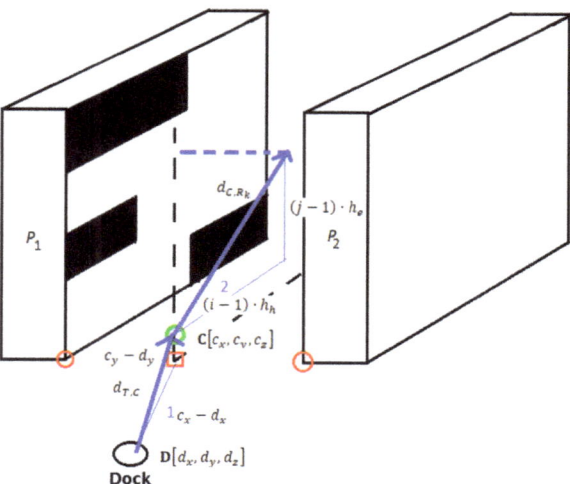

Figure 6. Route and guides. The green circle is the start position of the examination; the blue line is the route of drone; the red square is the center of the corridor (reference point). The red circles are referece points. (source: self-edited figure).

3.4.1. The Journey and Time from the Dock to the Starting Point

It consists of three parts (Figure 6):
- Step 1. the drone travels from the charger to the starting point between the shelves (as indicated by the green circle);
- Step 2. the drone travels to the first compartment to be processed;
- Step 3. its camera is turned in the correct direction.

Step 1. Time to reach the starting position of the shelves
Distance of compartment $R_k = R_k(i,j)$ from charger:

$$d_{T,R_k(i,j)} = d_{T,C} + d_{C,R_k}. \tag{25}$$

$R_k = R_k(i,j)$ compartment access time from charger:

$$t_{T,R_k(i,j)} = t_{T,C} + t_{C,R_k}, \tag{26}$$

where $d_{T,C}$ is the path between the docking station and the starting position of the middle guide path between the two shelves to the green square.

$$d_{T,C_k} = \sqrt{\left(\frac{h_e}{2}\right)^2 + (c_{kx} - d_x)^2 + \left(c_{ky} - d_y\right)^2} \tag{27}$$

$t_{T,C}$ is the time required to reach the starting position of the middle guide path between the Dock and the two shelves:

$$t_{T,C_k} = \frac{h_e}{2V_a} + \frac{\sqrt{(c_{kx} - d_x)^2 + \left(c_{ky} - d_y\right)^2}}{V_h}. \tag{28}$$

Step 2. Distance and time from the starting position of the shelves to the starting compartment.

Distance and time from the center to the starting compartment:

$$d_{C_k,R_k} = \sqrt{((j-1) \cdot h_h)^2 + ((i-1) \cdot h_e)^2} \tag{29}$$

$$t_{C_k,R_k} = \frac{d_{C_k,R_k}}{V((j-1) \cdot h_h, (i-1) \cdot h_e)} + \frac{90}{V_r} + T_{PH} \tag{30}$$

Step 3. The camera
Where $\frac{90}{V_r}$ is the camera rotation time.
The way to the starting position:

$$t_{T,R_k(i,j)} = t_{T,C_k} + t_{C_k,R_k} = \\ = \frac{h_e}{2V_a} + \frac{\sqrt{(c_{kx}-d_x)^2+\left(c_{ky}-d_y\right)^2}}{V_h} + \frac{\sqrt{((j-1)\cdot h_h)^2+((i-1)\cdot h_e)^2}}{V((j-1)\cdot h_h,(i-1)\cdot h_e)} + \frac{90}{V_r} + T_{PH} \tag{31}$$

3.4.2. The Time to Travel to the Dock from a Given Point Can Be Determined Similarly

This is the reverse of the previous since
- Step 1—first, rotate the camera to the home position.
- Step 2—go to the starting point of the shelving system.
- Step 3—go to the charger.

Summarized as follows:

$$t_{R_k(i,j),T} = t_{R_k,c} + t_{C_k,T} =$$

$$= \frac{90}{V_r} + \frac{\sqrt{((j-1)\cdot h_h)^2 + ((i-1)\cdot h_e)^2}}{V((j-1)\cdot h_h, (i-1)\cdot h_e)} + \frac{h_e}{2V_d} + \frac{\sqrt{(c_{kx}-d_x)^2 + (c_{ky}-d_y)^2}}{V_h} \quad (32)$$

3.4.3. The Length and Time of a Point-To-Point Route

The path and time between the next two compartments are determined as shown in Figure 7. Due to the middle plane, it is sufficient to determine the distance between the two compartments by creating a Pythagorean theorem. It is enough to calculate the speed for the time and by dividing the distance we obtain the time. In addition, the camera can rotate if necessary (180°). This can be determined by subtracting the position of the shelf system of the two compartments and then taking the absolute value. This is 0 if the 2 cells are in the same shelving system and 1 if the two compartments are in a separate shelving system. If the rotation time is multiplied by this value, it will either rotate or not as per our need. At the end, the time of photography is added.

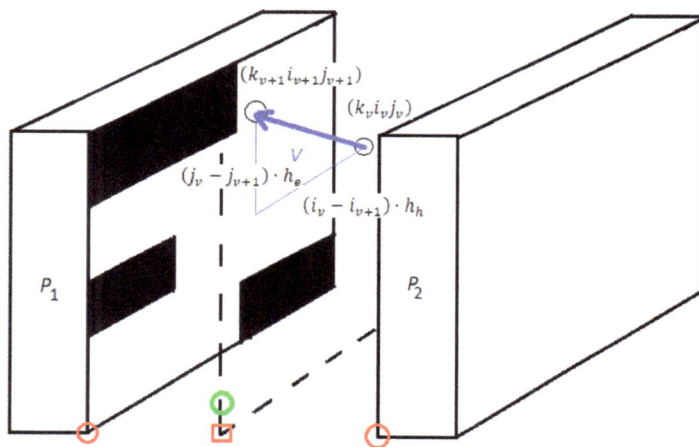

Figure 7. Compartment to compartment. The green circle is the start position of the examination; the blue line is the route of drone; the red square is the center of the corridor (reference point). The red circles are referece points. (source: self-edited figure).

Let us take $(k_v i_v j_v), (k_{v+1} i_{v+1} j_{v+1})$ as the two points. Their distance is:

$$d((k_v i_v j_v), (k_v i_{v+1} j_{v+1})) = \sqrt{((j_v - j_{v+1})\cdot h_h)^2 + ((i_v - i_{v+1})\cdot h_e)^2} \quad (33)$$

Time spent on this route by the drone:

$$t_{P_1}((k_v i_v j_v), (k_{v+1} i_{v+1} j_{v+1})) =$$

$$= \frac{\sqrt{((j_v - j_{v+1})\cdot h_h)^2 + ((i_v - i_{v+1})\cdot h_e)^2}}{V((j_v - j_{v+1})\cdot h_h, (i_v - i_{v+1})\cdot h_e)} + \frac{abs(k_v - k_{v+1})\cdot 180}{V_r} + T_{PH} \quad (34)$$

where

$$\frac{abs(k_1 - k_2)\cdot 180}{V_r} \quad (35)$$

is the rotation of the camera.

3.4.4. From One Compartment to Another Compartment

When considering change from one compartment in one row to another compartment in another row, we used the following steps (See Figure 8):

- Step 1—first, the drone moves to the starting point of the shelving system;
- Step 2—then, it moves to the starting point of the next shelving system;
- Step 3—then, it moves to the starting compartment of the queue.

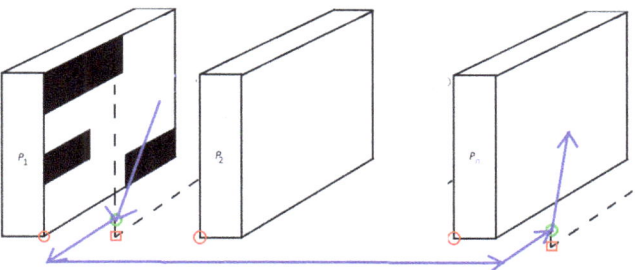

Figure 8. From compartment to compartment to another row. The green circle is the start position of the examination; the blue line is the route of drone; the red square is the center of the corridor (reference point). The red circles are referece points.

The situation is similar if the change is made at the other end of the shelving system. Let

$$a(j) = \begin{cases} j-1, & \text{if } C \text{ is the point under test} \\ n-j, & \text{if } \overline{C} \text{ is the point under test} \end{cases} \tag{36}$$

$$T_{R_{k_1}(i_1,j_1),R_{k_2}(i_2,j_2)}(C) = t_{R_{k_1},C_{k_1}} + t_{C_{k_1},C_{k_2}} + t_{C_{k_1},R_{k_1}} =$$
$$= \frac{d_{R_{k_1},C_{k_1}}}{V(a(j_1)\cdot h_h,(i_1-1)\cdot h_e)} + \frac{90}{V_r} + \frac{\frac{h_c}{2}+\text{abs}(k_1-k_2)\cdot(h_w+h_d)+\frac{h_c}{2}}{v_h} +$$
$$+ \frac{d_{C_{k_2},R_{k_2}}}{V(a(j_1)\cdot h_h,(i_2-1)\cdot h_e)} =$$
$$= \frac{d_{R_{k_1},C_{k_1}}}{V(a(j_1)\cdot h_h,(i_1-1)\cdot h_e)} + \frac{h_c+\text{abs}(k_1-k_2)\cdot(h_w+h_d)}{v_h} +$$
$$+ \frac{d_{C_{k_2},R_{k_2}}}{V(a(j_2)\cdot h_h,(i_2-1)\cdot h_e)} + \frac{90}{V_r} + T_{PH} \tag{37}$$

Similar to the optimal path, calculate the

$$T_{R_{k_1}(i_1,j_1),R_{k_2}(i_2,j_2)}(\overline{C}) = t_{R_{k_1},\overline{C}_{k_1}} + t_{\overline{C}_{k_1},\overline{C}_{k_2}} + t_{\overline{C}_{k_1},R_{k_1}} \tag{38}$$

Let

$$t_{R_{k_1}(i_1,j_1),R_{k_2}(i_2,j_2)} = \min\left(T_{R_{k_1}(i_1,j_1),R_{k_2}(i_2,j_2)}(C), T_{R_{k_1}(i_1,j_1),R_{k_2}(i_2,j_2)}(\overline{C})\right) \tag{39}$$

Taking into account that there may be two consecutive compartments to being examined within a row or between different rows, the function t_P is composed of two parts, of which only the current one is always included. If there are two opposing shelving systems, then if $k_{v+1} = k_v + 1$ and $mod(k_v,2) = 1$, or $k_v = k_{v+1} + 1$ and $mod(k_v,2) = 0$, or $k_{v+1} = k_v$, then

$$t_P((k_v i_v j_v),(k_{v+1}i_{v+1}j_{v+1})) = t_{P_1}((k_v i_v j_v),(k_{v+1}i_{v+1}j_{v+1})) \tag{40}$$

otherwise

$$t_P((k_v i_v j_v),(k_{v+1}i_{v+1}j_{v+1})) = t_{R_{k_v}(i_v,j_v),R_{k_{v+1}}(i_{v+1},j_{v+1})} \tag{41}$$

Execution time of the $Ś_u$ sub-sequence (without docking):

$$t_P(Ś_u) = \sum_{v=p}^{q-1} t_P((k_v i_v j_v), (k_{v+1} i_{v+1} j_{v+1})). \tag{42}$$

$$T_f(Ś_u) = t_{T,R_k(i,j)} + t_P(Ś_u) + t_{R_k(i,j),T} \tag{43}$$

3.5. The Constraints

Based on the above, the sum of the compartment variables is exactly the sum of the number of cells from 0 to the number of cells -1.

Two conditions must be provided in the model's conditional framework:
1. Each number of compartments must be different;
2. The row numbers must take all values starting from 0 up to the total number of cells (i.e., the row numbers must increase one by one);

This can be specified by two group conditions. The value of the variable cells must not be negative (since it is an entry sequence); therefore,

$$0 \leq x_{kij}. \tag{44}$$

The value of x_{kij} can be clearly bounded from above:

$$x_{kij} \leq r \cdot m \cdot n. \tag{45}$$

Each number must be different if you are looking at different compartments:

$$k, k_1 \in [1, \ldots, r], \; i, i_1 \in [1, \ldots, m], j, j_1 \in [1, \ldots, n]. \tag{46}$$

If (i.e., two compartments are different), then

$$1000k_1 + 100i_1 + j_1 \neq 1000k_2 + 100i_2 + j_2, \\ x_{k_1,i_1,j_1} \neq x_{k_2,i_2,j_2}. \tag{47}$$

In summary, the mathematical model

$$k, k_1 \in [1, \ldots, r], \; i, i_1 \in [1, \ldots, m], j, j_1 \in [1, \ldots, n] \\ 0 \leq x_{kij} \leq r \cdot m \cdot n \\ x_{kij} \neq x_{k_2,i_2,j_2} \; if \; 1000k + 100i + j \neq 1000k_1 + 100i_1 + j_1, \\ T = \sum_{u=1}^{p} T_f(Ś_u) \to min! \tag{48}$$

4. The Solution Method

The computational model can be further simplified by

$$0 \leq x_{kij} \leq r \cdot m \cdot n \tag{49}$$

The constraint can be replaced by the

$$0 \leq x_{kij} \leq mtp \cdot r \cdot m \cdot n \tag{50}$$

(e.g., may be $mtp = 100$), and use the following routine as the nonlinear constraint. This is important for the genetic algorithm. Then, it is sufficient that all values are different.

4.1. The Objective Generation Algorithm (OGA)

Step 1.
Construct a random set of

$$S = S((k_1 i_1 j_1), (k_2 i_2 j_2), \ldots, (k_{2mn} i_{2mn} j_{2mn})) \tag{51}$$

compartments where

$$(k_{l_1} i_{l_1} j_{l_1}) \neq (k_{l_2} i_{l_2} j_{l_2}), \text{ if } l_1 \neq l_2. \tag{52}$$

Each compartment should be tested once and only once.
Step 2.
Let $u = 0$, $S_v = \varnothing$,
and $g = (k_1 i_1 j_1)$ the first item in the series (if any).
Step 3.
If there are no more items in the series, continue from Step 5.
If there are, then

$$\begin{aligned} u &:= u + 1 \\ \acute{S}_u &= \varnothing \end{aligned} \tag{53}$$

Step 4.
Add element g of the series to the subsequence.

$$\acute{S}_u := \acute{S}_u + \{g\} \tag{54}$$

Calculate the value of

$$T_f(\acute{S}_u) \tag{55}$$

If

$$T_w - T_f(\acute{S}_u) > \Delta t \tag{56}$$

take the next element g and continue from Step 4.
If

$$T_w - T_f(\acute{S}_u) \leq 0 \tag{57}$$

i.e., the drone would not return with the addition of the new element, then

$$\begin{aligned} \acute{S}_u &:= \acute{S}_u - \{g\} \\ T &:= T + T_f(\acute{S}_u) \\ S_v &:= S_v + \{\mathbf{D}, \acute{S}_u\} \end{aligned} \tag{58}$$

Then proceed to Step 3.
If

$$0 \leq T_w - T_f(\acute{S}_u) \leq \Delta t \tag{59}$$

Then take the next item g and continue from Step 3.

$$\begin{aligned} T &:= T + T_f(\acute{S}_u) \\ S_v &:= S_v + \{\mathbf{D}, \acute{S}_u\} \end{aligned} \tag{60}$$

Step 5.
Let

$$S_v := S_v + \{\mathbf{D}\} \tag{61}$$

At this point, the task list was completed with the charges, and the total processing time T was obtained.

4.2. Determining the Optimal Route

We used an evolutionary algorithm for the solution.

Step 1. Set the initial parameters (population number, number of steps, etc.).
The formation of the initial population, i.e., each chromosome, will be one

$$S = S((k_1i_1j_1), (k_2i_2j_2), \ldots, (k_{2mn}i_{2mn}j_{2mn})) \tag{62}$$

series.

Step 2.

Run the algorithm by determining the fitness value for each individual in the population using the Target Function Generation Algorithm (OGA). This should also be built into factory algorithms.

Step 3.

After stopping the algorithm, we evaluate the result and program the obtained optimal solution (S_v) into the drone together with the necessary camera rotations and photography.

5. Results

The model and procedure described above leads to the following results.

The first result is in an enclosed double-bay warehouse that does not have a satellite positioning system nor an IoT positioning system; the inventory can be checked automatically using a mid-range drone. It follows that the above model generally handles the movement of the drone in the aisles of a double-bay warehouse between the charging station (dock) and the corresponding starting compartment, and the last compartment and the dock. The outlined procedure provides a near-optimal route-planning method that can scan as many compartments as possible relative to the operating time of the drone and ensures a safe return to the starting point. Since the warehouse solution does not require a complete optimal solution, a well-tested OGA device can clearly be used.

The results can be divided into two parts: in the first part, a route-optimizing model was created. The characteristics of the warehouse were considered, such as the unified double-shelf system structure and the resolution of a compartment up to three parts. The drone was able to take photos from the middle of the aisle, so there was no need to move out of the bisecting plane towards the shelving systems. This was a simplifying condition discovered during the study in the logistics decenter. The drone was not responsible for finding the QR codes associated with the compartments, nor was it responsible for evaluating whether there were any goods placed in it. All these tasks can be easily performed by employing software to evaluate the photos, which could further accelerate the process. Another possible option is to take a picture of two opposite compartments in a row by rotating the camera, provided that it happens in a shorter time. This is influenced by specific values of the parameters. The first result obtained is the route optimization; this should be the procedure carried out prior to the launch of the drone.

The second result is on-the-fly control: after launching the drone from the dock, it receives instructions where to go, how to get there, and what activities to perform there (if camera rotation and photography are needed). The drone is instructed in real time for the next task for each position, while (of course) internal energy level monitoring is also performed.

6. Discussion

During our research of the literature, we came across several solutions related to optimal road planning. Most of them solve the problem with the help of neural networks. In their paper, Andrey V. Gavrilov and Artem Lenskiy propose a model for a new biologically inspired mobile robot navigation system. The novelty of their work is the combination of short-term memory and online neural-network learning using the event history stored in this memory. The neural network is trained with a modified error backpropagation algorithm that uses the principle of reward and punishment when interacting with the environment [18]. The robot navigation mechanism is one of the most challenging research topics in mobile robots, which requires the robot to find the right path and travel from its current position to the target position without encountering obstacles. In their paper,

Cheng and Cheng use the intelligent method of reinforcement learning to find a solution to the abovementioned problem. It considers the distances detected by a laser beam and the relative movement angle as the input of the neural network model, and the action posture of the robot as the output. This neural network model is trained by a deep Q-learning network (DQN) algorithm through positive and negative feedback rewards defined by task-specific learning goals. In this sense, the trained model helps the robot determine the appropriate steps to take in each state to safely reach the target without manual intervention. According to the results achieved on the simulation platform, the trained neural network model successfully moves the robot from a random starting point to a random destination, which proves the effectiveness of the DQN algorithm in the field of robotic navigation. [19] These models could also be applied to our problem, but it should be considered that the drone must not move in a plane, but in space. This would greatly complicate the solution. In fact, the solution we provide provides a simpler, more efficient solution. In particular, the application of neural networks would have required many examples, which we did not have at our disposal.

Another task from the research was to create an image processing and inventory analysis and a recording software that can be used for the task. The first task in Image Processing is to recognize the QR code itself and to identify the specific compartment. The identification of the compartment is provided by the routing model, and the route itself must be known to the processing application. Hence, automatically received photos are taken according to the route activities. The shelf system and the compartment where the photo was taken can be assigned to each photo by the application. This is a simple synchronization task.

The processing of the images is not very complicated, as most QR code readers are able to validate, and of course, interpret the data in the code. However, the fact that a compartment may be divided into several sub-compartments in a manner not previously known, so that several QR codes may have to be recognized, complicates the situation. It is also important that the QR code of another compartment should not be included in the photo and should not be handled by the recognizing application either. This can be easily prevented, as the shelf system is uniformly colored in most logistics centers—there were blue columns and red shelves in the warehouse we examined. With the help of these colors, the cells can be delimited, and the division can be determined based on the expected size by linear image processing. In other words, based on the image, one can see how many QR codes to search for, which can be easily carried out with the QR code search procedure. (Focusing was included into the shooting time of the drone).

The final processing application checks whether the actual unit load in the given compartment meets the requirements based on the position and QR code and indicates the compliance or deviations to the warehouse operator accordingly.

7. Conclusions

In this paper, we presented a model of a drone-driven inventory control solution. As a result of the method and with the help of the implemented application, the time of inventory testing can be greatly reduced, and the task can be performed with the help of an average human resource. A task that had once taken several days to complete can now be completed in about two days with this solution. In addition, the platform solution currently used, which endangers personal safety, can be avoided. It is obvious that in the case of the entire warehouse, the use of several drones can further reduce this time, and erroneous picking due to human errors can be eliminated by frequent inspections, so that the use of drones can also reduce the resulting losses.

Determining location based on QR code recognition is not a viable option, and one of the best known and most widely used methods is the Viola–Jones object detection framework. The mentioned framework provides an efficient way to focus the detection process on specific parts of the image. Based on our solution design, the initial state already shows a possible solution, and the intermediate states will always be possible solutions and a good GA procedure is sufficient to apply a parameter reduction solution. In reality, there are many "good" paths to choose from. However, our tests show that the path depends significantly on the relationship between the underlying data.

At the beginning of our article, a full parameter exploration was performed. The range of data was defined with the help of practitioners, and then the basic collected data were grouped according to their role. Once the required parameters had been selected, it was important to record their dimensions. Next, we created a parametric model of the warehouse and the factory parameters of the drone to be used, improved with the data we had found. We created a manageable, simplified motion and speed. The next step was to develop a practical positioning strategy. Then, we created a mathematical model of the operation and assigned the theorems and determined environment needed for optimization.

Author Contributions: Conceptualization, M.G.; methodology, M.G.; writing—review and editing, L.S.; visualization, L.R.; investigation, J.U. All authors have read and agreed to the published version of the manuscript.

Funding: This research project was funded by Budapest Business School Research Fund.

Institutional Review Board Statement: Not applicable.

Informed Consent Statement: Not applicable.

Data Availability Statement: Not applicable.

Acknowledgments: This research project was carried out within the framework of Centre of Excellence for Future Value Chains of Budapest Business School.

Conflicts of Interest: The authors declare no conflict of interest.

References

1. Bányai, T.; Illés, B.; Gubán, M.; Gubán, A.; Schenk, F.; Bányai, A. Optimization of Just-In-Sequence Supply: A Flower Pollination Algorithm-Based Approach. *Sustainability* **2019**, *11*, 3850. [CrossRef]
2. An, R.; Guo, S.; Zheng, L.; Hirata, H.; Gu, S. Uncertain moving obstacles avoiding method in 3D arbitrary path planning for a spherical underwater robot. *Robot. Auton. Syst.* **2022**, *151*, 104011. [CrossRef]
3. Fülöp, M.T.; Gubán, M.; Gubán, A.; Avornicului, M. Application Research of Soft Computing Based on Machine Learning Production Scheduling. *Processes* **2022**, *10*, 520. [CrossRef]
4. Pehlivanoglu, Y.V.; Pehlivanoglu, P. An enhanced genetic algorithm for path planning of autonomous UAV in target coverage problems. *Appl. Soft Comput.* **2021**, *112*, 107796. [CrossRef]
5. Benes, F.; Stasa, P.; Svub, J.; Alfian, G.; Kang, Y.-S.; Rhee, J.-T. Investigation of UHF Signal Strength Propagation at Warehouse Management Applications Based on Drones and RFID Technology Utilization. *Appl. Sci.* **2022**, *12*, 1277. [CrossRef]
6. Gerwen, J.V.-V.; Geebelen, K.; Wan, J.; Joseph, W.; Hoebeke, J.; De Poorter, E. Indoor Drone Positioning: Accuracy and Cost Trade-Off for Sensor Fusion. *IEEE Trans. Veh. Technol.* **2021**, *71*, 961–974. [CrossRef]
7. Rhiat, A.; Chalal, L.; Saadane, A. A Smart Warehouse Using Robots and Drone to Optimize Inventory Management. In *Proceedings of the Future Technologies Conference (FTC) 2021*; Springer: Berlin/Heidelberg, Germany, 2021; Volume 1, pp. 475–483.
8. Liu, H.; Chen, Q.; Pan, N.; Sun, Y.; An, Y.; Pan, D. UAV Stocktaking Task-Planning for Industrial Warehouses Based on the Improved Hybrid Differential Evolution Algorithm. *IEEE Trans. Ind. Inform.* **2021**, *18*, 582–591. [CrossRef]
9. Szegedi, Z. *Raktározáslogisztika*; AMEROPA Kiadó: Budapest, Hungary, 2010.
10. Rjeb, A.; Gayon, J.-P.; Norre, S. Sizing of a homogeneous fleet of robots in a logistics warehouse. *IFAC-PapersOnLine* **2021**, *54*, 552–557. [CrossRef]
11. eyesee-drone.com. Available online: https://eyesee-drone.com/eyesee-the-inventory-drone-solution/ (accessed on 10 March 2022).
12. Jácome, R.N.; Huertas, H.L.; Procel, P.C.; Garcés, A.G. Fuzzy Logic for Speed Control in Object Tracking Inside a Restricted Area Using a Drone. In *Developments and Advances in Defense and Security*; Springer: Berlin/Heidelberg, Germany, 2019; pp. 135–1456.
13. Paredes, J.A.; Álvarez, F.J.; Aguilera, T.; Aranda, F.J. Precise drone location and tracking by adaptive matched filtering from a top-view ToF camera. *Expert Syst. Appl.* **2019**, *141*, 112989. [CrossRef]
14. Li, F.; Zlatanova, S.; Koopman, M.; Bai, X.; Diakité, A. Universal path planning for an indoor drone. *Autom. Constr.* **2018**, *95*, 275–283. [CrossRef]
15. Sacramento, D.; Pisinger, D.; Ropke, S. An adaptive large neighborhood search metaheuristic for the vehicle routing problem with drones. *Transp. Res. Part C: Emerg. Technol.* **2019**, *102*, 289–315. [CrossRef]
16. Dhein, G.; Zanetti, M.S.; de Araújo, O.C.B.; Cardoso, G., Jr. Minimizing dispersion in multiple drone routing. *Comput. Oper. Res.* **2019**, *109*, 28–42. [CrossRef]

17. Morocho-Cayamcela, M.E.; Lim, W.; Maier, M. An optimal location strategy for multiple drone base stations in massive MIMO. *ICT Express* **2021**, *8*, 230–234. [CrossRef]
18. Gavrilov, A.V.; Lenskiy, A. Mobile Robot Navigation Using Reinforcement Learning Based on Neural Network with Short Term Memory. In *ICIC 2011: Advanced Intelligent Computing*; Springer: Berlin/Heidelberg, Germany, 2011; pp. 210–217.
19. Cheng, C.; Chen, Y. A Neural network based mobile robot navigation approach using reinforcement learning parameter tuning mechanism. In Proceedings of the 2021 China Automation Congress (CAC), Beijing, China, 22–24 October 2021.

Article

Scheduling with Resource Allocation, Deteriorating Effect and Group Technology to Minimize Total Completion Time

Jia-Xuan Yan, Na Ren, Hong-Bin Bei, Han Bao and Ji-Bo Wang *

School of Science, Shenyang Aerospace University, Shenyang 110136, China
* Correspondence: wangjibo@sau.edu.cn

Abstract: This paper studies a single-machine problem with resource allocation (RA) and deteriorating effect (DE). Under group technology (GT) and limited resource availability, our goal is to determine the schedules of groups and jobs within each group such that the total completion time is minimized. For three special cases, polynomial time algorithms are given. For a general case, a heuristic, a tabu search algorithm, and an exact (i.e., branch-and-bound) algorithm are proposed to solve this problem.

Keywords: resource allocation; group technology; deterioration effect; scheduling

MSC: 90B35

1. Introduction

With the development of economy, the research on the group technology (denoted by GT) problem involves a variety of fields, especially in the supply chain management, information processing, computer systems, and other industries (see Ham et al. [1], Wang et al. [2]). Yang [3] and Bai et al. [4] investigated single-machine GT scheduling with learning and deterioration effects. Lu et al. [5] studied the single-machine problem with GT and time-dependent processing times (i.e., time-dependent scheduling), i.e., the processing time of jobs and setup time of groups are time-dependent. For the makespan minimization subject to release dates, they presented a polynomial time algorithm. Wang et al. [6] examined the single-machine problem with GT and shortening job processing times. For the makespan minimization with ready times, they demonstrated that some special cases were optimally solved in polynomial time. Liu et al. [7] studied the single-machine problem with GT and deterioration effects (denoted by DE), i.e., the processing time of jobs are time-dependent and setup time of groups are constants. For the makespan minimization with ready times, they proposed a branch-and-bound algorithm. Zhu et al. [8] discussed the single-machine problem with GT, resource allocation (denoted by RA), and learning effects. For the weighted sum minimization of makespan and total resource consumption, Zhu et al. [8] proved that the problem remains polynomially solvable. In 2018, Zhang et al. [9] discussed the single-machine problem with GT and position-dependent processing times. In 2020, Liao et al. [10] considered the two-competing scheduling problem with GT and learning effects. In 2021, Lv et al. [11] addressed single-machine slack due date assignment problems with GT, RA, and learning effects. In 2021, Xu et al. [12] investigated the single-machine problem with GT, nonperiodical maintenance, and DE. For the makespan minimization, they proposed some heuristic algorithms.

Recently, Oron [13] and Li and Wang [14] considered a single-machine scheduling model combining RA and DE. Later, Wang et al. [15] discussed a scheduling model combining GT, RA, and DE. Under the single-machine setting, the objective is to minimize the weighted sum of makespan and total resource consumption. Wang et al. [15] showed that some special cases remain polynomially solvable. In 2020, Liang et al. [16] considered the same model as Wang et al. [15] for the general case; they provided heuristic and

Citation: Yan, J.-X.; Ren, N.; Bei, H.-B.; Bao, H.; Wang, J.-B. Scheduling with Resource Allocation, Deteriorating Effect and Group Technology to Minimize Total Completion Time. *Mathematics* **2022**, *10*, 2983. https://doi.org/10.3390/math10162983

Academic Editors: Zsolt Tibor Kosztyán and Zoltán Kovács

Received: 19 July 2022
Accepted: 16 August 2022
Published: 18 August 2022

Publisher's Note: MDPI stays neutral with regard to jurisdictional claims in published maps and institutional affiliations.

Copyright: © 2022 by the authors. Licensee MDPI, Basel, Switzerland. This article is an open access article distributed under the terms and conditions of the Creative Commons Attribution (CC BY) license (https://creativecommons.org/licenses/by/4.0/).

branch-and-bound algorithms. In 2019, Wang and Liang [17] studied the single-machine problem with GT, RA, and DE concurrently. For the makespan minimization under the constraint that total resource consumption cannot exceed an upper bound, they proved that some special cases remain polynomially solvable. For the general case, they provided heuristic and branch-and-bound algorithms.

This paper conducts a further study on the problem with GT, RA, and DE, but the objective cost is to minimize the total completion time under the constraint that total resource consumption cannot exceed an upper bound. For three special cases, polynomial algorithms are given. For the general case, upper and lower bounds of the problem are given, then the branch-and-bound algorithm is proposed. In addition, a tabu search algorithm and numerical simulation analysis are given.

The rest of this paper is organized as follows: Section 2 presents a formulation of the problem. Section 3 gives some basic properties. Section 4 studies some special cases. Section 5 considers the general case, and we propose some algorithms to solve this problem. Section 6 presents the numerical simulations. The conclusions are given in Section 7.

2. Problem Statement

The following notation (see Table 1) will be used throughout this paper. There are $\tilde{n}$ independent jobs. In order to exploit GT in production (see Ji et al. [18]), all the jobs are classified into $\tilde{m}$ ($\tilde{m} \geq 2$) groups (i.e., $\Omega_1, \Omega_2, \ldots, \Omega_{\tilde{m}}$) in advance according to their processing similarities. All the jobs in the same group must be processed in succession on a single machine. Assume that the single machine and all jobs are available at time zero. Let J_{hj} be the job j in group Ω_h, and the number of jobs in group Ω_h is $\tilde{n}_h$, i.e., $\sum_{h=1}^{\tilde{m}} \tilde{n}_h = \tilde{n}$. The actual processing time of J_{hj} is:

$$p_{hj}^{Apt} = \left(\frac{\varsigma_{hj}}{\tilde{r}_{hj}}\right)^{\eta} + \theta t, \tag{1}$$

where ς_{hj} (resp. $\tilde{r}_{hj} \geq 0$) is a workload (respective amount of resource) of J_{hj}, $\eta > 0$ is a constant, $\theta \geq 0$ is a common deterioration rate, and $t \geq 0$ is its starting time. The actual setup time of Ω_h is:

$$s_h^{Apt} = \left(\frac{o_h}{\tilde{r}_h}\right)^{\eta} + \mu t, \tag{2}$$

where o_h (respectively, $\tilde{r}_h$) is a workload (amount of resource) of Ω_h, and $\mu \geq 0$ is a common deterioration rate. Obviously, the parameters $\tilde{n}, \tilde{m}, \varsigma_{hj}, \tilde{n}_h, o_h, \eta, \theta$, and μ are given in advance, and the resource allocation $\tilde{r}_{hj}$ and $\tilde{r}_h$ are decision variables. Our goal is to find the optimal group schedule $\bar{\pi}_\Omega^*$, job schedule $\bar{\pi}_h^*$ ($h = 1, \cdots, \tilde{m}$) within Ω_h, and resource allocation R^* (i.e., $\tilde{r}_{hj}$ and $\tilde{r}_h$) such that a total completion time,

$$\widehat{tct}(\bar{\pi}_\Omega, \bar{\pi}_h | h = 1, \cdots, \tilde{m}, R) = \sum_{h=1}^{\tilde{m}} \sum_{j=1}^{\tilde{n}_h} \tilde{C}_{hj} \tag{3}$$

is minimized subject to $\sum_{h=1}^{\tilde{m}} \sum_{j=1}^{\tilde{n}_h} \tilde{r}_{hj} \leq \tilde{V}$, $\sum_{h=1}^{\tilde{m}} \tilde{r}_h \leq \tilde{U}$, where $\tilde{V}$ and $\tilde{U}$ are given constants (there is not any constraint between the $\tilde{r}_{hj}$ variables and the $\tilde{r}_h$ variables, and $\sum_{h=1}^{\tilde{m}} \sum_{j=1}^{\tilde{n}_h} \tilde{r}_{hj}$ and $\sum_{h=1}^{\tilde{m}} \tilde{r}_h$ are independent from each other). By using the three-field notation (see Gawiejnowicz [19]), the problem can be denoted by

$$1\left|p_{hj}^{Apt}=\left(\frac{\varsigma_{hj}}{\widetilde{r}_{hj}}\right)^{\eta}+\theta t, s_{h}^{Apt}=\left(\frac{o_{h}}{\widetilde{r}_{h}}\right)^{\eta}+\mu t, \sum_{h=1}^{\widetilde{m}}\sum_{j=1}^{\widetilde{n}_{h}}\widetilde{r}_{hj}\leq\widetilde{V}, \sum_{h=1}^{\widetilde{m}}\widetilde{r}_{h}\leq\widetilde{U}, GT\right|\widehat{tct},$$

where 1 denotes the single machine, the middle field is the job and group characteristics, and $\widehat{tct}$ is the objective function (this problem is abbreviated as $P_{\widehat{tct}}$). Wang et al. [15] and Liang et al. [16] considered the problem

$$1\left|p_{hj}^{Apt}=\left(\frac{\varsigma_{hj}}{\widetilde{r}_{hj}}\right)^{\eta}+\theta t, s_{h}^{Apt}=\left(\frac{o_{h}}{\widetilde{r}_{h}}\right)^{\eta}+\mu t, GT\right|\alpha_1\times C_{\max}+\alpha_2\sum_{h=1}^{\widetilde{m}}\sum_{j=1}^{\widetilde{n}_{h}}\widetilde{r}_{hj}+\alpha_3\sum_{h=1}^{\widetilde{m}}\widetilde{r}_{h},$$

where $\alpha_l \geq 0$ ($l = 1, 2, 3$) is a given constant and $C_{\max} = \max\{\bar{C}_{hj}|h = 1, \ldots, \widetilde{m}; j = 1, \ldots, \widetilde{n}_h\}$. Wang and Liang [17] studied the problem

$$1\left|p_{hj}^{Apt}=\left(\frac{\varsigma_{hj}}{\widetilde{r}_{hj}}\right)^{\eta}+\theta t, s_{h}^{Apt}=\left(\frac{o_{h}}{\widetilde{r}_{h}}\right)^{\eta}+\mu t, \sum_{h=1}^{\widetilde{m}}\sum_{j=1}^{\widetilde{n}_{h}}\widetilde{r}_{hj}\leq\widetilde{V}, \sum_{h=1}^{\widetilde{m}}\widetilde{r}_{h}\leq\widetilde{U}, GT\right|C_{\max}.$$

Table 1. Symbols.

Notation	Meaning
$\widetilde{n}$ (resp. $\widetilde{m}$)	number of jobs (respective groups)
Ω_h	group h
$\widecheck{J}_{hj}$	job j at group Ω_h
$\widetilde{n}_h$	number of jobs belonging to Ω_h, i.e., $\sum_{h=1}^{\widetilde{m}}\widetilde{n}_h = \widetilde{n}$
ς_{hj}	workload of $\widecheck{J}_{hj}$ (a positive value which represents job parameter)
$\widetilde{r}_{hj}$	amount of resource assigned to $\widecheck{J}_{hj}$
p_{hj}^{Apt}	actual processing time of $\widecheck{J}_{hj}$
o_h	workload of Ω_h (a positive value which represents group parameter), $h = 1, 2, \ldots, \widetilde{m}$,
$\widetilde{r}_h$	amount of resource allocated to Ω_h
s_h^{Apt}	actual setup time of Ω_h
$\bar{C}_{hj}$	completion time of $\widecheck{J}_{hj}$
$[j]$	jth position in a schedule
$\widehat{tct} = \sum_{i=1}^{\widetilde{m}}\sum_{j=1}^{\widetilde{n}_h}\bar{C}_{ij}$	total completion time
$\bar{\pi}_\Omega$	group schedule
$\bar{\pi}_h$	job schedule in Ω_h
Π	schedule of jobs and groups, i.e., $\Pi = (\bar{\pi}_\Omega, \bar{\pi}_h|h = 1, \ldots, \widetilde{m})$

3. Basic Results

For a given schedule Π, stemming from Wang et al. [15] and Liang et al. [16], by a mathematical induction, we have

$$
\begin{aligned}
\bar{C}_{[1][1]} &= \left(\frac{o_{[1]}}{\widetilde{r}_{[1]}}\right)^{\eta} + \left(\frac{\varsigma_{[1][1]}}{\widetilde{r}_{[1][1]}}\right)^{\eta} + \theta\left(\frac{o_{[1]}}{\widetilde{r}_{[1]}}\right)^{\eta} = \left(\frac{\varsigma_{[1][1]}}{\widetilde{r}_{[1][1]}}\right)^{\eta} + (1+\theta)\left(\frac{o_{[1]}}{\widetilde{r}_{[1]}}\right)^{\eta}, \\
\bar{C}_{[1][2]} &= \bar{C}_{[1][1]} + \left(\frac{\varsigma_{[1][2]}}{\widetilde{r}_{[1][2]}}\right)^{\eta} + \theta \bar{C}_{[1][1]} \\
&= \left(\frac{\varsigma_{[1][2]}}{\widetilde{r}_{[1][2]}}\right)^{\eta} + (1+\theta)\left(\frac{\varsigma_{[1][1]}}{\widetilde{r}_{[1][1]}}\right)^{\eta} + (1+\theta)^2 \left(\frac{o_{[1]}}{\widetilde{r}_{[1]}}\right)^{\eta}, \\
&\vdots \\
\bar{C}_{[1][\widetilde{n}_1]} &= \sum_{j=1}^{\widetilde{n}_{[1]}} (1+\theta)^{\widetilde{n}_{[1]}-j} \left(\frac{\varsigma_{[1][j]}}{\widetilde{r}_{[1][j]}}\right)^{\eta} + (1+\theta)^{\widetilde{n}_{[1]}} \left(\frac{o_{[1]}}{\widetilde{r}_{[1]}}\right)^{\eta}, \\
\bar{C}_{[2][1]} &= \bar{C}_{[1][\widetilde{n}_1]} + \left(\frac{o_{[2]}}{\widetilde{r}_{[2]}}\right)^{\eta} + \mu \bar{C}_{[1][\widetilde{n}_1]} + \left(\frac{\varsigma_{[2][1]}}{\widetilde{r}_{[2][1]}}\right)^{\eta} + \theta\left(\bar{C}_{[1][\widetilde{n}_1]} + \left(\frac{o_{[2]}}{\widetilde{r}_{[2]}}\right)^{\eta} + \mu \bar{C}_{[1][\widetilde{n}_1]}\right) \\
&= \sum_{j=1}^{\widetilde{n}_{[1]}} (1+\mu)(1+\theta)^{\widetilde{n}_{[1]}-j+1} \left(\frac{\varsigma_{[1][j]}}{\widetilde{r}_{[1][j]}}\right)^{\eta} + (1+\mu)(1+\theta)^{\widetilde{n}_{[1]}+1} \left(\frac{o_{[1]}}{\widetilde{r}_{[1]}}\right)^{\eta} \\
&\quad + (1+\theta)\left(\frac{o_{[2]}}{\widetilde{r}_{[2]}}\right)^{\eta} + \left(\frac{\varsigma_{[2][1]}}{\widetilde{r}_{[2][1]}}\right)^{\eta}, \\
\bar{C}_{[2][2]} &= \bar{C}_{[2][1]} + \left(\frac{\varsigma_{[2][2]}}{\widetilde{r}_{[2][2]}}\right)^{\eta} + \theta \bar{C}_{[2][1]} \\
&= \sum_{j=1}^{\widetilde{n}_{[1]}} (1+\mu)(1+\theta)^{\widetilde{n}_{[1]}-j+2} \left(\frac{\varsigma_{[1][j]}}{\widetilde{r}_{[1][j]}}\right)^{\eta} + (1+\mu)(1+\theta)^{\widetilde{n}_{[1]}+2} \left(\frac{o_{[1]}}{\widetilde{r}_{[1]}}\right)^{\eta} \\
&\quad + (1+\theta)^2 \left(\frac{o_{[2]}}{\widetilde{r}_{[2]}}\right)^{\eta} + (1+\theta)\left(\frac{\varsigma_{[2][1]}}{\widetilde{r}_{[2][1]}}\right)^{\eta} + \left(\frac{\varsigma_{[2][2]}}{\widetilde{r}_{[2][2]}}\right)^{\eta}, \\
&\vdots \\
\bar{C}_{[2][\widetilde{n}_2]} &= \sum_{j=1}^{\widetilde{n}_{[1]}} (1+\mu)(1+\theta)^{\widetilde{n}_{[1]}+\widetilde{n}_{[2]}-j} \left(\frac{\varsigma_{[1][j]}}{\widetilde{r}_{[1][j]}}\right)^{\eta} + (1+\mu)(1+\theta)^{\widetilde{n}_{[1]}+\widetilde{n}_{[2]}} \left(\frac{o_{[1]}}{\widetilde{r}_{[1]}}\right)^{\eta} \\
&\quad + \sum_{j=1}^{\widetilde{n}_{[2]}} (1+\theta)^{\widetilde{n}_{[2]}-j} \left(\frac{\varsigma_{[2][j]}}{\widetilde{r}_{[2][j]}}\right)^{\eta} + (1+\theta)^{\widetilde{n}_{[2]}} \left(\frac{o_{[2]}}{\widetilde{r}_{[2]}}\right)^{\eta}, \\
&\vdots \\
\bar{C}_{[\widetilde{m}][\widetilde{n}_m]} &= \sum_{h=1}^{\widetilde{m}} \sum_{j=1}^{\widetilde{n}_{[h]}} (1+\mu)^{\widetilde{m}-h}(1+\theta)^{\sum_{l=h}^{\widetilde{m}} \widetilde{n}_{[l]}-j} \left(\frac{\varsigma_{[h][j]}}{\widetilde{r}_{[h][j]}}\right)^{\eta} \\
&\quad + \sum_{h=1}^{\widetilde{m}} (1+\mu)^{\widetilde{m}-h}(1+\theta)^{\sum_{l=h}^{\widetilde{m}} \widetilde{n}_{[l]}} \left(\frac{o_{[h]}}{\widetilde{r}_{[h]}}\right)^{\eta}.
\end{aligned}
$$

According to the above equations, we have

$$\begin{aligned}
\widehat{tct} &= \sum_{i=1}^{\widetilde{m}} \sum_{j=1}^{\widetilde{n}_h} \bar{C}_{[i][j]} \\
&= \sum_{h=1}^{\widetilde{m}} \sum_{j=1}^{\widetilde{n}_h} \left[\sum_{l=j}^{\widetilde{n}_{[h]}} (1+\theta)^{l-j} + \sum_{k=h+1}^{\widetilde{m}} (1+\mu)^{k-h} \sum_{l=1}^{\widetilde{n}_{[k]}} (1+\theta)^{l-j-\widetilde{n}_{[k]}+\sum_{\xi=h}^{k} \widetilde{n}_{[\xi]}} \right] \left(\frac{\varsigma_{[i][j]}}{\widetilde{r}_{[i][j]}} \right)^{\eta} \\
&\quad + \sum_{h=1}^{\widetilde{m}} \left[\sum_{k=h}^{\widetilde{m}} (1+\mu)^{k-h} \sum_{l=1}^{\widetilde{n}_{[k]}} (1+\theta)^{l-\widetilde{n}_{[k]}+\sum_{\xi=h}^{k} \widetilde{n}_{[\xi]}} \right] \left(\frac{o_{[h]}}{\widetilde{r}_{[h]}} \right)^{\eta}.
\end{aligned}$$ (4)

Lemma 1. *For a given schedule* Π *of* $P_{\widehat{tct}}$*, the optimal resource allocation* $R^*(\bar{\pi}_\Omega, \bar{\pi}_h | h = 1, \cdots, \widetilde{m})$ *is*

$$\widetilde{r}^*_{[h][j]} = \frac{\left[\sum_{l=j}^{\widetilde{n}_{[h]}} (1+\theta)^{l-j} + \sum_{k=h+1}^{\widetilde{m}} (1+\mu)^{k-h} \sum_{l=1}^{\widetilde{n}_{[k]}} (1+\theta)^{l-j-\widetilde{n}_{[k]}+\sum_{\xi=h}^{k} \widetilde{n}_{[\xi]}} (\varsigma_{[h][j]})^\eta \right]^{\frac{1}{\eta+1}}}{\sum_{h=1}^{\widetilde{m}} \sum_{j=1}^{\widetilde{n}_h} \left[\sum_{l=j}^{\widetilde{n}_{[h]}} (1+\theta)^{l-j} + \sum_{k=h+1}^{\widetilde{m}} (1+\mu)^{k-h} \sum_{l=1}^{\widetilde{n}_{[k]}} (1+\theta)^{l-j-\widetilde{n}_{[k]}+\sum_{\xi=h}^{k} \widetilde{n}_{[\xi]}} (\varsigma_{[h][j]})^\eta \right]^{\frac{1}{\eta+1}}} \times \widetilde{V}$$ (5)

for $h = 1, \cdots, \widetilde{m}; j = 1, \cdots, \widetilde{n}_i$, *and*

$$\widetilde{r}^*_{[h]} = \frac{\left[\sum_{k=h}^{\widetilde{m}} (1+\mu)^{k-h} \sum_{l=1}^{\widetilde{n}_{[k]}} (1+\theta)^{l-\widetilde{n}_{[k]}+\sum_{\xi=h}^{k} \widetilde{n}_{[\xi]}} (o_{[h]})^\eta \right]^{\frac{1}{\eta+1}}}{\sum_{h=1}^{\widetilde{m}} \left[\sum_{k=h}^{\widetilde{m}} (1+\mu)^{k-h} \sum_{l=1}^{\widetilde{n}_{[k]}} (1+\theta)^{l-\widetilde{n}_{[k]}+\sum_{\xi=h}^{k} \widetilde{n}_{[\xi]}} (o_{[h]})^\eta \right]^{\frac{1}{\eta+1}}} \times \widetilde{U}$$ (6)

for $h = 1, \cdots, \widetilde{m}$.

Proof. Obviously, Equation (4) is a convex function with respect to $\widetilde{r}_{[h][j]}$ and $\widetilde{r}_{[h]}$. It is obvious that in the optimal solution all resources should be consumed, i.e., $\sum_{h=1}^{\widetilde{m}} \sum_{j=1}^{\widetilde{n}_h} \widetilde{r}_{[h][j]} - \widetilde{V} = 0$ and $\sum_{h=1}^{\widetilde{m}} \widetilde{r}_{[h]} - \widetilde{U} = 0$. As in Wang and Liang [17], Shabtay and Kaspi [20], and Wang and Wang [21], for a given schedule, the optimal resource allocation of the problem $P_{\widehat{tct}}$ can be solved by the Lagrange multiplier method. The Lagrangian function is

$$\begin{aligned}
Q(\kappa, v, R) &= \sum_{h=1}^{\widetilde{m}} \sum_{j=1}^{\widetilde{n}_h} \bar{C}_{[h][j]} + \kappa \left(\sum_{h=1}^{\widetilde{m}} \sum_{j=1}^{\widetilde{n}_h} \widetilde{r}_{[h][j]} - \widetilde{V} \right) + v \left(\sum_{h=1}^{\widetilde{m}} \widetilde{r}_{[h]} - \widetilde{U} \right) \\
&= \sum_{h=1}^{\widetilde{m}} \sum_{j=1}^{\widetilde{n}_h} \left[\sum_{l=j}^{\widetilde{n}_{[h]}} (1+\theta)^{l-j} + \sum_{k=h+1}^{\widetilde{m}} (1+\mu)^{k-h} \sum_{l=1}^{\widetilde{n}_{[k]}} (1+\theta)^{l-j-\widetilde{n}_{[k]}+\sum_{\xi=h}^{k} \widetilde{n}_{[\xi]}} \right] \left(\frac{\varsigma_{[h][j]}}{\widetilde{r}_{[h][j]}} \right)^\eta \\
&\quad + \sum_{h=1}^{\widetilde{m}} \left[\sum_{k=h}^{\widetilde{m}} (1+\mu)^{k-h} \sum_{l=1}^{\widetilde{n}_{[k]}} (1+\theta)^{l-\widetilde{n}_{[k]}+\sum_{\xi=h}^{k} \widetilde{n}_{[\xi]}} \right] \left(\frac{o_{[h]}}{\widetilde{r}_{[h]}} \right)^\eta \\
&\quad + \kappa \left(\sum_{h=1}^{\widetilde{m}} \sum_{j=1}^{\widetilde{n}} \widetilde{r}_{[h][j]} - \widetilde{V} \right) + v \left(\sum_{h=1}^{\widetilde{m}} \widetilde{r}_{[h]} - \widetilde{U} \right),
\end{aligned}$$ (7)

where $\kappa \geq 0$ and $v \geq 0$ are the Lagrangian multipliers. Differentiating Equation (7) with respect to $\widetilde{r}_{[h][j]}$ and κ, then

$$\begin{aligned}
\frac{\partial Q(\kappa, v, R)}{\partial \widetilde{r}_{[i][j]}} &= \delta - \eta \left[\sum_{l=j}^{\widetilde{n}_{[i]}} (1+\theta)^{l-j} + \sum_{k=h+1}^{\widetilde{m}} (1+\mu)^{k-h} \sum_{l=1}^{\widetilde{n}_{[k]}} (1+\theta)^{l-j-\widetilde{n}_{[k]}+\sum_{\xi=h}^{k} \widetilde{n}_{[\xi]}} \right] \\
&\quad \times \frac{(\varsigma_{[h][j]})^\eta}{(\widetilde{r}_{[h][j]})^{\eta+1}} \\
&= 0
\end{aligned}$$ (8)

and
$$\frac{\partial Q(\kappa, \upsilon, R)}{\partial \kappa} = \sum_{h=1}^{\widetilde{m}} \sum_{j=1}^{\widetilde{n}_h} \widetilde{r}_{[h][j]} - \widetilde{V} = 0. \tag{9}$$

By using Equations (8) and (9), it follows that

$$\widetilde{r}_{[h][j]} = \left[\frac{\eta \left(\sum_{l=j}^{\widetilde{n}_{[h]}} (1+\theta)^{l-j} + \sum_{k=h+1}^{\widetilde{m}} (1+\mu)^{k-h} \sum_{l=1}^{\widetilde{n}_{[k]}} (1+\theta)^{l-j-\widetilde{n}_{[k]}+\sum_{\zeta=h}^{k}\widetilde{n}_{[\zeta]}} \right)}{\kappa} \right]^{\frac{1}{\eta+1}} \times \left(\zeta_{[h][j]} \right)^{\frac{\eta}{\eta+1}} \tag{10}$$

and

$$\kappa^{\frac{1}{\eta+1}} = \frac{\sum_{h=1}^{\widetilde{m}} \sum_{j=1}^{\widetilde{n}_h} \left[\eta \left(\sum_{l=j}^{\widetilde{n}_{[h]}} (1+\theta)^{l-j} + \sum_{k=h+1}^{\widetilde{m}} (1+\mu)^{k-i} \sum_{l=1}^{\widetilde{n}_{[k]}} (1+\theta)^{l-j-\widetilde{n}_{[k]}+\sum_{\zeta=h}^{k}\widetilde{n}_{[\zeta]}} \right) \left(\zeta_{[h][j]} \right)^{\eta} \right]^{\frac{1}{\eta+1}}}{\widetilde{V}}. \tag{11}$$

From Equations (10) and (11), then

$$\widetilde{r}^*_{[h][j]} = \frac{\left[\sum_{l=j}^{\widetilde{n}_{[h]}} (1+\theta)^{l-j} + \sum_{k=h+1}^{\widetilde{m}} (1+\mu)^{k-h} \sum_{l=1}^{\widetilde{n}_{[k]}} (1+\theta)^{l-j-\widetilde{n}_{[k]}+\sum_{\zeta=h}^{k}\widetilde{n}_{[\zeta]}} (\zeta_{[h][j]})^{\eta} \right]^{\frac{1}{\eta+1}}}{\sum_{h=1}^{\widetilde{m}} \sum_{j=1}^{\widetilde{n}_h} \left[\sum_{l=j}^{\widetilde{n}_{[h]}} (1+\theta)^{l-j} + \sum_{k=h+1}^{\widetilde{m}} (1+\mu)^{k-h} \sum_{l=1}^{\widetilde{n}_{[k]}} (1+\theta)^{l-j-\widetilde{n}_{[k]}+\sum_{\zeta=h}^{k}\widetilde{n}_{[\zeta]}} (\zeta_{[h][j]})^{\eta} \right]^{\frac{1}{\eta+1}}} \times \widetilde{V}.$$

Similarly, Equation (6) can be obtained. □

By Lemma 1, substituting Equations (5) and (6) into $\widehat{tct} = \sum_{h=1}^{\widetilde{m}} \sum_{j=1}^{\widetilde{n}_h} \bar{C}_{hj}$, we have

$$\begin{aligned}
\widehat{tct} &= \sum_{h=1}^{\widetilde{m}} \sum_{j=1}^{\widetilde{n}_h} \left[\sum_{l=j}^{\widetilde{n}_{[h]}} (1+\theta)^{l-j} + \sum_{k=h+1}^{\widetilde{m}} (1+\mu)^{k-h} \sum_{l=1}^{\widetilde{n}_{[k]}} (1+\theta)^{l-j-\widetilde{n}_{[k]}+\sum_{\zeta=h}^{k}\widetilde{n}_{[\zeta]}} \right] \left(\frac{\zeta_{[h][j]}}{\widetilde{r}_{[h][j]}} \right)^{\eta} \\
&+ \sum_{h=1}^{\widetilde{m}} \left[\sum_{k=h}^{\widetilde{m}} (1+\mu)^{k-h} \sum_{l=1}^{\widetilde{n}_{[k]}} (1+\theta)^{l-\widetilde{n}_{[k]}+\sum_{\zeta=h}^{k}\widetilde{n}_{[\zeta]}} \right] \left(\frac{o_{[h]}}{\widetilde{r}_{[h]}} \right)^{\eta} \\
&= \widetilde{V}^{-\eta} \left(\sum_{h=1}^{\widetilde{m}} \sum_{j=1}^{\widetilde{n}_h} \left(\sum_{l=j}^{\widetilde{n}_{[h]}} (1+\theta)^{l-j} + \sum_{k=h+1}^{\widetilde{m}} (1+\mu)^{k-h} \sum_{l=1}^{\widetilde{n}_{[k]}} (1+\theta)^{l-j-\widetilde{n}_{[k]}+\sum_{\zeta=h}^{k}\widetilde{n}_{[\zeta]}} \right)^{\frac{1}{\eta+1}} (\zeta_{[h][j]})^{\frac{\eta}{\eta+1}} \right)^{\eta+1} \\
&+ \widetilde{U}^{-\eta} \left(\sum_{h=1}^{\widetilde{m}} \left(\sum_{k=h}^{\widetilde{m}} (1+\mu)^{k-h} \sum_{l=1}^{\widetilde{n}_{[k]}} (1+\theta)^{l-\widetilde{n}_{[k]}+\sum_{\zeta=h}^{k}\widetilde{n}_{[\zeta]}} \right)^{\frac{1}{\eta+1}} (o_{[h]})^{\frac{\eta}{\eta+1}} \right)^{\eta+1}.
\end{aligned} \tag{12}$$

Lemma 2. *For $P_{\widehat{tct}}$, the optimal job schedule $\bar{\pi}^*_h$ within group $\Omega_h (h = 1, \cdots, \widetilde{m})$ is the non-decreasing order of $\zeta_{h\langle j \rangle}$, i.e., $\zeta_{h\langle 1 \rangle} \leq \zeta_{h\langle 2 \rangle} \leq \cdots \zeta_{h\langle \widetilde{n}_h \rangle}$.*

Proof. From Equation (12), for group $\Omega_{[h]}$, the objective cost is:

$$\sum_{j=1}^{\widetilde{n}_h} \left(\sum_{l=j}^{\widetilde{n}_{[h]}} (1+\theta)^{l-j} + \sum_{k=h+1}^{\widetilde{m}} (1+\mu)^{k-h} \sum_{l=1}^{\widetilde{n}_{[k]}} (1+\theta)^{l-j-\widetilde{n}_{[k]}+\sum_{\zeta=h}^{k}\widetilde{n}_{[\zeta]}} \right)^{\frac{1}{\eta+1}} (\zeta_{[h][j]})^{\frac{\eta}{\eta+1}} = \sum_{j=1}^{\widetilde{n}_h} x_{[h][j]} y_{[h][j]},$$

where $x_{[h][j]} = \left(\sum_{l=j}^{\tilde{n}_{[h]}} (1+\theta)^{l-j} + \sum_{k=h+1}^{\tilde{m}} (1+\mu)^{k-h} \sum_{l=1}^{\tilde{n}_{[k]}} (1+\theta)^{l-j-\tilde{n}_{[k]}+\sum_{\xi=h}^{k} \tilde{n}_{[\xi]}} \right)^{\frac{1}{\eta+1}}$ and $y_{[h][j]} = (\varsigma_{[h][j]})^{\frac{\eta}{\eta+1}}$. The term $x_{[h][j]}$ is a monotonically decreasing function of j, by the HLP rule (Hardy et al. [22], i.e., the term $\sum_{j=1}^{\tilde{n}_h} x_{[h][j]} y_{[h][j]}$ is minimized if sequence $x_{[h][1]}, x_{[h][2]}, \ldots, x_{[h][\tilde{n}_h]}$ is ordered non-decreasingly and sequence $y_{[h][1]}, y_{[h][2]}, \ldots, y_{[h][\tilde{n}_h]}$ is ordered non-increasingly or vice versa), for the group $\Omega_{[h]}$ ($h = 1, \cdots, \tilde{m}$), if ς_{hj} is a non-decreasing order, i.e., $\varsigma_{h\langle 1 \rangle} \leq \varsigma_{h\langle 2 \rangle} \leq \cdots \varsigma_{h\langle \tilde{n}_h \rangle}$, the result can be obtained. □

4. Special Cases

By Lemma 2, for group Ω_h, the optimal schedule $\bar{\pi}_h^*$ is the non-decreasing order of $\varsigma_{h\langle j \rangle}$, i.e., $\varsigma_{h\langle 1 \rangle} \leq \varsigma_{h\langle 2 \rangle} \leq \cdots \varsigma_{h\langle \tilde{n}_h \rangle}$. From Equation (12), let

$$X = \tilde{U}^{-\eta} \left(\sum_{h=1}^{\tilde{m}} \left(\sum_{k=h}^{\tilde{m}} (1+\mu)^{k-h} \sum_{l=1}^{\tilde{n}_{[k]}} (1+\theta)^{l-\tilde{n}_{[k]}+\sum_{\xi=h}^{k} \tilde{n}_{[\xi]}} \right)^{\frac{1}{\eta+1}} (o_{[h]})^{\frac{\eta}{\eta+1}} \right)^{\eta+1}$$

and

$$Y = \tilde{V}^{-\eta} \left(\sum_{h=1}^{\tilde{m}} \sum_{j=1}^{\tilde{n}_h} \left(\sum_{l=j}^{\tilde{n}_{[h]}} (1+\theta)^{l-j} + \sum_{k=h+1}^{\tilde{m}} (1+\mu)^{k-h} \sum_{l=1}^{\tilde{n}_{[k]}} (1+\theta)^{l-j-\tilde{n}_{[k]}+\sum_{\xi=h}^{k} \tilde{n}_{[\xi]}} \right)^{\frac{1}{\eta+1}} (\varsigma_{[h][j]})^{\frac{\eta}{\eta+1}} \right)^{\eta+1}.$$

In this section, we study some special cases (i.e., the cases of parameters ς_{hj}, o_h, and $\tilde{n}_h$ have some relationship, then X (Y) is minimized or a constant) which can be solved in polynomial time. The special cases stemmingfrom the parameters ς_{hj}, o_h, and $\tilde{n}_h$ have some relationship.

4.1. Case 1

If $o_h = o$ and $\tilde{n}_h = \frac{\tilde{n}}{\tilde{m}} = \ddot{n}$ ($h = 1, \cdots, \tilde{m}$), from Equation (12), it follows that

$$\tilde{U}^{-\eta} \left(\sum_{h=1}^{\tilde{m}} \left(\sum_{k=h}^{\tilde{m}} (1+\mu)^{k-h} \sum_{l=1}^{\tilde{n}_{[k]}} (1+\theta)^{l-\tilde{n}_{[k]}+\sum_{\xi=h}^{k} \tilde{n}_{[\xi]}} \right)^{\frac{1}{\eta+1}} (o_{[h]})^{\frac{\eta}{\eta+1}} \right)^{\eta+1}$$

$$= \tilde{U}^{-\eta} o^{\eta} \left(\sum_{h=1}^{\tilde{m}} \left(\sum_{k=h}^{\tilde{m}} (1+\mu)^{k-h} \sum_{l=1}^{\ddot{n}} (1+\theta)^{l+(k-h)\ddot{n}} \right)^{\frac{1}{\eta+1}} \right)^{\eta+1}$$

is a constant (i.e., $\tilde{U}, o, \eta, \mu, \theta, \ddot{n}$, and $\tilde{m}$ are given constants, and this term is independent of these parameters). Let

$$Y_{h\rho} = \begin{cases} 1, & \text{if } \Omega_h \text{ is assigned to } \rho\text{th position} \\ 0, & \text{otherwise} \end{cases} \quad (13)$$

and

$$\Theta_{h\rho} = \sum_{j=1}^{\ddot{n}} \left(\sum_{l=j}^{\ddot{n}} (1+\theta)^{l-j} + \sum_{k=\rho+1}^{\tilde{m}} (1+\mu)^{k-\rho} \sum_{l=1}^{\ddot{n}} (1+\theta)^{l-j+(k-\rho)\ddot{n}} \right)^{\frac{1}{\eta+1}} (\varsigma_{h\langle j \rangle})^{\frac{\eta}{\eta+1}}. \quad (14)$$

The optimal group schedule can be translated into the following assignment problem:

$$\text{Min} \quad \sum_{h=1}^{\widetilde{m}} \sum_{\rho=1}^{\widetilde{m}} \Theta_{h\rho} Y_{h\rho} \tag{15}$$

$$\text{s.t.} \quad \sum_{\rho=1}^{\widetilde{m}} Y_{h\rho} = 1, h = 1, \ldots, \widetilde{m}, \tag{16}$$

$$\sum_{h=1}^{\widetilde{m}} Y_{h\rho} = 1, \rho = 1, \ldots, \widetilde{m}, \tag{17}$$

$$Y_{h\rho} = 0 \text{ or } 1, h, \rho = 1, \ldots, \widetilde{m}. \tag{18}$$

Thus, for the special case $o_h = o$ and $\widetilde{n}_h = \frac{\widetilde{n}}{\widetilde{m}} = \ddot{n}$ ($h = 1, \cdots, \widetilde{m}$), the problem $P_{\widehat{fct}}$ can be solved by:

Theorem 1. *If $o_h = o$ and $\widetilde{n}_h = \frac{\widetilde{n}}{\widetilde{m}} = \ddot{n}$ ($h = 1, \cdots, \widetilde{m}$), $P_{\widehat{fct}}$ is solvable by Algorithm 1 in $O(\widetilde{n}^3)$ time.*

Algorithm 1: Case 1

Step 1. For group Ω_h ($h = 1, \ldots, \widetilde{m}$), optimal job schedule $\bar{\pi}_h^*$ can be determined by Lemma 2, i.e., $\varsigma_{h\langle 1\rangle} \leq \varsigma_{h\langle 2\rangle} \leq \cdots \varsigma_{h\langle \widetilde{n}_h\rangle}$.
Step 2. Calculate $\Theta_{h\rho}$ ($h, \rho = 1, \ldots, \widetilde{m}$), and determine optimal group schedule $\bar{\pi}_\Omega^*$ by using Equations (15)–(18).
Step 3. Optimal resource allocations $\widetilde{r}_{hj}^*$ and $\widetilde{r}_h^*$ are calculated by Equations (5) and (6) (see Lemma 1).

Proof. Time of Step 1 is $O(\sum_{h=1}^{m}(\widetilde{n}_h \log \widetilde{n}_h)) \leq O(\widetilde{n} \log \widetilde{n})$. Steps 3 needs $O(\widetilde{n})$ time. For an assignment problem, Step 2 needs $O(\widetilde{m}^3) \leq O(\widetilde{n}^3)$ time. Thus, the total time is $O(\widetilde{n}^3)$. □

4.2. Case 2

If $\varsigma_{hj} = \varsigma$ and $\widetilde{n}_h = \frac{\widetilde{n}}{\widetilde{m}} = \ddot{n}, h = 1, \cdots, \widetilde{m}, j = 1, 2, \cdots, \widetilde{n}_h$, we have:

Lemma 3. *For $P_{\widehat{fct}}$, if $\varsigma_{hj} = \varsigma$ and $\widetilde{n}_h = \frac{\widetilde{n}}{\widetilde{m}} = \ddot{n}$ ($h = 1, \cdots, \widetilde{m}; j = 1, \cdots, \widetilde{n}_h$), then the optimal group schedule $\bar{\pi}_\Omega^*$ is the non-decreasing order of o_h, i.e., $o_{(1)} \leq o_{(2)} \leq \ldots \leq o_{(\widetilde{m})}$.*

Proof. From Equation (12), if $\varsigma_{hj} = \varsigma$ and $\widetilde{n}_h = \frac{\widetilde{n}}{\widetilde{m}} = \ddot{n}$,

$$\widetilde{V}^{-\eta} \left(\sum_{h=1}^{\widetilde{m}} \sum_{j=1}^{\widetilde{n}_h} \left(\sum_{l=j}^{\widetilde{n}_{[h]}} (1+\theta)^{l-j} + \sum_{k=h+1}^{\widetilde{m}} (1+\mu)^{k-h} \sum_{l=1}^{\widetilde{n}_{[k]}} (1+\theta)^{l-j-\widetilde{n}_{[k]}+\sum_{\zeta=h}^{k} \widetilde{n}_{[\zeta]}} \right)^{\frac{1}{\eta+1}} (\varsigma_{[h][j]})^{\frac{\eta}{\eta+1}} \right)^{\eta+1}$$

$$= \widetilde{V}^{-\eta} \varsigma^{\eta} \left(\sum_{h=1}^{\widetilde{m}} \sum_{j=1}^{\ddot{n}} \left(\sum_{l=j}^{\ddot{n}} (1+\theta)^{l-j} + \sum_{k=h+1}^{\widetilde{m}} (1+\mu)^{k-h} \sum_{l=1}^{\ddot{n}} (1+\theta)^{l-j+(k-h)\ddot{n}} \right)^{\frac{1}{\eta+1}} \right)^{\eta+1}$$

is a constant (i.e., $\widetilde{V}, \varsigma, \eta, \mu, \theta, \ddot{n}$, and $\widetilde{m}$ are given constants, and this term is independent of these parameters).

From Equation (12) and the above analysis, it can be proved that minimizing $\widehat{fct}$ is equal to minimizing the following expression:

$$\begin{aligned}
&\widetilde{U}^{-\eta}\left(\sum_{h=1}^{\widetilde{m}}\left(\sum_{k=h}^{\widetilde{m}}(1+\mu)^{k-h}\sum_{l=1}^{\widetilde{n}_{[k]}}(1+\theta)^{l-\widetilde{n}_{[k]}+\sum_{\zeta=h}^{k}\widetilde{n}_{[\zeta]}}\right)^{\frac{1}{\eta+1}}(o_{[h]})^{\frac{\eta}{\eta+1}}\right)^{\eta+1}\\
&=\widetilde{U}^{-\eta}\left(\sum_{h=1}^{\widetilde{m}}\left(\sum_{k=h}^{\widetilde{m}}(1+\mu)^{k-h}\sum_{l=1}^{\widetilde{n}}(1+\theta)^{l-\widetilde{n}+\sum_{\zeta=h}^{k}\widetilde{n}}\right)^{\frac{1}{\eta+1}}(o_{[h]})^{\frac{\eta}{\eta+1}}\right)^{\eta+1} \quad (19)\\
&=\widetilde{U}^{-\eta}\left(\sum_{h=1}^{\widetilde{m}}\left(\sum_{k=h}^{\widetilde{m}}(1+\mu)^{k-h}\sum_{l=1}^{\widetilde{n}}(1+\theta)^{l+(k-h)\widetilde{n}}\right)^{\frac{1}{\eta+1}}(o_{[h]})^{\frac{\eta}{\eta+1}}\right)^{\eta+1}.
\end{aligned}$$

Similar to Lemma 2, $\left(\sum_{k=h}^{\widetilde{m}}(1+\mu)^{k-h}\sum_{l=1}^{\widetilde{n}}(1+\theta)^{l+(k-h)\widetilde{n}}\right)^{\frac{1}{\eta+1}}$ is a monotonically decreasing function of h, and by the HLP rule (Hardy et al. [22]), Equation (19) can be minimized by arranging groups in the non-decreasing order of o_h; this completes the proof. □

Thus, for the special case $\varsigma_{hj}=\varsigma$ and $\widetilde{n}_h=\frac{\widetilde{n}}{\widetilde{m}}=\widetilde{n}$ ($i=1,\cdots,\widetilde{m};j=1,\cdots,\widetilde{n}_h$), the problem $P_{\widehat{fct}}$ can be solved by:

Theorem 2. *If $\varsigma_{hj}=\varsigma$ and $\widetilde{n}_h=\frac{\widetilde{n}}{\widetilde{m}}=\widetilde{n}$ ($h=1,\cdots,\widetilde{m}$), $P_{\widehat{fct}}$ is solvable by Algorithm 2 in $O(\widetilde{n}\log\widetilde{n})$ time.*

Algorithm 2: Case 2

Step 1. For group Ω_h ($h=1,\cdots,\widetilde{m}$), optimal job schedule can be obtained in any order.
Step 2. Optimal group schedule π_Ω^* is the non-decreasing order of o_h.
Step 3. Optimal resource allocations $\widetilde{r}_{hj}^*$ and $\widetilde{r}_h^*$ are calculated by Equations (5) and (6) (see Lemma 1).

4.3. Case 3

For any groups Ω_x and Ω_y, if $o_x \leq o_y$ implies $\widetilde{n}_x \geq \widetilde{n}_y$, we have:

Lemma 4. *For any groups Ω_x and Ω_y of $P_{\widehat{fct}}$, if $o_x \leq o_y$ implies $\widetilde{n}_x \geq \widetilde{n}_y$, the optimal group schedule π_Ω^* is non-decreasing order of o_h.*

Proof. Similar to the proof of Liang et al. [6] (see Equation (12)). □

For this special case, i.e., for any groups Ω_x and Ω_y, if $o_x \leq o_y$ implies $\widetilde{n}_x \geq \widetilde{n}_y$, $P_{\widehat{fct}}$ can be solved by:

Theorem 3. *For any groups Ω_x and Ω_y, if $o_x \leq o_y$ implies $\widetilde{n}_x \geq \widetilde{n}_y$, $P_{\widehat{fct}}$ is solvable by Algorithm 3 in $O(\widetilde{n}\log\widetilde{n})$ time.*

Algorithm 3: Case 3

Step 1. For group Ω_h ($h=1,\ldots,\widetilde{m}$), the optimal job schedule $\widetilde{\pi}_h^*$ can be determined by Lemma 2, i.e., $\varsigma_{h\langle 1\rangle}\leq\varsigma_{h\langle 2\rangle}\leq\cdots\varsigma_{h\langle\widetilde{n}_h\rangle}$.
Step 2. The optimal group schedule π_Ω^* is the non-decreasing order of o_h.
Step 3. The optimal resource allocations $\widetilde{r}_{hj}^*$ and $\widetilde{r}_h^*$ are calculated by Equations (5) and (6) (see Lemma 1).

---

5. A General Case

For $P_{\widehat{fct}}$, we cannot find a polynomially optimal algorithm, and the complexity of determining the optimal group schedule is still an open problem; we conjecture that this problem is NP-hard. Thus, B&B (i.e., branch-and-bound, where we need a lower bound and a upper bound) and heuristic algorithms might be a good way to solve $P_{\widehat{fct}}$.

5.1. Upper Bound

For the $\widehat{fct}$ minimization, any feasible solution can be proposed as a upper bound (denoted by UB). Similar to Section 3, the group sorting method can be used as the heuristic and then this solution is improved by using the pairwise interchange method.

For a better comparison, an alternative or complementary to Algorithm 4 is proposed, a tabu search (denoted by $\widetilde{ts}$) algorithm (i.e., Algorithm 5) can be used to solve $P_{\widehat{fct}}$.

Algorithm 4: Upper Bound

Step 1. For group Ω_h ($h = 1, \cdots, \widetilde{m}$), an internal optimal job schedule π_h^* (Lemma 2) is: $\varsigma_{h\langle 1 \rangle} \leq \varsigma_{h\langle 2 \rangle} \leq \cdots \varsigma_{h\langle \widetilde{n}_h \rangle}$.

Step 2. Groups are scheduled by the non-decreasing order of o_h, i.e., $o_{(1)} \leq o_{(2)} \leq \ldots \leq o_{(\widetilde{m})}$.

Step 3. Groups are scheduled by the non-increasing order of $\widetilde{n}_h$, i.e., $\widetilde{n}_{<<1>>} \geq \widetilde{n}_{<<2>>} \geq \cdots \geq \widetilde{n}_{<<\widetilde{m}>>}$.

Step 4. From Steps 2 and 3, the smallest value $\widehat{fct}$ (see Equation (12)) is selected as an original group schedule $\bar{\pi}_\Omega$.

Step 5. Set $k = 1$.

Step 6. Set $s = k + 1$.

Step 7. The new group schedule can be obtained by exchanging the kth and sth groups (denoted as $\bar{\pi}_\Omega^*$), and when $\widehat{fct}$ of $\bar{\pi}_\Omega^*$ is smaller than $\bar{\pi}_\Omega$, $\bar{\pi}_\Omega$ is updated by $\bar{\pi}_\Omega^*$.

Step 8. If $s < \widetilde{m}$, then set $s = s + 1$, go to step 7.

Step 9. If $k < \widetilde{m} - 1$, then set $k = k + 1$, go to step 6; otherwise, STOP. Output the group schedule $\bar{\pi}_\Omega^*$ of the best group schedule found by the heuristic algorithm and its objective value $\widehat{fct}$.

Step 10. According to Lemma 1, calculate the resource allocation by Equations (5) and (6).

Algorithm 5: $\widetilde{ts}$

Step 1. For group $\Omega_h (h = 1, \cdots, \widetilde{m})$, an internal optimal job schedule π_h^* can be obtained by Lemma 2, i.e., $\varsigma_{h\langle 1 \rangle} \leq \varsigma_{h\langle 2 \rangle} \leq \cdots \varsigma_{h\langle \widetilde{n}_h \rangle}$.

Step 2. Let the tabu list be empty and the iteration number be zero.

Step 3. Choose an initial group schedule by the Steps 2–4 of Algorithm 4, calculate its value $\widehat{fct}$ (see Equation (12)) and set the current group schedule as the best solution $\bar{\pi}_\Omega^*$.

Step 4. Search the associated neighborhood of the current group schedule and resolve if there is a group schedule $\bar{\pi}_\Omega^{**}$ with the smallest objective value in associated neighborhood and it is not in the tabu list, where the neighborhood is generated by the random exchange of any two groups.

Step 5. If $\widehat{fct}(\bar{\pi}_\Omega^{**}) < \widehat{fct}(\bar{\pi}_\Omega^*)$, then let $\bar{\pi}_\Omega^* = \bar{\pi}_\Omega^{**}$. Update the tabu list and the iteration number.

Step 6. If there is not a group schedule in associated neighborhood but it is not in the tabu list or the maximum number of iterations is reached, output the local optimal group schedule $\bar{\pi}_\Omega$ and $\widehat{fct}(\bar{\pi}_\Omega)$. Otherwise, update tabu list and go to Step 4.

Step 7. According to Lemma 1, calculate the resource allocation by Equations (5) and (6).

5.2. Lower Bound

Let $\tilde{\pi}_\Omega = (\tilde{\pi}_{\Omega p}, \tilde{\pi}_{\Omega u})$ be a group schedule, where $\tilde{\pi}_{\Omega p}$ (respectively $\tilde{\pi}_{\Omega u}$) is the scheduled (respectively unscheduled) part, and there are r groups in $\tilde{\pi}_{\Omega p}$. From Equation (12) and Lemma 4, the lower bound (denoted by LB) of $P_{\widehat{tct}}$ is

$$LB = \tilde{V}^{-\eta} \left(\sum_{h=1}^{r} \sum_{j=1}^{\tilde{n}_h} \left(\begin{array}{l} \sum_{l=j}^{\tilde{n}_{[h]}} (1+\theta)^{l-j} + \sum_{k=h+1}^{r} (1+\mu)^{k-h} \sum_{l=1}^{\tilde{n}_{[k]}} (1+\theta)^{l-j-\tilde{n}_{[k]} + \sum_{\xi=h}^{k} \tilde{n}_{[\xi]}} + \\ \sum_{k=r+1}^{\tilde{m}} (1+\mu)^{k-h} \sum_{l=1}^{\tilde{n}_{<<k>>}} (1+\theta)^{l-j-\tilde{n}_{<<k>>} + \sum_{\xi=h}^{r} \tilde{n}_{[\xi]} + \sum_{\xi=r+1}^{k} \tilde{n}_{<<\xi>>}} \end{array} \right)^{\frac{1}{\eta+1}} (\varsigma_{[h]\langle j \rangle})^{\frac{\eta}{\eta+1}} \right)^{\eta+1}$$

$$+ \sum_{h=r+1}^{\tilde{m}} \sum_{j=1}^{\tilde{n}_h} \left(\begin{array}{l} \sum_{l=j}^{\tilde{n}_{[h]}} (1+\theta)^{l-j} + \\ \sum_{k=h+1}^{\tilde{m}} (1+\mu)^{k-h} \sum_{l=1}^{\tilde{n}_{<<k>>}} (1+\theta)^{l-j-\tilde{n}_{<<k>>} + \sum_{\xi=h}^{k} \tilde{n}_{<<\xi>>}} \end{array} \right)^{\frac{1}{\eta+1}} (\varsigma_{(h)\langle j \rangle})^{\frac{\eta}{\eta+1}}$$

$$+ \tilde{U}^{-\eta} \left(\sum_{h=1}^{r} \left(\begin{array}{l} \sum_{k=h}^{r} (1+\mu)^{k-h} \sum_{l=1}^{\tilde{n}_{[k]}} (1+\theta)^{l-\tilde{n}_{[k]} + \sum_{\xi=h}^{k} \tilde{n}_{[\xi]}} + \\ \sum_{k=r+1}^{\tilde{m}} (1+\mu)^{k-h} \sum_{l=1}^{\tilde{n}_{<<k>>}} (1+\theta)^{l-\tilde{n}_{<<k>>} + \sum_{\xi=h}^{r} \tilde{n}_{[\xi]} + \sum_{\xi=r+1}^{k} \tilde{n}_{<<\xi>>}} \end{array} \right)^{\frac{1}{\eta+1}} (o_{[h]})^{\frac{\eta}{\eta+1}} \right)^{\eta+1}$$

$$+ \sum_{h=r+1}^{\tilde{m}} \left(\sum_{k=h}^{\tilde{m}} (1+\mu)^{k-h} \sum_{l=1}^{\tilde{n}_{<<k>>}} (1+\theta)^{l-\tilde{n}_{<<k>>} + \sum_{\xi=h}^{k} \tilde{n}_{<<\xi>>}} \right)^{\frac{1}{\eta+1}} (o_{(h)})^{\frac{\eta}{\eta+1}} \right), \quad (20)$$

where $\varsigma_{h\langle 1 \rangle} \leq \varsigma_{h\langle 2 \rangle} \leq \cdots \varsigma_{h\langle \tilde{n}_h \rangle}$, $o_{(r+1)} \leq o_{(r+2)} \leq \cdots \leq o_{(\tilde{m})}$ and $\tilde{n}_{<<r+1>>} \geq \tilde{n}_{<<r+2>>} \geq \cdots \geq \tilde{n}_{<<\tilde{m}>>}$ (remark: $o_{(h)}$ and $\tilde{n}_{<<h>>}$ ($h = r+1, \ldots, \tilde{m}$) do not necessarily correspond to identical group).

From the UB (see Algorithm 4) and LB (see Equation (20)), a standardized $B\&B$ algorithm can be given.

6. Computational Result

A series of computational experiments were performed to evaluate the effectiveness of the UB, $B\&B$, and $\widehat{ts}$ algorithms, and the $\widehat{ts}$ algorithm was terminated after 2000 iterations. The proposed algorithms were coded in the C++ language and performed on a desktop computer with CPUInter®Corei5-10500 3.10 GHz, 8 GB RAM on Windows® 10 operating system. The following parameters were randomly generated: ζ_{hj} is uniformly distributed in $[1, 100]$; o_h is uniformly distributed in $[1, 50]$; θ and μ are uniformly distributed in $(0, 0.5)$, $(0.5, 1)$; $\tilde{U} = \tilde{V} = 500$; $\tilde{n} = 100, 150, 200, 250, 300$; $\tilde{m} = 12, 13, 14, 15, 16$ (at least one job per group); $\eta = 2$. For each combination ($\tilde{n}$, $\tilde{m}$, and $\theta(\mu)$), there were 10 randomly generated replicas and the maximum $\widehat{cpu}$ time for each instance was set to 3600 s. For the $B\&B$ algorithm, average and maximum $\widehat{cpu}$ time (in seconds), and average and maximum node numbers were given. The error bound of UB and $\widehat{ts}$ algorithms is given by:

$$\frac{\widehat{tct}(Y) - \widehat{tct}(Opt)}{\widehat{tct}(Opt)},$$

where $Y \in \{UB, \widehat{ts}\}$, $\widehat{tct}(Y)$ is a value $\widehat{tct}$ by Y, and $\widehat{tct}(Opt)$ is an optimal value by a $B\&B$ algorithm. The computational results are given in Tables 2 and 3. From Tables 2 and 3, it is easy to see that the $B\&B$ can solve up to 300 jobs in a reasonable amount of time, and UB performs very well compared to $\widehat{ts}$ in terms of error bound. When $\tilde{n} \leq 300$, the maximum error bound is less than 0.001559 (i.e., relative error $\leq 0.1559\%$).

Table 2. Results of algorithms for $\theta, \mu \sim (0, 0.5)$.

$\tilde{n}$	$\tilde{m}$	B&B-$\widetilde{cpu}$ (s)		Node Number of B&B		UB-$\widetilde{cpu}$ (s)		Error Bound of UB		$\widehat{ts}$-$\widetilde{cpu}$ (s)		Error Bound of $\widehat{ts}$	
		Mean	Max	Mean	Max	Mean	Max	Mean	Max	Mean	Max	Mean	Max
100	12	135.024	221.776	1,809,907.670	2,159,443	0.016	0.017	0.000095	0.000187	20.779	20.851	3.834449	7.624277
	13	487.759	689.564	3,549,270.333	5,082,238	0.026	0.027	0.000156	0.000268	27.917	27.931	1.732993	2.020046
	14	922.643	1522.268	13,107,200.333	15,310,034	0.039	0.040	0.000801	0.000857	36.547	36.851	2.649336	3.713691
	15	2194.031	2700.565	27,285,725.333	29,086,172	0.06	0.066	0.000958	0.001559	46.688	46.716	2.817131	3.046495
	16	3600	3600	31,359,296.667	35,393,226	0.089	0.091	0	0	59.426	59.502	4.264297	5.401098
150	12	207.987	342.972	2,341,793.000	3,117,957	0.018	0.019	0.000027	0.000078	20.801	21.24	1.514108	1.621744
	13	542.599	801.597	6,761,302.333	9,380,258	0.024	0.025	0	0	27.637	27.713	1.385886	2.443091
	14	945.239	1546.23	12,394,620.667	16,056,940	0.038	0.039	0.000023	0.000062	36.417	36.447	2.669022	3.621472
	15	2253.448	2792.626	21,252,555.333	28,365,609	0.058	0.059	0.000044	0.000083	46.842	46.884	2.305773	2.829561
	16	3600	3600	3,216,807.333	35,946,209	0.084	0.086	0.000078	0.000165	59.635	59.732	2.348701	3.032307
200	12	244.069	401.384	2,977,588.333	4,496,930	0.019	0.024	0	0	20.679	20.701	1.159309	1.440431
	13	603.216	898.287	7,165,875.333	9,493,651	0.025	0.026	0.000035	0.000071	27.631	27.626	1.273332	1.786464
	14	998.154	1702.5569	10,620,850.667	18,113,633	0.039	0.04	0	0	36.339	36.386	1.895725	2.250205
	15	2256.669	2899.45	25,283,619.350	29,882,329	0.058	0.059	0.000336	0.000512	46.892	46.941	1.741518	2.476327
	16	3600	3600	30406061.000	34993966	0.083	0.084	0	0	59.634	59.691	2.173201	3.408911
250	12	315.999	511.48	4,632,641.000	7,187,564	0.018	0.019	0.000726	0.000937	20.606	20.611	0.849315	1.063118
	13	649.96	998.95	7,359,686.667	9,993,712	0.026	0.026	0.000012	0.000053	27.674	27.727	1.177795	1.975853
	14	1052.236	1798.635	10,615,423.970	15,492,118	0.038	0.040	0.000225	0.000429	35.369	36.441	2.132518	5.285686
	15	2348.584	3022.158	23,198,516.333	26,916,519	0.061	0.063	0	0	46.182	46.886	2.195878	3.378249
	16	3600	3600	31,985,126.350	39,841,545	0.085	0.087	0.000047	0.000096	59.642	60.662	1.080341	2.231895
300	12	372.965	602.478	6,529,516.270	8,874,654	0.019	0.021	0.000264	0.000418	20.228	21.678	2.132238	3.441628
	13	700.648	1096.126	9,534,255.360	10,346,347	0.028	0.029	0	0	27.432	28.344	3.041866	4.726763
	14	1125.267	1900.597	18,285,356.330	20,378,676	0.042	0.043	0.000241	0.000358	35.636	36.359	2.508975	3.354484
	15	2411.266	3098.486	23,166,586.555	29,786,776	0.061	0.063	0.000074	0.000085	45.856	46.612	1.456993	2.018688
	16	3600	3600	33,064,597.980	36,268,497	0.086	0.088	0	0	59.202	60.342	2.665422	3.625572

Table 3. Results of algorithms for $\theta, \mu \sim (0.5, 1)$.

$\tilde{n}$	$\tilde{m}$	B&B-$\widetilde{cpu}$ (s) Mean	Max	Node Number of B&B Mean	Max	UB-$\widetilde{cpu}$ (s) Mean	Max	Error Bound of UB Mean	Max	$\widetilde{t_s}$ -$\widetilde{cpu}$ (s) Mean	Max	Error Bound of $\widetilde{t_s}$ Mean	Max
100	12	111.759	203.165	1,772,325.333	2,006,440	0.018	0.022	0.000342	0.000361	20.636	20.663	2.151314	2.733541
	13	514.284	720.05	5,192,266.570	8,375,900	0.036	0.057	0.000023	0.000097	27.71	27.724	2.302026	2.604564
	14	899.152	1511.534	10,440,786.667	15,534,053	0.041	0.044	0.000056	0.000089	38.454	41.59	3.211589	4.194101
	15	2231.154	2691.187	21,511,386.670	28,404,113	0.062	0.071	0	0	47.426	47.484	3.053645	3.928604
	16	3600	3600	32,304,624.333	34,845,329	0.086	0.087	0.000154	0.000203	60.495	60.688	4.714135	6.396946
150	12	197.605	301.479	2,269,584.670	3,575,833	0.017	0.018	0.000977	0.000995	20.896	20.912	1.417686	1.890114
	13	570.153	807.542	6,764,995.435	10,027,994	0.025	0.026	0.000089	0.0000138	28.125	28.213	1.023524	1.151338
	14	966.147	1632.498	10,816,813.000	17,165,408	0.039	0.04	0.000135	0.000185	36.918	36.995	1.383139	1.714258
	15	2265.154	2823.396	64,825,309.666	20,264,395	0.07	0.094	0	0	47.613	47.704	1.918044	3.053374
	16	3600	3600	33,081,125.000	38,287,571	0.086	0.091	0.000235	0.000304	59.542	59.622	2.339585	3.275121
200	12	251.663	412.269	3,364,810.333	4,354,750	0.016	0.017	0.000322	0.000358	20.588	20.619	0.679119	1.162433
	13	632.148	910.214	7,692,721.250	12,135,354	0.038	0.064	0.000014	0.000039	27.675	27.737	0.843637	0.974668
	14	1021.267	1741.637	10,359,758.667	18,262,014	0.040	0.041	0	0	36.342	37.353	1.094559	1.495353
	15	2303.264	2935.348	24,840,981.000	29,871,474	0.057	0.058	0.000055	0.000083	46.872	46.91	1.243455	1.642072
	16	3600	3600	36,074,135.333	39,275,374	0.083	0.084	0	0	59.671	59.794	1.942357	2.492556
250	12	310.286	507.549	3,193,303.333	5,195,728	0.017	0.018	0	0	20.627	20.651	0.578495	1.212256
	13	669.297	1032.756	7,887,726.555	13,510,556	0.025	0.026	0.000327	0.000449	27.716	28.722	0.971304	1.540024
	14	1077.954	1901.25	11,022,935.550	20,161,905	0.042	0.043	0.000087	0.000126	38.265	41.688	1.464696	2.107542
	15	2363.186	3102.583	24,480,723.980	32,108,671	0.08	0.092	0.000355	0.000421	47.464	48.424	1.073162	1.436231
	16	3600	3600	35,416,920.000	37,899,764	0.092	0.096	0.000039	0.000058	60.474	61.622	1.607212	2.647154
300	12	372.261	611.365	4,028,462.640	6,779,955	0.021	0.022	0.000022	0.000073	20.858	21.996	0.770591	1.264125
	13	726.314	1143.348	8,899,027.570	13,410,513	0.036	0.057	0	0	28.135	29.234	1.661815	2.354942
	14	1132.706	2008.646	14,693,257.000	23,608,109	0.059	0.061	0.0000068	0.000112	36.936	38.599	0.702051	1.018678
	15	2546.264	3348.345	30,358,453.333	35,337,815	0.084	0.085	0	0	47.341	48.502	1.670674	2.166306
	16	3600	3600	35,362,523.000	39,764,582	0.086	0.092	0.000034	0.000086	58.245	60.262	1.247154	1.626366

7. Conclusions

This paper investigated the group problem with deterioration effects and resource allocation. The goal was to determine $\bar{\pi}_{\Omega}^*$, $\bar{\pi}_h^*$ ($h = 1, \cdots, \widetilde{m}$) in Ω_h and R^* such that $\widehat{tct}$ is minimized under $\sum_{i=1}^{\widetilde{m}} \sum_{j=1}^{\widetilde{n}_h} \widetilde{r}_{ij} \leq \widetilde{V}$ and $\sum_{i=1}^{\widetilde{m}} \widetilde{r}_i \leq \widetilde{U}$. For some special cases, we demonstrated that this problem remains polynomially solvable. For the general case, we proposed some algorithms to solve this problem. As a future extension, it is interesting to deal with group scheduling with two scenarios based on processing times (see Wu et al. [23]) and delivery times (see Qian and Zhan [24]).

Author Contributions: Conceptualization, J.-X.Y. and H.-B.B.; methodology, J.-X.Y. and N.R.; software, J.-X.Y., H.-B.B. and H.B.; formal analysis, J.-X.Y. and J.-B.W.; investigation, J.-B.W.; writing—original draft preparation, J.-X.Y. and J.-B.W.; writing—review and editing, J.-X.Y. and J.-B.W. All authors have read and agreed to the published version of the manuscript.

Funding: This Work was supported by LiaoNing Revitalization Talents Program (Grant No. XLYC2002017) and Natural Science Foundation of LiaoNing Province, China (Grant No. 2020-MS-233).

Institutional Review Board Statement: Not applicable.

Informed Consent Statement: Not applicable.

Data Availability Statement: The data used to support this paper are available from the corresponding author upon request.

Conflicts of Interest: The authors declare no conflict of interest.

References

1. Ham, I.; Hitomi, K.; Yoshida, T. Group Technology: Applications to Production Management. Available online: https://link.springer.com/book/10.1007/978-94-009-4976-8 (accessed on 17 July 2022).
2. Wang, J.B.; Guo, A.X.; Shan, F.; Jiang, B.; Wang, L.Y. Single machine group scheduling under decreasing linear deterioration. *J. Appl. Math. Comput.* **2007**, *24*, 283–293. [CrossRef]
3. Yang, S.J. Group scheduling problems with simultaneous considerations of learning and deterioration effects on a single-machine. *Appl. Math. Model.* **2011**, *35*, 4008–4016. [CrossRef]
4. Bai, J.; Li, Z.R.; Huang, X. Single-machine group scheduling with general deterioration and learning Eff. *Appl. Math. Model.* **2012**, *36*, 1267–1274. [CrossRef]
5. Lu, Y.Y.; Wang, J.J.; Wang, J.B. Single machine group scheduling with decreasing time-dependent processing times subject to release dates. *Appl. Math. Comput.* **2014**, *234*, 286–292. [CrossRef]
6. Wang, J.B.; Liu, L.; Wang, J.J.; Li, L. Makespan minimization scheduling with ready times, group technology and shortening job processing times. *Comput. J.* **2018**, *61*, 1422–1428. [CrossRef]
7. Liu, F.; Yang, J.; Lu, Y.Y. Solution algorithms for single-machine group scheduling with ready times and deteriorating jobs. *Eng. Optim.* **2019**, *51*, 862–874. [CrossRef]
8. Zhu, Z.G.; Sun, L.Y.; Chu, F.; Liu, M. Single-machine group scheduling with resource allocation and learning effect. *Comput. Ind. Eng.* **2011**, *60*, 148–157. [CrossRef]
9. Zhang, X.; Liao, L.; Zhang, W.; Cheng, T.C.E.; Tan, Y.; Ji, M. Single-machine group scheduling with new models of position-dependent processing times. *Comput. Ind. Eng.* **2018**, *117*, 1–5. [CrossRef]
10. Liao, B.; Wang, X.; Zhu, X.; Yang, S.; Pardalos, P.M. Less is more approach for competing groups scheduling with different learning effects. *J. Comb. Optim. Vol.* **2020**, *39*, 33–54. [CrossRef]
11. Lv, D.Y.; Luo, S.W.; Xue, J.; Xu, J.X.; Wang, J.B. A note on single machine common flow allowance group scheduling with learning effect and resource allocation. *Comput. Ind. Eng.* **2021**, *151*, 106941. [CrossRef]
12. Xu, H.Y.; Li, X.P.; Ruiz, R.B.; Zhu, H.H. Group scheduling with nonperiodical maintenance and deteriorating effects. *IEEE Trans. Syst. Man Cybern. Syst.* **2021**, *51*, 2860–2872. [CrossRef]
13. Oron, D. Scheduling controllable processing time jobs in a deteriorating environment. *J. Of The Oper. Res. Soc.* **2014**, *64*, 49–56. [CrossRef]
14. Li, L.; Wang, J.-J. Scheduling jobs with deterioration effect and controllable processing time. *Neural Comput. Appl.* **2018**, *29*, 1163–1170. [CrossRef]
15. Wang, D.; Huo, Y.; Ji, P. Single-machine group scheduling with deteriorating jobs and allotted resource. *Optim. Lett.* **2014**, *8*, 591–605. [CrossRef]
16. Liang, X.X.; Liu, M.Q.; Feng, Y.B.; Wang, J.B.; Wen, L.S. Solution algorithms for single-machine resource allocation scheduling with deteriorating jobs and group technology. *Eng. Optim.* **2020**, *52*, 1184–1197. [CrossRef]

17. Wang, J.B.; Liang, X.X. Group scheduling with deteriorating jobs and allotted resource under limited resource availability constraint. *Eng. Optim.* **2019**, *51*, 231–246. [CrossRef]
18. Ji, M.; Chen, K.; Ge, J.; Cheng, T.C.E. Group scheduling and job-dependent due window assignment based on a common flow allowance. *Comput. Ind. Eng.* **2014**, *68*, 35–41. [CrossRef]
19. Gawiejnowicz, S. *Models and Algorithms of Time-Dependent Scheduling*; Springer: Berlin/Heidelberg, Germany, 2020.
20. Shabtay, D.; Kaspi, M. Minimizing the total weighted flow time in a single machine with controllable processing times. *Comput. Oper. Res.* **2004**, *31*, 2279–2289. [CrossRef]
21. Wang, J.B.; Wang, M.Z. Single-machine scheduling to minimize total convex resource consumption with a constraint on total weighted flow time. *Comput. Oper. Res.* **2012**, *39*, 492–497. [CrossRef]
22. Hardy, G.-H.; Littlewood, J.-E.; Polya, G. *Inequalities*, 2nd ed.; Cambridge University Press: Cambridge, UK, 1967.
23. Wu, C.C.; Bai, D.; Chen, J.H.; Lin, W.C.; Xing, L.; Lin, J.C.; Cheng, S.-R. Several variants of simulated annealing hyper-heuristic for a single-machine scheduling with two-scenario-based dependent processing times. *Swarm Evol. Comput.* **2021**, *60*, 100765. [CrossRef]
24. Qian, J.; Zhan, Y. The due date assignment scheduling problem with delivery times and truncated sum-of-processing-times-based learning effect. *Mathematics* **2021**, *9*, 3085. [CrossRef]

Article

Multipurpose Aggregation in Risk Assessment

Zoltán Kovács [1,*], Tibor Csizmadia [2], István Mihálcz [3,4] and Zsolt T. Kosztyán [3]

1. Department of Supply Chain Management, Institute of Management, Faculty of Business Administration and Economics, University of Pannonia, 8200 Veszprem, Hungary
2. Department of Management, Institute of Management, Faculty of Business Administration and Economics, University of Pannonia, 8200 Veszprem, Hungary
3. Department of Quantitative Methods, Institute of Management, Faculty of Business Administration and Economics, University of Pannonia, 8200 Veszprem, Hungary
4. Siix Hungary, 2750 Nagykőrös, Hungary
* Correspondence: kovacs.zoltan@gtk.uni-pannon.hu

Abstract: Risk-mitigation decisions in risk-management systems are usually based on complex risk indicators. Therefore, aggregation is an important step during risk assessment. Aggregation is important when determining the risk of components or the overall risk of different areas or organizational levels. In this article, the authors identify different aggregation scenarios. They summarize the requirements of aggregation functions and characterize different aggregations according to these requirements. They critique the multiplication-based risk priority number (RPN) used in existing applications and propose the use of other functions in different aggregation scenarios. The behavior of certain aggregation functions in warning systems is also examined. The authors find that, depending on the aggregation location within the organization and the purpose of the aggregation, considerably more functions can be used to develop complex risk indicators. The authors use different aggregations and seriation and biclustering to develop a method for generating corrective and preventive actions. The paper provides contributions for individuals, organizations, and or policy makers to assess and mitigate the risks at all levels of the enterprise.

Keywords: risk assessment; flexibility; multilevel structure

MSC: 91B05

Citation: Kovács, Z.; Csizmadia, T.; Mihálcz, I.; Kosztyán, Z.T. Multipurpose Aggregation in Risk Assessment. *Mathematics* **2021**, *10*, 3166. https://doi.org/10.3390/math10173166

Academic Editor: Constantin Zopounidis

Received: 1 August 2022
Accepted: 27 August 2022
Published: 2 September 2022

Publisher's Note: MDPI stays neutral with regard to jurisdictional claims in published maps and institutional affiliations.

Copyright: © 2022 by the authors. Licensee MDPI, Basel, Switzerland. This article is an open access article distributed under the terms and conditions of the Creative Commons Attribution (CC BY) license (https://creativecommons.org/licenses/by/4.0/).

1. Introduction

Risk aggregation plays an important role in various risk-assessment processes [1,2]. Risks can be aggregated for several purposes. It can happen at the lowest level of the systems (processes, products) during the calculation of a complex indicator from the factors. The overall risk value of certain areas can be formed, but risk can also be aggregated along the organizational hierarchy. In the following, we present a novel methodology of aggregation that can be used for different purposes. Aggregation can be considered a method for combining a list of numerical values into a single representative value [3,4]. Traditionally, the risk value is calculated based on a fixed number of risk components. Failure mode and effect analysis (FMEA), which is a widely used risk-assessment method, includes three risk components: the occurrence (O), detectability (D), and severity (S) [5–7]. Various methods that increase the number of risk components have been introduced in the literature. The use of four risk components was proposed by Karasan et al. [8] and Maheswaran and Loganathan [9], and Ouédraogo et al. [10] and Yousefi et al. [11] used five risk components. In contrast to the use of a fixed number of components, Bognár and Hegedűs [12] developed the partial risk map (PRISM) method, which flexibly considers only the FMEA components that are actually needed in the risk-assessment process. The total risk evaluation framework (TREF) method generalizes this idea and can flexibly handle an arbitrary number of risk components [13].

In addition, various methods and analyses for aggregating risk components have been proposed, such as the *vIsekriterijumska optimizacija i kompromisno resenje* (VIKOR) method [14,15], the technique for order preference by similarity to the ideal solution (TOPSIS) method [16,17], the elimination and choice expressing the reality (ELECTRE) method [18,19], the evaluation based on the distance from the average solution (EDAS) method [20,21], the preference ranking organization method for enrichment evaluations (PROMETHEE) method [22,23], the Gray relational analysis (GRA) method [24,25], the MULTIMOORA method [26,27], the TODIM (Portuguese acronym for interactive multi-criteria decision making) method [28,29], and the sum of ranking differences (SRD) method [30,31]. These methods use different perspectives and various procedures to aggregate the values of distinct risk components into a single representative risk value.

Conventional risk management systems evaluate risk by calculating the risk priority number (RPN) as an aggregated risk indicator.

Risk indicators can be aggregated further through additional steps. These aggregations can be performed along the hierarchy of the organization, the hierarchy of the processes, or other logical operations.

In terms of aggregation, a common feature of the methods is that these methods provide aggregated values at only one level. The TREF method [13] and the new FMEA [32] consider two levels: the risk-component level and the aggregated value level. No existing methods can handle more than two levels; however, in practice, there are often more than two aggregation levels, and different types of corrective/preventive actions may be needed at the risk component level and the aggregated value level.

Moreover, one of the main constraints of existing methods is that these approaches do not consider risks in different levels of the process hierarchy. However, corrective/preventive actions can be prescribed at each hierarchy level, and different corrective/preventive actions may be needed at various process hierarchy levels. In summary, because the relationships between the process hierarchy levels (causes and effects across levels) are not addressed by existing methods, flexible, total system-level risk assessments have not yet been addressed. There is no work in the literature that deals with the multilevel case in general, as it is presented in this paper. Filipović [33] dealt with the multilevel case, but the domain was limited to the insurance area and the standard (Solvecy II) solution. Bjørnsen and Aven [2] provide a good summary of the general issue of aggregation; however, they do not deal with corrective and preventive actions [2]. They have presented different (oil and gas industry, stock investment, national, societal) cases.

In general, it can be concluded that none of the publications in the literature deals with the general approach as it is described in this paper. The most frequently missing components are as follows.

- Risks are aggregated, however, only on two (error mode and functional error, effect) or on three (cause, error mode, effect) levels. This is the general approach in risk-management of production systems.
- Although there is a hierarchical (vertical) aggregation, the model is not suitable for area-based (horizontal) aggregation and the opposite.
- The model is specific to a given area, for example insurance, bankruptcy risk, and production.
- Model/framework does not establish a link between the aggregation of risks and the generation of corrective, preventive measures. For this reason, the previous aggregation methods (including FMEA) can be considered as a special case of the aggregation model presented in this paper.

Motivated by the above analyses and literature reviews, we highlight the contributions of this study to existing risk-assessment methods as follows:

C_1 A multilevel framework known as the enterprise-level matrix (ELM), which consists of three matrices, is proposed to evaluate risk at different enterprise levels. The three matrices are the risk-level matrix (RLM), the threshold-level matrix (TLM), and the action-level matrix (ALM).

C_2 The proposed framework aggregates not only the risk components but also the overall risk indicators of the process components at all levels of the corporate process hierarchy. Thus, appropriate corrective/preventive actions can be prescribed at each process hierarchy level, as different types of corrective/preventive actions may be needed at the process and corporate levels.

C_3 We use data-mining methods such as seriation and biclustering techniques to simultaneously identify risk components/warnings and process components to select an appropriate set of corrective/preventive actions.

The remainder of this paper is structured as follows. Section 2 introduces the preliminary details and the requirements and characterizations of the aggregation functions. Section 3 demonstrates a practical example of the proposed approach. Section 4 summarizes the paper.

2. Preliminaries

We use the following terminology throughout this work.

Risk component: the input of the aggregation. The risk components can be primary data, such as the occurrence, severity, and detection, which are often called factors. (The term "factor" refers to the most commonly used aggregation method: multiplication.) The components can also be aggregated values, such as vertical risk aggregation in an organization. This case is the mean of the RPNs of a product, process, or organization.

Aggregated value: the result of the aggregation. The aggregated value is typically a scalar value; however, it can also be a vector, such as when the risk cannot be characterized by one number.

2.1. The Set of Enterprise-Level Matrices (ELM)

This study proposes three multilevel matrices: the risk-level matrix (RLM), threshold-level matrix (TLM), and action-level matrix (ALM). These matrices are all multidimensional matrices, with the columns representing the risk components and their aggregations at all levels and the rows representing the process components and their aggregations at all levels. The risk-level matrix (RLM) specifies the risk values of all risk and process components. For all risk values (i.e., for each cell) in the RLM, a threshold value is specified in the threshold-level matrix. The threshold-level matrix includes specific thresholds for all risk values; however, a generic threshold can also be specified for all process and risk components. A corrective/preventive action occurs if a risk value is greater than or equal to the specific threshold value. The action-level matrix contains the specific corrective/preventive actions for mitigating the risk values; these actions can be specific for the given process and risk component or generic for each process and risk component.

The proposed set of multilevel matrices, denoted as the enterprise-level matrix (ELM), helps decision-makers evaluate and assess risk at all levels of the enterprise. In addition, data-mining methods, such as seriation and biclustering, are used to select the set of corrective/preventive tasks.

2.1.1. Risk-Level Matrix

Table 1 specifies the structure of the hierarchical risk-evaluation matrix, hereafter denoted as the risk-level matrix (RLM), where the columns specify the risk components and the rows specify the process components. The rows and columns can both be aggregated; therefore, the aggregation level can be specified for both the rows, such as process component $\Rightarrow$ process $\Rightarrow$ process area $\Rightarrow \ldots \Rightarrow$ enterprise-level process, and the columns, such as risk component $\Rightarrow$ aspect $\Rightarrow \ldots \Rightarrow$ enterprise-level risk component.

Definition 1. Denote I (J) as the aggregation level of a row (column). Denote $\mathbf{R}_{I,J} \in \mathbb{R}_+^{(n_I \times m_J)}$ as an $n_I \times m_J$ risk-level matrix, where n_I (m_J) is the number of rows (columns) in aggregation level I (J).

Definition 2. Let $\mathbf{R}_{I,J}$ be a risk-level matrix and denote $r_{I,J}(i,j)$ as the risk value of risk component $j = 1, 2, \ldots, m_J$ of process component $i = 1, 2, \ldots, n_I$ in process level I and factor level J. Denote $r_{I,J}(i, \cdot)$ as the set of risk components (in process level I and factor level J); $r_{I,J}(\cdot, j)$ as the set of processes in process level I and factor level J; $r_{I,\cdot}(i, j_{I,\cdot})$ as the set of factor levels; and $r_{\cdot,J}(i,j)$ as the set of process levels ($I = 1, 2, \ldots, N$, $J = 1, 2, \ldots, M$).

The elements of the next level of the RLM can be calculated as follows:

$$r_{I+1,J}(i,j) = S_I(r_{I,J}(\cdot, j), \mathbf{v}) \tag{1}$$

$$r_{I,J+1}(i,j) = S_J(r_{I,J}(i, \cdot), \mathbf{w}) \tag{2}$$

where S_I and S_J are at least monotonous aggregation functions and $\mathbf{v}$ and $\mathbf{w}$ are weight vectors.

Table 1 shows a risk-level matrix with two risk components, two process components, two factor levels, and two process levels.

Table 1. The structure of a risk-level matrix.

				Aspects				
				a_1 = Quality			a_2 = Environment	
	Risk-Level Matrix			Risk Components		Aggr.	Risk Components		Aggr.
				f_1	f_2		f_3	f_4	
Process	p_1	Process Components	c_1	$r_{1,1}(1,1)$	$r_{1,1}(1,2)$	$r_{1,2}(1,1)$	$r_{1,1}(1,3)$	$r_{1,1}(1,4)$	$r_{1,2}(1,2)$
			c_2	$r_{1,1}(2,1)$	$r_{1,1}(2,2)$	$r_{1,2}(2,1)$	$r_{1,1}(2,3)$	$r_{1,1}(2,4)$	$r_{1,2}(2,2)$
		Aggregated values		$r_{2,1}(1,1)$	$r_{2,1}(1,2)$	$r_{2,2}(1,1)$	$r_{2,1}(1,3)$	$r_{2,1}(1,4)$	$r_{2,2}(1,2)$
	p_2	Process Components	c_3	$r_{1,1}(3,1)$	$r_{1,1}(3,2)$	$r_{1,2}(3,1)$	$r_{1,1}(3,3)$	$r_{1,1}(3,4)$	$r_{1,2}(3,2)$
			c_4	$r_{1,1}(4,1)$	$r_{1,1}(4,2)$	$r_{1,2}(4,1)$	$r_{1,1}(4,3)$	$r_{1,1}(4,4)$	$r_{1,2}(4,2)$
		Aggregated values		$r_{2,1}(2,1)$	$r_{2,1}(2,2)$	$r_{2,2}(2,1)$	$r_{2,1}(2,3)$	$r_{2,1}(2,4)$	$r_{2,2}(2,2)$

Example 1. Following the structure of this multilevel matrix, arbitrary factor and process levels and arbitrary numbers of risk and process components can be specified. For example, in the case of the traditional FMEA method, let I be an arbitrary process level and J be an arbitrary factor level. Suppose that the FMEA can be calculated at process level I and factor level J. In this case, we have $m_J = 3$, namely, the severity (S), occurrence (O), and detection (D). Suppose $\forall i \in \{1, 2, \ldots, n_I\}$ and $\forall j \in \{1, 2, \ldots, m_J\}$, $v_i = w_j := 1$, $r_{I,J}(i,j) \in \{1, 2, \ldots, 10\}$, $i := 1, \ldots, n$; then,

$$r_{I,J+1}(i,j) = \prod_{j:=1}^{m_J} r_{I,J}(i,j) \tag{3}$$

$$r_{I+1,J}(i,j) = \prod_{i:=1}^{n_I} r_{I,J}(i,j), \tag{4}$$

where $r_{I,J+1}(i,j)$ is the vertical aggregation of risk component i in process level I, and $r_{I+1,J}(i,j)$ is the horizontal aggregation of risk component i in process level I. In this case, the traditional risk priority number indicates the process risk in process level $I + 1$ for an arbitrary risk factor j.

It should be noted that the RLM extends traditional risk-evaluation techniques, such as the FMEA method, to model all levels of process and risk components as one matrix. The RLM allows different kinds of aggregation functions; however, to compare the risk values in different aggregation levels, aggregated values should be used to normalize the values to the same scale as the risk values. The FMEA approach considers only two levels, and only risk components can be aggregated (i.e., multiplied) into an RPN. Hierarchical frameworks, such as the total risk evaluation framework (TREF), consider risk components in multiple aggregation levels.

Example 2. *The TREF approach considers $m_J \in \{2,3,4,5,6\}$, $v_i, w_j \in \mathbb{R}^+$, $r_{I,J}(i,j) \in \{1,2,\ldots,10\}$, $\sum_{i:=1}^{n} v_i = 1$, and $i := 1,\ldots,n$ and uses four types of functions:*

- $S_I^{(1)}(\mathbf{R_{I,J}}, \mathbf{v}) = \prod_{i:=1}^{n_I} r_{I,J}(i,j)^{v_i}$ *is the weighted geometric mean of the process components.*
- $S_I^{(2)}(\mathbf{R_{I,J}}, \mathbf{1}) = max(\{r_{I,J}(1,j),\ldots,r_{I,J}(n_I,j)\})$ *is the maximum value of the process risks.*
- $S_I^{(3)}(\mathbf{R}_{I,J}, \mathbf{v}) = Median(\{\mathbf{R}_{I,J}, \mathbf{v}\})$ *is the weighted median of the process risks.*
- $S_I^{(4)}(\mathbf{R}_{I,J}, \mathbf{v}) = \sqrt{\sum_{i:=1}^{n_I} v_i r_{I,J}(i,j)^2}$ *is the weighted radial distance of the process risks.*

In the case of $\forall i,j, v_i = 1/n_I$, the aggregation functions $S_\cdot^{(1)}$, $S_\cdot^{(3)}$ and $S_\cdot^{(4)}$ produce the unweighted geometric mean, unweighted median and unweighted radial distance of the risk components.

The TREF approach considers more than three risk components and multiple aggregation functions. However, the RLM can be applied to extend the TREF because the RLM specifies aggregations for both risk components and process levels.

Definition 3. *Let $\mathbf{R}_{I,J}$ be a risk-level matrix. Denote $\mathbf{T}_{I,J} \in \mathbb{R}_+^{(n_I \times m_J)}$ as a threshold-level matrix. A risk event occurs in process i of risk factor j if $\mathbf{R}_{I,J}(i,j) \geq \mathbf{T}_{I,J}(i,j)$. Formally, the risk event matrix (REM) is $\mathbf{E}_{I,J} \in \{0,1\}^{(n_I \times m_J)}$, with*

$$e_{I,J}(i,j) = \begin{cases} 1, \mathbf{e}_{I,J}(i,j) \geq \mathbf{t}_{I,J}(i,j) \\ 0, \mathbf{e}_{I,J}(i,j) < \mathbf{t}_{I,J}(i,j) \end{cases}. \quad (5)$$

A corrective/preventive task should be prescribed if $\sum_i \sum_j e_{I,J}(i,j) \geq \mu_{I,J}$, where $\mu_{I,J} \in \mathbb{Z}$, with $I = 1,2,\ldots,N$ and $J = 1,2,\ldots,M$.

Remark 1. *Threshold values can be arbitrary positive values; however, they should be specified within a specified quantile of risk values.*

Definition 4. *Denote $a_{I,J}(i,j) \in \mathcal{A}$ as the i,j cell of the corrective/preventive task at process level I and factor level J, where $\mathcal{A}$ is the set of corrective/preventive tasks. Each $a_{I,J}(i,j) \in \mathcal{A}$ specifies a quadruplet: $a_{I,J}(i,j) = (p_{I,J}(i,j), t_{I,J}(i,j), c_{I,J}(i,j), \mathcal{R}_{I,J}(i,j))$, where $0 \leq p_{I,J}(i,j) \leq 1$ is the relative priority of the corrective/preventive task (e.g., if and only if the impacts of the risk events should be mitigated: $p_{I,J}(i,j) \leftarrow e_{I,J}(i,j)$), where $t, c, \mathcal{R}$ denote the time (t), cost (c), and resource ($\mathcal{R}$) demands, respectively.*

Example 3.

1. *In the case of the traditional FMEA approach, thresholds are specified only in the second level. Furthermore, the same threshold is usually specified for all processes. If the risk values are between [1, 10], the critical RPN is usually defined as the product of the average risk factors, $5 \times 5 \times 5 = 125$ [34,35]. Formally, we have $T_{1,2}(.,.) = 125$. Different corrective/preventive actions can be specified for each process component. However, in this case, the aim of these corrective/preventive actions is to mitigate the RPN, and distinct corrective/preventive actions are not specified for each risk component. Formally, we have $a_{I,J+1}(i,.) = a_{I,J}(i,.)$.*
2. *The TREF method specifies the thresholds of the risk components in the first factor level and their aggregations in the second level; however, these thresholds are the same for all processes. This method proposes the use of six risk factors in the first level. Formally, we have $[T_{1,1}(.,1), T_{1,1}(.,2), \ldots, T_{1,1}(.,6)] = [t_1, t_2, \ldots, t_6]$. This method proposes several aggregation approaches, and, similar to the traditional FMEA technique, this method specifies*

the threshold of the next factor level. Formally, $T_{1,2}(.,.) = t_{1,2}$. A warning is generated if either a risk-component value or the aggregated value is greater than the threshold. In addition, the TREF method allows warnings to be generated manually due to a seventh factor, namely, the criticality factor, where a value of 1 indicates that the process is critical process that must be corrected regardless of the risk value.

Due to the column-specific thresholds, different corrective/preventive actions can be specified to mitigate each risk component and its aggregations. Nevertheless, in this case, common corrective/preventive actions are specified to mitigate the risk components.

3. On the one hand, the new FMEA method considers three factors in the first factor level. On the other hand, the new FMEA method specifies the threshold for the first factor level; however, corrective preventive tasks are carried out if at least two factors are greater than a threshold (based on the action priority logic [36]).

4. The ELM can be used to specify cell-specific corrective/preventive actions. In general, these actions can be row-specific (process component-specific), such as in the FMEA method, or column-specific, such as in the TREF method; importantly, different corrective/preventive tasks can be specified for various cells.

Theoretically, the FMEA and TREF methods can both be used in different process levels; however, neither of these methods aggregate the risk values of the processes. The vertical aggregation, which is performed by all risk-assessment techniques, indicates which processes must be corrected. In addition, if the TREF method is followed, corrective/preventive tasks can be specified to decrease the risk-component value. In other words, different corrective/preventive tasks can be specified to decrease the severity or occurrence of a process risk. However, no existing methods provide the general severity or occurrence of the processes performed by a company. The proposed RLM and REM allow us to specify:

- specific thresholds for all processes; and
- specific thresholds for all risk components simultaneously.

These thresholds can be specific for all factor and process levels. The vertical aggregation result indicates the aggregated value of the risk component. The horizontal aggregation result indicates the aggregated value of the process risks.

Traditional methods, the new FMEA approach, and the TREF method can all be modeled by the ELM. In addition, the ELM allows a company to determine specific thresholds and corrective/preventive actions for each risk value and risk event. Corrective/preventive actions can be prioritized, allowing sets of different activities to be incorporated into existing processes. Another advantage of the ELM is that all risk levels are included in the same matrix; therefore, complex improvement projects or processes can be specified to simultaneously mitigate risks at all levels.

2.1.2. Specific Processes

An improvement process is a set of corrective/preventive tasks. This study focuses on the first phase of developing an improvement process, namely, process screening. In this phase, the set of tasks in the improvement process with the greatest impact on risk mitigation is specified. In the proposed algorithm, we have the following steps.

step 1 The risk priorities of all corrective/preventive tasks are specified.

step 2 The seriation technique [37] is used to simultaneously reorder the rows (process components) and columns (risk components), yielding a set of risk and process components with high risk priorities.

step 3 The biclustering technique, which uses a bicluster to specify the mitigated risk and process components, is proposed. This set of corrective/preventive actions specifies the set of tasks included in the improvement process.

step 4 After screening, conventional process and project management methods are used to schedule the correction tasks according to time, cost, and resource constraints.

In our study, multilevel matrix representations and data-mining techniques, such as seriation and biclustering, are integrated into screening and scheduling algorithms to determine the set of corrective/preventive tasks that mitigate enterprise risks at all aggregation levels. Although these algorithms performed well in general cases, this is the first study that attempts to combine these techniques to improve the whole risk-assessment process.

Step 1—Specification of the task priority matrix

Definition 5. *Let $\mathbf{P} = \mathbf{P}_{I,J} \in [0,1]^{n_I, m_J}, I = 1, 2, \ldots, N, J = 1, 2, \ldots, M$ be a (task) priority matrix. Depending on the decision, $p_{I,J}(i,j)$ is either $p_{I,J}(i,j) = e_{I,J}(i,j)$, or*

$$p_{I,J}(i,j) = \begin{cases} 1 & \text{, if } r_{I,J}(i,j) > t_{I,J}(i,j) \\ (t_{I,J}(i,j) - r_{I,J}(i,j))/r_{I,J}^{\max} & \text{, otherwise} \end{cases}$$

where $r_{I,J}^{\max}$ is the maximal possible risk value at aggregation level (I, J).

The task priority matrix $\mathbf{P}$ is either binarized or 0–1 normalized, with greater numbers indicating higher priority tasks at all aggregation levels. In step 2, seriation is applied, which uses combinatorial data analysis to find a linear arrangement of the objects in a set according to a loss function. The main goal of this process is to reveal the structural information [37].

Step 2—Seriation of the task priority matrix

In general, the goal of a seriation problem is to find a permutation function Ψ^* that optimizes the value of a given loss function L in an $n \times m$ dissimilarity matrix $\mathbf{D}$:

$$\Psi^* = \arg\min_{\Psi} L(\Psi(\mathbf{D})). \tag{6}$$

In this study, the loss function is the Euclidean distance between neighboring cells. Simultaneous row and column permutations to minimize a loss function is an NP-complete problem, which is directly traceable to a traveling salesman problem [37]; therefore, hierarchical clustering [38], which is a fast approximation method, is used to specify blocks of similar risky processes and risk components. Seriation identifies a set of risky processes and risk components; however, it does not delimit these blocks.

Step 3—Specification of risky blocks in the task priority matrix

Definition 6. *A block is a submatrix of the task priority matrix that specifies risky processes (as rows) and risk components (as columns) simultaneously. A selected block in which the median of the cell elements is significantly greater than both the nonselected processes and risk components represents a risky block.*

Risky blocks are identified with the iterative binary biclustering of gene sets (iBBiG) [39] algorithm. This algorithm assumes that the utilized dataset is a binary dataset; if this assumption is not valid, the first step is to binarize the dataset based on a given threshold (τ). Because $\mathbf{E}$ is a binary matrix, if $\mathbf{P} = \mathbf{E}$, then $\mathbf{P}$ is also a binary matrix; otherwise, the threshold is based on the judgment of the decision makers.

The applied iBBiG algorithm balances the homogeneity (in this case, the entropy) of the selected submatrix with the size of the risky block. Formally, the iBBiG algorithm maximizes the following target function, with the binarized dataset of matrix $\mathbf{P}$ denoted as $\mathbf{B}$,

$$\max \leftarrow score := (1 - H_\mathcal{B})^\alpha \begin{cases} \sum_i \sum_j [\mathcal{B}]_{i,j} & \text{, if } tr(\mathcal{B}) > \tau \\ 0 & \text{, if } Med(\mathcal{B}) \leq \tau \end{cases}, \tag{7}$$

where $score$ is the score value of the submatrix (bicluster, risky block) $\mathcal{B} \subseteq \mathbf{B}$. $H_\mathcal{B}$ is the entropy of submatrix $\mathcal{B}$, $tr = Med(\mathcal{B})$ is the median of bicluster $\mathcal{B}$, $\alpha \in [0,1]$ is the exponent, and τ is the threshold. If τ or α increases, we obtain a smaller but more homogeneous submatrix. Previous studies [39] have suggested that the balance exponent (α) should be set to 0.3.

Risky blocks may overlap. However, based on the score value of the risky blocks, they must be ordered.

Step 4—Specification of corrective/preventive processes

The risky blocks specify the set of risky processes and risk components that must be mitigated simultaneously across all aggregation levels, as well as the set of corrective/preventive tasks in the activity-level matrix.

If there is more than one risky block, the scores of the risky blocks can be ranked. If the set of corrective/preventive tasks and their demands are specified, the task order is a scheduling problem that can be solved with the method described in [40].

Step 1 ensures that risks are addressed at all aggregation levels. Step 2 identifies risky blocks, and step 3 specifies the set of risky processes and risk components in all aggregation levels. Finally, step 4 specifies the set of processes, and the process proposed in [40] is used to schedule these processes according to time, cost, and resource constraints.

2.2. Requirements of the Aggregation Functions

To evaluate and assess risks at all aggregation levels, appropriate aggregation functions must be selected. We limit our analysis to scalar aggregation values. Several content and mathematical requirements can be set for different aggregation functions.

1. **Objectives**: What are the objectives of risk management? The aggregated value is an indicator that reflects the basis underlying managerial or engineering decisions. Different aggregation functions have distinct component risk scales. As a result, a top-to-bottom approach is proposed instead of the traditional bottom-to-top approach when scale definition is an early step. This requirement can be used to classify aggregation functions, such as summation type (total risk), average type (mean or median risk), or distance (from a given value) type aggregated risk indicators. This expectation indicates that there is usually no best or worst aggregation function, and the applied aggregation function depends on the situation and the purpose of the aggregation.
2. **Validity**: The validity is determined according to the nature of the components and processes via the aggregated risk of the components. For example, in the case of extremely high severity, such as nuclear disasters, natural disasters, or war, the severity is excluded, and the probability is used as the primary risk indicator. In more frequent cases, the 'severity $\times$ probability' is calculated as the expected value. In this case, the aggregation is either the most characteristic value (no aggregation) or an estimation of the expected value. The 'expected' value can be interpreted in broader terms that extend beyond probability theory approaches [41–45]. Another scenario is when the risk in multiple areas is combined. In this case, the expected total risk is the sum of the risks in the areas, as discussed above. The traditional RPN calculation (occurrence $\times$ severity $\times$ detection) can be viewed as an expected value if the occurrence and detection are independent. The introduction of additional components (such as multiplication factors) might cause difficulties in interpreting the aggregated value as an indicator. Smart weighting can be used to address this problem.

Next, we formulate the mathematical requirements. The mathematical requirements guarantee a lack of distortion.

3. **Monotonicity**: When one component has a higher risk value than the other components, the aggregated risk value cannot be less than the largest risk value [41,44].
4. **Symmetry**: When the components' risk values have symmetric distributions with the same mean, the distribution of the aggregated values is also symmetric [41,44].
5. **Uniformity, linearity**: When the components have a uniform distribution, the distribution of the aggregated values should also be uniform [41,44].

The above requirements appear to be logical; however, the requirements are difficult to satisfy, and it is not certain that these requirements are adequate, contrary to the literature. For example, in the case of additive or multiplicative models, the values near the mean appear more frequently because these values originate from not only medium-medium risk value combinations but also small–large and large–small risk value combinations.

6. **Scale fit**: Aggregation operations should be performed with the applied scale values [46].
7. **Scale end point identity**: The result should be in the same interval as the components (if they are equal) or a common scale if the components have different scales. On the one hand, this requirement helps in assessing the resulting risk, which is a psychological advantage. On the other hand, successive aggregations between different hierarchal levels may distort the result if the components have different scales [47].

2.3. Characterization of Potential Aggregation Functions

In practice, the characteristics of the applied aggregation function must be considered when determining w_i. For example, how the applied aggregation function handles distribution asymmetry and component outliers must be considered. The properties of some aggregation functions were described by [48].

A preliminary evaluation of various aggregation functions is included in Table 2. We assume that the components have a scale of [1, 10] and that the number of components is n.

Table 2. Characterization of risk aggregation functions.

Aggregation Function	Advantages	Disadvantages
Sum	Easy to calculate and relatively good linearity.	Fits additive components only. The resulting scale is not identical to the scale of the components ([1, 10]), which can be an advantage in determining the total risk. The result is a sum rather than an average, and the resulting value is greater than the components' risks when there are more areas or processes. This characteristic is critical for managing the risks of several or a few areas in managerial work.
Arithmetic mean	Easy to calculate and relatively good linearity. The resulting scale is identical to the components' scale ([1, 10]).	Fits additive components only. The components must be measured on the same interval scale. This function does not return the full risk; for example, it does not take into account the need to manage the risks of several or a few areas.
Product	Fits with multiplicative models, such as the expected values of the probability (occurrence) and severity. This is the most commonly used aggregation method	Poor linearity. Does not map to the original [1, 10] scale and instead maps to the interval $[1, 10^n]$.
Product/10^{n-1}	Correction to the product function. The resulting scale ([$1/10^{n-1}$, 10]) is close to the original scale (e.g., [1, 10]).	Poor linearity; mapping to almost the same scale does not help. This function tends to output extremely small values.
Geometric mean	Normalizes values in different ranges; thus, various scale intervals can be applied. The resulting scale is identical to the components' scale ([1, 10]).	Not easy to calculate in practice. This function fits better with multiplicative models than with other models.
Radial distance /$\sqrt{n}$	Moderately good linearity when compared to the linearity of other functions.	The calculation is not easy in practice.
Median	The resulting scale is the same as the components' scale, and this function can also be used on ordinal scales.	The calculation is not easy in practice. The scale is relatively rough and can be considered correct only for homogeneous risk components.

Table 2. *Cont.*

Aggregation Function	Advantages	Disadvantages
Maximum	Easy to calculate. The large values focus attention on critical areas.	Poor representation of the total risk population.
Minimum	Easy to calculate.	Poor representation of the total risk population.
Number of values over threshold	Easy to calculate. This method focuses attention on critical areas.	Poor representation of the total risk population.
Range and standard deviation	Easy to calculate. These approaches show the range or dispersion of the risk components.	Does not output the risk level.
Quantile	Outputs the top occurrence values	Does not output the risk level.

3. Practical Example

Our example shows the risk-management system used by a real company. At the request of the company, we have changed some information.

3.1. Research Plan

The research objective was to test different aggregation functions in various aggregation situations. We evaluated functions that approximately satisfied the requirements discussed in Section 2.2. To select the aggregation functions, we considered the results of a previous study [13]. The basis of the examination is shown in Table 1. Due to the large number of possible cases, we analyzed only the cases shown in Table 3. The focus of each risk component is referred to as its "component"; at the lowest aggregation level, these components can be a part of a product or process.

At higher aggregation levels, the risk component is the result of lower-level aggregations, e.g., the RPN.

Table 3. Examination plan.

No.	Aggregation Situation	Number of Components	Function	Remark
1	Aggregation of different risk components of the same entity (process or product component) at the lowest level. (The horizontal aggregation is shown in Table 2, 1a.).	Number of risk components: 6, namely, the occurrence, severity, detection, control, information, and range.	Arithmetic mean, corrected product, geometric mean, radial distance, median, minimum, maximum, range, number of values over warning threshold, and sum.	This is the most commonly used aggregation method for calculating the RPN of the components of a product or process. This approach shows the overall risk of a subprocess or product component.
2	Aggregation of the same risk components of different entities (process or product component) at the lowest level. (The vertical aggregation is shown in Table 2, 2a.).	Number of entities (subprocesses or product components): 1–4.	Same as in 1.	This method shows the overall risk in specific levels.
3	Further (vertical) aggregation of 1a (1b).	The aggregated values from 1, namely, the number of entities (subprocesses or product components)	Sum, arithmetic mean, and number of values over threshold.	This method shows the total risk in a certain level (within the limitations of the applied function).

Table 3. *Cont.*

No.	Aggregation Situation	Number of Components	Function	Remark
4	Further (horizontal) aggregation of 2a (2b).	The aggregated values from 2; thus, there are 6 risk components, namely, the occurrence, severity, detection, control, information, and range.	Sum, arithmetic mean, and number of values over threshold.	This method shows the total risk in a certain level (within the limitations of the applied function).
5	Aggregation of all risk components at higher levels (Figures 1 and 2).	Number of risk components: 6; number of entities (subprocesses or product components): 1–4.:	Arithmetic mean, geometric mean, radial distance, median, number of values over warning threshold, and sum	This method shows the total risk in a certain level (within the limitations of the applied function).
5	Aggregation of warnings (Figure 3).	Number of entities.	Sum and number of values over threshold	This method shows the total risk in a certain level (within the limitations of the applied function).
6	Generating preventive actions (Figure 4).	Number of entities.	Arithmetic mean, geometric mean, median, maximum, and corr. product	This step selects the threshold for the optimal preventive action.

3.2. Process Hierarchy

To demonstrate the proposed matrix-based risk analysis, we use a three-level hierarchy. The detailed hierarchy is described below:

4. Production
    4.1. Customer orders - order processing
        4.1.1. Start processing order
        4.1.2. Entry production control form
    4.5. Production preparation
        4.5.1. Product engineering
        4.5.2. Product planning
5. Logistics
    5.1. Purchasing
        5.1.1. Offer request
        5.1.2. Demand form
        5.1.3. Place order
        5.1.4. Receive material on time
    5.2. Warehouse management
        5.2.1. Vehicle arrival
        5.2.2. Unloading
        5.2.3. Unwrapping, inspection.

In this example, each subprocess has 2–4 failure modes. At the lowest level, we used six risk components (namely, the occurrence (O), severity (S), detection (D), control (C), information (I), and range (R)) to describe the risk.

3.3. Results of the Matrix-Based Risk Assessment

3.3.1. Bidirectional Aggregation

The results obtained at the lowest level are shown in Figure 1.

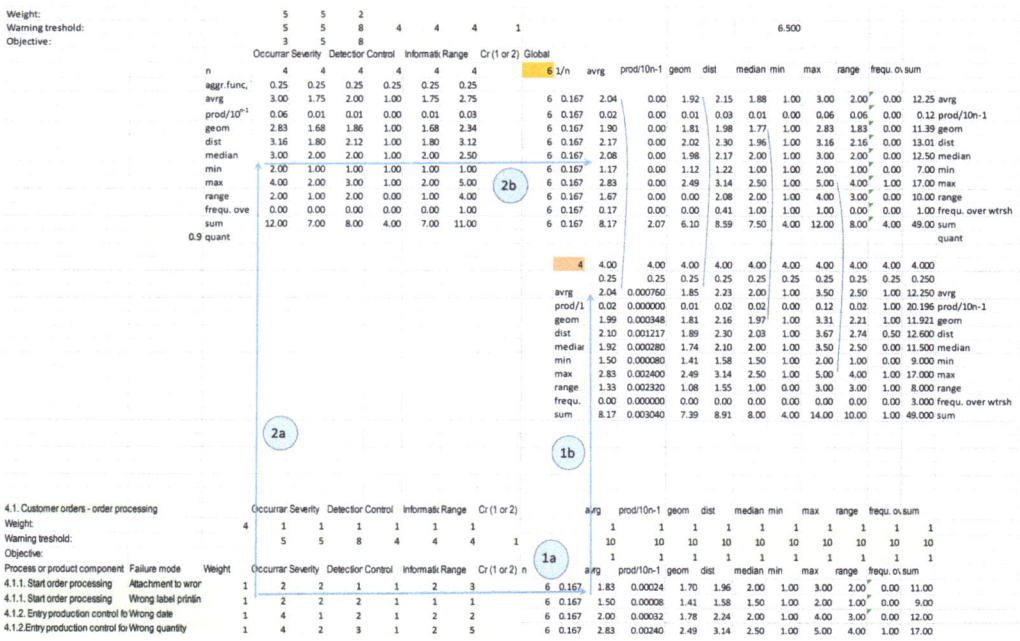

Figure 1. Results of bidirectional aggregation at the lowest level.

In Figure 1, the aggregation directions are indicated by the arrows. In one case, we first performed horizontal aggregation (1a). This approach is consistent with common practice: the RPN is typically calculated as a product function by using risk components such as the occurrence and severity. These RPNs can be aggregated further (1b). The other case is the opposite scenario. First, we aggregated the same risk components for different subprocesses (2a); then, the resulting indicators were aggregated by using different functions (2b). There are two interesting ways to view the results:
1. Determining which functions should be used in different aggregation situations; and
2. Comparing the results of the two aggregation directions.

Ad1. The aggregated values obtained from the same data by using different functions differ significantly. Due to the limited extent of this paper, it is not possible to interpret all the results. However, we discuss some important results. No linear results were obtained with the product and corrected product (interval $[1/10^{n-1}, 10]$) functions. Based on preliminary theoretical considerations, it is still interesting to determine how the results deviate from the aggregated values. In this respect, the arithmetic, geometric mean, and median methods appear to perform better. However, because the risk components at this level differ, additive models (such as the sum, mean, and median approaches) cannot be applied. Thus, our recommendation is to use the geometric mean method. When aggregating values in the next levels, we work with homogeneous data; thus, the indicators provided by aggregation functions based on the additive model (such as the sum, mean, median, and frequency) can be interpreted.

Ad2. The values of the two aggregation direction were compared.

In Figure 1, we connected the corresponding data obtained with different aggregation directions. For example, the arithmetic mean is 1.96–1.96, the geometric mean is 1.86–1.8, and the median is 1.77–1.97. Surprisingly, the two aggregation directions led to nearly identical results. However, this finding cannot be generalized, as it depends on the data. The next level of aggregation is combining production and logistics. The aggregation results along the entire hierarchy are shown in Figure 2.

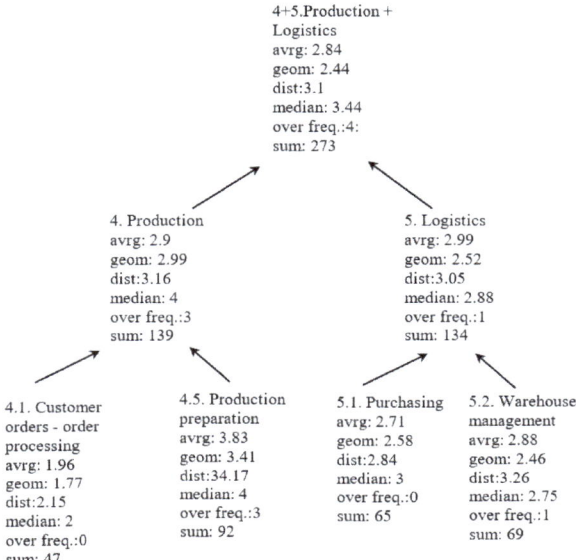

Figure 2. Results of multilevel aggregation.

3.3.2. Aggregating Warnings

Warnings can also be aggregated. We aggregated the warnings along the hierarchy, as shown in Figure 3.

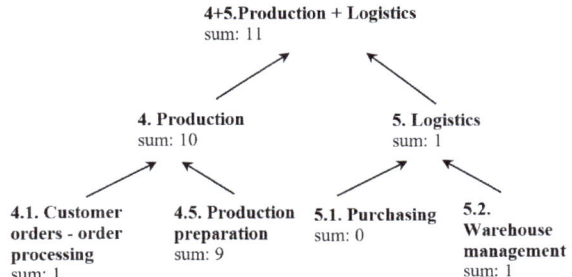

Figure 3. Results of multilevel warning aggregation.

The function results can be summarized as follows:

One issue with the product function is apparent: strong bias. As a result, warnings may result in Type I or Type II errors. Normalization of the product to the interval $[1/10^{n-1}, 10]$ is not a good solution because this distortion remains. Although 10, as the largest scale value, is psychologically advantageous for judging the risk, in practice, small aggregated risk values are generated, even if there are only a few small values among the component risks. This result can be observed in the prod/10^{n-1} lines in Figure 1. These low values lead to cumulative bias during further aggregations. Thus, for expected value-type aggregated risk values or heterogeneous components, we recommend the geometric mean or potentially the radial distance as opposed to the product. As a result of the above findings, horizontal aggregation is proposed for the lowest level, while vertical aggregation is proposed for higher levels. As it can be seen in the Figures 2 and 3, the multi-level aggregation can be implemented with risk values and warnings as well. Combining this with the two-way (horizontal and vertical) aggregation directions offers a versatile, multipurpose application opportunity that cannot be found in the literature. A further option to use this hierarchical structure is to generate risk mitigation countermeasures.

3.3.3. Generating Preventive Actions

Following the four steps of the proposed method (Section 2.1.2), first, the aggregated risk values were calculated by using the six risk components and the failure modes in the lowest evaluation level. Five aggregation methods, namely, (1) the (arithmetic) mean, (2) geometric mean, (3) median, (4) maximum, (5) and product normalized to the interval [1, 10] methods, were used to calculate the values of the rows (process components) and columns (risk components). The processes, subprocesses, and failure modes are highlighted in Figure 4. In addition, the background color of each cell indicates the risk level, with red cells indicating higher risk values and green cells indicating lower risk values.

The aggregated values are calculated in two ways, as shown in Figure 4. The left side of Figure 4 shows the first method, in which the risk values of the process components are aggregated first, whereas the right side of Figure 4 shows the opposite calculation method.

| Row | Process | Failure mode / aggregation mode | \multicolumn{11}{c}{Horizontal => vertical aggregation} | \multicolumn{11}{c}{Vertical => horizontal aggregation} |
			O	S	D	I	C	R	Mean	Geom. mean	Median	Max.	Prod/10^n+1	O	S	D	I	C	R	Mean	Geom. mean	Median	Max.	Prod/10^n+1
1	4.1.1. Start order processing	Attachment to wrong order	2.00	2.00	1.00	1.00	2.00	3.00	1.83	1.70	2.00	3.00	1.00	2.00	2.00	1.00	1.00	2.00	3.00	1.83	1.70	2.00	3.00	1.00
2	4.1.1. Start order processing	Wrong label printing	2.00	2.00	2.00	1.00	1.00	1.00	1.50	1.41	1.50	2.00	1.00	2.00	2.00	2.00	1.00	1.00	1.00	1.50	1.41	1.50	2.00	1.00
3	4.1.1. Start order processing	Mean	2.00	2.00	1.50	1.00	1.50	2.00	1.67	1.62	1.75	2.00	1.00	2.00	2.00	1.50	1.00	1.50	2.00	1.67	1.56	1.75	2.50	1.00
4	4.1.1. Start order processing	Geom. mean	2.00	2.00	1.41	1.00	1.41	1.73	1.59	1.55	1.57	2.00	1.00	2.00	2.00	1.41	1.00	1.41	1.73	1.66	1.55	1.73	2.45	1.00
5	4.1.1. Start order processing	Median	2.00	2.00	1.50	1.00	1.50	2.00	1.67	1.62	1.75	2.00	1.00	2.00	2.00	1.50	1.00	1.50	2.00	1.67	1.56	1.75	2.50	1.00
6	4.1.1. Start order processing	Max	2.00	2.00	2.00	1.00	2.00	3.00	1.91	2.00	2.00	3.00	1.00	2.00	2.00	2.00	1.00	2.00	3.00	1.83	1.70	2.00	3.00	1.00
7	4.1.1. Start order processing	Prod/10^n+1	1.40	1.40	1.20	1.10	1.20	1.30	1.27	1.26	1.25	1.40	1.00	1.40	1.40	1.20	1.10	1.20	1.30	1.28	1.24	1.30	1.60	1.10
8	4.1.2. Entry production control form	Wrong date	4.00	1.00	2.00	1.00	2.00	2.00	2.00	1.78	2.00	4.00	1.00	4.00	1.00	2.00	1.00	2.00	2.00	2.00	1.78	2.00	4.00	1.00
9	4.1.2. Entry production control form	Wrong quantity	4.00	2.00	3.00	1.00	2.00	5.00	2.83	2.49	2.50	5.00	1.02	4.00	2.00	3.00	1.00	2.00	5.00	2.83	2.49	2.50	5.00	1.02
10	4.1.2. Entry production control form	Mean	4.00	1.50	2.50	1.00	2.00	3.50	2.42	2.17	2.25	4.00	1.01	4.00	1.50	2.50	1.00	2.00	3.50	2.42	2.14	2.25	4.50	1.01
11	4.1.2. Entry production control form	Geom. mean	4.00	1.41	2.45	1.00	2.00	3.16	2.34	2.11	2.22	4.00	1.01	4.00	1.41	2.45	1.00	2.00	3.16	2.38	2.11	2.24	4.47	1.01
12	4.1.2. Entry production control form	Median	4.00	1.50	2.50	1.00	2.00	3.50	2.42	2.17	2.25	4.00	1.01	4.00	1.50	2.50	1.00	2.00	3.50	2.42	2.14	2.25	4.50	1.01
13	4.1.2. Entry production control form	Max	4.00	2.00	3.00	1.00	2.00	5.00	2.83	2.49	2.50	5.00	1.02	4.00	2.00	3.00	1.00	2.00	5.00	2.83	2.49	2.50	5.00	1.02
14	4.1.2. Entry production control form	Prod/10^(n-1)	2.60	1.20	1.60	1.10	1.40	2.00	1.65	1.58	1.50	2.60	1.00	2.60	1.20	1.60	1.10	1.40	2.00	1.57	1.44	1.50	3.00	1.10
15	4.1. Customer orders - order processing	Mean	3.00	1.75	2.00	1.00	1.75	2.75	2.04	1.92	1.88	3.00	1.01	3.00	1.75	2.00	1.00	1.75	2.75	2.04	1.85	2.00	3.50	1.01
16	4.1. Customer orders - order processing	Geom. mean	2.83	1.68	1.86	1.00	1.68	2.34	1.90	1.81	1.77	2.83	1.00	2.83	1.68	1.86	1.00	1.68	2.34	1.99	1.81	1.97	3.31	1.01
17	4.1. Customer orders - order processing	Median	3.00	1.75	2.00	1.00	1.75	2.75	2.04	1.92	1.88	3.00	1.01	3.00	1.75	2.00	1.00	1.75	2.75	2.04	1.85	2.00	3.50	1.01
18	4.1. Customer orders - order processing	Max	4.00	2.00	3.00	1.00	2.00	5.00	2.83	2.49	2.50	5.00	1.02	4.00	2.00	3.00	1.00	2.00	5.00	2.83	2.49	2.50	5.00	1.02
19	4.1. Customer orders - order processing	Prod/10^(n-1)	1.36	1.17	1.19	1.12	1.17	1.26	1.21	1.21	1.18	1.36	1.00	1.36	1.17	1.19	1.12	1.17	1.26	1.20	1.18	1.20	1.48	1.12
20	4.5.1. Product engineering	Poor customer communication	4.00	3.00	1.00	7.00	2.00	4.00	3.50	2.96	3.50	7.00	1.07	4.00	3.00	1.00	7.00	2.00	4.00	3.50	2.96	3.50	7.00	1.07
21	4.5.1. Product engineering	Poor internal communication	4.00	3.00	1.00	7.00	2.00	4.00	3.50	2.96	3.50	7.00	1.07	4.00	3.00	1.00	7.00	2.00	4.00	3.50	2.96	3.50	7.00	1.07
22	4.5.1. Product engineering	Mean	4.00	3.00	1.00	7.00	2.00	4.00	3.50	2.96	3.50	7.00	1.07	4.00	3.00	1.00	7.00	2.00	4.00	3.50	2.96	3.50	7.00	1.07
23	4.5.1. Product engineering	Geom. mean	4.00	3.00	1.00	7.00	2.00	4.00	3.50	2.96	3.50	7.00	1.07	4.00	3.00	1.00	7.00	2.00	4.00	3.50	2.96	3.50	7.00	1.07
24	4.5.1. Product engineering	Median	4.00	3.00	1.00	7.00	2.00	4.00	3.50	2.96	3.50	7.00	1.07	4.00	3.00	1.00	7.00	2.00	4.00	3.50	2.96	3.50	7.00	1.07
25	4.5.1. Product engineering	Max	4.00	3.00	1.00	7.00	2.00	4.00	3.50	2.96	3.50	7.00	1.07	4.00	3.00	1.00	7.00	2.00	4.00	3.50	2.96	3.50	7.00	1.07
26	4.5.1. Product engineering	Prod/10^(n-1)	2.60	1.90	1.10	5.90	1.40	2.60	2.58	2.21	2.25	5.90	1.01	2.60	1.90	1.10	5.90	1.40	2.60	2.23	1.88	2.23	5.90	1.11
27	4.5.2. Production engineering	Missing documents	3.00	4.00	2.00	5.00	5.00	5.00	4.00	3.80	4.50	5.00	1.30	3.00	4.00	2.00	5.00	5.00	5.00	4.00	3.80	4.50	5.00	1.30
28	4.5.2. Production engineering	Wrong schedule	3.00	6.00	2.00	5.00	5.00	5.00	4.33	4.06	5.00	6.00	1.45	3.00	6.00	2.00	5.00	5.00	5.00	4.33	4.06	5.00	6.00	1.45
29	4.5.2. Production engineering	Mean	3.00	5.00	2.00	5.00	5.00	5.00	4.17	3.94	5.00	5.00	1.38	3.00	5.00	2.00	5.00	5.00	5.00	4.17	3.93	4.75	5.50	1.38
30	4.5.2. Production engineering	Geom. mean	3.00	4.90	2.00	5.00	5.00	5.00	4.15	3.93	4.95	5.00	1.37	3.00	4.90	2.00	5.00	5.00	5.00	4.16	3.93	4.74	5.48	1.37
31	4.5.2. Production engineering	Median	3.00	5.00	2.00	5.00	5.00	5.00	4.17	3.94	5.00	5.00	1.38	3.00	5.00	2.00	5.00	5.00	5.00	4.17	3.93	4.75	5.50	1.38
32	4.5.2. Production engineering	Max	3.00	6.00	2.00	5.00	5.00	5.00	4.33	4.06	5.00	6.00	1.45	3.00	6.00	2.00	5.00	5.00	5.00	4.33	4.06	5.00	6.00	1.45
33	4.5.2. Production engineering	Prod/10^(n-1)	1.90	3.40	1.40	3.50	3.50	3.50	2.87	2.70	3.45	3.50	1.04	1.90	3.40	1.40	3.50	3.50	3.50	2.73	2.54	3.25	4.00	1.19
34	4.5 Production preparation	Mean	3.50	4.00	1.50	6.00	3.50	4.50	3.83	3.54	3.75	6.00	1.20	3.50	4.00	1.50	6.00	3.50	4.50	3.83	3.45	4.13	6.25	1.22
35	4.5 Production preparation	Geom. mean	3.46	3.83	1.41	5.92	3.16	4.47	3.71	3.41	3.65	5.92	1.16	3.46	3.83	1.41	5.92	3.16	4.47	3.82	3.41	4.07	6.19	1.21
36	4.5 Production preparation	Median	3.50	4.00	1.50	6.00	3.50	4.50	3.83	3.54	3.75	6.00	1.20	3.50	4.00	1.50	6.00	3.50	4.50	3.83	3.45	4.13	6.25	1.22
37	4.5 Production preparation	Max	4.00	6.00	2.00	7.00	5.00	5.00	4.83	4.51	5.00	7.00	1.84	4.00	6.00	2.00	7.00	5.00	5.00	4.33	4.06	5.00	7.00	1.45
38	4.5 Production preparation	Prod/10^(n-1)	1.49	1.65	1.15	3.07	1.49	1.91	1.79	1.71	1.57	3.07	1.00	1.49	1.65	1.15	3.07	1.49	1.91	1.61	1.48	1.72	3.36	1.13
39	4. Production	Mean	3.25	2.88	1.75	3.50	2.63	3.63	2.94	2.86	3.06	3.63	1.05	3.25	2.88	1.75	3.50	2.63	3.63	2.94	2.65	3.06	4.88	1.11
40	4. Production	Geom. mean	3.13	2.54	1.62	2.43	2.31	3.24	2.54	2.48	2.49	3.24	1.02	3.13	2.54	1.62	2.43	2.31	3.24	2.75	2.48	2.83	4.53	1.10
41	4. Production	Median	3.25	2.88	1.75	3.50	2.63	3.63	2.94	2.86	3.06	3.63	1.05	3.25	2.88	1.75	3.50	2.63	3.63	2.94	2.65	3.06	4.88	1.11
42	4. Production	Max	4.00	6.00	3.00	7.00	5.00	5.00	5.00	4.82	5.00	7.00	2.26	4.00	6.00	3.00	7.00	5.00	5.00	4.33	4.06	5.00	7.00	1.45
43	4. Production	Prod/10^(n-1)	1.20	1.19	1.14	1.34	1.17	1.24	1.22	1.21	1.20	1.34	1.00	1.20	1.19	1.14	1.34	1.17	1.21	1.17	1.21	1.50	1.13

Figure 4. Risk-level matrix for production processes.

A comparison of the results shown in Figure 4 indicates that the different aggregation methods result in the same trends in the aggregated risk values. This finding was confirmed by the seriation results, in which the process and risk components were calculated at the same level, and the biclustering results, in which the sets of risk and process components were selected simultaneously. Therefore, only the first aggregation mode was considered.

To specify the set of risk/process components that must be mitigated, we use two methods. In the first approach, which is an unsupervised method, a predefined threshold matrix is not necessary. In this case, we want to identify the set of risk/process components and their aggregations that are greater than a specified quantile. In contrast, a threshold matrix is specified in the supervised risk evaluation method, with the risk event matrix specifying the risk values of the risk and process components to be mitigated. However, because the risk and process components have common corrective/preventive tasks, this set should also be collected by seriation and biclustering methods.

Figure 5 shows the seriation (step 3) and biclustering (step 4) results for two thresholds ($\tau = 0.5$ (Med) and $\tau = 0.75$ (Q1)).

Figure 5. The unsupervised risk evaluation results. The seriated and biclustered risk-level matrices with $\tau = 0.5$ (Med) and $\tau = 0.75$ (Q1) are shown.

Figure 5 identifies two overlapping $\tau = 0.5$ (Med) biclusters and one overlapping $\tau = 0.75$ (Q1) bicluster. Increasing the value of τ leads to smaller, cleaner biclusters. Because the risk/process components and their aggregations are both considered, the selected and omitted rows and columns must discussed.

The seriation and biclustering results indicate the set of risk and process components and their aggregations. The results show that the risk values in the production preparation process (4.5) and the risk components during the product engineering (4.5.1) and production engineering (4.5.2) processes should both be mitigated. However, the customer orders (4.1) and their subprocesses were not selected. Although both biclusters identified risk component information (I), neither specified the detection (D) value. The maximum aggregation metric, which identifies the riskiest process and risk components, is always applied to the bicluster; however, the production metric, which is used in the FMEA approach, is never applied. The results also show that if there are several risky processes in a higher aggregation level, the mean and median cannot be used to identify the risks to be mitigated.

Figure 6 shows specific thresholds for the risk components and their aggregations. A risk value should be mitigated (red background cells) if its value is greater than or equal to the threshold value. In this example, thresholds are specified for the risk components and their aggregations; however, thresholds are not specified for the process components and their aggregations. Therefore, common thresholds are assumed for all kinds of processes.

Figure 6. The supervised risk evaluation results. The seriated and biclustered risk-level matrices for different risk events are shown.

Figure 6 shows the seriated and biclustered risk-level matrices for different risk events. In this case, two overlapping biclusters can be specified for both the $\alpha = 0.3$ and $\alpha = 1.0$ parameters that indicate the sets of risk components and their aggregations, as well as the sets of process components and their aggregations. If the risk-level matrix is seriated and biclustered according to the binary values of the risk event matrix, the set of specified risk/process components is similar to the set generated by the unsupervised risk evaluation method (see Figure 5). Additionally, in this case, two overlapping biclusters can be identified. However, the Q1 and Med biclusters are identical. In this case, the purity can be increased by increasing the value of the α parameter. Regardless of whether the threshold matrix is included or excluded, the identified risk values that should be mitigated specify the set of corrective/preventive improvement tasks (see Figure 7). Figure 7 shows part of the matrix of corrective/preventive actions. Five tasks, namely, (1) feedback on customer communication, (2) feedback on internal communication, (3) meeting deadlines and faster recognition, (4) more frequent updates, and (5) improving forecasts, are considered in the failure mode level, whereas the maintaining requirements and increasing discipline, training, and bonuses tasks are considered in the aggregated levels. It is important to note that corrective/preventive actions do not need to be specified for all cells. Because the maximal values are corrected if and only if one of the risk/process components must be corrected, corrective/preventive actions should be specified only for the risk/process components.

Figure 7 shows the selected cells for parameters $\alpha = 0.3$ and $\alpha = 1.0$.

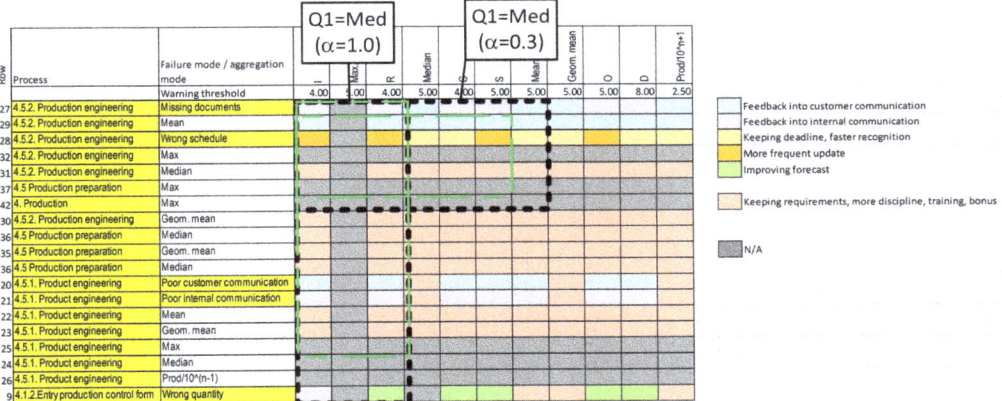

Figure 7. The matrix of corrective/preventive actions for $\alpha = 0.3$ and $\alpha = 1.0$.

In this practical example, both selections required aggregated corrective/preventive tasks, such as *maintaining requirements and increasing discipline, training, and bonuses*. This result indicates that not only should failures be corrected or prevented but also that these failures should be prevented at higher risk and process levels.

4. Summary and Conclusions

A real-world example is used to demonstrate the proposed novel multilevel matrix-based risk assessment method for mitigating risk. The paper contributes three key findings to the literature. (C_1) The proposed set of multilevel matrices, known as the enterprise-level matrix (ELM), supports the whole risk assessment process, including identifying the risks (e.g., the RLM), evaluating the risks (e.g., the TLM), and determining the corrective/preventive actions for risk mitigation (e.g., the ALM). (C_2) The multilevel matrix structure allows decision makers to address the process and risk components and their multipurpose aggregations in the same matrix. As a result, the process components, all levels of the process and risk components, the aggregated risk values and the risk areas in all levels of the enterprise can be evaluated simultaneously. The proposed matrix-based method does not limit the number of risk components or the number of levels in the aggregation hierarchy. In addition, to the best of our knowledge, this is the first method that aggregates both the risk and process components to evaluate risks at different process levels. (C_3) By employing seriation and biclustering methods, the risk-level and threshold-level matrices can both be reordered to identify warnings or risks for the process and risk components simultaneously. If more than one aggregation method is employed to aggregate the risk/process components, the employed data mining method, namely, the biclustering and seriation method, selects the appropriate aggregation functions, which indicate the risks in higher process and risk aggregation levels. The employed data-mining method specifies multilevel submatrices that identify the process components, processes, process areas, risk components and risk areas simultaneously. According to the proposed multilevel submatrices, including the RLM and TLM, the appropriate corrective/preventive actions can be proposed based on the ALM matrix to mitigate risks at different levels.

In this work, we ignored the case where there is a dependency between risk components. This is a limitation compared to real cases and opens research opportunities in the future. In the practical example, we omitted the weighting of the risks. However, this limitation can be easily solved by using formulas containing weights. A practical implementation limitation is that the choice between two types of aggregation direction and several functions is a time-consuming process.

Author Contributions: Conceptualization, Z.K.; Methodology, Z.T.K.; Validation, T.C. and I.M.; Writing–original draft, Z.K. and Z.T.K. All authors have read and agreed to the published version of the manuscript.

Funding: This work has been implemented by the TKP2021-NVA-10 project with the support provided by the Ministry of Culture and Innovation of Hungary from the National Research, Development and Innovation Fund, financed under the 2021 Thematic Excellence Programme funding scheme.

Data Availability Statement: Not applicable.

Conflicts of Interest: The authors declare no conflict of interest.

Nomenclature

AHP	Analytical Hierarchy Process
ALM	Action-Level Matrix
ANP	Analytical Network Process
Cr	Criticality factor
CI	Consistency Index
CR	Consistency Ratio
f	Vector of risk factors
EDAS	Evaluation Based on the Distance from the Average Solution
ELECTRE	Elimination and Choice Expressing the Reality
ELM	Enterprise-Level Matrix
FMEA	Failure Mode and Effects Analysis
Fuzzy FMEA	Fuzzy Failure Mode and Effects Analysis
GRA	Grey Relational Analysis
ISO	International Standardization Organization
K	Invention function
MULTIMOORA	Multiplicative Form of the Multiobjective Optimization by Ratio Analysis
n	Number of risk factors
PROMETHEE	Preference Ranking Organization Method for Enrichment Evaluations
RAP	Risk Aggregation Protocol
RI	Random Consistency Index
RLM	Risk-Level Matrix

RPN	Risk Priority Number
SRD	Sum of Ranking Differences
T	Threshold vector
TLM	Threshold-Level Matrix
TODIM	TOmada de Decisao Iterativa Multicriterio
TOPSIS	Technique for Order Preference by Similarity to the Ideal Solution
TREF	Total Risk Evaluation Framework
$S(f, \mathbf{w})$	Risk aggregation function
VIKOR	VIsekriterijumska optimizacija i KOmpromisno Resenje
w	Vector of weights
$(\mathbf{W1}) - (\mathbf{W3})$	Warning rules
WS	Warning System

References

1. Bani-Mustafa, T.; Zeng, Z.; Zio, E.; Vasseur, D. A new framework for multi-hazards risk aggregation. *Saf. Sci.* **2020**, *121*, 283–302. [CrossRef]
2. Bjørnsen, K.; Aven, T. Risk aggregation: What does it really mean? *Reliab. Eng. Syst. Saf.* **2019**, *191*, 106524. [CrossRef]
3. Pedraza, T.; Rodríguez-López, J. Aggregation of L-probabilistic quasi-uniformities. *Mathematics* **2020**, *8*, 1980. [CrossRef]
4. Pedraza, T.; Rodríguez-López, J. New results on the aggregation of norms. *Mathematics* **2021**, *9*, 2291. [CrossRef]
5. Fattahi, R.; Khalilzadeh, M. Risk evaluation using a novel hybrid method based on FMEA, extended MULTIMOORA, and AHP methods under fuzzy environment. *Saf. Sci.* **2018**, *102*, 290–300. [CrossRef]
6. Liu, H.C.; Liu, L.; Liu, N. Risk evaluation approaches in failure mode and effects analysis: A literature review. *Expert Syst. Appl.* **2013**, *40*, 828–838. [CrossRef]
7. Spreafico, C.; Russo, D.; Rizzi, C. A state-of-the-art review of FMEA/FMECA including patents. *Comput. Sci. Rev.* **2017**, *25*, 19–28. [CrossRef]
8. Karasan, A.; Ilbahar, E.; Cebi, S.; Kahraman, C. A new risk assessment approach: Safety and Critical Effect Analysis (SCEA) and its extension with Pythagorean fuzzy sets. *Saf. Sci.* **2018**, *108*, 173–187. [CrossRef]
9. Maheswaran, K.; Loganathan, T. A novel approach for prioritization of failure modes in FMEA using MCDM. *Int. J. Eng. Res. Appl.* **2013**, *3*, 733–739.
10. Ouédraogo, A.; Groso, A.; Meyer, T. Risk analysis in research environment–part II: weighting lab criticity index using the analytic hierarchy process. *Saf. Sci.* **2011**, *49*, 785–793. [CrossRef]
11. Yousefi, S.; Alizadeh, A.; Hayati, J.; Baghery, M. HSE risk prioritization using robust DEA-FMEA approach with undesirable outputs: A study of automotive parts industry in Iran. *Saf. Sci.* **2018**, *102*, 144–158. [CrossRef]
12. Bognár, F.; Hegedűs, C. Analysis and Consequences on Some Aggregation Functions of PRISM (Partial Risk Map) Risk Assessment Method. *Mathematics* **2022**, *10*, 676. [CrossRef]
13. Kosztyán, Z.T.; Csizmadia, T.; Kovács, Z.; Mihálcz, I. Total risk evaluation framework. *Int. J. Qual. Reliab. Manag.* **2020**, *37*, 575–608. [CrossRef]
14. Wang, J.; Wei, G.; Lu, M. An extended VIKOR method for multiple criteria group decision making with triangular fuzzy neutrosophic numbers. *Symmetry* **2018**, *10*, 497. [CrossRef]
15. Wei, G.; Zhang, N. A multiple criteria hesitant fuzzy decision making with Shapley value-based VIKOR method. *J. Intell. Fuzzy Syst.* **2014**, *26*, 1065–1075. [CrossRef]
16. Kutlu, A.C.; Ekmekçioğlu, M. Fuzzy failure modes and effects analysis by using fuzzy TOPSIS-based fuzzy AHP. *Expert Syst. Appl.* **2012**, *39*, 61–67. [CrossRef]
17. Wei, G.W. Extension of TOPSIS method for 2-tuple linguistic multiple attribute group decision making with incomplete weight information. *Knowl. Inf. Syst.* **2010**, *25*, 623–634. [CrossRef]
18. Chen, N.; Xu, Z. Hesitant fuzzy ELECTRE II approach: a new way to handle multi-criteria decision making problems. *Inf. Sci.* **2015**, *292*, 175–197. [CrossRef]
19. Figueira, J.R.; Greco, S.; Roy, B.; Słowiński, R. An overview of ELECTRE methods and their recent extensions. *J. Multi-Criteria Decis. Anal.* **2013**, *20*, 61–85. [CrossRef]
20. Ghorabaee, M.K.; Zavadskas, E.K.; Amiri, M.; Turskis, Z. Extended EDAS method for fuzzy multi-criteria decision-making: an application to supplier selection. *Int. J. Comput. Commun. Control* **2016**, *11*, 358–371. [CrossRef]
21. Zindani, D.; Maity, S.R.; Bhowmik, S. Fuzzy-EDAS (evaluation based on distance from average solution) for material selection problems. In *Advances in Computational Methods in Manufacturing*; Springer: Berlin, Germany, 2019; pp. 755–771. [CrossRef]
22. Liao, H.; Xu, Z. Multi-criteria decision making with intuitionistic fuzzy PROMETHEE. *J. Intell. Fuzzy Syst.* **2014**, *27*, 1703–1717. [CrossRef]
23. Vetschera, R.; De Almeida, A.T. A PROMETHEE-based approach to portfolio selection problems. *Comput. Oper. Res.* **2012**, *39*, 1010–1020. [CrossRef]
24. Li, X.; Wei, G. GRA method for multiple criteria group decision making with incomplete weight information under hesitant fuzzy setting. *J. Intell. Fuzzy Syst.* **2014**, *27*, 1095–1105. [CrossRef]

25. Sun, G.; Guan, X.; Yi, X.; Zhou, Z. Grey relational analysis between hesitant fuzzy sets with applications to pattern recognition. *Expert Syst. Appl.* **2018**, *92*, 521–532. [CrossRef]
26. Liu, H.C.; Fan, X.J.; Li, P.; Chen, Y.Z. Evaluating the risk of failure modes with extended MULTIMOORA method under fuzzy environment. *Eng. Appl. Artif. Intell.* **2014**, *34*, 168–177. [CrossRef]
27. Liu, H.C.; You, J.X.; Lu, C.; Shan, M.M. Application of interval 2-tuple linguistic MULTIMOORA method for health-care waste treatment technology evaluation and selection. *Waste Manag.* **2014**, *34*, 2355–2364. [CrossRef] [PubMed]
28. Huang, Y.H.; Wei, G.W. TODIM method for Pythagorean 2-tuple linguistic multiple attribute decision making. *J. Intell. Fuzzy Syst.* **2018**, *35*, 901–915. [CrossRef]
29. Wang, J.; Wei, G.; Lu, M. TODIM method for multiple attribute group decision making under 2-tuple linguistic neutrosophic environment. *Symmetry* **2018**, *10*, 486. [CrossRef]
30. Héberger, K. Sum of ranking differences compares methods or models fairly. *TrAC Trends Anal. Chem.* **2010**, *29*, 101–109. [CrossRef]
31. Héberger, K.; Kollár-Hunek, K. Sum of ranking differences for method discrimination and its validation: comparison of ranks with random numbers. *J. Chemom.* **2011**, *25*, 151–158. [CrossRef]
32. Gueorguiev, T.; Kokalarov, M.; Sakakushev, B. Recent trends in FMEA methodology. In Proceedings of the 2020 7th International Conference on Energy Efficiency and Agricultural Engineering (EE&AE), Ruse, Bulgaria, 2–14 November 2020; pp. 1–4. [CrossRef]
33. Filipović, D. Multi-level risk aggregation. *ASTIN Bull. J. IAA* **2009**, *39*, 565–575. [CrossRef]
34. Ayyub, B.M. *Risk Analysis in Engineering and Economics*; Chapman and Hall/CRC: Boca Raton, FL, USA, 2014; p. 640.
35. Keskin, G.A.; Özkan, C. An alternative evaluation of FMEA: Fuzzy ART algorithm. *Qual. Reliab. Eng. Int.* **2008**, *25*, 647–661. [CrossRef]
36. AIAG-VDA. *Failure Mode and Effects Analysis—FMEA Handbook*; Verband der Automobilindustrie, Southfild, Michigan Automotive Industry Action Group: Berlin, Germany, 2019; Volume 1.
37. Hahsler, M.; Hornik, K.; Buchta, C. Getting Things in Order: An Introduction to the R Package seriation. *J. Stat. Softw.* **2008**, *25*, 1–34. [CrossRef]
38. Bar-Joseph, Z.; Gifford, D.K.; Jaakkola, T.S. Fast optimal leaf ordering for hierarchical clustering. *Bioinformatics* **2001**, *17*, S22–S29. [CrossRef]
39. Gusenleitner, D.; Howe, E.A.; Bentink, S.; Quackenbush, J.; Culhane, A.C. iBBiG: Iterative binary bi-clustering of gene sets. *Bioinformatics* **2012**, *28*, 2484–2492. [CrossRef] [PubMed]
40. Kosztyán, Z.T.; Pribojszki-Németh, A.; Szalkai, I. Hybrid multimode resource-constrained maintenance project scheduling problem. *Oper. Res. Perspect.* **2019**, *6*, 100129. [CrossRef]
41. Calvo, T.; Kolesárová, A.; Komorníková, M.; Mesiar, R. Aggregation Operators: Properties, Classes and Construction Methods. In *Aggregation Operators*; Physica-Verlag HD: Heidelberg, Germany, 2002; pp. 3–104. [CrossRef]
42. Beliakov, G.; Pradera, A.; Calvo, T. *Aggregation Functions: A Guide for Practitioners*; Springer-Verlag GmbH: Berlin, Germany, 2008.
43. Kolesarova, A.; Mesiar, R. On linear and quadratic constructions of aggregation functions. *Fuzzy Sets Syst.* **2015**, *268*, 1–14. [CrossRef]
44. Grabisch, M.; Marichal, J.L.; Mesiar, R.; Pap, E. *Aggregation Functions*; Cambridge University Press: Cambridge, UK, 2009; Volume 127.
45. Grabisch, M.; Marichal, J.L.; Mesiar, R.; Pap, E. Aggregation functions: means. *Inf. Sci.* **2011**, *181*, 1–22. [CrossRef]
46. Marichal, J.L.; Mesiar, R. Meaningful aggregation functions mapping ordinal scales into an ordinal scale: A state of the art. *Aequationes Math.* **2009**, *77*, 207–236. [CrossRef]
47. Zotteri, G.; Kalchschmidt, M.; Caniato, F. The impact of aggregation level on forecasting performance. *Int. J. Prod. Econ.* **2005**, *93*, 479–491. [CrossRef]
48. Malekitabar, H.; Ardeshir, A.; Sebt, M.H.; Stouffs, R.; Teo, E.A.L. On the calculus of risk in construction projects: Contradictory theories and a rationalized approach. *Saf. Sci.* **2018**, *101*, 72–85. [CrossRef]

Article

Multi-Trip Time-Dependent Vehicle Routing Problem with Split Delivery

Jie Zhang, Yifan Zhu, Xiaobo Li, Mengjun Ming, Weiping Wang and Tao Wang *

College of Systems Engineering, National University of Defense Technology, Changsha 410073, China
* Correspondence: wangtao1976@nudt.edu.cn

Abstract: Motivated by some practical applications of post-disaster supply delivery, we study a multi-trip time-dependent vehicle routing problem with split delivery (MTTDVRP-SD) with an unmanned aerial vehicle (UAV). This is a variant of the VRP that allows the UAV to travel multiple times; the task nodes' demands are splittable, and the information is time-dependent. We propose a mathematical formulation of the MTTDVRP-SD and analyze the pattern of the solution, including the delivery routing and delivery quantity. We developed an algorithm based on the simulation anneal (SA) framework. First, the initial solution is generated by an improved intelligent auction algorithm; then, the stochastic neighborhood of the delivery route is generated based on the SA algorithm. Based on this, the model is simplified to a mixed-integer linear programming model (MILP), and the CPLEX optimizer is used to solve for the delivery quantity. The proposed algorithm is compared with random–simulation anneal–CPLEX (R-SA-CPLEX), auction–genetic algorithm–CPLEX (A-GA-CPLEX), and auction–simulation anneal–CPLEX (A-SA) on 30 instances at three scales, and its effectiveness and efficiency are statistically verified. The proposed algorithm significantly differs from R-SA-CPLEX at a 99% confidence level and outperforms R-SA-CPLEX by about 30%. In the large-scale case, the computation time of the proposed algorithm is about 30 min shorter than that of A-SA. Compared to the A-GA-CPLEX algorithm, the performance and efficiency of the proposed algorithm are improved. Furthermore, compared to a model that does not allow split delivery, the objective function values of the solution of the MTTDVRP-SD model are reduced by 52.67%, 48.22%, and 34.11% for the three scaled instances, respectively.

Keywords: multi-trip; split delivery; auction mechanism; simulated annealing; mixed-integer linear programming model

MSC: 90C11

Citation: Zhang, J.; Zhu, Y.; Li, X.; Ming, M.; Wang, W.; Wang, T. Multi-Trip Time-Dependent Vehicle Routing Problem with Split Delivery. *Mathematics* **2022**, *10*, 3527. https://doi.org/10.3390/math10193527

Academic Editors: Zsolt Tibor Kosztyán and Zoltán Kovács

Received: 21 August 2022
Accepted: 23 September 2022
Published: 27 September 2022

Publisher's Note: MDPI stays neutral with regard to jurisdictional claims in published maps and institutional affiliations.

Copyright: © 2022 by the authors. Licensee MDPI, Basel, Switzerland. This article is an open access article distributed under the terms and conditions of the Creative Commons Attribution (CC BY) license (https://creativecommons.org/licenses/by/4.0/).

1. Introduction

The purpose of any post-disaster relief activity is to deliver requested (or even urgent) supplies and services to a place and within the time frame needed while trying to ensure minimal costs [1]. A disaster often results in road destruction or special traffic control, which poses great challenges for ground transportation and rescue. Therefore, the use of UAVs may be a good choice. The development of many technologies has made it feasible for rescue organizations to implement UAV delivery. Carbon fiber has enabled the development of lightweight airframes [2]. Lithium polymer batteries have a relatively high energy density, effectively increasing the flight time of UAVs [3]. GPS can be used for UAV navigation [4]. Technologies such as light detection and image processing can identify obstacles and targets [5]. In fact, a number of large enterprises have begun to use UAVs to complete deliveries, such as Amazon, Google, and Alibaba.

This study is motivated by the use of UAVs for the emergency delivery of supplies to a disaster area for post-disaster relief. Each disaster camp has a demand and urgency for supplies. Rescue supplies are centrally stored in a depot on the outskirts of the disaster area. UAVs bring relief supplies to the disaster camps for delivery. Each UAV needs to perform multiple trips due to its limited single-load capacity and battery power, resulting in the need to constantly return to the depot to replenish supplies and batteries. When a UAV runs out of power, the depot replaces the battery with a new fully charged one [6,7], ensuring that the UAV can be dispatched again with negligible time consumption in the process. Another challenging issue is that the urgent needs of disaster camps for supplies vary continuously over time and are discrete with supply delivery work. In fact, this is similar to a soft time window constraint, where different moments and different delivery quantities gain different revenues and have different costs for the UAV. We model this new variant as a multi-trip time-dependent vehicle routing problem with split delivery, which is based on the classic multi-trip vehicle routing problem (MTVRP), which also takes into account the following characteristics: multiple trips per UAV, time-dependent urgency, split delivery, and a UAV battery power limit.

For the vehicle routing problem with multiple trips, Taillard et al. [8] first introduced multiple trips into the vehicle routing problem (VRP) and proposed a tabu search heuristic algorithm for this problem. They proposed the MTVRP in order to extend the standard VRP and obtain high-quality solutions for a series of test problems. Salhi et al. [9] proposed a new hybrid genetic algorithm for the MTVRP problem with encouraging results. Mingozzi et al. [10] argued that the MTVRP was proposed because of the consideration of vehicle capacity constraints and maximum travel time constraints, and they proposed an exact solution algorithm that divided the solution into two parts—the feasible route for the vehicle and the travel departure schedule. In fact, exact approaches for the MTVRP and its variants are rare, and a discussion thereof is omitted due to space constraints. Interested readers are referred to [11–13]. Paradiso et al. [14] also focused on the MTVRP with time windows and proposed an exact solution framework that relied on column generation, column enumeration, and cutting planes. However, they proposed a significant point: that MTVRPs with different side constraints require special formulations and solution methods to solve them, which means that MTVRPs themselves generate different variants depending on different constraints, and each variant requires special models to model, as well as special approaches to its solution.

The studies cited above only investigated the vehicle routing problem while considering multiple trips. The time-dependent characteristic and split delivery were not taken into consideration in their studies. However, the MTVRP is the basis for the study of such variant problems.

The time-dependent characteristic has different interpretations. Donati et al. [15] and Ichoua et al. [16] described travel speed as time-dependent, or rather, travel time as time-dependent. Sun et al. [17] improved a time-dependent travel speed model in the background of delivery services under city congestion. They verified the realism and superiority of the proposed model through an experimental case study. There are many more studies investigating time-dependent travel time [18,19], and some other studies describing costs as time-dependent [20]. However, the time-dependent characteristic considered in this paper—from the practical point of UAV emergency supply delivery—is that the information of the task is time-varying, while the speed of the UAV is constant. The relationship between speed, load, and power consumption of UAVs was thoroughly studied by Liu et al. [21]. Similarly, Nguyen et al. [22] proposed a time-dependent characterization of demand and described it with two conditional assumptions. They proposed a taboo search metaheuristic algorithm that introduced an elite solution set and a frequency-based memory diversification strategy with encouraging results. Later, they added constraints for both the inbound and outbound traffic with success in [23]. However, they did not describe the dependence of the task demand on time and whether demand can be met multiple times much. These points are necessary for consideration in the UAV emergency supply delivery problem.

The introduction of a split-delivery constraint in the VRP problem was first proposed by Dror and Trudeau [24], who used a heuristic algorithm to find a cost reduction of almost 14% with split deliveries. Nowak et al. [25] pointed out that split delivery means delivering certain loads in multiple trips rather than one trip. Their study also focused on analyzing the extent to which the benefits of split delivery are related to the size of the load, the cost of the load, and the frequency of the load destination. Some other researchers limited split delivery to specific dimensions, such as the demand for a single task being satisfied in at most two [26] or three [27,28] times. Lai et al. [29] investigated the problem of unlimited times of split delivery in city services and developed a tabu search algorithm by combining dynamic programming, neighborhood search, and perturbation processes. They also analyzed the impact of split delivery on the back of the favorable results achieved by the algorithm. Naturally, the main focus of their study was on the combination of split delivery and the VRP, which may not describe the actual situation in disaster relief well.

The MTTDVRP-SD problem is NP-hard because it contains the MTVRP as its special case, and the MTVRP is NP-hard [30]. It is interesting to note that this problem develops its unique characteristics and difficulties by modeling various practical features together, and that this is a blind spot in the current research. Now, we briefly analyze the difficulties of the MTTDVRP-SD model. First, the solution should include not only the delivery routing order, but also the delivery quantity. At the same time, the delivery routing order implicitly includes the arrival time of the UAV. Therefore, the solution computation process includes two layers of optimization for the delivery routing and delivery quantity, leading to a huge solution search space. In particular, as the size of the problem increases, it is difficult for traditional algorithms to achieve a trade-off between solution quality and computation time. Second, the feasibility check for trips includes the demand constraint of the disaster camp, the load constraint of the UAV, and the maximum battery power constraint. It is possible to make infeasible trips to deliver to remote camps that exceed the battery power that is feasible if the UAV is loaded with a small quantity of supplies, but then it is necessary to check that the camps' supply demands are met. The feasibility check of the solution requires a thorough evaluation of the UAV's trip allocation and careful scheduling of the UAV's routing and dispatch of supplies. These challenging characteristics necessitate a rigorous investigation of the problem in order to propose suitable models and design tailored algorithms.

Considering both the use of delivery vehicles (i.e., UAVs) in the practical transportation industry and the theoretical gap in terms of modeling in the current study, we investigate a problem model that is more adapted to the emergency rescue scenario. Due to the complexity of the problem, we try to design a new heuristic algorithm (named A-SA-CPLEX) based on the intelligent auction mechanism, the simulated annealing (SA) algorithm, and the CPLEX optimizer. Specifically, the main contributions of this paper can be summarized as follows.

- A formal description of the UAV emergency supply delivery problem is provided. This problem is described as a new variant of the MTVRP problem, denoted as MTTDVRP-SD, and it is modeled as mixed-integer programming (MIP). MTTDVRP-SD considers the actual problem characteristics more comprehensively and defines the time-dependent urgency function explicitly as a piecewise linear function. The solution to the MTTDVRP-SD problem (i.e., the UAV's delivery pattern) consists of the delivery routing and delivery quantity, i.e., it contains two decision variables.
- The A-SA-CPLEX algorithm is proposed. Firstly, an intelligent auction mechanism that integrates single-task auctions and a pre-authorization mechanism are developed to construct a feasible and better solution in a short time. Then, the combination of the SA algorithm with the CPLEX optimizer is proposed to further improve the quality of the solution. This can effectively improve the efficiency of the iteration of solutions.
- In SA, the transformation of the MILP model can be achieved by first generating a random delivery routing and then bringing it into the MTTDVRP-SD model. At this point, the CPLEX optimizer can be used to find the optimal solution of the MILP model, which is the optimal delivery quantity under random delivery routing. The combination of the delivery routing and the delivery quantity constitutes the new solution, and the iteration continues.

- Experiments were carried out under an emergency supply delivery scenario. Then, we derived a large number of random instances of three different sizes for testing the proposed algorithm and compared it with three other algorithms. The experimental results show that our approach can efficiently solve the problem. Lastly, we additionally investigated the advantages of the MTTDVRP-SD model.

The remainder of this paper is organized as follows. Section 2 provides the formal description and a mathematical model of the problem. The heuristic algorithm is explained in Section 3, followed by extensive descriptions of the experimental results in Section 4. Finally, the conclusion and possible directions of future studies are discussed in Section 5.

2. Problem Definition and Formulation

In this section, we describe the MTTDVRP-SD in detail and present a mathematical model of the problem.

2.1. Basic Definition

Let $V = \{1, 2, \ldots, N_V\}$ denote the set of disaster camps (i.e., task nodes) and let $\{0\}$ denote the supply depot node, which is the starting or ending point of a trip. The MTTDVRP-SD is defined over a complete directed graph $G = (V', E)$, with node set $V' = V \cup \{0\}$ and arc set $E = \{(i,j) : i, j \in V, i \neq j\}$. Each node $i \in V$ is associated with a supply demand m_i, an urgency for supply demand e_i, and a two-dimensional coordinate (x_i, y_i). Note that the supply demand of the node changes with the step-by-step delivery of UAVs, and the urgency is additionally affected by time, which is described in detail later. Additionally, each arc $(i, j) \in E$ that can be traveled by UAVs is associated with a Euclidean distance D_{ij}.

Let G denote UAVs with a speed S, a rated load capacity L, a rated battery power W, and self-weight G. Note that the energy consumption of the UAV's battery depends on its self-weight and the load that it carries, which will become smaller step by step once the supplies have been delivered to the task nodes. Specifically, the energy consumption can be viewed to vary linearly with loading and self-weight [31,32]. Additionally, during the delivery task, the speed of the UAV is constant.

A trip is defined as a sequence of node visits that starts from the depot, progresses along a sequence of task nodes, and returns to the depot. After selecting the appropriate sub-route and assigning a delivery task, the UAV will load the corresponding supplies in order and exchange the batteries at the depot. Then, it will go to visit the assigned nodes and deliver the supplies one by one. For each trip, UAVs have constraints on the rated weight and rated battery power. Therefore, multiple trips are necessary with the limited UAVs available. Let R denote the set of possible trips for a UAV, and let the pair $(k, r), k \in U, r \in R$ denote the r-th trip of the k-th UAV.

2.2. Time-Dependent Task Information

In fact, many types of supplies are needed in a disaster relief situation, including food, water, medicine, etc. However, in order to facilitate emergency response and effective implementation of rescue, we do not over-calculate the need for various types of supplies, nor do we conduct precise delivery. It is a more common practice to synthesize various supplies into a single rescue package [33], i.e., to integrate them into a single supply delivery operation. To simplify the problem, the supply demand of task nodes is unitized. Considering that the maximum loading capacity of a UAV may be smaller than the supply demand of a single node, we propose a splittable delivery method for demand, i.e., the supply demand of a single node may be satisfied in multiple trips. Figure 1a shows that the supply demand of a task node is satisfied with three deliveries.

In the aftermath of a large-scale natural disaster, the urgency of supply demands can vary between task nodes due to differences in casualties, degree of house destruction, and economic levels [34]. On the other hand, the urgency of the task node becomes progressively greater over time, which may be due to secondary injuries caused by hunger, cold, and aggravation of conditions. As relief supplies are gradually replenished, the urgency decreases again. Figure 1b shows the change in urgency when the supply demands of a task node are met with three deliveries.

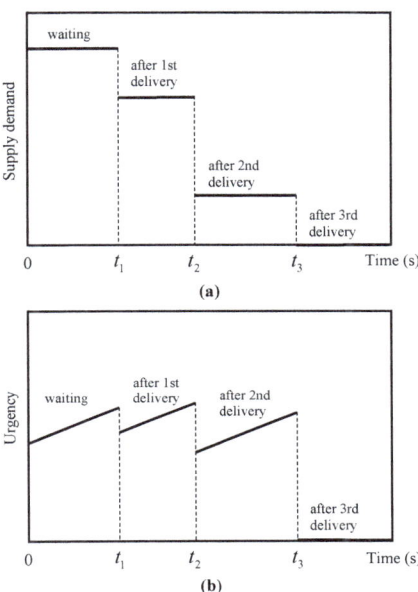

Figure 1. Illustration of the task information changes in the process with three deliveries. (a) Changes in the demand in the delivery process. (b) Changes in the urgency in the delivery process.

The supply demand $m_i(t)$ of the task node i will not change until the supplies are received, but the urgency $e_i(t)$ will increase linearly with time; at the moment of receiving the supplies, such as the moment t_1, t_2, t_3, the supply demand and urgency of the task node will decrease accordingly, but the decrease in urgency is related to the amount of supplies delivered q_i^{kr} and the initial urgency $e_i(0)$. Note that, at the moment t_3, the supply demands of the task node i are all satisfied, the delivery task of the node is considered to be completed, and the urgency becomes 0 directly. The formula is expressed in Equations (1) and (2). In fact, the delivery and reception of supplies and the change in node information are not done in the same instant, which is due to the time delay in the process of the delivery of supplies and the distribution of supplies, but this is not considered in this paper.

$$m_i(t^+) = \begin{cases} m_i(t^-) - q_i^{kr}, & x_i^{kr} = 1, \\ m_i(t^-), & \text{others.} \end{cases} \quad (1)$$

$$e_i(t^+) = \begin{cases} 0, & m_i(t^+) = 0, \\ e_i(t^-) - \frac{e_i(0)}{m_i(0)} \times q_i^{kr}, & m_i(t^+) > 0 \text{ and } x_i^{kr} = 1, \\ e_i(t_0) + a \times (t - t_0), & \text{others.} \end{cases} \quad (2)$$

where t_0 denotes the moment when the last supply demand of the task node was met; t^- and t^+ mathematically denote the left and right convergence of moment t, respectively.

The objective of the model is to find the minimal-cost solution that satisfies the task nodes' demand constraints, maximum loading constraints, and maximum battery power constraints. Unlike the usual objective function of the VRP and its variant problems, which considers minimizing the total travel distance or working time, the cost is defined as the damage duration of the task node, which is calculated with the urgency and rescue waiting time.

2.3. Mathematical Formulation

In this section, we formulate the MTTDVRP-SD as an MIP model to optimize the UAV delivery patterns (in terms of delivery routing and delivery quantity). The decision variables are defined by $i, j \in V', k \in U, r \in R$. To simplify the model formulation, the binary decision variable x_{ij}^{kr} is used to denote the delivery route, but a transformation is required. If $x_{ij}^{kr} = 1$, indicating that the trip (k, r) visits node j from i, then node j is added to the delivery route of UAV k; otherwise, it is not added. The delivery quantity corresponding to the delivery routing is denoted by discrete decision variables q_j^{kr}.

The MIP model will discussed in detail below.

$$f = \min\{\max_{i \in V} \int_0^{T_i^{end}} e_i(t)\,dt\} \tag{3}$$

$$t \in N \tag{4}$$

$$\sum_{k \in U} \sum_{r \in R} q_j^{kr} = m_j(0), \forall j \in V \tag{5}$$

$$N_R^k \geq 1, \forall k \in U \tag{6}$$

$$0 \leq l_k^r(t) < L_k, \forall k \in U, r \in R, t \tag{7}$$

$$l_k^r(st_k^r) > 0, \forall k \in U, r \in R \tag{8}$$

$$T_j^{kr} = x_{ij}^{kr} \times T_i^{kr} + x_{ij}^{kr} \times D_{ij}/S_k, \forall i, j \in V', k \in U, r \in R \tag{9}$$

$$et_k^r = st_k^r + \sum_{i \in V'} \sum_{j \in V'} x_{ij}^{kr} \times D_{ij}/S_k = T_0^{kr}, \forall k \in U, r \in R, i \neq j \tag{10}$$

$$st_k^{r+1} = \begin{cases} et_k^r, & \forall r \in R \\ 0, & \forall r \notin R \end{cases}, \forall k \in U, r+1 \in R \tag{11}$$

$$0 \leq w_k^r(t) \leq W_k, \forall k \in U, r \in R, t \tag{12}$$

$$w_k^r(t) = \int_{t_k^r}^{t} \delta \times (l_k^r(\tau) + G)d\tau, \forall k \in U, r \in R, t \tag{13}$$

$$\sum_{i \in V' \setminus \{j\}} x_{ij}^{kr} = \{0, 1\}, \forall j \in V, k \in U, r \in R \tag{14}$$

$$\sum_{j \in V' \setminus \{i\}} x_{ij}^{kr} = \{0, 1\}, \forall i \in V, k \in U, r \in R \tag{15}$$

$$\sum_{j \in V} x_{0j}^{kr} = 1, \forall k \in U, r \in R \tag{16}$$

$$\sum_{i \in V} x_{i0}^{kr} = 1, \forall k \in U, r \in R \tag{17}$$

$$\sum_{k \in U} \sum_{r \in R} \sum_{i \in V^i \setminus \{j\}} x_{ij}^{kr} \geq 1, \forall j \in V \tag{18}$$

$$\sum_{k \in U} \sum_{r \in R} \sum_{j \in V' \setminus \{i\}} x_{ij}^{kr} \geq 1, \forall i \in V \tag{19}$$

$$0 < q_j^{kr} \leq L_k, \forall j \in V, k \in U, r \in R \tag{20}$$

$$q_j^{kr} \leq m_j, \forall j \in V, k \in U, r \in R \tag{21}$$

$$x_{ij}^{kr} \in \{0,1\}, \forall i,j \in V, k \in U, r \in R \tag{22}$$

Equation (3) is used to minimize the maximum duration damage among all task nodes, which is calculated by the integral of the urgency over time. Equation (4) represents time as a set of discrete sequences belonging to natural numbers. Equation (5) ensures that all task nodes' demands are met. Equation (6) indicates that all UAVs belong to at least one trip.

Equation (7) guarantees that the loading of the UAV does not exceed its limit at any moment. Equation (8) indicates that the loading of the UAV at the start of any trip is strictly greater than 0. Equation (9) represents the calculation of the arrival time for node j during the r-th trip of the k-th UAV, which is a recursive formula. Equations (10) and (11) represent the calculation of the end and start time of a trip, respectively.

Equation (12) ensures that the UAV can go back safely, i.e., the energy consumed at any given moment does not exceed the limit. Equation (13) represents the calculation of the energy consumption of the UAV. Under the condition of constant UAV speed, the power is linearly related to the loading and self-weight, while the loading changes with the delivery of supplies, so it is a segmented linear function. Energy consumption is the product of power and time. More details can be found in the work of Liu et al. [21].

Equations (14) and (15) require that all nodes, including the depot, will be arrived at and left at most once during a trip. Equations (16) and (17) ensure that all trips start and end at the depot. Equations (18) and (19) guarantee that all task nodes will be arrived at and left at most once during the whole rescue process. Equations (20)–(22) define the ranges of the decision variables.

3. Approaches

This section proposes a solution algorithm based on SA. An initial solution is first constructed by a developed auction algorithm that integrates single-task auctions and a pre-authorization mechanism. Then, the SA algorithm combined with the CPLEX optimizer is applied to improve the initial solution.

3.1. Solution Representation

The delivery route and delivery quantity are the fundamental building blocks of the solution representation. In Section 2.3, the transformation from a binary decision variable x_{ij}^{kr} into a delivery route was described. Each UAV has multiple sub-trips, and the quantity of supplies delivered to each node is determined. Each sub-trip of the UAV has a schedule that is directly related to the objective function and can be computed recursively by Equation (9) with the time complexity of $O(|R|)$. The test regarding the feasibility of the solution must include two aspects, namely, the schedule corresponding to each sub-trip and the corresponding quantity of supplies to be delivered. An example of a solution to the MTTDVRP-SR is depicted in Figure 2, including some brief descriptions.

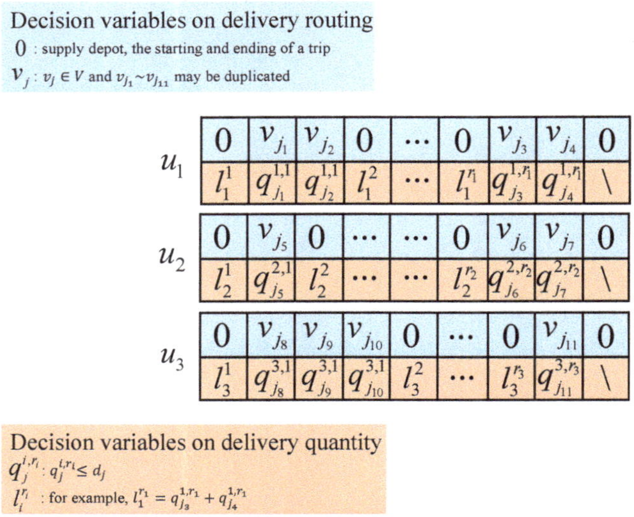

Decision variables on delivery routing
0 : supply depot, the starting and ending of a trip
$v_j : v_j \in V$ and $v_{j_1} \sim v_{j_{11}}$ may be duplicated

u_1
0	v_{j_1}	v_{j_2}	0	...	0	v_{j_3}	v_{j_4}	0
l_1^1	$q_{j_1}^{1,1}$	$q_{j_2}^{1,1}$	l_1^2	...	$l_1^{r_1}$	$q_{j_3}^{1,r_1}$	$q_{j_4}^{1,r_1}$	\

u_2
0	v_{j_5}	0	...	...	0	v_{j_6}	v_{j_7}	0
l_2^1	$q_{j_5}^{2,1}$	l_2^2	...	...	$l_2^{r_2}$	$q_{j_6}^{2,r_2}$	$q_{j_7}^{2,r_2}$	\

u_3
0	v_{j_8}	v_{j_9}	$v_{j_{10}}$	0	...	0	$v_{j_{11}}$	0
l_3^1	$q_{j_8}^{3,1}$	$q_{j_9}^{3,1}$	$q_{j_{10}}^{3,1}$	l_3^2	...	$l_3^{r_3}$	$q_{j_{11}}^{3,r_3}$	\

Decision variables on delivery quantity
$q_j^{i,r_i} : q_j^{i,r_i} \leq d_j$
$l_i^{r_i}$: for example, $l_1^{r_1} = q_{j_3}^{1,r_1} + q_{j_4}^{1,r_1}$

Figure 2. Example of a solution with three UAVs and less than 11 nodes.

3.2. Auction for Constructing the Initial Solution

3.2.1. Designed Mechanism

In the auction process, there are mainly two kinds of roles, i.e., an announcer and bidders. The work of the announcer is to publish tasks and assign them, and the bidders' work is to bid on the tasks and accept them. Consequently, we will focus on the interactions between the different roles to illustrate the auction mechanism.

Considering the problem of task assignment in the UAV swarm, the key point is to allocate each task to the proper UAV at the right time. In this work, we use an auction mechanism to determine the delivery routing and quantity for each UAV. As is the case in auction activities, the first step is to analyze the task requirements and determine the number and type of UAVs, and we carry out this work in the preparation stage. The following stages are announcing, bidding, pre-authorization, and authorization.

1. Announcing.

   The main work of this phase is for the announcer to delete the assigned tasks and update the information about the unassigned tasks. Note that the task information includes the price after constantly bidding for, in addition to the two-dimensional coordinates, supply demand, and urgency of the task mentioned in the model. Finally, they are published for all bidders.

2. Bidding.

   In this stage, each bidder (i.e., UAV) calculates the bidding value based on its status parameters (including the current position, speed, loading, remaining battery, completion time of the last task) and task information. Different loadings of UAVs lead to different energy consumption levels, so UAVs may obtain different rewards for the same task. In addition, the calculation should obey the common predefined rules. After getting the bidding value, bidders send the values to the announcer for bidding. The timing of a UAV's request for auction is the completion of the currently assigned task.

3. Pre-authorization.

   After the announcer receives the bidder's bid value, it selects the appropriate UAV for contract pre-authorization according to the predefined selection strategy. Since there are multiple UAVs bidding for the same task, the pre-authorization phase ends with all UAVs getting a task that they are satisfied with. Then, the announcer sends the complete task information to the winning UAV and records the result of this pre-assignment. The UAV will also be involved in the next auction after receiving a pre-authorized task and can be re-selected for a task with a higher revenue, but there can only be one pre-authorized task at a time.

4. Authorization.

The UAV is not considered authorized to perform the task until it receives authorization for that task. In this stage, UAVs need to verify that they have been pre-authorized. If a pre-authorization has been obtained, then it is directly transformed into an authorization; otherwise, an auction is requested from the announcer. Note that the UAV is only authorized for one task until the deadline for the completion of the authorized task.

3.2.2. Bidding Value

In the auction mechanism mentioned before, the announcer selects the proper UAV based on the bidding values. Consequently, the calculation of the bidding values is significant for the efficiency. In the bidding process, whether a candidate UAV can satisfy the energy constraint is the most important factor, and we describe this effect with a step function.

$$\phi(w_k^r(t) - pw) = \begin{cases} 1, & w_k^r(t) - pw \geq 0, \\ 0, & \text{others}. \end{cases} \quad (23)$$

where pw is the estimated power consumption.

Another factor that should be taken into consideration is the duration damage of tasks, and it should be as small as possible. In addition, the urgency decreases when the supply requirements of the task node are delivered. The greater the delivery, the greater the decrease in urgency and the greater the revenue. Therefore, we calculate the revenue $revenue_i^{kr}$ of UAV u_k for the task v_i at r-th trip with the following equation.

$$revenue_i^{kr} = \phi(w_k^r(t) - pw) \times \left(\int_0^t e_i(\tau)d\tau + \frac{e_i(0)}{m_i(0)} \times q_i^{kr} \right) \quad (24)$$

As a bidder, the UAV will choose the task i with the highest net revenue for bidding. In addition to the value of the revenue, the bidding value bid_i^{kr} for the task i also needs to consider the price of the task itself with the following equation.

$$bid_i^{kr} = revenue_i^{kr} - \max_{j \in V \setminus \{i\}} \{revenue_j^{kr} - p_j\} + \varepsilon \quad (25)$$

3.2.3. Selection Strategies

In the pre-authorization phase, the announcer receives the bid information from the UAV and completes the assignment of tasks. In the auction process, the announcer will pre-authorize different tasks for different UAVs. The key to this phase is the selection strategy for task assignment. The announcer receives all UAVs' bids and constructs a set BID. Then, the announcer selects the bidder with the maximal bidding value for task i. If bid_i^{kr} is selected, it must meet the following constraint.

$$bid_i^{kr} \geq bid_i^{k'r'}, \forall bid_i^{kr}, bid_i^{k'r'} \in BID \quad (26)$$

In the auction process, what we need to pay attention to is that when the bidding value is 0, the corresponding UAV will not be treated as a valid bidder, and it will not be added to the BID set. When a UAV k is pre-authorized for task i, the price p_i of task i is updated to its bid value with following equation.

$$p_i = bid_i^{kr} \quad (27)$$

A case exists with more than two UAVs bidding for the same task, but the task can only be pre-authorized for one UAV. At this moment, the UAV that is not pre-authorized needs to go back to the bidding stage and re-enter the bidding based on the latest task prices, while the pre-authorized UAV does not have to.

3.3. Simulated Annealing Integrated with CPLEX

We propose simulated annealing integrated with CPLEX (SA-CPLEX) to further improve the quality of the initial solution. The outline of SA-CPLEX is presented in Algorithm 1. The SA algorithm was first proposed to solve combinatorial optimization problems by Kirkpatrick et al. [35], and it provides an effective way of solving the TSP and VRP problems, which are difficult to deal with when using traditional methods [36]. The SA algorithm is a stochastic search algorithm based on the Monte Carlo iterative solution strategy, and its main idea is based on the similarity between the annealing process of solids in physics and general combinatorial optimization problems. Stochasticity is reflected in accepting a worse solution with a certain probability instead of accepting only the current optimal solution. With random factors introduced into the search process, it can avoid being prematurely trapped in a local minimum, and the global optimal solution can possibly be obtained.

Algorithm 1: Proposed Algorithm.

Input : $(V', E), U, R; T_0, T', \beta, MaxInnerIter$;
Output: SOL^*, f^*.

1 Constructing Initial Solution SOL_0, including SOL_Route_0 and $SOL\_Quantity_0$;
2 Initial: $inneriter \leftarrow 0$, and $SOL^*, SOL' \leftarrow SOL_0$;
3 Calculate f^*, f' from SOL_0;
4 $temp \leftarrow T_0$;
5 **while** $temp > T'$ **do**
6   Search SOL_Route in the neighborhood of SOL_Route';
7   Calculate $SOL\_Quantity$ from SOL_Route by CPLEX;
8   **while** $SOL\_Quantity$ is no solution **do**
9   **if** $inneriter == MaxInnerIter$ **then**
10             $SOL\_Route \leftarrow SOL\_Route^*$;
11             $SOL\_Quantity \leftarrow SOL\_Quantity^*$;
12   **break**;
13         $inneriter \leftarrow inneriter + 1$;
14   Calculate $SOL\_Quantity$ from SOL_Route by CPLEX;
15     $SOL \leftarrow SOL\_Route, SOL\_Quantity$;
16   Calculate f from SOL;
17     $delta\_f = f - f'$;
18   **if** $delta\_f < 0$ **then**
19         $SOL' \leftarrow SOL$;
20         $f' \leftarrow f$;
21   **if** $f < f^*$ **then**
22             $SOL^* \leftarrow SOL$;
23             $f^* \leftarrow f$;
24   **else if** $rand < \exp(delta\_f/temp)$ **then**
25         $SOL' \leftarrow SOL$;
26         $f' \leftarrow f$;
27     $temp \leftarrow temp \times \beta$;

Four parameters—T_0, T', β, and $MaxInnerIter$—are defined for the SA algorithm. T_0, T', and $\beta (0 < \beta < 1)$ are the typical parameters used in SA for, respectively, the initial temperature, the final temperature, and the cooling factor. *MaxInnerIter* represents a threshold of the number of non-solutions at a particular temperature. The general structure of SA comes from Kirkpatrick et al. [35].

First, the initial solution SOL_0 is constructed by an improved auction algorithm. We initialize *inneriter*, SOL^*, SOL', f^*, f', *temp* as shown in lines 2~4, and all of them will be updated in the following calculation process. When the current temperature *temp* is greater than the final temperature T, the search process will continue. As mentioned previously, the solution SOL is composed of the delivery route SOL_Route and the delivery quantity $SOL\_Quantity$, but only the former generates a new neighborhood solution according to different search operators (as described in Section 3.3.1). $SOL\_Quantity$ is based on the determination to convert the model into an MILP, and the optimal delivery quantity is found by the CPLEX optimizer (as described in Section 3.3.2).

Due to the specificity of the model, including the multiple trips and separable demands, the solution space is huge, which leads to the generation of many infeasible neighborhood solutions and the consumption of an unnecessarily large amount of computing power, i.e., after the new SOL_Route is determined, no feasible $SOL\_Quantity$ can be found, so internal iterations such as those in lines 7~14 are necessary. However, when the number of internal iterations reaches the threshold of *MaxInnerIter*, we reset the neighborhood solution to the current optimal solution and reduce the temperature to avoid the deadlock phenomenon.

When the new neighborhood solution SOL is generated, we compute its objective function value f and cause it to differ from the initial value f' of the current temperature, which is denoted as *delta_f* (line 17). If the objective function value is improved (*delta_f* is less than 0), SOL' is replaced by SOL. If the current optimal objective function value f^* is improved ($f < f^*$), SOL^* and f^* will be replaced by SOL and f, respectively (lines 18~23).

If SOL is worse than SOL', a random number *rand* ($0 < rand < 1$) is generated and compared with $\exp(delta\_f/temp)$ (line 24). This operation introduces a stochastic factor to the search process, which can effectively prevent it from being trapped in a local optimum. If *rand* is less than $\exp(delta\_f/temp)$, we will accept SOL and update SOL', f' according to lines 25~26. At the end of the search round, we need to decrease the temperature and continue iterating.

3.3.1. Random Search of Delivery Routing

The proposed algorithm uses a random neighborhood structure that features seven types of moving operators, including *Swap-Single*, *Move*, *Insert*, *Delete*, *Swap-All*, *2-Swap-Single*, and *2-Swap-All*. Figure 3 illustrates how we implement all moves in the solution representation to generate a new neighborhood delivery routing. In Figure 3, black dots indicate the depot, light blue indicates the task nodes, and red and blue indicate the task nodes that are about to perform the moving operators.

The first operator is focused on the swap of two routing nodes on the same UAV and randomly selects only one UAV. However, for *Swap-All*, all UAVs will perform *Swap-Single*, *2-Swap-Single* focuses on swapping four different routing nodes on the same UAV, and *2-Swap-All* means that all UAVs will perform *2-Swap-Single*. *Move* is done by selecting one position randomly and moving it into the position before another randomly selected position, but the node being moved cannot be a depot. The following two operators are *Insert* and *Delete*. *Insert* is used by selecting a random node and converting it into a random position. *Delete* is similar to it, but the deleted node cannot be a depot or a node that has only been visited once in the current solution.

The search intensity of these seven operators gradually increases, and all of them are used randomly and repeatedly until no further improvement is obtained. Implementing these moves will change the solution structure. It is not only limited to the route sequence, but also the times at which nodes are visited (as explicitly done by *Insert* and *Delete*). When the delivery route is determined, the time for the UAV to visit each node is also determined.

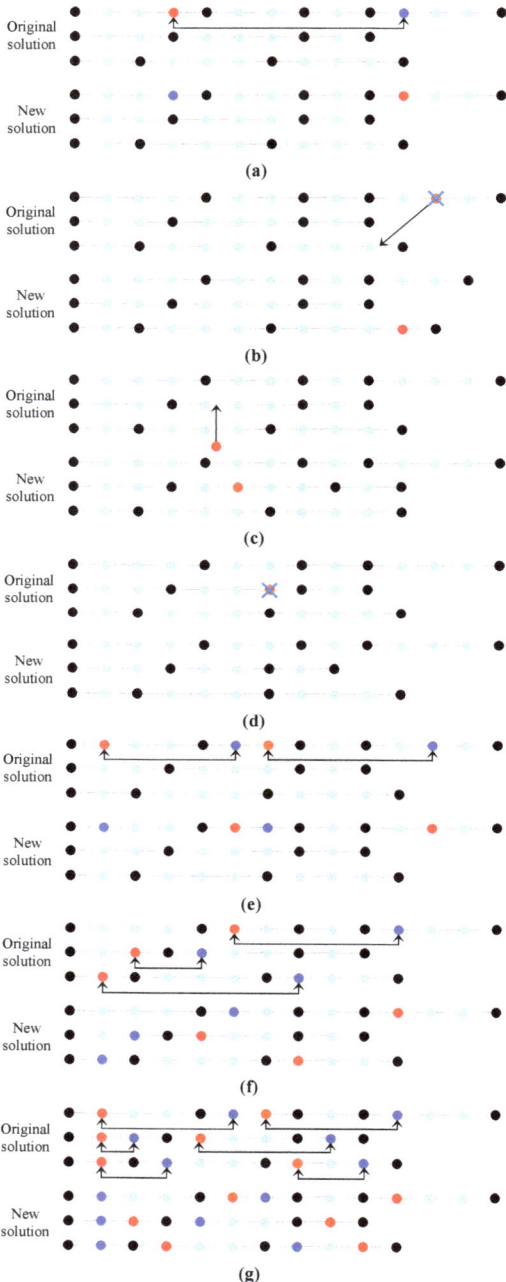

Figure 3. Illustration of the creation of a new delivery routing sequence using seven operators. (**a**) *Swap-Single*. (**b**) *Move*. (**c**) *Insert*. (**d**) *Delete*. (**e**) *Swap-All*. (**f**) *2-Swap-Single*. (**g**) *2-Swap-All*.

3.3.2. Exact Search of Delivery Quantity

In Section 2.3, there are two types of decision variables for the MTTDVRP-SD. If both decision variables are considered together, the solution search process can be very difficult. In Section 3.3.1, we first generate a new *SOL_Route* with seven moving operators. When *SOL_Route* is determined, the value of the decision variable x_{ij}^{kr} can be determined based on the representation of the solution shown in Figure 2. Then, by bringing x_{ij}^{kr} into the MTTDVRP-SD, a simplification of the MILP model is achieved and can be solved directly by the CPLEX optimizer. At this time, the optimal delivery quantity under this delivery route can be found, and the combination of the delivery route and delivery quantity forms a new neighborhood solution, which then participates in the next iteration round.

The degraded model is composed of Equations (3), (5), (7), (8), (12), (13), (20), and (21). However, the objective function (Equation (3)) needs to be rewritten, as shown in the following.

$$f = \min\{\max_{j \in V} \sum_{n=1}^{n_j} (e_j(T_j^n) + e_j(T_j^{n-1})) \times (T_j^n - T_j^{n-1})/2\} \qquad (28)$$

where n_j denotes the times at which node j was visited; T_j^n denotes the time at which node j was visited for the n-th time, and $T_j^0 = 0, j \in V$. According to Equation (2), $e_j(T_j^n)$ can be calculated as follows.

$$e_j(T_j^n) = e_j(T_j^{n-1}) + \alpha \times (T_j^n - T_j^{n-1}) - \frac{e_j(0)}{m_j(0)} \times q_j^n \qquad (29)$$

where q_j^n denotes the delivery quantity of node j accepted for the n-th time, and it is different from the definition of q_j^{kr}. However, they can be transformed into each other. When *SOL_Route* is determined, we can calculate how many times each node is visited, the time of the the visits, and the number of q_j^n. Then, we sort the multiple visit times of node j, and we can establish the relationship between $(k.r)$ and n. Based on this relationship, the transformation between q_j^n and q_j^{kr} can be achieved.

Until now, this simplified model has still not become a standard MILP model. We need to introduce a new decision variable C to convert the Minimax of the objective function into a minimum value problem. Then, we reformulate the objective function of Equation (3) as shown in Equation (30) and add $N_V + 1$ constraints, as in Equation (31).

$$f = \min c \qquad (30)$$

$$\begin{cases} \sum_{n=1}^{n_1} (e_1(T_1^n) + e_1(T_1^{n-1})) \times (T_1^n - T_1^{n-1})/2 \leq c \\ \vdots \\ \sum_{n=1}^{n_{N_V}} (e_{N_V}(T_{N_V}^n) + e_{N_V}(T_{N_V}^{n-1})) \times (T_{N_V}^n - T_{N_V}^{n-1})/2 \leq c \\ c \in R \end{cases} \qquad (31)$$

Using the above method, the model is successfully degraded to a standard MILP model, which can be solved exactly by the CPLEX optimizer. This can quickly find the optimal *SOL_Quantity* under a new *SOL_Route* or demonstrate that there is no feasible solution while favorably reducing the computational resources of the search process.

4. Experiments and Discussion

The proposed algorithm was coded in C++, and the MILP model was solved with IBM ILOG CPLEX Optimization Studio 22.1.0.0. All of the experiments were conducted using Visual Studio 2022 platform, the CPU was an Intel(R) Core (TM) i7-9700 CPU @ 3.00GHz 3.00GHz, and the OS was Windows 7.

4.1. Test Instances for the MTTDVRP-SD

To illustrate how the MTTDVRP-SD behaves in general, we averaged the results of some randomly generated instances of each scenario. The scenarios were conducted on three different scales, which are displayed in Table 1. Each instance consisted of a rectangular area of 4000 × 4000 m. We generated 10 random instances for each scale of the scenario. In each instance, the disaster camps were uniformly distributed throughout the area and were given a uniform random demand of 6~10 units; the initial urgency of the disaster camps was a random value in the range of 0.1~0.4, and the parameter of urgency changed over time $\alpha = 0.0002$; the depot was randomly located at the boundary location of the area. We ran the A-SA-CPLEX algorithm 30 times per instance and calculated the average, standard deviation, and average runtime for these 30 runs. The same was true for the implementation of the comparison algorithm and the comparison model.

Table 1. Parameters of instances.

Scale	Number of Task Nodes (N_V)	Number of UAVs (N_U)
Small	30	3
Medium	50	5
Large	100	10

The parameters of the UAVs were derived from some public sources and scaled accordingly to fit the case scenario. The maximum capacity of each UAV was in the range of 14~17 units, which included the payload and self-weight, with the self-weight $G = 2$ units. The average speed of each UAV during the task was constant, between 15~20; the maximum battery capacity was a random value between 6000~7000. In this section, unless mentioned otherwise, when running the SA part, the initial temperature was $Y = 500$, the final temperature was $Y' = 0.1$, the cooling factor was $\Delta = 0.999$, and the number of rounds was $\Lambda = 10{,}000$.

4.2. Results of the A-SA-CPLEX Algorithm

In this section, we use the instance s_1 as an example to illustrate the solution process of the A-SA-CPLEX algorithm and to show the optimal solution. Figure 4 shows the convergence trend of the A-SA-CPLEX algorithm. The objective function values in the figure are the solutions after each iteration of the algorithm, instead of recording only the optimal solution for the current iteration. As can be seen, the algorithm experiences an intense oscillation in the early stages, which is because the SA algorithm has a higher probability of accepting poorer solutions at the beginning of the iteration, which helps to jump out of the local optimal solution. After about 5000 iterations, the algorithm reaches a plateau and obtains a current iterative optimal solution with an objective function value below 400.

Figure 5 gives information about the optimal delivery routing and delivery quantity found by the A-SA-CPLEX algorithm, and the arrival time of the task node is implicitly represented by the delivery routing. In Figure 5, the three lines together consist of the solution, and they represent the execution schemes of UAVs u_1, u_2, and u_3, respectively. The red circles indicate depots, the blue circles indicate task nodes, and the numbers in the circles are the serial numbers of the nodes. The numbers below the red circles indicate the quantities of supplies loaded from the depot for this trip, and the numbers inside the brackets indicate the maximum loading capacity of that UAV. The numbers below the blue circles indicate the quantity of supplies delivered to that task node. Under this optimal dispatching strategy, the maximum duration damage is 359.71 among all task nodes. From the solutions, each UAV made multiple trips, with UAV u_1 making six trips, u_2 making four trips, and u_3 making five trips. On the other hand, the supply demands of the existent task nodes were distributed and delivered; for example, task nodes v_{10}, v_{12}, v_{13}, v_{17}, v_{18}, and v_{24} were split into two deliveries.

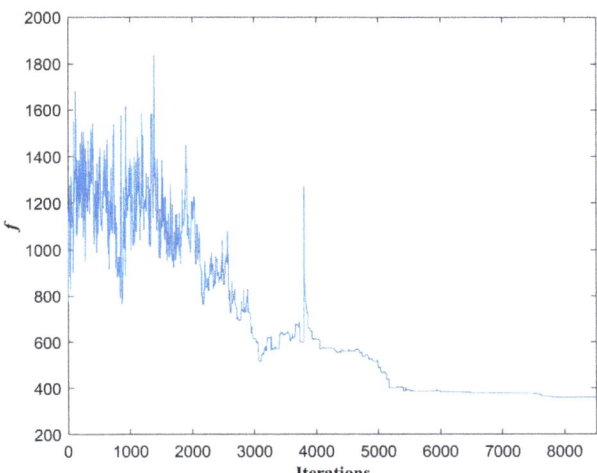

Figure 4. Convergence trend of the A-SA-CPLEX algorithm in the instance s_1.

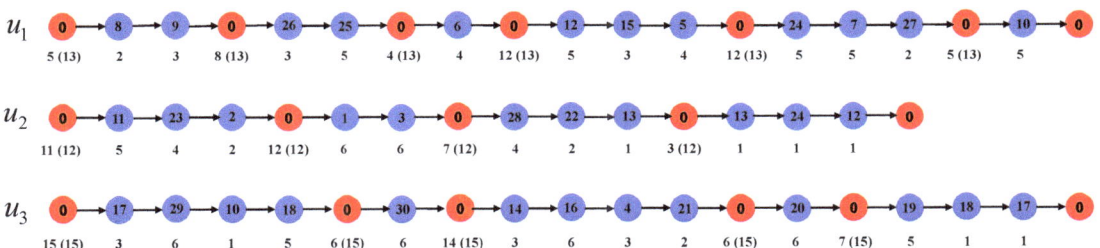

Figure 5. Solution of the instance s_1.

4.3. Comparative Analysis of the Algorithms

To explore the performance of the algorithm, ten instances for each different scale were randomly generated with the method described above and used to conduct the experiment. For each instance, the results of the proposed algorithm were used for a comparison with the results of other algorithms. The compared algorithms included the R-SA-CPLEX algorithm, A-SA algorithm, and A-GA-CPLEX algorithm. The R-SA-CPLEX algorithm is an improvement of the random initial feasible solution using the proposed SA-CPLEX method. The A-SA algorithm optimizes the initial solution constructed by the proposed auction method using only SA. The A-GA-CPLEX algorithm uses the GA framework for solving; however, the initial population is composed of the initial solution constructed by the proposed auction method and some random feasible solutions.

Table 2 presents all of the experimental results obtained by the four algorithms for 30 instances in three scales. Each algorithm was run 30 times, and the average results are displayed. The first column of the table contains the three scales of the instance. The second column contains the names of all instances. Column 3~5, 6~8, 9~11, and 12~14 show the statistical results, which include the average and standard deviation of the objective function value, as well as the average runtimes of the four algorithms. The last three columns show the relative reduction in the average value of the objective function for each of the two compared algorithms with respect to the proposed algorithm. The subsequent tables have similar meanings.

Before analyzing the results of the four algorithms further, we performed a statistical analysis of the performance of the A-SA-CPLEX algorithm and the comparison algorithms.

Although presenting the results of multiple optimizations of an algorithm as an average and standard deviation is a valuable way to proceed, statistical analysis is important for the investigation of significant differences in performance between algorithms and to overcome randomness [37]. Therefore, in this paper, the Wilcoxon rank-sum test was used to perform nonparametric statistical tests to test the significance of the results for all 30 instances of the three scales mentioned above.

The p-value is a form of output from the Wilcoxon rank-sum test. If the p-value of two random datasets after the Wilcoxon rank-sum test is less than 0.01, the two datasets can be considered statistically significant at the 99% confidence level, i.e., significantly different; conversely, the two datasets are not accepted as significantly different at the 99% confidence level. The results of the Wilcoxon rank-sum test are shown in Table 3. In all instances, the p-values of the results of the A-SA-CPLEX and R-SA-CPLEX algorithms were less than 0.01, while the p-values with the A-SA algorithm were greater than 0.01. For the A-GA-CPLEX algorithm, there were two large-scale instances with p-values greater than 0.01, while those of all other instances were less than 0.01. Therefore, it can be concluded that at a 99% confidence level, it can be considered that A-SA-CPLEX is significantly different from the R-SA-CPLEX algorithm, while it is not significantly different from the A-SA algorithm. For most instances, the A-GA-CPLEX can be considered significantly different from the R-SA-CPLEX algorithm at the 99% confidence level. In the following, we further analyze the performance of the different algorithms.

For small-scale instances, the proposed algorithm in this paper shows a decrease of 27.11% to 39.39% in the objective function value compared to the solution of the conventional R-SA-CPLEX algorithm. For the other two scale instances, this decrease is also significant. In the medium-sized instances, this decrease ranges from 28.30% to 44.25%, while in the large scale, it ranges from 14.41% to 35.63%. Since the value of the objective function decreases by around 30% for the solutions at the three scales, it can be demonstrated that the proposed algorithm has a great advantage over the conventional R-SA-CPLEX algorithm in terms of the quality of the solutions. The probable reason is that, for the MTTDVRP-SD model, which includes a two-layer optimization of delivery routing and delivery quantity, the solution space is large, and the form of the solution has a great influence on the solution search.

The performance improvement of the proposed algorithm is also significant compared to that of the A-GA-CPLEX algorithm. In small-scale instances, the objective function value of the A-SA-CPLEX algorithm decreases by 21.42%~31.54% compared to the A-GA-CPLEX algorithm. Similarly, in the medium-scale instances, there is a decrease of 28.46%~41.34%. However, in the large-scale instances, there are two instances (l_5 and l_10) where both algorithms have the same performance. This is because both algorithms cannot continue optimizing the initial solution constructed by the auction algorithm. Further, in comparison with the R-SA-CPLEX algorithm, the computational results of the A-GA-CPLEX algorithm are shown to be superior in 22 instances. This is because with the design of the A-GA-CPLEX algorithm, the initial population contains an initial solution constructed by the auction algorithm. However, for the R-SA-CPLEX algorithm, the initial solution is constructed randomly. This indicates that the initial solution is important in the MTTDVRP-SD.

On the other hand, we can see that the quality of the solution of the proposed algorithm is basically not improved compared to that of the A-SA algorithm. This is because we transformed the problem model into an MILP model when we determined the neighborhood solution of the delivery route using the SA method. In terms of the quality of the solution, it is about the same at this point to use the SA method or the CPLEX optimizer to determine the delivery quantity; the main difference may be the computing time.

Table 2. Results of comparing the four algorithms under three scale instances.

Scale	Name	R-SA-Cplex			A-GA-CPLEX			A-SA			A-SA-Cplex			Comparison		
		Avg. f	Std. f	Time (s)	Avg. f	Std. f	Time (s)	Avg. f	Std. f	Time (s)	Avg. f	Std. f	Time (s)	(R-SA-CPLEX - A-SA-CPLEX) /R-SA-CPLEX	(A-GA-CPLEX - A-SA-CPLEX) /A-GA-CPLEX	(A-SA - A-SA-CPLEX) /A-SA
Small Scale	s_1	584.17	157.32	48.93	531.94	46.24	101.68	388.15	35.82	206.97	379.94	33.54	62.89	33.56%	28.57%	2.12%
	s_2	515.50	44.37	36.58	497.54	51.00	100.67	375.74	31.55	205.90	389.44	36.56	52.14	27.11%	21.73%	−3.65%
	s_3	565.84	287.07	47.71	483.10	48.53	108.80	363.92	36.93	231.88	379.61	42.26	56.47	35.68%	21.42%	−4.31%
	s_4	496.90	228.20	57.05	415.17	42.73	107.29	301.18	35.19	234.67	308.69	33.85	59.36	39.39%	25.65%	−2.49%
	s_5	661.49	271.12	48.22	618.07	75.64	105.85	407.49	30.34	238.68	423.13	31.31	63.12	38.40%	31.54%	−3.84%
	s_6	458.67	36.66	37.42	439.72	50.45	103.62	323.29	26.67	224.58	327.07	24.55	57.45	29.52%	25.62%	−1.17%
	s_7	545.72	160.79	48.44	506.67	98.68	170.28	370.83	38.15	244.68	380.34	32.91	72.79	32.05%	24.93%	−2.56%
	s_8	548.25	123.49	48.48	524.49	49.81	92.98	378.68	26.11	229.12	377.18	28.39	63.35	30.93%	28.09%	0.39%
	s_9	515.34	53.43	36.94	474.37	50.10	102.28	363.76	28.63	242.74	367.75	32.46	58.44	29.41%	22.48%	−1.10%
	s_10	522.21	139.29	49.48	520.00	71.31	109.73	379.37	26.21	231.80	359.30	32.59	61.17	27.35%	30.90%	5.29%
Medium Scale	m_1	717.40	43.87	51.65	754.15	46.96	116.90	487.82	39.84	521.60	494.73	42.15	70.99	32.00%	34.40%	−1.42%
	m_2	806.94	225.66	80.20	783.41	48.35	117.28	511.23	55.41	547.05	503.44	42.38	76.18	36.65%	35.74%	1.52%
	m_3	695.63	67.77	48.20	774.51	63.40	170.49	449.99	33.35	565.60	454.33	44.68	78.15	35.31%	41.34%	−0.97%
	m_4	726.29	211.56	78.18	794.52	69.43	108.52	479.91	33.95	581.31	470.72	35.24	76.01	33.92%	40.75%	1.92%
	m_5	722.52	101.66	56.88	693.08	33.62	108.81	487.76	36.44	552.68	486.28	50.02	70.91	32.49%	29.84%	0.30%
	m_6	879.41	381.35	94.43	707.23	39.97	124.69	490.30	44.08	582.47	505.97	38.13	72.44	42.49%	28.46%	−3.20%
	m_7	827.99	186.05	64.02	840.53	58.18	108.14	530.51	51.71	568.87	523.73	44.76	79.34	35.93%	37.69%	1.28%
	m_8	648.55	145.98	58.41	655.82	37.80	129.69	464.98	55.22	592.54	447.71	48.42	70.84	28.30%	31.73%	3.71%
	m_9	851.94	217.45	62.87	871.43	50.81	116.90	551.53	44.46	581.77	558.33	55.95	73.75	35.26%	35.93%	−1.23%
	m_10	829.19	334.25	100.29	711.84	52.42	118.64	475.71	43.00	551.32	482.05	46.48	89.90	42.63%	32.28%	−1.33%
Large Scale	l_1	919.96	68.54	75.21	829.61	50.17	697.23	605.15	34.49	2294.73	616.36	38.67	141.19	34.22%	25.70%	−1.85%
	l_2	989.16	90.38	74.69	971.47	42.34	938.39	664.30	57.07	2346.96	676.99	49.94	158.01	32.84%	30.31%	−1.91%
	l_3	1248.19	87.70	75.62	1171.94	13.78	1002.05	809.52	56.16	1415.81	799.10	65.71	172.20	35.14%	31.81%	1.29%
	l_4	1015.97	64.15	74.88	941.38	47.89	718.53	653.98	44.88	1397.94	653.81	37.81	145.75	35.63%	30.55%	0.03%
	l_5	934.31	66.13	75.23	727.50	0.00	1042.44	727.50	0.00	1799.83	727.50	0.00	141.48	22.13%	0.00%	0.00%
	l_6	949.17	70.86	75.20	816.56	41.36	694.05	625.93	45.23	2260.12	630.77	53.80	628.22	34.06%	22.75%	−0.77%
	l_7	1038.95	69.43	75.06	1067.85	51.26	837.51	703.96	60.47	2383.37	717.09	60.83	152.97	32.24%	32.85%	−1.87%
	l_8	1139.70	88.37	76.69	1271.90	9.83	1010.65	802.30	58.45	1414.42	789.39	51.37	167.56	29.60%	37.94%	1.61%
	l_9	1051.74	77.10	76.27	938.61	39.95	705.22	699.09	55.40	2336.35	713.99	48.66	142.03	33.53%	23.93%	−2.13%
	l_10	952.91	46.35	75.78	815.60	0.00	949.62	815.60	0.00	2746.52	815.60	0.00	526.58	14.41%	0.00%	0.00%

Note: Avg. is an abbreviation for average and Std. is an abbreviation for standard deviation.

Table 3. Results from the Wilcoxon test.

Scale	Name	p-Value		
		R-SA-CPLEX vs. A-SA-CPLEX	A-GA-CPLEX vs. A-SA-CPLEX	A-SA vs. A-SA-CPLEX
Small Scale	s_1	<0.01	<0.01	0.27
	s_2	<0.01	<0.01	0.14
	s_3	<0.01	<0.01	0.72
	s_4	<0.01	<0.01	1.00
	s_5	<0.01	<0.01	0.00
	s_6	<0.01	<0.01	0.72
	s_7	<0.01	<0.01	0.14
	s_8	<0.01	<0.01	0.72
	s_9	<0.01	<0.01	1.00
	s_10	<0.01	<0.01	0.07
Medium Scale	m_1	<0.01	<0.01	1.00
	m_2	<0.01	<0.01	0.47
	m_3	<0.01	<0.01	0.72
	m_4	<0.01	<0.01	0.47
	m_5	<0.01	<0.01	0.72
	m_6	<0.01	<0.01	0.47
	m_7	<0.01	<0.01	0.14
	m_8	<0.01	<0.01	0.27
	m_9	<0.01	<0.01	0.47
	m_10	<0.01	<0.01	1.00
Large Scale	l_1	<0.01	<0.01	0.27
	l_2	<0.01	<0.01	0.14
	l_3	<0.01	<0.01	0.47
	l_4	<0.01	<0.01	0.72
	l_5	<0.01	1.00	1.00
	l_6	<0.01	<0.01	1.00
	l_7	<0.01	<0.01	0.47
	l_8	<0.01	<0.01	0.72
	l_9	<0.01	<0.01	0.14
	l_10	<0.01	1.00	1.00

Analyzing the computation time of the four algorithms in different scale instances, we can see that the computation time of the R-SA-CPLEX algorithm is less than that of the proposed algorithm. However, in the small- and medium-scale instances, this computing time advantage is only about 15 s. In the large-scale instances, this advantage is about three times faster, close to 2 min. To some extent, it shows that the disadvantage of the computational speed of the proposed algorithm compared to the R-SA-CPLEX algorithm becomes more and more obvious as the problem size increases, but it is still within an acceptable range. For the A-GA-CPLEX algorithm, the runtime is longer compared to that of the A-SA-CPLEX algorithm. In both the small- and medium-scale instances, this runtime disadvantage is less pronounced, at less than 1 min. However, at a large scale, this disadvantage is more than 10 min. Unfortunately, the disadvantage of the computational speed of the A-SA algorithm becomes very obvious. As the scale of the problem increases, the computing time of the A-SA algorithm increases exponentially. In the large-scale instances, the computation time of the A-SA algorithm is about nine times greater than that of the A-SA-CPLEX algorithm, and the average time taken is about 34 min. This is unacceptable for emergency rescue problems.

Furthermore, by analyzing the standard deviation of the objective function for each instance, we can clearly conclude that the A-SA-CPLEX and A-SA algorithms are more stable than the R-SA-CPLEX algorithm. The stability of the solution is also very important for life-related optimization problems, such as an emergency rescue.

4.4. Comparative Analysis of the Models

In a previous paper, we learned that the main innovations of the MTTDVRP-SD model are the multiple trips of UAV, the time dependence of task information, and split delivery. In the following, we will illustrate the practicality and superiority of the MTTDVRP-SD model in terms of theoretical analysis or experimental validation. The superiority of using multiple trips is obvious. First, the cost of manufacturing UAVs is expensive in comparison. Under a fixed cost, the problem may not find a solution if a UAV is not reused [31]. Second, in the emergency rescue environment, rescue teams often have a higher capacity for raising life supplies than UAVs. This makes it difficult to find enough UAVs to enable a single departure, meaning that the sum of all task demands is less than the single-load capacity of all UAVs. Regarding the time dependence of the task information, this is a mathematical description of an earthquake disaster area and it is necessary. On the other hand, regarding the necessity of split delivery, we intend to conduct an experimental verification. The 30 instances of different scales from the previous subsection were still chosen and solved with the proposed A-SA-CPLEX algorithm. The experiment was repeated 30 times for each instance, and the average, standard deviation, and average runtime were calculated. The difference was that the comparison model did not allow split delivery, and the comparison model can be noted as MTTDVRP.

Table 4 shows the benefits of allowing split delivery. We can see that in all 30 random instances, allowing split delivery produces a solution that is less damaging to the task nodes, with at least a 20% reduction in this damage. The standard deviations of the objective functions of the two models were also analyzed, and it was found that the standard deviation of the MTTDVRP-SD model was relatively smaller and more stable. However, the runtime of the algorithm under the MTTDVRP model was longer, although the difference in solution time between the two models is not obvious from the results in Table 4.

The model comparison results for the three different scale instances were analyzed separately and represented in the form of box plots [38], as shown in Figure 6. We can see that as the instance went from a small and a medium to a large scale, the median results of the two model comparisons decreased from 52.67% to 48.22%, and then to 34.11%. To a certain extent, this indicates that the superiority of the MTTDVRP-SD model over the MTTDVRP gradually decreases as the problem's scale increases. However, in large-scale instances, there is still an advantage of about 34%. The reason for this phenomenon may be that as the problem size increases, the number of UAVs and tasks increases, but the area of the region remains the same, which leads to a greater spatial density of tasks and, later, partially offsets the advantage of split delivery a bit.

Table 4. Results of comparing the two models under three scale instances.

Scale	Name	MTTDVRP			MTTDVRP-SD			Comparison
		Avg. f	Std. f	Runtime (s)	Avg. f	Std. f	Runtime (s)	(MTTDVRP-MTTDVRP-SD)/MTTDVRP
Small Scale	s_1	796.58	199.13	43.90	379.94	33.54	62.89	52.30%
	s_2	778.40	98.70	40.88	389.44	36.56	52.14	49.97%
	s_3	780.39	128.11	39.93	379.61	42.26	56.47	51.36%
	s_4	683.31	112.03	41.06	308.69	33.85	59.36	54.82%
	s_5	988.15	151.05	44.11	423.13	31.31	63.12	57.18%
	s_6	667.37	126.28	39.91	327.07	24.55	57.45	50.99%
	s_7	922.82	0.00	37.63	380.34	32.91	72.79	58.79%
	s_8	803.23	136.57	42.21	377.18	28.39	63.35	53.04%
	s_9	704.70	138.34	41.23	367.75	32.46	58.44	47.81%
	s_10	767.07	100.14	41.63	359.30	32.59	61.17	53.16%
Medium Scale	m_1	932.62	83.57	56.53	494.73	42.15	70.99	46.95%
	m_2	1031.15	149.39	52.02	503.44	42.38	76.18	51.18%
	m_3	818.79	69.40	48.11	454.33	44.68	78.15	44.51%
	m_4	993.61	122.41	47.04	470.72	35.24	76.01	52.63%
	m_5	826.90	92.17	47.26	486.28	50.02	70.91	41.19%
	m_6	902.68	143.82	46.46	505.97	38.13	72.44	43.95%
	m_7	1117.83	112.30	47.40	523.73	44.76	79.34	53.15%
	m_8	794.84	106.87	49.55	447.71	48.42	70.84	43.67%
	m_9	1105.22	135.88	45.93	558.33	55.95	73.75	49.48%
	m_10	972.37	135.99	46.65	482.05	46.48	89.90	50.43%
Large Scale	l_1	1015.89	104.89	96.20	616.36	38.67	141.19	39.33%
	l_2	1028.96	95.56	99.79	676.99	49.94	158.01	34.21%
	l_3	1210.82	128.89	100.10	799.10	65.71	172.20	34.00%
	l_4	1003.74	96.57	101.56	653.81	37.81	145.75	34.86%
	l_5	963.91	56.80	99.06	727.50	0.00	628.22	24.53%
	l_6	990.26	112.83	91.14	630.77	53.80	141.48	36.30%
	l_7	1028.96	100.01	97.89	717.09	60.83	152.97	30.31%
	l_8	1177.57	86.40	102.51	789.39	51.37	167.56	32.96%
	l_9	1103.27	109.39	96.21	713.99	48.66	142.03	35.28%
	l_10	1026.62	121.50	95.62	815.60	0.00	526.58	20.55%

Note: Avg. is an abbreviation for average and Std. is an abbreviation for standard deviation.

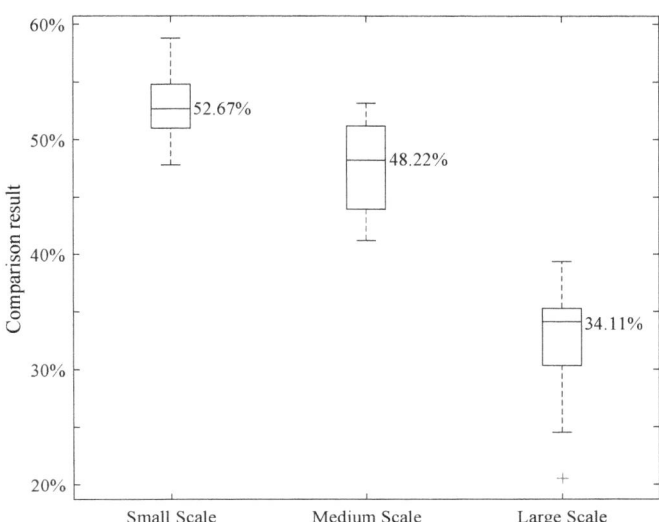

Figure 6. A box plot showing the model comparison results for the three scale instances.

5. Conclusions

In this paper, we consider a variant model of the VRP (i.e., MTTDVRP-SD) that is more suitable for post-disaster emergency delivery scenarios. Based on the VRP, new conditions, such as multiple trips of a UAV, task information changing over time, and splittable task demands, are considered. It is also necessary to satisfy the UAV loading and maximum power constraints. We propose a mathematical description of the MTTDVRP-SD based on undirected graphs and decompose the optimization process into two layers of optimization—delivery routing and delivery quantity—but both of them are related. Based on the SA framework, we developed an efficient A-SA-CPLEX algorithm to further optimize the initial solution generated by the improved intelligent auction algorithm. We first determined the random delivery routing neighborhood based on the SA algorithm, and then mathematically transformed the original model into an MILP problem that can be solved quickly by the CPLEX optimizer, thus greatly improving the computational efficiency. Finally, numerical experiments were conducted. Instance s_1 was used as an example to illustrate the solution process of the A-SA-CPLEX algorithm and to show the optimal solution. The effectiveness and efficiency of the proposed algorithm were verified by comparing four algorithms in 30 examples of three scales: small, medium, and large. The results of the Wilcoxon rank-sum test showed that the proposed algorithm was significantly better than the R-SA-CPLEX algorithm and the A-GA-CPLEX algorithm, and that it was comparable to the A-SA algorithm at the 99% confidence level. On the other hand, the computational efficiency of the proposed algorithm was better compared to that of the R-GA-CPLEX algorithm and was slightly weaker compared to that of the R-SA-CPLEX algorithm, but still within an acceptable range. However, the computational efficiency of the A-SA algorithm was significantly lower than that of the proposed algorithm and decreased exponentially as the problem's scale increased. We also explored the advantages of the MTTDVRP-SD model, theoretically analyzed the advantages of multiple trips and time dependence, experimentally analyzed the advantages of split delivery, and attained some valuable conclusions.

There are more powerful algorithms that can be developed to effectively solve the MTTDVRP-SD. Naturally, for each particular problem, we need more realistic modeling for the details of the problem in order to generate higher application value. In the future, we will consider conducting research on such problems in dynamic scenarios while taking more practical aspects, such as hardware, into account.

Author Contributions: Conceptualization, J.Z. and Y.Z.; methodology, J.Z.; software, J.Z.; validation, J.Z., T.W., and W.W.; formal analysis, X.L.; investigation, X.L.; resources, M.M.; data curation, Y.Z.; writing—original draft preparation, J.Z.; writing—review and editing, T.W.; visualization, M.M. All authors have read and agreed to the published version of the manuscript.

Funding: This work was supported in part by the National Natural Science Foundation of China under Grant 72101263.

Institutional Review Board Statement: Not applicable.

Informed Consent Statement: Not applicable.

Data Availability Statement: The data presented in this study are available on request from the corresponding author.

Acknowledgments: The authors acknowledge the National University of Defense Technology.

Conflicts of Interest: The authors declare no conflict of interest.

Notations

Some of the parameters involved in the model and their meanings are as follows.

Indices

i, j	Index of task nodes' serial numbers, $i, j \in V$
k	Index of UAVs' serial numbers, $k \in U$
r	Index of UAV departures, $r \in R$

Sets

U	Set of UAVs
V	Set of task nodes
V'	Set of nodes, a supply depot node is added compared to V
R	Set of UAV trips

Parameters

N_U	Number of all UAVs
N_V	Number of all task nodes
N_R^k	The maximum number of trips of the UAV k
D_{ij}	Euclidean distance between task nodes i and j
(x_i, y_i)	The two-dimensional coordinates of the task node i
(x_0, y_0)	The two-dimensional coordinates of the depot 0
α	Parameters of urgency over time
W_k	The maximum safety energy of the UAV k
L_k	Upper limit of the loading capacity of the UAV k
G	Self-weight of the UAV k
δ	Parameters of UAV's energy consumption with time and weight
S_k	Speed of the UAV k

Variables

t	Discrete time series
T_i^{kr}	The moment when node i is visited in the r-th trip of UAV k
T_i^{end}	The moment when the supply demands of node i are fully satisfied
$m_i(t)$	The supply demand of the task node i at moment t
$e_i(t)$	The urgency of the task node i at moment t
st_k^r	Start time of the r-th trip of the UAV k
et_k^r	Finish time of the r-th trip of the UAV k
d_i^k	Euclidean distance from the UAV k to the task node i
$w_k^r(t)$	The remaining energy of the r-th trip of the UAV k at moment t
$l_k^r(t)$	The loading of the r-th trip of the UAV k at moment t
$(x_k(t), y_k(t))$	Two-dimensional coordinates of the UAV k at t moments
x_{ij}^{kr}	Binary decision variable, if the UAV k makes its r-th trip from node i to node j, $x_{ij}^{kr}=1$; otherwise, $x_{ij}^{kr}=0$
q_j^{kr}	Decision variables, the quantity of supply delivered by the UAV k on its r-th trip to task node i

References

1. Molina, J.; López-Sánchez, A.; Hernández-Díaz, A.G.; Martínez-Salazar, I. A Multi-start Algorithm with Intelligent Neighborhood Selection for solving multi-objective humanitarian vehicle routing problems. *J. Heuristics* **2018**, *24*, 111–133. [CrossRef]
2. Park, S.J.; Kim, B.J. Carbon fibers and their composites. In *Carbon Fibers*; Springer: Berlin/Heidelberg, Germany, 2015; pp. 275–317.
3. Beard, K.W. *Linden's Handbook of Batteries*; McGraw-Hill Education: New York, NY, USA, 2019.
4. Chen, D.; Gao, G.X. Probabilistic graphical fusion of LiDAR, GPS, and 3D building maps for urban UAV navigation. *Navigation* **2019**, *66*, 151–168. [CrossRef]
5. Karpenko, S.; Konovalenko, I.; Miller, A.; Miller, B.; Nikolaev, D. UAV control on the basis of 3D landmark bearing-only observations. *Sensors* **2015**, *15*, 29802–29820. [CrossRef]
6. Ure, N.K.; Chowdhary, G.; Toksoz, T.; How, J.P.; Vavrina, M.A.; Vian, J. An automated battery management system to enable persistent missions with multiple aerial vehicles. *IEEE/ASME Trans. Mechatron.* **2014**, *20*, 275–286. [CrossRef]
7. Fujii, K.; Higuchi, K.; Rekimoto, J. Endless flyer: A continuous flying drone with automatic battery replacement. In Proceedings of the 2013 IEEE 10th International Conference on Ubiquitous Intelligence and Computing and 2013 IEEE 10th International Conference on Autonomic and Trusted Computing, Vietri sul Mare, Italy, 18–21 December 2013; pp. 216–223.
8. Taillard, E.D.; Laporte, G.; Gendreau, M. Vehicle routeing with multiple use of vehicles. *J. Oper. Res. Soc.* **1996**, *47*, 1065–1070. [CrossRef]
9. Salhi, S.; Petch, R. A GA based heuristic for the vehicle routing problem with multiple trips. *J. Math. Model. Algorithms* **2007**, *6*, 591–613. [CrossRef]
10. Mingozzi, A.; Roberti, R.; Toth, P. An exact algorithm for the multitrip vehicle routing problem. *INFORMS J. Comput.* **2013**, *25*, 193–207. [CrossRef]
11. Azi, N.; Gendreau, M.; Potvin, J.Y. An exact algorithm for a single-vehicle routing problem with time windows and multiple routes. *Eur. J. Oper. Res.* **2007**, *178*, 755–766. [CrossRef]
12. Macedo, R.; Alves, C.; de Carvalho, J.V.; Clautiaux, F.; Hanafi, S. Solving the vehicle routing problem with time windows and multiple routes exactly using a pseudo-polynomial model. *Eur. J. Oper. Res.* **2011**, *214*, 536–545. [CrossRef]
13. Hernandez, F.; Feillet, D.; Giroudeau, R.; Naud, O. A new exact algorithm to solve the multi-trip vehicle routing problem with time windows and limited duration. *4or* **2014**, *12*, 235–259. [CrossRef]
14. Paradiso, R.; Roberti, R.; Laganá, D.; Dullaert, W. An exact solution framework for multitrip vehicle-routing problems with time windows. *Oper. Res.* **2020**, *68*, 180–198. [CrossRef]
15. Donati, A.V.; Montemanni, R.; Casagrande, N.; Rizzoli, A.E.; Gambardella, L.M. Time dependent vehicle routing problem with a multi ant colony system. *Eur. J. Oper. Res.* **2008**, *185*, 1174–1191. [CrossRef]
16. Ichoua, S.; Gendreau, M.; Potvin, J.Y. Vehicle dispatching with time-dependent travel times. *Eur. J. Oper. Res.* **2003**, *144*, 379–396. [CrossRef]
17. Sun, Y.; Wang, D.; Lang, M.; Zhou, X. Solving the time-dependent multi-trip vehicle routing problem with time windows and an improved travel speed model by a hybrid solution algorithm. *Clust. Comput.* **2019**, *22*, 15459–15470. [CrossRef]
18. Sun, P.; Veelenturf, L.P.; Hewitt, M.; Van Woensel, T. The time-dependent pickup and delivery problem with time windows. *Transp. Res. Part B Methodol.* **2018**, *116*, 1–24. [CrossRef]
19. Dabia, S.; Ropke, S.; Van Woensel, T.; De Kok, T. Branch and price for the time-dependent vehicle routing problem with time windows. *Transp. Sci.* **2013**, *47*, 380–396. [CrossRef]
20. Liu, S.; Qin, S.; Zhang, R. A branch-and-price algorithm for the multi-trip multi-repairman problem with time windows. *Transp. Res. Part E Logist. Transp. Rev.* **2018**, *116*, 25–41. [CrossRef]
21. Liu, Y.; Liu, Z.; Shi, J.; Wu, G.; Pedrycz, W. Two-echelon routing problem for parcel delivery by cooperated truck and drone. *IEEE Trans. Syst. Man Cybern. Syst.* **2020**, *51*, 7450–7465. [CrossRef]
22. Nguyen, P.K.; Crainic, T.G.; Toulouse, M. A tabu search for time-dependent multi-zone multi-trip vehicle routing problem with time windows. *Eur. J. Oper. Res.* **2013**, *231*, 43–56. [CrossRef]
23. Nguyen, P.K.; Crainic, T.G.; Toulouse, M. Multi-trip pickup and delivery problem with time windows and synchronization. *Ann. Oper. Res.* **2017**, *253*, 899–934. [CrossRef]
24. Dror, M.; Trudeau, P. Savings by split delivery routing. *Transp. Sci.* **1989**, *23*, 141–145. [CrossRef]
25. Nowak, M.; Ergun, Ö.; White, C.C., III. Pickup and delivery with split loads. *Transp. Sci.* **2008**, *42*, 32–43. [CrossRef]
26. Ji, B.; Zhou, S.; Samson, S.Y.; Wu, G. An enhanced neighborhood search algorithm for solving the split delivery vehicle routing problem with two-dimensional loading constraints. *Comput. Ind. Eng.* **2021**, *162*, 107720. [CrossRef]
27. Bortfeldt, A.; Yi, J. The split delivery vehicle routing problem with three-dimensional loading constraints. *Eur. J. Oper. Res.* **2020**, *282*, 545–558. [CrossRef]
28. Chen, Z.; Yang, M.; Guo, Y.; Liang, Y.; Ding, Y.; Wang, L. The split delivery vehicle routing problem with three-dimensional loading and time Windows constraints. *Sustainability* **2020**, *12*, 6987. [CrossRef]
29. Lai, Q.; Zhang, Z.; Yu, M.; Wang, J. Split-Delivery Capacitated Arc-Routing Problem With Time Windows. *IEEE Trans. Intell. Transp. Syst.* **2020**, *23*, 2882–2887. [CrossRef]
30. Cattaruzza, D.; Absi, N.; Feillet, D. Vehicle routing problems with multiple trips. *4or* **2016**, *14*, 223–259. [CrossRef]
31. Dorling, K.; Heinrichs, J.; Messier, G.G.; Magierowski, S. Vehicle routing problems for drone delivery. *IEEE Trans. Syst. Man. Cybern. Syst.* **2016**, *47*, 70–85. [CrossRef]

32. D'Andrea, R. Guest editorial can drones deliver? *IEEE Trans. Autom. Sci. Eng.* **2014**, *11*, 647–648. [CrossRef]
33. Song, J.M.; Chen, W.; Lei, L. Supply chain flexibility and operations optimisation under demand uncertainty: A case in disaster relief. *Int. J. Prod. Res.* **2018**, *56*, 3699–3713. [CrossRef]
34. Song, X.; Wang, J.; Chang, C. Nonlinear continuous consumption emergency scheduling model and algorithm based on demand urgency. *Inf. Control* **2014**, *43*, 9.
35. Kirkpatrick, S.; Gelatt, C.D., Jr.; Vecchi, M.P. Optimization by simulated annealing. *Science* **1983**, *220*, 671–680. [CrossRef] [PubMed]
36. Kaku, I.; Xiao, Y.; Xia, G. The deterministic annealing algorithms for vehicle routing problems. *Int. J. Smart Eng. Syst. Des.* **2003**, *5*, 327–339. [CrossRef]
37. Dehghani, M.; Montazeri, Z.; Hubálovskỳ, Š. GMBO: Group mean-based optimizer for solving various optimization problems. *Mathematics* **2021**, *9*, 1190. [CrossRef]
38. Tareen, A.D.K.; Nadeem, M.S.A.; Kearfott, K.J.; Abbas, K.; Khawaja, M.A.; Rafique, M. Descriptive analysis and earthquake prediction using boxplot interpretation of soil radon time series data. *Appl. Radiat. Isot.* **2019**, *154*, 108861. [CrossRef] [PubMed]

Article

A Flexible Robust Possibilistic Programming Approach toward Wood Pellets Supply Chain Network Design

Zaher Abusaq [1,*], Muhammad Salman Habib [2,*], Adeel Shehzad [3], Mohammad Kanan [1] and Ramiz Assaf [4]

1. Industrial Engineering Department, Jeddah College of Engineering, University of Business and Technology, Jeddah 21448, Saudi Arabia
2. Department of Industrial and Manufacturing Engineering, University of Engineering and Technology, Lahore 54890, Pakistan
3. Department of Mechanical Engineering, University of Engineering and Technology, Lahore 54890, Pakistan
4. Department of Industrial Engineering, An-Najah National University, Nablus P.O. Box 7, Palestine
* Correspondence: zaher@ubt.edu.sa (Z.A.); salmanhabib@uet.edu.pk (M.S.H.)

Abstract: Increasing energy demand and the detrimental environmental impacts of fossil fuels have led to the development of renewable energy sources. Rapid demand growth for wood pellets over the last decade has established wood pellets as a potential renewable energy source in a globally competitive energy market. Integrated decision making including all stakeholders in the wood pellet supply chain (WPSC) is essential for a smooth transition to commercially viable wood pellet production. In this aspect, this study aims to suggest a decision support system for optimizing biomass-based wood pellet production supply chain network design (WPP-SCND). The WPP-SCND decision system minimizes the total supply chain (SC) cost of the system while also reducing carbon emissions associated with wood pellet SC activities. All objective parameters, including biomass availability at the supply terminals, market demand, and biomass production, are considered fuzzy to account for epistemic uncertainty. A fuzzy flexible robust possibilistic programming (fuzzy-FRPP) technique is developed for solving the suggested uncertain WPP-SCND model. The case findings show that the imprecise nature of the parameters has a significant impact on the strategic and tactical decisions in the wood pellet SC. By investing almost 10% of the total cost, robust decisions within the wood pellet SC can be obtained. It is established that the fuzzy-FRPP technique successfully provides robust decisions and achieves a balance between transportation costs, emissions costs, and economies of scale when making capacity decisions. Although the suggested decision support system is used to manage the production and distribution of wood pellets, the insights and solution methodology may be extended to the production of other biofuels. The proposed research may be valuable to authorities involved in planning large-scale wood pellet-related production-distribution projects.

Keywords: fuzzy optimization techniques; wood pellet supply chain; flexible programming; linear programming

MSC: 90C05; 90C08; 90C11

1. Introduction

Major worldwide issues include the energy crisis, population growth, food scarcity, resource depletion, and global warming [1,2]. Given these conditions, recovering resources from waste is essential for reducing dependence on nonrenewable energy sources [3]. A circular economy (CE) plays a crucial role in this regard since it supports the transition from a linear to a circular framework defined by return operations of waste resources. CE seeks to make all operations circular, where no "disposable trash" is produced, and all outputs are inputs for other systems [4,5]. However, a CE alone may not be sustainable. Switching to a bioeconomy (BE) based on renewable resources in conjunction with circular economy (CE) will not only reduce environmental stress but also make CE feasible, resulting in a circular bioeconomy (CRBE) [6]. CRBE entails converting waste materials into products with added value, such as food, biomass, and bioenergy, in order to conserve virgin natural resources. CRBE has both economic and environmental benefits, as recovery of bio-based wastes or byproducts encourages potential reutilization, transforming wastes into marketable goods with added value and enabling economic growth [6,7].

Multiple studies have emphasized the potential importance of biomass in meeting the world energy need through CRBE [8–10]. The promotion of CRBE in the context of energy production is supported by the valorization of accessible biomass through biofuel production. Biofuels are carbon-neutral fuels that are more environmentally friendly than fossil fuels [11,12]. Governments throughout the world, however, are taking initiatives to reduce fossil fuel utilization and greenhouse gas (GHG) emissions [13]. In this context, wood pellets are considered a viable energy source due to their multiple advantages, including their high heat value, low moisture content, and portability [14]. Wood pellets are equivalent to other biofuels such as biodiesel and bioethanol in terms of traded volume and are one of the most commonly traded commodities in the world [10]. The market outlook for wood pellets is relatively optimistic: the worldwide pellet market is projected to reach 54 million tons by 2025 [13].

Historically, forest companies were able to profit from their massive harvesting operations, which pushed resources to wood pellet processing plants and then to other markets following a push production system. Now, the push production business strategy is economically unsustainable for both the industry and the forest-dependent communities in light of the current extremely volatile global economy [15]. In addition, sawmill waste, which is often used to manufacture wood pellets, is desired biomass for a range of processes and hence insufficient for meeting demand [13]. Therefore, manufacturers have had to discover new sources of biomass for the manufacturing of wood pellets. In this context, following the CRBE, biomass such as forest harvesting byproducts and agricultural leftovers (wheat straw, rice husk, and bagasse) has tremendous potential to replace sawmill waste. To compete in the market, these feedstock sources are often geographically distributed and must be supplied to wood pellet production facilities cost-effectively, since high production costs are the major barrier to the commercialization of wood pellets [16]. Furthermore, the transportation of biomass and wood pellets in a wood pellet supply chain (WPSC) contributes significantly to carbon emissions. As a result, effective WPSC network design is essential for a quick transition to a circular bioeconomy.

Additionally, wood pellet production SCs are more susceptible to parameter uncertainty than commercial SCs due to highly volatile business dynamics: Wood pellet feedstocks are dependent on primary goods that are largely seasonal, whereas biomass pricing, and logistics costs, are influenced by international variations in fossil fuel prices [17]. Most prior studies do not include the integration of uncertainties associated with biomass supply and transportation, wood pellet manufacturing, and market demand in the optimal design of WPSC. In contrast, most of the previous WPSC design literature has used deterministic methodologies (see: Boukherroub et al. [13], Méndez-Vázquez et al. [16], Mansuy et al. [18], Shabani et al. [19], Kanzian et al. [20], etc.). Failure to account for the uncertain environment during the planning phase may result in a WPSC design that is less than optimal or impractical. Effective uncertainty management related to the materials and operations utilized in the manufacture of wood pellets throughout the whole supply chain allows all stakeholders to enjoy additional economic advantages, which strengthens the operations' sustainability.

Keeping in mind the abovementioned challenges for a successful transition to a circular bioeconomy, this study addresses the following questions:

- Research question 1: How can an integrated decision support system that efficiently collects, transports, and converts massive quantities of various biomasses into wood pellets be developed in a sustainable manner to support the transition to a circular bioeconomy?

- Research question 2: How can robust decisions for strategic and tactical levels in a wood pellet SC be acquired in a highly uncertain environment?

To answer these research questions, a multi-period wood pellet production supply chain network design (WPP-SCND) model employing a linear programming approach is proposed. The purpose of the suggested optimization model is to minimize the value of the economic objective while taking into account the associated environmental impact costs. The suggested WPP-SCND model decreases the environmental effect and total cost of wood pellet production and distribution while fulfilling demand, resulting in a low-carbon bioeconomy.

The remainder of this research is structured as follows. The subsequent section surveys related works. Section 3 explains the research methodology adopted in this study. Section 4 provides the WPP-SCND optimization model and case study results analysis. The work is concluded in Section 5.

2. Research Context

Researchers and practitioners are focusing their attention on renewable energy generation because of the global energy crisis. As a result, there has been increased interest in incorporating circular bioeconomy principles into the development of wood waste-to-energy chains.

Given this context, several researchers have used mathematical modeling-based methods to apply principles of circular bioeconomy considering various types of wood waste. Méndez-Vázquez et al. [16] proposed a nonlinear mixed integer programming (MIP) model to efficiently locate biofuel pellet processing plants in a circular bioeconomy setting. The objectives of overall systems cost reduction and GHG emissions minimization were considered in designing a low-carbon WPSC network. The principles of circular bioeconomy were employed by Mansuy et al. [18] in using fire-killed forest trees in two Canadian forest management units to develop and optimize supply scenarios to meet different pellet plant capacities under multiple operational, ecological, and economic constraints. The authors provided their findings using a deterministic mixed-integer linear programming (MILP) model. Shabani et al. [19] examined various optimization methods for reducing total wood pellet production system costs, as well as conducting a comprehensive analysis of various wood pellet SC-related decisions such as location-allocation and capacity of wood pellet processing facilities, transportation modes, and optimal biomass mix. Kanzian et al. [20] developed a deterministic MILP model for minimizing total wood biomass supply costs to heating plants by considering transportation, processing, and storage costs. The optimization model provided decisions for allocating wood chips to the selected terminals and plants. An et al. [21] devised a strategic and tactical decision-making mathematical model for the design of the lignocellulosic biofuel supply chain, taking into account different types of wood waste as biomass. This study highlights the most economically significant aspects at all levels of the circular bioeconomy. Vasković et al. [22] used the VIKOR multi-criteria decision technique to rank the energy chain of wooden biomass supply and select the best variant in a circular bioeconomy. Cambero and Sowlati [23] proposed a deterministic multi-objective MILP forest-based biomass SC model that takes into account all three dimensions of sustainability to maximize net present value, CO_2 emissions savings, and societal welfare. Trochu et al. [24] address the circular bioeconomy under environmental policies by targeting recycled wood materials from the construction and demolition of buildings. The proposed MILP model minimizes the cost of the wood recycling SC by deciding the optimal locations and capacities of wood processing facilities. All aforementioned research addressing the circular bioeconomy by considering different types of wood waste-to-energy generation settings has presented solutions in a deterministic environment while neglecting the related uncertainties.

A few researchers have integrated uncertainty in the planning phase of designing a wood pellet supply chain. In this domain, Mobini et al. [25] developed a simulation model that takes into account the stochastic uncertainty of the environment to assist SC managers in planning a wood pellet SC by encompassing the entire echelon from biomass collection to wood pellet delivery to clients. Akhtari and Sowlati [26] also considered stochastic uncertainties in the wood pellet SC by proposing a hybrid simulation–optimization technique named recursive optimization-simulation. Using this solution approach, the authors integrated strategic, tactical, and operational plans for the wood pellet SC. Boukherroub et al. [13] adopted a generic approach using LogiLab simulation software to choose the best raw material, optimal quantity allocations, and most optimal locations of wood pellet production facilities in order to design a profitable wood pellet SC taking into account economies of scale. Yılmaz Balaman et al. [27] proposed a fuzzy approach-based framework for strategic and tactical level planning in waste biomass-based energy production investments that optimizes several forms of waste, including numerous types of production technologies, in consideration of circular economy principles. A summary of research related to WPSC network design is provided in Table 1.

Investigating wood pellet production-related studies demonstrates that these studies offer comprehensive systems for the wood pellet supply chain but that only a few of them have taken into account the uncertainties associated with biomass availability, transportation, production, and market demand. Because of these uncertainties, some of the supply chain configurations may be impractical or less than optimal. According to Pishvaee et al. [28], there are two types of uncertainties: stochastic and epistemic. Stochastic uncertainty is appropriate for instances when historical data on an uncertain parameter are available for accurately estimating probability distribution, which is not the case in the majority of cases involving wood waste management. As a result, the stochastic method is inappropriate for the considered problem. According to Torabi et al. [29], fuzzy programming is the most effective technique for dealing with imprecise parameters for which stochastic approaches are inapplicable. Keeping this in view, in this study, fuzzy possibilistic programming (FPP) is employed to manage the uncertain parameters of the WPP-SCND model. The FPP approach does not need historic information on ambiguous parameters; rather, a probability distribution for the uncertain parameter is built based on the experience of experts. Moreover, the concept of flexible programming is incorporated into FPP to relax the WPP-SCND model's uncertain constraints, such as biomass-to-pellet conversion, biomass availability, and wood pellet demand. Since the robustness of the strategic and tactical decisions of the WPP-SCND model is essential, fuzzy flexible robust possibilistic programming (fuzzy-FRPP) is proposed by combining the robust programming (RP) technique with flexible FPP.

To the best of the author's knowledge, Yılmaz Balaman et al. [27] are the only researchers to use a fuzzy solution approach to design a wood pellet SC network considering circular bioeconomy principles. Although epistemic uncertainty is adequately addressed in that research using a fuzzy technique, it does not claim to offer robust solutions in an uncertain environment, which is essential for the sustainability of the wood pellet SC. To bridge this research gap, this study presents a decision support system for a wood pellet production SC in an unpredictable environment and adds to the existing literature on the design of WPSC networks in the following ways:

- Proposing a multi-period WPP-SCND optimization model that takes into account epistemic uncertainty in input parameters to obtain reliable integrated strategic and tactical decisions that take into account the effects of WPSC activities on the environment and the economy.
- Proposing a fuzzy-FRPP solution to tackle the uncertain environment and obtain robust WPSC decisions by taking advantage of both flexible and robust programming techniques under a highly uncertain environment.

Providing a solution that allows for wood pellet SC management to quantify the economic impacts of carbon emissions associated with wood pellet SC activities in order to design policies accordingly.

Table 1. Summary of the research related to WPSC network design.

Author	Source	Type of Feedstock	Decision Levels	Method/Analysis	Uncertainty Handling Approach		Environmental Aspect	Economic Aspect	Supply Chain Decisions Considered			
					Stochastic	Fuzzy			LA	CP	FM	UN
Boukherroub et al. [13]	Forest and agriculture biomass	Wood chips	Strategic, tactical, operational	LogiLab simulation package				✓	✓	✓	✓	
Méndez-Vázquez et al. [16]	Residual biomass	Agriculture waste	Strategic, tactical, operational	Deterministic mixed-integer non-linear programming			✓	✓	✓	✓	✓	
Mansuy et al. [18]	Forest biomass	Fire killed trees	Strategic	Deterministic linear mathematical modeling			✓	✓	✓			
Shabani et al. [19]	Forest and agriculture biomass	Wood chips	Strategic, tactical	Comparative analysis of techniques			✓	✓	✓	✓	✓	
Kanzian et al. [20]	Forest biomass	Wood chips	Strategic, operational	Deterministic linear mathematical modeling				✓	✓			
Vasković et al. [22]	Agricultural biomass	Wood chips	Prioritization	VIKOR multi-criteria decision-making technique				✓				
Cambero and Sowlati [23]	Forest biomass	Wood chips	Strategic, tactical, operational	Multi-objective deterministic linear mathematical modeling			✓	✓	✓	✓	✓	
Trochu et al. [24]	Household wood waste	Construction and demolition of wood waste	Strategic, tactical, operational	Linear mathematical modeling				✓	✓	✓	✓	✓
Mobini et al. [25]	Agricultural biomass	Sawmill wood waste	Strategic	Discrete event simulation for modeling of SC for planning and analysis of SC model	✓		✓	✓	✓			✓
Akhtari and Sowlati [26]	Forest biomass	Forest waste and sawmills dust	Strategic, tactical operational	Recursive optimization-simulation approach	✓		✓	✓	✓	✓		✓
Yılmaz Balaman et al. [27]	Forest and agriculture	Mix wastes	Strategic, tactical,	Fuzzy multi-objective		✓	✓	✓	✓	✓	✓	✓
Van Dyken et al. [30]	Forest biomass	Wood chips	Strategic, operational	Deterministic linear mathematical modeling			✓	✓	✓	✓	✓	

Table 1. *Cont.*

Author	Source	Type of Feedstock	Decision Levels	Method/Analysis	Uncertainty Handling Approach		Environmental Aspect	Economic Aspect	Supply Chain Decisions Considered			
					Stochastic	Fuzzy			LA	CP	FM	UN
Vitale et al. [31]	Forest biomass	Sawdust, shaving, wood chip	Operational	Column generation method				✓	✓		✓	
De Laporte et al. [32]	Agriculture biomass	Switchgrass and miscanthus	Strategic	GIS-based empirical study				✓				
This study	Agricultural biomass	Sawdust, wheat straw, bagasse, Rice husk	Operational, strategic, tactical	Fuzzy flexible robust possibilistic programming approach		✓	✓	✓	✓	✓	✓	✓

LA—location allocation, CP—capacity planning, FM—flow of materials, UN—uncertainty.

3. Research Methodology

As discussed in the above section, this study aims to provide a decision support system for wood pellet production managers by integrating economic and environmental aspects in the background of a circular bioeconomy. That implies that the study should provide a comprehensive overview of SC performance in an uncertain environment for the optimization model objectives. The research methodology used in this study is provided in Figure 1.

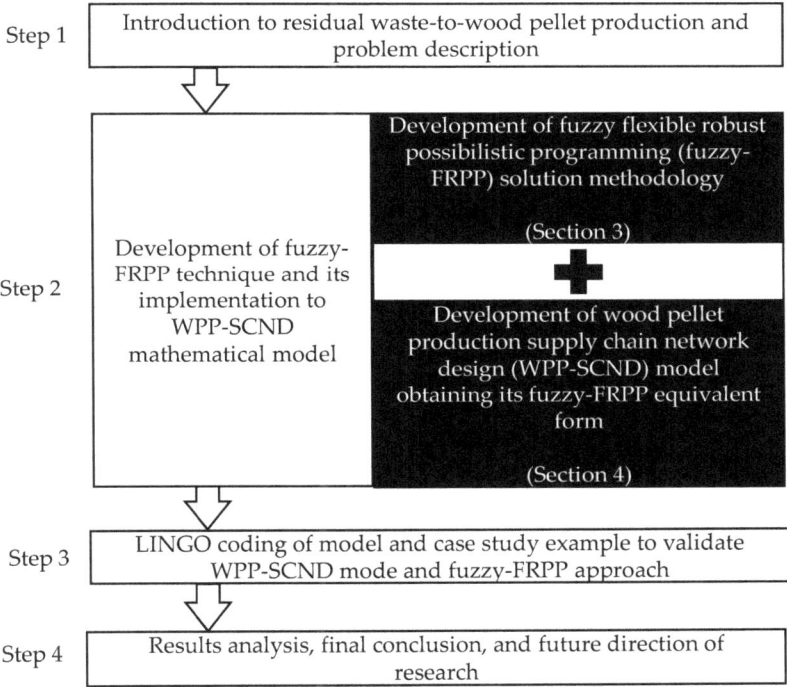

Figure 1. Research methodology employed for the study.

In the first step, the theoretical foundation for the investigation is established. This section provides a comprehensive explanation of essential principles and issues in a wood pellet manufacturing and distribution system, as well as determines the study's goals, which are described explicitly and simply in a problem statement. In light of the mentioned issues, the research questions are developed. The second step involves developing a mathematical model in line with the problem statement and research questions. The WPP-SCND model is designed in this stage to reduce the cost of wood pellet manufacturing as well as the environmental impact of the related operations. To handle the uncertainty in the WPP-SCND model, a fuzzy-FRPP solution combining FPP, flexible programming, and robust programming is proposed. After that, the fuzzy-FRPP equivalent form of the WPP-SCND model is coded in LINGO optimization software. In the third stage, to answer the research questions and validate the proposed mathematical model and solution approach, a comprehensive quantitative analysis is undertaken using a case study. Finally, at the last stage, the conclusion and limitations of the study, as well as future research directions, are provided.

3.1. Why Are Linear Programming and Fuzzy-FRPP the Most Appropriate Solution Strategies for the Proposed WPP-SCND Model?

In the first part of this study, a linear programming approach is used to achieve the aims of cost and carbon emissions reduction in a wood pellet SC in a circular bioeconomy scenario. The benefit of the linear programming approach is that it is based on simple algebraic formulations and provides better insights into complex systems by always guaranteeing global optimal solutions.

In the second part, to address the problem of an uncertain environment associated with the WPP-SCND model parameters, this study integrates FPP, RP, and flexible programming to develop fuzzy-FRPP. Each technique offers the following distinct advantages to deal with uncertainty:

- FPP is the best choice when there is epistemic uncertainty in the collected data and stochastic methodologies cannot be used because there are no previous data [33]. Epistemic uncertainty affects WPP-SCND model elements such as biomass-to-wood-pellet conversion, production costs, wood pellet demand, and biomass availability. To nullify the effect of uncertainty, FPP is best suited. However, FPP simply gives the average value of the unknown parameter and cannot account for fluctuations [28]. This drawback can be overcome by merging RP with FPP to form fuzzy robust possibilistic programming (fuzzy-RPP).
- Robust programming makes the WPP-SCND model objective independent of average value and also integrates feasibility and optimality robustness. Hence, the incorporation of FP within robust programming will form fuzzy-FRPP.
- Flexible programming enables managers to integrate flexibility into uncertain constraint goals. The level of flexibility in these soft constraints can be decided by the manager.

Hence, the fuzzy-FRPP approach can efficiently minimize the risk due to operational uncertainty/epistemic uncertainty.

3.2. Generic Formulation of Fuzzy-FRPP Solution Approach

To address the challenge of uncertainty linked with WPP-SCND model parameters, a solution called fuzzy-FRPP is proposed here. Generic form of fuzzy-FRPP approach is provided below:

3.2.1. Fuzzy Possibilistic Programming

A generalized version of an optimization model containing imprecise parameters is presented in Equation (1) to understand the composition of possibilistic programming:

$$\begin{aligned} \text{Min} \quad T = & \ \widetilde{F} \times g + \widetilde{H} \times o \\ \text{Subject to} \quad & D \times g \leq \widetilde{V}, \\ & E \times g = 0, \\ & S \times o \leq \widetilde{T} \times g, \\ & U \times o \geq 1, \\ & o \geq 0, \qquad g \in \{0,1\}, \end{aligned} \quad (1)$$

In Equation (1), F, H, V, and T are the parameters tainted with epistemic uncertainty and follow the trapezoidal fuzzy number (TFN). The membership function of $\widetilde{F}$ can be developed as follows:

$$\mu_{\widetilde{F}}(n) = \begin{cases} \frac{n-F_1}{F_2-F_1} & F_1 \leq n < F_2 \\ \frac{F_4-n}{F_4-F_3} & F_3 < n \leq F_4 \end{cases} \quad (2)$$

$$\mu_{\widetilde{F}}(n) = \begin{cases} 1 & \text{if } F_2 \leq n \leq F_3 \\ 0 & \text{otherwise,} \end{cases} \quad (3)$$

where $n \in \mathbb{R}$.

(a) Expected value (*ExV*)

Under the FPP technique, uncertain parameters of the objective are transformed into the crisp form using the *ExV* operator [34] as follows:

$$d(\tilde{F}, \tilde{0}_1) = \frac{1}{4}(F_1, F_2, F_3, F_4) \quad (4)$$

(b) *Me-measure*

Me-measure, proposed by Xu and Zhou [35], was applied to translate uncertain constraints into crisp form. Using *Me*, SC managers can interactively incorporate their preferences in the range of pessimistic and optimistic approaches as below:

$$Me\{\tilde{F} \geq n\} = Nec\{\tilde{F} \geq n\} + \Im \times \left[Pos\{\tilde{F} \geq n\} - Nec\{\tilde{F} \geq n\}\right] \quad (5)$$

In Equation (5), $\Im$ represents the preference of SC managers on the spectrum of pessimistic-optimistic. The *Me* for $\tilde{F} \leq n$ and $\tilde{F} \geq n$ is obtained as follows:

$$Me\{\tilde{F} \leq n\} = \begin{cases} \Im \times \frac{n - F_1}{n_2 - F_1}, & F_1 \leq n \leq F_2 \\ \Im + (1 - \Im) \times \frac{n - F_3}{n_4 - F_3}, & F_3 \leq n \leq F_4 \end{cases} \quad (6)$$

$$Me\{\tilde{F} \leq n\} = \begin{cases} 0, & n \leq F_1 \\ \Im, & \text{if } F_2 \leq n \leq F_3 \\ 1, & n \geq F_4 \end{cases} \quad (7)$$

$$Me\{\tilde{F} \geq n\} = \begin{cases} \Im + (1 - \Im) \times \frac{F_2 - n}{F_2 - h_1}, & F_1 \leq n \leq F_2 \\ \Im \times \frac{F_4 - n}{F_4 - h_3}, & F_3 \leq n \leq F_4 \end{cases} \quad (8)$$

$$Me\{\tilde{F} \geq n\} = \begin{cases} 1, & n \leq F_1 \\ \Im, & \text{if } F_2 \leq n \leq F_3 \\ 0, & n \geq F_4 \end{cases} \quad (9)$$

Using *Me*, the *ExV* of $\tilde{F}$ is obtained as:

$$EV^{Me}[F] = \int_0^{+\infty} Me\{F \geq n\} \times dn - \int_{-\infty}^{0} Me\{F \leq N\} \times dn \quad (10)$$

$$EV^{Me}[F] = \frac{1 - \Im}{2} \times (F_1 + F_2) + \frac{\Im}{2} \times (F_3 + F_4) \quad (11)$$

Using Equations (6)–(9), *Me* for $\tilde{F} \leq n$ and $\tilde{F} \geq n$ is obtained as:

$$Me\{\tilde{F} \leq n\} \geq J \Leftrightarrow \Im + (1 - \Im) \times \frac{n - F_3}{F_4 - F_3} \geq J \Leftrightarrow n \geq \frac{(J - \Im) \times F_4 + (1 - J) \times F_3}{1 - \Im}, \quad (12)$$

$$Me\{\tilde{F} \geq n\} \geq J \Leftrightarrow \Im + (1 - \Im) \times \frac{F_2 - n}{F_2 - F_1} \geq J \Leftrightarrow n \leq \frac{(J - \Im) \times F_1 + (1 - J) \times F_2}{1 - \Im}, \quad (13)$$

Using the *ExV* and *Me* provided in Equations (4), (12) and (13), the uncertain parameters of Equation (1) are transformed into a certain form as below:

$$\begin{aligned}
\text{Min} \quad & ExV[T] = \left[\frac{1-\Im}{2} \times (F_1 + F_2) + \frac{\Im}{2} \times (F_3 + F_4)\right] \times g + \left[\frac{1-\Im}{2} \times (H_1 + H_2) + \frac{\Im}{2} \times (H_3 + H_4)\right] \times o \\
\text{Subject to} \quad & D \times g \leq \left[\frac{(J_1 - \Im) \times V_1 + (1 - J_1) \times V_2}{1 - \Im}\right], \\
& E \times g = 0, \\
& S \times o \leq \left[\frac{(J_2 - \Im) \times T_1 + (1 - J_2) \times T_2}{1 - \Im}\right] \times g, \\
& U \times o \geq 1, \\
& o \geq 0,\ g \in \{0,1\},\ 0.5 \leq J_1, J_2 \leq 1,\ 0 \leq \Im \leq 1
\end{aligned} \quad (14)$$

3.2.2. Fuzzy Flexible Possibilistic Programming

In the next stage, the FPP equivalent form presented in Equation (14) is modified by integrating flexibility in its constraint. The modified FPP form is as below:

$$\begin{aligned}
\text{Min} \quad & ExV[T] = \left[\frac{1-\Im}{2} \times (F_1 + F_2) + \frac{\Im}{2} \times (F_3 + F_4)\right] \times g + \left[\frac{1-\Im}{2} \times (H_1 + H_2) + \frac{\Im}{2} \times (H_3 + H_4)\right] \times o \\
\text{Subject to} \quad & D \times g \mathrel{\widetilde{\leq}} \left[\frac{(J_1 - \Im) \times V_1 + (1 - J_1) \times V_2}{1 - \Im}\right], \\
& E \times g = 0, \\
& S \times o \mathrel{\widetilde{\leq}} \left[\frac{(J_2 - \Im) \times T_1 + (1 - J_2) \times T_2}{1 - \Im}\right] \times g, \\
& U \times o \geq 1, \\
& o \geq 0,\ g \in \{0,1\},\ 0.5 \leq J_1, J_2 \leq 1,\ 0 \leq \Im \leq 1
\end{aligned} \quad (15)$$

where $\Im$ is the pessimistic–optimistic parameter, J_1 and J_2 depict SC manager level of confidence, and $\widetilde{\leq}$ integrates flexibility in the uncertain constraints target.

$$\begin{aligned}
\text{Min} \quad & ExV[T] = \left[\frac{1-\Im}{2} \times (F_1 + F_2) + \frac{\Im}{2} \times (F_3 + F_4)\right] \times g + \left[\frac{1-\Im}{2} \times (H_1 + H_2) + \frac{\Im}{2} \times (H_3 + H_4)\right] \times o \\
\text{Subject} \quad & D \times g \leq \left[\frac{(J_1 - \Im) \times V_1 + (1 - J_1) \times V_2}{1 - \Im}\right] + \left[\frac{u_1 + u_2 + u_3 + u_4}{4}\right](1 - \lambda_1) \\
& E \times g = 0, \\
& S \times o \leq \left[\frac{(J_2 - \Im) \times T_1 + (1 - J_2) \times T_2}{1 - \Im}\right] \times g + \left[\left\{\frac{i_1 + i_2 + i_3 + i_4}{4}\right\}(1 - \lambda_2)\right] \times g \\
& U \times o \geq 1, \\
& o \geq 0,\ g \in \{0,1\},\ 0.5 \leq J_1, J_2 \leq 1,\ 0 \leq \Im \leq 1,\ 0 \leq \lambda_1, \lambda_2 \leq 1
\end{aligned} \quad (16)$$

Equation (16) is the equivalent form of the FPP approach for the uncertain model provided in Equation (1). The constraint target uncertainty sign $\widetilde{\leq}$ is substituted with $\left[\frac{u_1+u_2+u_3+u_4}{4}\right](1-\lambda_1)$ and $\left[\left\{\frac{i_1+i_2+i_3+i_4}{4}\right\}(1-\lambda_2)\right] \times g$ terms. In these terms, u_1, u_2, u_3, u_4 and i_1, i_2, i_3, i_4 are TFN for $\widetilde{u}$ and $\widetilde{i}$, respectively, and represent constraint flexibility margins. Further, λ_1 and λ_2 represent the level of confidence of the SC manager specifically for uncertain constraint flexibility margin parameters $\widetilde{u}$ and $\widetilde{i}$. The FPP formulation provided in Equation (16) perfectly tackles the operational uncertainty. Nevertheless, there are two drawbacks of the FPP method. First, the deviation of the objective from ExV of uncertain parameters cannot be controlled. Second, it will take longer to achieve global optimal as the number of flexible equations in the optimization model increases. A modified method called fuzzy RPP is suggested to address these problems.

3.2.3. Flexible Robust Possibilistic Programming (FRPP)

To address the shortcomings of flexible FPP, the RPP-II formulation developed by Pishvaee et al. [28] is further integrated into the flexible FPP formulation provided in Equation (16) as follows:

$$\begin{aligned}
\text{Min} \quad & ExV[T] + \Re(T_{\max} - ExV[T]) + \Phi_1\left[\left[\frac{(J_1-\Im)\times V_1+(1-J_1)\times V_2}{1-\Im}\right] - J_1\right] + \\
& \Phi_2\left[\left[\frac{(J_2-\Im)\times T_1+(1-J_2)\times T_2}{1-\Im}\right] - J_2\right] \times g + \pi_1\left[\left[\frac{u_1+u_2+u_3+u_4}{4}\right](1-\lambda_1)\right] + \pi_2\left[\left\{\frac{i_1+i_2+i_3+i_4}{4}\right\}(1-\lambda_2)\right] \times g \\
\text{Subject to} \quad & ExV[T] = \left[\frac{1-\Im}{2} \times (F_1 + F_2) + \frac{\Im}{2} \times (F_3 + F_4)\right] \times g + \left[\frac{1-\Im}{2} \times (H_1 + H_2) + \frac{\Im}{2} \times (H_3 + H_4)\right] \times o \\
& T_{\max} = F_4 \times g + H_4 \times o \\
& D \times g \leq \left[\frac{(J_1-\Im)\times V_1+(1-J_1)\times V_2}{1-\Im}\right] + \left[\frac{u_1+u_2+u_3+u_4}{4}\right](1-\lambda_1)
\end{aligned} \quad (17)$$

$$\begin{aligned}
& E \times g = 0, \\
& S \times o \leq \left[\frac{(J_2-\Im)\times T_1+(1-J_2)\times T_2}{1-\Im}\right] \times g + \left[\left\{\frac{i_1+i_2+i_3+i_4}{4}\right\}(1-\lambda_2)\right] \times g \\
& U \times o \geq 1, \\
& o \geq 0, \ g \in \{0,1\}, \ 0.5 \leq J_1, J_2 \leq 1, \ 0 \leq \Im \leq 1, \ 0 \leq \lambda_1, \lambda_2 \leq 1
\end{aligned}$$

In Equation (17), $T_{\max}$ represents the worst-case value of the objective, while the second term of the objective minimizes deviation for the worst case scenario, thus providing optimality robustness; $\Re$ is the scaling factor of optimality robustness, which can range between 0 and 1. The disparity between the worst possible value and the value utilized within uncertain constraints is minimized by the third and fourth terms, which incorporate feasibility robustness into the results. Finally, the fifth and sixth terms are the penalties for deviating from the soft constraint's target value.

4. Mathematical Model and Case Results

4.1. Working Framework of the WPP-SCND Model

The mathematical model of the wood pellet supply chain is described in this section. The WPP-SCND model reduces the overall system cost by first choosing the best locations for biomass processing facilities and then allocating the optimal amounts to facilities during each planning period. Biomass in the form of sawdust and agricultural waste is delivered from supply terminal a to pelletization plant b, where it is converted into wood pellets. Following that, wood pellets are provided from pelletization facility b to distribution center c, whence they are transferred to market m to meet energy demands. This model not only reduces the system cost but also accounts for the carbon emissions related to raw material collection, transportation to pelletization facilities, and transportation of wood pellets from pelletization plants to market centers in terms of carbon penalty.

Figure 2 illustrates the structure of the WPP-SCND model.

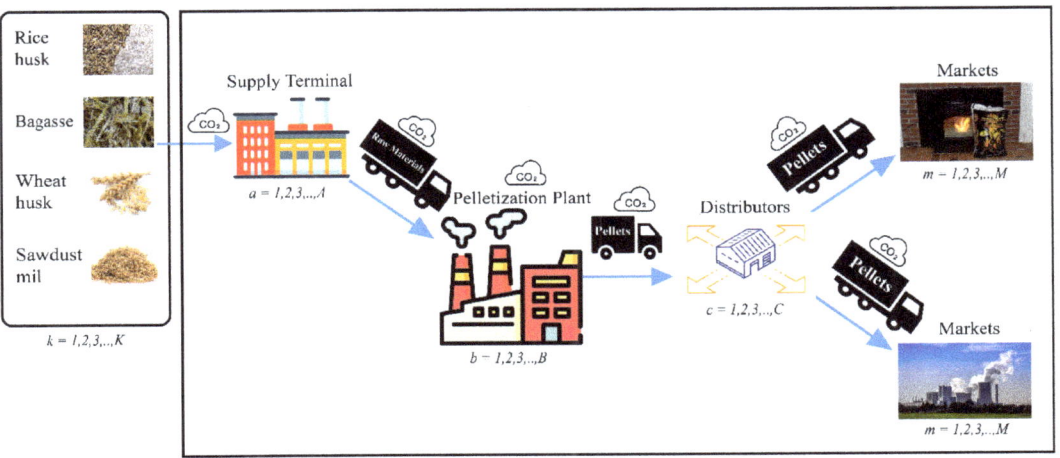

Figure 2. Working framework of WPP-SCND optimization model.

4.1.1. Notations

In this section, the notations used in the WPP-SCND model are presented.

Indices

k	Index for raw material types
a	Index for raw material collection points
b	Index for pelletization plant
c	Index for distribution center
m	Index for marketplace
q	Index for the capacity level of pelletization plant
r	Index for the capacity level of the distribution center
t	Index for the period

Decision Variables

Q_{abkt}	Amount of raw material type (k) transported from collection point (a) to pelletization plant (b) in time (t)
Q_{bct}	Amount of pellets transported from pelletization plant (b) to distributor (c) in the time period (t)
Q_{cmt}	Quantity of pellet supplied from the distributor (c) to marketplace (m) during the time (t)
X_a	0 if supply terminal (a) is not selected, 1 if supply terminal (a) is selected
Y_{bq}	0 if the plant (b) with capacity (q) is not selected, 1 if the plant (b) with capacity (q) is selected
Z_{cr}	0 if distribution center (c) with capacity (r) is not selected, 1 if distribution center (c) with capacity (r) is selected

Parameters

$\tilde{\partial}_a^{ins}$	Cost of constructing (a) biomass supply terminal (a)
$\tilde{\partial}_{bq}^{ins}$	Cost of constructing pelletizing facility (b) with capacity (q)
$\tilde{\partial}_{cr}^{ins}$	Cost of constructing distribution center (c) with capacity (r)
$\tilde{p}c_{akt}$	The purchasing cost of biomass (k) at supply terminal (a) in time (t)
$\tilde{\varepsilon}_a^{hnd}$	Quantity of CO_2 emissions during raw material handling at biomass supply terminal (a)
$\tilde{H}_a^{hnd}$	Cost of biomass handling at biomass supply terminal (a)
$\tilde{\varepsilon}_b$	Quantity of CO_2 emissions during raw pellet production at location (b)
e^{tax}	Carbon emission tax
$\tilde{sup}_{akt}$	The available quantity of raw material type (k) at the collection point (a) in time (t)
$\tilde{dem}_{mt}$	Pellets demand in market m during the period (t)
cap_{bq}	Production capacity of the pellets plant with level (q)
cap_{cr}	Storage capacity of the distribution center c with level (r)
$\tilde{\delta}$	The conversion factor for biomass to pellets
$\tilde{p}d_b$	Wood pellets production cost at pelletization plant (b)
$\tilde{\tau}_{ab}$	The shipping cost of supplying raw material from the supply terminal (a) to the pelletization plant (b)
$\tilde{\tau}_{bc}$	Transportation cost of moving pellets from pelletization plant (b) to distribution center (c)
$\tilde{\tau}_{cm}$	Transportation cost of moving pellets from the distribution center (c) to market (m)
$\tilde{\varepsilon}_{ab}$	Quantity of carbon emissions during raw material transportation from supply terminal (a) to pelletization plant (b)
$\tilde{\varepsilon}_{bc}$	Quantity of carbon emissions during transportation of pellets from pelletization plant (b) to distribution center (c)
$\tilde{\varepsilon}_{cm}$	Quantity of carbon emissions during transportation of pellets from the distribution center (c) to market (m)

4.1.2. Assumptions

- The homogenous fleet of vehicles is assumed to be available at all echelons of the supply chain.
- Allowable cargo is less than one truckload.
- The regional collection of biomass is assumed to be available at potential locations of supply terminals.
- The distances between the collecting points and the pelletization plants, as well as between the pelletization plants and the demand zones, are known.
- A CO_2 emission tax is imposed under local government policy for all stakeholders.

I. Objectives functions of the WPP-SCND model:

(a) Total supply chain cost objective

The first, second, and third terms of the objective function represent the costs of establishing a supply terminal, pelletization plant, and distribution center:

$$\sum_{a}^{A}(\widetilde{\partial}_{a}^{ins} \times X_a) + \sum_{b}^{B}\sum_{q}^{Q}(\widetilde{\partial}_{bq}^{ins} \times Y_{bq}) + \sum_{c}^{C}\sum_{r}^{R}(\widetilde{\partial}_{cr}^{ins} \times Z_{cr}) \qquad (18)$$

The fourth term of the objective function illustrates the cost of purchasing biomass, handling costs, and handling-related emissions penalties:

$$\sum_{a}^{A}\sum_{b}^{B}\sum_{k}^{K}\sum_{t}^{T}\left[(\widetilde{p}c_{akt}) + (\widetilde{\varepsilon}_{a}^{hnd} \times e^{tax}) + \widetilde{H}_{a}^{hnd}\right] \times Q_{abkt} \qquad (19)$$

The fifth term shows the total wood pellet production cost and the CO_2 emissions tax imposed during pellet production:

$$\sum_{a}^{A}\sum_{b}^{B}\sum_{k}^{K}\sum_{t}^{T}[\{(\widetilde{p}d_b) + (\widetilde{\varepsilon}_b \times e^{tax})\} \times Q_{abkt}] \qquad (20)$$

The sixth, seventh, and eighth terms illustrate the total SC transportation cost in the WPP-SCND model:

$$\sum_{a}^{A}\sum_{b}^{B}\sum_{k}^{K}\sum_{t}^{T}[\widetilde{\tau}_{ab} \times Q_{abkt}] + \sum_{b}^{B}\sum_{c}^{C}\sum_{t}^{T}[\widetilde{\tau}_{bc} \times Q_{bct}] + \sum_{c}^{C}\sum_{m}^{M}\sum_{t}^{T}[\widetilde{\tau}_{cm} \times Q_{cmt}] \qquad (21)$$

The total carbon emissions tax that is incurred during the transportation of raw material and wood pellets among processing facilities of the WPP-SCND model is provided in the ninth, tenth, and eleventh terms of the objective function:

$$\sum_{a}^{A}\sum_{b}^{B}\sum_{k}^{K}\sum_{t}^{T}[(\widetilde{\varepsilon}_{ab} \times e^{tax})] \times Q_{abkt} + \sum_{b}^{B}\sum_{c}^{C}\sum_{t}^{T}[(\widetilde{\varepsilon}_{bc} \times e^{tax})] \times Q_{bct} + \sum_{c}^{C}\sum_{m}^{M}\sum_{t}^{T}[(\widetilde{\varepsilon}_{cm} \times e^{tax}) \times Q_{cmt}] \qquad (22)$$

II. Constraints of the WPP-SCND model

The biomass supply constraint is provided by Equation (23). It represents that the amount of biomass type 'b' at a supply terminal should be greater than the amount of biomass carried from the supply terminal to pelletization facilities:

$$\sum_{b}^{B} Q_{abkt} \leq \widetilde{sup}_{akt} \times X_a \quad \forall a, k, t \qquad (23)$$

Equation (24) represents the biomass-to-wood pellet conversion constraints, which also limit the system in that the amount of wood pellets delivered to distributors should not exceed the total amount manufactured at a pelletization facility:

$$\sum_{a}^{A}\sum_{k}^{K} Q_{abkt} \times \widetilde{\delta} \geq \sum_{c}^{C} Q_{bct} \quad \forall b, t \qquad (24)$$

Equation (25) depicts demand constraints, which bound the system to fulfill the demand of all markets:

$$\sum_{c}^{C} Q_{cmt} \geq \widetilde{dem}_{mt} \quad \forall m, t \qquad (25)$$

Equation (26) requires that the total amount of wood pellets provided to market from a distribution center not exceed the entire amount of wood pellets supplied from a palletization factory to that distribution center:

$$\sum_{b}^{B} Q_{bct} \geq \sum_{m}^{M} Q_{cmt} \qquad \forall c, t \qquad (26)$$

Equations (27) and (28) represent the processing capacity and storage capacity restrictions of pelletization plants and distribution centers, respectively:

$$\sum_{a}^{A}\sum_{k}^{K} Q_{abkt} \leq \sum_{q}^{Q} cap_{bq} \times Y_{bq} \qquad \forall b, t \qquad (27)$$

$$\sum_{b}^{B} Q_{bct} \leq \sum_{r}^{R} cap_{cr} \times Z_{cr} \qquad \forall c, t \qquad (28)$$

Equations (29) and (30), respectively, limit the system to a single capacity level for all operational pelletization plants and distribution centers:

$$\sum_{q}^{Q} Y_{bq} \leq 1 \qquad \forall b \qquad (29)$$

$$\sum_{r}^{R} Z_{cr} \leq 1 \qquad \forall c \qquad (30)$$

Equations (31) and (32) are the non-negativity and binary constraints, respectively:

$$Q_{abkt}, Q_{bct}, Q_{cmt} \geq 0 \qquad \forall a, b, c, m, k, t \qquad (31)$$

$$X_a, Y_{bq}, Z_{cr} \in \{0,1\} \qquad \forall a, b, q, c, r \qquad (32)$$

4.1.3. Equivalent Fuzzy-FRPP Form of WPP-SCND Model

Using the systematic conversions of the uncertain model provided in Sections 3.2.1, 3.2.2, and 3.2.3, the equivalent fuzzy-FRPP form of the WPP-SCND model is provided below:

$$\begin{aligned}
\text{Minimize} \quad & Exp[f^{cost}] + \chi[f^{cost,MAX} - Exp[f^{cost}]] + \\
& p^{sup} \times \sum_{a}^{A}\sum_{k}^{K}\sum_{t}^{T} \left[\left\{ \frac{(\psi^{sup}-\lambda)sup_{akt(1)} + (1-\psi^{sup})sup_{akt(2)}}{1-\lambda} \right\} - sup_{akt(1)} \right] X_a + \\
& p^{dem} \times \sum_{m}^{M}\sum_{t}^{T} \left[dem_{mt(4)} - \left\{ \frac{(\psi^{dem}-\lambda)dem_{mt(4)} + (1-\psi^{dem})dem_{mt(3)}}{1-\lambda} \right\} \right] + \\
& \left[p^{conv} \times \left\{ \sum_{a}^{A}\sum_{k}^{K} Q_{abkt} \times \left(\frac{(\psi^{conv}-\lambda)\delta_{(1)} + (1-\psi^{conv})\delta_{(2)}}{1-\lambda} \right) - \delta_{(1)} \right\} \right]
\end{aligned} \qquad (33)$$

$$\begin{aligned}
Exp[f^{cost}] = & \sum_{a}^{A} \left[\left\{ \frac{1-\xi}{2}\left(\partial_{a(1)}^{ims} + \partial_{a(2)}^{ins}\right) + \frac{\xi}{2}\left(\partial_{a(3)}^{ims} + \partial_{a(4)}^{ins}\right) \right\} \times X_a \right] + \sum_{b}^{B}\sum_{q}^{Q} \left[\left\{ \frac{1-\xi}{2}\left(\partial_{bq(1)}^{ins} + \partial_{bq(2)}^{ims}\right) + \frac{\xi}{2}\left(\partial_{bq(3)}^{ims} + \partial_{bq(4)}^{ins}\right) \right\} \times Y_{bq} \right] + \\
& \sum_{c}^{C}\sum_{r}^{R} \left[\left\{ \frac{1-\xi}{2}\left(\partial_{cr(1)}^{inx} + \partial_{cr(2)}^{inx}\right) + \frac{\xi}{2}\left(\partial_{cr(3)}^{ins} + \partial_{cr(4)}^{ins}\right) \right\} \times Z_{cr} \right] + \\
& \sum_{a}^{A}\sum_{b}^{B}\sum_{k}^{K}\sum_{t}^{T} \left[\begin{array}{l} \left\{ \frac{1-\xi}{2}(pc_{akt(1)} + pc_{akt(2)}) + \frac{\xi}{2}(pc_{akt(3)} + pc_{akt(4)}) \right\} + \left\{ \left(\frac{1-\xi}{2}\left(\epsilon_{a(1)}^{hnd} + \epsilon_{a(2)}^{hnd}\right) + \frac{\xi}{2}\left(\epsilon_{a(3)}^{hnd} + \epsilon_{a(4)}^{hnd}\right) \right) \times e^{tax} \right\} + \\ \left(\frac{1-\xi}{2}\left(H_{a(1)}^{hnd} + H_{a(2)}^{hnd}\right) + \frac{\xi}{2}\left(H_{a(3)}^{hnd} + H_{a(4)}^{hnd}\right) \right) \end{array} \right] \times Q_{abkt} + \\
& \sum_{a}^{A}\sum_{b}^{B}\sum_{k}^{K}\sum_{t}^{T} \left[\left\{ \frac{1-\xi}{2}(pd_{b(1)} + pd_{b(2)}) + \frac{\xi}{2}(pd_{b(3)} + pd_{b(4)}) \right\} + \left\{ \left(\frac{1-\xi}{2}(\epsilon_{b(1)} + \epsilon_{b(2)}) + \frac{\xi}{2}(\epsilon_{b(3)} + \epsilon_{b(4)}) \right) \times e^{tax} \right\} \right] \times Q_{abkt} + \\
& \sum_{a}^{A}\sum_{b}^{B}\sum_{k}^{K}\sum_{t}^{T} \left[\left\{ \frac{1-\xi}{2}(\tau_{ab(1)} + \tau_{ab(2)}) + \frac{\xi}{2}(\tau_{ab(3)} + \tau_{ab(4)}) \right\} \times Q_{abkt} \right] + \sum_{b}^{B}\sum_{c}^{C}\sum_{t}^{T} \left[\left\{ \frac{1-\xi}{2}(\tau_{bc(1)} + \tau_{bc(2)}) + \frac{\xi}{2}(\tau_{bc(3)} + \tau_{bc(4)}) \right\} \times Q_{bct} \right] + \\
& \sum_{c}^{C}\sum_{m}^{M}\sum_{t}^{T} \left[\left\{ \frac{1-\xi}{2}(\tau_{cm(1)} + \tau_{cm(2)}) + \frac{\xi}{2}(\tau_{cm(3)} + \tau_{cm(4)}) \right\} \times Q_{cmt} \right] + \sum_{a}^{A}\sum_{b}^{B}\sum_{k}^{K}\sum_{t}^{T} \left[\left\{ \left(\frac{1-\xi}{2}(\epsilon_{ab(1)} + \epsilon_{ab(2)}) + \frac{\xi}{2}(\epsilon_{ab(3)} + \epsilon_{ab(4)}) \right) \times e^{tax} \right\} \times Q_{abkt} \right] + \\
& \sum_{b}^{B}\sum_{c}^{C}\sum_{t}^{T} \left[\left\{ \left(\frac{1-\xi}{2}(\epsilon_{bc(1)} + \epsilon_{bc(2)}) + \frac{\xi}{2}(\epsilon_{bc(3)} + \epsilon_{bc(4)}) \right) \times e^{tax} \right\} \times Q_{bct} \right] + \sum_{c}^{C}\sum_{m}^{M}\sum_{t}^{T} \left[\left\{ \left(\frac{1-\xi}{2}(\epsilon_{cm(1)} + \epsilon_{cm(2)}) + \frac{\xi}{2}(\epsilon_{cm(3)} + \epsilon_{cm(4)}) \right) \times e^{tax} \right\} \times Q_{cmt} \right]
\end{aligned} \qquad (34)$$

$$
\begin{aligned}
f^{cost,MAX} = & \sum_{a}^{A}\left[\left\{\partial_{a(4)}^{ins}\right\} \times X_a\right] + \sum_{b}^{B}\sum_{q}^{Q}\left[\partial_{bq(4)}^{ins} \times Y_{bq}\right] + \sum_{c}^{C}\sum_{r}^{R}\left[\partial_{cr(4)}^{ins} \times Z_{cr}\right] + \\
& \sum_{a}^{A}\sum_{b}^{B}\sum_{k}^{K}\sum_{t}^{T}\left[\{pc_{akt(4)}\} + \left\{e_{a(4)}^{hnd} \times e^{tax}\right\} + \left\{H_{a(4)}^{hnd}\right\}\right] \times Q_{abkt} + \sum_{a}^{A}\sum_{b}^{B}\sum_{k}^{K}\sum_{t}^{T}\left[pd_{b(4)} + \left\{\left(\varepsilon_{b(4)}\right) \times e^{tax}\right\}\right] \times Q_{abkt} + \\
& \sum_{a}^{A}\sum_{b}^{B}\sum_{k}^{K}\sum_{t}^{T}\left[\{\tau_{ab(4)}\} \times Q_{abkt}\right] + \sum_{b}^{B}\sum_{c}^{C}\sum_{t}^{T}\left[\{\tau_{bc(4)}\} \times Q_{bct}\right] + \sum_{c}^{C}\sum_{m}^{M}\sum_{t}^{T}\left[\{\tau_{cm(4)}\} \times Q_{cmt}\right] + \\
& \sum_{a}^{A}\sum_{b}^{B}\sum_{k}^{K}\sum_{t}^{T}\left[\left\{\left(\varepsilon_{ab(4)}\right) \times e^{tax}\right\} \times Q_{abkt}\right] + \sum_{b}^{B}\sum_{c}^{C}\sum_{t}^{T}\left[\left\{\left(\varepsilon_{bc(4)}\right) \times e^{tax}\right\} \times Q_{bct}\right] + \sum_{c}^{C}\sum_{m}^{M}\sum_{t}^{T}\left[\left\{\left(\varepsilon_{cm(4)}\right) \times e^{tax}\right\} \times Q_{cmt}\right]
\end{aligned}
\tag{35}
$$

$$
\sum_{b}^{B} Q_{abkt} \leq \left[\frac{(\psi^{sup} - \lambda)sup_{akt(1)} + (1 - \psi^{sup})sup_{akt(2)}}{1 - \lambda}\right] \times X_a + \left[\left(\frac{\vartheta_1 + \vartheta_2 + \vartheta_3 + \vartheta_4}{4}\right)(1 - \Omega^{sup})\right] \times X_a \quad \forall a,k,t \mid 0.5 \leq \psi^{sup} \leq 1 \tag{36}
$$

$$
\sum_{c}^{C} Q_{cmt} \geq \left[\frac{(\psi^{dem} - \lambda)dem_{mt(4)} + (1 - \psi^{dem})dem_{mt(3)}}{1 - \lambda}\right] - \left[\left(\frac{\mu_1 + \mu_2 + \mu_3 + \mu_4}{4}\right)(1 - \Omega^{dem})\right] \quad \forall m,t \mid 0.5 \leq \psi^{sup} \leq 1 \tag{37}
$$

$$
\sum_{c}^{C} Q_{bct} \leq \sum_{a}^{A}\sum_{k}^{K} Q_{abkt} \times \left[\frac{(\psi^{conv} - \lambda)\delta_{(1)} + (1 - \psi^{conv})\delta_{(2)}}{1 - \lambda}\right] + \left[\left(\frac{\Upsilon_1 + \Upsilon_2 + \Upsilon_3 + \Upsilon_4}{4}\right)(1 - \Omega^{conv})\right] \quad \forall b,t \mid 0.5 \leq \psi^{sup} \leq 1 \tag{38}
$$

and constraints (26)–(32).

4.2. Case Study to Validate Fuzzy-FRPP-Based WPP-SCND Model

To assess the efficacy of the WPP-SCND model and fuzzy-FRPP solution approach, a Pakistan-specific case study is presented in this section. Pakistan's economy is suffering as a result of a serious energy crisis. Utilities' electricity supply falls well short of demand. The current shortage surpasses 6000 megawatts. Natural gas, the country's second-largest fuel source after biofuels, is also becoming increasingly scarce. Generally, the shortage imposes substantial costs on the economy, estimated at around 2% of GDP each year, through reduced productivity, exports, and jobs. In this grim situation, using locally accessible second-generation biomass to generate energy can support the shrinking economy of the country. In this context, four types of locally available biomass are utilized to manufacture wood pellets that may be used to generate energy in a variety of ways. These biomasses include sawmill dust, rice husk, wheat straw, and bagasse. The Punjab province is chosen for this case because it is the most fertile region in Pakistan and meets the majority of the country's agricultural needs. For the given case, nine potential locations for biomass supply terminals, four possible sites for pelletization plants, and three potential sites for distribution hubs are considered to meet the energy demands of five major markets of the province. Furthermore, 2 capacity levels are considered for each pelletization plant, 35 and 50 thousand tons, while 2 capacity levels are evaluated for each distribution center, 40 and 60 thousand tons. The following are the key tactical and strategic decisions provided by the WPP-SCND model: minimum number of operational supply terminals, pelletization plants, and distribution hubs; capacity levels of operational pelletization plants and distribution hubs; and optimal quantities of allocated biomass from supply terminals to pelletization plants, wood pellets to be supplied from plants to distribution hubs, and pellets transported to demand zones from distribution hubs.

The WPP-SCND model efficiently provides answers to the following questions while designing the wood pellet supply chain:

- Which supply terminals should be selected to purchase biomass?
- What are the optimal quantities and mix of biomass (sawmill waste, wheat straw, rice husk, and bagasse) to supply to the production plant in each planning period?
- Where should wood production plants and distribution centers be located considering the economies of scale?
- What quantity is produced/processed at each operational facility in each planning period?

Figure 3 shows all potential wood pellet production SC sites for the given case study.

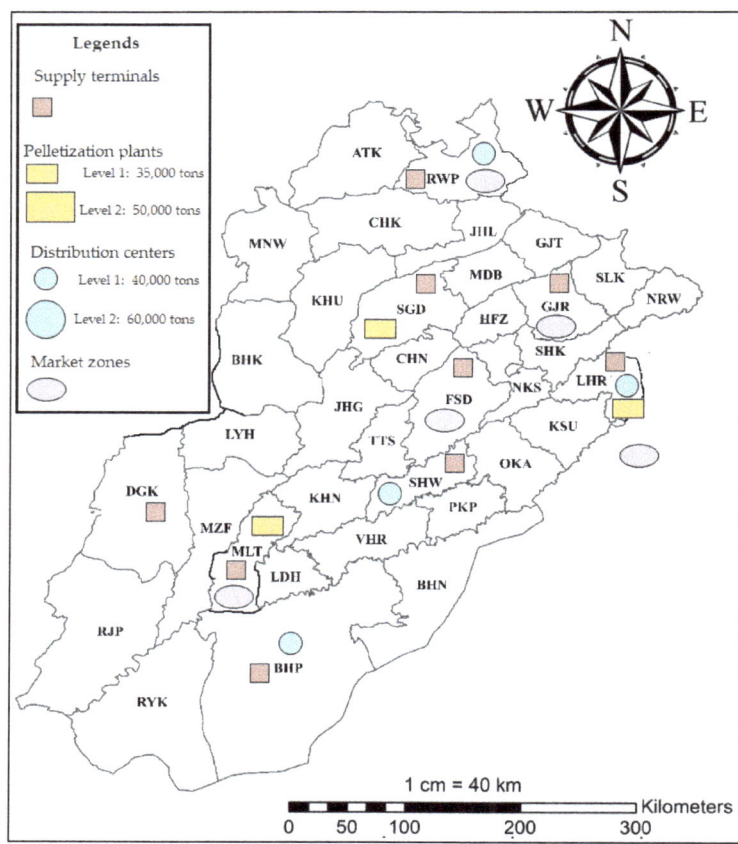

Figure 3. Potential wood pellet production SC sites for the given case.

4.2.1. Data Collection and Analysis for the WPP-SCND Model

For the proposed WPP-SCND model, datasets are mostly collected from regional government departments. The availability of rice husk, wheat straw, and bagasse biomass in each division of the province is acquired from the federal agriculture marketing department (http://www.amis.pk/, accessed on 10 May 2021) Pakistan. The potential of sawdust production is estimated after analyzing the reports provided by the provincial agriculture department (https://agripunjab.gov.pk/, accessed on 10 May 2021) and the forest, wildlife, and fisheries department (https://fwf.punjab.gov.pk/, accessed on 10 May 2021). The purchase cost of biomass and its handling costs are decided based on the locally collected information. Further, input parameters such as the construction cost of the pelletization plant and distribution hub were decided after analyzing published articles and regional industries [36,37]. Since railways infrastructure is not very reliable, only the roadway mode of transportation is assumed for the given case. The transportation matrix for each tier is obtained from Google Maps and is also considered an imprecise parameter in the computational analysis. Transportation costs among wood pellet processing facilities were decided in consultation with local logistics companies. The considered wood pellet SC comprises the shipping of biomass among supply terminals and pelletization plants and the handling of supplied biomass at each pelletization plant. It also entails the transportation of wood pellets from production plants to the distribution hub and then from the distribution hub to the wood pellet markets. Further, a homogenous fleet of vehicles with 45 tons of load-carrying capacity is considered. Emissions during transportation between wood pellet production sites are adapted from Gonela et al. [38]. A government tax of USD 10/ton is assumed following a report by the World Bank [39].

In this research, all objective parameters, including biomass availability at the supply terminals, market demand, and biomass production, are considered fuzzy to account for epistemic uncertainty. For each uncertain parameter, a TFN is developed. In order to obtain a TFN for each uncertain parameter, 4 random numbers (a_1, a_2, a_3, a_4) between 0.25 and 0.75 following uniform distribution are generated. Using these random numbers, the TFN of an uncertain parameter is obtained according to Equations (39)–(42). For instance, if $\widetilde{F}$ is a parameter having trapezoidal distribution, four points TFN of $\widetilde{F}$ are obtained using the following set of Equations (39)–(42) [40,41]:

$$F_1 = (1 - a_1) \times F^{most} \tag{39}$$

$$F_2 = \{1 - (a_1 \times a_2)\} \times F^{most} \tag{40}$$

$$F_3 = \{1 + (a_3 \times a_4)\} \times F^{most} \tag{41}$$

$$F_4 = (1 + a_4) \times F^{most} \tag{42}$$

Appendix A includes the most likely datasets utilized for the computational analysis of the WPP-SCND optimization model.

4.2.2. Results and Discussion on Research Questions

(a) Research question 1: How can an integrated decision support system that efficiently collects, transports, and converts massive quantities of various biomasses into wood pellets be developed in a sustainable manner to support the transition to a circular bioeconomy?

The first research question, which aims to provide a decision support system for the efficient design of WPSC, is discussed here. To answer this research question, first, a WPP-SCND optimization model is proposed, and then, a fuzzy-FRPP solution is suggested. After that, the collected datasets and corresponding fuzzy-FRPP form of the WPP-SCND model given in Equations (26)–(38) are solved using the LINGO optimization solver. As previously stated, the fuzzy-FRPP approach comprises several interactive parameters such as χ (scaling multiplier for optimality robustness), λ (constraints optimistic-pessimistic factor), ξ (objective optimistic-pessimistic factor), ψ^{sup}, ψ^{dem}, ψ^{conv} (confidence level for constraint parameters), Ω^{sup}, Ω^{dem}, Ω^{conv} (soft constrain margins), and p^{sup}, p^{dem}, p^{conv} (penalties for violating uncertain constraints). All of these parameters are defined following the real-time environment. The value of the scaling multiplier for optimality robustness (χ) controls the deviation over and above the ExV of the WPP-SCND model and may vary between 0 and 1. Further, the value of the optimistic–pessimistic parameter (λ) decides the inclination of the manager between the two extremes of the worst-case scenario and best-case scenario. If $\lambda = 0$, then the approach of the manager is pessimistic, and Me becomes equal to Nec. If $\lambda = 0.5$, then the attitude of the manager is compromising, and Me becomes equal to Cr. Lastly, if $\lambda = 1$, then the manager is more inclined toward the optimistic side, and Me becomes equal to Pos. Finally, the values of the target violation penalties (ψ^{sup}, ψ^{dem}, ψ^{conv}, p^{sup}, p^{dem}, p^{conv}) are decided based on real-time information. Considering a scaling multiplier for optimality robustness of 0.5 and a confidence interval of 0.75 for uncertain constraints and objective parameters, and adopting an optimistic approach, results of the WPP-SCND model are obtained to answer the following research questions:

For the given values of the parameters, a minimum total cost of USD 113,137,700 for both planning periods is obtained. For the given set of parameters, ExV cost of USD 102,773,900 is attained. However, ExV cost only computes results based on the average value of an imprecise parameter, which is not reliable. Therefore, the fuzzy-FRPP method given in Equation (33) is utilized to obtain robust results. According to this methodology, the robustness of results is enhanced by adding penalties for the violation of the target value due to uncertainty. For the given case, USD 6,909,209 is incurred as a penalty to increase the optimality, while a penalty of USD 3,454,605 is imposed to enhance the feasibility of the WPP-SCND model. The analysis of the total cost of the considered wood pellet supply chain system is shown in Table 2.

Table 2. Breakdown of the total cost of the wood pellet SC according to the fuzzy-FRPP approach.

ExV Cost (Thousand USD)	Optimality Robustness Cost (USD)	Feasibility Robustness Cost (USD)	Total Cost (USD)
102,773,900	6,909,209	3,454,605	113,137,700

$\lambda = 1.0$, ψ^{sup}, ψ^{dem}, $\psi^{conv} = 0.75$.

Comprehensive results for the specified settings of parameters depicting all strategic and tactical level decisions are illustrated in Figure 4. The obtained findings show that seven potential biomass supply terminals have been chosen out of nine. Because the supply terminals in Lahore and Multan have the greatest facility installation costs of all, they are not operational. The Rawalpindi supply terminal gathers biomass from the southern districts of the Punjab, whilst Sargodha and Faisalabad cover the center and western portions. Gujranwala mostly serves the western portions of Punjab, whereas DG Khan and Bahawalpur serve the southern regions. It is also found that to reduce the SC cost in terms of transportation and emissions due to transportation, supply terminals having the maximum potential of biomass are made operational.

All four of the pelletization facilities in Rawalpindi, Bahawalpur, Lahore, and Sahiwal are chosen for the second echelon of the wood pellet SC. One of these, the Lahore plant, was put into operation with a 50,000-ton processing capacity. The other plants were all installed with a 30,000-ton processing capacity. The Rawalpindi supply terminal supplies all biomass to its pelletization plant. Because the Lahore pelletization plant is designed to operate with the maximum pelletization capacity/period biomass, supplies from the biomass supply terminals in Sargodha, Faisalabad, and Gujranwala are sent to Lahore during both planning periods. The Sahiwal biomass terminal also supplies all of its biomass to its pelletization plant. Lastly, supplies from the DG Khan and Bahawalpur supply points also send their biomass to the pelletization plant located in Bahawalpur. Decisions made in the second tier of the supply chain show that to reduce the cost associated with emissions and transportation, the optimization model preferably chose all the pelletization plants located closest to their supply locations. It is also noticed that among the four types of available biomass, sawmill dust was the least preferred due to its high purchase cost.

In the third tier, the Rawalpindi pelletization facility sent its wood pellets to the Multan distribution center in the first planning period and the Lahore distribution center in the second planning period. Further, in the first planning period, Bahawalpur did not manufacture any pellets, but in the second period, it delivered pellets to the distribution centers in Sargodha and Multan. Lahore only produced wood pellets during the first planned period, sending them to its own distribution facility and the Sargodha distribution center. During the first planning period, the Sahiwal pelletization facility delivered its pellets to Sargodha and Lahore, whereas during the second, it sent all of its pellets to the Lahore distribution center. For the final echelon of WPSC, the distribution facilities in Lahore and Sargodha were made operational with higher capacity levels, while Multan's facility was chosen with a lower capacity level. Wood pellets from the Lahore distribution center met the energy needs of its market zone as well as the Gujranwala market. The Sargodha distribution facility sent wood pellets to the market zones of Faisalabad and Rawalpindi. Finally, Multan's distribution hub meets the energy demands of its market zone as well as the market in Faisalabad.

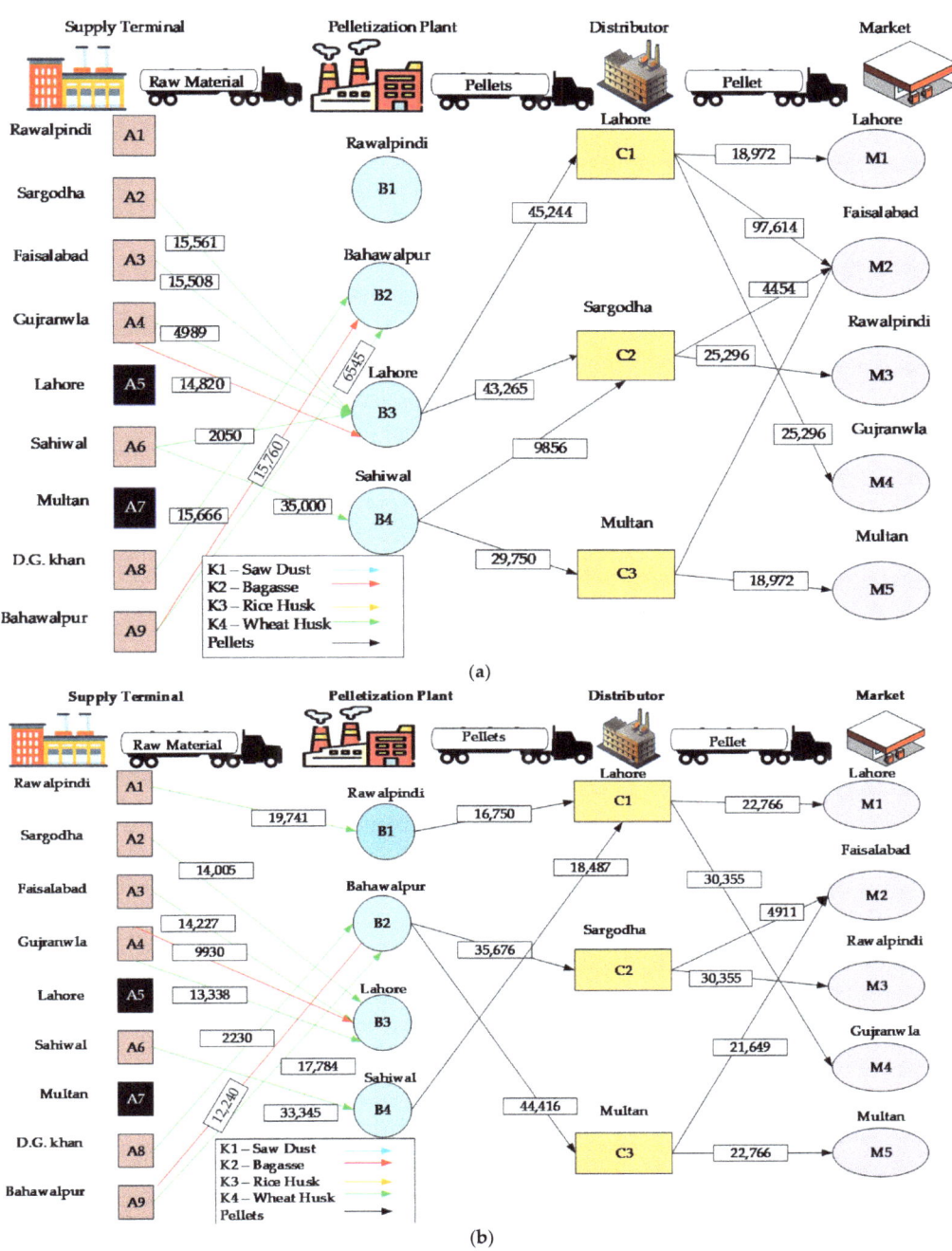

Figure 4. WPP-SCND model decisions using fuzzy-FRPP during (**a**) first time period t_1 (**b**) second time period t_2.

(b) Research question 2: How can robust decisions for strategic and tactical levels in a wood pellet SC be acquired in a highly uncertain environment?

Herein, the second research question aims to deal with an uncertain environment and provide robust decisions for strategic and tactical planning for a WPSC network design. To attain this goal, the fuzzy-FRPP approach is proposed that provides not only robust but also cost-efficient optimal solutions under uncertain environments. To evaluate the quality of the results provided by the fuzzy-FRPP approach, its results are compared with a counterpart solution methodology named FRPP. Further, an explanation of how a subjective approach to dealing with risk impacts the results of the fuzzy-FRPP technique is also provided in this section.

I. Comparative analysis of FPP and fuzzy-FRPP approach to analyze the impact of robustness

In this part, a comparison of the FPP and fuzzy-FRPP approaches is presented for evaluating the impact of robustness. As described in Section 3.2, the FPP approach makes decisions based on the ExV of imprecise parameters of the objective, but fuzzy-FRPP considers costs of flexibility margins in constraints, as well as feasibility and optimality robustness. A comparison of the two methodologies demonstrates that high-cost location decisions, such as pelletization plant installation and distribution hubs, do not vary. However, in terms of capacity decisions, the decisions regarding the two approaches differ. This is because fuzzy-FRPP adds resilience to model decisions by selecting wood pellet production facilities with larger aggregate capacities. In order to achieve the goal of a higher aggregate capacity, either small-capacity facilities in several locations or larger-capacity facilities in fewer sites are chosen. Additionally, it was demonstrated that when making capacity decisions, the fuzzy-FRPP approach successfully strikes an equilibrium between transportation costs, emissions costs, and economies of scale.

A detailed analysis of the results shows that the majority of the location decisions made by the two methodologies are similar. In the first echelon, instead of Multan, the Rawalpindi biomass supply terminal is made operational in FPP. Further, the Rawalpindi pelletization facility was not chosen for the second tier of the WPP-SCND model; instead, the Bahawalpur pelletization facility was placed into operation with a greater capacity level. Finally, in the last tier of FPP decisions, all three distribution centers were chosen, with the Multan distribution center becoming operational with a lower processing capacity. The FPP technique operates with lower aggregate capacity, and therefore, the total cost is lower than the fuzzy-FRPP approach.

II. Impact of change in objective and constraint pessimistic–optimistic (λ) factor on the total cost of the WPP-SCND model

Since the values of the interactive parameters are decided based on real-time dynamics, therefore, a sensitivity analysis for multiple scenarios is provided to establish the effectiveness of provided model and solution technique. For this purpose, a comprehensive analysis is provided to examine the impact of combined variation in the objective pessimistic-optimistic factor (ξ) and constraints pessimistic–optimistic (λ) factor on the total cost of the WPP-SCND model. Using various combinations of these interactive parameters multiple global optimal solutions are provided in Table 3. Pessimistic–optimistic factor (λ) is one of the key parameters that provide information about the attitude of the decision maker in an uncertain environment. If the value of $\lambda = 0$, then the decision maker has adopted a risk aversion approach and they are planning for the best-case scenario, and if $\lambda = 0.99$, then the decision makers are planning by keeping the best-case scenario; $\lambda = 0.5$ provides a compromise between the two extremes. The results provided in Table 3 are in line with this proposition. Analysis of the results shows that as λ increases from 0.1 to 0.9 for each value of the confidence level of the decision maker, the overall system cost of the WPP-SCND model decreases. This is because higher values of λ provide an optimistic approach as a results model provides the minimum possible cost. It is also seen that as the value of the objective pessimistic–optimistic factor (ξ) increases, the total SC cost also increases.

Table 3. Effect of variation in objective pessimistic–optimistic factor (ξ) and constraint pessimistic-optimistic (λ) factor on the objective of the WPP-SCND model.

Objective Pessimistic–Optimistic Factor (ξ)	Constraint Pessimistic–Optimistic Factor (λ)				
	0.1	0.3	0.5	0.7	0.9
	Total Supply Chain Cost for WPP-SCND Model ($)				
0.1	110,558,900	107,803,400	102,954,400	92,339,250	51,491,180
0.3	112,457,100	110,077,900	106,041,300	97,033,580	61,243,520
0.5	114,465,400	112,753,700	109,570,000	102,617,700	73,082,560
0.7	116,655,000	115,383,100	112,368,000	108,399,400	86,763,080
0.9	118,495,700	117,913,800	116,871,600	114,465,400	102,617,700

III. Impact of uncertainty handling technique on the WPP-SCND model facilities capacity level decision and scalability aspect

Strategic planning decisions regarding facility placement and capacity are crucial for determining the performance of the system. Therefore, the WPP-SCND model considers the capacity level decisions in the wood pelletization plant echelon and distribution and storage echelon of the WPSC. The suggested model aims to find the optimal tradeoff between the capacity levels and the total number of facilities in each supply chain tier. In addition, it is also important to strike a balance between logistics costs and economies of scale to make WPSC decisions that are both cost-effective and environmentally sustainable. For instance, increasing the number of low-capacity facilities (wood pelletization plant and distribution and storage center) can lower transportation costs, but ignoring economies of scale may raise total system costs. On the contrary, economies of scale will be more advantageous if fewer facilities with more capacity are placed into operation. In this instance, nevertheless, longer distances between facilities may result in higher system costs overall.

Herein, the impact of a specific type of uncertainty handling of the WPP-SCND model facility capacity level decision is observed. Each solution provides capacity decisions by striking a balance between the robustness of the solutions and the objective value of the WPP-SCND model. In this background, a comparative analysis of WPP-SCND model capacity decisions for the following three solution approaches is provided: (i) deterministic approach, (ii) FPP approach, and (iii) fuzzy-FRPP approach. Figure 5 shows the operational number and capacity levels of wood pelletization plants and distribution and storage facilities against each solution. The results indicate that the WPP-SCND model with a deterministic approach chooses the fewest number of facilities and the lowest capacity levels in each wood pellet SC tier. This is because neither penalties for constraint violation nor a flexibility margin is included in the deterministic method, and the model only attempts to find an efficient balance between economies of scale and transportation costs; the deterministic approach thus has the lowest overall WPSC costs. For the second solution, FPP, the WPP-SCND approach yields greater overall costs than the deterministic method. This is because the FPP approach acknowledges epistemic uncertainty by using a possibilistic distribution for each uncertain parameter that may vary within a certain range, but it does not also include the constraint violation penalty factor. As a consequence, the overall WPSC cost is more than that of the deterministic approach but lower than that of the fuzzy-FRPP approach. Finally, the fuzzy-FRPP methodology has the greatest overall cost of all available solution approaches. This is because fuzzy-FRPP takes into consideration not just the epistemic uncertainty in the WPP-SCN D model's uncertain parameters but also the constraints violation penalties. In order to decrease the surge in overall WPSC costs, the model chooses wood pellet processing facilities with greater capacities. This approach not only allows the WPP-SCND model to avoid constraint violation penalties but also minimizes the system's overall logistics cost.

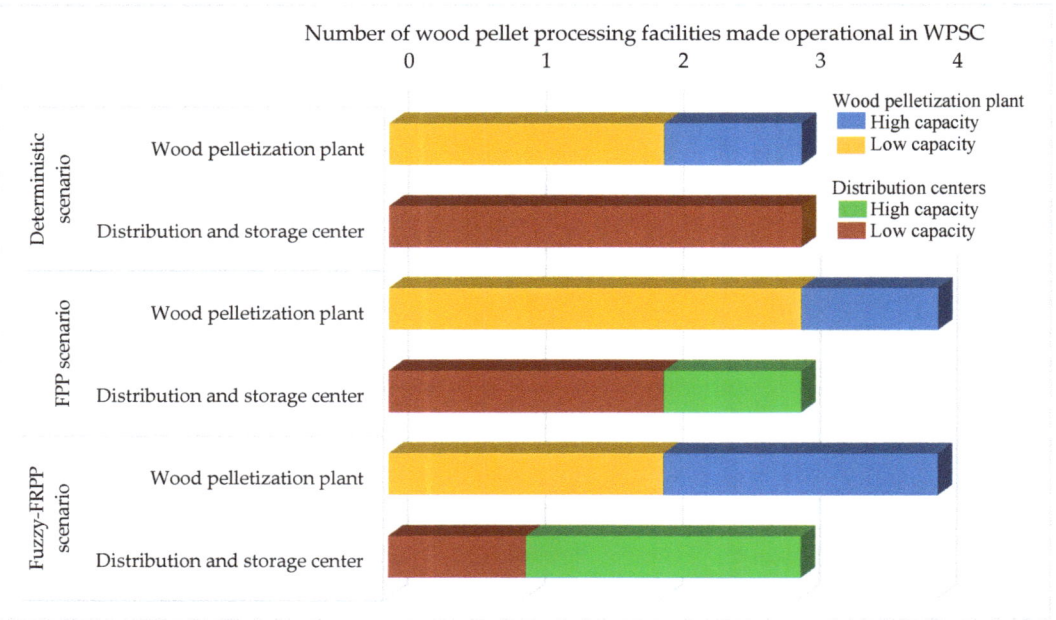

Figure 5. Impact of specific uncertainty handling technique on the WPP-SCND model's facility capacity level decision.

The uncertainty associated with critical WPP-SCND model parameters further hampers the scalability of wood pellet production. Analyses of the results indicate that the scalability of wood pellet production is significantly dependent on biomass type, biomass cost, biomass availability, biomass yield, and scalable wood pellet production method. For instance, the production yield of wood pellets is highly dependent on the kind of biomass and its manufacturing process. In this context, the suggested WPP-SCND model accounts for the uncertainty regarding biomass supply and biomass production. In line with this, the fuzzy-FRPP technique provides efficient solutions by including the biomass supply and yields penalty violations into the objective function of the optimization model. In addition to the previously indicated critical factor for the scalability of wood pellet manufacturing, the robust design of the logistics network is a crucial aspect in the biofuels sector. The disruption of the logistics network may be caused by both natural and man-made disasters. Wood pellet biomass supply disruptions may impact biomass production (e.g., natural disasters), material processing capacity (e.g., underinvestment), transportation network (e.g., damaged roads), and biomass demand for competing sectors (e.g., increased demand due to material competition).

5. Conclusions, Limitations, and Future Research Directions

This research proposed a multi-period wood pellet production distribution using residual wastes as biomass. The provided optimization model aims to minimize the environmental effect and total cost of wood pellet collection, manufacturing, and supply while satisfying the target market's need for wood pellets for the sustainable growth of a wood waste-based bioeconomy. Because biomass used for wood pellets is a residual product that is primarily seasonal, and because biomass purchasing and transportation costs are related to fossil fuels, a very dynamic environment exists. To deal with this uncertain environment, a fuzzy-FRPP technique is developed. The fuzzy-FRPP technique not only permits flexibility in the target of constraints with imprecise parameters but also incorporates resilience into the WPP-SCND model results. Fuzzy-FRPP is an interactive solution that contains 12 parameters. The scope of the suggested approach is significantly expanded since choosing the values of the parameters would allow decision makers to make decisions in line with their preferences. Although the proposed decision support system is employed to manage wood pellet production and distribution, the results and solution may be used for the synthesis of other biofuels (bioethanol, biodiesel, biomethane, etc.). The most important findings of this study are as follows:

- It is observed that for situations where epistemic uncertainty is largely associated with the collected dataset, the fuzzy-FRPP approach will always provide robust decisions with a slight increase in overall system cost. According to the computational analysis of the case study, the outcomes may be protected against uncertainty by spending an additional 10%.
- Comparing the results of the FPP and fuzzy-FRPP approaches shows that the latter favors adopting a centralized SC structure by making fewer facilities with a greater capacity level operational, while the former favors decentralizing the wood pellet SC structure.
- It was also discovered that the two largest expenses associated with WPSC were the installation of the wood pellet plant and the cost of producing wood pellets. This demonstrates that by exploring alternative, cost-effective wood pellet manufacturing processes, wood pellet fuels may be made more economically competitive with fossil fuels.

This study also has some limitations that give a roadmap for future research in this field. This study does not explore any form of contract mechanism that may play a key role in overcoming uncertainty among WPSC stakeholders. The consideration of a contract mechanism between suppliers of wood-based biomass and wood pellet-manufacturing plants is therefore another way to broaden the scope of this research. Additionally, cooperation across WPSC stakeholders is essential for reducing the uncertainty associated with biomass supply and enhancing the economic viability of wood pellets in comparison with fossil fuels, and extending this research by employing LCA-based environmental impact assessment could be valuable. In addition, for the scalable production of wood pellets, it is essential to address the uncertainties associated with biomass supply, biomass yields, and wood pellet production technology. However, the uncertainty associated with pellet production technology is not addressed in this study. This investigation may be expanded by addressing the scalability of cost-effective wood pellet production technologies. Further, this research does not consider the risk associated with the disruption perspective. The integration of SC disruption within the proposed model will also enhance the utilization of this research in practical scenarios. Furthermore, the utilization of this research can be enhanced by considering sustainability.

Author Contributions: Z.A.: Conceptualization, Writing—original draft, Methodology, Investigation, Funding. M.S.H.: Conceptualization, Writing—original draft, Writing—revised draft, Investigation, Software, Supervision. A.S.: Software and Investigation, Data collection. M.K.: Conceptualization, Writing—original draft, Supervision, Project administration, Funding. R.A.: Software and Investigation. All authors have read and agreed to the published version of the manuscript.

Funding: This research received no external funding.

Institutional Review Board Statement: Not applicable.

Informed Consent Statement: Not applicable.

Data Availability Statement: Not applicable.

Conflicts of Interest: The authors declare no conflict of interest.

Appendix A

Tables A1–A7 provide the most likely values of the input parameters of the WPP-SCND model. Due to space limitations, only information about key parameters is provided.

Table A1. Quantity of raw material available at each supply terminal in period t (tons).

	K1 (Straw Mil)		K2 (Bagasse)		K3 (Rice Husk)		K4 (Wheat Husk)	
	T1	T2	T1	T2	T1	T2	T1	T2
A1	7800	7540	9230	17,260	21,190	29,878	35,880	32,292
A2	7800	7280	6760	12,641	42,900	60,489	16,380	14,742
A3	5200	5720	5252	9821	20,020	28,228	16,640	14,976
A4	4160	3900	5252	9821	24,700	34,827	15,600	14,040
A5	7800	8320	10,400	19,448	26,000	36,660	10,400	9360
A6	5200	5850	7280	13,614	33,800	47,658	39,000	35,100
A7	10,400	10,400	9880	18,476	7800	10,998	41,600	37,440
A8	5200	6500	6760	12,641	35,100	49,491	26,000	23,400
A9	5200	6240	6890	12,884	39,000	54,990	20,800	18,720

Table A2. Pelletization capacity of the plant (tons/period).

	Q1	Q2
B1	35,000	50,000
B2	35,000	50,000
B3	35,000	50,000
B4	35,000	50,000

Table A3. Distribution center storage capacity (tons/period).

	R1	R2
C1	40,000	60,000
C2	40,000	60,000
C3	40,000	60,000

Table A4. Pellet demand in each market zone (tons).

	T1	T2
M1	12,000	14,400
M2	14,000	16,800
M3	16,000	19,200
M4	16,000	19,200
M5	12,000	14,400

Table A5. Transportation cost of biomass between biomass supply terminal and pelletization plants (USD/ton-km).

		B1 (Pelletization Plant)	B2 (Pelletization Plant)	B3 (Pelletization Plant)	B4 (Pelletization Plant)
RAWALPINDI	A1	6	574	359	401
SARGODHA	A2	232	370	188	186
FAISALABAD	A3	301	321	181	102
GUJRANWALA	A4	212	474	92	363
LAHORE	A5	359	413	10	171
SAHIWAL	A6	401	243	171	5
MULTAN	A7	520	100	338	180
D.G. KHAN	A8	615	183	438	279
BAHAWALPUR	A9	599	8	430	244

Table A6. Transportation cost of wood pellets between pelletization plants and distribution centers (USD/ton-km).

		C1	C2	C3
RAWALPINDI	B1	332	218	517
BAHAWALPUR	B2	427	381	100
LAHORE	B3	10	188	338
SAHIWAL	B4	171	230	181

Table A7. Transportation cost of wood pellets between pelletization plants and distribution centers (USD/ton-km).

		M1	M2	M3	M4	M5
LAHORE	C1	10	181	331	92	338
SARGODHA	C2	187	91	232	221	291
MULTAN	C3	338	242	520	395	8

References

1. Habib, M.S.; Tayyab, M.; Zahoor, S.; Sarkar, B. Management of animal fat-based biodiesel supply chain under the paradigm of sustainability. *Energy Convers. Manag.* **2020**, *225*, 113345. [CrossRef]
2. Munir, M.A.; Habib, M.S.; Hussain, A.; Shahbaz, M.A.; Qamar, A.; Masood, T.; Sultan, M.; Abbas, M.M.; Imran, S.; Hasan, M. Blockchain adoption for sustainable supply chain management: An economic, environmental, and social perspective. *Front. Energy Res.* **2022**, *613*, 899632. [CrossRef]
3. Habib, M.S.; Omair, M.; Ramzan, M.B.; Chaudhary, T.N.; Farooq, M.; Sarkar, B. A robust possibilistic flexible programming approach toward a resilient and cost-efficient biodiesel supply chain network. *J. Clean. Prod.* **2022**, *366*, 132752. [CrossRef]
4. D'adamo, I.; Sassanelli, C. Biomethane Community: A Research Agenda towards Sustainability. *Sustainability* **2022**, *14*, 4735. [CrossRef]
5. Taddei, E.; Sassanelli, C.; Rosa, P.; Terzi, S. Circular supply chains in the era of industry 4.0: A systematic literature review. *Comput. Ind. Eng.* **2022**, *170*, 108268. [CrossRef]
6. Salvador, R.; Puglieri, F.N.; Halog, A.; Andrade, F.G.D.; Piekarski, C.M.; De Francisco, A.C. Key aspects for designing business models for a circular bioeconomy. *J. Clean. Prod.* **2021**, *278*, 124341. [CrossRef]
7. D'Adamo, I.; Gastaldi, M.; Morone, P.; Rosa, P.; Sassanelli, C.; Settembre-Blundo, D.; Shen, Y. Bioeconomy of Sustainability: Drivers, Opportunities and Policy Implications. *Sustainability* **2022**, *14*, 200. [CrossRef]
8. Kanan, M.; Habib, M.S.; Habib, T.; Zahoor, S.; Gulzar, A.; Raza, H.; Abusaq, Z. A Flexible Robust Possibilistic Programming Approach for Sustainable Second-Generation Biogas Supply Chain Design under Multiple Uncertainties. *Sustainability* **2022**, *14*, 11597. [CrossRef]

9. Raimondo, M.; Caracciolo, F.; Cembalo, L.; Chinnici, G.; Pappalardo, G.; D'Amico, M. Moving towards circular bioeconomy: Managing olive cake supply chain through contracts. *Sustain. Prod. Consum.* **2021**, *28*, 180–191. [CrossRef]
10. Yun, H.; Wang, H.; Clift, R.; Bi, X. The role of torrefied wood pellets in the bio-economy: A case study from Western Canada. *Biomass Bioenergy* **2022**, *163*, 106523. [CrossRef]
11. Habib, M.S.; Asghar, O.; Hussain, A.; Imran, M.; Mughal, M.P.; Sarkar, B. A robust possibilistic programming approach toward animal fat-based biodiesel supply chain network design under uncertain environment. *J. Clean. Prod.* **2021**, *278*, 122403. [CrossRef]
12. Kanan, M.; Habib, M.S.; Shahbaz, A.; Hussain, A.; Habib, T.; Raza, H.; Abusaq, Z.; Assaf, R. A Grey-Fuzzy Programming Approach towards Socio-Economic Optimization of Second-Generation Biodiesel Supply Chains. *Sustainability* **2022**, *14*, 10169. [CrossRef]
13. Boukherroub, T.; LeBel, L.; Lemieux, S. An integrated wood pellet supply chain development: Selecting among feedstock sources and a range of operating scales. *Appl. Energy* **2017**, *198*, 385–400. [CrossRef]
14. Hughes, N.M.; Shahi, C.; Pulkki, R. A Review of the Wood Pellet Value Chain, Modern Value/Supply Chain Management Approaches, and Value/Supply Chain Models. *J. Renew. Energy* **2014**, *2014*, 654158. [CrossRef]
15. Mobtaker, A.; Ouhimmou, M.; Audy, J.F.; Rönnqvist, M. A review on decision support systems for tactical logistics planning in the context of forest bioeconomy. *Renew. Sustain. Energy Rev.* **2021**, *148*, 111250. [CrossRef]
16. Méndez-Vázquez, M.A.; Gómez-Castro, F.I.; Ponce-Ortega, J.M.; Serafín-Muñoz, A.H.; Santibañez-Aguilar, J.E.; El-Halwagi, M.M. Mathematical optimization of a supply chain for the production of fuel pellets from residual biomass. *Clean Technol. Environ. Policy* **2017**, *19*, 721–734. [CrossRef]
17. Ghaderi, H.; Moini, A.; Pishvaee, M.S. A multi-objective robust possibilistic programming approach to sustainable switchgrass-based bioethanol supply chain network design. *J. Clean. Prod.* **2018**, *179*, 368–406. [CrossRef]
18. Mansuy, N.; Thiffault, E.; Lemieux, S.; Manka, F.; Paré, D.; Lebel, L. Sustainable biomass supply chains from salvage logging of fire-killed stands: A case study for wood pellet production in eastern Canada. *Appl. Energy* **2015**, *154*, 62–73. [CrossRef]
19. Shabani, N.; Akhtari, S.; Sowlati, T. Value chain optimization of forest biomass for bioenergy production: A review. *Renew. Sustain. Energy Rev.* **2013**, *23*, 299–311. [CrossRef]
20. Kanzian, C.; Holzleitner, F.; Stampfer, K.; Ashton, S. Regional energy wood logistics–optimizing local fuel supply. *Silva Fenn.* **2009**, *43*, 113–128. [CrossRef]
21. An, H.; Wilhelm, W.E.; Searcy, S.W. A mathematical model to design a lignocellulosic biofuel supply chain system with a case study based on a region in Central Texas. *Bioresour. Technol.* **2011**, *102*, 7860–7870. [CrossRef]
22. Vasković, S.; Halilović, V.; Gvero, P.; Medaković, V.; Musić, J. Multi-criteria optimization concept for the selection of optimal solid fuels supply chain from wooden biomass. *Croat. J. For. Eng. J. Theory Appl. For. Eng.* **2015**, *36*, 109–123.
23. Cambero, C.; Sowlati, T. Incorporating social benefits in multi-objective optimization of forest-based bioenergy and biofuel supply chains. *Appl. Energy* **2016**, *178*, 721–735. [CrossRef]
24. Trochu, J.; Chaabane, A.; Ouhimmou, M. Reverse logistics network redesign under uncertainty for wood waste in the CRD industry. *Resour. Conserv. Recycl.* **2018**, *128*, 32–47. [CrossRef]
25. Mobini, M.; Sowlati, T.; Sokhansanj, S. A simulation model for the design and analysis of wood pellet supply chains. *Appl. Energy* **2013**, *111*, 1239–1249. [CrossRef]
26. Akhtari, S.; Sowlati, T. Hybrid optimization-simulation for integrated planning of bioenergy and biofuel supply chains. *Appl. Energy* **2020**, *259*, 114124. [CrossRef]
27. Yılmaz Balaman, Ş.; Wright, D.G.; Scott, J.; Matopoulos, A. Network design and technology management for waste to energy production: An integrated optimization framework under the principles of circular economy. *Energy* **2018**, *143*, 911–933. [CrossRef]
28. Pishvaee; Razmi, J.; Torabi, S.A. Robust possibilistic programming for socially responsible supply chain network design: A new approach. *Fuzzy Sets Syst.* **2012**, *206*, 1–20. [CrossRef]
29. Torabi; Namdar, J.; Hatefi, S.; Jolai, F. An enhanced possibilistic programming approach for reliable closed-loop supply chain network design. *Int. J. Prod. Res.* **2016**, *54*, 1358–1387. [CrossRef]
30. Van Dyken, S.; Bakken, B.H.; Skjelbred, H.I. Linear mixed-integer models for biomass supply chains with transport, storage and processing. *Energy* **2010**, *35*, 1338–1350. [CrossRef]
31. Vitale, I.; Dondo, R.G.; González, M.; Cóccola, M.E. Modelling and optimization of material flows in the wood pellet supply chain. *Appl. Energy* **2022**, *313*, 118776. [CrossRef]
32. De Laporte, A.V.; Weersink, A.J.; McKenney, D.W. Effects of supply chain structure and biomass prices on bioenergy feedstock supply. *Appl. Energy* **2016**, *183*, 1053–1064. [CrossRef]
33. Pishvaee; Torabi, S.A. A possibilistic programming approach for closed-loop supply chain network design under uncertainty. *Fuzzy Sets Syst.* **2010**, *161*, 2668–2683. [CrossRef]
34. Habib, M.S.; Sarkar, B. A multi-objective approach to sustainable disaster waste management. In Proceedings of the International Conference on Industrial Engineering and Operations Management, Paris, France, 26–27 July 2018; pp. 1072–1083.
35. Xu, J.; Zhou, X. Approximation based fuzzy multi-objective models with expected objectives and chance constraints: Application to earth-rock work allocation. *Inf. Sci.* **2013**, *238*, 75–95. [CrossRef]
36. Visser, L.; Hoefnagels, R.; Junginger, M. Wood pellet supply chain costs—A review and cost optimization analysis. *Renew. Sustain. Energy Rev.* **2020**, *118*, 109506. [CrossRef]

37. Pirraglia, A.; Gonzalez, R.; Saloni, D. Techno-economical analysis of wood pellets production for US manufacturers. *BioResources* **2010**, *5*, 2374–2390.
38. Gonela, V.; Zhang, J.; Osmani, A.; Onyeaghala, R. Stochastic optimization of sustainable hybrid generation bioethanol supply chains. *Transp. Res. Part E Logist. Transp. Rev.* **2015**, *77*, 1–28. [CrossRef]
39. World Bank. *Carbon Tax Guide: A Handbook for Policy Makers*; World Bank Open Knowledge: Washington, DC, USA, 2017.
40. Habib, M.S. Robust Optimization for Post-Disaster Debris Management in Humanitarian Supply Chain: A Sustainable Recovery Approach. Ph.D. Thesis, Hanyang University, Seoul, Korea, 2018.
41. Habib, M.S.; Maqsood, M.H.; Ahmed, N.; Tayyab, M.; Omair, M. A multi-objective robust possibilistic programming approach for sustainable disaster waste management under disruptions and uncertainties. *Int. J. Disaster Risk Reduct.* **2022**, *75*, 102967. [CrossRef]

MDPI
St. Alban-Anlage 66
4052 Basel
Switzerland
Tel. +41 61 683 77 34
Fax +41 61 302 89 18
www.mdpi.com

Mathematics Editorial Office
E-mail: mathematics@mdpi.com
www.mdpi.com/journal/mathematics

www.ingramcontent.com/pod-product-compliance
Lightning Source LLC
LaVergne TN
LVHW070144100526
838202LV00015B/1889